FILM PRODUCERS, STUDIOS, AGENTS AND CASTING DIRECTORS

GUIDE

Second Edition

FILM PRODUCERS, STUDIOS, AGENTS AND CASTING DIRECTORS GUIDE

Second Edition

Compiled and Edited by
Susan Avallone & Jack Lechner

(First Edition by Kate Bales)

LONE EAGLE

**FILM PRODUCERS, STUDIOS, AGENTS
and CASTING DIRECTORS GUIDE
SECOND EDITION**

LONE EAGLE PUBLISHING CO.
9903 Santa Monica Blvd.
Beverly Hills, CA 90212
213/471-8066

Printed in the United States of America

Book designed by Liz Ridenour & Heidi Frieder

This book was entirely typeset using an Apple Macintosh Plus, Apple Macintosh II, LaserwriterPlus, Microsoft Word, Microsoft Excel, and Aldus Pagemaker.

Printed by McNaughton & Gunn, Saline, Michigan 48176

ISBN: 0-943728-28-2

NOTE: We have made every reasonable effort to ensure that the information contained herein is as accurate as possible. However, errors and omissions are sure to occur and neither the publishers nor the editors can take responsibility for them. We would appreciate your notifying us of any which you may find so that we may correct them in future editions.

* Lone Eagle Publishing is a division of Lone Eagle Productions, Inc.

LETTER FROM THE PUBLISHERS

It is with great pride and pleasure that we present the Second Annual Edition of the FILM PRODUCERS, STUDIOS, AGENTS and CASTING DIRECTORS GUIDE. This revised edition has been a long time coming, and we are sure you will find it is well worth the wait.

After our first edition came out, we asked you to tell us what you wanted to see in a second edition, and you told us *more—more* listings, *more* credits, and *more* contact information. Susan Avallone and Jack Lechner, our new co-editors, worked overtime to ensure this second edition meets (and, hopefully, surpasses) your expectations. It has doubled in size and is much broader in scope than the last edition. There is also a whole new section on casting directors which we think you will find useful. As we know this directory (as well as the other ones we publish) is used for hiring purposes as well as for research, Susan and Jack pestered agents, combed through mounds of research materials, and called many of you on the phone to get current contact information. Still, that is the one area in which we always need your help. Please include our office on your change of address/change of agent notices.

As always, we appreciate your comments and suggestions.

Joan V. Singleton and Ralph S. Singleton
Publishers

THE HENRY HIGGINS OF HOLLYWOOD, INC.

ROBERT EASTON

(213) 463-4811

THE DIALECT DOCTOR

Accents Cured – Dialects Strengthened

has taught: DON ADAMS, JENNY AGUTTER, ANA ALICIA, STEVE ALLEN, FERNANDO ALLENDE, MARIA CONCHITA ALONSO, ANTHONY ANDREWS, ANN-MARGRET, ADAM ANT, ANNE ARCHER, EVE ARDEN, JEAN-PIERRE AUMONT, MARGARET AVERY, CANDICE AZZARA, BARBARA BACH, CATHERINE BACH, JIM BACKUS, JOE DON BAKER, IAN BANNEN, ADRIENNE BARBEAU, DREW BARRYMORE, PETER BARTON, BELINDA BAUER, STEVE BAUER, STEPHANIE BEACHAM, BONNIE BEDELIA, JIM BELUSHI, BARBI BENTON, CRYSTAL BERNARD, KEN BERRY, BIJAN, BARBARA BILLINGSLEY, JACQUELINE BISSET, SUSAN BLAKELY, PETER BONERZ, KLAUS MARIA BRANDAUER, EILEEN BRENNAN, BEAU BRIDGES, LLOYD BRIDGES, DANIELLE BRISEBOIS, JAMES BRODERICK, JAMES BROLIN, PIERCE BROSNAN, BRYAN BROWN, GEORG STANFORD BROWN, IAN BUCHANAN, TOM BURLINSON, DELTA BURKE, RAYMOND BURR, LeVAR BURTON, RUTH BUZZI, CORINNE CALVET, KIRK CAMERON, COLLEEN CAMP, VIRGINIA CAPERS, HARRY CAREY, JR., GEORGE CARLIN, DAVID CARRADINE, KEITH CARRADINE, BARBARA CARRERA, THOMAS CARTER, VERONICA CARTWRIGHT, SHAUN CASSIDY, MAXWELL CAULFIELD, RICHARD CHAMBERLAIN, STOCKARD CHANNING, LORRAINE CHASE, JOAN CHEN, LOIS CHILES, CANDY CLARK, JAMES COBURN, IMOGENE COCA, DENNIS COLE, DABNEY COLEMAN, DIDI CONN, MICHAEL CONRAD, ROBERT CONRAD, ALEX CORD, BUD CORT, MICHAEL CRAWFORD, MARY CROSBY, TOM CRUISE, JOAN CUSACK, JIM DALE, TONY DANZA, PATTI DAVIS, PAM DAWBER, FELICITY DEAN, OLIVIA DE HAVILLAND, REBECCA DE MORNAY, PATRICK DEMPSEY, ROBERT DE NIRO, BRIAN DENNEHY, BO DEREK, LAURA DERN, DANNY DE VITO, ALISON DOODY, ROBYN DOUGLASS, BRAD DOURIF, LESLEY-ANNE DOWN, DAVID DUKES, ROBERT DUVALL, SHEENA EASTON, ANITA EKBERG, HECTOR ELIZONDO, STEPHEN ELLIOTT, RON ELY, LINDA EVANS, PETER FALK, STEPHANIE FARACY, TOVAH FELDSHUH, LUPITA FERRER, SHIRLEY ANN FIELD, LINDA FIORENTINO, PETER FIRTH, FIONNULA FLANAGAN, LOUISE FLETCHER, NINA FOCH, JANE FONDA, ROBERT FOXWORTH, TONY FRANCIOSA, GENIE FRANCIS, JAMES FRANCISCUS, KATHLEEN FREEMAN, TERESA GANZEL, TERRI GARBER, ANDY GARCIA, CHRISTOPHER GEORGE, LYNDA DAY GEORGE, RICHARD GERE, MEL GIBSON, SIR JOHN GIELGUD, ROBERT GINTY, ALEXANDER GODUNOV, TRACEY GOLD, JOHN GOODMAN, MARJOE GORTNER, GERRITT GRAHAM, ERIN GRAY, LINDA GRAY, MELANIE GRIFFITH, MOSES GUNN, STEVE GUTTENBERG, SHELLEY HACK, GENE HACKMAN, VERONICA HAMEL, MARK HAMILL, NICHOLAS HAMMOND, TOM HANKS, DARYL HANNAH, ED HARRIS, RUTGER HAUER, PATRICIA HAYES, GINA HECHT, MARIEL HEMINGWAY, LANCE HENRIKSEN, PAMELA HENSLEY, BARBARA HERSHEY, HOWARD HESSEMAN, CHARLTON HESTON, ANNE HEYWOOD, JOHN HILLERMAN, POLLY HOLLIDAY, EARL HOLLIMAN, ANTHONY HOPKINS, BO HOPKINS, DENNIS HOPPER, BOB HOSKINS, JOAN HOTCHKIS, BETH HOWLAND, SEASON HUBLEY, FINOLA HUGHES, GARY IMHOFF, JILL IRELAND, KATE JACKSON, HERB JEFFERSON JR., GLYNIS JOHNS, ELAINE JOYCE, KATY JURADO, WILLIAM KATT, JAMES KEACH, HARVEY KEITEL, MARTHE KELLER, SALLY KELLERMAN, LINDA KELSEY, LANCE KERWIN, MARGOT KIDDER, RICHARD KIEL, VAL KILMER, PERRY KING, NASTASSJA KINSKI, SWOOSIE KURTZ, RON LACEY, CHRISTOPHER LAMBERT, TED LANGE, CLORIS LEACHMAN, EVA LeGALLIENNE, ANNIE LENNOX, JAY LENO, FIONA LEWIS, SHARI LEWIS, EMILY LLOYD, GARY LOCKWOOD, ROBERT LOGGIA, LYNN LORING, DOLPH LUNDGREN, KARL MALDEN, NICK MANCUSO, MONTE MARKHAM, MILLICENT MARTIN, MARSHA MASON, MARY ELIZABETH MASTRANTONIO, TIM MATHESON, ROBERTA MAXWELL, ANDREW McCARTHY, PEGGY McCAY, RODDY McDOWALL, DOROTHY McGUIRE, DOUG McKEON, FRANK McRAE, JAYNE MEADOWS, HEATHER MENZIES, BETTE MIDLER, JULIET MILLS, LYNNE MOODY, DEMI MOORE, MARY TYLER MOORE, TERRY MOORE, MICHAEL MORIARTY, DONNY MOST, PATRICIA NEAL, LIAM NEESON, SAM NEILL, CRAIG T. NELSON, BARRY NEWMAN, HAING NGOR, DUSTIN NGUYEN, JULIA NICKSON, MICHAEL NOURI, GLYNNIS O'CONNOR, SIR LAURENCE OLIVIER, EDWARD JAMES OLMOS, JENNIFER O'NEILL, CATHERINE OXENBERG, AL PACINO, JOANNA PACULA, JAMESON PARKER, BARBARA PARKINS, MANDY PATINKIN, GREGORY PECK, LISA PELIKAN, JOHN BENNETT PERRY, MARIA PERSCHY, PENNY PEYSER, MICHELLE PFEIFFER, DONALD PLEASENCE, JOAN PLOWRIGHT, AMANDA PLUMMER, STEFANIE POWERS, LAWRENCE PRESSMAN, LEE PURCELL, RANDY QUAID, KATHLEEN QUINLAN, BEULAH QUO, DEBORAH RAFFIN, STEVE RAILSBACK, JOHN RAITT, DAVID RASCHE, JOHN RATZENBERGER, ALYSON REED, LEE REMICK, ALEJANDRO REY, CYNTHIA RHODES, NATASHA RICHARDSON, JACK RILEY, MOLLY RINGWALD, JOHN RITTER, TANYA ROBERTS, PAUL RODRIGUEZ, TRISTAN ROGERS, JOHN RUBINSTEIN, JOHN RUSSELL, EVA MARIE SAINT, EMMA SAMMS, JOHN SAXON, GRETA SCACCHI, JACK SCALIA, ANNE SCHEDEEN, AVERY SCHREIBER, RICKY SCHRODER, ARNOLD SCHWARZENEGGER, JEAN BRUCE SCOTT, MARTHA SCOTT, CONNIE SELLECCA, CAROLINE SEYMOUR, JANE SEYMOUR, YOKO SHIMADA, WIL SHRINER, DWIGHT SHULTZ, GREGORY SIERRA, JONATHAN SILVERMAN, JEAN SIMMONS, MADGE SINCLAIR, JACLYN SMITH, JIMMY SMITS, ANN SOTHERN, DAVID SOUL, SISSY SPACEK, SYLVESTER STALLONE, ANDREW STEVENS, CONNIE STEVENS, FISHER STEVENS, PARKER STEVENSON, DEAN STOCKWELL, MADELYN STOWE, PETER STRAUSS, GAIL STRICKLAND, DONALD SUTHERLAND, PATRICK SWAYZE, JACK THOMPSON, SIGRID THORNTON, CHARLENE TILTON, LILY TOMLIN, LIZ TORRES, CONSTANCE TOWERS, TOMMY TUNE, TWIGGY, SUSAN TYRRELL, CICELY TYSON, ROBERT URICH, PAVLA USTINOV, MONIQUE VAN DE VEN, MERETE VAN KAMP, DICK VAN PATTEN, JOYCE VAN PATTEN, ROBERT VAUGHN, CHICK VENNERA, SAL VISCUSO, LINDSAY WAGNER, ROBERT WAGNER, DEE WALLACE, SHANI WALLIS, RAY WALSTON, JESSICA WALTER, RACHEL WARD, LESLEY ANN WARREN, DENZEL WASHINGTON, CARLENE WATKINS, DENNIS WEAVER, LISA WHELCHEL, FORREST WHITAKER, CINDY WILLIAMS, BRUCE WILLIS, FLIP WILSON, MARIE WINDSOR, JAMES WOODS, JANE WYATT, JANE WYMAN, RICHARD YNIGUEZ, MICHAEL YORK, SUSANNAH YORK, ALAN YOUNG, JOHNNY YUNE, DAPHNE ZUNIGA

. . . and over two thousand others.

INTRODUCTION

Welcome to the second edition of the **FILM PRODUCERS, STUDIOS, AGENTS and CASTING DIRECTORS GUIDE.** Because circumstances change so quickly in the film industry, it's been a formidable task to keep the credits in this book up-to-date and accurate. Inevitably, any current film reference can only provide a kind of snapshot of the way things stand at the time of publication. Producers' credits are always subject to adjustment by lawsuit; contact numbers are often just a way to get a forwarding address; and the perils of listing studio executive rosters are legendary.

Happily, we feel assured that the new edition is as reliable as the changing winds of Hollywood permit. Each existing listing has been revised, updated, and checked for accuracy against a number of sources. We have added thousands of new entries to the book, and deleted earlier entries that were in error.

The book consists of four sections:

FILM PRODUCERS lists credits for producers of feature films released in the United States over the last few decades. Not listed are most foreign films; short films; films made for television; films produced by people who have long since left the industry, or are deceased; grade-Z exploitation films, including pornographic films; and (with some exceptions) films that were released directly on videocassette. We have chosen not to include any listing we could not verify, so while there are undoubtedly omissions—both of producers and of films—there should be no outright errors.

We have also omitted any names listed on a film's credits as "Presented By" or "In Association With," as well as Associate Producers who have no prior or subsequent credits in some other producing capacity. We realize the former does a disservice to several legitimate producers whose credits are often listed this way (most notably Dino De Laurentiis), and the latter to some *de facto* line producers — but we had to draw the line somewhere. Our profound apologies if we drew it across your face.

The section is organized alphabetically by producer, and indexed alphabetically by film title.

Alternate or foreign titles are listed in italics after the primary U.S. title. Please be aware that when a co-producer is listed in parentheses at the start of a producer entry, all credits without an asterisk are shared. (This does not necessarily mean that the two people are business partners, either past or present.) Please refer to the KEY TO ABBREVIATIONS on page x if you need help deciphering any of the symbols in the listings.

ACADEMY AWARD INFORMATION

You will notice when going through the listing sections, that we have indicated Oscar nominations (★) and wins (★★). We have deviated a bit from the Academy's listing and have put these stars by everyone's name who was a producer on those films as this award is actually for Best Picture, not Best Producer. This is not to indicate that those people actually have a golden statuette on their mantels, but merely to recognize their contribution to the award or nomination. For a list of the actual nominees and winners, please refer to page two.

AGENTS lists talent agents and agencies serving the film industry in Los Angeles and New York. To the best extent possible, we have listed the names of agents who deal primarily with the film industry, e.g., theatrical agents.

STUDIOS lists current personnel and contact information for major studios, "mini-majors," independent distributors, and selected production companies. Many smaller production companies are not listed, but can be found under their principals' headings in the Producers Guide.

CASTING DIRECTORS lists active casting directors for film and television in Los Angeles and New York.

Our thanks go to the stalwart crew at Lone Eagle Publishing, who slave year-round over hot Macs to bring industry directories to the world: Joan and Ralph Singleton, future information junkie Katie Singleton, Mike Green, Beth Wetzel, and the flying fingers of Steve LuKanic. Another deserved tip of the hat to our colleague Michael Singer, whose FILM DIRECTORS: A Complete Guide sets the standard for this obscure literary genre, and who gave of his massive information banks constantly ... if sometimes unknowingly. We're also indebted to the wonderful people at the Academy of Motion Picture Arts and Sciences Margaret Herrick Library and the AFI Louis B. Mayer Library, who made everything easier. And to all the people at the agencies and numerous production companies who helped us compile and confirm this information — you know who you are, and we're awfully glad we know, too.

Susan thanks Jack (again and again and again) for taking over the incredible and life-changing task of putting this book together; Kate Bales for seeing the need for this kind of reference and for passing the reins to us; and my husband Carr D'Angelo, family and friends for continued support and encouragement while my time got eaten up by "the book."

Jack thanks Susan; Erik Huber, who is available for your next open writing assignment; Alan Parker and Robert F. Colesberry, for being all-around *mensches*; Art Linson, for keeping me off the streets; John H. Williams and David V. Picker, without whom; my family, who still don't believe I can make a living in this business (and who may yet be right); and my indescribably delicious wife Sam Maser, who somehow refrained from kicking me out of the house when the dining room was hip-deep in old copies of *Variety*. That's true love.

Our aim is to make this book ever more complete until bookstore shelves collapse under its weight. Please help support the shelf manufacturers of America by letting us know how our listings can be improved for future editions—especially if your name is included within these pages. We're happy if you're happy. Let's do lunch. Ciao!

Susan Avallone and Jack Lechner
Los Angeles, California
June 1990

TABLE OF CONTENTS

LETTER FROM THE PUBLISHERS v

INTRODUCTION vii

KEY TO ABBREVIATIONS & SYMBOLS x

LISTING SECTIONS
- Producers 1
- Studios 205
- Agents 237
- Casting Directors 257

INDEX OF FILM TITLES
- Producers 169

ACADEMY AWARD INFORMATION
- Producers 2

INDEX OF ADVERTISERS 277

ABOUT THE EDITORS 278

KEY TO ABBREVIATIONS

EP	=	Executive Producer
CP	=	Co-Producer
SP	=	Supervising Producer
LP	=	Line Producer
AP	=	Associate Producer
FD	=	Feature Documentary
AF	=	Animated Feature
w/	=	sharing the same credit with

KEY TO SYMBOLS

★	=	after a film title denotes an Academy Award nomination
★★	=	after a film titles denotes an Academy Award win.
†	=	denotes deceased person
*	=	credit not shared

EDITORS NOTES

NOTE: As we were going to press, we were informed that Paramount had the audacity to change their phone number. Therefore, please substitute the prefix 956 for 468 when dialing a Paramount number, e.g., the new main number for Paramount is 213/956-5000.

NOTE #2: If a producer has no contact information listed, please contact the Producers Guild at the following address.

PRODUCERS GUILD OF AMERICA
400 South Beverly Drive
Beverly Hills, CA 90212
Tel. 213/557-0807

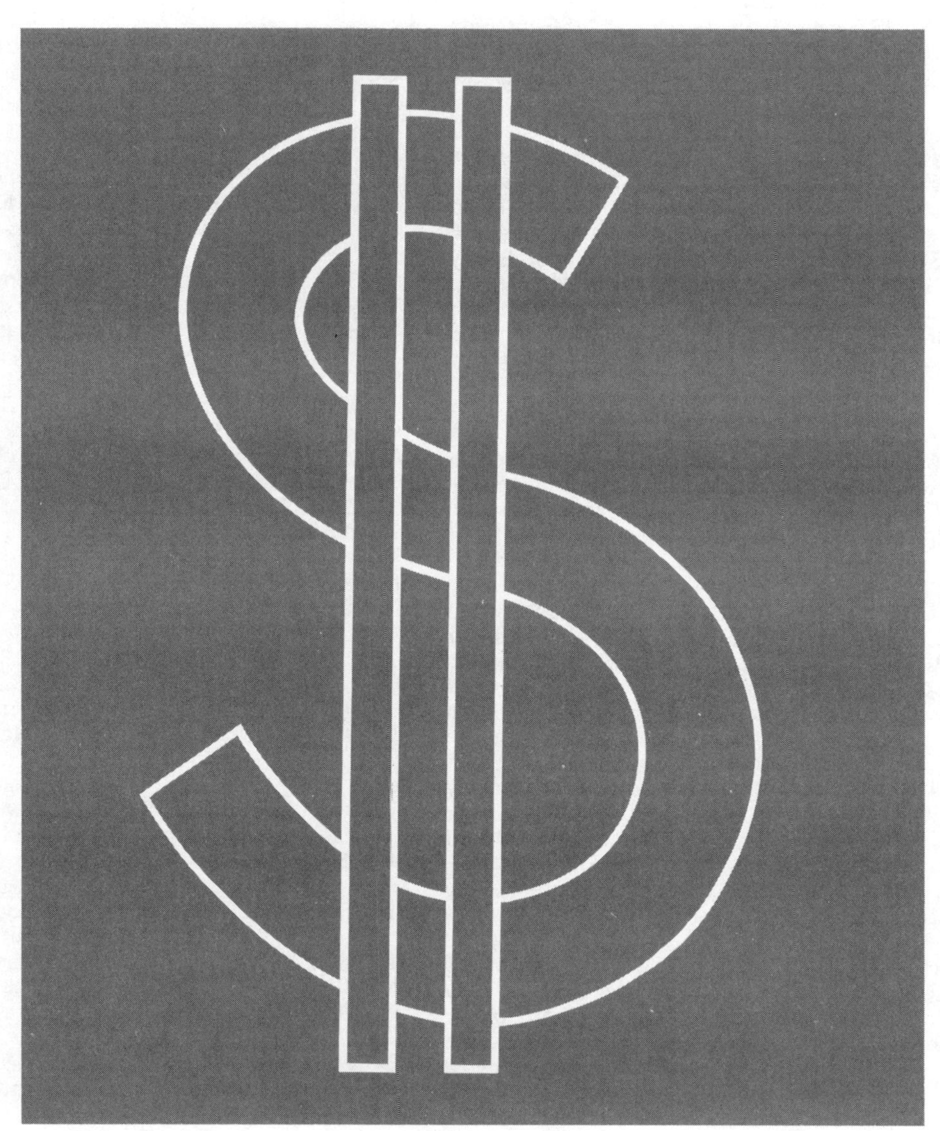

FILM PRODUCERS, STUDIOS, AGENTS & CASTING DIRECTORS GUIDE

P R O D U C E R S

PRODUCERS AWARDS AND NOMINATIONS 1977-1989

★★ = Winner in the category

1977
ANNIE HALL .... Charles H. Joffe★★
THE GOODBYE GIRL .... Ray Stark
JULIA .... Richard Roth
STAR WARS .... Gary Kurtz
THE TURNING POINT .... Herbert Roass and
.... Arthur Laurents

1978
COMING HOME .... Jerome Hellman
THE DEER HUNTER .... Barry Spikings,
.... Michael Deeley, Michael Cimino
.... and John Peverall★★
HEAVEN CAN WAIT .... Warren Beatty
MIDNIGHT EXPRESS .... Alan Marshall and
.... David Puttnam
AN UNMARRIED WOMAN .... Paul Mazursky and
.... Tony Ray

1979
ALL THAT JAZZ .... Robert Alan Aurthur
APOCALYPSE NOW .... Francis Coppola
BREAKING AWAY .... Peter Yates
KRAMER VS. KRAMER .... Stanley R. Jaffe★★
NORMA RAE .... Tamara Asseyev and Alex Rose

1980
COAL MINER'S DAUGHTER .... Bernard Schwartz
THE ELEPHANT MAN .... Jonathan Sanger
ODINARY PEOPLE .... Ronald L. Schwary★★
RAGING BULL .... Irwin Winkler and Robert Chartoff
TESS .... Calude Berri and Timothy Burrill

1981
ATLANTIC CITY .... Denis Heroux and John Kemeny
CHARIOTS OF FIRE .... David Puttnam★★
ON GOLDEN POND .... Bruce Gilbert
RAIDERS OF THE LOST ARK .... Frank Marshall
REDS .... Warren Beatty

1982
E.T. THE EXTRA-TERRESTRIAL .... Steven Spielberg
.... and Kathleen Kennedy
GANDHI .... Richard Attenborough★★
MISSING .... Edward Lewis and Mildred Lewis
TOOTSIE .... Sydney Pollack and Dick Richards
THE VERDICT ... Richard D. Zanuck and David Brown

1983
THE BIG CHILL .... Michael Shamberg
THE DRESSER .... Peter Yates
THE RIGHT STUFF .... Irwin Winkler and
.... Robert Chartoff
TENDER MERCIES .... Philip S. Hobel
TERMS OF ENDEARMENT .... James L. Brooks★★

1984
AMADEUS .... Saul Zaentz★★
THE KILLING FIELDS .... David Puttnam
A PASSAGE TO INDIA .... John Brabourne and
.... Richard Goodwin
PLACES IN THE HEART .... Arlene Donovan
A SOLDIER'S STORY .... Norman Jewison,
.... Ronald L. Schwary and Patrick Palmer

1985
THE COLOR PURPLE .... Steven Spielberg,
.... Kathleen Kennedy, Frank Marshall
.... and Quincy Jones
KISS OF THE SPIDER WOMAN .... David Weisman
OUT OF AFRICA .... Sydney Pollack★★
PRIZZI'S HONOR .... John Foreman
WITNESS .... Edward S. Feldman

1986
CHILDREN OF A LESSER GOD .... Burt Sugarman
.... andPatrick Palmer
HANNAH AND HER SISTERS .... Robert Greenhut
THE MISSION ...... Fernando Ghia and David Puttnam
PLATOON .... Arnold Kopelson★★
A ROOM WITH A VIEW ....,. Ismail Merchant

1987
BROADCAST NEWS .... James L. Brooks
FATAL ATTRACTION .... Stanley R. Jaffe and
.... Sherry Lansing
HOPE AND GLORY .... John Boorman
THE LAST EMPEROR .... Jeremy Thomas★★
MOONSTRUCK .... Norman Jewison

1988
ACCIDENTAL TOURIST .... Lawrence Kasden,
.... Charles Okun and Michael Grillo
DANGEROUS LIASONS .... Norma Heymaand
.... Hank Moonjean
MISSISSIPPI BURNING .... Frederick Zollo and
.... Robert F. Colesberry
RAINMAN .... Mark Johnson★★
WORKING GIRL .... Douglas Wick

1989
BORN ON THE FOURTH OF JULY .... Oliver Stone
.... and A. Kitman Ho
DEAD POETS SOCIETY .... Steven Haft,
.... Tony Thomasand Paul Junger Witt
DRIVING MISS DAISY .... Lili Fini Zanuck
.... andRichard D. Zanuck★★
FIELD OF DREAMS .... Charles Gordon
.... andLawrence Gordon

ELLIOT ABBOTT
Business: c/o 20th Century-Fox, 10201 W. Pico Blvd., Los Angeles, CA, 90035, 213/203-3631

HOME OF THE BRAVE (FD) Cinecom, 1986, EP
AWAKENINGS Columbia, 1990, EP w/Arne L. Schmidt

STEVE ABBOTT
Business: Prominent Features Ltd., 68A Delancey St., London NW1 7RY, England, 01/284-1004

A FISH CALLED WANDA MGM/UA, 1988, EP w/John Cleese

NICK ABDO
Agent: David Shapira & Associates - Sherman Oaks, 818/906-9845
Contact: Directors Guild of America - Los Angeles, 213/289-2000

YOUNG DOCTORS IN LOVE 20th Century-Fox, 1982, AP w/Jeffrey Ganz
THE FLAMINGO KID 20th Century-Fox, 1984, AP
NOTHING IN COMMON Tri-Star, 1986, AP
OVERBOARD MGM, 1987, AP
BEACHES Buena Vista, 1988, CP

JIM ABRAHAMS
Agent: ICM - Los Angeles, 213/550-4000
Business: Abrahams Boy, Inc., 11777 San Vicente Blvd., Suite 600, Los Angeles, CA, 90049, 213/820-1942

AIRPLANE! Paramount, 1980, EP w/David Zucker & Jerry Zucker
THE NAKED GUN: FROM THE FILES OF POLICE SQUAD! Paramount, 1988, EP w/David Zucker & Jerry Zucker
CRY-BABY Universal, 1990, EP w/ Brian Grazer

MORT ABRAHAMS
GOODBYE, MR. CHIPS MGM, 1969, AP
THE CHAIRMAN 20th Century-Fox, 1969
BENEATH THE PLANET OF THE APES 20th Century-Fox, 1970, AP
TO FIND A MAN *THE BOY NEXT DOOR/SEX AND THE TEENAGER* Columbia, 1972, EP
LUTHER American Film Theatre, 1974, EP
THE MAN IN THE GLASS BOOTH American Film Theatre, 1975, EP
THE GREEK TYCOON Universal, 1978, EP w/Peter Howarth & Les Landau
THE HOLCROFT COVENANT Universal, 1985, EP
SEVEN HOURS TO JUDGMENT Trans World Entertainment, 1988

JACK ABRAMOFF
RED SCORPION Shapiro Glickenhaus, 1989

ROBERT ABRAMOFF
RED SCORPION Shapiro Glickenhaus, 1989, EP w/Paul Erickson & Daniel Sklar

GERALD W. ABRAMS
Business: King-Phoenix Entertainment, 310 N. San Vicente Blvd., #300, Los Angeles, CA, 90048, 213/657-7502

HEARTS OF FIRE Lorimar, 1988, EP w/Doug Harris

PETER ABRAMS
THE KILLING TIME New World, 1987, w/Robert L. Levy

RICHARD GILBERT ABRAMSON
(credit w/William E. McEuen)

PEE-WEE'S BIG ADVENTURE Warner Bros., 1985, w/Robert Shapiro*
BIG TOP PEE-WEE Paramount, 1988, EP
THE BIG PICTURE Columbia, 1989, EP

CATLIN ADAMS
Agent: Triad Artists, Inc. - Los Angeles, 213/556-2727
Contact: Directors Guild of America - Los Angeles, 213/289-2000

STICKY FINGERS Spectrafilm, 1988, w/Melanie Mayron

TONY ADAMS
Business: Blake Edwards Entertainment, 9336 W. Washington Blvd., Culver City, CA, 90230, 213/202-3375

RETURN OF THE PINK PANTHER United Artists, 1975, AP
THE PINK PANTHER STRIKES AGAIN United Artists, 1976, AP
REVENGE OF THE PINK PANTHER United Artists, 1978, EP
10 Orion/Warner Bros., 1979, w/Blake Edwards
S.O.B. Lorimar/Paramount, 1981, w/Blake Edwards
VICTOR/VICTORIA MGM/UA, 1982, w/Blake Edwards
TRAIL OF THE PINK PANTHER MGM/UA, 1982, w/Blake Edwards
CURSE OF THE PINK PANTHER MGM/UA, 1983, w/Blake Edwards
THE MAN WHO LOVED WOMEN Columbia, 1983, w/Blake Edwards
MICKI & MAUDE Columbia, 1984
A FINE MESS Columbia, 1986
THAT'S LIFE! Columbia, 1986
BLIND DATE Tri-Star, 1987
SUNSET Tri-Star, 1988
SKIN DEEP 20th Century-Fox, 1989

KEITH ADDIS
Business: Addis-Wechsler & Associates, 8444 Wilshire Blvd., 5th Floor, Beverly Hills, CA, 90211, 213/653-8867

BREATHLESS Orion, 1983, EP
THE BRIDE Columbia, 1985, EP

GARY ADELSON
Business: Adelson-Baumgarten Productions, 10000 W. Washington Blvd., Suite 4900, Culver City, CA, 90232, 213/287-2620

THE LAST STARFIGHTER Universal, 1984, w/Edward O. DeNault
THE BOY WHO COULD FLY Lorimar, 1986
IN THE MOOD Lorimar, 1987, w/Karen Mack

TAP Tri-Star, 1989, w/Richard Vane
HARD TO KILL Warner Bros., 1990, w/Joel Simon & Bill Todman, Jr.

MERV ADELSON
(credit w/Lee Rich)

TWILIGHT'S LAST GLEAMING Allied Artists, 1977*
THE CHOIRBOYS Universal, 1977
WHO IS KILLING THE GREAT CHEFS OF EUROPE? Warner Bros., 1978, EP
THE BIG RED ONE United Artists, 1980, EP

MICHELE ADER
Contact: Directors Guild of America - Los Angeles, 213/289-2000

TURNER & HOOCH Buena Vista, 1989, CP

MISHAAL KAMAL ADHAM
THE NEW ADVENTURES OF PIPPI LONGSTOCKING Columbia, 1988, EP

ALLEN ADLER
MAKING LOVE 20th Century-Fox, 1982, w/Daniel Melnick

GILBERT ADLER
BASIC TRAINING Moviestore, 1985, w/Otto Salamon
CERTAIN FURY New World, 1985

LOU ADLER
Business Manager: Dick Deblois, Ernst & Whinney, 1875 Century Park East, Los Angeles, CA, 90067, 213/553-2800
Contact: Directors Guild of America - Los Angeles, 213/289-2000

BREWSTER MCCLOUD MGM, 1970
THE ROCKY HORROR PICTURE SHOW 20th Century-Fox, 1976, EP
UP IN SMOKE Paramount, 1978, w/Lou Lombardo
SHOCK TREATMENT 20th Century-Fox, 1981, EP w/Michael White

ELEONORE ADLON
(credit w/Percy Adlon)
Contact: German Film & TV Academy, Pommernallee 1, 1 Berlin 19, 0311/302-6096

BAGDAD CAFE Island Pictures, 1988
ROSALIE GOES SHOPPING Four Seasons, 1990

PERCY ADLON
(credit w/Eleonore Adlon)
Contact: German Film & TV Academy, Pommernallee 1, 1 Berlin 19, 0311/302-6096

BAGDAD CAFE Island Pictures, 1988
ROSALIE GOES SHOPPING Four Seasons, 1990

STAFAN AHRENBERG
Business: Electric Pictures, 8539 Sunset Blvd., Suite 4-109, Los Angeles, CA, 90069, 213/856-2949

WAXWORK Vestron, 1988

JOSEPH L. AKERMAN
Business: Vidmark Entertainment, 2901 Ocean Park Blvd., Suite 123, Santa Monica, CA, 90405, 213/399-8877

ERNEST SAVES CHRISTMAS Buena Vista, 1988, EP w/ Martin Erlichman

MOUSTAPHA AKKAD
Business: Trancas International Films, Inc., 9229 Sunset Blvd., Suite 415, Los Angeles, CA, 90069, 213/657-7670

LION OF THE DESERT UFD, 1981
APPOINTMENT WITH DEATH Galaxy, 1985, EP
HALLOWEEN 4: THE RETURN OF MICHAEL MYERS Galaxy, 1988, EP
HALLOWEEN 5: THE REVENGE OF MICHAEL MYERS Galaxy, 1989, EP

NORMAN ALADJEM
FIREWALKER Cannon, 1986, EP w/Jeffrey M. Rosenbaum

RICHARD L. ALBERT
THE FORBIDDEN DANCE Columbia, 1990, w/Marc S. Fischer

ROBERT ALDEN
STREETWALKIN' Concorde, 1985
SATISFACTION 20th Century-Fox, 1988, EP w/Armyan Bernstein

WILLIAM ALDRICH
WHO IS KILLING THE GREAT CHEFS OF EUROPE? Warner Bros., 1978
...ALL THE MARBLES MGM/UA, 1981

JEAN-PIERRE ALESSANDRI
TO KILL A PRIEST Columbia, 1990, EP

JANE ALEXANDER
Business: Altion Productions, c/o Viacom Productions, 10 Universal City Plaza, Universal City, CA, 91608, 818/505-7619
Agent: William Morris Agency - Beverly Hills, 213/274-7451

SQUARE DANCE *HOME IS WHERE THE HEART IS* Island Pictures, 1987, EP w/Charles Haid

LES ALEXANDER
Business: Barry & Enright Productions, 201 Wilshire Blvd., 2nd Floor, Santa Monica, CA, 90404, 213/556-1000

NEXT OF KIN Warner Bros., 1989, w/Don Enright

MALIK B. ALI
HENRY: PORTRAIT OF A SERIAL KILLER Greycat Films, 1990, EP w/Waleed B. Ali

WALEED B. ALI
HENRY: PORTRAIT OF A SERIAL KILLER Greycat Films, 1990, EP w/Malik B. Ali

DEDE ALLEN
Agent: Bauer Benedek Agency - Los Angeles, 213/275-2421

REDS ★ Paramount, 1981, EP w/Simon Relph

IRWIN ALLEN
Business: Irwin Allen Productions, 4000 Warner Blvd., Burbank, CA, 91505, 818/954-3601
Agent: William Morris Agency - Beverly Hills, 213/274-7451

THE ANIMAL WORLD Warner Bros., 1956
THE STORY OF MANKIND Warner Bros., 1957
THE LOST WORLD 20th Century-Fox, 1960
VOYAGE TO THE BOTTOM OF THE SEA 20th Century-Fox, 1961
FIVE WEEKS IN A BALLOON 20th Century-Fox, 1962
THE POSEIDON ADVENTURE 20th Century-Fox, 1972
THE TOWERING INFERNO ★ 20th Century-Fox/ Warner Bros., 1974
THE SWARM Warner Bros., 1978
BEYOND THE POSEIDON ADVENTURE Warner Bros., 1979
WHEN TIME RAN OUT Warner Bros., 1980

JAY PRESSON ALLEN
Agent: ICM - New York, 212/556-5600

IT'S MY TURN Columbia, 1980, EP
JUST TELL ME WHAT YOU WANT Warner Bros., 1980, w/Sidney Lumet
PRINCE OF THE CITY Orion/Warner Bros., 1981, EP
DEATHTRAP Warner Bros., 1982, EP

LEWIS ALLEN
Business: Lewis Allen Productions, 1500 Broadway, New York, NY, 10036, 212/221-2400

FARENHEIT 451 Universal, 1967
FORTUNE AND MEN'S EYES MGM, 1971, w/Lester Persky
NEVER CRY WOLF Buena Vista, 1983, w/Jack Couffer & Joseph Strick
1918 Cinecom, 1985, EP w/Peter Newman
ON VALENTINE'S DAY Angelika, 1986, EP w/Lindsay Law, Ross E. Milloy & Peter Newman
SWIMMING TO CAMBODIA Cinecom, 1987, EP w/Ira Deutchman, Amir J. Malin & Peter Newman
O. C. AND STIGGS MGM/UA, 1987, EP
END OF THE LINE Orion Classics, 1987, w/Peter Newman
MISS FIRECRACKER Corsair, 1989, EP w/Ross E. Milloy
LORD OF THE FLIES Castle Rock/Columbia, 1990, EP w/Peter Newman

DAN ALLINGHAM
Contact: Directors Guild of America - Los Angeles, 213/289-2000

THE CHICKEN CHRONICLES Avco Embassy, 1977, AP
REUBEN, REUBEN 20th Century-Fox International Classics, 1983, AP
A BREED APART Orion, 1984, AP
INTO THE NIGHT Universal, 1985, EP
COMMUNION New Line Cinema, 1989, w/Philippe Mora & Whitley Strieber

BRIAN ALLMAN
Business: Evenstar Pictures, 8233 Manchester Ave., #5, Playa del Rey, CA, 90293, 213/306-0368

APARTMENT ZERO Skouras Pictures, 1989, CP

WILLIAM ALLYN
Business: McNeil-Allyn Films, 12031 Ventura Blvd., #3, Studio City, CA, 91604, 818/763-0771

RICH & FAMOUS MGM/UA, 1981
COUSINS Paramount, 1989

MELANIE J. ALSCHULER
PRETTY SMART New World, 1987, CP

HOWARD ALSTON
Business: Marstar Productions, 20th Century-Fox, 10201 W. Pico Blvd., Los Angeles, CA, 90035, 213/203-3970
Contact: Directors Guild of America - Los Angeles, 213/289-2000

CODE NAME: EMERALD MGM/UA, 1985, CP w/Jonathan Sanger
MASK Universal, 1985, CP

ROBERT ALTMAN
Business: Sand Castle 5 Productions, 502 Park Ave., Suite 156, New York, NY, 10022, 212/826-6641
Contact: Writers Guild of America - Los Angeles, 213/550-1000

THE DELINQUENTS United Artists, 1957
THE JAMES DEAN STORY Warner Bros., 1957, w/George W. George
NIGHTMARE IN CHICAGO Universal, 1964
MCCABE & MRS. MILLER Warner Bros., 1971, EP
CALIFORNIA SPLIT Columbia, 1974, w/Joseph Walsh
NASHVILLE ★ Paramount, 1975
BUFFALO BILL & THE INDIANS or SITTING BULL'S HISTORY LESSON United Artists, 1976
THE LATE SHOW Warner Bros., 1977
WELCOME TO L.A. United Artists, 1977
3 WOMEN 20th Century-Fox, 1977
A WEDDING 20th Century-Fox, 1978
REMEMBER MY NAME Columbia, 1978
QUINTET 20th Century-Fox, 1979
A PERFECT COUPLE 20th Century-Fox, 1979
RICH KIDS United Artists, 1979, EP
HEALTH 20th Century-Fox, 1980
STREAMERS United Artists Classics, 1983, w/Nick J. Mileti
SECRET HONOR Cinecom, 1985
O. C. AND STIGGS MGM/UA, 1987, w/Peter Newman

CARLOS ALVAREZ
WALKER Universal, 1987, LP

JENNIFER ALWARD
Business: King-Phoenix Entertainment, 310 N. San Vicente Blvd., #300, Los Angeles, CA, 90048, 213/657-7502

HEARTS OF FIRE Lorimar, 1988, w/Richard Marquand & Jennifer Miller

ROD AMATEAU
Agent: CAA - Los Angeles, 213/288-4545
Contact: Directors Guild of America - Los Angeles, 213/289-2000

THE GARBAGE PAIL KIDS MOVIE Atlantic Entertainment, 1987

YORAM BEN-AMI
(see Yoram BEN-Ami)

ALAN AMIEL
COMMANDO SQUAD Trans World Entertainment, 1987

GIDEON AMIR
SURVIVAL GAME Trans World Entertainment, 1987

TARAK BEN AMMAR
(see Tarak BEN Ammar)

ANDY ANDERSON
Agent: Triad Artists, Inc. - Los Angeles, 213/556-2727

POSITIVE I.D. Universal, 1987

BILL ANDERSON
THIRD MAN ON THE MOUNTAIN Buena Vista, 1959
SWISS FAMILY ROBINSON Buena Vista, 1960
THE SIGN OF ZORRO Buena Vista, 1960
MOON PILOT Buena Vista, 1962, CP
SAVAGE SAM Buena Vista, 1963, CP
A TIGER WALKS Buena Vista, 1964, CP
THE MOON-SPINNERS Buena Vista, 1964, CP
THE FIGHTING PRINCE OF DONEGAL Buena Vista, 1966, CP
THE ADVENTURES OF BULLWHIP GRIFFIN Buena Vista, 1967, CP
THE HAPPIEST MILLIONAIRE Buena Vista, 1967, CP
THE ONE & ONLY GENUINE ORIGINAL FAMILY BAND Buena Vista, 1968
SMITH! Buena Vista, 1969
THE COMPUTER WORE TENNIS SHOES Buena Vista, 1969
THE BAREFOOT EXECUTIVE Buena Vista, 1971
THE $1,000,000 DUCK Buena Vista, 1971
THE BISCUIT EATER Buena Vista, 1972
CHARLEY AND THE ANGEL Buena Vista, 1973
SUPERDAD Buena Vista, 1973
THE STRONGEST MAN IN THE WORLD Buena Vista, 1975
THE APPLE DUMPLING GANG Buena Vista, 1975
DR. SYN, ALIAS THE SCARECROW Buena Vista, 1975, CP
TREASURE OF MATECUMBE Buena Vista, 1976
THE SHAGGY D.A. Buena Vista, 1976

KURT ANDERSON
PARTY LINE SVS Films, 1988, w/Thomas S. Byrnes & William Webb

KEN ANNAKIN
Business Manager: Cappel, Coyne & Co., 2121 Avenue of the Stars, Los Angeles, CA, 90067, 213/553-0310
Agent: William Morris Agency - Beverly Hills, 213/274-7451

THE NEW ADVENTURES OF PIPPI LONGSTOCKING Columbia, 1988, CP

DEE ANTHONY
SGT. PEPPER'S LONELY HEARTS CLUB BAND Universal, 1978, EP

TONY ANTHONY
WILD ORCHID Triumph, 1990, w/Mark Damon

LOU ANTONIO
Agent: InterTalent Agency, Inc. - Los Angeles, 213/271-0600
Contact: DIrectors Guild of America - Los Angeles, 213/289-2000

MICKI & MAUDE Columbia, 1984, EP w/Jonathan D. Krane

MICHAEL APTED
Business: Michael Apted Film Company,1800 Century Park East, Suite 300, Los Angeles, CA, 90067, 213/203-0777
Agent: CAA - Beverly Hills, 213/288-4545

THE RIVER RAT Paramount, 1984, EP

SHIMON ARAMA
Business: Nova International Films, Inc., 1801 Century Park East, Suite 1400, Los Angeles, CA, 90067, 213/551-0240

TRIUMPH OF THE SPIRIT Triumph, 1989, w/Arnold Kopelson

PAUL ARATOW
SHEENA Columbia, 1984

BEN ARBEID
ENIGMA Embassy, 1983, w/Andre Pergament & Peter Shaw

MANUEL ARCE
CROSSOVER DREAMS Miramax, 1985

ALAN ARKIN
Agent: ICM - Los Angeles, 213/550-4000
Contact: Directors Guild of America - New York, 212/581-0370

THE IN-LAWS Warner Bros., 1979, EP

LOUIS S. ARKOFF
Business: Arkoff International Pictures, The Burbank Studios, Producers 2, Suite 1103A, Burbank, CA, 91505, 818/954-3091

UP THE CREEK Orion, 1984, EP w/Samuel Z. Arkoff

SAMUEL Z. ARKOFF
Business: Arkoff International Pictures, The Burbank Studios, Producers 2, Suite 1103A, Burbank, CA, 91505, 818/954-3091

THE PIT & THE PENDULUM American International, 1961, EP w/ James H. Nicholson
TALES OF TERROR American International, 1962, EP w/ James H. Nicholson
THE RAVEN American International, 1963, EP w/ James H. Nicholson
X — THE MAN WITH X-RAY EYES American International, 1963, EP w/ James H. Nicholson
BEACH PARTY American International, 1963
BIKINI BEACH American International, 1964, w/James H. Nicholson
MUSCLE BEACH PARTY American International, 1964, EP
BEACH BLANKET BINGO American International, 1965, w/ James H. Nicholson
WILD IN THE STREETS American International, 1968, w/James H. Nicholson

THE DUNWICH HORROR American International, 1970, w/James H. Nicholson
CRY OF THE BANSHEE American International, 1970
BLOODY MAMA American International, 1970, EP w/James H. Nicholson
DILLINGER American International, 1973, w/Lawrence Gordon
LITTLE CIGARS American International, 1973, EP
FOOD OF THE GODS American International, 1976
A MATTER OF TIME American International, 1976, EP w/Guilio Sbarigia
ONE SUMMER LOVE American International, 1976, EP
FUTUREWORLD American International, 1976, EP
THE FOOD OF THE GODS American International, 1976, EP
DRAGONFLY American International, 1976, EP
THE GREAT SCOUT & CATHOUSE THURSDAY American International, 1976, EP
EMPIRE OF THE ANTS American International, 1977, EP
OUR WINNING SEASON American International, 1978, EP
FORCE 10 FROM NAVARONE American International, 1978
CALIFORNIA DREAMING American International, 1979, EP
C.H.O.M.P.S. American International, 1979, EP
THE AMITYVILLE HORROR American International, 1979, EP
HOW TO BEAT THE HIGH COST OF LIVING American International, 1980, EP
DRESSED TO KILL Filmways, 1980, EP
UNDERGROUND ACES Filmways, 1981, EP
UP THE CREEK Orion, 1984, EP w/Louis S. Arkoff

ALICE ARLEN
Agent: ICM - New York, 212/556-5600

COOKIE Warner Bros., 1989, EP w/Nora Ephron & Susan Seidelman
A SHOCK TO THE SYSTEM Corsair, 1990, AP

RICHARD ARLOOK
AFTER MIDNIGHT MGM/UA, 1989, w/Peter Greene, Jim Wheat, & Ken Wheat

MARK ARMSTRONG
HELLRAISER New World, 1987, EP w/David Saunders & Christopher Webster

J. GORDON ARNOLD
THE RETURN OF THE SOLDIER European Classics, 1985, EP w/John Quested & Edward Simons

AMI ARTZI
PURGATORY New Star Entertainment, 1989
THE FORBIDDEN DANCE Columbia, 1990, EP w/Menahem Golan

WILLIAM ASHER
Agent: Leading Artists, Inc. - Beverly Hills, 213/858-1999
Contact: DIrectors Guild of America - Los Angeles, 213/289-2000

MOVERS & SHAKERS MGM/UA, 1985, w/Charles Grodin

HOWARD ASHMAN
Agent: William Morris Agency - New York, 212/586-5100

THE LITTLE MERMAID (AF) Buena Vista, 1989, w/John Musker

TAMARA ASSEYEV
Business: Tamara Asseyev Productions, 10 Universal City Plaza, Universal City, CA, 91608, 818/505-7566

THE WILD RACERS American International, 1968, AP
PADDY Allied Artists, 1970
THE AROUSERS *SWEET KILL* New World, 1970
DRIVE-IN Columbia, 1976, w/Alex Rose
I WANNA HOLD YOUR HAND Universal, 1978, w/Alex Rose
BIG WEDNESDAY Warner Bros., 1978, EP w/Alex Rose
NORMA RAE ★ 20th Century-Fox, 1979, w/Alex Rose & Martin Ritt

OBIDIO G. ASSONITIS
Business: Cannon Productions, 5757 Wilshire Blvd., Suite 721, Los Angeles, CA, 90036, 213/965-0901

BEYOND THE DOOR FVI, 1975
PIRANHA II *THE SPAWNING* Saturn International, 1983, EP
CHOKE CANYON United Films, 1986
IRON WARRIOR Trans World Entertainment, 1987 (under the pseudonym "Sam Sill")
THE CURSE Trans World Entertainment, 1987

NAIM ATTALLAH
Business: Namara Films, Ltd., 45 Poland St., London W1V 4AV, England

BRIMSTONE AND TREACLE United Artists Classics, 1982, EP

RICHARD ATTENBOROUGH
Business: Beaver Lodge, Richmond Green, Surrey, England, 01/940-7234
Agent: CAA - Beverly Hills, 213/288-4545

THE L-SHAPED ROOM Columbia, 1963, w/Sir John Woolf
GANDHI ★★ Columbia, 1982
CRY FREEDOM Universal, 1987

GABRIEL AUER
SALAAM BOMBAY! Cinecom, 1988, EP w/Michael Nozik, Cherie Rodgers & Anil Tejani

JEFFREY AUERBACH
Business: Blake Edwards Entertainment, 9336 W. Washington Blvd., Culver City, CA, 90230, 213/202-3375

JUDGMENT IN BERLIN New Line Cinema, 1988, EP w/William R. Greenblatt & Martin Sheen

BOB AUGUR
Attorney: Frank Gruber - Los Angeles, 213/274-5638

THE TROUBLE WITH DICK Fever Dream Production Company, 1989, w/Gary Walkow

JOE AUGUSTYN
Business: Paragon Arts International, 6777 Hollywood Blvd., Suite 700, Hollywood, CA, 90028, 213/465-5355

NIGHT OF THE DEMONS International Film Marketing, 1988

CARLOS AURED
ALIEN PREDATOR Trans World Entertainment, 1987, w/Deran Sarafian

BUD AUSTIN
MIKEY & NICKY Paramount, 1976, EP
JOHNNY DANGEROUSLY 20th Century-Fox, EP w/Harry Colomby

FRANKIE AVALON
BACK TO THE BEACH Paramount, 1987, EP w/Annette Funicello

JOHN G. AVILDSEN
Agent: Bauer Benedek Agency - Los Angeles, 213/275-2421

LEAN ON ME Warner Bros., 1989, EP

JON AVNET
Business: Avnet-Kerner Company, 505 N. Robertson Blvd., Los Angeles, CA, 90048, 213/271-7408

COAST TO COAST Paramount, 1980, w/Steve Tisch
RISKY BUSINESS The Geffen Company/ Warner Bros., 1983, w/Steve Tisch
DEAL OF THE CENTURY Warner Bros., 1983, EP w/Paul Brickman & Steve Tisch
LESS THAN ZERO 20th Century-Fox, 1987, w/Jordan Kerner
MEN DON'T LEAVE The Geffen Company/ Warner Bros., 1990

IRVING AXELRAD
THE COLOR OF MONEY Buena Vista, 1986, w/Barbara DeFina

DAVID R. AXELROD
WINNERS TAKE ALL Apollo, 1987, EP

DAN AYKROYD
Attorney: Alan Hergott - Los Angeles, 213/859-6800
Agent: CAA - Beverly Hills, 213/288-4545

ONE MORE SATURDAY NIGHT Columbia, 1986, EP

GERALD AYRES
Agent: Broder-Kurland-Webb-Uffner Agency - Los Angeles, 213/656-9262

CISCO PIKE Columbia, 1972
THE LAST DETAIL Columbia, 1973
FOXES United Artists, 1980, w/David Puttnam

IRVING AZOFF
Business: Azoff Entertainment, 345 N. Maple Dr., Suite 205, Beverly Hills, CA, 90210, 213/288-5500

URBAN COWBOY Paramount, 1980, w/Robert Evans
FAST TIMES AT RIDGEMONT HIGH Universal, 1982, w/Art Linson

B

BETH B
SALVATION! Circle Releasing, 1987, w/Michael Shamberg

DANIEL F. BACANER
Business: Fremont II, 8489 W. 3rd St., Los Angeles, CA, 90048, 213/852-0934

BLOOD SIMPLE Circle Releasing Corporation, 1985, EP
SCARED STIFF International Film Marketing, 1987

STEVEN BACH
MR. BILLION 20th Century-Fox, 1976, w/Ken Friedman
BUTCH & SUNDANCE: THE EARLY DAYS 20th Century-Fox, 1979, w/Gabriel Katzka

LAWRENCE P. BACHMANN
WHOSE LIFE IS IT ANYWAY? MGM, 1981

DORO BACHRACH
Business: 250 W. 57th St., #1905, New York, NY,10019, 212/582-5689

DIRTY DANCING Vestron, 1987, AP
LOVE HURTS Tri-Star, 1990

JOHN D. BACKE
Business: Tomorrow Entertainment, 327 East 50th St., New York, NY,10022, 212/355-7737

BRENDA STARR New World, 1987, EP
A KILLING AFFAIR Hemdale, 1988, EP w/Myron A. Hyman

PETER BACSO
LILY IN LOVE New Line Cinema, 1985, EP w/Robert Halmi Jr.

BILL BADALATO
Business: Keith Barish Productions, 8285 Sunset Blvd., #8, Hollywood, CA, 90046, 213/650-7086
Agent: Triad Artists, Inc., - Los Angeles, 213/556-2727

BANG THE DRUM SLOWLY Paramount, 1973, AP
TOP GUN Paramount, 1986, EP
WEEDS DEG, 1987
1969 Atlantic Entertainment, 1988, w/Daniel Grodnik

SUE BADEN-POWELL
CHATTAHOOCHEE Hemdale, 1990, CP

JOHN BADHAM
Business: Badham-Cohen Group, 100 Universal City Plaza, Universal City, CA, 91608, 818/777-3166
Agent: Triad Artists, Inc. - Los Angeles, 213/556-2727

STAKEOUT Buena Vista, 1987, EP
DISORGANIZED CRIME Buena Vista, 1989, EP w/Rob Cohen
BIRD ON A WIRE Universal, 1990, w/Rob Cohen

THOMAS BAER
Business: Orion Pictures, 1888 Century Park East, Los Angeles, CA, 90067, 213/282-2715

LOST ANGELS Orion, 1989, w/Howard Rosenman

JERRY A. BAERWITZ
Contact: Directors Guild of America - Los Angeles, 213/289-2000

FRIGHT NIGHT Columbia, 1985, AP
STEWARDESS SCHOOL Columbia, 1987, CP w/Michael Kane
LISTEN TO ME WEG/Columbia, 1989, CP
COUPE DE VILLE Universal, 1990, AP

PATRICK BAILEY
Agent: Smith-Freedman & Associates - Beverly Hills, 213/852-4777
Contact: Directors Guild of America - Los Angeles, 213/289-2000

SPACECAMP 20th Century-Fox, 1986, w/Walter Coblenz

ROY BAIRD
WOMEN IN LOVE United Artists, 1969, AP
THE DEVILS Warner Bros., 1971, AP
THE MUSIC LOVERS United Artists, 1971, EP
THAT'LL BE THE DAY EMI, 1974, EP
THE LAST DAYS OF MAN ON EARTH *THE FINAL PROGRAMME* New World, 1974, EP w/Michael Moorcock & David Puttnam
MAHLER Mayfair, 1974
LISZTOMANIA Warner Bros., 1975, w/David Puttnam
STARDUST Columbia, 1975, EP
QUADROPHENIA World Northal, 1979, w/Bill Curbishley
McVICAR Crown International, 1982, w/Bill Curbishley & Roger Daltrey

RALPH BAKSHI
Business Manager: Howard Bernstein, Kaufman & Bernstein, 1900 Avenue of the Stars, Suite 2270, Los Angeles, CA, 90067, 213/277-1900
Business: Ralph Bakshi Productions, 8125 Lankershim Blvd., North Hollywood, CA, 91605

WIZARDS (AF) 20th Century- Fox, 1977
AMERICAN POP (AF) Paramount, 1981, w/Martin Ransohoff
HEY GOOD LOOKIN' (AF) Warner Bros., 1982
FIRE AND ICE (AF) 20th Century-Fox, 1983, w/Frank Frazetta

HOWARD L. BALDWIN
Business: Indian Neck Productions, 202 N. Canon Dr., 2nd Floor, Beverly Hills, CA, 90210, 213/276-7067

BILLY GALVIN Vestron, 1986, EP w/Stuart Benjamin, Lindsay Law & William Minot
FROM THE HIP DEG, 1987, EP w/William Minot & Brian Russell
SPELLBINDER MGM/UA, 1988, EP w/Richard Cohen

HAIG BALIAN
THE GIRL WITH THE RED HAIR United Artists Classics, 1983, w/Chris Brouwer

DAVID BALL
CREEPSHOW 2 New World, 1987

MARK BALSAM
MATEWAN Cinecom, 1987, EP w/Amir J. Malin & Jerry Silva

MICHAEL BALSON
BAT 21 Tri-Star, 1988, w/David Fisher & Gary A. Neill

ALBERT BAND
Business: Full Moon Entertainment, 9200 Sunset Blvd., #530, Los Angeles, CA, 90069, 213/859-1040

LITTLE CIGARS American International, 1973
TERRORVISION Empire, 1986
TROLL Empire, 1986
GHOST WARRIOR Empire, 1986, EP w/Efrem Harkham, Uri Harkham & Arthur H. Maslansky

CHARLES BAND
Business: Full Moon Entertainment, 9200 Sunset Blvd., #530, Los Angeles, CA, 90069, 213/859-1040

PARASITE Embassy, 1982
FUTURE COP Empire, 1985
THE DUNGEONMASTER Empire, 1985
FROM BEYOND Empire, 1986, EP
ZONE TROOPERS Empire, 1986, EP
TERRORVISION Empire, 1986, EP
ELIMINATORS Empire, 1986
GHOST WARRIOR Empire, 1986
ENEMY TERRITORY Empire, 1987, EP
DOLLS Empire, 1987, EP
PRISON Empire, 1988, EP
DEADLY WEAPON Empire, 1988, EP
GHOST TOWN Trans World Entertainment, 1988, EP
BUY & CELL Empire, 1989, EP

MIRRA BANK
ENORMOUS CHANGES AT THE LAST MINUTE TC Films International, 1985

TOM BARAD
Business: Paramount Pictures, 5555 Melrose Ave., Hollywood, CA, 90035, 213/468-5000

CRAZY PEOPLE Paramount, 1990

GARY BARBER
Business: Morgan Creek Productions, 1875 Century Park East, Suite 200, Los Angeles, CA, 90067, 213/284-8884

MIDNIGHT CROSSING Vestron, 1988, EP w/Gregory Cascante, Dan Ireland & Wanda S. Rayle
COMMUNION New Line Cinema, 1989, EP w/Paul Redshaw

JOSEPH BARBERA
Business: Hanna-Barbera Productions, Inc., 3400 Cahuenga Blvd. West, Los Angeles, CA, 90068, 213/851-5000

C.H.O.M.P.S. American International, 1979

BEN BARENHOLTZ
Business: Circle Releasing, 239 1/2 East 32nd St., New York, NY, 10016, 212/686-0822

MILLER'S CROSSING 20th Century-Fox, 1990, EP

KEITH BARISH
Business: Keith Barish Productions, 8285 Sunset Blvd., #8, Hollywood, CA, 90046, 213/650-7086

ENDLESS LOVE Universal, 1981, EP
SOPHIE'S CHOICE Universal, 1982, w/Alan J. Pakula
MISUNDERSTOOD MGM/UA, 1984, EP w/Craig Baumgarten
9 1/2 WEEKS MGM/UA, 1986, EP w/Frank Konigsberg & F. Richard Northcott
BIG TROUBLE IN LITTLE CHINA 20th Century-Fox, 1986, EP w/Paul Monash
LIGHT OF DAY Tri-Star, 1987, w/Rob Cohen
THE MONSTER SQUAD Tri-Star, 1987, EP w/Rob Cohen & Peter Hyams
THE RUNNING MAN Tri-Star, 1987, EP w/Rob Cohen
IRONWEED Tri-Star, 1987, w/Marcia Nasatir
THE SERPENT & THE RAINBOW Universal, 1988, EP w/Rob Cohen
HER ALIBI Warner Bros., 1989

MOSHE BARKAT
(co-producers: Moshe Diamant & Sunil R. Shah)
Business: Trans World Entertainment, 3330 W. Cahuenga Blvd., Suite 500, Los Angeles, CA, 90058, 213/969-2800

PRAY FOR DEATH American Distribution Group, 1986, EP
RAGE OF HONOR Trans World Entertainment, 1987, EP

CLIVE BARKER
Agent: CAA - Beverly Hills, 213/288-4545

HELLBOUND: HELLRAISER II New World, 1988, EP w/Christopher Webster

LYNN BARKER
VICIOUS SVS Films, 1988, LP

JOHN BARNETT
STRANGE BEHAVIOR World Northal, 1981, w/Antony I. Ginnane
WILD HORSES Satori, 1984

ALAN BARNETTE
OFF LIMITS 20th Century-Fox, 1988

EARL BARRET
Business Manager: Jamner, Pariser & Meschures - Los Angeles, 213/652-0222

SEE NO EVIL, HEAR NO EVIL Tri-Star, 1989, EP w/Burtt Harris & Arne Sultan

BRUNO BARRETO
Business: Producoes Cinematograficas L.C. Barreto Ltd., Rua Visconde De Caravelas, 28-Botafogos, Rio de Janeiro, Brazil, 021/286-7186

WHERE THE RIVER RUNS BLACK MGM/UA, 1986, LP w/Flavio R. Tambellini

ERIC BARRETT
I'M GONNA GIT YOU SUCKA MGM/UA, 1989, CP w/Tamara Rawitt

GEORGE BARRIE
THE CLASS OF MISS MacMICHAEL Brut Productions, 1979, EP

LISA BARSAMIAN
FRIDAY THE 13TH PART 2 Paramount, 1981, EP w/Tom Gruenberg
FRIDAY THE 13TH PART 3 Paramount, 1982, EP
OFF THE WALL Jensen Farley Pictures, 1983, EP
MEATBALLS PART II Tri-Star, EP

PETER BART
Business: *Variety*, 475 Park Ave. South, New York, NY, 10016, 212/779-1100

ISLANDS IN THE STREAM Paramount, 1977, w/Max Palevsky
REVENGE OF THE NERDS 20th Century-Fox, 1984, EP w/David Obst
YOUNGBLOOD MGM/UA, 1986, w/Patrick C. Wells
REVENGE OF THE NERDS II 20th Century-Fox, 1987, w/Robert W. Cort & Ted Field

HALL BARTLETT
Business: Hall Bartlett Films, Inc., 9200 Sunset Blvd., Suite 908, Los Angeles, CA, 90069, 213/278-8883

CHANGES Cinerama Releasing Corporation, 1969
THE WILD PACK American International, 1972
JONATHAN LIVINGSTON SEAGULL Paramount, 1973
THE CHILDREN OF SANCHEZ Lone-Star, 1978

GEOF BARTZ
STRIPPER (FD) 20th Century-Fox, 1986, w/Melvyn J. Estrin & Jerome Gary

HAL BARWOOD
Contact: DGA - Los Angeles, 213/289-2000
Agent: ICM - Los Angeles, 213/550-4000

CORVETTE SUMMER MGM/UA, 1978
DRAGONSLAYER Paramount, 1981

KENT BATEMAN
Agent: ICM - Los Angeles, 213/550-4000
Contact: Directors Guild of America - Los Angeles, 213/289-2000

TEEN WOLF TOO Atlantic Entertainment, 1987

CAROL BAUM
Business: Sandollar Productions, 8730 Sunset Blvd., Penthouse, Los Angeles, CA, 90069, 213/659-5933

DEAD RINGERS 20th Century-Fox, 1988, EP w/Sylvio Tabet
JACKNIFE Cineplex Odeon, 1989, w/Robert Schaffel
GROSS ANATOMY Buena Vista, 1989, EP w/Sandy Gallin

FRED BAUM
UP THE CREEK Orion, 1984, CP

CRAIG BAUMGARTEN

Business: Adelson-Baumgarten Productions, 10000 W. Washington Blvd., Suite 4900, Culver City, CA, 90232, 213/287-2620

MISUNDERSTOOD MGM/UA, 1984, EP w/Keith Barish

ROBERT BAYLIS

AGENCY Jensen Farley, 1981, AP
DEATH HUNT 20th Century-Fox, 1981, AP
SILENCE OF THE NORTH Universal, 1982, CP
LOVE SONGS Spectrafilm, 1986, w/Elie Chouraqui
MARIA CHAPDELAINE Moviestore, 1986, w/Murray Shostak

PETER BEALE

Business: Showscan Film Corporation, 3939 Landmark St., Culver City, CA, 90230, 213/558-0150

FIVE DAYS ONE SUMMER Warner Bros., 1982, EP

RAY BEATTIE

YOUNG EINSTEIN Warner Bros., 1989, EP w/Graham Burke

WARREN BEATTY

Business Manager: Traubner & Flynn, 2029 Century Park East, Los Angeles, CA, 90067
Contact: Directors Guild of America - Los Angeles, 213/289-2000

BONNIE & CLYDE ★ Warner Bros., 1967
SHAMPOO Columbia, 1975
HEAVEN CAN WAIT ★ Paramount, 1978
REDS ★ Paramount, 1981
ISHTAR Columbia, 1987
DICK TRACY Buena Vista, 1990

JOSEPH BEAUBIEN

ATLANTIC CITY ★ Paramount, 1981, EP w/Gabriel Boustani

WILLIAM BEAUDINE, JR.

Contact: Directors Guild of America - Los Angeles, 213/289-2000

COUNTRY Buena Vista, 1984, LP

STANLEY BECK

STRAIGHT TIME Warner Bros., 1978, w/Tim Zinnemann
DEATH VALLEY Universal, 1982, CP w/Richard Rothstein
MAN, WOMAN & CHILD Paramount, 1983, EP

RICHARD BECKER

BAD INFLUENCE Triumph, 1990, EP w/ Morrie Eisenman

BARRY BECKERMAN

Contact: Writers Guild of America - Beverly Hills, 213/550-1000

RED DAWN MGM/UA, 1984, w/Buzz Feitshans

SIDNEY BECKERMAN

LAST SUMMER Allied Artists, 1969, w/Alfred W. Crown
MARLOWE MGM, 1969, w/Gabriel Katzka
KELLY'S HEROES MGM, 1970, w/Gabriel Katzka
JOE KIDD Universal, 1972
MARATHON MAN Paramount, 1976, w/Robert Evans
THE RIVER NIGER Cine Artists, 1976, w/Isaac L. Jones
SIDNEY SHELDON'S BLOODLINE Paramount, 1979, w/David V. Picker
SERIAL Paramount, 1980
BLOOD BEACH Jerry Gross Organization, 1981, EP
A STRANGER IS WATCHING MGM/UA, 1982
THE ADVENTURES OF BUCKAROO BANZAI ACROSS THE EIGHTH DIMENSION 20th Century-Fox, 1984, EP
RED DAWN MGM/UA, 1984, EP
INSIDE OUT Hemdale, 1986
THE SICILIAN 20th Century-Fox, 1987, EP

RON BECKMAN

Business: Apollo Pictures, 6071 Bristol Parkway, Culver City, CA, 90230, 213/568-8282

THE CHALLENGE Embassy, 1982, w/Robert L. Rosen
CAN'T BUY ME LOVE Buena Vista, 1987, EP w/Jere Henshaw

DAVID BEGELMAN

Business: Gladden Entertainment, 10100 Santa Monica Blvd., #600, Los Angeles, CA, 90067, 213/282-7500

WHOLLY MOSES! Columbia, 1980

JEFF BEGUN

HARDBODIES Columbia, 1984, w/Ken Dalton
PRETTY SMART New World, 1987, w/Ken Solomon

DON BEHRNS

Contact: Directors Guild of America - Los Angeles, 213/289-2000

FRIDAY THE 13TH, PART VI: JASON LIVES Paramount, 1986

HARRY BELAFONTE

Agent: Triad Artists, Inc. - Los Angeles, 213/556-2727

BEAT STREET Orion, 1984, w/David V. Picker

GRAHAM BELIN

UNION CITY Kinesis, 1980

ALAN BELKIN

Business: Alan Belkin Productions, Inc., 720 N. Seward St., Hollywood, CA, 90038, 213/465-9815
Contact: Directors Guild of America - Los Angeles, 213/289-2000

A DIFFERENT STORY Avco Embassy, 1978
A FORCE OF ONE American Cinema, 1980
THE OCTAGON American Cinema, 1980, EP w/Michael C. Leone
CHARLIE CHAN & THE CURSE OF THE DRAGON QUEEN American Cinema, 1981, EP w/Michael C. Leone
THAT WAS THEN...THIS IS NOW Paramount, 1985, EP w/Brandon K. Phillips
GETTING EVEN American Distribution Group, 1986, EP

TOM BELLAGIO

CHAMPIONS FOREVER (FD) Ion, 1989, EP w/Hollister Whitworth

DAVINA BELLING
(credit w/Clive Parsons)
Business: Film & General Productions, Ltd., 10 Pembridge Place, London W2 4XB, England, 01/221-1141

INSERTS United Artists, 1976
SCUM Berwick Street Films, 1979
THAT SUMMER Columbia, 1979
BREAKING GLASS Paramount, 1980
BRITTANIA HOSPITAL United Artists Classics, 1982
GREGORY'S GIRL Samuel Goldwyn Company, 1982
COMFORT AND JOY Universal, 1984

DONALD BELLISARIO
Business: Belisarius Productions, 100 Universal City Plaza, Universal City, CA, 91608, 818/777-3381
Agent: Broder/Kurland/Webb/Uffner - Los Angeles, 213/274-8921

LAST RITES MGM/UA, 1988, w/Patrick McCormick

HERCULES BELLVILLE
STRANGERS KISS Orion Classics, 1984, CP

HENRI BELOLO
CAN'T STOP THE MUSIC AFD, 1980, w/Allan Carr & Jacques Morali

JERRY BELSON
Agent: CAA - Beverly Hills, 213/288-4545
Contact: Directors Guild of America - Los Angeles, 213/289-2000

HOW SWEET IT IS! National General, 1968, w/Garry Marshall
STUDENT BODIES Paramount, 1981, EP w/Harvey Miller
FOR KEEPS Tri-Star, 1988, w/Walter Coblenz

LESLIE BELZBERG
INTO THE NIGHT Universal, 1985, AP
SPIES LIKE US Warner Bros., 1985, AP
COMING TO AMERICA Paramount, 1988, EP w/Mark Lipsky

YORAM BEN-AMI
Business: Triumph Pictures, Inc., 6111 Shirley Ave., Tarzana, CA, 91356, 818/708-1384
Agent: Gorfaine/Schwartz/Roberts - Los Angeles, 213/858-1144

LONE WOLF MCQUADE Orion, 1982
SHEENA Columbia, 1984, EP

TARAK BEN AMMAR
LA TRAVIATA Universal Classics, 1983
MISUNDERSTOOD MGM/UA, 1984
PIRATES Cannon, 1986

MICHAEL BENDER
BEETLEJUICE Warner Bros., 1988, w/Richard Hashimoto & Larry Wilson

BILL BENENSON
Business: Bill Benenson Productions, 321 Hampton Dr., Suite 209, Venice, CA, 90291, 213/399-7793

BOULEVARD NIGHTS Warner Bros., 1979
THE LIGHTSHIP Castle Hill, 1986, w/Moritz Borman

STUART BENJAMIN
Business: New Visions Entertainment Corporation, 5750 Wilshire Blvd., 6th Floor, Los Angeles, CA, 90036, 213/965-2500

BILLY GALVIN Vestron, 1986, EP w/Howard L. Baldwin, Lindsay Law & William Minot
LA BAMBA Columbia, 1987, EP
EVERYBODY'S ALL-AMERICAN Warner Bros., 1988, EP
ROOFTOPS New Visions, 1989, EP w/Taylor Hackford

HARRY BENN
THE BOY FRIEND MGM, 1971, AP
SAVAGE MESSIAH MGM, 1972, AP
TOMMY Columbia, 1975, AP
INSERTS United Artists, 1976, AP
THE RAZOR'S EDGE Columbia, 1984, w/Robert P. Marcucci
YOUNG SHERLOCK HOLMES Paramount, 1985, AP
GOOD MORNING, VIETNAM Buena Vista, 1987, CP w/Ben Moses

BILL BENNETT
Agent: William Morris Agency - Beverly Hills, 213/274-7451

BACKLASH Samuel Goldwyn Company, 1987

HARVE BENNETT
Business: Paramount Pictures, 5555 Melrose Ave., Los Angeles, CA, 90038, 213/468-5796
Attorney: Ziffren, Brittenham & Branca - Los Angeles, 213/552-3388

STAR TREK II: THE WRATH OF KHAN Paramount, 1982, EP
STAR TREK III: THE SEARCH FOR SPOCK Paramount, 1984
STAR TREK IV: THE VOYAGE HOME Paramount, 1986
STAR TREK V: THE FINAL FRONTIER Paramount, 1989

JOHN B. BENNETT
TULIPS Avco Embassy, 1981, EP w/Harold Greenberg

STEPHANIE BENNETT
Business: Delilah Pictures, c/o The Mount Company, 3723 W. Olive Ave., Burbank, CA, 91505, 818/846-1500

THE COMPLEAT BEATLES (FD) TeleCulture, 1984, w/Patrick Montgomery
CHUCK BERRY: HAIL! HAIL! ROCK 'N' ROLL! (FD) Universal, 1987, w/Chuck Berry

GRAHAM BENSON
QUEEN OF HEARTS Cinecom, 1989, EP

JAY BENSON
THE STEPFATHER New Century/Vista, 1987

MARK BENTLEY
RESTLESS NATIVES Orion Classics, 1986, EP

KATE BENTON
SPELLBINDER MGM/UA, 1988, CP w/Steve Berman, Todd Black & Mickey Borofsky

ROBERT BENTON
Business: 110 W. 57th St., 5th Floor, New York, NY, 10019, 212/247-5652
Agent: Sam Cohn, ICM - New York, 212/556-5600

THE HOUSE ON CARROLL STREET Orion, 1988, EP w/Arlene Donovan

OBIE BENZ
HEAVY PETTING (FD) Skouras Pictures, 1989

BENJAMIN BERG
LATINO Cinecom, 1986

DICK BERG
Business: Stonehenge Productions, 10202 W. Washington Blvd., Culver City, CA, 90232, 213/280-7350
Contact: Writers Guild of America - Los Angeles, 213/550-1000

SHOOT Avco Embassy, 1976, EP
FRESH HORSES WEG/Columbia, 1988

ANDREW BERGMAN
Business: Lobell-Bergman Productions, 9336 W. Washington Blvd., Culver City, CA, 90230, 213/202-3362
Agent: ICM - New York, 212/556-5600

CHANCES ARE Tri-Star, 1989, EP w/Neil Machlis

JULIE BERGMAN
MAJOR LEAGUE Paramount, 1989, CP

MEL BERGMAN
SURVIVAL RUN Film Ventures International, 1980, EP w/Ruben Broido
REMO WILLIAMS: THE ADVENTURE BEGINS... Orion, 1985, EP w/Dick Clark

ELEANOR BERGSTEIN
Agent: CAA - Beverly Hills, 213/288-4545

DIRTY DANCING Vestron, 1987, CP

ROGER BERLIND
BEYOND THERAPY New World, 1987, EP

GERALD BERMAN
THE GUEST RM Productions, 1984

STEVEN E. BERMAN
Business: Indian Neck Productions, 202 N. Canon Dr., 2nd Floor, Beverly Hills, CA, 90210, 213/276-7067

SPELLBINDER MGM/UA, 1988, CP w/Kate Benton, Todd Black, & Mickey Borofsky

JUDD BERNARD
Agent: CAA - Beverly Hills, 213/288-4545

DOUBLE TROUBLE MGM, 1967, w/ Irwin Winkler
POINT BLANK MGM, 1967, w/Robert Chartoff
BLUE Paramount, 1968, w/Irwin Winkler
ENTER THE NINJA Cannon, 1981, w/Yoram Globus

SAM BERNARD
Agent: The Gage Group - Los Angeles, 213/859-8777

RAD Tri-Star, 1986, CP

YANNICK BERNARD
BABAR: THE MOVIE New Line Cinema, 1989, EP w/Pierre Bertrand-Jaume & Stephane Sperry

BARRY BERNARDI
Agent: The Gersh Agency - Beverly Hills, 213/274-6611
Contact: Directors Guild of America - Los Angeles, 213/289-2000

ESCAPE FROM NEW YORK Avco Embassy, 1981, AP
CHRISTINE Columbia, 1983, AP
STARMAN Columbia, 1984, CP
WANTED DEAD OR ALIVE New World, 1986, CP
POLTERGEIST III MGM/UA, 1988

GUSTAVE BERNE
PHANTOM OF THE PARADISE 20th Century-Fox, 1974, EP

FRED BERNER
Business: Berner/Schlamme Productions, 1619 Broadway, 9th Floor, New York, NY, 10019, 212/603-0609

MISS FIRECRACKER Corsair, 1989

HARVEY BERNHARD
Business: Bernhard-Robson Entertainment, 8439 Sunset Blvd., #308, Los Angeles, CA, 90069, 213/654-4500

THE MACK Cinerama Releasing Corporation, 1973
THE OMEN 20th Century-Fox, 1976
DAMIEN - OMEN II 20th Century-Fox, 1978
THE FINAL CONFLICT 20th Century-Fox, 1981
THE BEAST WITHIN MGM/UA, 1982, w/Gabriel Katzka
LADYHAWKE Warner Bros., 1985, EP
THE GOONIES Warner Bros., 1985, w/Richard Donner
THE LOST BOYS Warner Bros., 1987

STEVEN BERNHARDT
Contact: Directors Guild of America - Los Angeles, 213/289-2000

GET TO KNOW YOUR RABBIT Warner Bros., 1972, w/Paul Gaer
THE FUNHOUSE Universal, 1981, w/Derek Power
TEMPEST Columbia, 1982, CP w/Pato Guzman

ALAIN BERNHEIM
Contact: Alma Productions, 9219 Cordell Drive, Los Angeles, CA, 90069, 213/550-7603

BUDDY BUDDY MGM, 1981, EP
YES, GIORGIO MGM, 1982, EP w/Herbert H. Breslin
RACING WITH THE MOON Paramount, 1984, w/John Kohn

HARMON BERNS
NATIONAL LAMPOON'S CLASS REUNION 20th Century-Fox, 1982, w/Peter V. Herald

ARMYAN BERNSTEIN
Agent: CAA - Beverly Hills, 213/288-4545

ONE FROM THE HEART Columbia, 1982, CP
SATISFACTION 20th Century-Fox, 1988, EP w/Robert Alden

JACK B. BERNSTEIN
Business: MGM Pictures, 10000 W. Washington Blvd., Culver City, CA, 90232, 213/280-6000
Agent: The Gersh Agency - Beverly Hills, 213/274-6611

THE FURY 20th Century-Fox, 1978, AP
NORTH DALLAS FORTY Paramount, 1979, EP
UNFAITHFULLY YOURS 20th Century-Fox, 1984, AP

JAY BERNSTEIN
Business: Jay Bernstein Productions, P.O. Box 1148, Beverly Hills, CA, 90213, 818/954-3791

SUNBURN Paramount, 1979, EP w/John Quested
NOTHING PERSONAL American International, 1980, EP w/Alan Hamel & Norman Hirschfield

JONATHAN BERNSTEIN
Contact: Directors Guild of America - Los Angeles, 213/289-2000

THE CHOSEN 20th Century-Fox International Classics, 1982
TESTAMENT Paramount, 1983, w/Lynne Littman
ONE MORE SATURDAY NIGHT Columbia, 1986, w/Robert Kosberg & Tova Laiter

CHUCK BERRY
Agent: William Morris Agency - Beverly Hills, 213/274-7451

CHUCK BERRY: HAIL! HAIL! ROCK 'N' ROLL! (FD) Universal, 1987, w/Stephanie Bennett

PIERRE BERTRAND-JAUME
BABAR: THE MOVIE (AF) New Line Cinema, 1989, EP w/Yannick Bernard & Stephane Sperry

ROBERTO BESSI
Business: Trans World Entertainment, 3330 Cahuenga Blvd. West, Suite 500, Los Angeles, CA, 90068, 213/969-2800

WARRIORS OF THE LOST WORLD Vista, 1985, w/Frank E. Hildebrand
FROM BEYOND Empire, 1986, LP

DAN BESSIE
EXECUTIVE ACTION National General, 1973, CP w/Gary Horowitz

JUST BETZER
Business: Just Betzer Films, Inc., c/o Raleigh Studios, 530o Melrose Ave., Suite 250B, Los Angeles, CA, 90038, 213/960-4026

BABETTE'S FEAST Orion Classics, 1987, EP
THE MISFIT BRIGADE *WHEELS OF TERROR* Trans World Entertainment, 1987, w/Benni Korzen
THE GIRL IN A SWING Millimeter Films, 1989

CURTIS BEUSMAN
TRUST ME Cinecom, 1989, EP

TIM BEVAN
Business: Working Title Ltd., 10 Livonia St., London W1V 3PH, 01/439-2424

MY BEAUTIFUL LAUNDRETTE Orion Classics, 1986, w/Sarah Radclyffe
PERSONAL SERVICES Vestron, 1987
SAMMY & ROSIE GET LAID Cinecom, 1987, w/Sarah Radclyffe
A WORLD APART Atlantic Entertainment, 1988, EP w/Graham Bradstreet
PAPERHOUSE Vestron, 1989, w/Sarah Radclyffe
FOR QUEEN & COUNTRY Atlantic Entertainment, 1989
DARK OBSESSION Circle Releasing, 1990
THE TALL GUY Miramax, 1990, EP
CHICAGO JOE AND THE SHOWGIRL New Line Cinema, 1990

JERRY BICK
THE LONG GOODBYE United Artists, 1973
THIEVES LIKE US United Artists, 1974, w/George Litto
RUSSIAN ROULETTE Avco Embassy, 1975
FAREWELL, MY LOVELY Avco Embassy, 1975, EP w/Elliott Kastner
SWING SHIFT Warner Bros., 1984
AGAINST ALL ODDS Columbia, 1984, EP

RICK BIEBER
Business: Stonebridge Productions, Columbia Pictures, Studio Plaza, 3400 Riverside Dr., Burbank, CA, 91505, 818/972-8808

THE FLATLINERS Columbia, 1990, w/ Michael Douglas

LYNN BIGELOW
Business: Kouf-Bigelow Productions, Walt Disney Pictures, 500 S. Buena Vista St., Burbank, CA, 91521, 818/560-5103

DISORGANIZED CRIME Buena Vista, 1989

DAN BIGGS
Business: Millennium Pictures, Inc., 2580 N.W. Upshur, Portland, OR, 97210, 503/227-7041

SHADOW PLAY New World, 1986, w/Susan Shadburne & Will Vinton

TONY BILL
Business: Tony Bill Productions, 73 Market St., Venice, CA, 90291, 213/396-5937
Agent: Martha Luttrell, ICM - Los Angeles, 213/550-4000

STEELYARD BLUES Warner Bros., 1973, w/Julia & Michael Phillips
THE STING ★★ Universal, 1973, w/Julia & Michael Phillips
HEARTS OF THE WEST United Artists, 1975
HARRY & WALTER GO TO NEW YORK Columbia, 1976, EP
GOING IN STYLE Warner Bros., 1979, w/Fred T. Gallo
BOULEVARD NIGHTS Warner Bros., 1979, EP
THE LITTLE DRAGONS Aurora, 1980, EP w/Robert S. Bremson

DEADHEAD MILES Paramount, 1982, w/Vernon Zimmerman
FIVE CORNERS Cineplex Odeon, 1988, w/Forrest Murray

MIKE BINDER
COUPE DE VILLE Universal, 1990, CP

MACK BING
Agent: The Gersh Agency - Beverly Hills, 213/274-6611
Contact: Directors Guild of America - Los Angeles, 213/289-2000

HARD COUNTRY AFD, 1981, w/David Greene
LICENSE TO DRIVE 20th Century-Fox, 1988, AP

THOMAS BIRD
DEAR AMERICA (FD) Corsair, 1988, w/Bill Couturié

ROGER BIRNBAUM
Business: 20th Century-Fox Film Corporation, 10201 W. Pico Blvd., Los Angeles, CA, 90035, 213/277-2111

THE SURE THING Embassy, 1985
WHO'S THAT GIRL Warner Bros., 1987, EP w/Peter Guber & Jon Peters

TONY BISHOP
FRIDAY THE 13TH PART 3 Paramount, 1982, CP
MEATBALLS PART II Tri-Star, 1984, w/Stephen Poe

MICHAEL BITTINS
DAS BOOT Columbia, 1982, CP

CAROL BLACK
Business: The Black/Marlens Company, 1440 S. Sepulveda Blvd., Los Angeles, CA, 90025, 213/444-8100
Agent: Leading Artists, Inc. - Los Angeles, 213/858-1999

SOUL MAN New World, 1986, CP w/Neal Marlens

NOEL BLACK
Agent: The Chasin Agency - Beverly Hills, 213/278-7505
Contact: Directors Guild of America - Los Angeles, 213/289-2000

MISCHIEF 20th Century-Fox, 1985, EP

SARAH RYAN BLACK
Business: Act III Communications, 1800 Century Park East, Suite 200, Los Angeles, CA, 90067, 213/553-3636

BREAKING IN Samuel Goldwyn Company, 1989, EP w/Andrew Meyer

TODD BLACK
(credit w/Mickey Borofsky)
Business: Wizan/Black Films, 11999 San Vicente Blvd., Suite 450, Los Angeles, CA, 90049, 213/472-6133

SPELLBINDER MGM/UA, 1988, CP w/Kate Benton & Steve Berman
SPLIT DECISIONS New Century/Vista, 1988, CP
THE GUARDIAN Universal, 1990, CP w/Dan Greenburg & Mickey Borofsky
SHORT TIME 20th Century-Fox, 1990*

BARRY BLACKMORE
DANNY BOY Triumph/Columbia, 1984

CHRIS BLACKWELL
Business: Island Pictures, 9000 Sunset Blvd., Suite 700, Los Angeles, CA, 90069, 213/276-4500
Contact: The Howard Brandy Company, Inc. - Los Angeles, 213/657-8320

GOOD TO GO Island Pictures, 1986, EP w/Jeremy Thomas
BIG TIME (FD) Island Pictures, 1988, EP

GREGORY S. BLACKWELL
TAKE THIS JOB AND SHOVE IT Embassy, 1981
UNDER THE BOARDWALK New World, 1989, w/Steven H. Chanin

BILL BLAKE
RHINESTONE 20th Century-Fox, 1984, CP w/Richard M. Spitalny

GRACE BLAKE
STAR 80 The Ladd Company/Warner Bros., 1983, AP
SCHOOL DAZE Columbia, 1988, EP

DANIEL H. BLATT
Business: Daniel H. Blatt Productions, 10202 W. Washington Blvd., Culver City, CA, 90230, 213/280-5170

I NEVER PROMISED YOU A ROSE GARDEN New World, 1977, w/Terence F. Deane & Michael Hausman
THE AMERICAN SUCCESS COMPANY *SUCCESS* Columbia, 1979, w/Edgar J. Scherick
THE HOWLING Avco Embassy, 1980, EP w/Steven A. Lane
INDEPENDENCE DAY Warner Bros., 1983, w/Robert Singer
CUJO Warner Bros., 1983, w/Robert Singer
LET'S GET HARRY Tri-Star, 1986, w/Robert Singer
THE BOOST Hemdale, 1988

WILLIAM PETER BLATTY
Agent: Tony Fantozzi, William Morris Agency - Beverly Hills, 213/274-7451

THE EXORCIST ★ Warner Bros., 1973
THE NINTH CONFIGURATION *TWINKLE, TWINKLE, "KILLER" KANE* Warner Bros., 1979

ANDRE BLAY
Business: Palisades Pictures, 1875 Century Park East, 3rd Floor, Los Angeles, CA, 90067, 213/785-3100

PRINCE OF DARKNESS Universal, 1987, EP w/Shep Gordon
THEY LIVE Universal, 1988, EP w/Shep Gordon
BRAIN DAMAGE Palisades Entertainment, 1988, EP w/Al Eicher
THE BLOB Tri-Star, 1988, EP
A CHORUS OF DISAPPROVAL South Gate Entertainment, 1989, EP w/Elliott Kastner

WILLIAM WARREN BLAYLOCK
GRANDVIEW, U.S.A. Warner Bros., 1984, w/Peter W. Rea

CHARLES B. BLOCH
THE FOG Avco Embassy, 1980, EP

IVAN BLOCH
THE STONE BOY 20th Century-Fox, 1984, w/Joe Roth

DAVID BLOCKER
Business: Raincity Inc., 550 N. Larchmont Blvd., Suite 202, Los Angeles, CA, 90004, 213/461-0195
Contact: Directors Guild of America - Los Angeles, 213/289-2000

CHOOSE ME Island Alive, 1984, w/Carolyn Pfeiffer
TROUBLE IN MIND Alive Films, 1985, w/Carolyn Pfeiffer
MADE IN HEAVEN Lorimar, 1987, w/Bruce A. Evans & Raynold Gideon
THE MODERNS Alive Films, 1988, w/Carolyn Pfeiffer
LOVE AT LARGE Orion, 1990

ALAN C. BLOMQUIST
Contact: Directors Guild of America - Los Angeles, 213/289-2000

EVERYBODY'S ALL-AMERICAN Warner Bros., 1988, CP

JIM BLOOM
Business: Blue Iris, Inc., 850 Keeler Ave., Berkeley, CA, 94708, 415/526-1996
Contact: Directors Guild of America - Los Angeles, 213/289-2000

THE EMPIRE STRIKES BACK 20th Century-Fox, 1980, AP w/Robert Watts
RETURN OF THE JEDI 20th Century-Fox, 1983, CP w/Robert Watts
WARNING SIGN 20th Century-Fox, 1985
FIRES WITHIN Pathe, 1990, EP

JOHN BLOOMGARDEN
DEAD OF WINTER MGM/UA, 1987, w/Marc Shmuger

PHILIPPE BLOT
THE ARROGANT Cannon, 1987

DENIS BLOUIN
IRONWEED Tri-Star, 1987, EP w/Rob Cohen & Joseph H. Kanter

DEBORAH BLUM
(credit w/Tony Ganz)
Business: Blum-Ganz Productions, c/o ITC Productions, 12711 Ventura Blvd., Studio City, CA, 91604, 818/760-2110

GUNG HO Paramount, 1986
VIBES Columbia, 1988
CLEAN AND SOBER Warner Bros., 1988

HARRY N. BLUM
Business: The Blum Group, 494 Tuallitan Road, Los Angeles, CA, 90049, 213/476-2229

OBSESSION Columbia, 1976, w/George Litto
THE MAGICIAN OF LUBLIN Cannon, 1979, EP

LEN BLUM
Agent: Rand Holston, CAA - Beverly Hills, 213/288-4545

FEDS Warner Bros., 1988, w/Ilona Herzberg

ROBERT F. BLUMOFE
Contact: 1100 Alta Loma Drive, Los Angeles, CA, 90069, 213/657-7000

BOUND FOR GLORY ★ United Artists, 1976, w/Harold Leventhal

DON BLUTH
(credit w/Gary Goldman & John Pomeroy)
Business: Sullivan/Bluth Studios, 3800 W. Alameda Ave., Suite 1120, Burbank, CA, 91505, 818/840-9446

THE SECRET OF N.I.M.H. (AF) MGM/UA, 1982
AN AMERICAN TAIL (AF) Universal, 1986
THE LAND BEFORE TIME (AF) Universal, 1988
ALL DOGS GO TO HEAVEN (AF) Universal, 1989

BRUCE BODNER
Business: Cornelius Productions, 2916 Main St., #200, Santa Monica, CA, 90405, 213/392-8501

FUNNY FARM Warner Bros., 1988, EP w/Patrick Kelley
FLETCH LIVES Universal, 1989, EP w/Robert Larson

ALLAN F. BODOH
GOOD GUYS WEAR BLACK American Cinema, 1978
GO TELL THE SPARTANS Avco Embassy, 1978, w/Mitchell Cannold
THE GREAT SMOKEY ROADBLOCK *THE LAST OF THE COWBOYS* Dimension, 1978

YUREK BOGAYEVICZ
Agent: CAA - Beverly Hills, 213/288-4545

ANNA Vestron, 1987, w/Zanne Devine

PETER BOGDANOVICH
Business: 2040 Avenue of the Stars, Suite 400, Los Angeles, CA, 90067, 213/203-8055
Agent: CAA - Beverly Hills, 213/288-4545

TARGETS Paramount, 1968
WHAT'S UP, DOC? Warner Bros., 1972
PAPER MOON Paramount, 1973
DAISY MILLER Paramount, 1974
AT LONG LAST LOVE 20th Century-Fox, 1975
ILLEGALLY YOURS DEG, 1988
TEXASVILLE Columbia, 1990, w/Henry T. Weinstein & Robert Whitmore

ANDRE BOISSIER
BROTHERS IN ARMS Ablo, 1988, EP w/Jan Erik Lunde

EDGAR BOLD
STEEL DAWN Vestron, 1987, AP
OPTIONS Vestron, 1989, CP w/Conrad Hool

CRAIG BOLOTIN
Agent: Rosalie Swedlin, CAA - Beverly Hills, 213/288-4545
Contact: Writers Guild of America - Los Angeles, 213/550-1000

BLACK RAIN Paramount, 1989, EP w/Julie Kirkham

LOIS BONFIGLIO
Business: Fonda Films, P.O. Box 491355, Los Angeles, CA, 90049, 213/458-4545

THE MORNING AFTER 20th Century-Fox, 1986, AP w/Wolfgang Glattes
OLD GRINGO Columbia, 1989

JOHN BOORMAN
Business: 9696 Culver Blvd., Suite 203, Culver City, CA, 90232, 213/558-8110
Agent: Jeff Berg, ICM - Los Angeles, 213/550-4000

DELIVERANCE ★ Warner Bros., 1972
ZARDOZ 20th Century-Fox, 1974
EXORCIST II: THE HERETIC Warner Bros., 1977, w/Richard Lederer
EXCALIBUR Orion/Warner Bros., 1981
DANNY BOY Triumph/Columbia, 1984, EP
THE EMERALD FOREST Embassy, 1985
HOPE AND GLORY ★ Columbia, 1987
WHERE THE HEART IS Buena Vista, 1990

JON BOORSTIN
Agent: Camden Artists, Ltd. - Los Angeles, 213/556-2022

DREAM LOVER MGM/UA, 1986, w/Alan J. Pakula

MARGARET BOOTH
THE SLUGGER'S WIFE Columbia, 1985, EP

PHIL BORACK
CHATTANOOGA CHOO CHOO April Fools, 1984, EP

JOSE LUIS BORAU
Business: El Iman S.A., Alberto Aleocer 42, Madrid 16, Spain, 01/250-5534

ON THE LINE Miramax, 1987, w/Steven Kovacs

DONALD P. BORCHERS
ANGEL New World, 1984, w/Roy Watts
CHILDREN OF THE CORN New World, 1984, w/Terrence Kirby
TUFF TURF New World, 1985
VAMP New World, 1986
TWO MOON JUNCTION Lorimar, 1988
FAR FROM HOME Vestron, 1989

BILL BORDEN
Business: New Visions Entertainment Corporation, 5750 Wilshire Blvd., 6th Floor, Los Angeles, CA, 90036, 213/965-2500

AGAINST ALL ODDS Columbia, 1984, AP
WHITE NIGHTS Columbia, 1985, AP
LA BAMBA Columbia, 1987, w/Taylor Hackford

LIZZIE BORDEN
BORN IN FLAMES First Run Features, 1983
WORKING GIRLS Miramax, 1987, w/Andi Gladstone

MORITZ BORMAN
UNDER THE VOLCANO Universal, 1984, w/Wieland Schulz-Keil
THE LIGHTSHIP Castle Hill, 1986, w/Bill Benenson
HOMER AND EDDIE Skouras, 1990, w/James Cady

MICKEY BOROFSKY
(credit w/Todd Black)
Business: Wizan/Black Films, 11999 San Vicente Blvd., Suite 450, Los Angeles, CA, 90049, 213/472-6133

JUNIOR BONNER ABC/Cinerama, 1972, AP*
SPELLBINDER MGM/UA, 1988, CP w/Kate Benton & Steve Berman
SPLIT DECISIONS New Century/Vista, 1988, CP
THE GUARDIAN Universal, 1990, CP w/Todd Black & Dan Greenburg
SHORT TIME 20th Century-Fox, 1990, EP w/Joe Wizan*

PHILLIP BORSOS
Business: 1800 Century Park East, Suite 300, Los Angeles, CA, 90067, 213/203-0777
Agent: Bauer Benedek Agency - Los Angeles, 213/275-2421

THE GREY FOX United Artists Classics, 1983, CP w/Barry Healey
ONE MAGIC CHRISTMAS Buena Vista, 1985, EP

SIMON BOSANQUET

NUNS ON THE RUN 20th Century-Fox, 1990, CP

FREDERIC BOURBOULON
WAITING FOR THE MOON Skouras Pictures, 1987, LP

GABRIEL BOUSTANI
ATLANTIC CITY ★ Paramount, 1981, EP w/Joseph Beaubien
DEATHWATCH Quartet, 1982, w/Janine Rubeiz

TOM BOUTROSS
APPOINTMENT WITH DEATH Galaxy, 1985

JOHN R. BOWEY
Business: Howard International, 6565 Sunset Blvd., Suite 400, Hollywood, CA, 90028, 213/463-2226

PRETTYKILL Spectrafilm, 1987, w/Martin Walters
TIME OF THE BEAST Liberty Films, 1989, EP

KENNETH BOWSER
Agent: Lucy Kroll Agency - New York, 212/877-0627

IN A SHALLOW GRAVE Skouras Pictures, 1988, w/Barry Jossen

DON BOYD
HONKY TONK FREEWAY Universal/AFD, 1981, w/Howard W. Koch Jr.
SCRUBBERS Orion Classics, 1984
ARIA Miramax, 1988
WAR REQUIEM Anglo International, 1988

JOE BOYD
Business: Carthage Records, Inc., P.O. Box 667, Rocky Hill, NJ 08553, 609/466-9320

SCANDAL Miramax, 1989, EP w/Nik Powell Bob Weinstein & Harvey Weinstein

ROBERT BOYETT
Business: Miller-Boyett Productions, 10202 W. Washington Blvd., Culver City, CA, 90232, 213/558-6555

THE BEST LITTLE WHOREHOUSE IN TEXAS Universal, 1982, w/Edward K. Milkis & Thomas L. Miller

BARBARA BOYLE
Business: Sovereign Pictures, Inc., 11845 W. Olympic Blvd., #1055, Los Angeles, CA, 90064, 213/312-1001

CAMPUS MAN Paramount, 1987, EP w/Marc E. Platt
EIGHT MEN OUT Orion, 1988, EP w/Jerry Offsay

MARC BOYMAN
THE INCUBUS FIlm Ventures International, 1982, w/John M. Eckert
THE FLY 20th Century-Fox, 1986, CP w Kip Ohman
DEAD RINGERS 20th Century-Fox, 1988, w/David Cronenberg

RON BOZMAN
Contact: Directors Guild of America - New York, 212/581-0370

SOMETHING WILD Orion, 1986, AP
MARRIED TO THE MOB Orion, 1988, AP
MIAMI BLUES Orion, 1990, CP w/Kenneth Utt
WAITING FOR THE LIGHT Triumph, 1990, w/Caldecott Chubb

LORD JOHN BRABOURNE
(credit w/Richard Goodwin)
Business: G.W. Films, Ltd., 41 Montpelier Walk, London SW7 1JH, England, 01/589-8829

ROMEO & JULIET ★ Paramount, 1968, w/Anthony Havelock-Allan*
THE DANCE OF DEATH Paramount, 1968*
PETER RABBIT AND TALES OF BEATRIX POTTER MGM, 1971, EP*
MURDER ON THE ORIENT EXPRESS Paramount, 1974
DEATH ON THE NILE Paramount, 1978
STORIES FROM A FLYING TRUNK EMI, 1979
THE MIRROR CRACK'D AFD, 1980
EVIL UNDER THE SUN Universal/AFD, 1982
A PASSAGE TO INDIA ★ Columbia, 1984
LITTLE DORRIT Cannon, 1988

JACOB BRACKMAN
Agent: ICM - New York, 212/556-5600

DAYS OF HEAVEN Paramount, 1978, EP
TIMES SQUARE AFD, 1980, w/Robert Stigwood

GRAHAM BRADSTREET
A WORLD APART Atlantic Entertainment, 1988, EP w/Tim Bevan

DAVID H. BRADY
THE GREY FOX United Artists Classics, 1983, EP

RICHARD BRANSON
Business: The Virgin Group, 328 Kensal Rd., London, W10 5XJ, 01/968-8888

ELECTRIC DREAMS MGM/UA, 1984, EP

ZEV BRAUN
Business: Zev Braun Pictures, 1440 S. Sepulveda Blvd., Los Angeles, CA, 90025, 213/444-8457

ANGELA Embassy, 1984, EP
WHERE ARE THE CHILDREN Columbia, 1986

ARTUR BRAUNER
THE ROSE GARDEN Cannon, 1989

ANDREW BRAUNSBERG
WONDERWALL Cinecenta, 1969
MACBETH Columbia, 1971
WHAT? Avco Embassy, 1973, EP
ANDY WARHOL'S DRACULA Bryanston, 1974, w/Carlo Ponti & Jean Pierre Rassam
ANDY WARHOL'S FRANKENSTEIN Bryanston, 1974, w/Carlo Ponti & Jean Pierre Rassam
THE TENANT Paramount, 1976
BEING THERE United Artists, 1979
THE HOUND OF THE BASKERVILLES Atlantic Entertainment, 1979, EP w/Michael White
THE POSTMAN ALWAYS RINGS TWICE Paramount, 1981, EP
LOOKIN' TO GET OUT Paramount, 1982, EP
ALPHABET CITY Atlantic Entertainment, 1984
CRUSOE Island Pictures, 1989
DRIVING ME CRAZY (FD) First Run Features, 1990

GEORGE BRAUNSTEIN
(credit w/Ron Hamady)

FADE TO BLACK American Cinema, 1980
SURF II International Films, 1984
AND GOD CREATED WOMAN Vestron, 1988
OUT COLD Hemdale, 1989
THE BOYFRIEND SCHOOL Hemdale, 1990

WILLIAM BRAUNSTEIN
Business: Bima Entertainment, Ltd., 2049 Century Park East, Suite 4050, Los Angeles, CA, 90067, 213/203-8488

SLIPSTREAM Entertainment Films, 1989, EP w/Nigel Green & Arthur Maslansky

PHILIP M. BREEN
Business: Rolling Hills Productions, 204 South Beverly Dr., #166, Beverly Hills, CA, 90212, 213/275-0872

SWORD OF THE VALIANT Cannon, 1984, EP w/Michael J. Kagan
THE NATURAL Tri-Star, 1984, EP w/Roger Towne

MARTIN BREGMAN
Business: Martin Bregman Productions, 100 Universal City Plaza, Universal City, CA, 91608, 818/777-4950; 642 Lexington Ave., Suite 1400, New York, NY,10022, 212/421-6161
Agent: Bauer Benedek Agency - Los Angeles, 213/275-2421

SERPICO Paramount, 1973
DOG DAY AFTERNOON ★ Warner Bros., 1975, w/Martin Elfand
THE NEXT MAN Allied Artists, 1976
THE SEDUCTION OF JOE TYNAN Universal, 1979
SIMON Orion/Warner Bros., 1980
THE FOUR SEASONS Universal, 1981
VENOM Paramount, 1982

SCARFACE Universal, 1983
SWEET LIBERTY Universal, 1986
REAL MEN MGM/UA, 1987
A NEW LIFE Paramount, 1988
LISTEN TO ME WEG/Columbia, 1989, EP
SEA OF LOVE Universal, 1989, w/Louis A. Stroller

MARIO BREGUI
Business: Produzioni Atlas Consorziate SRL, Viale Rigina Margherita 279, 00198 Roma, Italy, 06-4403797

THE CHOIRBOYS Universal, 1977, EP w/Pietro Bregui & Mark Damon

PIETRO BREGUI
Business: Produzioni Atlas Consorziate SRL, Viale Rigina Margherita 279, 00198 Roma, Italy, 06-4403797

THE CHOIRBOYS Universal, 1977, EP w/Mario Bregui & Mark Damon

ROBERT S. BREMSON
OBSESSION Columbia, 1976, EP
THE LITTLE DRAGONS Aurora, 1980, EP w/Tony Bill

HERBERT H. BRESLIN
YES, GIORGIO MGM, 1982, EP w/Alain Bernheim

KEVIN BRESLIN
UHF Orion, 1989, CP w/Deren Getz

MARTIN BREST
Business: City Lights Films, c/o Universal Pictures, 100 Universal City Plaza, Universal City, CA, 91608, 818/777-1325
Agent: CAA - Beverly Hills, 213/288-4545

MIDNIGHT RUN Universal, 1988

JASON BRETT
Business: Jason Brett Productions, c/o New World Entertainment, 1440 S. Sepulveda Blvd., Los Angeles, CA, 90025, 213/444-8100
Agent: Bauer Benedek Agency - Los Angeles, 213/275-2421

ABOUT LAST NIGHT... Tri-Star, 1986, w/Stuart Oken

JONATHAN BRETT
SHE-DEVIL Orion, 1989, w/Susan Seidelman

ALAN BREWER
PLAYING FOR KEEPS Universal, 1986, w/Bob Weinstein & Harvey Weinstein

COLIN M. BREWER
THE KEEP Paramount, 1983, EP

LARRY BREZNER
Business: Rollins-Morra-Brezner, 801 Westmount Dr., Los Angeles, CA, 90069, 213/657-5384

THROW MOMMA FROM THE TRAIN Orion, 1987
GOOD MORNING, VIETNAM Buena Vista, 1987, w/Mark Johnson
THE 'BURBS Universal, 1989, w/Michael Finnell
COUPE DE VILLE Universal, 1990, w/Paul Schiff

MARSHALL BRICKMAN
Agent: ICM - Los Angeles, 213/550-4000
Contact: Directors Guild of America - Los Angeles, 213/289-2000

THE MANHATTAN PROJECT 20th Century-Fox, 1986, w/Jennifer Ogden

PAUL BRICKMAN
Agent: CAA - Beverly Hills, 213/288-4545
Contact: Directors Guild of America - Los Angeles, 213/289-2000

CITIZENS BAND *HANDLE WITH CARE* Paramount, 1977, AP
DEAL OF THE CENTURY Warner Bros., 1983, EP w/Jon Avnet & Steve Tisch
MEN DON'T LEAVE The Geffen Company/Warner Bros., 1990, EP

HOWARD M. BRICKNER
SIDEWALK STORIES Island Pictures, 1989, EP w/Vicki Lebenbaum

JAMES BRIDGES
Agent: CAA - Beverly Hills, 213/288-4545
Contact: Directors Guild of America - Los Angeles, 213/289-2000

PERFECT Columbia, 1985

JACK BRIGGS
EAT & RUN New World, 1987

RICHARD S. BRIGHT
TRIBUTE 20th Century-Fox, 1980, EP w/David Foster & Lawrence Turman

JOHN BRILEY
Agent: ICM - Los Angeles, 213/550-4000
Contact: Writers Guild of America - Los Angeles, 213/550-1000

CRY FREEDOM Universal, 1987, CP w/Norman Spencer

BERNIE BRILLSTEIN
Business: The Brillstein Company, 9200 Sunset Blvd., Suite 428, Los Angeles, CA, 90069, 213/275-6135

THE BLUES BROTHERS Universal, 1980, EP
MAD MAGAZINE PRESENTS UP THE ACADEMY Warner Bros., 1980, EP
CONTINENTAL DIVIDE Universal, 1981, EP w/Steven Spielberg
NEIGHBORS Columbia, 1981, EP w/Irving Paul Lazar
DOCTOR DETROIT Universal, 1983, EP
GHOSTBUSTERS Columbia, 1984, EP
SUMMER RENTAL Paramount, 1985, EP
SPIES LIKE US Warner Bros., 1985, EP
DRAGNET Universal, 1987, EP
GHOSTBUSTERS II Columbia, 1989, EP w/Michael C. Gross & Joe Medjuck

BO BRINKMAN
ICE HOUSE Upfront Films, 1989

TOM BROADBRIDGE
VICIOUS SVS Films, 1988, EP
NIGHT VISITOR MGM/UA, 1989, EP w/Shelley E. Reid

ALBERT R. BROCCOLI
Business: Warfield Productions, 10000 W. Washington Blvd., Culver City, CA, 90232, 213/280-6565

RED BERET *PARATROOPER* 1954, w/Irving Allen & Anthony Bushell
THE BLACK KNIGHT Columbia, 1954, w/Irving Allen & Phil C. Samuel
HELL BELOW ZERO Columbia, 1954, w/Irving Allen & George W. Willoughby
PRIZE OF GOLD Columbia, 1955, w/Irving Allen
ODONGO Columbia, 1956, EP w/Irving Allen
THE COCKLESHELL HEROES Columbia, 1956, w/Irving Allen
SAFARI Columbia, 1956, EP w/Irving Allen
ZARAK Columbia, 1957, w/Irving Allen
FIRE DOWN BELOW Columbia, 1957, w/Irving Allen
PICKUP ALLEY Columbia, 1957, w/Irving Allen
HIGH FLIGHT Columbia, 1958, w/Irving Allen
THE MAN INSIDE Columbia, 1958, w/Irving Allen
HOW TO MURDER A RICH UNCLE Columbia, 1958, EP w/Irving Allen
NO TIME TO DIE *TANK FORCE* Columbia, 1958, w/Irving Allen
THE BANDIT OF ZHOBE Columbia, 1959, w/Irving Allen
KILLERS OF KILIMANJARO Columbia, 1960, EP w/Irving Allen
JAZZ BOAT Columbia, 1960, w/Irving Allen
THE TRIALS OF OSCAR WILDE Kingsley International, 1960, EP w/Irving Allen
PLAY IT COOLER Columbia, 1961, EP w/Irving Allen
DR. NO United Artists, 1962, w/Harry Saltzman
CALL ME BWANA United Artists, 1963, w/Harry Saltzman
FROM RUSSIA WITH LOVE United Artists, 1963, w/Harry Saltzman
GOLDFINGER United Artists, 1964, w/Harry Saltzman
YOU ONLY LIVE TWICE United Artists, 1967, w/Harry Saltzman
CHITTY CHITTY BANG BANG United Artists, 1968
ON HER MAJESTY'S SECRET SERVICE United Artists, 1969, w/Harry Saltzman
DIAMONDS ARE FOREVER United Artists, 1971, w/Harry Saltzman
LIVE AND LET DIE United Artists, 1973, w/Harry Saltzman
THE MAN WITH THE GOLDEN GUN United Artists, 1974, w/Harry Saltzman
THE SPY WHO LOVED ME United Artists, 1977
MOONRAKER United Artists, 1979
FOR YOUR EYES ONLY United Artists, 1981
OCTOPUSSY MGM/UA, 1983
A VIEW TO A KILL MGM/UA, 1985, w/Michael G. Wilson
THE LIVING DAYLIGHTS MGM/UA, 1987, w/Michael G. Wilson
LICENCE TO KILL MGM/UA, 1989, w/Michael G. Wilson

THOMAS H. BRODEK
Contact: Directors Guild of America - Los Angeles, 213/289-2000

TRANSYLVANIA 6-5000 New World, 1985, w/Mace Neufeld
THE AVIATOR MGM/UA, 1985, w/Mace Neufeld
THE BOSS' WIFE Tri-Star, 1986
THE PRINCIPAL Tri-Star, 1987

JACK BRODSKY
Business: JBRO Productions, c/o 20th Century-Fox Film Corporation, 10201 W. Pico Blvd., Los Angeles, CA, 90035, 213/277-2111

LITTLE MURDERS 20th Century-Fox, 1971
EVERYTHING YOU ALWAYS WANTED TO KNOW ABOUT SEX* (*BUT WERE AFRAID TO ASK) United Artists, 1972, EP
SUMMER WISHES, WINTER DREAMS Columbia, 1973
ROMANCING THE STONE 20th Century-Fox, 1984, CP w/Joel Douglas
THE JEWEL OF THE NILE 20th Century-Fox, 1985, CP w/Joel Douglas
DANCERS Cannon, 1987, EP w/Nora Kaye

DENNIS BRODY
3:15 THE MOMENT OF TRUTH Dakota Entertainment, 1986, w/Robert Kenner

RUBEN BROIDO
SURVIVAL RUN Film Ventures International, 1980, EP w/Mel Bergman

CARY BROKAW
Business: Avenue Entertainment, 12100 Wilshire Blvd., Suite 1650, Los Angeles, CA, 90066, 213/442-2200

TROUBLE IN MIND Alive Films, 1985, EP
NOBODY'S FOOL Island Pictures, 1986, EP
DOWN BY LAW Island Pictures, 1986, EP w/Otto Grokenberger
SLAMDANCE Island Pictures, 1987, EP
PASCALI'S ISLAND Avenue Pictures, 1988, EP
STRAIGHT TO HELL Island Pictures, 1988, EP w/Scott Millaney
SIGNS OF LIFE Avenue Pictures, 1989, EP w/Lindsay Law
COLD FEET Avenue Pictures, 1989, EP
DRUGSTORE COWBOY Avenue Pictures, 1989, EP

EDGAR BRONFMAN, JR.
Business: Joseph E. Seagram & Sons, Inc., 375 Park Avenue, New York, NY, 10152, 212/572-7000

THE BORDER Universal, 1982

JAMES L. BROOKS
Business: Gracie Films, 20th Century-Fox, 10201 W. Pico Blvd., Los Angeles, CA, 90035, 213/203-3770
Agent: ICM - Los Angeles, 213/550-4000

STARTING OVER Paramount, 1979, w/Alan J. Pakula
TERMS OF ENDEARMENT ★★ Paramount, 1983
BROADCAST NEWS ★ 20th Century-Fox, 1987
BIG 20th Century-Fox, 1988, w/Robert Greenhut
SAY ANYTHING 20th Century-Fox, 1989, EP
WAR OF THE ROSES 20th Century-Fox, 1989, w/Arnon Milchan

MEL BROOKS
Business: Brooksfilms, Ltd., P.O. Box 900, Beverly Hills, CA, 90213, 213/203-1375
Contact: Directors Guild of America - Los Angeles, 213/289-2000

HIGH ANXIETY 20th Century-Fox, 1977
THE HISTORY OF THE WORLD - PART I 20th Century-Fox, 1981

TO BE OR NOT TO BE   20th Century-Fox, 1983
THE DOCTOR AND THE DEVILS   20th Century-Fox, 1985, EP
84 CHARING CROSS ROAD   Columbia, 1987, EP
SPACEBALLS   MGM/UA, 1987

MITCHELL BROWER
MCCABE & MRS. MILLER   Warner Bros., 1971, w/David Foster
THE GETAWAY   National General, 1972, w/David Foster

CHRIS BROUWER
THE GIRL WITH THE RED HAIR   United Artists Classics, 1983, w/Haig Balian

ANDREW BROWN
PRICK UP YOUR EARS   Samuel Goldwyn Company, 1987
DEALERS   Skouras Pictures, 1989, EP w/John Hambley

BRUCE W. BROWN
WELCOME TO 18   American Distribution Group, 1986, EP

CHRIS BROWN
Business: Palace Pictures, 16/17 Wardour Mews, London W1, England, 01/734-7060 or 8170 Beverly Blvd., Suite 203, Los Angeles, CA, 90048, 213/655-1114

THE COMPANY OF WOLVES   Cannon, 1985, w/Stephen Woolley
ABSOLUTE BEGINNERS   Orion, 1986, w/Stephen Woolley
MONA LISA   Island Pictures, 1986, CP w/Ray Cooper
SIESTA   Lorimar, 1987, CP

DAVID BROWN
(credit w/Richard D. Zanuck)
Business: The Manhattan Project, Tri-Star Pictures, 711 Fifth Ave., New York, NY, 10022, 212/702-6055

Sssssss   Universal, 1973, EP
WILLIE DYNAMITE   Universal, 1974
THE SUGARLAND EXPRESS   Universal, 1974
THE GIRL FROM PETROVKA   Universal, 1974
THE BLACK WINDMILL   Universal, 1974
THE EIGER SANCTION   Universal, 1974, EP
JAWS ★   Universal, 1975
MACARTHUR   Universal, 1977, EP
JAWS II   Universal, 1978
THE ISLAND   Universal, 1980
NEIGHBORS   Columbia, 1981
THE VERDICT ★   20th Century-Fox, 1982
COCOON   20th Century-Fox, 1985, w/Lili Fini Zanuck
TARGET   Warner Bros., 1985
COCOON: THE RETURN   20th Century-Fox, 1988, w/Lili Fini Zanuck
DRIVING MISS DAISY   Warner Bros., 1989, EP w/Jake Eberts*

G. MAC BROWN
Contact: Directors Guild of America - New York, 212/581-0370

HELLO AGAIN   Buena Vista, 1987, CP w/Thomas Folino, Susan Isaacs & Martin Mickelson
SHE-DEVIL   Orion, 1989, CP

HOWARD BROWN
CHEECH & CHONG'S NEXT MOVIE   Universal, 1980
CHEECH & CHONG'S NICE DREAMS   Columbia, 1981
THINGS ARE TOUGH ALL OVER   Columbia, 1982

PETER BROWN
SPARKLE   Warner Bros., 1976, EP w/Beryl Vertue

ROBERT LATHAM BROWN
Contact: Directors Guild of America - Los Angeles, 213/289-2000

HOWARD THE DUCK   Universal, 1986, CP

JAMES D. BRUBAKER
Business: Sidewalk Productions, 1640 S. Sepulveda Blvd., #208, Los Angeles, CA, 90025, 213/478-4282
Contact: Directors Guild of America - Los Angeles, 213/289-2000

TRUE CONFESSIONS   United Artists, 1981, AP
THE RIGHT STUFF ★   The Ladd Company/Warner Bros., 1983, EP
RHINESTONE   20th Century-Fox, 1984, AP
ROCKY IV   MGM/UA, 1985, EP w/Arthur Chobanian
BEER   Orion, 1986, EP
COBRA   Warner Bros., 1986, EP
OVER THE TOP   Cannon, 1987, EP
PATTY HEARST   Atlantic Entertainment, 1988, LP

BONNIE BRUCKHEIMER-MARTELL
Business: All-Girl Pictures, Walt Disney Pictures, 500 S. Buena Vista St., Burbank, CA, 91521, 818/560-5000

BEACHES   Buena Vista, 1988, w/Bette Midler & Margaret Jennings South

JERRY BRUCKHEIMER
(credit w/Don Simpson)
Business: Simpson-Bruckheimer Productions, Paramount Pictures, 5555 Melrose Ave., Los Angeles, CA, 90038, 213/468-4518

FAREWELL, MY LOVELY   Avco Embassy, 1975, w/George Pappas*
RAFFERTY & THE GOLD DUST TWINS   Warner Bros., 1975, AP*
MARCH OR DIE   Columbia, 1977, w/Dick Richards*
AMERICAN GIGOLO   Paramount, 1980*
DEFIANCE   American International, 1980, w/William S. Gilmore*
THIEF   United Artists, 1981, w/Ronnie Caan*
CAT PEOPLE   Universal, 1982, EP*
YOUNG DOCTORS IN LOVE   20th Century-Fox, 1982*
FLASHDANCE   Paramount, 1983
BEVERLY HILLS COP   Paramount, 1984
THIEF OF HEARTS   Paramount, 1984
TOP GUN   Paramount, 1986
BEVERLY HILLS COP II   Paramount, 1987
DAYS OF THUNDER   Paramount, 1990

PIETER JAN BRUGGE
Contact: Directors Guild of America - Los Angeles, 213/289-2000

MY DEMON LOVER   New Line Cinema, 1987, LP
GLORY   Tri-Star, 1989, CP

STANLEY F. BUCHTHAL
Business: Buckeye Entertainment, 1414 Avenue of the Americas, 6th Floor, New York, NY, 10019, 212/888-9115

HAIRSPRAY New Line Cinema, 1988, CP w/John Waters

RONALD L. BUCK
Agent: William Morris Agency - Beverly Hills, 213/274-7451

BREAKOUT Columbia, 1975, EP
HARRY & SON Orion, 1984, w/Paul Newman

ANTHONY BUCKLEY
BLISS New World, 1986

JEFF BUHAI
(credit w/David Obst & Steve Zacharias)
Agent: Bauer Benedek Agency - Los Angeles, 213/275-2421

THE WHOOPEE BOYS Paramount, 1986, EP
JOHNNY BE GOOD Orion, 1988, EP

ANDREW BULLIANS
(credit w/Jean Bullians)

3:15 THE MOMENT OF TRUTH Dakota Entertainment, 1986, EP w/Sandy Climan & Charles C. Thieriot
THE BIKINI SHOP *THE MALIBU BIKINI SHOP* International Film Marketing, 1987, EP w/Sandy Climan & Charles C. Thieriot
BORN TO RACE MGM/UA, 1988

JEAN BULLIANS
(credit w/Andrew Bullians)

3:15 THE MOMENT OF TRUTH Dakota Entertainment, 1986, EP w/Sandy Climan & Charles C. Thieriot
THE BIKINI SHOP *THE MALIBU BIKINI SHOP* International Film Marketing, 1987, EP w/Sandy Climan & Charles C. Thieriot
BORN TO RACE MGM/UA, 1988

MARK BUNTZMAN
Business: Artists Alliance Productions, Inc., 1800 N. Highland, #316, Los Angeles, CA, 90028, 213/465-9160
Contact: 818/980-3007

EXTERMINATOR 2 Cannon, 1984

MARK BURG
Business: Island Pictures, 8920 Sunset Blvd., 2nd Floor, Los Angeles, CA, 90069, 213/276-4500

CAN'T BUY ME LOVE Buena Vista, 1987, CP
BULL DURHAM Orion, 1988, w/Thom Mount

GRAHAM BURKE
YOUNG EINSTEIN Warner Bros., 1989, EP w/Ray Beattie

STEVEN E. BURMAN
THE CELLAR Moviestore, 1990, w/Patrick C. Wells & John Woodward

ALLAN BURNS
Agent: John Gaines, APA - Los Angeles, 213/273-0744

JUST BETWEEN FRIENDS Orion, 1986, w/Edward Teets

MICHAEL BURNS
THRESHOLD 20th Century-Fox International Classics, 1983, w/Jon Slan

WILLIAM BURR
STEPFATHER II Millimeter, 1989, w/Darin Scott

PETER BURRELL
Contact: Directors Guild of America - Los Angeles, 213/289-2000

SMOKEY & THE BANDIT II Universal, 1980, AP
ZOOT SUIT Universal, 1982
DEATH OF AN ANGEL 20th Century-Fox, 1986
STACKING Spectrafilm, 1987, CP w/Patrick Markey

TIMOTHY BURRILL
Business: Burrill Productions, 19 Cranbury Road, London SW6 2NS, 01-736-8673

PRIVILEGE Universal, 1967, AP
MACBETH Columbia, 1971
ALPHA BETA Cine III, 1976
TESS ★ Columbia, 1980, CP
THE PIRATES OF PENZANCE Universal, 1983, CP
ANOTHER TIME, ANOTHER PLACE Samuel Goldwyn Company, 1984, EP
SUPERGIRL Warner Bros., 1984
THE FOURTH PROTOCOL Lorimar, 1987
TO KILL A PRIEST Columbia, 1990, SP

GEOFF BURROWES
Contact: Australian Film Commission, 9229 Sunset Blvd., Los Angeles, CA, 90069, 213/275-7074

THE MAN FROM SNOWY RIVER 20th Century-Fox, 1983
RETURN TO SNOWY RIVER Buena Vista, 1988
BACKSTAGE Hoyts, 1988

CHRIS BURT
REVOLUTION Warner Bros., 1985, EP

SCOTT BUSHNELL
Business: Sand Castle 5 Productions, 502 Park Ave., Suite 156, New York, NY, 10022, 212/826-6641

NASHVILLE ★ Paramount, 1975, AP
BUFFALO BILL & THE INDIANS or SITTING BULL'S HISTORY LESSON United Artists, 1976, AP
3 WOMEN 20th Century-Fox, 1977, AP
A WEDDING 20th Century-Fox, 1978, AP
A PERFECT COUPLE 20th Century-Fox, 1979, AP
RICH KIDS United Artists, 1979, EP
HEALTH 20th Century-Fox, 1980, AP
POPEYE Paramount/Buena Vista, 1980, AP
COME BACK TO THE 5 & DIME, JIMMY DEAN, JIMMY DEAN Cinecom, 1982
STREAMERS United Artists Classics, 1983, AP
SECRET HONOR Cinecom, 1985, EP
FOOL FOR LOVE Cannon, 1986, AP
BEYOND THERAPY New World, 1987, AP
O.C. AND STIGGS MGM/UA, 1987, AP

MICHAEL BUTLER
HAIR United Artists, 1979, w/Lester Persky

DANN BYCK
Business: Byck/Lancaster Productions, 2427 Cazaux Pl., Los Angeles, CA, 90068, 213/856-9025

'NIGHT, MOTHER Universal, 1986, EP w/David Lancaster

MARK BYERS
STRIPPED TO KILL Concorde, 1987, w/Matt Leipzig & Andy Ruben

BILL BYRNE
FROM HOLLYWOOD TO DEADWOOD Island Pictures, 1989, EP

THOMAS S. BYRNES
PARTY LINE SVS Films, 1988, w/Kurt Anderson & William Webb
TO SLEEP WITH ANGER SVS Films, 1990, w/Caldecott Chubb & Darin Scott

C

RONNIE CAAN
THIEF United Artists, 1981, w/Jerry Bruckheimer

JAMES CADY
Contact: Directors Guild of America - Los Angeles, 213/289-2000

HOMER AND EDDIE Skouras, 1990, w/Moritz Borman

BARRY CAHN
THE HILLS HAVE EYES II Castle Hill, 1985, w/Peter Locke

CHRISTOPHER CAIN
Agent: CAA - Beverly Hills, 213/288-4545
Contact: Directors Guild of America - Los Angeles, 213/289-2000

YOUNG GUNS 20th Century-Fox, 1988, w/Joe Roth

MICHAEL CAINE
Agent: ICM - Los Angeles, 213/550-4000

THE FOURTH PROTOCOL Lorimar, 1987, EP w/Frederick Forsyth & Wafic Said

JOHN CALLEY
Contact: Firefly Farn, P.O. Box 446, Washington Depot, CT, 06795

THE CINCINNATI KID MGM, 1965, AP
ICE STATION ZEBRA MGM, 1968, w/Martin Ransohoff
CASTLE KEEP Columbia, 1969, w/Martin Ransohoff
CATCH 22 Paramount, 1970, w/Martin Ransohoff
FAT MAN AND LITTLE BOY Paramount, 1989, EP
POSTCARDS FROM THE EDGE Columbia, 1990, w/Mike Nichols

DAVID CALLOWAY
WILD THING Atlantic Entertainment, 1987, w/Nicolas Clermont

BEVERLY J. CAMHE
THE BELIEVERS Orion, 1987, w/Michael Childers & John Schlesinger
THE PACKAGE Orion, 1989, w/Tobie Haggerty

ALIDA CAMP
BODY CHEMISTRY Concorde, 1990

CAROLYN CAMP
Business: Mulberry Square Productions, One Glen Lakes, 8140 Walnut Hill Lane, Suite 301, Dallas, TX, 75231, 214/369-2430
Contact: Directors Guild of America - Los Angeles, 213/289-2000

BENJI THE HUNTED Buena Vista, 1987, SP

BRUCE CAMPBELL
Business: Renaissance MotionPictures, Inc., 28 East 10th St., New York, NY, 10003, 212/477-0432

THE EVIL DEAD New Line Cinema, 1983, EP w/Samuel M. Raimi
EASY WHEELS Fries Entertainment, 1989, EP w/Robert Tapert

JOHN CANDY
Agent: APA - Los Angeles, 213/273-0744

WHO'S HARRY CRUMB? Tri-Star, 1989, EP

JAMES CANNADY
THE WHITE GIRL Tony Brown Prods., 1990

SHERYL CANNADY
THE WHITE GIRL Tony Brown Prods., 1990, EP

MITCHELL CANNOLD
(credit w/Steven Reuther)
Business: Vestron Pictures, 60 Long Ridge Rd., Stamford, CT, 06907, 203/978-5400

GO TELL THE SPARTANS Avco Embassy, 1978, w/Allan F. Bodoh*
CHINA GIRL Vestron, 1987, EP
DIRTY DANCING Vestron, 1987, EP
AND GOD CREATED WOMAN Vestron, 1988, EP w/Ruth Vitale
CALL ME Vestron, 1988, EP w/Ruth Vitale
BIG MAN ON CAMPUS Vestron, 1989, EP
PARENTS Vestron, 1989, EP
LITTLE MONSTERS MGM/UA, 1989, EP w/Dori B. Wasserman*

LARRY CANO
SILKWOOD 20th Century-Fox, 1983, EP w/Buzz Hirsch

STANLEY S. CANTER
ST. IVES Warner Bros., 1976, w/Pancho Kohner
GREYSTOKE: THE LEGEND OF TARZAN, LORD OF THE APES Warner Bros., 1984, w/Hugh Hudson

ELIZABETH CANTILLON
HOW I GOT INTO COLLEGE 20th Century-Fox, 1989, CP

MARIE CANTIN
Contact: Directors Guild of America - Los Angeles, 213/289-2000

HEART CONDITION New Line Cinema, 1990, CP w/Bernie Goldmann

NEIL CANTON
Contact: Amblin Entertainment, 818/777-4600

BLOOD BEACH Jerry Gross Organization, 1981, AP
THE ADVENTURES OF BUCKAROO BANZAI ACROSS THE EIGHTH DIMENSION 20th Century-Fox, 1984, w/W. D. Richter
BACK TO THE FUTURE Universal, 1985, w/Bob Gale
THE WITCHES OF EASTWICK Warner Bros., 1987, w/Peter Guber & Jon Peters
CADDYSHACK II Warner Bros., 1988, w/Peter Guber & Jon Peters
BACK TO THE FUTURE II Universal, 1989, w/Bob Gale
BACK TO THE FUTURE III Universal, 1990, w/Bob Gale

LEE CAPLIN
Business: Caplin Productions, 8274 Grand View, Los Angeles, CA, 90046, 213/650-1882

TO DIE FOR Skouras Pictures, 1989, EP w/Greg H. Sims

SYD CAPPE
FRIENDS, LOVERS & LUNATICS Fries Entertainment, 1989, EP

FRANK CAPRA, JR.
Business: Bonjo Productions, Ltd., One Transglobal Square, P.O. Box 7005, Long Beach, CA, 90807, 213/426-3622
Agent: The Gersh Agency - Beverly Hills, 213/274-6611

MAROONED Columbia, 1969, AP
BATTLE FOR THE PLANET OF THE APES 20th Century-Fox, 1973, AP
BILLY JACK GOES TO WASHINGTON Taylor- Laughlin, 1978
BORN AGAIN Avco Embassy, 1978
THE BLACK MARBLE Avco Embassy, 1980
AN EYE FOR AN EYE Avco Embassy, 1981
THE SEDUCTION Avco Embassy, 1982, EP w/Chuck Russell & Joseph Wolf
VICE SQUAD Avco Embassy, 1982, EP w/Sandy Howard & Bob Rehme
FIRESTARTER Universal, 1984
MARIE MGM/UA, 1985

JIM CARABATSOS
Agent: Martin Shapiro, Shapiro-Lichtman, Inc., - Los Angeles, 213/859-8877

NO MERCY Tri-Star, 1986, CP
HAMBURGER HILL Paramount, 1987, w/Marcia Nasatir

JOSEPH M. CARACCIOLO
Contact: Directors Guild of America - Los Angeles, 213/289-2000

A CHORUS LINE Columbia, 1985, AP
BRIGHTON BEACH MEMOIRS Universal, 1986, AP
THE GLASS MENAGERIE Cineplex Odeon, 1987, AP
THE SECRET OF MY SUCCESS Universal, 1987, LP
BILOXI BLUES Universal, 1988, EP w/Marykay Powell
THE DREAM TEAM Universal, 1989, EP
PARENTHOOD Universal, 1989, EP
SECOND SIGHT Warner Bros., 1989, EP
AUNT JULIA & THE SCRIPTWRITER Cinecom, 1990, EP

JOANN CARELLI
THE DEER HUNTER Universal, 1978, AP
HEAVEN'S GATE United Artists, 1980
THE SICILIAN 20th Century-Fox, 1987, w/Michael Cimino

TOPPER CAREW
Contact: Directors Guild of America - Los Angeles, 213/289-2000

D.C. CAB Universal, 1983

ED CARLIN
BATTLE BEYOND THE STARS New World, 1980

MARK CARLINER
Business: Mark Carliner Productions, 11700 Laurelwood Dr., Studio City, CA, 91604, 818/763-4783

HEAVEN HELP US Tri-Star, 1985, w/Dan Wigutow
CROSSROADS Columbia, 1986

PHYLLIS CARLYLE
Business: Carlyle Productions, 639 N. Larchmont Dr., 2nd Floor, Los Angeles, CA, 90038, 213/469-3086

THE ACCIDENTAL TOURIST ★ Warner Bros., 1988, EP w/John Malkovich

DON CARMODY
TULIPS Avco Embassy, 1981
PORKY'S 20th Century-Fox, 1982, w/Bob Clark
PORKY'S II: THE NEXT DAY 20th Century-Fox, 1983, w/Bob Clark
SPACEHUNTER: ADVENTURES IN THE FORBIDDEN ZONE Columbia, 1983, w/John Dunning & Andre Link
MEATBALLS III Moviestore, 1986, w/John Dunning
THE BIG TOWN Columbia, 1987, CP
SWITCHING CHANNELS Tri-Star, 1988, EP
PHYSICAL EVIDENCE Columbia, 1988
WELCOME HOME Columbia, 1989, EP

JULIO CARO
Business: Siren Pictures, 10 East 22nd St., New York, NY, 10010, 212/254-9770

SIESTA Lorimar, 1987, EP w/Zalman King & Nik Powell
STATIC MCEG, 1988, EP

JOHN CARPENTER
Agent: Jim Wiatt, ICM - Los Angeles, 213/550-4000

DARK STAR Jack H. Harris Enterprises, 1974
HALLOWEEN II Universal, 1981, w/Debra Hill
HALLOWEEN III: SEASON OF THE WITCH Universal, 1982, w/Debra Hill
THE PHILADELPHIA EXPERIMENT New World, 1984, EP

ALLAN CARR
Business: Allan Carr Enterprises, P.O. Box 691670, Los Angeles, CA, 90069, 213/278-2490

THE FIRST TIME United Artists, 1969, w/Roger Smith
C.C. & COMPANY Avco Embassy, 1970, w/Roger Smith

GREASE Paramount, 1978, w/Robert Stigwood
CAN'T STOP THE MUSIC AFD, 1980, w/Henri Belolo & Jacques Morali
GREASE 2 Paramount, 1982, w/Robert Stigwood
WHERE THE BOYS ARE '84 Tri-Star, 1984
CLOAK & DAGGER Universal, 1984

RON CARR

BURNING SECRET Vestron, 1988, SP

TERRY CARR

Agent: CAA - Beverly Hills, 213/288-4545
Contact: Directors Guild of America - Los Angeles, 213/289-2000

THE BAD NEWS BEARS GO TO JAPAN Paramount, 1977, AP
AN ALMOST PERFECT AFFAIR Paramount, 1979
COAST TO COAST Paramount, 1980, EP
YES, GIORGIO MGM, 1982, AP

PAUL CARRAN

WIRED Taurus, 1989, EP w/P. Michael Smith

MICHAEL CARRERAS

THE LADY VANISHES Rank, 1979, EP w/Arlene Sellers & Alex Winitsky

GORDON CARROLL

Business: Brandywine Films, 1211 N. Wetherly Dr., Los Angeles, CA, 90069

HOW TO MURDER YOUR WIFE United Artists, 1965, EP
LUV Columbia, 1967, EP
COOL HAND LUKE Warner Bros., 1967
THE APRIL FOOLS National General, 1969
PAT GARRETT & BILLY THE KID MGM, 1973
ALIEN 20th Century-Fox, 1979, w/David Giler & Walter Hill
BLUE THUNDER Columbia, 1983
THE BEST OF TIMES Universal, 1986
ALIENS 20th Century-Fox, 1986, EP w/David Giler & Walter Hill
RED HEAT Tri-Star, 1988, w/Walter Hill

WILLARD CARROLL

Business: Hyperion Entertainment, 837 Traction Ave., #402, Los Angeles, CA, 90013, 213/625-2921

NUTCRACKER Atlantic Entertainment, 1986, w/Donald Kushner, Peter Locke & Thomas L. Wilhite

WILLIAM P. CARTLIDGE

EDUCATING RITA Columbia, 1983, CP
NOT QUITE PARADISE New World, 1986, CP
CONSUMING PASSIONS Samuel Goldwyn Company, 1988
DEALERS Skouras Pictures, 1989

FRED CARUSO

Business: Warner Bros., 4000 Warner Blvd., Producers Bldg. 5, Suite 114, Burbank, CA, 91522, 818/954-3382
Agent: Bauer Benedek Agency - Los Angeles, 213/275-2421

NETWORK ★ United Artists, 1976, AP
WINTER KILLS Avco Embassy, 1979
DRESSED TO KILL Filmways, 1980, AP
BLOW OUT Filmways, 1981, EP
BLUE VELVET DEG, 1986
THE PRESIDIO Paramount, 1988, CP
CASUALTIES OF WAR Columbia, 1989, CP
WE'RE NO ANGELS Paramount, 1989, CP

GREGORY CASCANTE

Business: August Entertainment, 838 N. Fairfax Ave., Los Angeles, CA, 90046, 213/658-8888

MIDNIGHT CROSSING Vestron, 1988, EP w/Gary Barber, Dan Ireland & Wanda S. Rayle
WAXWORK Vestron, 1988, EP w/Dan Ireland, William J. Quigley & Mario Sotela

EUGENE C. CASHMAN

RETURN OF THE LIVING DEAD PART II Lorimar, 1988, EP

PATRICK CASSAVETTI

BRAZIL Universal, 1985, CP
MONA LISA Island Pictures, 1986, w/Stephen Woolley
PARIS BY NIGHT Cineplex Odeon, 1990

T. J. CASTRONOVO

DOUBLE REVENGE Smart Egg Releasing, 1988, w/John S. Curran

GILBERT CATES

Business: Film-Jamel Productions, 195 S. Beverly Dr., Suite 412, Beverly Hills, CA, 90212, 213/273-7773
Agent: William Morris Agency - Beverly Hills, 213/274-7451

DRAGONFLY American International, 1976, CP
THE LAST MARRIED COUPLE IN AMERICA Universal, 1980, EP w/Joseph Cates

JOSEPH CATES

Business: Cates Films, 57 E. 74th St., New York, NY 10021, 212/517-7100
Contact: Directors Guild of America - Los Angeles, 213/289-2000

THE LAST MARRIED COUPLE IN AMERICA Universal, 1980, EP w/Gilbert Cates

ROBERT CAVALLO

(credit w/Steven Fargnoli & Joseph Ruffalo)
Business: Roven-Cavallo Entertainment, Raleigh Studios, 650 Bronson Ave., Suite 218 West, Los Angeles, CA, 90038, 213/960-4921

PURPLE RAIN Warner Bros., 1984
UNDER THE CHERRY MOON Warner Bros., 1986
SIGN O' THE TIMES Cineplex Odeon, 1987

SUSAN CAVAN

THE BAY BOY Orion, 1985, EP w/Frank Jacobs

ALAIN CHAMMAS

THE BUDDY SYSTEM 20th Century-Fox, 1984

GREGG CHAMPION

Agent: Joe Rosenberg, ICM - Los Angeles, 213/550-4000
Contact: Directors Guild of America - Los Angeles, 213/289-2000

BLUE THUNDER Columbia, 1983, AP
AMERICAN FLYERS Warner Bros., 1985, AP

SHORT CIRCUIT Tri-Star, 1986, SP
STAKEOUT Buena Vista, 1987, SP

DAVID CHAN
Business: Golden Harvest Films, Inc., 9884 Santa Monica Blvd., Beverly Hills, CA, 90212, 213/203-0722

THE PROTECTOR Golden Harvest, 1985
TEENAGE MUTANT NINJA TURTLES New Line Cinema, 1990, w/Kim Dawson & Simon Fields

JOHN K. CHAN
Business: C.I.M. Productions, 665 Bush St., San Francisco, CA, 94108, 415/433-2342

EAT A BOWL OF TEA Columbia, 1989, EP w/Lindsay Law
LIFE IS CHEAP Far East Stars, 1990, EP w/Wayne Wang

WARREN CHANEY
ALOHA SUMMER Spectrafilm, 1988, EP

STEVEN H. CHANIN
UNDER THE BOARDWALK New World, 1989, w/Gregory S. Blackwell

SIMON CHANNING-WILLIAMS
HIGH HOPES Skouras Pictures, 1989, w/Victor Glynn
WHEN THE WHALES CAME 20th Century-Fox, 1989

DOUG CHAPIN
Business: Krost/Chapin Productions, 4000 Warner Blvd., Burbank, CA, 91522, 818/954-6526

WHEN A STRANGER CALLS United Artists, 1979, w/Steve Feke
PANDEMONIUM MGM/UA, 1982
AMERICAN DREAMER Warner Bros., 1984
AMERICAN ANTHEM Columbia, 1986, w/Robert Schaffel

SAUL CHAPLIN
Business: 8969 Sunset Blvd., Los Angeles, 90069, 213/271-2904

THE SOUND OF MUSIC 20th Century-Fox, 1965, AP
STAR! 20th Century-Fox, 1968
MAN OF LA MANCHA United Artists, 1972, AP
THAT'S ENTERTAINMENT, PART 2 MGM/UA, 1976, w/Daniel Melnick

CHRISTIAN CHARRET
WAIT UNTIL SPRING, BANDINI Orion, 1990, EP w/Cyril de Rouvre, Amadeo Pagani & Giorgio Silvago

ROBERT CHARTOFF
(credit w/Irwin Winkler)
Business: Robert Chartoff Productions, 10125 W. Washington Blvd., Culver City, CA, 90230, 213/204-0474

POINT BLANK MGM, 1967, w/Judd Bernard*
THE SPLIT MGM, 1968
THEY SHOOT HORSES, DON'T THEY? Cinerama Releasing Corporation, 1969, w/Sydney Pollack
LEO THE LAST United Artists, 1970
THE STRAWBERRY STATEMENT MGM, 1970
BELIEVE IN ME MGM, 1971
THE GANG THAT COULDN'T SHOOT STRAIGHT MGM, 1971
THE MECHANIC United Artists, 1972
THE NEW CENTURIONS Columbia, 1972
THUMB TRIPPING Avco Embassy, 1972
UP THE SANDBOX National General, 1972
BUSTING United Artists, 1974
S*P*Y*S 20th Century-Fox, 1974
BREAKOUT Columbia, 1975
THE GAMBLER Paramount, 1974
PEEPER 20th Century-Fox, 1976
NICKELODEON Columbia, 1976
ROCKY ★★ United Artists, 1976
NEW YORK, NEW YORK United Artists, 1977
VALENTINO United Artists, 1977
COMES A HORSEMAN United Artists, 1978, EP
UNCLE JOE SHANNON United Artists, 1978
ROCKY II United Artists, 1979
RAGING BULL ★ United Artists, 1980
TRUE CONFESSIONS United Artists, 1981
ROCKY III MGM/UA, 1982
THE RIGHT STUFF ★ The Ladd Company/ Warner Bros., 1983
ROCKY IV MGM/UA, 1985
BEER Orion, 1986*

STANLEY CHASE
HIGH-BALLIN' American International, 1978, EP w/William Hayward
MACK THE KNIFE 21st Century, 1989

DAVID CHASMAN
BRIGHTON BEACH MEMOIRS Universal, 1986, EP
THE SECRET OF MY SUCCESS Universal, 1987, EP

JULIA CHASMAN
Business: Universal Pictures, 445 Park Ave., New York, NY, 10022, 212/759-7500

SHAG: THE MOVIE Hemdale, 1989, w/Stephen Woolley

AMIN Q. CHAUDHRI
Business: Continental Film Group, Ltd., Park St., Sharon, PA, 16146, 412/981-3456

TIGER WARSAW Sony Pictures, 1988
AN UNREMARKABLE LIFE SVS Films, 1989

JOHN CHAVEZ
MEET THE HOLLOWHEADS Moviestore, 1989, w/Joseph Grace

STEPHEN G. CHEIKES
THE HEAVENLY KID Orion, 1985, EP w/Gabe Sumner

JEFFREY CHERNOV
Business: Walt Disney Pictures, 500 S. Buena Vista St., Burbank, CA, 91521, 818/840-1000
Contact: Directors Guild of America - Los Angeles, 213/289-2000

CUTTER'S WAY United Artists Classics, 1981, AP
EDDIE MURPHY RAW Paramount, 1987, CP

CHRIS CHESSER
Business: 4212 Costello Ave., Sherman Oaks, CA, 91423, 818/789-0851

MAJOR LEAGUE Paramount, 1989, w/Irby Smith
WAR PARTY Hemdale, 1989, EP w/Franc Roddam

GIRAUD CHESTER
COME BACK TO THE 5 & DIME, JIMMY DEAN, JIMMY DEAN Cinecom, 1982, EP

RANDOLPH CHEVELDAVE
FRIDAY THE 13TH PART VIII — JASON TAKES MANHATTAN Paramount, 1989

DEVEN CHIERIGHINO
THE WIZARD OF SPEED AND TIME Shapiro-Glickenhaus Entertainment, 1989, w/Richard Kaye

MICHAEL CHILDERS
Contact: Directors Guild of America - Los Angeles, 213/289-2000

THE BELIEVERS Orion, 1987, w/Beverly J. Camhe & John Schlesinger

MICHAEL CHINICH
Business: Hughes Entertainment, 100 Universal Plaza, Universal City, CA, 91608, 818/777-6363

THE BINGO LONG TRAVELING ALL-STARS AND MOTOR KINGS Universal, 1976, AP
PRETTY IN PINK Paramount, 1986, EP w/John Hughes
FERRIS BUELLER'S DAY OFF Paramount, 1986, EP
SOME KIND OF WONDERFUL Paramount, 1987, EP w/Ronald Colby
PLANES, TRAINS AND AUTOMOBILES Paramount, 1987, EP w/Neil Machlis

DAVID CHISOLM
Agent: CAA - Beverly Hills, 213/288-4545

THE WIZARD Universal, 1989, w/Ken Topolsky

ARTHUR CHOBANIAN
ROCKY IV MGM/UA, 1985, EP w/James D. Brubaker

ELIE CHOURAQUI
Contact: French Film Office, 745 Fifth Ave., New York, NY, 10151, 212/832-8860

LOVE SONGS Spectrafilm, 1986, w/Robert Baylis

MARIE-CHRISTINE CHOURAQUI
Contact: French Film Office, 745 Fifth Ave., New York, NY, 10151, 212/832-8860

LOVE SONGS Spectrafilm, 1986, EP w/Murray Shostak

RAYMOND CHOW
Business: Golden Harvest Films, Inc., 9884 Santa Monica Blvd., Beverly Hills, CA, 90212, 213/203-0722

THE CANNONBALL RUN 20th Century-Fox, 1981, EP
DEATH HUNT 20th Century-Fox, 1981, EP w/Albert S. Ruddy
MEGAFORCE 20th Century-Fox, 1982, EP
BETTER LATE THAN NEVER Warner Bros., 1983, EP
HIGH ROAD TO CHINA Warner Bros., 1983, EP
LASSITER Warner Bros., 1984, EP w/Andre Morgan
THE PROTECTOR Golden Harvest, 1985, EP
TEENAGE MUTANT NINJA TURTLES New Line Cinema, 1990, EP

BO CHRISTENSEN
BABETTE'S FEAST Orion Classics, 1987

BRIAN CHRISTIAN
RETRIBUTION Taurus Entertainment, 1988, EP w/Scott Lavin

ROBERT CHRISTIANSEN
(credit w/Rick Rosenberg)
Business: Chris-Rose Productions, 4000 Warner Blvd., Producers 2, #1104-A, Burbank, CA, 91522, 818/954-1748

ADAM AT SIX A.M. National General, 1970
HIDE IN PLAIN SIGHT MGM/UA, 1980

CALDECOTT CHUBB
Business: Edward R. Pressman Film Corporation, 4000 Warner Blvd., Prod. 5, Room 114, Burbank, CA, 91522, 818/954-3315

GOOD MORNING BABYLON Vestron, 1987, AP w/Lloyd Fonvielle
CHERRY 2000 Orion, 1988, w/Edward R. Pressman
TO SLEEP WITH ANGER SVS Films, 1990, w/Thomas S. Byrnes & Darin Scott
WAITING FOR THE LIGHT Triumph, 1990, w/Ron Bozman

MICHAEL CIMINO
Attorney: Barry Hirsch, Armstrong & Hirsch, 1888 Century Park East, Los Angeles, CA, 90067, 213/553-0305
Business Manager: Alan Cohen & Co. - New York, 212/755-0750

THE DEER HUNTER ★★ Universal, 1978, w/Michael Deeley, John Peverall & Barry Spikings
THE SICILIAN 20th Century-Fox, 1987, w/Joann Carelli

TONY CINCIRIPINI
THE LAWLESS LAND Concorde, 1988, w/Larry Leahy

LUIGI CINGOLANI
Business: Smart Egg Pictures, 7080 Hollywood Blvd., Suite 518, Hollywood, CA, 90028, 213/463-8937

OMEGA SYNDROME New World, 1987
DOUBLE REVENGE Smart Egg Releasing, 1988, EP w/George Zecevic
CAMERON'S CLOSET SVS Films, 1989
SPACED INVADERS Buena Vista, 1990

ANNETTE CIRILLO
THE RETURN OF SWAMP THING Miramax, 1989, CP

AL CLARK
(credit w/Robert Devereux)
Business: Virgin Vision Ltd., 328 Kensal Rd., London W10 5XJ, England, 01/968-8888

1984 Atlantic Entertainment, 1985, CP
ABSOLUTE BEGINNERS Orion, 1986, EP w/Nik Powell

GOTHIC Vestron, 1987, EP
ARIA Miramax, 1988, CP w/Mike Watts

BOB CLARK
Business Manager: Harold D. Cohen - Los Angeles, 213/550-0570
Contact: Directors Guild of America - Los Angeles, 213/289-2000

BREAKING POINT 20th Century-Fox, 1976, w/Claude Héroux
PORKY'S 20th Century-Fox, 1982, w/Don Carmody
PORKY'S II: THE NEXT DAY 20th Century-Fox, 1983, w/Don Carmody
A CHRISTMAS STORY MGM/UA, 1983, w/Rene Dupont
FROM THE HIP DEG, 1987, w/Rene Dupont

DICK CLARK
Business: Dick Clark Productions, Inc., 3003 W. Olive Ave., Burbank, CA, 91510, 818/954-8609

REMO WILLIAMS: THE ADVENTURE BEGINS... Orion, 1985, EP w/Mel Bergman

GREYDON CLARK
JOYSTICKS Jensen-Farley, 1983

LOUISE CLARK
A WINTER TAN Circle Releasing, 1989

NIGEL STAFFORD-CLARK
(see Nigel STAFFORD-Clark)

FRANK CLARKE
LETTER TO BREZHNEV Circle Releasing, 1985, EP

DOUG CLAYBOURNE
Business: Claybourne Productions, 848 Fuller Ave., Los Angeles, CA, 90046, 213/930-1112
Contact: Directors Guild of America - Los Angeles, 213/289-2000

THE ESCAPE ARTIST Orion/Warner Bros., 1982, w/Buck Houghton
RUMBLE FISH Universal, 1983, w/Fred Roos
THE BLACK STALLION RETURNS MGM/UA, 1983, w/Fred Roos & Tom Sternberg
LIGHT OF DAY Tri-Star, 1987, EP
THE SERPENT & THE RAINBOW Universal, 1988, w/David Ladd
ERNEST SAVES CHRISTMAS Buena Vista, 1988, w/Stacy Williams
THE WAR OF THE ROSES 20th Century-Fox, 1989, EP w/Polly Platt

JOHN CLEESE
Business: Prominent Features Ltd., 68A Delancey St., London NW1 7RY, England, 01/284-1004

A FISH CALLED WANDA MGM/UA, 1988, EP w/ Steve Abbott

TERENCE CLEGG
CAL Warner Bros., 1984, EP
OUT OF AFRICA ★★ Universal, 1985, CP
CRY FREEDOM Universal, 1987, EP
GORILLAS IN THE MIST Universal, 1988, w/Arnold Glimcher

RENE CLEITMAN
THE BAY BOY Orion, 1985, CP

DICK CLEMENT
Agent: Elliot Webb, Broder-Kurland-Webb-Uffner Agency - Los Angeles, 213/656-9262
Contact: Directors Guild of America - Los Angeles, 213/289-2000

VICE VERSA Columbia, 1988, w/Ian La Frenais

NICOLAS CLERMONT
WILD THING Atlantic Entertainment, 1987, w/David Calloway

GRAEME CLIFFORD
Agent: Lou Pitt, ICM - Los Angeles, 213/550-4000
Contact: Directors Guild of America - Los Angeles, 213/289-2000

BURKE & WILLS Hemdale, 1987, w/John Sexton

SANDY CLIMAN
(credit w/Charles C. Thieriot)

ALMOST YOU 20th Century-Fox, 1984, EP w/Stephen J. Levin
3:15 THE MOMENT OF TRUTH Dakota Entertainment, 1986, EP w/Andrew Bullians & Jean Bullians
THE BIKINI SHOP *THE MALIBU BIKINI SHOP* International Film Marketing, 1987, EP w/Andrew Bullians & Jean Bullians

LEON CLORE
MORGAN; A SUITABLE CASE FOR TREATMENT Cinema 5, 1966
ALL NEAT IN BLACK STOCKINGS National General, 1969
THE FRENCH LIEUTENANT'S WOMAN United Artists, 1981

WALTER COBLENZ
Business: Bellisle Productions, 2348 Apollo Dr., Los Angeles, CA, 90046, 213/469-0896
Contact: Directors Guild of America - Los Angeles, 213/289-2000

THE CANDIDATE Warner Bros., 1972
ALL THE PRESIDENT'S MEN ★ Warner Bros., 1976
THE ONION FIELD Avco Embassy, 1979
THE LEGEND OF THE LONE RANGER Universal/ AFD, 1981
STRANGE INVADERS Orion, 1983
SPACECAMP 20th Century-Fox, 1986, w/Patrick Bailey
FOR KEEPS Tri-Star, 1988, w/Jerry Belson
SISTER SISTER New World, 1988
18 AGAIN New World, 1988

MICHAEL CODRON
CLOCKWISE Universal, 1986

EDWARD COE
GHOST FEVER Miramax, 1987, w/Ron Rich

ETHAN COEN
Agent: Leading Artists, Inc. - Beverly Hills, 213/858-1999

BLOOD SIMPLE Circle Releasing Corporation, 1985

RAISING ARIZONA 20th Century-Fox, 1987
MILLER'S CROSSING 20th Century-Fox, 1990, w/Graham Place & Mark Silverman

JONATHAN COHEN
MARIGOLDS IN AUGUST RM Productions, 1984, w/Mark Forstater

LARRY COHEN
Attorney: Skip Brittenham, Ziffren, Brittenham & Branca, 2049 Century Park East, Los Angeles, CA, 90067, 213/552-3388
Agent: Robert Littman, The Robert Littman Company - Los Angeles, 213/278-1572

Q UFD, 1982
THE STUFF New World, 1985, EP
FULL MOON HIGH Orion, 1986
IT'S ALIVE III: ISLAND OF THE ALIVE Warner Bros., 1987, EP
WICKED STEPMOTHER MGM/UA, 1989, EP

LAWRENCE J. COHEN
Agent: CAA - Beverly Hills, 213/288-4545

THE BIG BUS Paramount, 1976, w/Fred Freeman

MARTIN B. COHEN
Business: Martin B. Cohen Productions, Inc., 9962 Durant Dr., Beverly Hills, CA, 90212, 213/552-2958
Agent: Abby Greshler, Diamond Artists, Ltd. - Los Angeles, 213/278-8146

HUMANOIDS FROM THE DEEP New World, 1980, w/Hunt Lowry

NAT COHEN
CLOCKWISE Universal, 1986, EP w/Verity Lambert

NORMAN I. COHEN
Business: Co-Star Entertainment, 216 E. 45th St., New York, NY, 10017, 212/557-0404

TRACKS Castle Hill, 1976, w/Ted Shapiro & Howard Zucker
THE GIG Castle Hill, 1985
THE LUCKIEST MAN IN THE WORLD Castle Hill, 1989

RICHARD COHEN
SPELLBINDER MGM/UA, 1988, EP w/Howard Baldwin

ROB COHEN
Business: Badham-Cohen Group, 100 Universal City Plaza, Universal City, CA, 91608, 818/777-3166
Agent: Leading Artists - Beverly Hills, 213/858-1999

MAHOGANY Paramount, 1975, w/Jack Ballard
THE BINGO LONG TRAVELING ALL-STARS & MOTOR KINGS Universal, 1976
SCOTT JOPLIN Universal, 1977, EP
THE WIZ Universal, 1978
THANK GOD IT'S FRIDAY Columbia, 1978
ALMOST SUMMER Universal, 1978
THE RAZOR'S EDGE Columbia, 1984, EP
THE LEGEND OF BILLIE JEAN Tri-Star, 1985
LIGHT OF DAY Tri-Star, 1987, w/Keith Barish
THE MONSTER SQUAD Tri-Star, 1987, EP w/Keith Barish & Peter Hyams
THE RUNNING MAN Tri-Star, 1987, EP w/Keith Barish
THE WITCHES OF EASTWICK Warner Bros., 1987, EP w/Don Devlin
IRONWEED Tri-Star, 1987, EP w/Denis Blouin & Joseph H. Kanter
THE SERPENT & THE RAINBOW Universal, 1988, EP w/Keith Barish
DISORGANIZED CRIME Buena Vista, 1989, EP w/John Badham
BIRD ON A WIRE Universal, 1990, w/John Badham

RONALD I. COHEN
Business: Ronald I. Cohen Productions Inc., 1155 Blvd. René-Lévesque, Suite 4103, Montreal, Quebec H3B 3V6, Canada, 514/397-1511

RUNNING Universal, 1979, w/Robert Cooper
MIDDLE AGE CRAZY 20th Century-Fox, 1980, w/Robert Cooper
TICKET TO HEAVEN United Artists Classics, 1981, EP
CROSS COUNTRY New World, 1983, EP
HARRY TRACY Quartet/Films, Inc., 1983

RONALD COLBY
Contact: Directors Guild of America - Los Angeles, 213/289-2000

THE RAIN PEOPLE Warner Bros., 1969, w/Bart Patton
HAMMETT Orion/Warner Bros., 1982, w/Don Guest & Fred Roos
SOME KIND OF WONDERFUL Paramount, 1987, EP w/Michael Chinich
SHE'S HAVING A BABY Paramount, 1988, EP

STEPHEN J. COLE
APARTMENT ZERO Skouras Pictures, 1989, EP

STAN COLEMAN
BORN IN EAST L.A. Universal, 1987, EP

THOMAS COLEMAN
(credit w/Michael Rosenblatt)

VALLEY GIRL Atlantic Entertainment, 1983, EP
ROADHOUSE 66 Atlantic Entertainment, 1984, EP
TEEN WOLF Atlantic Entertainment, 1985, EP
THE MEN'S CLUB Atlantic Entertainment, 1986, EP w/John Harada
EXTREMITIES Atlantic Entertainment, 1986, EP
NUTCRACKER Atlantic Entertainment, 1986, EP
SUMMER HEAT Atlantic Entertainment, 1987, EP
STEEL JUSTICE Atlantic Entertainment, 1987, EP
WILD THING Atlantic Entertainment, 1987, EP
THE GARBAGE PAIL KIDS MOVIE Atlantic Entertainment, 1987, EP
TEEN WOLF TOO Atlantic Entertainment, 1987, EP
COP Atlantic Entertainment, 1988, EP
PATTY HEARST Atlantic Entertainment, 1988, EP
1969 Atlantic Entertainment, 1988, EP*

ROBERT F. COLESBERRY
Business: 7720 Sunset Blvd., Los Angeles, CA, 90046, 213/969-0969
Contact: Directors Guild of America - New York, 212/581-0370

TATTOO 20th Century-Fox, 1981, AP
BABY, IT'S YOU Paramount, 1983, AP
THE KING OF COMEDY 20th Century-Fox, 1983, AP

FALLING IN LOVE Paramount, 1984, AP
THE NATURAL Tri-Star, 1984, AP
AFTER HOURS The Geffen Company/Warner Bros., 1985, w/Griffin Dunne & Amy Robinson
HOUSEKEEPING Columbia, 1987
THE HOUSE ON CARROLL STREET Orion, 1988, w/Peter Yates
MISSISSIPPI BURNING ★ Orion, 1988, w/Frederick Zollo
COME SEE THE PARADISE 20th Century-Fox, 1990

PAUL COLICHMAN

(credit w/Miles A. Copeland III)

Business: I.R.S. World Media, 8335 Sunset Blvd., Los Angeles, CA, 90069, 213/650-8010

THE DECLINE OF WESTERN CIVILIZATION PART II: THE METAL YEARS (FD) New Line Cinema, 1988, EP
A SINFUL LIFE New Line Cinema, 1989, EP

RICHARD COLL

MISS FIRECRACKER Corsair, 1989, CP

DAVID COLLINS

EAT THE PEACH Skouras Pictures, 1987, EP

PETER COLLISTER

KGB: THE SECRET WAR Cinema Group, 1986, EP

HARRY COLOMBY

Agent: Coxson & Carleton - Los Angeles, 213/924-2028

MR. MOM 20th Century-Fox, 1983, CP
JOHNNY DANGEROUSLY 20th Century-Fox, EP w/Bud Austin
THE SQUEEZE Tri-Star, 1987, EP w/David Shamroy Hamburger
TOUCH AND GO Tri-Star, 1987, EP

FRANCO COMMITTERI

MACARONI Paramount, 1985, w/Aurelio & Luigi De Laurentiis

JON CONNOLLY

Agent: CAA - Beverly Hills, 213/288-4545
Contact: Writers Guild of America - Los Angeles, 213/550-1000

THE DREAM TEAM Universal, 1989, CP w/David Loucka

JACK CONRAD

THE HOWLING Avco Embassy, 1980, w/Michael Finnell

D. CONSTANTINE CONTE

CONAN THE BARBARIAN Universal, 1982, EP w/Edward R. Pressman
FIGHTING BACK Paramount, 1982
48 HOURS Paramount, 1982, EP
HARD TO HOLD Universal, 1984
NO MERCY Tri-Star, 1986
THE PRESIDIO Paramount, 1988
ANOTHER 48 HOURS Paramount, 1990, CP

JOAN GANZ COONEY

Business: Children's Television Workshop, One Lincoln Plaza, 4th Floor, New York, NY, 10023, 212/595-3456

SESAME STREET PRESENTS: FOLLOW THAT BIRD Warner Bros., 1985, EP

RAY COONEY

WHOSE LIFE IS IT ANYWAY? MGM, 1981, EP w/Martin C. Schute

HARRY COOPER

HEARTBREAKERS Orion, 1985, EP w/Joseph Franck & Lee Muhl

NESSA COOPER

LAST RESORT Concorde, 1986, EP

RAY COOPER

Business: HandMade Films, Ltd., 26 Cadogan Square, London SW1X 0JP, England, 01/584-8345 or 7400 Beverly Blvd., #210, Los Angeles, CA, 90036, 213/936-8050

MONA LISA Island Pictures, 1986, CP w/Chris Brown
THE ADVENTURES OF BARON MUNCHAUSEN Columbia, 1989, CP
HOW TO GET AHEAD IN ADVERTISING Warner Bros., 1989, CP

ROBERT COOPER

Business: Home Box Office, 2049 Century Park East, Suite 4100, Los Angeles, CA, 90067, 213/201-9200

RUNNING Universal, 1979, w/Ronald I. Cohen
MIDDLE AGE CRAZY 20th Century-Fox, 1980, w/Ronald I. Cohen

MILES A. COPELAND III

Business: I.R.S. World Media, 8335 Sunset Blvd., Los Angeles, CA, 90069, 213/650-8010

LUCKY STIFF New Line Cinema, 1988, EP w/Laurie Perlman, Derek Power & Pat Proft
THE DECLINE OF WESTERN CIVILIZATION PART II: THE METAL YEARS (FD) New Line Cinema, 1988, EP w/Paul Colichman
A SINFUL LIFE New Line Cinema, 1989, EP w/Paul Colichman

FRANCIS FORD COPPOLA

Business: Zoetrope Studios, Sentinel Bldg., 916 Kearny St., San Francisco, CA, 94133, 415/789-7500
Agent: ICM - Los Angeles, 213/550-4000

TONIGHT FOR SURE Premier Pictures, 1962
THE TERROR American International, 1963, AP
THX 1138 Warner Bros., 1970, EP
AMERICAN GRAFFITI ★ Universal, 1973
THE CONVERSATION ★ Paramount, 1974, w/Fred Roos
THE GODFATHER - PART II ★★ Paramount, 1974
APOCALYPSE NOW ★ United Artists, 1979
THE BLACK STALLION United Artists, 1979, EP
HAMMETT Orion/Warner Bros., 1982, EP
THE ESCAPE ARTIST Orion/Warner Bros., 1982, EP w/Fred Roos
PARSIFAL Triumph/Columbia, 1983
THE BLACK STALLION RETURNS MGM/UA, 1983, EP

RUMBLE FISH Universal, 1983, EP
MISHIMA: A LIFE IN FOUR CHAPTERS Warner Bros., 1985, EP w/George Lucas
GARDENS OF STONE Tri-Star, 1987, w/Michael I. Levy
TOUGH GUYS DON'T DANCE Cannon, 1987, EP w/Tom Luddy
LION HEART Orion, 1987, EP w/Jack Schwartzman

PENNY CORKE

GOTHIC Vestron, 1987
SALOME'S LAST DANCE Vestron, 1988

CIS CORMAN

Business: Barwood Films, 75 Rockefeller Plaza, #1709, New York, NY, 10019, 212/484-7300

NUTS Warner Bros., 1987, EP w/Teri Schwartz

GENE CORMAN

Business: 21st Century Film Corporation, 8200 Wilshire Blvd., Beverly Hills, CA, 90211, 213/658-3000

YOU CAN'T WIN 'EM ALL Columbia, 1970
VON RICHTHOFEN & BROWN United Artists, 1971
PRIVATE PARTS MGM, 1972
COOL BREEZE MGM, 1972
HIT MAN MGM, 1972
I ESCAPED FROM DEVIL'S ISLAND United Artists, 1973, w/Roger Corman
THE SLAMS MGM, 1973
VIGILANTE FORCE United Artists, 1976
F.I.S.T. United Artists, 1978, EP
TARGET: HARRY ABC Pictures International, 1979, EP
THE BIG RED ONE United Artists, 1980
IF YOU COULD SEE WHAT I HEAR Jensen Farley Pictures, 1982, EP w/Dale Falconer
A MAN CALLED SARGE Cannon, 1990

JULIE CORMAN

Business: Concorde Films, 11600 San Vicente Blvd., Los Angeles, CA, 90049, 213/820-6733

MOVING VIOLATION 20th Century-Fox, 1976
THE LADY IN RED New World, 1979
SATURDAY THE 14TH New World, 1981
THE DIRT BIKE KID Concorde, 1985
CHOPPING MALL Concorde, 1986
LAST RESORT Concorde, 1986
DA FilmDallas, 1988
NIGHTFALL Concorde, 1989
NOWHERE TO RUN *TEMPTATION BLUES* Concorde, 1989
SATURDAY THE 14TH STRIKES BACK Concorde, 1989
PATHFINDER Concorde, 1989
BRAIN DEAD Concorde, 1990
A CRY IN THE WILD CONCORDE, 1990

ROGER CORMAN

Business: Concorde Films, 11600 San Vicente Blvd., Los Angeles, CA, 90049, 213/820-6733

HIGHWAY DRAGNET Allied Artists, 1954, AP
CRY BABY KILLER American International, 1954
THE MONSTER FROM THE OCEAN FLOOR American International, 1954
THE FAST AND THE FURIOUS American International, 1954
STAKEOUT ON DOPE STREET American International, 1958
HIGH SCHOOL BIG SHOT American International, 1958
T-BIRD GANG American International, 1958
THE WILD RIDE American International, 1960
THE BATTLE OF BLOOD ISLAND American International, 1960
LITTLE SHOP OF HORRORS Filmgroup, 1960
BATTLE BEYOND THE SUN American International, 1962
THE MAGIC VOYAGE OF SINBAD American International, 1962
DEMENTIA 13 American International, 1963
PIT STOP American International, 1963
MOVING VIOLATION American International, 1963
BEACH BALL American International, 1965
QUEEN OF BLOOD American International, 1965
TARGETS American International, 1967, EP
DEVIL'S ANGELS American International, 1967
THE WILD RACERS American International, 1967
BLOODY MAMA American International, 1970
THE DUNWICH HORROR American International, 1970, EP
GAS-S-S-S! American International, 1970
THE STUDENT NURSES American International, 1970, EP
BOXCAR BERTHA American International, 1972
I ESCAPED FROM DEVIL'S ISLAND United Artists, 1973, w/Gene Corman
BIG BAD MAMA New World, 1974
BORN TO KILL *COCKFIGHTER* New World, 1974
DEATH RACE 2000 New World, 1975
CAPONE 20th Century-Fox, 1975
MOVING VIOLATION 20th Century-Fox, 1976, EP
JACKSON COUNTY JAIL United Artists/New World, 1976, EP
FIGHTING MAD 20th Century-Fox, 1976
EAT MY DUST New World, 1976
I NEVER PROMISED YOU A ROSE GARDEN New World, 1977, EP w/Edgar J. Scherick
THUNDER & LIGHTNING 20th Century-Fox, 1977
GRAND THEFT AUTO New World, 1978, EP
PIRANHA New World, 1978, EP w/Jeff Schechtman
DEATHSPORT New World, 1978
AVALANCHE New World, 1978
SAINT JACK New World, 1979
TARGET: HARRY ABC Pictures International, 1979
FAST CHARLIE...THE MOONBEAM RIDER Universal, 1979, w/Saul Krugman
ROCK 'N' ROLL HIGH SCHOOL New World, 1979, EP
BATTLE BEYOND THE STARS New World, 1980, EP
SMOKEY BITES THE DUST New World, 1981
GALAXY OF TERROR New World, 1981
FORBIDDEN WORLD New World, 1982
LOVE LETTERS New World, 1983
COCAINE WARS Concorde, 1985, w/Alex Sessa
STREETWALKIN' Concorde, 1985, EP
MUNCHIES Concorde, 1987
BIG BAD MAMA II Concorde, 1987
STRIPPED TO KILL Concorde, 1987, EP
SWEET REVENGE Concorde, 1987, EP
HOUR OF THE ASSASSIN Concorde, 1987, EP
DADDY'S BOYS Concorde, 1988
THE DRIFTER Concorde, 1988, EP
WATCHERS Tri-Star, 1988, EP
CRIME ZONE Concorde, 1988, EP
THE LAWLESS LAND Concorde, 1988, EP w/Juan Forch
THE TERROR WITHIN Concorde, 1989
LORDS OF THE DEEP Concorde, 1989
STRIPPED TO KILL 2 Concorde, 1989, EP
TRANSYLVANIA TWIST Concorde, 1989, EP
BLOODFIST Concorde, 1989
STREETS Concorde, 1990, EP

FRANKENSTEIN UNBOUND 20th Century-Fox, 1990, w/Kobi Jaeger & Thom Mount
THE HAUNTING OF MORELLA Concorde, 1990
ANDY AND THE AIRWAVE RANGERS Concorde, 1990, EP

JOHN CORNELL

Business: Paramount Pictures, 5555 Melrose Ave., Los Angeles, CA, 90038, 213/468-5796

"CROCODILE" DUNDEE Paramount, 1986
CROCODILE DUNDEE II Paramount, 1988, w/Jane Scott

STUART CORNFELD

Business: Baltimore Pictures, c/o Tri-Star Pictures, Studio Plaza, 3400 Riverside Dr., Burbank, CA, 91505, 818/954-3710

FATSO 20th Century-Fox, 1980
THE ELEPHANT MAN ★ Paramount, 1980, EP
THE HISTORY OF THE WORLD - PART I 20th Century-Fox, 1981, AP
GIRLS JUST WANT TO HAVE FUN New World, 1985, EP
NATIONAL LAMPOON'S EUROPEAN VACATION Warner Bros., 1985, CP
THE FLY 20th Century-Fox, 1986
MOVING Warner Bros., 1988
THE FLY II 20th Century-Fox, 1989, EP
HIDER IN THE HOUSE Vestron, 1989, CP w/Lem Dobbs

ROBERT W. CORT

(credit w/Ted Field)

Business: Interscope Communications, 10900 Wilshire Blvd., Suite 1400, Los Angeles, CA, 90024, 213/208-8525

TURK 182 20th Century-Fox, 1985, EP w/Peter Samuelson*
REVENGE OF THE NERDS II 20th Century-Fox, 1987, w/Peter Bart
OUTRAGEOUS FORTUNE Buena Vista, 1987
THREE MEN AND A BABY Buena Vista, 1987
CRITICAL CONDITION Paramount, 1987
COLLISION COURSE DEG, 1988
THE SEVENTH SIGN Tri-Star, 1988
COCKTAIL Buena Vista, 1988
BILL & TED'S EXCELLENT ADVENTURE Orion, 1989, EP w/Stephen Deutsch
RENEGADES Universal, 1989, EP w/James G. Robinson & Joe Roth
AN INNOCENT MAN Buena Vista, 1989
BLIND FURY Tri-Star, 1990, EP w/David Madden*
THE FIRST POWER Orion, 1990, w/David Madden
BIRD ON A WIRE Universal, 1990, EP

ROBERT CORTES

CRACKERS Universal, 1984, w/Edward Lewis
THE RIVER Universal, 1984, w/Edward Lewis

FRANCESCO CORTI

THE URANIUM CONSPIRACY Noah Films, 1978, w/Yoram Globus

BILL COSBY

Business: SAH Enterprises, Inc., 205 Hill St., Santa Monica, CA, 90405, 213/457-8023
Agent: Norman Brokaw, William Morris Agency - Beverly Hills, 213/274-7451

MAN & BOY Levitt-Pickman, 1972, EP
LEONARD PART 6 Columbia, 1987

DAC COSCARELLI

PHANTASM II Universal, 1988, EP
SURVIVAL QUEST MGM/UA, 1990, EP

KEVIN COSTNER

Business: Tig Productions, Raleigh Studios, 650 N. Bronson, Suite 211, Los Angeles, CA, 90004, 213/874-4401
Agent: CAA - Beverly Hills, 213/288-4545

REVENGE Columbia, 1990, EP
DANCES WITH WOLVES Orion, 1990, EP

GRAHAM COTTLE

Contact: Directors Guild of America - Los Angeles, 213/289-2000

UNDER THE CHERRY MOON Warner Bros., 1986, AP
MIRACLE MILE Hemdale, 1989, CP
TEENAGE MUTANT NINJA TURTLES New Line Cinema, 1990, CP

JACK COUFFER

Agent: ICM - Los Angeles, 213/550-4000
Contact: Directors Guild of America - Los Angeles, 213/289-2000

NEVER CRY WOLF Buena Vista, 1983, w/Lewis Allen & Joseph Strick

JEROME COURTLAND

Agent: Sanford-Beckett/Tobias-Skouras - Los Angeles, 213/208-2100
Contact: Directors Guild of America - Los Angeles, 213/289-2000

ESCAPE TO WITCH MOUNTAIN Buena Vista, 1975
RIDE A WILD PONY Buena Vista, 1975
PETE'S DRAGON Buena Vista, 1977, w/Ron Miller
RETURN FROM WITCH MOUNTAIN Buena Vista, 1978, w/Ron Miller
THE DEVIL AND MAX DEVLIN Buena Vista, 1981
AMY Buena Vista, 1981

JAMES A. COURTNEY

MOONTRAP Shapiro-Glickenhaus Entertainment, 1989, EP w/Brian C. Manoogian & Alan M. Solomon

BILL COUTURIÉ

Agent: CAA - Beverly Hills, 213/288-4545

TWICE UPON A TIME (AF) Warner Bros., 1983
DEAR AMERICA (FD) Corsair, 1988, w/Thomas Bird

PAUL COWAN

ANOTHER TIME, ANOTHER PLACE Samuel Goldwyn Company, 1984, AP
DANCE WITH A STRANGER Samuel Goldwyn Company, 1985, AP

RIDERS OF THE STORM *THE AMERICAN WAY* Miramax, 1987, w/Laurie Keller
WE THINK THE WORLD OF YOU Cinecom, 1989, CP

PENNY FINKELMAN COX
Contact: Directors Guild of America - Los Angeles, 213/289-2000

TERMS OF ENDEARMENT Paramount, 1983, CP w/Martin Jurow
BROADCAST NEWS 20th Century-Fox, 1987, CP
HONEY, I SHRUNK THE KIDS Buena Vista, 1989
WELCOME HOME, ROXY CARMICHAEL ITC, 1990

RONNY COX
RAW COURAGE *COURAGE* New World, 1984, w/Robert L. Rosen

MALCOLM CRADDOCK
PING PONG Samuel Goldwyn Company, 1987, w/Michael Guest

CARL CRAIG
HOLLYWOOD SHUFFLE Samuel Goldwyn Company, 1987, EP
I'M GONNA GIT YOU SUCKA MGM/UA, 1989, w/Peter McCarthy

STUART CRAIG
CAL Warner Bros., 1984, w/David Puttnam

JENNY CRAVEN
ORDEAL BY INNOCENCE Cannon, 1985

WES CRAVEN
Business: Wes Craven Films, 8271 Melrose Ave., Los Angeles, CA, 90046, 213/852-1100
Agent: Andrea Eastman, ICM - Los Angeles, 213/550-4000

A NIGHTMARE ON ELM STREET 3: DREAM WARRIORS New Line Cinema, 1987, EP w/Stephen Diener
SHOCKER Universal, 1989, EP w/Shep Gordon

ROBERT L. CRAWFORD
Business: Pan Arts Productions, 4000 Warner Blvd., Burbank, CA, 91522, 818/954-3631

THE STING Universal, 1973, AP
THE GREAT WALDO PEPPER Universal, 1975, AP
SLAP SHOT Universal, 1977, AP
A LITTLE ROMANCE Orion/Warner Bros., 1979, w/Yves Rousset-Rouard
THE WORLD ACCORDING TO GARP Warner Bros., 1982, w/George Roy Hill
THE LITTLE DRUMMER GIRL Warner Bros., 1984
DEADLY FRIEND Warner Bros., 1986, CP
FUNNY FARM Warner Bros., 1988

WAYNE CRAWFORD
(credit w/Andrew Lane)
Business: Crawford-Lane Productions, 14101 Valleyheart Dr., #205, Sherman Oaks, CA, 91423, 818/501-2076
Agent: Paul Kohner, Inc. - Los Angeles, 213/559-1060

VALLEY GIRL Atlantic Entertainment, 1983
NIGHT OF THE COMET Atlantic Entertainment, 1984
JAKE SPEED New World, 1986, w/William Fay
MORTAL PASSIONS MGM/UA, 1990, EP w/Joel Levine

FRANCO CRISTALDI
AMARCORD New World, 1974
THE NAME OF THE ROSE 20th Century-Fox, 1986, CP w/Alexandre Mnouchkine
CINEMA PARADISO Miramax, 1990

DAVID CRONENBERG
Business: 217 Avenue Rd., Toronto, Ontario M5R 2J3, Canada, 416/961-3432
Agent: Mike Marcus, CAA - Beverly Hills, 213/288-4545

DEAD RINGERS 20th Century-Fox, 1988, w/Marc Boyman

BILLY CROSS
WEEDS DEG, 1987, EP w/Mel Pearl

EMILIA CROW
AND GOD CREATED WOMAN Vestron, 1988, CP w/Robert Crow

ROBERT CROW
AND GOD CREATED WOMAN Vestron, 1988, CP w/Emilia Crow

CAMERON CROWE
Agent: Judy Scott-Fox, William Morris Agency - Beverly Hills, 213/274-7451

THE WILD LIFE Universal, 1984, w/Art Linson

PATRICK CROWLEY
Contact: Directors Guild of America - Los Angeles, 213/289-2000

TRUE BELIEVER Columbia, 1989, CP
ROBOCOP II Orion, 1990, EP

ALFRED W. CROWN
LAST SUMMER Allied Artists, 1969, w/Sidney Beckerman

OWEN CRUMP
Contact: Directors Guild of America - Los Angeles, 213/289-2000

DARLING LILI Paramount, 1970, EP

BILLY CRYSTAL
Agent: ICM - Los Angeles, 213/550-4000

MEMORIES OF ME MGM/UA, 1988, w/Michael Hertzberg & Alan King

GREGORY M. CUMMINS
PATTI ROCKS FilmDallas, 1988, w/Gwen Field

GENE CUNNINGHAM
FORBIDDEN ZONE Samuel Goldwyn Company, 1980, EP

JERE CUNNINGHAM
THE LAST OF THE FINEST Orion, 1990, EP

SEAN S. CUNNINGHAM

Agent: ICM - Los Angeles, 213/550-4000
Contact: Directors Guild of America - Los Angeles, 213/289-2000

LAST HOUSE ON THE LEFT Hallmark Releasing Corporation, 1973
HERE COME THE TIGERS American International, 1978, w/Stephen Miner
FRIDAY THE 13TH Paramount, 1980
SPRING BREAK Columbia, 1983
THE NEW KIDS Columbia, 1985, w/Andrew Fogelson
HOUSE New World, 1986
HOUSE II: THE SECOND STORY New World, 1987
THE HORROR SHOW MGM/UA, 1989
DEEPSTAR SIX Tri-Star, 1989, w/Patrick Markey

MIKE CURB

Business: Curb-Musifilm, 3907 W. Alameda Ave., Burbank, CA, 91505, 818/843-2872

BODY SLAM DEG, 1987, w/Shel Lytton

BILL CURBISHLEY

QUADROPHENIA World Northal, 1979, w/Roy Baird
McVICAR Crown International, 1982, w/Roy Baird & Roger Daltrey

JOHN S. CURRAN

Contact: Directors Guild of America - Los Angeles, 213/289-2000

DOUBLE REVENGE Smart Egg Releasing, 1988, w/T.J. Castronovo
CAMERON'S CLOSET SVS Films, 1989, LP

BRUCE COHN CURTIS

CHATTERBOX American International, 1977
ROLLER BOOGIE United Artists, 1979
HELL NIGHT Aquarius, 1981, w/Irwin Yablans
THE SEDUCTION Avco Embassy, 1982, w/Irwin Yablans
DREAMSCAPE 20th Century-Fox, 1984
FEAR CITY Zupnik-Curtis Enterprises, 1985

DAN CURTIS

Business: Dan Curtis Productions Inc., 10000 W. Washington Blvd., Suite 3014, Culver City, CA, 90232, 213/280-6567
Business Manager: Michael Rutman, Breslauer, Jacobson & Rutman, 10880 Wilshire Blvd., Los Angeles, CA, 90024, 213/553-1707

HOUSE OF DARK SHADOWS MGM, 1970
NIGHT OF DARK SHADOWS MGM, 1971
BURNT OFFERINGS United Artists, 1976

DOUGLAS CURTIS

THE PHILADELPHIA EXPERIMENT New World, 1984, w/ Joel B. Michaels
BLACK MOON RISING New World, 1986, w/Joel B. Michaels
NICE GIRLS DON'T EXPLODE New World, 1987, w/John Wells

TOM CURTIS

DREAMSCAPE 20th Century-Fox, 1984, EP w/Stanley R. Zupnik

JOHN H. CUSHINGHAM

THE EXTRAORDINARY SEAMAN MGM, 1968, CP

JOSEPH CUSUMANO

THE COTTON CLUB Orion, 1984, LP w/Barrie M. Osborne

D

ROBERT DALEY

Business: 1900 Avenue of the Stars, Suite 2270, Los Angeles, CA, 90067, 213/277-1900
Contact: Directors Guild of America - Los Angeles, 213/289-2000

DIRTY HARRY Warner Bros., 1971, EP
PLAY MISTY FOR ME Universal, 1971
JOE KIDD Universal, 1972, EP
HIGH PLAINS DRIFTER Universal, 1973
BREEZY Universal, 1973
MAGNUM FORCE Warner Bros., 1973
THUNDERBOLT & LIGHTFOOT United Artists, 1974
THE EIGER SANCTION Universal, 1974
THE OUTLAW JOSEY WALES Warner Bros., 1976
THE ENFORCER Warner Bros., 1976
THE GAUNTLET Warner Bros., 1977
EVERY WHICH WAY BUT LOOSE Warner Bros., 1978
ESCAPE FROM ALCATRAZ Paramount, 1979
BRONCO BILLY Warner Bros., 1980, EP
ANY WHICH WAY YOU CAN Warner Bros., 1980, EP
STICK Universal, 1985, EP w/William Gordean
REAL GENIUS Tri-Star, 1985, EP

KEN DALTON

HARDBODIES Columbia, 1984, w/Jeff Begun

RICHARD DALTON

JESUS Warner Bros., 1979, CP
MARTIN'S DAY MGM/UA, 1985, w/Roy Krost

ROBIN DALTON

MADAME SOUSATZKA Cineplex Odeon, 1988

ROGER DALTREY

Agent: The Lantz Office - New York, 212/586-0200

McVICAR Crown International, 1982, w/Roy Baird & Bill Curbishley

JOHN DALY

(credit w/Derek Gibson)

Business: Hemdale Film Corporation, 1118 N. Wetherly Dr., Los Angeles, CA, 90069, 213/550-6894

SUNBURN Paramount, 1979, w/Gerald Green*
CARBON COPY Avco Embassy, 1981, EP*
CATTLE ANNIE & LITTLE BRITCHES Universal, 1981, EP
STRANGE BEHAVIOR World Northal, 1981, EP w/William Fayman & David Hemmings
GOING APE! Paramount, 1981, EP*
HIGH RISK American Cinema, 1981, EP*
YELLOWBEARD Orion, 1983, EP*
DEADLY FORCE Embassy, 1983, EP*

A BREED APART Orion, 1984
THE TERMINATOR Orion, 1984, EP
RETURN OF THE LIVING DEAD Orion, 1985, EP
THE FALCON & THE SNOWMAN Orion, 1985, EP*
AT CLOSE RANGE Orion, 1986, EP
SALVADOR Hemdale, 1986, EP
HOOSIERS Orion, 1986, EP
PLATOON ★★ Orion, 1986, EP
RIVER'S EDGE Island Pictures, 1987, EP
BEST SELLER Orion, 1987, EP
BUSTER Hemdale, 1988, EP
THE BOOST Hemdale, 1988, EP
MADE IN U.S.A. Tri-Star, 1988, EP
LOVE AT STAKE Tri-Star, 1988, EP
SHAG: THE MOVIE Hemdale, 1989, EP w/Nik Powell
MIRACLE MILE Hemdale, 1989
CRIMINAL LAW Hemdale, 1989, EP
WAR PARTY Hemdale, 1989, w/Bernard Williams
VAMPIRE'S KISS Hemdale, 1989, EP
OUT COLD Hemdale, 1989, EP
STAYING TOGETHER Hemdale, 1989, EP
THE BOYFRIEND SCHOOL Hemdale, 1990, EP

MARK DAMON

Business: Vision International, 3330 W. Cahuenga Blvd., Suite 500, Los Angeles, CA, 90068, 213/969-2900

THE CHOIRBOYS Universal, 1977, EP w/Mario Bregui & Pietro Bregui
DAS BOOT Columbia, 1982, EP w/John Hyde & Edward R. Pressman
THE NEVERENDING STORY Warner Bros., 1984, EP w/John Hyde
FLIGHT OF THE NAVIGATOR Buena Vista, 1986, EP w/Malcolm R. Harding, John Hyde & Jonathan Sanger
THE CLAN OF THE CAVE BEAR Warner Bros., 1986, EP w/Peter Guber, John Hyde, Sidney Kimmel & Jon Peters
SHORT CIRCUIT Tri-Star, 1986, EP w/John Hyde
THE LOST BOYS Warner Bros., 1987, EP w/Richard Donner & John Hyde
BAT 21 Tri-Star, 1988, CP w/David Saunders
HIGH SPIRITS Tri-Star, 1988, EP w/Moshe Diamant & Eduard Sarlui
MAC & ME Orion, 1988, EP w/William B. Kerr
WILD ORCHID Triumph Releasing, 1990, w/Tony Anthony

GEORGES DANCIGERS

(credit w/Alexandre Mnouchkine)

THAT MAN FROM RIO Lopert, 1964
DEAR DETECTIVE *DEAR INSPECTOR* Cinema 5, 1978
JUPITER'S THIGH Quartet, 1981
LA BALANCE Spectrafilm, 1983

JAY DANIEL

Agent: William Morris Agency - Beverly Hills, 213/274-7451
Contact: Directors Guild of America - Los Angeles, 213/289-2000

CLEAN AND SOBER Warner Bros., 1987, CP

JEFF DANNENBAUM

(credit w/Kathleen Dowdey)

Business: Five Point Films, Inc., 915 Highland View N.E., Suite B, Atlanta, GA 30306, 404/875-6076

BLUE HEAVEN Vestron/ShapiroEntertainment, 1985, EP

PHILIP D'ANTONI

Contact: Directors Guild of America - New York, 212/581-0370

BULLITT Warner Bros., 1968
THE FRENCH CONNECTION ★★ 20th Century- Fox, 1971
THE SEVEN-UPS 20th Century-Fox, 1973

JOHN DARK

HALF A SIXPENCE Paramount, 1967, EP
SLAYGROUND Universal, 1984, w/Gower Frost
SHIRLEY VALENTINE Paramount, 1989, EP

STEPHEN DART

THE HANOI HILTON Cannon, 1987, EP

PASCALE DAUMAN

THE COOK, THE THIEF, HIS WIFE & HER LOVER Miramax, 1990, CP w/Daniel Toscan duPlantier & Denis Wigman

PIERRE DAVID

Business: The Image Organization, 9000 Sunset Blvd., Suite 915, Los Angeles, CA, 90069, 213/278-8751

THE BROOD New World, 1979, EP w/Victor Solnicki
HOG WILD Avco Embassy, 1980, EP w/Victor Solnicki & Stephen Miller
SCANNERS Avco Embassy, 1981, EP wVictor Solnicki
DIRTY TRICKS Avco Embassy, 1981, EP w/Arnold Kopelson & Victor Solnicki
GAS Paramount, 1981, EP w/Victor Solnicki
VISITING HOURS 20th Century-Fox, 1982, EP w/Victor Solnicki
VIDEODROME Universal, 1983, EP w/Victor Solnicki
THE FUNNY FARM New World, 1983, EP
GOING BERSERK Universal, 1983, EP
OF UNKNOWN ORIGIN Warner Bros., 1983, EP
COVERGIRL New World, 1984, EP w/Victor Solnicki
QUIET COOL New Line Cinema, 1986, EP w/Arthur Sarkissian & Larry Thompson
HOT PURSUIT Paramount, 1987, w/Theodore R. Parvin
MY DEMON LOVER New Line Cinema, 1987, EP w/Larry Thompson
INTERNAL AFFAIRS Paramount, 1990, EP w/René Malo & David Streit

GORDON DAVIDSON

Business: Mark Taper Forum, 135 N. Grand Ave., Los Angeles, CA, 90012, 213/972-7353
Agent: Michael Peretzian, William Morris Agency - Beverly Hills, 213/274-7451

ZOOT SUIT Universal, 1982, EP

JAY DAVIDSON

HEADHUNTER Academy Entertainment, 1989

MARTIN DAVIDSON
Agent: Melinda Jason, Columbia Pictures, Studio Plaza, 3400 Riverside Dr., Burbank, CA, 91505
Contact: Directors Guild of America - Los Angeles, 213/289-2000

HEART OF DIXIE Orion, 1989, EP

ANDREW DAVIS
Attorney: Peter Dekom, Bloom & Dekom, 9255 Sunset Blvd., Los Angeles, CA, 90069, 213/278-8622
Agent: The Agency - Los Angeles, 213/551-3000

STONY ISLAND World Northal, 1980, w/Tamar Simon Hoffs
ABOVE THE LAW Warner Bros., 1988, w/Steven Seagal
THE PACKAGE Orion, 1989, CP w/Dennis Haggerty

ANDREW Z. DAVIS
LOST ANGELS Orion, 1989, LP

JOHN A. DAVIS
Business: Davis Entertainment, 20th Century-Fox, 10201 W. Pico Blvd., Los Angeles, CA, 90035, 213/203-3540

PREDATOR 20th Century-Fox, 1987, w/Lawrence Gordon & Joel Silver
THREE O'CLOCK HIGH Universal, 1987, CP w/Neil Israel
TAFFIN MGM/UA, 1988, AP
LICENSE TO DRIVE 20th Century-Fox, 1988, EP
LITTLE MONSTERS United Artists, 1989, w/Andrew Licht & Jeffrey Mueller
THE LAST OF THE FINEST Orion, 1990

PETER S. DAVIS
(credit w/William N. Panzer)
Business: Davis-Panzer Productions, 1438 N. Gower St., Suite 573, Los Angeles, CA, 90028, 213/463-2343

STUNTS New Line Cinema, 1977, EP w/Robert Shaye
STEEL World Northal, 1980
ST. HELENS Parnell, 1981, AP
THE OSTERMAN WEEKEND 20th Century-Fox, 1983
O'HARA'S WIFE Enfield, 1984
HIGHLANDER 20th Century-Fox, 1986
FREEWAY New World, 1988

RICHARD DAVIS
PHAR LAP 20th Century-Fox, 1984, EP

JON DAVISON
Business: Tobor Pictures, The Culver Studios, 9336 W. Washington Blvd., Culver City, CA, 90230, 213/202-3385

HOLLYWOOD BOULEVARD New World, 1977
GRAND THEFT AUTO New World, 1978
PIRANHA New World, 1978
AIRPLANE! Paramount, 1980
WHITE DOG *TRAINED TO KILL* Paramount, 1982
TWILIGHT ZONE — THE MOVIE Warner Bros., 1983, AP
TOP SECRET! Paramount, 1984, w/Hunt Lowry
ROBOCOP Orion, 1987, EP
ROBOCOP 2 Orion, 1990

KIM DAWSON
TEENAGE MUTANT NINJA TURTLES New Line Cinema, 1990, w/David Chan & Simon Fields

RAYMOND DAY
KNIGHTS & EMERALDS Warner Bros., 1986, w/Susan Richards

JONATHAN DAYTON
THE DECLINE OF WESTERN CIVILIZATION PART II: THE METAL YEARS (FD) New Line Cinema, 1988, w/Valerie Faris

JOEL DEAN
SUMMER LOVERS Filmways, 1982, EP

TERENCE F. DEANE
I NEVER PROMISED YOU A ROSE GARDEN New World, 1977, w/Michael Hausman & Daniel H. Blatt

WILLIAM DEAR
Agent: CAA - Beverly Hills, 213/288-4545
Contact: Directors Guild of America - Los Angeles, 213/289-2000

HARRY AND THE HENDERSONS Universal, 1987, w/Richard Vane

GERALD B. DEARING
CANDY MOUNTAIN International Film Exchange, 1988, EP

ALEX DeBENEDETTI
FIGHTING BACK Paramount, 1982, CP w/David Lowe
PUMPKINHEAD United Artists, 1988, EP

ALLEN DeBEVOISE
BREAKIN' Cannon, 1984, w/David Zito

LISA DEDMOND
HENRY: PORTRAIT OF A SERIAL KILLER Greycat Films, 1990, w/John McNaughton

MICHAEL DEELEY
Business: Consolidated Entertainment, 9000 Sunset Blvd., Suite 415, Los Angeles, CA, 90069, 213/275-5719

THE KNACK - AND HOW TO GET IT United Artists, 1965, AP
WHERE'S JACK? Paramount, 1969, EP
MURPHY'S WAR Paramount, 1971
CONDUCT UNBECOMING Allied Artists, 1975, w/Barry Spikings
THE MAN WHO FELL TO EARTH Cinema 5, 1976, w/Barry Spikings
CONVOY United Artists, 1978, EP w/Barry Spikings
THE DEER HUNTER ★★ Universal, 1978, w/Michael Cimino, John Peverall & Barry Spikings
BLADE RUNNER The Ladd Company/Warner Bros., 1982

BARBARA De FINA
Business: Scorsese Productions, 1619 Broadway, New York, NY, 10019, 212/603-0617

SPRING BREAK Columbia, 1983, AP
THE NEW KIDS Columbia, 1985, AP
THE COLOR OF MONEY Buena Vista, 1986, w/Irving Axelrad

THE LAST TEMPTATION OF CHRIST Universal, 1988
NEW YORK STORIES "Life Lessons" Buena Vista, 1989
GOOD FELLAS Warner Bros., 1990, EP

THIERRY De GANAY
SOMEONE TO WATCH OVER ME Columbia, 1987, w/Harold Schneider

CARTER De HAVEN
Attorney: Eric Weissman, Weissman, Wolff, 9655 Wilshire Blvd., Beverly Hills, CA, 90212, 213/858-7888
Contact: Directors Guild of America - Los Angeles, 213/289-2000

A WALK WITH LOVE AND DEATH 20th Century-Fox, 1969
THE KREMLIN LETTER 20th Century-Fox, 1970, w/Sam Wiesenthal
THE LAST RUN MGM, 1971
ULZANA'S RAID Universal, 1972
THE OUTFIT MGM, 1973
OPERATION DAYBREAK Warner Bros., 1975
SENIORS Cinema Shares Inernational, 1978, w/Stanley Shapiro
CARBON COPY Avco Embassy, 1981, w/Stanley Shapiro
YELLOWBEARD Orion, 1983
SCANDALOUS Orion, 1984, EP
SPECIAL EFFECTS New Line Cinema, 1984, EP
PERFECT STRANGERS New Line Cinema, 1984
MAXIE Orion, 1985
HOOSIERS Orion, 1986, w/AngeloPizzo
BEST SELLER Orion, 1987
THE EXORCIST: 1990 20th Century-Fox, 1990

DONNA DEITCH
Business: Desert Heart Productions, 685 Venice Blvd., Venice, CA, 90291, 213/827-1515
Agent: Martha Luttrell, ICM - Los Angeles, 213/550-4000

DESERT HEARTS Samuel Goldwyn Company, 1986

RICHARD DeKOKER
JUGGERNAUT United Artists, 1974

AURELIO De LAURENTIIS
(credit w/Luigi De Laurentiis)
Business: De Laurentiis Ricordi Video, Via Berchet 2, 20121 Milano, Italy, 02-8881

MACARONI Paramount, 1985, w/Franco Committeri
LEVIATHAN MGM/UA, 1989

DINO De LAURENTIIS
Business: De Laurentiis Communications, 8670 WIlshire Blvd., 3rd Floor, Beverly Hills, CA, 90211, 213/289-6100

THE BIBLE 20th Century-Fox, 1966
BARBARELLA Paramount, 1968
WATERLOO Paramount, 1971
A MAN CALLED SLEDGE Columbia, 1971
THE VALACHI PAPERS Columbia, 1972
MANDINGO Paramount, 1975
THE SHOOTIST Paramount, 1976, EP
DRUM United Artists, 1976, EP
LIPSTICK Paramount, 1976, EP
KING KONG Paramount, 1976
ORCA Paramount, 1976, w/Luciano Vincenzoni
KING OF THE GYPSIES Paramount, 1978, EP
THE SERPENT'S EGG Paramount, 1977
HURRICANE Paramount, 1979
FLASH GORDON Universal, 1980
RAGTIME Paramount, 1981
YEAR OF THE DRAGON MGM/UA, 1985

LUIGI De LAURENTIIS
(credit w/Aurelio De Laurentiis)
Business: De Laurentiis Ricordi Video, Via Berchet 2, 20121 Milano, Italy, 02-8881

MACARONI Paramount, 1985, w/Franco Committeri
LEVIATHAN MGM/UA, 1989

RAFFAELLA De LAURENTIIS
Business: Rafaella Productions, Universal Pictures, 100 Universal City Plaza, Bungalow 121-C, Universal City, CA, 91608, 818/777-2655

BEYOND THE REEF Universal, 1981
CONAN THE BARBARIAN Universal, 1982, w/Buzz Feitshans
DUNE Universal, 1984
CONAN THE DESTROYER Universal, 1984
JAMES CLAVELL'S TAI-PAN DEG, 1986
PRANCER Orion, 1989

ROBERT DeLAURENTIS
Agent: BBMW - Los Angeles, 213/277-4998

A LITTLE SEX Universal, 1982, w/Bruce Paltrow

MARCUS DeLEON
BORDER RADIO Coyote Films, 1987

WANDA DELL
Business: Dell Films, 1905 Powers Ferry Rd., Suite 260, Atlanta, GA, 30067, 404/955-6924

THE PRIVATE EYES New World, 1981, w/Lang Elliott
MARVIN AND TIGE *LIKE FATHER AND SON* Fox International Classics, 1985

BOB DEMCHUK
Business: Scene East Productions, Ltd., 153 Mercer St., New York, NY, 10012, 212/226-6525
Contact: Directors Guild of America - New York, 212/581-0370

WHATEVER IT TAKES Aquarius Films, 1986

PAUL DeMEO
Agent: Robinson, Weintraub, Gross - Los Angeles, 213/653-5802

ZONE TROOPERS Empire, 1986
THE WRONG GUYS New World, 1988, CP

JONATHAN DEMME
Business: Clinica Estetico Ltd., 1600 Broadway, #503, New York, NY, 10019, 212/262-2777
Agent: Rick Nicita, CAA - Beverly Hills, 213/288-4545

ANGELS HARD AS THEY COME New World, 1972, w/Joe Viola
SOMETHING WILD Orion, 1986, w/Kenneth Utt
MIAMI BLUES Orion, 1990, w/Gary Goetzman

EDWARD O. DeNAULT
Contact: Directors Guild of America - Los Angeles, 213/289-2000

THE LAST STARFIGHTER Universal, 1984, w/Gary Adelson

GIULIANI DeNEGRI
GOOD MORNING BABYLON Vestron, 1987

ROBERT DeNIRO
Business: Tribeca Productions, 375 Greenwich St., New York, NY, 10013, 212/941-4040
Agent: Fred Specktor, CAA - Beverly Hills, 213/288-4545

WE'RE NO ANGELS Paramount, 1989, EP

ALLAN DENNIS
Contact: Directors Guild of America - New York, 212/581-0370

AFTER MIDNIGHT MGM/UA, 1989, EP w/Barry J. Hirsch

JON S. DENNY
NOBODY'S FOOL Island Pictures, 1986, w/James C. Katz

PEN DENSHAM
(credit w/John Watson)
Business: Trilogy Entertainment Group, 1875 Century Park East, #1090, Los Angeles, CA, 90067, 213/277-5662
Agent: Mike Simpson, William Morris Agency - Beverly Hills, 213/274-7451

THE ZOO GANG New World, 1985
THE KISS Tri-Star, 1988

BRIAN DePALMA
Agent: Bauer Benedek Agency - Los Angeles, 213/275-2421
Contact: Directors Guild of America - New York, 212/581-0370

BODY DOUBLE Columbia, 1984

CYNTHIA DePAULA
ENEMY TERRITORY Empire, 1987, w/Tim Kincaid
NECROPOLIS Empire, 1987, w/Tim Kincaid
SHE'S BACK Vestron, 1989

BO DEREK
Agent: CAA - Beverly Hills, 213/288-4545

TARZAN, THE APE MAN MGM/UA, 1981
BOLERO Cannon, 1984
GHOSTS CAN'T DO IT Trans World Entertainment, 1990

CYRIL De ROUVRE
WAIT UNTIL SPRING, BANDINI Orion, 1990, EP w/Christian Charret, Amadeo Pagani & Giorgio Silvago

NAVIN DESAI
Business: Continental Film Group, Ltd., Park Street, Sharon, PA, 16146, 412/981-3456

TIGER WARSAW Sony Pictures, 1988, EP w/Gay Mayer & Watson Warriner

DAVID De SILVA
FAME MGM/UA, 1980, w/Alan Marshall

IRA DEUTCHMAN
SWIMMING TO CAMBODIA Cinecom, 1987, EP w/Lewis Allen, Amir J. Malin & Peter Newman
MATEWAN Cinecom, 1987, AP
SCENES FROM THE CLASS STRUGGLE IN BEVERLY HILLS Cinecom, 1989, EP w/Amir J. Malin

DAVID DEUTSCH
A DAY IN THE DEATH OF JOE EGG Columbia, 1970
THE DAY OF THE JACKAL Universal, 1973, w/Julien Derode & Sir John Woolf

STEPHEN DEUTSCH
Business: Summerland Productions, 10000 W. Washington Blvd., Culver City, CA, 90232, 213/280-6000

SOMEWHERE IN TIME Universal, 1980
ALL THE RIGHT MOVES 20th Century-Fox, 1983
RUSSKIES New Century/Vista, 1987, EP w/Mort Engelberg
BILL & TED'S EXCELLENT ADVENTURE Orion, 1989, EP w/Robert W. Cort & Ted Field
SHE'S OUT OF CONTROL WEG/Columbia, 1989

ROBERT DEVEREUX
(credit w/Al Clark)
Business: Virgin Vision Ltd., 328 Kensal Rd., London W10 5XJ, England, 01/968-8888

1984 Atlantic Entertainment, 1985, CP
ABSOLUTE BEGINNERS Orion, 1986, EP w/Nik Powell
GOTHIC Vestron, 1987, EP
ARIA Miramax, 1988, CP w/Mike Watts

ZANNE DEVINE
Business: North Winds Entertainment, 1223 Wilshire Blvd., Suite 565, Santa Monica, CA, 90403, 213/558-4504

ANNA Vestron, 1987, w/Yurek Bogayevicz
PRISONERS OF INERTIA North Winds Entertainment, 1989

DON DEVLIN
PETULIA Warner Bros./7 Arts, 1968, EP
THE FORTUNE Columbia, 1975, w/Mike Nichols
HARRY & WALTER GO TO NEW YORK Columbia, 1976, w/Harry Gittes
MY BODYGUARD 20th Century-Fox, 1980
THE WITCHES OF EASTWICK Warner Bros., 1987, EP w/Rob Cohen

GARY DeVORE
Agent: ICM - Los Angeles, 213/550-4000

TRAXX DEG, 1988

LARRY De WAAY
Business: Paramount Pictures, 5555 Melrose Ave., Los Angeles, CA, 90038, 213/468-4824
Contact: Directors Guild of America - Los Angeles, 213/289-2000

YENTL MGM/UA, 1983, EP
THE DOGS OF WAR United Artists, 1981

ELECTRIC DREAMS MGM/UA, 1984, w/Rusty Lemorande
HAMBURGER HILL Paramount, 1987, CP
NEXT OF KIN Warner Bros., 1989, EP
THE HUNT FOR RED OCTOBER Paramount, 1990, EP w/Jerry Sherlock

MATTHIAS DEYLE
OUT OF ORDER Sandstar Releasing, 1985, w/Thomas Schuehly

MOSHE DIAMANT
Business: Trans World Entertainment, 3330 W. Cahuenga Blvd., Suite 500, Los Angeles, CA, 90068, 213/969-2800

PRAY FOR DEATH American Distribution Group, 1986, EP w/Moshe Barkat & Sunil R. Shah
CATCH THE HEAT Trans World Entertainment, 1987, EP w/Stirling Silliphant
THE CURSE Trans World Entertainment, 1987, EP
RAGE OF HONOR Trans World Entertainment, 1987, EP w/Moshe Barkat & Sunil R. Shah
SURVIVAL GAME Trans World Entertainment, 1987, EP
KANSAS Trans Word Entertainment, 1988, CP
HIGH SPIRITS Tri-Star, 1988, EP w/Mark Damon & Eduard Sarlui
FULL MOON IN BLUE WATER Trans World Entertainment, 1988, EP w/Eduard Sarlui
THE FURTHER ADVENTURES OF TENNESSEE BUCK Trans World Entertainment, 1988
NIGHT GAME Trans World Entertainment, 1989, EP w/Eduard Sarlui
TEEN WITCH Trans World Entertainment, 1989, EP w/Eduard Sarlui

RON DIAMOND
SORORITY HOUSE MASSACRE Concorde, 1987

STEPHEN DIENER
Business: New Line Cinema, 116 N. Robertson Blvd., Suite 808, Los Angeles, CA, 90048, 213/854-5811

A NIGHTMARE ON ELM STREET 2: FREDDY'S REVENGE New Line Cinema, 1985, EP w/Stanley Dudelson
THE HIDDEN New Line Cinema, 1987, EP w/Dennis Harris, Jeffrey Klein & Lee Muhl
A NIGHTMARE ON ELM STREET 3: DREAM WARRIORS New Line Cinema, 1987, EP w/Wes Craven
NIGHTMARE ON ELM STREET 4: THE DREAM MASTER New Line Cinema, 1988, EP w/Sara Risher

DOUGLAS DILGE
STRANGERS KISS Orion Classics, 1984
GOOD TO GO Island Pictures, 1986, w/Sean Ferrer

ROBERT DILLON
Agent: CAA - Beverly Hills, 213/288-4545

MUSCLE BEACH PARTY American International, 1964, w/ James H. Nicholson

DENISE DiNOVI
Business: TIm Burton Productions, c/o Warner Brothers, 1041 N. Formosa, Writers Bldg., #10, West Hollywood, CA, 90046, 213/850-2665

GOING BERSERK Universal, 1983, AP
FRATERNITY VACATION New World, 1985, EP
HEATHERS New World, 1989
MEET THE APPLEGATES New World, 1989

MARK DiSALLE
KICKBOXER Cannon, 1989

ROY EDWARD DISNEY
Business: The Walt Disney Company, 500 S. Buena Vista St., Burbank, CA, 91521, 818/560-1000
Contact: Directors Guild of America - Los Angeles, 213/289-2000

CHEETAH Buena Vista, 1989, EP

LESLIE DIXON
Agent: ICM - Los Angeles, 213/550-4000

LOVERBOY Tri-Star, 1989, EP w/Tom Ropelewski
MADHOUSE Orion, 1990

DALE DJERASSI
'68 New World, 1988, w/Steven Kovacs & Isabel Maxwell

BOSKO DJORDJEVIC
MARIA'S LOVERS Cannon, 1984, w/Lawrence Mortorff

LEM DOBBS
Agent: David Kanter, Bauer Benedek Agency - Los Angeles, 213/275-2421
Contact: Writers Guild of America - Los Angeles, 213/550-1000

HIDER IN THE HOUSE Vestron, 1989, CP w/Stuart Cornfeld

NEAL DOBROFSKY
WANDA NEVADA United Artists, 1979
BRONCO BILLY Warner Bros., 1980, w/Dennis Hackin

E. L. DOCTOROW
Agent: ICM - New York, 212/556-5600

DANIEL Paramount, 1983, EP w/Sidney Lumet

TOM DONALD
HIGH HOPES Skouras Pictures, 1989, EP

ROGER DONALDSON
Agent: CAA - Beverly Hills, 213/288-4545
Contact: Directors Guild of America - Los Angeles, 213/289-2000

SMASH PALACE ARC, 1981
CADILLAC MAN Orion, 1990

STANLEY DONEN
Agent: William Morris Agency - Beverly Hills, 213/274-7451
Contact: Directors Guild of America - Los Angeles, 213/289-2000

CHARADE Universal, 1963
ARABESQUE Universal, 1966
BEDAZZLED 20th Century-Fox, 1967
TWO FOR THE ROAD 20th Century-Fox, 1967
THE LITTLE PRINCE Paramount, 1974
MOVIE MOVIE Warner Bros., 1978
SATURN 3 AFD, 1980
BLAME IT ON RIO 20th Century-Fox, 1984

LAUREN SHULER-DONNER
(see Lauren SHULER-Donner)

RICHARD DONNER
Business: Richard Donner Productions, Warner Bros., 4000 Warner Blvd., Burbank, CA, 91522, 818/954-4437
Business Manager: Gerald Breslauer, Breslauer, Jacobson & Rutman, 213/879-0167
Agent: CAA - Beverly Hills, 213/288-4545

THE FINAL CONFLICT 20th Century-Fox, 1981, EP
THE GOONIES Warner Bros., 1985, w/Harvey Bernhard
LADYHAWKE Warner Bros., 1985, w/Lauren Shuler-Donner
LETHAL WEAPON Warner Bros., 1987, w/Joel Silver
THE LOST BOYS Warner Bros., 1987, EP w/Mark Damon & John Hyde
SCROOGED Paramount, 1988, w/Art Linson
LETHAL WEAPON 2 Warner Bros., 1989, w/Joel Silver

ARLENE DONOVAN
Business: 110 W. 57th St., 5th Floor, New York, NY, 10019, 212/247-5652

STILL OF THE NIGHT MGM/UA, 1982
PLACES IN THE HEART ★ Tri-Star, 1984
NADINE Tri-Star, 1987
THE HOUSE ON CARROLL STREET Orion, 1988, EP w/Robert Benton

MARTIN DONOVAN
APARTMENT ZERO Skouras Pictures, 1989, w/David Koepp

ROBIN DOUET
WINTER FLIGHT Cinecom, 1986, w/Susan Richards
MR. LOVE Warner Bros., 1986, w/Susan Richards
SHANGHAI SURPRISE MGM, 1986, CP
DEFENSE OF THE REALM Hemdale, 1987, w/Lynda Myles
WONDERLAND Vestron, 1988, CP

MARION DOUGHERTY
Business: Warner Bros., 4000 Warner Blvd., Burbank, CA, 91522, 818/954-3021

SMILE United Artists, 1975, EP w/David V. Picker

JOEL DOUGLAS
ROMANCING THE STONE 20th Century-Fox, 1984, CP w/Jack Brodsky
TORCHLIGHT UCO Films, 1985
THE JEWEL OF THE NILE 20th Century-Fox, 1985, CP w/Jack Brodsky
COURAGE MOUNTAIN Triumph, 1990, EP

KIRK DOUGLAS
Business: The Bryna Company, 141 El Camino Dr., Beverly Hills, CA, 90212, 213/274-5294
Agent: CAA - Beverly Hills, 213/288-4545

SPARTACUS Universal, 1960, EP

MICHAEL DOUGLAS
Business: Stonebridge Productions, Columbia Pictures, StudioPlaza, 3400 Riverside Dr., Burbank, CA, 91505, 818/972-8808
Agent: CAA - Beverly Hills, 213/288-4545

ONE FLEW OVER THE CUCKOO'S NEST ★★ United Artists, 1975, w/Saul Zaentz
THE CHINA SYNDROME Columbia, 1979
RUNNING Universal, 1979
ROMANCING THE STONE 20th Century-Fox, 1984
STARMAN Columbia, 1984, EP
THE JEWEL OF THE NILE 20th Century-Fox, 1985
THE FLATLINERS Columbia, 1990, w/Rick Bieber

PETER VINCENT DOUGLAS
Business: UniversalPictures, Bldg. 473, 2nd Flr., UniversalCity, CA, 91408, 818/777-3138
Agent: CAA - Beverly Hills, 213/288-4545

THE FINAL COUNTDOWN United Artists, 1980
SOMETHING WICKED THIS WAY COMES Buena Vista, 1983
FLETCH Universal, 1985, w/Alan Greisman
A TIGER'S TALE Atlantic Entertainment, 1988
FLETCH LIVES Universal, 1989, w/Alan Greisman

NED DOWD
(credit w/Randy Ostrow)

THINGS CHANGE Columbia, 1988, AP*
LET IT RIDE Paramount, 1989, CP
STATE OF GRACE Orion, 1990

KATHLEEN DOWDEY
(credit w/Jeff Dannenbaum)
Business: Five Point Films, Inc., 915 Highland View N.E., Suite B, Atlanta, GA, 30306, 404/875-6076

A CELTIC TRILOGY (FD) First Run Features, 1979
BLUE HEAVEN Vestron/Shapiro Entertainment, 1985, CP

GARTH DRABINSKY
(credit w/Joel B. Michaels)
Business: Alive Entertainment Corporation of Canada, 1300 Young, 2nd Floor, Toronto, Ontario, M4T 1X2, 416/324-5800

THE SILENT PARTNER EMC Films/Aurora, 1979, EP
THE CHANGELING AFD, 1980
TRIBUTE 20th Century-Fox, 1980
THE AMATEUR 20th Century-Fox, 1981
LOSIN' IT Embassy, 1983, EP

BERT DRAGIN
SUBURBIA *THE WILD SIDE* New Horizons, 1984

VICTOR DRAI
Business: Victor Drai Productions, 2765 Woodstock Rd., Los Angeles, CA, 90046, 213/650-2203

THE WOMAN IN RED Orion, 1984
THE MAN WITH ONE RED SHOE 20th Century-Fox, 1985
THE BRIDE Columbia, 1985
WEEKEND AT BERNIE'S 20th Century-Fox, 1989

DOUG DRAIZIN
Business: The Irv Schechter Company, 9300 Wilshire Blvd., Suite 410, Beverly Hills, CA, 90212, 213/278-8070

MOVING VIOLATIONS 20th Century-Fox, 1985, EP w/Pat Proft

PAUL DRANE
THE MAN WHO SAW TOMORROW (FD) Warner Bros., 1981, w/Robert Guenette & Lee Kramer

SARA DRIVER
STRANGER THAN PARADISE Samuel Goldwyn Company, 1984

MICHAEL DRYHURST
Agent: Barrett, Benson, McCartt, Weston - Los Angeles, 213/553-2600 or 213/277-4998

THE TERMINAL MAN Warner Bros., 1974, AP
EXCALIBUR Orion/Warner Bros., 1981, AP
NEVER SAY NEVER AGAIN Warner Bros., 1983, AP
THE EMERALD FOREST Embassy, 1985, CP
HOPE AND GLORY ★ Columbia, 1987, CP

RANI DUBÉ
GANDHI ★★ Columbia, 1982, CP

STANLEY DUDELSON
Business: Artist Entertainment Group, Inc., 5455 Wilshire Blvd., Suite 1715, Los Angeles, CA, 90036, 213/933-7496

A NIGHTMARE ON ELM STREET New Line Cinema, 1984, EP w/Joseph Wolf
A NIGHTMARE ON ELM STREET 2: FREDDY'S REVENGE New Line Cinema, 1985, EP w/Stephen Diener

GRIFFIN DUNNE
(credit w/Amy Robinson)
Business: Double Play Productions, 1250 Broadway, New York, NY, 10019, 212/643-1077

CHILLY SCENES OF WINTER *HEAD OVER HEELS* United Artists, 1979, w/Mark Metcalf
BABY IT'S YOU Paramount, 1983
AFTER HOURS The Geffen Company/Warner Bros., 1985, w/Robert F. Colesberry
RUNNING ON EMPTY Warner Bros., 1988

JOHN DUNNING
(credit w/Andre Link)
Business: Cinepix Inc., 8275 Mayrand St., Montreal, Quebec H4P 2C8, Canada, 514/342-2340

THEY CAME FROM WITHIN Trans-America, 1976, w/Alfred Pariser
THE HOUSE BY THE LAKE American International, 1977, EP
RABID New World, 1977*
MEATBALLS Paramount, 1979, EP
MY BLOODY VALENTINE Paramount, 1981, w/Stephen Miller
HAPPY BIRTHDAY TO ME Columbia, 1981
SPACEHUNTER: ADVENTURES IN THE FORBIDDEN ZONE Columbia, 1983, w/Don Carmody
MEATBALLS III Moviestore, 1986, w/Don Carmody*

DANIEL TOSCAN duPLANTIER
THE COOK, THE THIEF, HIS WIFE & HER LOVER Miramax, 1990, CP w/Pascale Dauman & Denis Wigman

RENE DUPONT
SILVER DREAM RACER Almi Cinema 5, 1980
A CHRISTMAS STORY MGM/UA, 1983, w/Bob Clark
TURK 182 20th Century-Fox, 1985, w/Ted Field
FROM THE HIP DEG, 1987, w/Bob Clark
COLLISION COURSE DEG, 1988, EP
LOOSE CANNONS Tri-Star, 1990, EP

ALLAN L. DURAND
BELIZAIRE THE CAJUN Skouras Pictures, 1986, w/Glen Pitre

RUDY DURAND
Business: Koala Productions, Ltd., 361 N. Canon Dr., Beverly Hills, CA, 90212, 213/476-1949
Contact: Directors Guild of America - Los Angeles, 213/289-2000

TILT Warner Bros., 1979

MICHEL DUVAL
SALVATION! Circle Releasing, 1987, EP w/Irving Ong & Ned Richardson

ROBERT DUVALL
Agent: Bill Robinson, ICM - Los Angeles, 213/550-4000

TENDER MERCIES ★ Universal, 1983, CP w/Horton Foote

JAMES DYER
Contact: Directors Guild of America - Los Angeles, 213/289-2000

WILD ORCHID Triumph Releasing, 1990, EP w/David Saunders

ROBERT DYKE
MOONTRAP Shapiro Glickenhaus Entertainment, 1989

E

BRIAN EASTMAN
WHOOPS APOCALYPSE MGM, 1986

GRAHAM EASTON
STRIKE IT RICH Miramax, 1989, w/Christine Oestricher

CLINT EASTWOOD

Business: Malpaso Productions, 4000 Warner Blvd., Burbank, CA, 91522, 818/954-2567
Agent: Leonard Hirshan, William Morris Agency - Beverly Hills, 213/274-7451

FIREFOX Warner Bros., 1982
HONKY TONK MAN Warner Bros., 1982
SUDDEN IMPACT Warner Bros., 1983
TIGHTROPE Warner Bros., 1984, w/Fritz Manes
PALE RIDER Warner Bros., 1985
HEARTBREAK RIDGE Warner Bros., 1986
BIRD Warner Bros., 1988
THELONIOUS MONK: STRAIGHT, NO CHASER (FD) Warner Bros., 1988, EP
WHITE HUNTER, BLACK HEART Warner Bros., 1990, EP

JAKE EBERTS

THE NAME OF THE ROSE 20th Century-Fox, 1986, EP w/Thomas Schuehly
HOPE & GLORY Columbia, 1987, EP w/Edgar F. Gross
THE ADVENTURES OF BARON MUNCHAUSEN Columbia, 1989, EP
DRIVING MISS DAISY ★ Warner Bros., 1989, EP w/David Brown
ME AND HIM Columbia, 1989, AP
TEXASVILLE Columbia, 1990, EP w/Bill Peiffer

JOHN M. ECKERT

Business: John M. Eckert Productions Ltd., 385 Carlton St., Toronto, Ontario M5A 2M3, Canada, 416/960-4961

RUNNING Universal, 1979, CP
THE INCUBUS FIlm Ventures International, 1982, w/Marc Boyman
HOME IS WHERE THE HART IS Atlantic Entertainment, 1987
MILLENNIUM 20th Century-Fox, 1989, SP

MICHAEL EDGLEY

THE MAN FROM SNOWY RIVER 20th Century-Fox, 1983, EP w/Simon Wincer

BOBBIE EDRICK

Business: Artists Circle Entertainment, 8955 Norma Place, Los Angeles, CA, 90069, 213/275-6330

DADDY'S DYIN' MGM/UA, 1990, EP w/Del Shores

BLAKE EDWARDS

Business: Blake Edwards Entertainment, 9336 W. Washington Blvd., Culver City, CA, 90230, 213/202-3375
Agent: Triad Artists, Inc. - Los Angeles, 213/556-2727

DARLING LILI Paramount, 1970
THE WILD ROVERS MGM, 1971, w/Ken Wales
RETURN OF THE PINK PANTHER United Artists, 1975
THE PINK PANTHER STRIKES AGAIN United Artists, 1976
REVENGE OF THE PINK PANTHER United Artists, 1978
10 Orion/Warner Bros., 1979, w/Tony Adams
S.O.B. Lorimar/Paramount, 1981, w/Tony Adams
VICTOR/VICTORIA MGM/UA, 1982, w/Tony Adams
TRAIL OF THE PINK PANTHER MGM/UA, 1982, w/Tony Adams
CURSE OF THE PINK PANTHER MGM/UA, 1983, w/Tony Adams
THE MAN WHO LOVED WOMEN Columbia, 1983, w/Tony Adams

GEORGE EDWARDS

Business: Desert Wind Productions, Raleigh Studios, 5300 Melrose Ave., Los Angeles, CA, 90038, 213/464-3082
Agent: Artists Group, Inc. - Los Angeles, 213/552-1100

FROGS American International, 1972, w/Peter Thomas
CHATTANOOGA CHOO CHOO April Fools, 1984, w/Jill Griffith
TRUST ME Cinecom, 1989

R. BEN EFRAIM

STRIKING BACK Film Ventures International, 1981, EP
PRIVATE LESSONS Jensen Farley, 1981
PRIVATE SCHOOL Universal, 1983, w/Don Enright

MEL EFROS

Contact: Directors Guild of America - Los Angeles, 213/289-2000

STAR TREK V: THE FINAL FRONTIER Paramount, 1989, CP

AL EICHER

BRAIN DAMAGE Palisades Entertainment, 1988, EP w/Andre Blay

BERND EICHINGER

Business: Neue Constantin Film, GmbH & Co, Verleih KG, Kaiserstraße 39, D-8000 München 40, West Germany, 38-60-90

CHRISTIANE F. New World, 1982, w/Hans Weth
THE NEVERENDING STORY Warner Bros., 1984, w/Dieter Giessler
THE NAME OF THE ROSE 20th Century-Fox, 1986
ME AND HIM Columbia, 1989
LAST EXIT TO BROOKLYN Cinecom, 1990

MARY EILTS

Contact: Directors Guild of America - Los Angeles, 213/289-2000

WATCHERS Universal, 1988, CP

D. E. EISENBERG

DREAM A LITTLE DREAM Vestron, 1989, w/Marc Rocco

MORRIE EISENMAN

Business: Proder Representatives Organization, 11849 W. Olympic Blvd., Suite 200, Los Angeles, CA, 90064, 213/478-5159

BAD INFLUENCE Triumph, 1990, EP w/Richard Becker

RAFAEL EISENMAN

I, MADMAN Trans World Entertainment, 1989
TEEN WITCH Trans World Entertainment, 1989, w/Alana H. Lambros

ED ELBERT

THE MIGHTY QUINN MGM/UA, 1989, w/Marion Hunt & Sandy Lieberson

KEVIN ELDERS
IRON EAGLE Tri-Star, 1986, EP

MARTIN ELFAND
Business: Martin Elfand Productions, Warner Bros., 4000 Warner Blvd., Bldg. 81, #208, Burbank, CA, 91522, 818/954-3505

KANSAS CITY BOMBER MGM, 1972
DOG DAY AFTERNOON ★ Warner Bros., 1975, w/Martin Bregman
IT'S MY TURN Columbia, 1980
AN OFFICER & A GENTLEMAN Paramount, 1982
KING DAVID Paramount, 1985
CLARA'S HEART Warner Bros., 1988
HER ALIBI Warner Bros., 1989, EP

RICHARD ELFMAN
Business: Richard Elfman Productions, 723 Ocean Front Walk, Venice, CA, 90291, 213/399-9118

FORBIDDEN ZONE Samuel Goldwyn Company, 1980

LANG ELLIOTT
Business: P. O. Box 7419, Thousand Oaks, CA, 91359, 818/707-9797
Contact: Directors Guild of America - Los Angeles, 213/289-2000

THE PRIVATE EYES New World, 1981, w/Wanda Dell
THE LONGSHOT Orion, 1986
CAGE New Century/Vista, 1989

CASSIAN ELWES
Business: 547 Westmount Dr., Los Angeles, CA, 90048, 213/785-3100

OXFORD BLUES MGM/UA, 1984, w/Elliott Kastner
NOMADS Atlantic Entertainment, 1986, w/George Pappas
WHITE OF THE EYE Palisades Entertainment, 1987, w/Brad Wyman
ZOMBIE HIGH Cinema Group, 1987, EP
NEVER ON TUESDAY Palisades Entertainment, 1987, EP
COLD FEET Avenue Entertainment, 1989
WARM SUMMER RAIN Trans World Entertainment, 1990, w/Lionel Wigram

JAY EMMETT
GARDENS OF STONE Tri-Star, 1987, EP w/Fred Roos, David Valdes & Stan Weston

MICHAEL S. ENDLER
BACK TO SCHOOL Orion, 1986, EP w/Estelle Endler & Harold Ramis

MORT ENGELBERG
Business: The Vista Organization, 8439 Sunset Blvd., #200, Los Angeles, CA, 90069, 213/656-9130

SMOKEY & THE BANDIT Universal, 1977
HOT STUFF Columbia, 1979
THE VILLAIN Columbia, 1979
THE HUNTER Paramount, 1980
NOBODY'S PERFEKT Columbia, 1981
SMOKEY & THE BANDIT PART 3 *SMOKEY IS THE BANDIT* Universal, 1983
THE HEAVENLY KID Orion, 1985
THE BIG EASY Columbia, 1987, EP
MAID TO ORDER New Century/Vista, 1987, w/Herb Jaffe
RUSSKIES New Century/Vista, 1987, w/Stephen Deutsch
THREE FOR THE ROAD New Century/Vista, 1987, w/Herb Jaffe
FRIGHT NIGHT PART 2 New Century/Vista, 1988, w/Herb Jaffe
PASS THE AMMO New Century/Vista, 1988, w/Herb Jaffe
DUDES New Century/Vista, 1988, EP
RENTED LIPS CineWorld Enterprises, 1988, w/Martin Mull
TRADING HEARTS New Century/Vista, 1988, EP w/Herb Jaffe

ROBERT ENGELMAN
Contact: Directors Guild of America - Los Angeles, 213/289-2000

LEATHERFACE: THE TEXAS CHAINSAW MASSACRE III New Line Cinema, 1990

IRA ENGLANDER
RUNNING BRAVE Buena Vista, 1983

GEORGE ENGLUND
Agent: CAA - Beverly Hills, 213/288-4545
Contact: Directors Guild of America - Los Angeles, 213/289-2000

DARK OF THE SUN *THE MERCENARIES* MGM, 1968
THE SHOES OF THE FISHERMAN MGM, 1968
ZACHARIAH Cinerama, 1970

DAN ENRIGHT
Business: Barry & Enright Productions, 201 Wilshire Blvd., 2nd Floor, Santa Monica, CA, 90404, 213/556-1000

PRIVATE LESSONS Jensen Farley, 1981, EP w/Jack Barry
MAKING MR. RIGHT Orion, 1987, EP w/Susan Seidelman

DON ENRIGHT
Business: Barry & Enright Productions, 201 Wilshire Blvd., 2nd Floor, Santa Monica, CA, 90404, 213/556-1000
Agent: ICM - Los Angeles, 213/550-4000

PRIVATE SCHOOL Universal, 1983, w/R. Ben Efraim
NEXT OF KIN Warner Bros., 1989, w/Les Alexander

ANDROS EPAMINONDAS
GIVE MY REGARDS TO BROAD STREET 20th Century-Fox, 1984
STEALING HEAVEN Scotti Bros., 1989, w/Simon MacCorkindale

NORA EPHRON
Agent: ICM - New York, 212/556-5600

COOKIE Warner Bros., 1989, EP w/Alice Arlen & Susan Seidelman

JULIUS J. EPSTEIN
Agent: ICM - Los Angeles, 213/550-4000

PETE 'N' TILLIE Universal, 1972
REUBEN, REUBEN 20th Century-Fox International Classics, 1983, CP

MITCH EPSTEIN
SALAAM BOMBAY! Cinecom, 1988, CP

C. O. ERICKSON
Business: Paramount Pictures, 5555 Melrose Ave., Los Angeles, CA, 90038, 213/468-5729
Agent: The Gersh Agency - Beverly Hills, 213/274-6611
Contact: Directors Guild of America - Los Angeles, 213/289-2000

BUONA SERA, MRS. CAMPBELL United Artists, 1968, EP
THERE WAS A CROOKED MAN Warner Bros., 1970, EP
CHINATOWN Paramount, 1974, AP
MAGIC 20th Century-Fox, 1978, EP
URBAN COWBOY Paramount, 1980, EP
POPEYE Paramount/Buena Vista, 1980, EP
ZORRO, THE GAY BLADE 20th Century-Fox, 1981, w/George Hamilton
FAST TIMES AT RIDGEMONT HIGH Universal, 1982, EP
THE LONELY GUY Universal, 1984, EP w/William E. McEuen
CLOAK & DAGGER Universal, 1984, EP
THE WILD LIFE Universal, 1984, EP
SECRET ADMIRER Orion, 1985, EP
PROJECT X 20th Century-Fox, 1987, EP
IRONWEED Tri-Star, 1987, CP w/Gene Kirkwood

PAUL ERICKSON
RED SCORPION Shapiro Glickenhaus, 1989, EP w/Robert Abramoff & Daniel Sklar

MARTIN ERLICHMAN
UP THE SANDBOX National General, 1972, AP
FOR PETE'S SAKE Columbia, 1974, w/Stanley Shapiro
COMA United Artists, 1978
BREATHLESS Orion, 1983
ERNEST GOES TO CAMP Buena Vista, 1987, EP w/Elmo Williams
ERNEST SAVES CHRISTMAS Buena Vista, 1988, EP w/Joseph L. Akerman
ERNEST GOES TO JAIL Buena Vista, 1990, EP

MOCTESUMA ESPARZA
ONLY ONCE IN A LIFETIME Movietime Films, 1979
THE BALLAD OF GREGORIO CORTEZ Embassy, 1983, w/Michael Hausman
RADIOACTIVE DREAMS DEG, 1986, w/Tom Karnowski
THE TELEPHONE New World, 1988, w/Robert Katz
THE MILAGRO BEANFIELD WAR Universal, 1988, w/Robert Redford

KAREN ESSEX
THE IN CROWD Orion, 1988, CP w/Jeffrey Hornaday

MELVYN J. ESTRIN
STRIPPER (FD) 20th Century-Fox, 1986, w/Geof Bartz & Jerome Gary

JOE ESZTERHAS
(credit w/Hal W. Polaire)
Agent: Guy McElwaine, ICM - Los Angeles, 213/550-4000
Contact: Writers Guild of America - Los Angeles, 213/550-1000

BETRAYED MGM/UA, 1988, EP
MUSIC BOX Tri-Star, 1989, EP

BRUCE A. EVANS
(credit w/Raynold Gideon)
Business: Evans-Gideon Productions, Universal Studios, 100 Universal City Plaza, Universal City, CA, 91608, 818/777-3121
Agent: CAA - Beverly Hills, 213/288-4545

STARMAN Columbia, 1984, AP
STAND BY ME Columbia, 1986, w/Andrew Scheinman
MADE IN HEAVEN Lorimar, 1987, w/David Blocker

CHARLES EVANS
TOOTSIE ★ Columbia, 1982, EP
MONKEY SHINES Orion, 1988

MICHAEL STANLEY-EVANS
(see Michael STANLEY-Evans)

ROBERT EVANS
Business: Robert Evans Productions, 1032 Beverly Dr., Beverly Hills, CA, 90210, 213/854-4187

CHINATOWN ★ Paramount, 1974
MARATHON MAN Paramount, 1976, w/Sidney Beckerman
BLACK SUNDAY Paramount, 1976
PLAYERS Paramount, 1979
URBAN COWBOY Paramount, 1980, w/Irving Azoff
POPEYE Paramount/Buena Vista, 1980
THE COTTON CLUB Orion, 1984
THE TWO JAKES Paramount, 1990, w/Harold Schneider

STEPHEN EVANS
HENRY V Samuel Goldwyn Company, 1989, EP

TED EVANSON
WHAT COMES AROUND W.O. Associates, 1986

DALE FALCONER
IF YOU COULD SEE WHAT I HEAR Jensen Farley Pictures, 1982, EP w/Gene Corman

HAMPTON FANCHER
Agent: Jim Berkus, Leading Artists, Inc. - Beverly Hills, 213/858-1999
Contact: Writers Guild of America - Los Angeles, 213/550-1000

BLADE RUNNER The Ladd Company/Warner Bros., 1982, EP w/Brian Kelly

WILLIAM FARALLA
Contact: Directors Guild of America - Los Angeles, 213/289-2000

THE BALLAD OF CABLE HOGUE Warner Bros./7 Arts, 1970, CP

STEVEN FARGNOLI
(credit w/Robert Cavallo & Joseph Ruffalo)

PURPLE RAIN Warner Bros., 1984
UNDER THE CHERRY MOON Warner Bros., 1986
SIGN O' THE TIMES Cineplex Odeon, 1987

VALERIE FARIS
THE DECLINE OF WESTERN CIVILIZATION PART II: THE METAL YEARS (FD) New Line Cinema, 1988, w/Jonathan Dayton

DAN FARRELL
WHERE THE RIVER RUNS BLACK MGM, 1986, CP

JOSEPH FARRELL
MANNEQUIN 20th Century-Fox, 1987, EP w/Edward Rugoff

MIKE FARRELL
Business: Farrell-Minoff Productions, 14755 Ventura Blvd., #203, Sherman Oaks, CA, 91403, 818/789-5766
Contact: Directors Guild of America - Los Angeles, 213/289-2000

DOMINICK & EUGENE Orion, 1988, w/Marvin Minoff

WILLIAM FAY
JAKE SPEED New World, 1986, w/Wayne Crawford & Andrew Lane

DODI FAYED
Business: Allied Stars, 55 Park Lane, London W1Y 3DH, England

BREAKING GLASS Paramount, 1980, EP
CHARIOTS OF FIRE ★★ The Ladd Company/Warner Bros., 1981, EP
F/X Orion, 1986, w/Jack Wiener

WILLIAM FAYMAN
STRANGE BEHAVIOR World Northal, 1981, EP w/John Daly & David Hemmings
HARLEQUIN New Image, 1983, EP

IRVING FEIN
OH, GOD! YOU DEVIL Warner Bros., 1984, EP
18 AGAIN New World, 1988, EP w/Michael Jaffe

BUZZ FEITSHANS
Business: Carolco Pictures, 8800 Sunset Blvd., Los Angeles, CA, 90069, 213/850-8800

DILLINGER American International, 1973
FOXY BROWN American International, 1974
BIG WEDNESDAY Warner Bros., 1978
HARDCORE Columbia, 1979
1941 Columbia/Universal, 1979
CONAN THE BARBARIAN Universal, 1982, w/Raffaella De Laurentiis
FIRST BLOOD Orion, 1982
UNCOMMON VALOR Paramount, 1983, w/John Milius
RED DAWN MGM/UA, 1984, w/Barry Beckerman
RAMBO: FIRST BLOOD PART II Tri-Star, 1985
EXTREME PREJUDICE Tri-Star, 1987
RAMBO III Carolco, 1988
TOTAL RECALL Tri-Star, 1990, w/Ronald Shusett

STEPHEN J. FEKE
Business: Parnassus Productions, 10000 W. Washington Blvd., #3007, Culver City, CA, 90232, 213/280-6538
Agent: Camden Artists, Ltd. - Los Angeles, 213/556-2022

WHEN A STRANGER CALLS United Artists, 1979, w/Doug Chapin

DENNIS J. FELDMAN
Agent: ICM - Los Angeles, 213/550-4000
Contact: Writers Guild of America - Los Angeles, 213/550-1000

THE GOLDEN CHILD Paramount, 1986, CP

EDWARD S. FELDMAN
Business: The Edward S. Feldman Company, 9454 Wilshire Blvd., #701, Beverly Hills, CA, 90212, 213/859-7050

WHAT'S THE MATTER WITH HELEN? United Artists, 1971
FUZZ United Artists, 1972, EP
SAVE THE TIGER Paramount, 1973, EP
THE OTHER SIDE OF THE MOUNTAIN Universal, 1975
TWO-MINUTE WARNING Universal, 1976
THE OTHER SIDE OF THE MOUNTAIN - PART 2 Universal, 1978
THE LAST MARRIED COUPLE IN AMERICA Universal, 1980, w/John Herman Shaner
SIX PACK 20th Century-Fox, 1982, EP w/Ted Witzer
THE SENDER Paramount, 1982
HOT DOG MGM/UA, 1984
WITNESS ★ Paramount, 1985
EXPLORERS Paramount, 1985, w/David Bombyk
THE HITCHER Tri-Star, 1986, EP w/Charles R. Meeker
HAMBURGER: THE MOTION PICTURE FM Entertainment, 1986, w/Charles R. Meeker
THE GOLDEN CHILD Paramount, 1986, w/Robert D. Wachs
NEAR DARK DEG, 1987, EP w/Charles R. Meeker
WIRED Taurus, 1989, w/Charles R. Meeker

PHIL FELDMAN
YOU'RE A BIG BOY NOW 7 Arts, 1966
THE WILD BUNCH Warner Bros./7 Arts, 1969
THE BALLAD OF CABLE HOGUE Warner Bros./7 Arts, 1970, EP
FOR PETE'S SAKE Columbia, 1974, EP
THE TOY Columbia, 1982
BLUE THUNDER Columbia, 1983, EP w/Andrew Fogelson
STEWARDESS SCHOOL Columbia, 1987

ERIC FELLNER
SID & NANCY Samuel Goldwyn Company, 1986
STRAIGHT TO HELL Island Pictures, 1987
PASCALI'S ISLAND Avenue Entertainment, 1988
THE RACHEL PAPERS United Artists, 1989, EP w/James T. Roe III

JON FELTHEIMER
Business: New World Television, 1440 S. Sepulveda Blvd., Los Angeles, CA, 90025, 213/444-8100

BODY ROCK New World, 1984, EP w/Phil Ramone & Charles J. Weber

ANDREW J. FENADY
Business: Fenady Associates, Inc., 249 N. Larchmont Blvd., Suite 6, Los Angeles, CA, 90004, 213/466-6375
Agent: ICM - Los Angeles, 213/550-4000

THE MAN WITH BOGART'S FACE *SAM MARLOW, PRIVATE EYE* 20th Century-Fox, 1980

ROBERT FENTRESS
DEAD & BURIED Avco Embassy, 1981, w/Ronald Shusett

SEAN FERRER
STRANGERS KISS Orion Classics, 1984, AP
GOOD TO GO Island Pictures, 1986, w/Douglas Dilge

BETH FERRIS
HEARTLAND Levitt-Pickman, 1979, w/Michael Hausman

CHRISTIAN FERRY
SHEENA Columbia, 1984, AP
RED SONJA MGM/UA, 1985

PETER FETTERMAN
Business: Peter Fetterman Productions, 818 21st St., Suite B, Santa Monica, CA, 90403, 213/453-6463

THE HAUNTING OF JULIA Discovery, 1981, w/Alfred Pariser
YES, GIORGIO MGM/UA, 1982

CY FEUER
CABARET Allied Artists, 1972
PIAF — THE EARLY YEARS 20th Century-Fox International Classics, 1982
A CHORUS LINE Columbia, 1985, w/Ernest Martin

JOSEPH FEURY
Business: Joseph Feury Productions, 120 Riverside Dr., #5-E, New York, NY, 10024, 212/877-7700
Contact: Directors Guild of America - Los Angeles, 213/289-2000

STAYING TOGETHER Hemdale, 1989

JOHN FIEDLER
Business: Rastar/Indieprod, 8800 Sunset Blvd., Los Angeles, CA, 90069

THE BEAST Columbia, 1988
AUNT JULIA & THE SCRIPTWRITER Cinecom, 1990, w/Mark Tarlov

DAVID M. FIELD
Business: Paramount Pictures, 5555 Melrose Ave., Los Angeles, CA, 90038, 213/468-4706
Agent: William Morris Agency - Beverly Hills, 213/274-7451

AMAZING GRACE AND CHUCK Tri-Star, 1987

GWEN FIELD
Contact: Paul Sandberg, c/o Sinclair-Tennenbaum, 335 N. Maple Dr., Suite 352, Beverly Hills, CA, 90210, 213/285-6222

PATTI ROCKS FilmDallas, 1988, w/Gregory M. Cummins
MORTAL PASSIONS MGM/UA, 1990

TED FIELD
(credit w/Robert W. Cort)
Business: Interscope Communications, 10900 Wilshire Blvd., Suite 1400, Los Angeles, CA, 90024, 213/208-8525

REVENGE OF THE NERDS 20th Century-Fox, 1984, w/Peter Samuelson*
TURK 182 20th Century-Fox, 1985, w/Rene Dupont*
REVENGE OF THE NERDS II 20th Century-Fox 1987, w/Peter Bart
OUTRAGEOUS FORTUNE Buena Vista, 1987
CRITICAL CONDITION Paramount, 1987
THREE MEN & A BABY Buena Vista, 1987
THE SEVENTH SIGN Tri-Star, 1988
COLLISION COURSE DEG, 1988
COCKTAIL Buena Vista, 1988
BILL & TED'S EXCELLENT ADVENTURE Orion, 1989, EP w/Stephen Deutsch
RENEGADES Universal, 1989, EP w/James G. Robinson & Joe Roth
AN INNOCENT MAN Buena Vista, 1989
THE FIRST POWER Orion, 1990, w/David Madden
BIRD ON A WIRE Universal, 1990, EP

ADAM FIELDS
VISION QUEST Warner Bros., 1985, EP w/Stan Weston
THE WHOOPEE BOYS Paramount, 1986, w/Peter MacGregor-Scott
JOHNNY BE GOOD Orion, 1988
GREAT BALLS OF FIRE Orion, 1989
JOURNEY TO THE CENTER OF THE EARTH Cannon, 1989, EP w/Avi Lerner &Tom Udell

FREDDIE FIELDS
Business: Freddie Fields Productions,152 N. La Peer Dr., Los Angeles, CA, 90048, 213/276-6555

LIPSTICK Paramount, 1976
CITIZENS BAND *HANDLE WITH CARE* Paramount, 1977
LOOKING FOR MR. GOODBAR Paramount, 1977
AMERICAN GIGOLO Paramount, 1980, EP
WHOLLY MOSES! Columbia, 1980
VICTORY Paramount, 1981
FEVER PITCH MGM/UA, 1985
POLTERGEIST II: THE OTHER SIDE MGM/UA, 1986, EP
AMERICAN ANTHEM Columbia, 1986, EP
CRIMES OF THE HEART DEG, 1986
MILLENNIUM 20th Century-Fox, 1989, EP w/John Foreman, P. Gael Mourant & Louis M. Silverstein
GLORY Tri-Star, 1989

SIMON FIELDS
Business: Limelight Productions, 1724 N. Whitley Ave., Los Angeles, CA, 90028, 213/464-5808

SIGN O' THE TIMES Cineplex Odeon, 1987, CP
TEENAGE MUTANT NINJA TURTLES New Line Cinema, 1990, w/David Chan & Kim Dawson

STEVEN FIERBERG
Business: 668 Washington St., #3A, New York, NY, 10014, 212/929-4199

FORTY-DEUCE Island Alive, 1982, AP
MIXED BLOOD Sara/Cinevista, 1985, w/Antoine Gannage

RONALD K. FIERSTEIN
TORCH SONG TRILOGY New Line Cinema, 1988, EP

CHRISTOPHER FIGG
HELLRAISER New World, 1987
HELLBOUND: HELLRAISER II New World, 1988
NIGHTBREED 20th Century-Fox, 1990

PETER FILARDI
Agent: InterTalent Agency - Los Angeles, 213/271-0600

THE FLATLINERS Columbia, 1990, EP w/Michael Rachmil & Scott Rudin

PENNY FINKELMAN COX
(see Penny Finkelman COX)

WILLIAM FINNEGAN
Business: Finnegan-Pinchuk Company, 4225 Coldwater Canyon, Studio City, CA, 91604, 818/508-5614

NIGHT OF THE CREEPS Tri-Star, 1986, EP
NORTH SHORE Universal, 1987
THE FABULOUS BAKER BOYS 20th Century-Fox, 1989, CP

MICHAEL FINNELL
Business: Renfield Productions, Warner Bros., 4000 Warner Blvd., Burbank, CA, 91522, 818/954-3670

ROCK 'N' ROLL HIGH SCHOOL New World, 1979, CP
THE HOWLING Avco Embassy, 1980, w/Jack Conrad
TWILIGHT ZONE — THE MOVIE Warner Bros., 1983, AP
GREMLINS Warner Bros., 1984
EXPLORERS Paramount, 1985, EP
INNERSPACE Warner Bros., 1987
THE 'BURBS Universal, 1988, w/Larry Brezner
GREMLINS 2: THE NEW BATCH Warner Bros., 1990

TOM FIORELLO
FORT APACHE, THE BRONX 20th Century-Fox, 1981, w/Martin Richards

MARC S. FISCHER
Business: 21st Century Film Corp., 8200 Wilshire Blvd., Beverly Hills, CA, 90211, 213/658-3000

THE FORBIDDEN DANCE Columbia, 1990, w/Richard L. Albert

RICHARD FISCHOFF
Business: Tri-Star Pictures, 3400 Riverside Dr., Burbank, CA, 91507, 818/972-7759

DESERT BLOOM Columbia, 1986, EP

DAVID FISHER
BAT 21 Tri-Star, 1988, w/Michael Balson & Gary A. Neill

MARY ANN FISHER
ANDROID Island Alive, 1984
HOUR OF THE ASSASSIN Concorde, 1987, CP

ROBERT FISHER
Contact: Directors Guild of America - New York, 212/581-0370

ROCKET GIBRALTAR Columbia, 1988, EP w/Geoffrey Mayo & Michael Ulick

ARNOLD FISHMAN
(credit w/Paul Lichtman)

OUT OF CONTROL New World, 1985, EP
TRANSYLVANIA 6-5000 New World, 1985, EP

JOAN FISHMAN
THE PRINCE OF PENNSYLVANIA New Line Cinema, 1988

KATHY FITZGERALD
WISE BLOOD New Line Cinema, 1980, w/Michael Fitzgerald

MICHAEL FITZGERALD
WISE BLOOD New Line Cinema, 1980, w/Kathy Fitzgerald
UNDER THE VOLCANO Universal, 1984, EP
THE PENITENT Cineworld, 1988

RODMAN FLENDER
Business: Concorde Films, 11600 San Vicente Blvd., Los Angeles, CA, 90049, 213/820-6733

LORDS OF THE DEEP Concorde, 1989, AP
STRIPPED TO KILL 2 Concorde, 1989, AP
THE TERROR WITHIN Concorde, 1989, CP w/Reid Shane
STREETS Concorde, 1990, AP
THE HAUNTING OF MORELLA Concorde, 1990
BODY CHEMISTRY Concorde, 1990, EP

ANGEL FLORES-MARINI
WALKER Universal, 1987, w/Lorenzo O'Brien
THE BLUE IGUANA Paramount, 1988, CP w/Othon Roffiel

ANDREW FOGELSON
WRONG IS RIGHT Columbia, 1982, EP
BLUE THUNDER Columbia, 1983, EP w/Phil Feldman
THE NEW KIDS Columbia, 1985, w/Sean S. Cunningham
JUST ONE OF THE GUYS Columbia, 1985

LAWRENCE D. FOLDES
Business: Star Cinema Production Group, Inc., 6253 Hollywood Blvd., Suite 927, Los Angeles, CA, 90028, 213/462-2000
Attorney: Ronald G. Gabler, 9606 Santa Monica Blvd., Beverly Hills, CA, 90210, 213/205-8908

MALIBU HIGH Crown International, 1979

THOMAS FOLINO

Business: Corsair Pictures, 1740 Broadway, 23rd Floor, New York, NY, 10019, 212/603-0652 or 1640 S. Sepulveda Blvd., #216, Los Angeles, CA, 90025, 213/479-8200

HELLO AGAIN Buena Vista, 1987, CP w/G. Mac Brown, Susan Isaacs & Martin Mickelson

GEORGE FOLSEY, JR.

Business: Universal Studios, 100 Universal City Plaza, #423, Universal City, CA, 91608, 818/777-1000
Contact: Directors Guild of America - Los Angeles, 213/289-2000

GLASS HOUSES Columbia, 1972
SCHLOCK Jack H. Harris Enterprises, 1973, EP
THE BLUES BROTHERS Universal, 1980, AP
AN AMERICAN WEREWOLF IN LONDON Universal, 1981
TWILIGHT ZONE - THE MOVIE Warner Bros., 1983, AP
TRADING PLACES Paramount, 1983, EP
INTO THE NIGHT Universal, 1985, w/Ron Koslow
SPIES LIKE US Warner Bros., 1985, w/Brian Grazer
CLUE Paramount, 1985, EP w/Peter Guber, John Landis & Jon Peters
THREE AMIGOS Orion, 1986, w/Lorne Michaels
AMAZON WOMEN ON THE MOON Universal, 1987, EP w/John Landis
COMING TO AMERICA Paramount, 1988, w/Robert D. Wachs

PETER FONDA

Business Manager: Lawrence J. Stern, Nanas, Stern, Biers & Company, 9434 Wilshire Blvd., Beverly Hills, CA, 90212, 213/273-2501
Contact: Directors Guild of America - Los Angeles, 213/289-2000

EASY RIDER Columbia, 1969

NAOMI FONER

Agent: CAA - Beverly Hills, 213/288-4545
Contact: Writers Guild of America - Los Angeles, 213/550-1000

RUNNING ON EMPTY Warner Bros., 1988, EP w/Burtt Harris

LLOYD FONVIELLE

Agent: ICM - Los Angeles, 213/550-4000
Contact: Writers Guild of America - Los Angeles, 213/550-1000

THE BRIDE Columbia, 1985, AP
GOOD MORNING BABYLON Vestron, 1987, AP w/Caldecott Chubb
CHERRY 2000 Orion, 1988, EP

HORTON FOOTE

Agent: Lucy Kroll Agency - New York, 212/877-0627
Contact: Writers Guild of America - New York, 212/245-6180

TENDER MERCIES ★ Universal, 1983, CP w/Robert Duvall
THE TRIP TO BOUNTIFUL Island Pictures, 1985, w/Sterling Van Wagenen

LILLIAN V. FOOTE

1918 Cinecom, 1985, w/Ross E. Milloy
ON VALENTINE'S DAY Angelika, 1986, w/Calvin Skaggs

DAVID FORBES

THE BIG SCORE Almi, 1983, EP w/Harry Hurwitz

JUAN FORCH

THE LAWLESS LAND Concorde, 1988, EP w/Roger Corman

JOHN FOREMAN

BUTCH CASSIDY AND THE SUNDANCE KID ★ 20th Century-Fox, 1969
WINNING Universal, 1969
WUSA Paramount, 1970, w/Paul Newman
PUZZLE OF A DOWNFALL CHILD Universal, 1970
SOMETIMES A GREAT NOTION Universal, 1971
THEY MIGHT BE GIANTS Universal, 1972, w/Paul Newman
THE LIFE & TIMES OF JUDGE ROY BEAN National General, 1972
POCKET MONEY National General, 1972
THE EFFECT OF GAMMA RAYS ON MAN-IN-THE-MOON MARIGOLDS 20th Century-Fox, 1972, EP
THE MACKINTOSH MAN Warner Bros., 1973
THE MAN WHO WOULD BE KING Allied Artists/Columbia, 1975
BOBBY DEERFIELD Columbia, 1977, EP
THE GREAT TRAIN ROBBERY United Artists, 1979
THE ICE PIRATES MGM/UA, 1984
EUREKA MGM/UA, 1984, EP
PRIZZI'S HONOR ★ 20th Century-Fox, 1985
MILLENNIUM 20th Century-Fox, 1989, EP w/Freddie Fields, P. Gael Mourant & Louis M. Silverstein

MARK FORSTATER

Business: Mark Forstater Productions, Ltd., 42a, Devonshire Close, Portland Place, London W.1., England, 01/631-0611

MONTY PYTHON AND THE HOLY GRAIL Cinema 5, 1974
XTRO New Line Cinema, 1983
KILLING HEAT Satori, 1984
NOT FOR PUBLICATION Samuel Goldwyn Company, 1984, EP
MARIGOLDS IN AUGUST RM Productions, 1984, w/Jonathan Cohen
PAINT IT BLACK Vestron, 1989, w/Anne Kimmel

BILL FORSYTH

Agent: CAA - Beverly Hills, 213/288-4545
Contact: Directors Guild of America - Los Angeles, 213/289-2000

THAT SINKING FEELING Samuel Goldwyn Company, 1984

FREDERICK FORSYTH

Agent: Perry Knowlton, Curtis Brown, Inc., 10 Astor Place, New York, NY, 10003, 212/473-5400

THE FOURTH PROTOCOL Lorimar, 1987, EP w/Michael Caine & Wafic Said

DAVID FOSTER
(credit w/Lawrence Turman)

Business: The Turman-Foster Company, 3400 Riverside Dr., 11th Floor, Burbank, CA, 91505, 818/972-7772

MCCABE & MRS. MILLER Warner Bros., 1971, w/Mitchell Brower*
THE GETAWAY National General, 1972, w/Mitchell Brower*
THE NICKEL RIDE 20th Century-Fox, 1974, EP
THE DROWNING POOL Warner Bros., 1975
FIRST LOVE Paramount, 1977
HEROES Universal, 1977
THE LEGACY Columbia, 1978
TRIBUTE 20th Century-Fox, 1980, EP w/Richard S. Bright
CAVEMAN United Artists, 1981
THE THING Universal, 1982
SECOND THOUGHTS Universal, 1983
MASS APPEAL Universal, 1984
THE MEAN SEASON Orion, 1985
SHORT CIRCUIT Tri-Star, 1986
RUNNING SCARED MGM, 1986
FULL MOON IN BLUE WATER Trans World Entertainment, 1988, w/John Turman
SHORT CIRCUIT II Tri-Star, 1988, w/Gary Foster
GLEAMING THE CUBE 20th Century-Fox, 1989

GARY FOSTER
Business: Gary Foster Productions, 3400 Riverside Dr., 11th Floor, Burbank, CA, 91505, 818/972-7785

SHORT CIRCUIT Tri-Star, 1986, AP
SHORT CIRCUIT II Tri-Star, 1988, w/David Foster & Lawrence Turman
LOVERBOY Tri-Star, 1989, w/Willie Hunt
SIDEOUT Tri-Star, 1990

PATRICIA FOULKROD
Business: 213/664-1408

BETTER WATCH OUT Carolco
WARM SUMMER RAIN Trans World Entertainment, 1990
KOOL BLUE Trans World Entertainment

PEGGY FOWLER
CAMPUS MAN Paramount, 1987, w/Jon Landau

ROBERT FOX
Business: World Film Services Ltd.,Pinewood Studios, Iver Heath, Bucks., SL0 0NH, England, 0753-651700

ANOTHER COUNTRY Orion Classics, 1984, EP w/Julian Seymour

TOM FOX
RETURN OF THE LIVING DEAD Orion, 1985
BLUE MONKEY Spectrafilm, 1987, EP
RETURN OF THE LIVING DEAD PART II Lorimar, 1988

JOSEPH FRANCK
HEARTBREAKERS Orion, 1985, EP w/Harry Cooper & Lee Muhl

LARRY J. FRANCO
Agent: The Gersh Agency - Beverly Hills, 213/274-6611
Contact: Directors Guild of America - Los Angeles, 213/289-2000

CUTTER'S WAY United Artists Classics, 1981, AP w/Jeffrey Chernov
ESCAPE FROM NEW YORK Avco Embassy, 1981, w/Debra Hill
THE THING Universal, 1982, AP
CHRISTINE Columbia, 1983, CP
STARMAN Columbia, 1984
BIG TROUBLE IN LITTLE CHINA 20th Century- Fox, 1986
PRINCE OF DARKNESS Universal, 1987
THEY LIVE Universal, 1988
TANGO & CASH Warner Bros., 1989, CP

JERRY FRANKEL
FAST BREAK Columbia, 1979, EP

BRIAN FRANKISH
Business: Paramount Pictures, 5555 Melrose Ave., Los Angeles, CA, 90038, 213/468-4427
Contact: Directors Guild of America - Los Angeles, 213/289-2000

VICE SQUAD Avco Embassy, 1982
STRANGE BREW MGM/UA, 1983, AP
THE BOY WHO COULD FLY Lorimar, 1986, AP
IN THE MOOD Lorimar, 1987, AP
FIELD OF DREAMS Universal, 1989, EP
FLIGHT OF THE INTRUDER Paramount, 1990, EP w/John McTiernan

JEFF FRANKLIN
Business: Jeff Franklin Productions, 10202 W. Washington Blvd., Culver City, CA, 90232, 213/280-5428
Agent: BBMW - Los Angeles, 213/277-4998

JUST ONE OF THE GUYS Columbia, 1985, EP
SUMMER SCHOOL Paramount, 1987, AP
THE IN CROWD Orion, 1988, EP w/John F. Roach

RICHARD FRANKLIN
Agent: The Daniel Ostroff Agency - Los Angeles, 213/278-1955
Contact: Directors Guild of America - Los Angeles, 213/289-2000

THE BLUE LAGOON Columbia, 1980, CP
ROAD GAMES Avco Embassy, 1981
LINK Cannon, 1986

FRANK FRAZETTA
FIRE & ICE (AF) 20th Century-Fox, 1983, w/Ralph Bakshi

RONALD E. FRAZIER
THE WRONG GUYS New World, 1988, w/Charles Gordon

GRAY FREDERICKSON
THE GODFATHER ★★ Paramount, 1972, AP
THE GODFATHER - PART II ★★ Paramount, 1974, CP w/Fred Roos
APOCALYPSE NOW ★ United Artists, 1979, CP w/Fred Roos

ONE FROM THE HEART Columbia, 1982, w/Fred Roos
THE OUTSIDERS Warner Bros., 1983, w/Fred Roos
UHF Orion, 1989, EP

WINNIE FREDRIKSZ
LIFE IS CHEAP Far East Stars, 1990

JOEL L. FREEDMAN
BRAINSTORM MGM/UA, 1983, EP

FRED FREEMAN
Agent: CAA - Beverly Hills, 213/288-4545
Contact: Writers Guild of America - Los Angeles, 213/550-1000

THE BIG BUS Paramount, 1976, w/Lawrence J. Cohen

JOEL FREEMAN
Agent: Triad Artists, Inc. - Los Angeles, 213/556-2727
Contact: Directors Guild of America - Los Angeles, 213/289-2000

CAMELOT Warner Bros., 1967, AP
FINIAN'S RAINBOW Warner Bros., 1968, AP
THE HEART IS A LONELY HUNTER Warner Bros., 1968, EP
SHAFT MGM, 1971
TROUBLE MAN 20th Century-Fox, 1972
LOVE AT FIRST BITE American International, 1979
THE OCTAGON American Cinema, 1980
THE KINDRED FM Entertainment, 1987, EP

PAUL FREEMAN
HALLOWEEN 4: THE RETURN OF MICHAEL MYERS Galaxy, 1988

ROBIN FRENCH
BLUE COLLAR Universal, 1978, EP

EUGENE FRENKE
THE LAST SUNSET Universal, 1961, w/Edward Lewis

KEN FRIEDMAN
Agent: Bauer Benedek Agency - Los Angeles, 213/275-2421
Contact: Writers Guild of America - Los Angeles, 213/550-1000

MR. BILLION 20th Century-Fox, 1976, w/Steven Bach

STEPHEN J. FRIEDMAN
Business: Kings Road Entertainment, 1901 Avenue of the Stars, Suite 605, Los Angeles, CA, 90067

THE LAST PICTURE SHOW ★ Columbia, 1971
LOVIN' MOLLY Columbia, 1974
SLAP SHOT Universal, 1977, w/Robert J. Wunsch
BLOODBROTHERS Warner Bros., 1979
FAST BREAK Columbia, 1979
HERO AT LARGE MGM/UA, 1980
LITTLE DARLINGS Paramount, 1980
EYE OF THE NEEDLE United Artists, 1981
THE INCUBUS Film Ventures International, 1982, EP
ALL OF ME Universal, 1984
ENEMY MINE 20th Century-Fox, 1985
CREATOR Universal, 1985
MORGAN STEWART'S COMING HOME New Century/Vista, 1987
TOUCH AND GO Tri-Star, 1987
THE BIG EASY Columbia, 1987

AVA OSTERN FRIES
Business: Fries Entertainment, 6922 Hollywood Blvd., 12th Floor, Hollywood, CA, 90028, 213/466-2266

TROOP BEVERLY HILLS WEG/Columbia, 1989

CHARLES FRIES
Business: Fries Entertainment, 6922 Hollywood Blvd., 12th Floor, Hollywood, CA, 90028, 213/466-2266

CAT PEOPLE Universal, 1982
THRASHIN' Fries Entertainment, 1986, EP w/Mike Rosenfeld
OUT OF BOUNDS Columbia, 1986, w/Mike Rosenfeld
TROOP BEVERLY HILLS WEG/Columbia, 1989, EP

THOMAS FRIES
FLOWERS IN THE ATTIC New World, 1987, w/Sy Levin

GIL FRIESEN
Contact: 770 Bonhill Road, Los Angeles, CA, 90049, 213/471-0514

THE BREAKFAST CLUB Universal, 1985, EP w/Andrew Meyer
BETTER OFF DEAD Warner Bros., 1985, EP w/Andrew Meyer
BRING ON THE NIGHT (FD) Samuel Goldwyn Company, 1985, EP w/Andrew Meyer
ONE CRAZY SUMMER Warner Bros., 1986, EP w/Andrew Meyer
THE BEAST Columbia, 1988, EP w/Dale Pollock
THE MIGHTY QUINN MGM/UA, 1989, EP w/Dale Pollock
WORTH WINNING 20th Century-Fox, 1989, w/Dale Pollock
BLAZE Buena Vista, 1989, w/Dale Pollock

GOWER FROST
SLAYGROUND Universal, 1984, w/John Dark

WILLIAM FRYE
AIRPORT '77 Universal, 1977
THE CONCORDE — AIRPORT '79 Universal, 1979
RAISE THE TITANIC AFD, 1980

ROBERT FRYER
THE BOYS FROM BRAZIL 20th Century-Fox, 1978, EP

FRED FUCHS
(credit w/Fred Roos)
Business: Zoetrope Studios, Sentinel Bldg., 916 Kearny St., San Francisco, CA, 94133, 415/789-7500

TUCKER: THE MAN AND HIS DREAM Paramount, 1988
NEW YORK STORIES "Life Without Zoe" Buena Vista, 1989

LEO L. FUCHS
SUNDAY LOVERS United Artists, 1981
JUST THE WAY YOU ARE MGM/UA, 1984
MALONE Orion, 1987

ANNETTE FUNICELLO
BACK TO THE BEACH Paramount, 1987, EP w/Frankie Avalon

SIDNEY J. FURIE
Business: Furie Productions, 9169 Sunset Blvd., Los Angeles, CA, 90069
Agent: Peter Rawley, ICM - Los Angeles, 213/550-4000

PURPLE HEARTS Warner Bros., 1984

JOHN FUSCO
Agent: William Morris Agency - Beverly Hills, 213/274-7451
Contact: Writers Guild of America - Los Angeles, 213/550-1000

YOUNG GUNS 20th Century-Fox, 1988, EP w/James G. Robinson

G

RICHARD GABOURIE
BUYING TIME MGM/UA, 1989

PAUL GAER
GET TO KNOW YOUR RABBIT Warner Bros., 1972, w/Steven Bernhardt

NICHOLAS GAGE
Contact: Writers Guild of America - New York, 212/245-6180

ELENI Warner Bros., 1985, w/Mark Pick & Nick Vanoff

LEONARD GAINES
GOING IN STYLE Warner Bros., 1979, EP

DEIRDRE GAINOR
ANNA Vestron, 1987, EP w/Julianne Gilliam

BOB GALE
Agent: Jack Rapke, CAA - Beverly Hills, 213/288-4545
Contact: Writers Guild of America - Los Angeles, 213/550-1000

I WANNA HOLD YOUR HAND Universal, 1977, AP
USED CARS Columbia, 1980
BACK TO THE FUTURE Universal, 1985, w/Neil Canton
BACK TO THE FUTURE II Universal, 1989, w/Neil Canton
BACK TO THE FUTURE III Universal, 1990, w/Neil Canton

MITCHELL GALIN
Business: Laurel Entertainment, Inc., 928 Broadway, New York, NY, 10010, 212/674-3800

PET SEMATARY Paramount, 1989, CP

SANDY GALLIN
Business: Sandollar Productions, 8730 Sunset Blvd., Penthouse, Los Angeles, CA, 90069, 213/659-5933

JACKNIFE Cineplex Odeon, 1989, EP
GROSS ANATOMY Buena Vista, 1989, EP w/Carol Baum

FRED T. GALLO
Business: Whitestone Productions, Warner Bros., 4000 Warner Blvd., Burbank, CA, 91522, 818/954-1881
Contact: Directors Guild of America - Los Angeles, 213/289-2000

LOVE AND DEATH United Artists, 1975, AP
GOING IN STYLE Warner Bros., 1979, w/Tony Bill
BODY HEAT Warner Bros., 1981

ANTOINE GANNAGE
MIXED BLOOD Sara Films/Cinevista, 1985, w/Steven Fierberg

BEN GANNON
TRAVELLING NORTH Cineplex Odeon, 1988

JEFFREY GANZ
Contact: Writers Guild of America - Los Angeles, 213/550-1000

YOUNG DOCTORS IN LOVE 20th Century-Fox, 1982, AP w/Nick Abdo
BAD MEDICINE 20th Century-Fox, 1985, CP

TONY GANZ
Business: Blum-Ganz Productions, c/o ITC Productions, 12711 Ventura Blvd., Studio City, CA, 91604, 818/760-2110
Contact: Directors Guild of America - Los Angeles, 213/289-2000

GUNG HO Paramount, 1986, w/Deborah Blum
NO MAN'S LAND Orion, 1987, EP w/Ron Howard
CLEAN & SOBER Warner Bros., 1988, w/Deborah Blum
VIBES Columbia, 1988, w/Deborah Blum

ERIC GARDNER
ELVIRA, MISTRESS OF THE DARK New World, 1988, w/Mark Pierson

ROBERT GARLAND
Agent: CAA - Beverly Hills, 213/288-4545
Contact: Writers Guild of America - Los Angeles, 213/550-1000

NO WAY OUT Orion, 1987, w/Laura Ziskin

TONY GARNETT
Business: Kestrel Films, 4000 Warner Blvd., Bldg. 81, Rm. 117, Burbank, CA, 91522, 818/954-1457
Attorney: Barry Hirsch - Los Angeles, 213/553-0305

KES United Artists, 1970
THE BODY Anglo-EMI, 1971
WEDNESDAY'S CHILD Cinema 5, 1972
DEEP IN THE HEART *HANDGUN* Warner Bros., 1984
SESAME STREET PRESENTS FOLLOW THAT BIRD Warner Bros., 1985

EARTH GIRLS ARE EASY Vestron, 1989
FAT MAN AND LITTLE BOY Paramount, 1989

HELEN GARVY
HARD TRAVELING New World, 1986

JEROME GARY
Agent: The Agency, 10351 Santa Monica Blvd., Suite 211, Los Angeles, CA, 90025, 213/551-3000
Contact: Directors Guild of America - New York, 212/581-0370

STRIPPER (FD) 20th Century-Fox, 1986, w/Geof Bartz & Melvyn J. Estrin

ANDREW GATY
Contact: Norman Rudman, Esq., Slaff, Mosk & Rudman, 9200 Sunset Blvd., Suite 825, Los Angeles, CA, 90069, 213/275-5351

HEART OF MIDNIGHT Samuel Goldwyn Company, 1988

BILL GAVIN
Business: Gavin Film Ltd., 120 Wardour St., London W1V 3LA, England

THE HOT SPOT Orion, 1990, EP w/Derek Power & Steve Ujlaki

MICHELE RAY-GAVRAS
(see Michele RAY-Gavras)

SARA GEATER
BUSINESS AS USUAL Cannon, 1988

DAVID GEFFEN
Business: The Geffen Company, 9130 Sunset Blvd., Los Angeles, CA, 90069, 213/278-9010

PERSONAL BEST Warner Bros., 1982, EP
LITTLE SHOP OF HORRORS The Geffen Company/ Warner Bros., 1986

ELLIOTT GEISINGER
Contact: Directors Guild of America - New York, 212/581-0370

CHILD'S PLAY MGM/UA, 1988, EP w/Barrie M. Osborne

LARRY GELBART
Business Manager: Barry Pollack - Los Angeles, 213/550-4525
Contact: Writers Guild of America - Los Angeles, 213/550-1000

BLAME IT ON RIO 20th Century-Fox, 1984, EP

RICHARD GELFAND
Contact: Directors Guild of America - Los Angeles, 213/289-2000

CALL ME Vestron, 1988, LP w/Mary Kane

ANDREW GELLIS
GRANDVIEW, U.S.A. Warner Bros., 1984, EP w/Jonathan T. Taplin

GERALD GEOFFRAY
Business: Paragon Arts International, 6777 Hollywood Blvd., Suite 700, Hollywood, CA, 90028, 213/465-5355

WITCHBOARD Cinema Group, 1987

GEORGE W. GEORGE
THE JAMES DEAN STORY Warner Bros., 1957 w/Robert Altman
TWISTED NERVE National General, 1969, w/Frank Granat
NIGHT WATCH Avco Embassy, 1973, w/Martin Poll
RICH KIDS United Artists, 1979, w/Michael Hausman
MY DINNER WITH ANDRE New Yorker, 1981, w/Beverly Karp

LOU GEORGE
Business: Arista Films, Inc., 16027 Ventura Blvd., Encino, CA, 91436, 818/907-7660

SURF II International Films, 1984, EP w/Frank D. Tolin

SUSAN GEORGE
Agent: APA - Los Angeles, 213/273-0744

STEALING HEAVEN Scotti Bros., 1989, EP

BILL GERBER
CRIMES OF THE HEART DEG, 1986, CP w/Arlyne Rothberg

PATRICIA GERRETSEN
NIGHT FRIEND Cineplex Odeon, 1988

WILLIAM C. GERRITY
Contact: Directors Guild of America - New York, 212/581-0370

SOPHIE'S CHOICE Universal, 1982, AP
DREAM LOVER MGM/UA, 1986, EP

JERRY GERSHWIN
Business: Winkast II Film Productions, 9507 Santa Monica Blvd., #224, Beverly Hills, CA, 90210, 213/285-9533

HARPER Warner Bros., 1966, w/Elliott Kastner
BREAKHEART PASS United Artists, 1976
NOMADS Atlantic Entertainment, 1986, EP

BERNARD GERSTEN
Business: Lincoln Center Theater, 150 W. 65th St., New York, NY, 10023, 212/362-7600

ONE FROM THE HEART Columbia, 1982, EP

DEREN GETZ
UHF Orion, 1989, CP w/Kevin Breslin

AZIZ GHAZAL
ZOMBIE HIGH Cinema Group, 1987, w/Marc Toberoff

FERNANDO GHIA
LADY CAROLINE LAMB United Artists, 1972
THE MISSION ★ Warner Bros., 1986, w/David Puttnam

STACEY GIACHINO
THE POWER Film Ventures International, 1984, AP
THE KINDRED FM Entertainment, 1987, CP

DEREK GIBSON

(credit w/John Daly)

Business: Hemdale Film Corporation, 1118 N. Wetherly Dr., Los Angeles, CA, 90069, 213/550-6894

JAGUAR LIVES! American International, 1979
DEATH SHIP Avco Embassy, 1980, w/Harold Greenberg*
A BREED APART Orion, 1984
THE TERMINATOR Orion, 1984, EP
TRIUMPHS OF A MAN CALLED HORSE Jensen Farley, 1984*
RETURN OF THE LIVING DEAD Orion, 1985, EP
AT CLOSE RANGE Orion, 1986, EP
SALVADOR Hemdale, 1986, EP
HOOSIERS Orion, 1986, EP
PLATOON ★★ Orion, 1986, EP
RIVER'S EDGE Island Pictures, 1987, EP
BEST SELLER Orion, 1987, EP
BUSTER Hemdale, 1988, EP
THE BOOST Hemdale, 1988, EP
MADE IN U.S.A. Tri-Star, 1988, EP
LOVE AT STAKE Tri-Star, 1988, EP
SHAG: THE MOVIE Hemdale, 1989, EP w/Nik Powell
MIRACLE MILE Hemdale, 1989
CRIMINAL LAW Hemdale, 1989, EP
WAR PARTY Hemdale, 1989, w/Bernard Williams
VAMPIRE'S KISS Hemdale, 1989, EP
OUT COLD Hemdale, 1989, EP
STAYING TOGETHER Hemdale, 1989, EP
THE BOYFRIEND SCHOOL Hemdale, 1990, EP

RAYNOLD GIDEON

(credit w/Bruce A. Evans)

Business: Evans-Gideon Productions, Universal Studios, 100 Universal City Plaza, Universal City, CA, 91608, 818/777-3121
Agent: CAA - Beverly Hills, 213/288-4545

STARMAN Columbia, 1984, AP
STAND BY ME Columbia, 1986, w/Andrew Scheinman
MADE IN HEAVEN Lorimar, 1987, w/David Blocker

DIETER GIESSLER

THE NEVERENDING STORY Warner Bros., 1984, w/Bernd Eichinger
THE NEVERENDING STORY II Warner Bros., 1990

BRUCE GILBERT

Business: American Filmworks, 3 Latimer Rd., Santa Monica, CA, 90402, 213/451-8521

THE CHINA SYNDROME Columbia, 1979, EP
NINE TO FIVE 20th Century-Fox, 1980
ROLLOVER Orion/Warner Bros., 1981
ON GOLDEN POND ★ Universal/AFD, 1981
THE MORNING AFTER 20th Century-Fox, 1986

LEWIS GILBERT

Business: c/o Baker Rooke, Clement House, 99 Aldwych, London WC2 BJY, England
Contact: Directors Guild of America - Los Angeles, 213/289-2000

ALFIE ★ Paramount, 1966
EDUCATING RITA Columbia, 1983
NOT QUITE PARADISE New World, 1986
SHIRLEY VALENTINE Paramount, 1989

DAVID GILER

Business: The Phoenix Company, Columbia Plaza, Producers 8, #205, Burbank, CA, 91505, 818/954-4905
Agent: ICM - Los Angeles, 213/550-4000

ALIEN 20th Century-Fox, 1979, w/Gordon Carroll & Walter Hill
SOUTHERN COMFORT 20th Century-Fox, 1981
RUSTLER'S RHAPSODY Paramount, 1985
ALIENS 20th Century-Fox, 1986, EP w/Gordon Carroll & Walter Hill
THE MONEY PIT Universal, 1986, EP w/Steven Spielberg
LET IT RIDE Paramount, 1989

JULIANNE GILLIAM

ANNA Vestron, 1987, EP w/Deirdre Gainor

TERRY GILLIAM

Business: 51 South Hill Park, London NW3, England
Agent: CAA - Beverly Hills, 213/288-4545

TIME BANDITS Avco Embassy, 1981

GARY GILLINGHAM

HAMBONE AND HILLIE New World, 1984, w/Sandy Howard

WILLIAM S. GILMORE

Business: Universal Studios, 100 Universal City Plaza, Bldg. 507, Universal City, CA, 91608, 818/777-1484
Contact: Directors Guild of America - Los Angeles, 213/289-2000

SOLDIER BLUE Avco Embassy, 1970, AP
THE LAST REMAKE OF BEAU GESTE Universal, 1977
DEFIANCE American International, 1980, w/Jerry Bruckheimer
DEADLY BLESSING United Artists, 1981
TOUGH ENOUGH 20th Century-Fox, 1983
AGAINST ALL ODDS Columbia, 1984, w/Taylor Hackford
WHITE NIGHTS Columbia, 1985, w/Taylor Hackford
LITTLE SHOP OF HORRORS The Geffen Company/ Warner Bros., 1986, LP
MIDNIGHT RUN Universal, 1988, EP
RETURN OF THE LIVING DEAD PART II Lorimar, 1988, CP

ANTONY I. GINNANE

Business: International Film Management Ltd., Level 4, 64 Stead St., South Melbourne, 3205 Australia, 03/699-6133

THIRST Greater Union Film Distribution, 1979
STRANGE BEHAVIOR World Northal, 1981, w/John Barnett
HARLEQUIN New Image, 1983
HIGH TIDE Tri-Star, 1987, EP w/Joseph Skrzynski
THE EVERLASTING SECRET FAMILY International Film Exchange, 1990, EP

VINCENT GIORDANO

TOUGHER THAN LEATHER New Line Cinema, 1988

HARRY GITTES

Business: Film Development Partners, Columbia Pictures, Studio Plaza, 3400 Riverside Dr., Burbank, CA, 91505, 818/954-3503

HARRY & WALTER GO TO NEW YORK Columbia, 1976, w/Don Devlin
GOIN' SOUTH Paramount, 1978, w/Harold Schneider
TIMERIDER: THE ADVENTURE OF LYLE SWANN Jensen Farley Pics, 1983
LITTLE NIKITA Columbia, 1988
BREAKING IN Samuel Goldwyn Company, 1989

FRANK GIUSTRA

BUSTER Tri-Star, 1988, EP w/Peter Strauss
BEST OF THE BEST Taurus, 1989, EP w/Michael Holzman & Jeff Ringler

ANDI GLADSTONE

WORKING GIRLS Miramax, 1987, w/Lizzie Borden

ALLAN GLASER

LUST IN THE DUST New World, 1985, w/Tab Hunter

WOLFGANG GLATTES

Contact: Directors Guild of America - Los Angeles, 213/289-2000

ALL THAT JAZZ 20th Century-Fox, 1979, AP w/Kenneth Utt
STILL OF THE NIGHT MGM/UA, 1982, AP w/Kenneth Utt
STAR 80 The Ladd Company/Warner Bros., 1983, w/Kenneth Utt
THE MORNING AFTER 20th Century-Fox, 1986, AP w/Lois Bonfiglio
POWER 20th Century-Fox, 1986, AP w/Kenneth Utt
WHITE WATER SUMMER Columbia, 1987, EP
NADINE Tri-Star, 1987, EP
SING Tri-Star, 1989, EP
THE HANDMAID'S TALE Cinecom, 1990, EP

EARL GLICK

STARSHIP INVASIONS Warner Bros., 1977, EP
CHILDREN OF THE CORN New World, 1984, EP w/Charles J. Weber

MICHAEL S. GLICK

Contact: Directors Guild of America - Los Angeles, 213/289-2000

BUSTIN' LOOSE Universal, 1981, w/Richard Pryor
LOCK UP Tri-Star, 1989, EP

NORMAN GLICK

STARSHIP INVASIONS Warner Bros., 1977, w/Ken Gord & Ed Hunt

JAMES GLICKENHAUS

Business: Shapiro-Glickenhaus Entertainment, 1619 Broadway, New York, NY, 10019, 212/265-1150
Agent: William Morris Agency - Beverly Hills, 213/274-7451

BASKET CASE 2 Shapiro-Glickenhaus Entertainment, 1990, EP

ARNOLD GLIMCHER

Agent: CAA - Beverly Hills, 213/288-4545

LEGAL EAGLES Universal, 1986, AP w/Sheldon Kahn
GORILLAS IN THE MIST Universal, 1988, w/Terence Clegg
THE GOOD MOTHER Buena Vista, 1988

TERRY GLINWOOD

Business: Glinwood Films, 8-12 Broadwick St., London W1V 1FH, England, 01/437-1181

MERRY CHRISTMAS, MR. LAWRENCE Universal, 1983, EP w/Masato Hara, Geoffrey Nethercott & Eiko Oshima
ERIK THE VIKING Orion, 1989, EP
EVERYBODY WINS Orion, 1990, EP w/Linda Yellen

YORAM GLOBUS

(credit w/Menahem Golan)

Business: Cannon Productions, 5757 Wilshire Blvd., Suite 721, Los Angeles, CA, 90036, 213/965-0901

THE URANIUM CONSPIRACY Noah Films, 1978, w/Francesco Corti*
IT'S A FUNNY FUNNY WORLD Noah Films, 1978
THE MAGICIAN OF LUBLIN Cannon, 1979
THE APPLE Cannon, 1980
THE HAPPY HOOKER GOES HOLLYWOOD Cannon, 1980
SCHIZOID Cannon, 1980
THE GODSEND Cannon, 1980
ENTER THE NINJA Cannon, 1981, w/Judd Bernard*
BODY AND SOUL Cannon, 1981
HOSPITAL MASSACRE Cannon, 1982
DEATH WISH II Filmways, 1982
THAT CHAMPIONSHIP SEASON Cannon, 1982
THE WICKED LADY Cannon, 1983
REVENGE OF THE NINJA Cannon, 1983
THE LAST AMERICAN VIRGIN Cannon, 1983
HERCULES Cannon, 1983
10 TO MIDNIGHT Cannon, 1983, EP
LOVE STREAMS Cannon, 1984
GRACE QUIGLEY *THE ULTIMATE SOLUTION OF GRACE QUIGLEY* Cannon, 1984
DEJA VU Cannon, 1984
SAHARA Cannon, 1984
THE NAKED FACE Cannon, 1984
BOLERO Cannon, 1984
MISSING IN ACTION
BREAKIN' MGM/UA/Cannon, 1984, EP
BREAKIN' 2: ELECTRIC BOOGALOO Tri-Star, 1984
HOUSE OF THE LONG SHADOWS Cannon, 1984
EXTERMINATOR 2 Cannon, 1984
NINJA III: THE DOMINATION Cannon, 1984
SWORD OF THE VALIANT Cannon, 1984
MISSING IN ACTION 2: THE BEGINNING Cannon, 1985
INVASION U.S.A. Cannon, 1985
DEATH WISH 3 Cannon, 1985
ORDEAL BY INNOCENCE Cannon, 1985, EP
KING SOLOMON'S MINES Cannon, 1985
FOOL FOR LOVE Cannon, 1985
RUNAWAY TRAIN Cannon, 1985
HOT RESORT Cannon, 1985
RAPPIN' Cannon, 1985
LIFEFORCE Tri-Star, 1985
AMERICAN NINJA Cannon, 1985
HOT CHILI Cannon, 1985

THE SEVEN MAGNIFICENT GLADIATORS Cannon, 1985
THE ASSISI UNDERGROUND Cannon, 1985
MARIA'S LOVERS Cannon, 1985, EP
THE AMBASSADOR Cannon, 1985
THE DELTA FORCE Cannon, 1986
THE NAKED CAGE Cannon, 1986, EP
AMERICA 3000 Cannon, 1986
DETECTIVE SCHOOL DROPOUTS *DUMB DICKS* Cannon, 1986
INVADERS FROM MARS Cannon, 1986
THE TEXAS CHAINSAW MASSACRE PART 2 Cannon, 1986
AVENGING FORCE Cannon, 1986
MURPHY'S LAW Cannon, 1986, EP
COBRA Warner Bros., 1986
P.O.W. THE ESCAPE Cannon, 1986
OTELLO Cannon, 1986
52 PICK-UP Cannon, 1986
FIREWALKER Cannon, 1986
DANGEROUSLY CLOSE Cannon, 1986, EP
ALLAN QUATERMAIN AND THE LOST CITY OF GOLD Cannon, 1987
NUMBER ONE WITH A BULLET Cannon, 1987
ASSASSINATION Cannon, 1987, EP
DOWN TWISTED Cannon, 1987
RUMPLESTILTSKIN Cannon, 1987
BEAUTY AND THE BEAST Cannon, 1987
AMERICAN NINJA 2 Cannon, 1987
HELL SQUAD Cannon, 1987, EP
TOO MUCH Cannon, 1987
DUET FOR ONE Cannon, 1987
MASTERS OF THE UNIVERSE Cannon, 1987
STREET SMART Cannon, 1987
OVER THE TOP Cannon, 1987
SUPERMAN IV: THE QUEST FOR PEACE Warner Bros., 1987
THE HANOI HILTON Cannon, 1987
BARFLY Cannon, 1987, EP
DANCERS Cannon, 1987
UNDER COVER Cannon, 1987
DUTCH TREAT Cannon, 1987
SURRENDER Warner Bros., 1987, EP
TOUGH GUYS DON'T DANCE Cannon, 1987
DEATH WISH 4: THE CRACKDOWN Cannon, 1987, EP
SHY PEOPLE Cannon, 1987
HANNA'S WAR Cannon, 1988
BRADDOCK: MISSING IN ACTION III Cannon, 1988
MESSENGER OF DEATH Cannon, 1988, EP
HERO AND THE TERROR Cannon, 1988, EP
A CRY IN THE DARK Warner Bros., 1988, EP
THE KITCHEN TOTO Cannon, 1988
POWAQQATSI Cannon, 1988
SALSA Cannon, 1988
APPOINTMENT WITH DEATH Cannon, 1988
KING LEAR Cannon, 1988
ALIEN FROM L.A. Cannon, 1988
BUSINESS AS USUAL Cannon, 1988, EP
HAUNTED SUMMER Cannon, 1989
PUSS IN BOOTS Cannon, 1989
KINJITE (FORBIDDEN SUBJECTS) Cannon, 1989, EP
THE ROSE GARDEN Cannon, 1989, EP w/Christopher Pearce*
CYBORG Cannon, 1989
MANIFESTO Cannon, 1989
DOIN' TIME ON PLANET EARTH Cannon, 1990
A MAN CALLED SARGE Cannon, 1990, EP w/Christopher Pearce*

DANNY GLOVER

Agent: William Morris Agency - Beverly Hills, 213/274-7451

TO SLEEP WITH ANGER SVS Films, 1990, EP w/Edward R. Pressman & Harris E. Tulchin

RICHARD GLOVER

NO HOLDS BARRED New Line Cinema, 1989, EP w/Hulk Hogan & Vince McMahon

VICTOR GLYNN

HIGH HOPES Skouras Pictures, 1989, w/Simon Channing-Williams

JANET GODDARD

LETTER TO BREZHNEV Circle Releasing, 1986

GARY GOETZMAN

Business: Clinica Estetico Ltd., 1600 Broadway, #503, New York, NY, 10019, 212/262-2777

STOP MAKING SENSE (FD) Cinecom, 1984
MODERN GIRLS Atlantic Entertainment, 1986
MIAMI BLUES Orion, 1990, w/Jonathan Demme

MENAHEM GOLAN

(credit w/Yoram Globus)

Business: 21st Century Film Corporation, 8200 Wilshire Blvd., Beverly Hills, CA, 90211, 213/658-3000

OPERATION THUNDERBOLT Cinema Shares International, 1977*
IT'S A FUNNY FUNNY WORLD Noah Films, 1978
THE MAGICIAN OF LUBLIN Cannon, 1979
THE APPLE Cannon, 1980
THE HAPPY HOOKER GOES HOLLYWOOD Cannon, 1980
SCHIZOID Cannon, 1980
THE GODSEND Cannon, 1980
BODY AND SOUL Cannon, 1981
HOSPITAL MASSACRE Cannon, 1982
DEATH WISH II Filmways, 1982
THAT CHAMPIONSHIP SEASON Cannon, 1982
THE WICKED LADY Cannon, 1983
10 TO MIDNIGHT Cannon, 1983, EP
REVENGE OF THE NINJA Cannon, 1983
THE LAST AMERICAN VIRGIN Cannon, 1983
HERCULES Cannon, 1983
LOVE STREAMS Cannon, 1984
GRACE QUIGLEY *THE ULTIMATE SOLUTION OF GRACE QUIGLEY* Cannon, 1984
DEJA VU Cannon, 1984
SAHARA Cannon, 1984
THE NAKED FACE Cannon, 1984
BOLERO Cannon, 1984
MISSING IN ACTION
BREAKIN' MGM/UA/Cannon, 1984, EP
BREAKIN' 2: ELECTRIC BOOGALOO Tri-Star, 1984
HOUSE OF THE LONG SHADOWS Cannon, 1984
EXTERMINATOR 2 Cannon, 1984
NINJA III: THE DOMINATION Cannon, 1984
SWORD OF THE VALIANT Cannon, 1984
MISSING IN ACTION 2: THE BEGINNING Cannon, 1985
INVASION U.S.A. Cannon, 1985
DEATH WISH 3 Cannon, 1985
ORDEAL BY INNOCENCE Cannon, 1985, EP
KING SOLOMON'S MINES Cannon, 1985
FOOL FOR LOVE Cannon, 1985

RUNAWAY TRAIN Cannon, 1985
HOT RESORT Cannon, 1985
RAPPIN' Cannon, 1985
LIFEFORCE Tri-Star, 1985
AMERICAN NINJA Cannon, 1985
HOT CHILI Cannon, 1985
THE SEVEN MAGNIFICENT GLADIATORS Cannon, 1985
THE ASSISI UNDERGROUND Cannon, 1985
MARIA'S LOVERS Cannon, 1985, EP
THE AMBASSADOR Cannon, 1985
THE DELTA FORCE Cannon, 1986
THE NAKED CAGE Cannon, 1986, EP
AMERICA 3000 Cannon, 1986
DETECTIVE SCHOOL DROPOUTS *DUMB DICKS* Cannon, 1986
INVADERS FROM MARS Cannon, 1986
THE TEXAS CHAINSAW MASSACRE PART 2 Cannon, 1986
AVENGING FORCE Cannon, 1986
MURPHY'S LAW Cannon, 1986, EP
COBRA Warner Bros., 1986
P.O.W. THE ESCAPE Cannon, 1986
OTELLO Cannon, 1986
52 PICK-UP Cannon, 1986
FIREWALKER Cannon, 1986
DANGEROUSLY CLOSE Cannon, 1986, EP
ALLAN QUATERMAIN AND THE LOST CITY OF GOLD Cannon, 1987
NUMBER ONE WITH A BULLET Cannon, 1987
ASSASSINATION Cannon, 1987, EP
DOWN TWISTED Cannon, 1987
BEAUTY AND THE BEAST Cannon, 1987
RUMPLESTILTSKIN Cannon, 1987
AMERICAN NINJA 2 Cannon, 1987
HELL SQUAD Cannon, 1987, EP
TOO MUCH Cannon, 1987
DUET FOR ONE Cannon, 1987
MASTERS OF THE UNIVERSE Cannon, 1987
STREET SMART Cannon, 1987
OVER THE TOP Cannon, 1987
SUPERMAN IV: THE QUEST FOR PEACE Warner Bros., 1987
THE HANOI HILTON Cannon, 1987
BARFLY Cannon, 1987, EP
DANCERS Cannon, 1987
UNDER COVER Cannon, 1987
DUTCH TREAT Cannon, 1987
SURRENDER Warner Bros., 1987, EP
TOUGH GUYS DON'T DANCE Cannon, 1987
DEATH WISH 4: THE CRACKDOWN Cannon, 1987, EP
SHY PEOPLE Cannon, 1987
HANNA'S WAR Cannon, 1988
BRADDOCK: MISSING IN ACTION III Cannon, 1988
MESSENGER OF DEATH Cannon, 1988, EP
HERO AND THE TERROR Cannon, 1988, EP
A CRY IN THE DARK Warner Bros., 1988, EP
THE KITCHEN TOTO Cannon, 1988
POWAQQATSI Cannon, 1988
SALSA Cannon, 1988
APPOINTMENT WITH DEATH Cannon, 1988
KING LEAR Cannon, 1988
ALIEN FROM L.A. Cannon, 1988
BUSINESS AS USUAL Cannon, 1988, EP
HAUNTED SUMMER Cannon, 1989
PUSS IN BOOTS Cannon, 1989
KINJITE (FORBIDDEN SUBJECTS) Cannon, 1989, EP
THE ROSE GARDEN Cannon, 1989, EP
CYBORG Cannon, 1989
MANIFESTO Cannon, 1989
DOIN' TIME ON PLANET EARTH Cannon, 1990
MACK THE KNIFE 21st Century, EP*
THE PHANTOM OF THE OPERA 21st Century, 1989, EP*
THE FORBIDDEN DANCE Columbia, 1990, EP w/Ami Artzi*

FREDERIC GOLCHAN

Business: Frederic Golchan Productions, The Burbank Studios, Producers Bldg. 1, Suite 211, Burbank, CA, 91505, 818/954-2418

QUICK CHANGE Warner Bros., 1990, EP

ERIC L. GOLD

I'M GONNA GIT YOU SUCKA MGM/UA, 1989, EP w/Raymond Katz

DAN GOLDBERG

Agent: Rand Holston, CAA - Beverly Hills, 213/288-4545

CANNIBAL GIRLS American International, 1973
MEATBALLS Paramount, 1979
STRIPES Columbia, 1981, w/Ivan Reitman

DANNY GOLDBERG

Business: Gold Mountain Entertainment, 3575 Cahuenga Blvd. West, Suite 470, Los Angeles, CA, 90068, 213/850-5660

NO NUKES (FD) Warner Bros., 1980, w/Julian Schlossberg

GARY DAVID GOLDBERG

Business: UBU Productions, 5555 Melrose Ave., Los Angeles, CA, 90038, 213/468-8625
Agent: The Jim Preminger Agency - Los Angeles, 213/475-9491

DAD Universal, 1989, w/Joseph Stern

LEONARD J. GOLDBERG

Business: The Leonard Goldberg Company, 5555 Melrose Ave., Hollywood, CA, 90038, 213/468-4813

CALIFORNIA SPLIT Columbia, 1974, EP w/Aaron Spelling
BABY BLUE MARINE Columbia, 1976, w/Aaron Spelling
THE BAD NEWS BEARS IN BREAKING TRAINING Paramount, 1977
WINTER KILLS Avco Embassy, 1979, EP w/Robert Sterling
ALL NIGHT LONG Universal, 1981, w/Jerry Weintraub
WARGAMES MGM/UA, 1983, EP
SPACECAMP 20th Century-Fox, 1986, EP

WARREN GOLDBERG

CITY LIMITS Atlantic Entertainment, 1985, EP

PHILLIP GOLDFARB

Business: Steven Bochco Productions, 20th Century Fox, 10201 W. Pico Blvd., Los Angeles, CA, 90035, 213/203-1711
Contact: Directors Guild of America - Los Angeles, 213/289-2000

ALL THE RIGHT MOVES 20th Century-Fox, 1983, CP

PHILLIP B. GOLDFINE

SKI PATROL Triumph Releasing, 1990, w/Donald L. West

GARY GOLDMAN

(credit w/Don Bluth & John Pomeroy)

Business: Sullivan/Bluth Studios, 3800 W. Alameda Ave., Suite 1120, Burbank, CA, 91505, 818/840-9446

THE SECRET OF N.I.M.H. (AF) MGM/UA, 1982
AN AMERICAN TAIL (AF) Universal, 1986
THE LAND BEFORE TIME (AF) Universal, 1988
ALL DOGS GO TO HEAVEN (AF) Universal, 1989

BERNIE GOLDMANN

HEART CONDITION New Line Cinema, 1990, CP w/Marie Cantin
BAD INFLUENCE Triumph, 1990, CP

ALLAN GOLDSTEIN

Agent: Devra Lieb, Triad Artists, Inc., 10100 Santa Monica Blvd., 16th Floor, Los Angeles, CA, 90067, 213/556-2727
Contact: Directors Guild of America - Los Angeles, 213/289-2000

ROOFTOPS New Visions, 1989, CP w/Sue Jett & Tony Mark

JUDY GOLDSTEIN

Business: Appledown, 9687 Olympic Blvd., Beverly Hills, CA, 90212, 213/552-1833

REMO WILLIAMS: THE ADVENTURE BEGINS... Orion, 1985, CP

MILTON GOLDSTEIN

Business: HKM Films, 1641 N. Ivar Ave., Hollywood, CA, 90028, 213/465-9191

PORKY'S REVENGE 20th Century-Fox, 1985, EP w/Melvin Simon
CAPTIVE HEARTS MGM/UA, 1987, EP

ROBERT A. GOLDSTON

RUNAWAY TRAIN Cannon, 1985, EP w/Henry T. Weinstein & Robert Whitmore

JOHN GOLDSTONE

Business: Prominent Features Ltd., 68A Delancey St., London NW1 7RY, England, 01/284-1004

THE THREE SISTERS American Film Theatre, 1973
THE LAST DAYS OF MAN ON EARTH *THE FINAL PROGRAMME* New World, 1974, w/Sandy Lieberson
MONTY PYTHON & THE HOLY GRAIL Cinema 5, 1974, EP
THE ROCKY HORROR PICTURE SHOW 20th Century-Fox, 1976, AP
JABBERWOCKY Cinema 5, 1977, EP
THE HOUND OF THE BASKERVILLES Atlantic Entertainment, 1979
MONTY PYTHON'S LIFE OF BRIAN Orion/Warner Bros., 1979
SHOCK TREATMENT 20th Century-Fox, 1981
MONTY PYTHON'S THE MEANING OF LIFE Universal, 1983
ERIK THE VIKING Orion, 1989

JOHN GOLDWYN

Business: MGM Pictures, 10000 W. Washington Blvd., Culver City, CA, 90232, 213/280-6000

POLICE ACADEMY 2: THEIR FIRST ASSIGNMENT Warner Bros., 1985, EP

SAMUEL GOLDWYN, JR.

Business: The Samuel Goldwyn Company, 10203 Santa Monica Blvd., Suite 500, Los Angeles, CA, 90067, 213/552-2255

COTTON COMES TO HARLEM United Artists, 1970
COME BACK CHARLESTON BLUE Warner Bros., 1972
THE GOLDEN SEAL Samuel Goldwyn Company, 1983
ONCE BITTEN Samuel Goldwyn Company, 1985, EP
MYSTIC PIZZA Samuel Goldwyn Company, 1988, EP
STELLA Samuel Goldwyn Company/Buena Vista, 1990

STEVEN GOLIN

(credit w/Sigurjon Sighvatsson)

Business: Propaganda Films, 940 N. Mansfield Ave., Los Angeles, CA, 213/462-6400

PRIVATE INVESTIGATIONS MGM, 1987
THE BLUE IGUANA Paramount, 1988
FEAR, ANXIETY, AND DEPRESSION Samuel Goldwyn Company, 1989, w/Stanley Wlodkowski
KILL ME AGAIN MGM/UA, 1989, w/David W. Warfield
DADDY'S DYIN' MGM/UA, 1990, w/Monty Montgomery
WILD AT HEART Samuel Goldwyn Company, 1990, w/Monty Montgomery

SY GOMBERG

THREE WARRIORS Fantasy Films, 1977, w/Saul Zaentz

STEVE GOMER

Contact: Directors Guild of America - New York, 212/581-0370

SWEET LORRAINE Angelika Films, 1987

GEORGE GOODMAN

Contact: Directors Guild of America - Los Angeles, 213/289-2000

COUSINS Paramount, 1989, EP

JOHNNY GOODMAN

BELLMAN AND TRUE Island Pictures, 1987, EP w/John Hambley, George Harrison & Denis O'Brien

R. W. GOODWIN

INSIDE MOVES AFD, 1980, w/Mark M. Tanz

RICHARD GOODWIN

(credit w/Lord John Brabourne)

Business: G.W. Films, Ltd., 41 Montpelier Walk, London SW7 1JH, England, 01/589-8829

THE DANCE OF DEATH Paramount, 1968, AP*
PETER RABBIT AND TALES OF BEATRIX POTTER MGM, 1971*
MURDER ON THE ORIENT EXPRESS Paramount, 1974
DEATH ON THE NILE Paramount, 1978
STORIES FROM A FLYING TRUNK EMI, 1979
THE MIRROR CRACK'D AFD, 1980
EVIL UNDER THE SUN Universal/AFD, 1982

BIDDY Sands Films Ltd., 1983*
A PASSAGE TO INDIA ★ Columbia, 1984
LITTLE DORRIT Cannon, 1988

KEN GORD

STARSHIP INVASIONS Warner Bros., 1977, w/Norman Glick & Ed Hunt
CRIMINAL LAW Hemdale, 1989, CP

WILLIAM GORDEAN

STICK Universal, 1985, EP w/Robert Daley

BERT I. GORDON

Business: Bert I. Gordon Films, 9640 Arby Dr., Beverly Hills, CA, 90210
Agent: Contemporary Artists Agency - Beverly Hills, 213.278-8250

FOOD OF THE GODS American International, 1976
EMPIRE OF THE ANTS American International, 1977

CHARLES GORDON

Business: Daybreak Productions, c/o 20th Century-Fox, 10201 W. Pico Blvd., Los Angeles, CA, 90035, 213/203-1715

NIGHT OF THE CREEPS Tri-Star, 1986
DIE HARD 20th Century-Fox, 1988, EP
THE WRONG GUYS New World, 1988, w/Ronald E. Frazier
K-9 Universal, 1989, w/Lawrence Gordon
FIELD OF DREAMS ★ Universal, 1989, w/Lawrence Gordon
LEVIATHAN MGM/UA, 1989, EP w/Lawrence Gordon
LOCK UP Tri-Star, 1989, w/Lawrence Gordon

JON GORDON

Business: 213/472-3439

RACE TO GLORY New Century/Vista, 1989, w/Daniel A. Sherkow
ALL'S FAIR Moviestore Entertainment, 1989

LAWRENCE GORDON

Business: Largo Entertainment, c/o 20th Century- Fox, 10201 W. Pico Blvd., Los Angeles, CA, 90035, 213/203-1715

DILLINGER American International, 1973, EP w/Samuel Z. Arkoff
IT'S NOT THE SIZE THAT COUNTS Joseph Brenner Associates, 1974, EP
HARD TIMES Columbia, 1975
ROLLING THUNDER American International, 1977, EP
THE DRIVER 20th Century-Fox, 1978
THE END United Artists, 1978
HOOPER Warner Bros., 1978, EP
THE WARRIORS Paramount, 1979
XANADU Universal, 1980
PATERNITY Paramount, 1981, w/Hank Moonjean
JEKYLL & HYDE...TOGETHER AGAIN Paramount, 1982
48 HOURS Paramount, 1982, w/Joel Silver
STREETS OF FIRE Universal, 1984, w/Joel Silver
BREWSTER'S MILLIONS Universal, 1985, w/Joel Silver
JUMPIN' JACK FLASH 20th Century-Fox, 1986, w/Joel Silver
PREDATOR 20th Century-Fox, 1987, w/John Davis & Joel Silver
THE COUCH TRIP Orion, 1988
DIE HARD 20th Century-Fox, 1988, w/Joel Silver
FIELD OF DREAMS ★ Universal, 1989, w/Charles Gordon
FAMILY BUSINESS Tri-Star, 1989
DIE HARD 2 20th Century-Fox, 1990, w/Joel Silver
ANOTHER 48 HOURS Paramount, 1990, w/Robert D. Wachs

MARK R. GORDON

(credit w/Chris Meledandri)

Business: Paramount Pictures, 5555 Melrose Ave., Los Angeles, CA, 90038, 213/468-5919

BROTHERS IN ARMS Ablo, 1988
OPPORTUNITY KNOCKS Universal, 1990

SHEP GORDON

Business: Alive Films, 8271 Melrose Ave., Los Angeles, CA, 90046, 213/852-1100

PRINCE OF DARKNESS Universal, 1987, EP w/Andre Blay
THE WHALES OF AUGUST Alive Films, 1987, EP
FAR NORTH Alive Films, 1988, EP
THEY LIVE Universal, 1988, w/Andre Blay
A TIME OF DESTINY Columbia, 1988, EP w/Carolyn Pfeiffer
THE MODERNS Alive Films, 1988, EP
SHOCKER Universal, 1989, EP w/Wes Craven

BERRY GORDY

Business: The Gordy Company, 6255 Sunset Blvd., Suite 1800, Los Angeles, CA, 90028, 213/461-9954
Contact: Directors Guild of America - Los Angeles, 213/289-2000

LADY SINGS THE BLUES Paramount, 1972, EP
THE BINGO LONG TRAVELING ALL-STARS & MOTOR KINGS Universal, 1976, EP
THE LAST DRAGON Tri-Star, 1985, EP

HOWARD GOTTFRIED

THE HOSPITAL United Artists, 1971
NETWORK ★ MGM/UA, 1976
ALTERED STATES Warner Bros., 1980
BODY DOUBLE Columbia, 1984, EP
THE MEN'S CLUB Atlantic Entertainment, 1986
TORCH SONG TRILOGY New Line Cinema, 1988

JOE GOTTFRIED

HARD TO HOLD Universal, 1984, EP

DEBORAH GOTTLIEB

THE HOT SPOT Orion, 1990, CP

LINDA GOTTLIEB

Business: Linda Gottlieb Productions, 1211 Avenue of the Americas, 20th Floor, New York, NY, 10036, 212/719-7522

DIRTY DANCING Vestron, 1987

MORTON GOTTLIEB

SAME TIME, NEXT YEAR Universal, 1978, w/Walter Mirisch
ROMANTIC COMEDY MGM/UA, 1983, w/Walter Mirisch

SAM GOWAN
A FLASH OF GREEN Spectrafilm, 1985, EP

JOSEPH GRACE
Business: Linden Productions, 10850 Wilshire Blvd., #250, Los Angeles, CA, 90024, 213/474-2234

MEET THE HOLLOWHEADS Moviestore, 1989, w/John Chavez

LORD LEW GRADE
THE MEDUSA TOUCH Warner Bros., 1978, w/Elliott Kastner & Arnon Milchan
FROM THE LIFE OF THE MARIONETTES Universal/AFD, 1980, EP w/Martin Starger

MICHAEL GRAIS
(credit w/Mark Victor)
Agent: CAA - Beverly Hills, 213/288-4545
Contact: Writers Guild of America - Los Angeles, 213/550-1000

POLTERGEIST II: THE OTHER SIDE MGM, 1986
GREAT BALLS OF FIRE Orion, 1989, EP

FRANK GRANAT
TWISTED NERVE National General, 1969, w/George W. George

DEREK GRANGER
A HANDFUL OF DUST New Line Cinema, 1988

BOB GRAY
LOOK WHO'S TALKING Tri-Star, 1989, LP

BRIAN GRAZER
Business: Imagine Entertainment, 1925 Century Park East, 23rd Floor, Los Angeles, CA, 90067, 213/277-1665

NIGHT SHIFT The Ladd Company/Warner Bros., 1982
SPLASH Buena Vista, 1984
REAL GENIUS Tri-Star, 1985
SPIES LIKE US Warner Bros., 1985, w/George Folsey, Jr.
ARMED & DANGEROUS Columbia, 1986, w/James Keach
LIKE FATHER, LIKE SON Tri-Star, 1987, w/David Valdes
PARENTHOOD Universal, 1989
OPPORTUNITY KNOCKS Universal, 1990, EP w/Brad Grey
CRY BABY Universal, 1990, EP w/Jim Abrahams

WENDY GREAN
SPEED ZONE Orion, 1989, LP
EDDIE & THE CRUISERS II: EDDIE LIVES Scotti Bros., 1989, LP

WILLIAM GREAVES
Business: William Greaves Productions, 80 8th Ave., New York, NY, 10011, 212/206-1213
Contact: Directors Guild of America - New York, 212/581-0370

BUSTIN' LOOSE Universal, 1981, EP

MIKE GRECO
ALOHA SUMMER Spectrafilm, 1988

DOUGLAS GREEN
Contact: Directors Guild of America - Los Angeles, 213/289-2000

GHOST STORY Universal, 1981, CP
HEARTBEEPS Universal, 1981, EP

GERALD GREEN
Business: Omniquest - Los Angeles, 213/854-5947

SUNBURN Paramount, 1979, w/John Daly & Derek Gibson
HIGH RISK American Cinema, 1981, w/Joe Raffill
SALVADOR Hemdale, 1986, w/Oliver Stone

HILTON A. GREEN
Contact: Directors Guild of America - Los Angeles, 213/289-2000

PSYCHO II Universal, 1983
SIXTEEN CANDLES Universal, 1984
PSYCHO III Universal, 1986

NIGEL GREEN
SLIPSTREAM Entertainment Films, 1989, EP w/William Braunstein & Arthur Maslansky

HAROLD GREENBERG
Business: Astral Film Enterprises, Inc., 175 Boul. Montpellier, Montreal, H4N 2G5, 514/748-6541; or 720 King St. West, Toronto M5V 2T3, 416/364-3894

IN PRAISE OF OLDER WOMEN Avco Embassy, 1978, w/Stephen J. Roth
TULIPS Avco Embassy, 1981, EP w/John B. Bennett
PORKY'S 20th Century-Fox, 1982, EP w/Melvin Simon
PORKY'S II: THE NEXT DAY 20th Century-Fox, 1983, EP w/Alan Landsburg & Melvin Simon
MARIA CHAPDELAINE Moviestore, 1986, EP

WILLIAM R. GREENBLATT
(credit w/Martin Sheen)
Business: Symphony Pictures, 5711 W. Slauson Blvd., #226, Culver City, CA, 90230, 213/649-3668

DA FilmDallas, 1988, EP w/Sam Grogg
JUDGMENT IN BERLIN New Line Cinema, 1988, EP w/Jeffery Auerbach

DAN GREENBURG
Agent: APA - Los Angeles, 213/273-0744
Contact: Writers Guild of America - Los Angeles, 213/550-1000

THE GUARDIAN Universal, 1990, CP w/Mickey Borofsky & Todd Black

MICHAEL GREENBURG
ALLAN QUATERMAIN & THE LOST CITY OF GOLD Cannon, 1987, LP

CAROL LYNN GREENE
BURNING SECRET Vestron, 1988, w/Norma Heyman & Eberhard Junkersdorf

PRODUCERS

DAVID GREENE
Agent: CAA - Beverly Hills, 213/288-4545
Contact: Directors Guild of America - Los Angeles, 213/289-2000

I START COUNTING United Artists, 1970
HARD COUNTRY AFD, 1981, w/Mack Bing

JUSTIS GREENE
ERNEST SAVES CHRISTMAS Buena Vista, 1988, CP w/Coke Sams

PETER GREENE
AFTER MIDNIGHT MGM/UA, 1989, w/Richard Arlook, Jim Wheat & Ken Wheat

ROBERT GREENHUT
Contact: Directors Guild of America - New York, 212/581-0370

LENNY ★ United Artists, 1974, AP
DOG DAY AFTERNOON Warner Bros., 1975, AP
ANNIE HALL ★★ United Artists, 1977, EP
INTERIORS United Artists, 1978, EP
HAIR United Artists, 1979, AP
MANHATTAN United Artists, 1979, EP
STARDUST MEMORIES United Artists, 1980
ARTHUR Orion/Warner Bros., 1981
A MIDSUMMER NIGHT'S SEX COMEDY Warner Bros./Orion, 1982
THE KING OF COMEDY 20th Century-Fox, 1983
ZELIG Orion/Warner Bros., 1983
BROADWAY DANNY ROSE Orion, 1984
THE PURPLE ROSE OF CAIRO Orion, 1985
HANNAH & HER SISTERS ★ Orion, 1986
HEARTBURN Paramount, 1986, w/Mike Nichols
RADIO DAYS Orion, 1987
SEPTEMBER Orion, 1987
ANOTHER WOMAN Orion, 1988
BIG 20th Century-Fox, 1988, w/James L. Brooks
WORKING GIRL ★ 20th Century-Fox, 1988, EP w/Laurence Mark
NEW YORK STORIES Buena Vista, 1989
CRIMES & MISDEMEANORS Orion, 1989
POSTCARDS FROM THE EDGE Columbia, 1990, EP w/Neil Machlis
QUICK CHANGE Warner Bros., 1990, w/Bill Murray

ROBERT GREENWALD
Business: Robert Greenwald Productions, 10510 Culver Blvd., Culver City, CA, 90232, 213/204-0404
Contact: Directors Guild of America - Los Angeles, 213/289-2000

SWEET HEARTS DANCE Tri-Star, 1988, EP w/Gabrielle Mandelik & Lauren Weissman

STEPHEN R. GREENWALD
AMITYVILLE II: THE POSSESSION Orion, 1982, w/Ira N. Smith

DAVID GREENWALT
Agent: Jim Wiatt, ICM - Los Angeles, 213/550-4000
Contact: Directors Guild of America - Los Angeles, 213/289-2000

MIRACLES Orion, 1986, EP

RICHARD GREGSON
DOWNHILL RACER Paramount, 1969

ALAN GREISMAN
Business: Aaron Spelling Productions, 1041 N. Formosa Ave., Los Angeles, CA, 90046, 213/850-2413

HEART BEAT Orion/Warner Bros., 1980, w/Michael Shamberg
MODERN PROBLEMS 20th Century-Fox, 1981, w/Michael Shamberg
WINDY CITY Warner Bros., 1984
FLETCH Universal, 1985, w/Peter Vincent Douglas
CLUB PARADISE Warner Bros., 1986, EP
'NIGHT, MOTHER Universal, 1986, w/Aaron Spelling
CROSS MY HEART Universal, 1987, EP w/Aaron Spelling
THREE O'CLOCK HIGH Universal, 1987, EP w/Aaron Spelling
SURRENDER Warner Bros., 1987, w/Aaron Spelling
SATISFACTION 20th Century-Fox, 1988, w/Aaron Spelling
FLETCH LIVES Universal, 1989, w/Peter Vincent Douglas
LOOSE CANNONS Tri-Star, 1990, w/Aaron Spelling

BRAD GREY
Business: The Brillstein Company, 9200 Sunset Blvd., Suite 428, Los Angeles, CA, 90069, 213/275-6135

OPPORTUNITY KNOCKS Universal, 1990, EP w/Brian Grazer

CHRIS GRIFFIN
EXPERIENCE PREFERRED...BUT NOT ESSENTIAL Samuel Goldwyn Company, 1983
KIPPERBANG *P'TANG YANG, KIPPERBANG* UA Classics, 1984
SECRETS Samuel Goldwyn Company, 1984
SHARMA & BEYOND Cinecom, 1986
FOREVER YOUNG Cinecom, 1986
THOSE GLORY, GLORY DAYS Cinecom, 1986
ARTHUR'S HALLOWED GROUND Cinecom, 1986

JILL GRIFFITH
Contact: Directors Guild of America - Los Angeles, 213/289-2000

CHATTANOOGA CHOO CHOO April Fools, 1984, w/George Edwards
84 CHARLIE MOPIC New Century/Vista, 1989, CP
ROSALIE GOES SHOPPING Four Seasons, 1990, LP

EDD GRILES
Contact: Directors Guild of America - New York, 212/581-0370

POUND PUPPIES & THE LEGEND OF BIG PAW (AF) Tri-Star, 1988, w/Ray Volpe

MICHAEL GRILLO
(credit w/Charles Okun)
Business: 650 N. Bronson Ave., Room 306, Hollywood, CA, 90004
Contact: Directors Guild of America - Los Angeles, 213/289-2000

SILVERADO Columbia, 1985, EP
CROSS MY HEART Universal, 1987, CP
THE ACCIDENTAL TOURIST ★ Warner Bros., 1988, w/Lawrence Kasdan
I LOVE YOU TO DEATH Tri-Star, 1990, EP

ALBERTO GRIMALDI

Business: P.E.A. Films, 9777 Wilshire Blvd., #912, Beverly Hills, CA, 90212, 213/858-6725

FOR A FEW DOLLARS MORE United Artists, 1967
THE GOOD, THE BAD & THE UGLY United Artists, 1968
A QUIET PLACE IN THE COUNTRY United Artists, 1968
SPIRITS OF THE DEAD American International, 1969
FELLINI SATYRICON United Artists, 1970
BURN! United Artists, 1970
THE DECAMERON United Artists, 1971
THE CANTERBURY TALES United Artists, 1972
MAN OF LA MANCHA United Artists, 1972, EP
LAST TANGO IN PARIS United Artists, 1973
THE ARABIAN NIGHTS United Artists, 1974
SALO: THE LAST 120 DAYS OF SODOM Zebra, 1975
ILLUSTRIOUS CORPSES United Artists, 1976
1900 Paramount, 1977
CASANOVA Universal, 1977
LOVERS AND LIARS Levitt-Pickman, 1979
HURRICANE ROSY United Artists, 1979
GINGER AND FRED MGM/UA, 1986

CHARLES GRODIN

Agent: Leading Artists, Inc. - Beverly Hills, 213/858-1999
Contact: Writers Guild of America - Los Angeles, 213/550-1000

MOVERS & SHAKERS MGM/UA, 1985, w/William Asher

DANIEL GRODNIK

Business: National Lampoon Films, 242 N. Canon Dr., Beverly Hills, CA, 90212, 213/445-5400

OUT OF CONTROL New World, 1985, w/Fred Weintraub
1969 Atlantic Entertainment, 1988, w/Bill Badalato
BLIND FURY Tri-Star, 1990, w/Tim Matheson

SAM GROGG

Business: Magic Pictures, 6842 Valjean, Van Nuys, CA, 91406, 818/781-3591

THE TRIP TO BOUNTIFUL Island Pictures, 1985, EP w/George Yaneff
PATTI ROCKS FilmDallas, 1987, EP
DA FilmDallas, 1988, EP w/William R. Greenblatt & Martin Sheen

OTTO GROKENBERGER

STRANGER THAN PARADISE Samuel Goldwyn Company, 1984, EP
DOWN BY LAW Island Pictures, 1986, EP w/Cary Brokaw

EDGAR F. GROSS

Business: 9696 Culver Blvd., Suite 203, Culver CIty, CA, 90232, 213/558-8110

THE EMERALD FOREST Embassy, 1985, EP
HOPE & GLORY Columbia, 1987, EP w/Jake Eberts
WHERE THE HEART IS Buena Vista, 1990, EP

MICHAEL C. GROSS

(credit w/Joe Medjuck)

Business: Ivan Reitman Productions, 4000 Warner Blvd., Burbank, CA, 91522, 213/954-1771

HEAVY METAL (AF) Columbia, 1981, AP w/Lawrence Nesis*
GHOSTBUSTERS Columbia, 1984, AP
LEGAL EAGLES Universal, 1986, EP
BIG SHOTS 20th Century-Fox, 1987
TWINS Universal, 1988, EP
GHOSTBUSTERS II Columbia, 1989, EP w/Bernie Brillstein

JACK GROSSBERG

Contact: Directors Guild of America - Los Angeles, 213/289-2000

PRETTY POISON 20th Century-Fox, 1968, AP
THE PRODUCERS Avco Embassy, 1968, AP
DON'T DRINK THE WATER Avco Embassy, 1969, AP
TAKE THE MONEY AND RUN Cinerama Releasing Corporation, 1969, AP
BANANAS United Artists, 1971
THE HOSPITAL United Artists, 1971, AP
EVERYTHING YOU ALWAYS WANTED TO KNOW ABOUT SEX* (*BUT WERE AFRAID TO ASK) United Artists, 1972, AP
SLEEPER United Artists, 1973
LEADBELLY Paramount, 1976, AP
THE BETSY Allied Artists, 1978, AP
FAST BREAK Columbia, 1979, AP
A STRANGER IS WATCHING MGM/UA, 1982, AP
STRANGE BREW MGM/UA, 1983, EP
THE EXPERTS Paramount, 1989, EP w/Jonathan D. Krane
LITTLE MONSTERS MGM/UA, 1989, SP

HOWARD K. GROSSMAN

Business: NorthernLights Entertainment, Ltd., Weston Woods, Weston, CT, 06883-1199, 203/226-5231

APPRENTICE TO MURDER New World, 1988

TOM GRUENBERG

FRIDAY THE 13TH PART 2 Paramount, 1981, EP w/Lisa Barsamian

PETER GRUNWALD

MONKEY SHINES Orion, 1988, EP w/Gerald S. Paonessa

MICHAEL GRUSKOFF

Business: The Gruskoff-Levy Company, 8737 Clifton Way, Beverly Hills, CA, 90211, 213/550-7302
Contact: The Howard Brandy Company, Inc., 755 N. La Cienega Blvd., Los Angeles, CA, 90069, 213/657-8320; 75 Rockfeller Plaza, Suite 1706, New York, NY, 10019

THE LAST MOVIE Universal, 1971, EP
SILENT RUNNING Universal, 1972
YOUNG FRANKENSTEIN 20th Century-Fox, 1974
LUCKY LADY 20th Century-Fox, 1975
RAFFERTY & THE GOLD DUST TWINS Warner Bros., 1975, w/Art Linson
QUEST FOR FIRE 20th Century-Fox, 1982, EP
MY FAVORITE YEAR MGM/UA, 1982
UNTIL SEPTEMBER MGM/UA, 1984
LOVE AT STAKE Tri-Star, 1988
PINK CADILLAC Warner Bros., 1989, EP

RICHARD GUAY
Business: Forward Films, 2445 Herring Ave., Bronx, NY, 10469

TRUE LOVE United Artists, 1989, w/Shelley Houis

PETER GUBER
(credit w/Jon Peters)
Business: Columbia Pictures, Studio Plaza, 3400 Riverside Dr., Burbank, CA, 91505, 818/972-7200

THE DEEP Columbia, 1977*
MIDNIGHT EXPRESS Columbia, 1978, EP*
AN AMERICAN WEREWOLF IN LONDON Universal, 1981, EP
SIX WEEKS Universal, 1982, EP
MISSING ★ Universal, 1983, EP
FLASHDANCE Paramount, 1983, EP
D.C. CAB Universal, 1983, EP
HEAD OFFICE Tri-Star, 1985, EP
VISION QUEST Warner Bros., 1985
THE LEGEND OF BILLIE JEAN Tri-Star, 1985, EP
CLUE Paramount, 1985, EP w/George Folsey Jr. & John Landis
THE COLOR PURPLE ★ Warner Bros., 1985, EP
THE CLAN OF THE CAVE BEAR Warner Bros., 1986, EP w/Mark Damon, John Hyde & Sidney Kimmel
YOUNGBLOOD MGM/UA, 1986, EP
THE WITCHES OF EASTWICK Warner Bros., 1987, w/Neil Canton
INNERSPACE Warner Bros., 1987, EP w/Kathleen Kennedy, Frank Marshall, & Steven Spielberg
WHO'S THAT GIRL Warner Bros., 1987, EP w/Roger Birnbaum
GORILLAS IN THE MIST Universal, 1988, EP
CADDYSHACK II Warner Bros., 1988, w/Neil Canton
RAIN MAN ★★ MGM/UA, 1988, EP
BATMAN Warner Bros., 1989
TANGO & CASH Warner Bros., 1989
MISSING LINK Universal, 1989, EP

ROBERT GUENETTE
Business: 1551 S. Robertson Blvd., #200, Los Angeles, CA, 90035, 213/785-9312
Contact: Directors Guild of America - Los Angeles, 213/289-2000
Contact: Writers Guild of America, 213/550-1000

THE MYSTERIOUS MONSTERS (FD) Sunn Classic, 1976, w/Charles E. Sellier Jr. & David L. Wolper
THE MAN WHO SAW TOMORROW (FD) Warner Bros., 1981, w/Paul Drane & Lee Kramer

JAMES WILLIAM GUERCIO
Business: Caribou Ranch, Nederland, CO, 80466, 303/258-3215
Agent: Jeff Berg, ICM - Los Angeles, 213/550-4000

ELECTRA GLIDE IN BLUE United Artists, 1973
SECOND HAND HEARTS *THE HAMSTER OF HAPPINESS* Lorimar/Paramount, 1981

J. P. GUERIN
THE KILLING TIME New World, 1987, EP

DON GUEST
Contact: Directors Guild of America - Los Angeles, 213/289-2000

BLUE COLLAR Universal, 1978
THE OSTERMAN WEEKEND 20th Century-Fox, 1983, AP
HAMMETT Orion/Warner Bros., 1982, w/Ronald Colby & Fred Roos
PARIS, TEXAS 20th Century-Fox, 1984
AT CLOSE RANGE Orion, 1986, w/Elliott Lewitt

MICHAEL GUEST
PING PONG Samuel Goldwyn Company, 1987, w/Malcolm Craddock

PAUL R. GURIAN
Business: Gurian Productions, c/o Tri-Star Pictures, 3400 Riverside Dr., Bungalow 3, Room 10, Burbank, CA, 91505, 818/954-5721

CUTTER'S WAY United Artists Classics, 1981
PEGGY SUE GOT MARRIED Tri-Star, 1986
THE SEVENTH SIGN Tri-Star, 1988, EP

PATO GUZMAN
Agent: The Gersh Agency - Beverly Hills, 213/274-6611

TEMPEST Columbia, 1982, CP w/Steven Bernhardt
MOSCOW ON THE HUDSON Columbia, 1984, CP
DOWN AND OUT IN BEVERLY HILLS Buena Vista, 1986, CP
MOON OVER PARADOR Universal, 1988, CP w/Geoffrey Taylor
ENEMIES, A LOVE STORY 20th Century-Fox, 1989, CP w/Irby Smith

H

TAYLOR HACKFORD
Business: New Visions Entertainment Corporation, 5750 Wilshire Blvd., 6th Floor, Los Angeles, CA, 90036, 213/965-2500
Agent: CAA - Beverly Hills, 213/288-4545

AGAINST ALL ODDS Columbia, 1984, w/William S. Gilmore
WHITE NIGHTS Columbia, 1985, w/William S. Gilmore
LA BAMBA Columbia, 1987, w/Bill Borden
EVERYBODY'S ALL-AMERICAN Warner Bros., 1988, w/Laura Ziskin & Ian Sander
ROOFTOPS New Visions, 1989, EP w/Stuart Benjamin

RONNIE HADAR
Business: Ronnie Hadar Productions, 1551 N. La Brea Ave., Hollywood, CA, 90028, 213/850-6110

THE TOMB Trans World Entertainment, 1986, w/Fred Olen Ray

MARILYN G. HAFT
IN A SHALLOW GRAVE Skouras Pictures, 1988, EP w/Lindsay Law

STEVEN M. HAFT
Business: Steven Haft Productions, 130 East 59th St., 10th Floor, New York, NY, 10022, 212/906-9518 or 20th Century-Fox, 10201 W. Pico Blvd., Los Angeles, CA, 90035, 213/203-2974

BEYOND THERAPY New World, 1987
MR. NORTH Samuel Goldwyn Company, 1988, w/Skip Steloff
DEAD POETS SOCIETY ★ Buena Vista, 1989, w/Tony Thomas & Paul Junger Witt

DENNIS HAGGERTY
THE PACKAGE Orion, 1989, CP w/Andrew Davis

TOBIE HAGGERTY
THE PACKAGE Orion, 1989, w/Beverly J. Camhe

CHARLES HAID
Agent: Writers & Artists Agency, 11726 San Vicente Blvd., Suite 300, Los Angeles, CA, 90049, 213/820-2240

SQUARE DANCE *HOME IS WHERE THE HEART IS* Island Pictures, 1987, EP w/Jane Alexander

DON HAIG
I'VE HEARD THE MERMAIDS SINGING Miramax, 1987, EP
NIGHT FRIEND Cineplex Odeon, 1988, EP
COMIC BOOK CONFIDENTIAL (FD) Cinecom, 1989, w/Martin Harbury & Ron Mann

JOE HALE
THE BLACK CAULDRON (AF) Buena Vista, 1985

JACK HALEY, JR.
Business: Jack Haley Jr. Productions, 8255 Beverly Blvd., Los Angeles, CA, 90048, 213/655-1106
Contact: Directors Guild of America - Los Angeles, 213/289-2000

THAT'S ENTERTAINMENT! (FD) MGM, 1974
BETTER LATE THAN NEVER Warner Bros., 1983, w/David Niven Jr.
THAT'S DANCING! (FD) MGM, 1985, w/David Niven Jr.

PETER HALEY
Business: Norstar Entertainment, Inc., 86 Bloor Street W., 5th Floor, Toronto, Ontario M5S 1M5, Canada, 416/961-6278

BULLIES Universal, 1986, EP
HELLO MARY LOU: PROM NIGHT II Samuel Goldwyn Company, 1987, EP

KATHY HALLBERG
THE SEVENTH SIGN Tri-Star, 1988, CP

ROBERT HALMI, JR.
Business: RHI, 720 5th Ave., 9th Floor, New York, NY, 10019, 212/977-9001
Contact: Directors Guild of America - Los Angeles, 213/289-2000

BRADY'S ESCAPE Satori, 1984, AP
LILY IN LOVE New Line Cinema, 1985, EP w/Peter Bacso

ROBERT HALMI, SR.
Business: RHI, 720 5th Ave., 9th Floor, New York, NY, 10019, 212/977-9001

BRADY'S ESCAPE Satori, 1984
THE ONE AND ONLY Paramount, 1978, EP
LILY IN LOVE New Line Cinema, 1985
CHEETAH Buena Vista, 1989

RON HAMADY
(credit w/George Braunstein)

FADE TO BLACK American Cinema, 1980
SURF II International Films, 1984
AND GOD CREATED WOMAN Vestron, 1988
OUT COLD Hemdale, 1989
THE BOYFRIEND SCHOOL Hemdale, 1990

JOHN HAMBLEY
BELLMAN AND TRUE Island Pictures, 1987, EP w/Johnny Goodman, George Harrison & Denis O'Brien
DEALERS Skouras Pictures, 1989, EP w/Andrew Brown

DAVID SHAMROY HAMBURGER
Contact: Directors Guild of America - Los Angeles, 213/289-2000

THE CANNONBALL RUN 20th Century-Fox, 1981, AP
MEGAFORCE 20th Century-Fox, 1982, AP
THE SQUEEZE Tri-Star, 1987, EP w/Harry Colomby

ALAN HAMEL
NOTHING PERSONAL American International, 1980, EP w/Jay Bernstein & Norman Hirschfield

GEORGE HAMILTON
Agent: APA - Los Angeles, 213/273-0744

LOVE AT FIRST BITE American International, 1979, EP w/Robert Kaufman
ZORRO, THE GAY BLADE 20th Century-Fox, 1981, w/C. O. Erickson

MICHAEL HAMLYN
U2: RATTLE & HUM (FD) Paramount, 1988

ANDRAS HAMORI
Business: Accent Entertainment, 8439 Sunset Blvd., Suite 302, Los Angeles, CA, 90069, 213/654-0231

HEAVENLY BODIES MGM/UA, 1985, AP
SEPARATE VACATIONS RSK Entertainment, 1986, AP
THE GATE New Century/Vista, 1987, CP
NOWHERE TO HIDE New Century/Vista, 1987
IRON EAGLE II Tri-Star, 1988, EP
FOOD OF THE GODS II Concorde, 1989, EP w/Robert Misiorowski

CHRISTOPHER HAMPTON
Agent: William Morris Agency - Beverly Hills, 213/274-7451

DANGEROUS LIAISONS ★ Warner Bros., 1988, CP

TIM HAMPTON
LEGEND Universal, 1986, CP
FRANTIC Warner Bros., 1988, w/Thom Mount

A DRY WHITE SEASON MGM, 1989, EP
THE NEVERENDING STORY II Warner Bros., 1990, EP

CHARLES HANNAH
VICIOUS SVS Films, 1988, w/David Hannay

DAVID HANNAH
VICIOUS SVS Films, 1988, w/Charles Hannah

GARY HANNAM
THE NAVIGATOR: AN ODYSSEY ACROSS TIME Circle Releasing, 1989, CP

LISA M. HANSEN
Business: CineTel Films, Inc., 3800 W. Alameda Ave., #825, Burbank, CA, 91505, 818/955-9551

ARMED RESPONSE CineTel, 1986, EP
BULLETPROOF CineTel, 1987, EP
COLD STEEL CineTel, 1987
976-EVIL New Line Cinema, 1989
HIT LIST New Line Cinema, 1989, EP
RELENTLESS New Line Cinema, 1989, EP w/Paul Hertzberg

BARRY HANSON
THE LONG GOOD FRIDAY Embassy, 1982
MORONS FROM OUTER SPACE Universal, 1985

JOHN HANSON
Business: New Front Films, 125 W. Richmond Ave., Point Richmond, CA, 94801, 415/231-0225
Agent: Scott Harris, Harris & Goldberg - Los Angeles, 213/553-5200

WILDROSE Troma, 1985, CP

MASATO HARA
MERRY CHRISTMAS, MR. LAWRENCE Universal, 1983, EP w/Terry Glinwood, Geoffrey Nethercott & Eiko Oshima
RAN Orion Classics, 1985, w/Serge Silberman

JOHN HARADA
THE MEN'S CLUB Atlantic Entertainment, 1986, EP w/Thomas Coleman & Michael Rosenblatt

MARTIN HARBURY
COMIC BOOK CONFIDENTIAL (FD) Cinecom, 1989, w/Don Haig & Ron Mann

MALCOLM R. HARDING
Contact: Directors Guild of America - Los Angeles, 213/289-2000

HARRY AND SON Orion, 1984, AP
FLIGHT OF THE NAVIGATOR Buena Vista, 1986, EP w/Mark Damon, John Hyde & Jonathan Sanger
FAR NORTH Alive Films, 1988, w/Carolyn Pfeiffer
WEEKEND AT BERNIE'S 20th Century-Fox, 1989, EP w/Robert Klane
SHORT TIME 20th Century-Fox, 1990, CP

STEWART HARDING
HAPPY BIRTHDAY TO ME Columbia, 1981, LP

JOHN HARDY
sex, lies, & videotape Miramax, 1989, w/Robert Newmyer

JOHN HARDY
QUEEN OF HEARTS Cinecom, 1989

SHARON HAREL
(credit w/Jacob Kotzky)
Business: Capitol Films, Ltd., 24 Upper Brook St., London W1Y 1PD, 01/872-0017

EVERY TIME WE SAY GOODBYE Tri-Star, 1986
IRON EAGLE II Tri-Star, 1988, w/John Kemeny

EFREM HARKHAM
(credit w/Uri Harkham)

GORKY PARK Orion, 1983, AP
GHOST WARRIOR Empire, 1986, EP w/Albert Band & Arthur H. Maslansky

URI HARKHAM
(credit w/Efrem Harkham)

GORKY PARK Orion, 1983, AP
GHOST WARRIOR Empire, 1986, EP w/Albert Band & Arthur H. Maslansky

JAN HARLAN
BARRY LYNDON Warner Bros., 1975, EP
FULL METAL JACKET Warner Bros., 1987, EP

J. BOYCE HARMAN, JR.
Contact: Directors Guild of America - New York, 212/581-0370

SHAKEDOWN Universal, 1988

KEN HARPER
THE WIZ Universal, 1978, EP

BURTT HARRIS
LITTLE MURDERS 20th Century-Fox, 1971, AP
CRUISING United Artists, 1980, AP
JUST TELL ME WHAT YOU WANT Warner Bros., 1980, EP
PRINCE OF THE CITY Orion/Warner Bros., 1981
DEATHTRAP Warner Bros., 1982
THE VERDICT ★ 20th Century-Fox, 1982, EP
DANIEL Paramount, 1983
GARBO TALKS MGM/UA, 1984, w/Elliott Kastner
D.A.R.Y.L. Paramount, 1985, CP w/Gabrielle Kelly
THE GLASS MENAGERIE Cineplex Odeon, 1987
RUNNING ON EMPTY Warner Bros., 1988, EP w/Naomi Foner
SEE NO EVIL, HEAR NO EVIL Tri-Star, 1989, EP w/Earl Barret & Arne Sultan
FAMILY BUSINESS Tri-Star, 1989, EP w/Jennifer Ogden
Q&A Tri-Star, 1990, w/Arnon Milchan

DENNIS HARRIS
THE HIDDEN New Line Cinema, 1987, EP w/Stephen Diener, Jeffrey Klein & Lee Muhl

DOUG HARRIS
HEARTS OF FIRE Lorimar, 1988, EP w/Gerald W. Abrams

JACK H. HARRIS
EYES OF LAURA MARS Columbia, 1978, EP
THE BLOB Tri-Star, 1988, w/Elliott Kastner

JAMES B. HARRIS
Business: James B. Harris Productions, 248 1/2 Lasky Dr., Beverly Hills, CA, 90212, 213/273-4270
Attorney: Louis C. Blau, Loeb & Loeb, 10100 Santa Monica Blvd., Los Angeles, CA, 90067, 213/552-7700
Agent: ICM - Los Angeles, 213/550-4000

THE KILLING United Artists, 1956
PATHS OF GLORY United Artists, 1957
LOLITA MGM, 1962
THE BEDFORD INCIDENT Columbia, 1965
SOME CALL IT LOVING Cine Globe, 1973
TELEFON MGM, 1977
FAST-WALKING Pickman, 1982
COP Atlantic Entertainment, 1988, w/James Woods

GEORGE HARRISON
(credit w/Denis O'Brien)
Business: HandMade Films, Ltd., 26 Cadogan Square, London SW1X 0JP, England, 01/584-8345 or 7400 Beverly Blvd., #210, Los Angeles, CA, 90036, 213/936-8050

LITTLE MALCOLM AND HIS STRUGGLE AGAINST THE EUNUCHS Multicetera Investments, 1974, EP*
MONTY PYTHON'S LIFE OF BRIAN Orion/Warner Bros., 1979, EP
TIME BANDITS Avco Embassy, 1981, EP
THE MISSIONARY Columbia, 1982, EP
PRIVATES ON PARADE Orion Classics, 1984, EP
SCRUBBERS Orion Classics, 1984, EP
BULLSHOT Island Alive, 1985, EP
A PRIVATE FUNCTION Island Alive, 1985, EP
MONA LISA Island Pictures, 1986, EP
SHANGHAI SURPRISE MGM, 1986, EP
WATER Atlantic Entertainment, 1986, EP
WITHNAIL & I Cineplex Odeon, 1987, EP
THE LONELY PASSION OF JUDITH HEARNE Island Pictures, 1987, EP
BELLMAN & TRUE Island Pictures, 1987, EP w/Johnny Goodman & John Hambley
FIVE CORNERS Cineplex Odeon, 1988, EP
TRACK 29 Island Pictures, 1988, EP
POWWOW HIGHWAY Warner Bros., 1989, EP
CHECKING OUT Warner Bros., 1989, EP
HOW TO GET AHEAD IN ADVERTISING Warner Bros., 1989, EP
NUNS ON THE RUN 20th Century-Fox, 1990, EP
THE RAGGEDY RAWNEY Four Seasons Entertainment, 1990, EP

KENNETH HARTFORD
HELL SQUAD Cannon, 1987

NEIL HARTLEY
Business: Woodfall Ltd., Hill House, 1 Little New St., London EC4A 3TR, England or 1478 N. Kings Rd., Los Angeles, CA, 90069

HAMLET Columbia, 1969
A DELICATE BALANCE American Film Theatre, 1973, EP
THE BORDER Universal, 1982, EP
THE HOTEL NEW HAMPSHIRE Orion, 1984

RAY HARTWICK
Contact: Directors Guild of America - Los Angeles, 213/289-2000

SO FINE Warner Bros., 1981, AP
PRINCE OF THE CITY Orion/Warner Bros., 1981, AP
OUT OF BOUNDS Columbia, 1986, EP w/John Tarnoff
THE UNTOUCHABLES Paramount, 1987, AP
VIBES Columbia, 1988, CP
SCROOGED Paramount, 1988, CP
OPPORTUNITY KNOCKS Universal, 1990, CP

RUPERT HARVEY
Business: Sho Films, 2300 Duane St., #9, Los Angeles, CA, 90039, 213/665-9088

ANDROID Island Alive, 1984, EP w/Barry Opper
CITY LIMITS Atlantic Entertainment, 1985, w/Barry Opper
CRITTERS New Line Cinema, 1986
SLAMDANCE Island Pictures, 1987, w/Barry Opper
THE BLOB Tri-Star, 1988, LP
A NIGHTMARE ON ELM STREET, PART 5: THE DREAM CHILD New Line Cinema, 1989, w/Robert Shaye

RICHARD HASHIMOTO
Contact: Directors Guild of America - Los Angeles, 213/289-2000

TOUGH GUYS Buena Vista, 1986, CP w/Jana Sue Memel
BEETLEJUICE Warner Bros., 1988, w/Michael Bender & Larry Wilson

SALAH M. HASSANEIN
Business: Warner Bros. International Theaters, 4000 Warner Blvd., Burbank, CA, 91522, 818/954-6000

KNIGHTRIDERS UFD, 1981, EP
CREEPSHOW Warner Bros., 1982, EP
DAY OF THE DEAD UFD, 1985, EP
COMPROMISING POSITIONS Paramount, 1985, EP
HELLO AGAIN Buena Vista, 1987, EP

GARY HAUNAN
WILD HORSES Satori, 1984, EP

MICHAEL HAUSMAN
Business: Cinehaus, 745 W. 55th St., Suite 1011, New York, NY, 10019, 212/245-9060
Contact: Directors Guild of America - New York, 212/581-0370

MIKEY AND NICKY Paramount, 1976
I NEVER PROMISED YOU A ROSE GARDEN New World, 1977, w/Daniel H. Blatt & Terence F. Deane
ALAMBRISTA! Bobwin/Film Haus, 1977, w/Irwin Young
HEARTLAND Levitt-Pickman, 1979, w/Beth Ferris
RICH KIDS United Artists, 1979, w/George W. George
ONE-TRICK PONY Warner Bros., 1980, CP
RAGTIME Paramount, 1981, EP w/Bernard Williams
SILKWOOD 20th Century-Fox, 1983, w/Mike Nichols
THE BALLAD OF GREGORIO CORTEZ Embassy, 1983, w/Moctesuma Esparza
PLACES IN THE HEART ★ Tri-Star, 1984, EP
AMADEUS ★★ Orion, 1984, EP w/Bertil Ohlsson
NO MERCY Tri-Star, 1986, EP
DESERT BLOOM Columbia, 1986

THE FLIGHT OF THE SPRUCE GOOSE Michael Hausman/Film Haus, 1986
HOUSE OF GAMES Orion, 1987
THINGS CHANGE Columbia, 1988
VALMONT Orion, 1989, w/Paul Rannam
STATE OF GRACE Orion, 1990, EP w/Ron Rotholz

ANTHONY HAVELOCK-ALLAN

ROMEO & JULIET ★ Paramount, 1968, w/Lord John Brabourne
RYAN'S DAUGHTER MGM, 1970

GOLDIE HAWN

Business: Hawn/Sylbert Productions, Hollywood Pictures, 500 S. Buena Vista St., Animation Bldg. 1-D-6, Burbank, CA, 91521, 818/560-6120

PRIVATE BENJAMIN Warner Bros., 1980, EP
PROTOCOL Warner Bros., 1984, EP

DENNIS HAYASHI

LIVING ON TOKYO TIME Skouras Pictures, 1987, w/Lynn O'Donnell

MATHEW HAYDEN

MIDNIGHT CROSSING Vestron, 1988

JEFFREY HAYES

Contact: Directors Guild of America - New York, 212/581-0370

ON THE EDGE Skouras Pictures, 1986, w/Rob Nilsson

TERRY HAYES

(credit w/Doug Mitchell)

Business: Kennedy Miller Productions, 30 Orwell St., Kings Cross, Sydney, Australia

MAD MAX BEYOND THUNDERDOME Warner Bros., 1985, CP
DEAD CALM Warner Bros., 1989, w/George Miller

WILLIAM HAYWARD

EASY RIDER Columbia, 1969, AP
THE HIRED HAND Universal, 1971
IDAHO TRANSFER Cinemation, 1975
HIGH-BALLIN' American International, 1978, EP w/Stanley Chase
WANDA NEVADA United Artists, 1979, EP
BLUE CITY Paramount, 1986, w/Walter Hill

PHILLIP HAZELTON

EYE OF THE CAT Universal, 1969, w/Bernard Schwartz

JOHN HEAD

Business: Broadway Video, 1619 Broadway, 9th Floor, New York, NY,10019, 212/265-7621

NOTHING LASTS FOREVER MGM/UA, 1984, CP

BARRY HEALEY

THE GREY FOX United Artists Classics, 1983, CP w/Phillip Borsos

HILARY HEATH

CRIMINAL LAW Hemdale, 1989, w/Robert MacLean

HUGH M. HEFNER

Business: Playboy, 919 N. Michigan Ave., Chicago, IL, 60611

THE CRAZY WORLD OF JULIUS VROODER 20th Century-Fox, 1974, EP
SAINT JACK New World, 1979, EP w/Edward L. Rissien

PAUL HELLER

Business: Paul Heller Productions, 1666 N. Beverly Dr., Beverly Hills, CA, 90210, 213/275-4477
Contact: Directors Guild of America - Los Angeles, 213/289-2000

DAVID & LISA Continental, 1962
THE EAVESDROPPER Royal Films International, 1966
SECRET CEREMONY Universal, 1969, EP
ENTER THE DRAGON Warner Bros., 1973, w/Fred Weintraub
BLACK BELT JONES Warner Bros., 1974, w/Fred Weintraub
TRUCK TURNER American International, 1974, w/Fred Weintraub
GOLDEN NEEDLES American International, 1974, w/Fred Weintraub
IT'S SHOWTIME United Artists, 1976, w/Fred Weintraub
HOT POTATO Warner Bros., 1976, w/Fred Weintraub
OUTLAW BLUES Warner Bros., 1977, EP w/Fred Weintraub
THE PACK Warner Bros., 1977, w/Fred Weintraub
CHECKERED FLAG OR CRASH Universal, 1978, w/Fred Weintraub
THE PROMISE Universal, 1979, w/Fred Weintraub
FIRST MONDAY IN OCTOBER Paramount, 1981, w/Martha Scott
WITHNAIL & I Cineplex Odeon, 1987, w/Lawrence Kirstein
MY LEFT FOOT ★ Miramax, 1989, EP w/Steve Morrison

ROSILYN HELLER

Business: Dresden Drive Productions, 2237 Nichols Canyon Rd., Los Angeles, CA, 90046, 213/876-2820

ICE CASTLES Columbia, 1979, EP
WHO'S THAT GIRL Warner Bros., 1987, w/Bernard Williams

JEROME HELLMAN

Business: Jerome Hellman Productions, 68 Malibu Colony Dr., Malibu, CA, 90265, 213/456-3361
Contact: Directors Guild of America - Los Angeles, 213/289-2000

THE WORLD OF HENRY ORIENT United Artists, 1964
A FINE MADNESS Warner Bros., 1966
MIDNIGHT COWBOY ★★ United Artists, 1969
THE DAY OF THE LOCUST Paramount, 1975
COMING HOME ★ United Artists, 1978
PROMISES IN THE DARK Orion/Warner Bros., 1979
THE MOSQUITO COAST Warner Bros., 1986

GEOFFREY HELMAN

THE FRENCH LIEUTENANT'S WOMAN United Artists, 1981, AP
KRULL Columbia, 1983, AP

THE DOCTOR AND THE DEVILS 20th Century-Fox, 1985, AP
84 CHARING CROSS ROAD Columbia, 1987

DAVID HELPERN
DEAD HEAT New World, 1988, w/Michael Meltzer

DAVID HEMMINGS
Business: A-L Productions, 3500 W. Olive, #650, Burbank, CA, 91505, 818/953-4114

STRANGE BEHAVIOR World Northal, 1981, EP w/John Daly & William Fayman

GRAHAM HENDERSON
Contact: Directors Guild of America - Los Angeles, 213/289-2000

BODY SLAM DEG, 1987, CP

DORIAN HENDRIX
MONDO NEW YORK 4th & Broadway, 1988, EP

LUTZ HENGST
KING, QUEEN, KNAVE Avco Embassy, 1972, w/David L. Wolper
DESPAIR New Line Cinema, 1979, EP w/Edward R. Pressman

KIM HENKEL
Contact: Writers Guild of America - Los Angeles, 213/550-1000

LAST NIGHT AT THE ALAMO Cinecom, 1984, w/Eagle Pennell

JERE HENSHAW
Business: Apollo Pictures, 6071 Bristol Parkway, Culver City, CA, 90230, 213/568-8282

CAN'T BUY ME LOVE Buena Vista, 1988, EP w/Ron Beckman

PAUL G. HENSLER
GOTCHA! Universal, 1985

JIM HENSON
Business: Henson Associates, c/o Walt Disney Studios, 500 S. Buena Vista St., Burbank, CA, 91521, 818/560-1000 or 117 East 69th St., New York, NY, 10021, 212/794-2400

THE MUPPET MOVIE AFD, 1979
THE DARK CRYSTAL Universal/AFD, 1982, w/Gary Kurtz
THE MUPPETS TAKE MANHATTAN Tri-Star, 1984, EP
THE WITCHES Warner Bros., 1989, EP

PETER V. HERALD
Agent: The Gersh Agency - Beverly Hills, 213/274-6611
Contact: Directors Guild of America - Los Angeles, 213.289-2000

MIRACLE OF THE WHITE STALLIONS Buena Vista, 1963, AP
EMIL & THE DETECTIVES Buena Vista, 1964, AP
NATIONAL LAMPOON'S CLASS REUNION 20th Century-Fox, 1982, CP w/Harmon Berns
DOCTOR DETROIT Universal, 1983, AP
D.C. CAB Universal, 1983, AP
OUTRAGEOUS FORTUNE Buena Vista, 1987, CP w/Scott Kroopf & Martin Mickelson

RICHARD HERLAND
SKY BANDITS Galaxy, 1986

NORMAN T. HERMAN
Contact: Directors Guild of America - Los Angeles, 213.289-2000

BLOODY MAMA American International, 1970, CP
FROGS American International, 1972, EP
ROLLING THUNDER American International, 1977
IN GOD WE TRUST Universal, 1980, EP

CLAUDE HÉROUX
BREAKING POINT 20th Century-Fox, 1976, w/Bob Clark
IN PRAISE OF OLDER WOMEN Avco Embassy, 1978, w/Robert Lantos
THE BROOD New World, 1979
CITY ON FIRE Avco Embassy, 1979
HOG WILD Avco Embassy, 1980
SCANNERS Avco Embassy, 1981
DIRTY TRICKS Avco Embassy, 1981
GAS Paramount, 1981
VISITING HOURS 20th Century-Fox, 1982
VIDEODROME Universal, 1983
GOING BERSERK Universal, 1983
THE FUNNY FARM New World, 1983
OF UNKNOWN ORIGIN Warner Bros., 1983
COVERGIRL New World, 1984
ANGELA Embassy, 1984, w/Julian Melzack

DENIS HEROUX
Business: Alliance Entertainment Corporation, 8439 Sunset Blvd., #404, Los Angeles, CA, 90069, 213/654-9488 or 920 Yonge Street, Suite 400, Toronto, Ontario, M4W 3C7, Canada, 416/967-1174

ATLANTIC CITY ★ Paramount, 1981
QUEST FOR FIRE 20th Century-Fox, 1982, w/John Kemeny
THE BAY BOY Orion, 1985, w/John Kemeny
EDDIE & THE CRUISERS II: EDDIE LIVES Scotti Bros., 1989, EP w/Victor Loewy, James L. Stewart & William Stuart

MICHAEL HERTZBERG
Contact: Directors Guild of America - Los Angeles, 213.289-2000

THE TWELVE CHAIRS UMC, 1970
BLAZING SADDLES Warner Bros., 1974
SILENT MOVIE 20th Century-Fox, 1976
JOHNNY DANGEROUSLY 20th Century-Fox, 1984
MEMORIES OF ME MGM/UA, 1988, w/Billy Crystal & Alan King
TURNER & HOOCH Buena Vista, 1989, EP w/Daniel Petrie Jr.

PAUL HERTZBERG
Business: CineTel Films, Inc., 3800 W. Alameda Ave., #825, Burbank, CA, 91505, 818/955-9551

ARMED RESPONSE CineTel, 1986

THE TOMB Trans World Entertainment, 1986, EP w/Richard Kaye
BULLETPROOF CineTel, 1987
CYCLONE CineTel, 1987
COLD STEEL CineTel, 1987, EP
976-EVIL New Line Cinema, 1989, EP
HIT LIST New Line Cinema, 1989
RELENTLESS New Line Cinema, 1989, EP w/Lisa M. Hansen

ILONA HERZBERG
FEDS Warner Bros., 1988, w/Len Blum
CASUAL SEX? Universal, 1980, w/Sheldon Kahn

JOHN HEYMAN
PRIVILEGE Universal, 1967
SECRET CEREMONY Universal, 1968
THE HERO Avco Embassy, 1970, w/Wolf Mankowitz
LOLA *TWINKY* American International, 1971, EP
THE GO-BETWEEN Columbia, 1971, w/Norman Priggen
JESUS Warner Bros., 1979
DANIEL Paramount, 1983, EP
D.A.R.Y.L. Paramount, 1985

NORMA HEYMAN
BEYOND THE LIMIT Paramount, 1983
BURNING SECRET Vestron, 1988, w/Carol Lynn Greene & Eberhard Junkersdorf
BUSTER Hemdale, 1988
DANGEROUS LIAISONS ★ Warner Bros., 1988, w/Hank Moonjean

JEAN HIGGINS
Contact: Directors Guild of America - Los Angeles, 213/289-2000

GETTING EVEN American Distribution Group, 1986, LP

PADDY HIGSON
COMFORT AND JOY Universal, 1984, AP
THE GIRL IN THE PICTURE Samuel Goldwyn Company, 1986

FRANK E. HILDEBRAND
VICE SQUAD Avco Embassy, 1982, AP
WARRIORS OF THE LOST WORLD Vista, 1985, w/Roberto Bessi
ONCE BITTEN Samuel Goldwyn Company, 1985, w/Dimitri Villard & Robby Wald

DEBRA HILL
Business: Debra Hill Productions, c/o Walt Disney Studios, 500 S. Buena Vista St., Burbank, CA, 91521, 818/560-1951

HALLOWEEN Compass International, 1978
THE FOG Avco Embassy, 1980
HALLOWEEN II Universal, 1981, w/John Carpenter
ESCAPE FROM NEW YORK Avco Embassy, 1981, w/Larry Franco
HALLOWEEN III: SEASON OF THE WITCH Universal, 1982, w/John Carpenter
THE DEAD ZONE Paramount, 1983
CLUE Paramount, 1985
HEAD OFFICE Tri-Star, 1985
ADVENTURES IN BABYSITTING Buena Vista, 1987, w/Lynda Obst
HEARTBREAK HOTEL Buena Vista, 1988, w/Lynda Obst
BIG TOP PEE-WEE Paramount, 1988, w/Paul Reubens
GROSS ANATOMY Buena Vista, 1989, w/Howard Rosenman

GEORGE ROY HILL
Business Manager: Edwins, Brown, McGladrey, Hendrickson & Pulle, 1133 Ave. of the Americas, New York, NY, 10019, 212/382-0024
Business: Pan Arts Productions, 4000 Warner Blvd., Burbank, CA, 91522, 818/954-3631

THE GREAT WALDO PEPPER Universal, 1975
THE WORLD ACCORDING TO GARP Warner Bros., 1982, w/Robert L. Crawford

WALTER HILL
Business: Paramount Pictures, 5555 Melrose Ave., Los Angeles, CA, 90038, 213/468-4805
Agent: ICM - Los Angeles, 213/550-4000

ALIEN 20th Century-Fox, 1979, w/Gordon Carroll & David Giler
BLUE CITY Paramount, 1986, w/William Hayward
ALIENS 20th Century-Fox, 1986, EP w/Gordon Carroll & David Giler
RED HEAT Tri-Star, 1988, w/Gordon Carroll

ARTHUR HILLER
Business: Walt Disney Studios, 500 S. Buena Vista St., Burbank, CA, 91521, 818/560-6397
Agent: Phil Gersh, The Gersh Agency - Beverly Hills, 213/274-6611

MAN OF LA MANCHA United Artists, 1972
THE CRAZY WORLD OF JULIUS VROODER 20th Century-Fox, 1974, w/Edward L. Rissien
THE IN-LAWS Warner Bros., 1979, w/William Sackheim
THE LONELY GUY Universal, 1984

KUNJIRO HIRATA
MYSTERY TRAIN Orion Classics, 1989, EP w/Hideaki Suda

BARRY J. HIRSCH
AFTER MIDNIGHT MGM/UA, 1989, EP w/Allan Dennis

BUZZ HIRSCH
SILKWOOD 20th Century-Fox, 1983, EP w/Larry Cano

CHARLES HIRSCH
Personal Manager: Carol Akiyama - Sherman Oaks, 818/906-3639
Contact: Writers Guild of America - Los Angeles, 213/550-1000

GREETINGS Sigma III, 1968
HI, MOM! Sigma III, 1970

NORMAN HIRSCHFIELD
NOTHING PERSONAL American International, 1980, EP w/Jay Bernstein & Alan Hamel

CHARLES HIRSCHHORN

Business: Walt Disney Studios, 500 S. Buena Vista St., Burbank, CA, 91521, 818/560-2795

DIRTY ROTTEN SCOUNDRELS Orion, 1988, EP w/Dale Launer

MICHAEL HIRSH

Business: Nelvana Ltd., 32 Atlantic Ave., Toronto, Ontario M6K 1X8, Canada, 416/588-5571 or 9000 Sunset Blvd., #911, Los Angeles, CA, 90069, 213/278-8466

THE CARE BEARS MOVIE (AF) Samuel Goldwyn Company, 1985, w/Patrick Loubert & Clive A. Smith
ROCK & RULE (AF) MGM/UA, 1985, w/Patrick Loubert
CARE BEARS MOVIE II: A NEW GENERATION (AF) Columbia, 1986, w/Patrick Loubert & Clive A. Smith
THE CARE BEARS ADVENTURE IN WONDERLAND (AF) Cineplex Odeon, 1987, w/Patrick Loubert & Clive A. Smith
BURGLAR Warner Bros., 1987, w/Kevin McCormick
BABAR: THE MOVIE (AF) New Line Cinema, 1989

RUPERT HITZIG

Business: 73 Market St., Venice, CA, 90201, 213/396-5937
Contact: Directors Guild of America - Los Angeles, 213.289-2000

ELECTRA GLIDE IN BLUE United Artists, 1973, EP
HAPPY BIRTHDAY, GEMINI United Artists, 1980
CATTLE ANNIE & LITTLE BRITCHES Universal, 1981, w/Alan King
WOLFEN Orion/Warner Bros., 1981
JAWS 3-D Universal, 1983
THE LAST DRAGON Tri-Star, 1985
THE SQUEEZE Tri-Star, 1987, w/Michael Tannen

A. KITMAN HO

Business: Ixtlan, Inc., 321 Hampton, Suite 105, Venice, CA, 90291, 213/399-2550
Contact: Directors Guild of America - Los Angeles, 213.289-2000

THE LOVELESS Atlantic Entertainment, 1984, w/Grafton Nunes
PLATOON ★★ Orion, 1986, CP
WALL STREET 20th Century-Fox, 1987, CP
TALK RADIO Universal, 1988, w/Edward R. Pressman
BORN ON THE FOURTH OF JULY ★ Universal, 1989, w/Oliver Stone

PHILIP HOBBS

FULL METAL JACKET Warner Bros., 1987, CP

PHILIP S. HOBEL

Business: Cinema Guild, 1697 Broadway, #802, New York, NY, 10019, 212/246-5522

TENDER MERCIES ★ Universal, 1983

MIKE HODGES

Contact: "Websley," Durweston, Blanford Farm, Doreset, England, 02/585-3188
Agent: Terence Baker, Hatton & Baker, 18 Jermyn St., London W1, England, 01/439-2971

THE TERMINAL MAN Warner Bros., 1974

PETER HOFFMAN

VALENTINO RETURNS Skouras Pictures, 1989, w/David Wisnievitz

TAMAR SIMON HOFFS

Agent: Phil Gersh, The Gersh Agency - Beverly Hills, 213/274-6611
Contact: Directors Guild of America - Los Angeles, 213.289-2000

STONY ISLAND World Northal, 1980, w/Andrew Davis
STAND ALONE New World, 1985, AP
THE ALLNIGHTER Universal, 1987

HULK HOGAN

Business: World Wrestling Federation, P.O. Box 3857, Stamford, CT, 06905

NO HOLDS BARRED New Line Cinema, 1989, EP w/Richard Glover & Vince McMahon

PAUL HOGAN

Business: Paramount Pictures, 5555 Melrose Ave., Hollywood, CA, 90067, 213/468-5796

CROCODILE DUNDEE II Paramount, 1988, EP

ARNOLD J. HOLLAND

Business: Lightyear Entertainment, 350 5th Ave., Suite 5101, New York, NY, 10118,

THE LEMON SISTERS Miramax, 1990, EP w/Tom Kuhn & Charles Mitchell

JULIAN HOLLOWAY

LOOPHOLE Almi Pictures, 1986, w/David Korda

HENRY HOLMES

THE TEXAS CHAINSAW MASSACRE PART 2 Cannon, 1986, EP w/James Jorgensen

MILTON HOLMES

A MATTER OF WHO MGM, 1962, w/Walter Shenson

MICHAEL HOLZMAN

BEST OF THE BEST Taurus, 1989, EP w/Frank Giustra & Jeff Ringler

RAY HOMER

Contact: Directors Guild of America - New York, 212/581-0370

AMERICAN GOTHIC Vidmark Entertainment, 1988, EP w/Michael Manley & George Walker

CONRAD HOOL

STEEL DAWN Vestron, 1987, w/Lance Hool
OPTIONS Vestron, 1989, CP w/Edgar Bold
DAMNED RIVER MGM/UA, 1989, w/Lance Hool

LANCE HOOL

Agent: William Morris Agency - Beverly Hills, 213/274-7451

10 TO MIDNIGHT Cannon, 1983, w/Pancho Kohner
MISSING IN ACTION Cannon, 1984, EP
STEEL DAWN Vestron, 1987, w/Conrad Hool
OPTIONS Vestron, 1989
DAMNED RIVER MGM/UA, 1989, w/Conrad Hool

TOBE HOOPER

Business Manager: Joel Behr - Los Angeles, 213/551-2320
Contact: Directors Guild of America - Los Angeles, 213/289-2000

THE TEXAS CHAINSAW MASSACRE Bryanston, 1974
THE TEXAS CHAINSAW MASSACRE PART 2 Cannon, 1986, CP

ROY HORAN

NO RETREAT, NO SURRENDER II Shapiro Glickenhaus, 1989

JEFFREY HORNADAY

Contact: Directors Guild of America - Los Angeles, 213/289-2000

THE IN CROWD Orion, 1988, CP w/Karen Essex

MARTIN HORNSTEIN

Contact: Directors Guild of America - Los Angeles, 213/289-2000

I, THE JURY 20th Century-Fox, 1982, AP
BAD BOYS Universal, 1983, AP
THE WOMEN'S CLUB Lightning, 1987, CP
PERMANENT RECORD Paramount, 1988, EP

TED HOROVITZ

ANDY AND THE AIRWAVE RANGERS Concorde, 1988

GARY HOROWITZ

Contact: Directors Guild of America - Los Angeles, 213/289-2000

EXECUTIVE ACTION National General, 1973, CP w/Dan Bessie

BUCK HOUGHTON

THE ESCAPE ARTIST Orion/Warner Bros., 1982, w/Doug Claybourne

SHELLEY HOUIS

TRUE LOVE MGM/UA, 1989, w/Richard Guay

MEL HOWARD

Contact: Directors Guild of America - Los Angeles, 213/289-2000

RENTED LIPS Cineworld, 1988, LP

RON HOWARD

Business: Imagine Entertainment, 1925 Century Park East, 23rd Floor, Los Angeles, CA, 90067, 213/277-1665
Agent: CAA - Beverly Hills, 213/288-4545

LEOAND LOREE United Artists, 1980, EP
GUNG HO Paramount, 1986, EP
NO MAN'S LAND Orion, 1987, EP w/Tony Ganz
CLEAN AND SOBER Warner Bros., 1988, EP
VIBES Columbia, 1988, EP

SANDY HOWARD

Business: World Entertainment & Business Network, Inc., 7060 Hollywood Blvd., Suite 1204, Los Angeles, CA, 90028, 213/467-4151

A MAN CALLED HORSE National General, 1970
RETURN OF A MAN CALLED HORSE United Artists, 1976, EP
METEOR American International, 1979, EP w/Gabriel Katzka
JAGUAR LIVES! American International, 1979, EP
CIRCLE OF IRON Avco Embassy, 1979, w/Paul Maslansky
DEATH SHIP Avco Embassy, 1980, EP
VICE SQUAD Avco Embassy, 1982, EP w/Frank Capra Jr. & Bob Rehme
DEADLY FORCE Embassy, 1983
TRIUMPHS OF A MAN CALLED HORSE Jensen Farley, 1984, EP
HAMBONE & HILLIE New World, 1984, w/Gary Gillingham
THE BOYS NEXT DOOR New World, 1985, w/Keith Rubinstein
AVENGING ANGEL New World, 1985, w/Keith Rubinstein
KGB: THE SECRET WAR Cinema Group, 1986, w/Keith Rubinstein
HOLLYWOOD VICE SQUAD Cinema Group, 1986, w/Arnold Orgolini
PRETTYKILL Spectrafilm, 1987, EP

JENNIFER HOWARTH

DISTANT VOICES, STILL LIVES Avenue Pictures, 1989

WARRINGTON HUDLIN

Agent: Triad Artists, Inc. - Los Angeles, 213/556-2727

HOUSE PARTY New Line Cinema, 1990

HUGH HUDSON

Business: Hudson Film, Ltd., 11 Queen's Gate Place Mews, London SW7 5BG, England, 01/581-3133
Agent: CAA - Beverly Hills, 213/288-4545

GREYSTOKE: THE LEGEND OF TARZAN, LORD OF THE APES Warner Bros., 1984, w/Stanley S. Canter

JOHN HUGHES

Business: Hughes Entertainment, 100 Universal Plaza, Universal City, CA, 91608, 818/777-6363
Agent: CAA - Beverly Hills, 213/288-4545

PRETTY IN PINK Paramount, 1986, EP w/Michael Chinich
FERRIS BUELLER'S DAY OFF Paramount, 1986, w/Tom Jacobson
SOME KIND OF WONDERFUL Paramount, 1987
PLANES, TRAINS & AUTOMOBILES Paramount, 1987
SHE'S HAVING A BABY Paramount, 1988

THE GREAT OUTDOORS Universal, 1988, EP w/Tom Jacobson
UNCLE BUCK Universal, 1989, w/Tom Jacobson
NATIONAL LAMPOON'S CHRISTMAS VACATION Warner Bros., 1989, w/Tom Jacobson

LENORA HUME

Business: Nelvana Ltd., 32 Atlantic Ave., Toronto, Ontario M6K 1X8, Canada, 416/588-5571

CARE BEARS MOVIE II: A NEW GENERATION (AF) Columbia, 1986, SP
THE CARE BEARS ADVENTURE IN WONDERLAND (AF) Cineplex Odeon, 1987, SP

ED HUNT

STARSHIP INVASIONS Warner Bros., 1977, w/Norman Glick & Ken Gord

JESSICA SALEH HUNT

Business: Angelika Films, 1974 Broadway, New York, NY, 10023, 212/769-1400

BAIL JUMPER Angelika Films, 1990, EP

MARION HUNT

SHE DANCES ALONE Continental, 1982, EP
THE MIGHTY QUINN MGM/UA, 1989, w/Ed Elbert & Sandy Lieberson

WILLIE HUNT

LOVERBOY Tri-Star, 1989, w/Gary Foster

JOHN HUNTER

JOHN AND THE MISSUS Cinema Group, 1987

TAB HUNTER

LUST IN THE DUST New World, 1985, w/Allan Glaser

GALE ANNE HURD

Business: Pacific Western Productions, 4000 Warner Blvd., Bungalow 1, Suite A, Burbank, CA, 91522, 818/954-3112

SMOKEY BITES THE DUST New World, 1981, CP
THE TERMINATOR Orion, 1984
ALIENS 20th Century-Fox, 1986
ALIEN NATION 20th Century-Fox, 1988, w/Richard Kobritz
BAD DREAMS 20th Century-Fox, 1988
THE ABYSS 20th Century-Fox, 1989
DOWNTOWN 20th Century-Fox, 1990, EP
TREMORS Universal, 1990, EP

HARRY HURWITZ

Business: RSM Productions, Inc., 450 N. Rossmore Ave., Los Angeles, CA, 90004, 213/466-5225; 42 West End Ave., New York, NY, 10024, 212/496-1357
Agent: Shapiro-Lichtman, Inc. - Los Angeles, 213/859-8877

THE PROJECTIONIST Maron Films Limited, 1971
THE COMEBACK TRAIL Dynamite Entertainment/ Rearguard Productions, 1971
CHAPLINESQUE, MY LIFE & HARD TIMES Xanadu, 1972
THE ROSEBUD BEACH HOTEL *THE BIG LOBBY* Almi, 1984, w/Irving Schwartz
THAT'S ADEQUATE That's Adequate Company, 1986, w/Irving Schwartz
THE BIG SCORE Almi, 1983, EP w/David Forbes

DALE HUTCHINSON

Contact: Directors Guild of America - Los Angeles, 213.289-2000

ELVIS: THAT'S THE WAY IT IS (FD) MGM, 1970

PETER HYAMS

Business: Peter Hyams, Inc., Paramount Pictures, 5555 Melrose Ave., Los Angeles, CA, 90038, 213/468-5977
Agent: CAA - Beverly Hills, 213/288-4545

2010 MGM/UA, 1984
RUNNING SCARED MGM, 1986, EP
THE MONSTER SQUAD Tri-Star, 1987, EP w/Keith Barish & Rob Cohen

JOHN HYDE

Business: Cinecorp, 4000 Warner Blvd., Producers Bldg. 1, Suite 103, Burbank, CA, 91522, 818/954-1677
Contact: The Howard Brandy Company, Inc. - Los Angeles, 213/657-8320

DAS BOOT Columbia, 1982, EP w/Mark Damon & Edward R. Pressman
FIRE & ICE (AF) 20th Century-Fox, 1983, EP w/Richard R. St. Johns
THE NEVERENDING STORY Warner Bros., 1984, EP w/Mark Damon
FLIGHT OF THE NAVIGATOR Buena Vista, 1986, EP w/Mark Damon, Malcolm R. Harding & Jonathan Sanger
THE CLAN OF THE CAVE BEAR Warner Bros., 1986, EP w/Mark Damon, Peter Guber, Sidney Kimmel & Jon Peters
SHORT CIRCUIT Tri-Star, 1986, EP w/Mark Damon
THE LOST BOYS Warner Bros., 1987, EP w/Mark Damon & Richard Donner
UHF Orion, 1989, w/Gene Kirkwood

MYRON A. HYMAN

BRENDA STARR New World, 1987
A KILLING AFFAIR Hemdale, 1988, EP w/John D. Backe

I

EDGAR IEVINS

Business: Ievins/Henenlotter, 443 W. 43rd St., #1, New York, NY, 10036, 212/265-2166

BASKET CASE Analysis Releasing, 1982
BRAIN DAMAGE Palisades Entertainment, 1988
BASKET CASE 2 Shapiro-Glickenhaus Entertainment, 1990

WILLIAM J. IMMERMAN

Business: Cannon Productions, 5757 Wilshire Blvd., Suite 721, Los Angeles, CA, 90036, 213/965-0901

SOUTHERN COMFORT 20th Century-Fox, 1981, EP
TAKE THIS JOB AND SHOVE IT Embassy, 1981, EP w/J. David Marks

BEVERLY IRBY
IN THE SPIRIT Castle Hill, 1990, w/Julian Schlossberg

DAN IRELAND
(credit w/William J. Quigley)
Business: Vestron Pictures, 2029 Century Park East, Suite 200, Los Angeles, CA, 90067, 213/551-1723

MIDNIGHT CROSSING Vestron, 1988, EP w/Gary Barber, Gregory Cascante & Wanda S. Rayle*
WAXWORK Vestron, 1988, EP w/Gregory Cascante & Mario Sotela
THE LAIR OF THE WHITE WORM Vestron, 1988, EP
PAPERHOUSE Vestron, 1989, EP w/M. J. Peckos*
THE RAINBOW Vestron, 1989, EP
TWISTER Vestron, 1990, EP

JILL IRELAND
Contact: Screen Actors Guild - Los Angeles, 213/465-4600

MURPHY'S LAW Cannon, 1986, CP

MATTHEW IRMAS
UNDER THE BOARDWALK New World, 1989, CP

SAM IRVIN
THE FIRST TIME New Line Cinema, 1982

RICH IRVINE
(credit w/James L. Stewart)

WHY WOULD I LIE? MGM/UA, 1980, EP
HEART LIKE A WHEEL 20th Century-Fox, 1983, EP
MAXIE Orion, 1985, EP

FRANK ISAAC
WIZARDS OF THE LOST KINGDOM Concorde, 1985, w/Alex Sessa
BARBARIAN QUEEN Concorde, 1985, w/Alex Sessa

LORD ANTHONY RUFUS ISAACS
(see Lord Anthony RUFUS Isaacs)

SUSAN ISAACS
Agent: William Morris Agency - New York, 212/586-5100

HELLO AGAIN Buena Vista, 1987, CP w/G. Mac Brown, Thomas Folino & Martin Mickelson

GERALD I. ISENBERG
Business: King-Phoenix Entertainment, 310 N. San Vicente Blvd., #300, Los Angeles, CA, 90048, 213/657-7502

THE CLAN OF THE CAVE BEAR Warner Bros., 1986

MARJORIE ISRAEL
WHY ME? Triumph, 1990

NANCY ISRAEL
Contact: Directors Guild of America - Los Angeles, 213/289-2000

THE ALLNIGHTER Universal, 1987, CP

NEIL ISRAEL
Agent: ICM - Los Angeles, 213/550-4000

TUNNELVISION World Wide, 1976, EP
THREE O'CLOCK HIGH Universal, 1987, CP w/John Davis

ROBERT ISRAEL
BACHELOR PARTY 20th Century-Fox, 1984, w/Ron Moler
MOVING VIOLATIONS 20th Century-Fox, 1985, CP

J

JAMES JACKS
Business: Universal Pictures, 100 Universal City Plaza, Universal City, CA, 91608, 818/777-1000

RAISING ARIZONA 20th Century-Fox, 1987, EP

GEORGE A. JACKSON
KRUSH GROOVE Warner Bros., 1985, EP w/Robert O. Kaplan
DISORDERLIES Warner Bros., 1987, w/Michael Jaffe & Michael Schultz

FRANK JACOBS
THE BAY BOY Orion, 1985, EP w/Susan Cavan

TOM JACOBSON
Business: 20th Century-Fox, 10201 W. Pico Blvd., Los Angeles, CA, 90035, 213/277-2211
Contact: Directors Guild of America - Los Angeles, 213/289-2000

FLASHDANCE Paramount, 1983, AP w/Lynda Obst
TOP SECRET! Paramount, 1984, AP
EXPLORERS Paramount, 1985, AP
THIEF OF HEARTS Paramount, 1985, AP
FERRIS BUELLER'S DAY OFF Paramount, 1986, w/John Hughes
BURGLAR Warner Bros., 1987, EP
THE GREAT OUTDOORS Universal, 1988, EP w/John Hughes
UNCLE BUCK Universal, 1989, w/John Hughes
NATIONAL LAMPOON'S CHRISTMAS VACATION Warner Bros., 1989, w/John Hughes

KOBI JAEGER
FRANKENSTEIN UNBOUND 20th Century-Fox, 1990, w/Roger Corman & Thom Mount

HERB JAFFE
Business: The Vista Organization, 8439 Sunset Blvd., #200, Los Angeles, CA, 90069, 213/656-9130

THE WIND & THE LION MGM, 1975
DEMON SEED MGM, 1977
WHO'LL STOP THE RAIN United Artists, 1978, w/Gabriel Katzka
TIME AFTER TIME Orion/Warner Bros., 1979
THOSE LIPS, THOSE EYES United Artists, 1980, EP
MOTEL HELL United Artists, 1980, EP
JINXED MGM/UA, 1982

THE LORDS OF DISCIPLINE Paramount, 1983, w/Gabriel Katzka
LITTLE TREASURE Tri-Star, 1985
FRIGHT NIGHT Columbia, 1985
MAID TO ORDER New Century/Vista, 1987, w/Mort Engelberg
THREE FOR THE ROAD New Century/Vista, 1987, w/Mort Engelberg
NIGHTFLYERS New Century/Vista, 1987, EP
TRADING HEARTS New Century/Vista, 1988, EP w/Mort Engelberg
FRIGHT NIGHT PART 2 New Century/Vista, 1988, w/Mort Engelberg
DUDES New Century/Vista, 1988, w/Miguel Tejada-Flores
PASS THE AMMO New Century/Vista, 1988, w/Mort Engelberg

HOWARD B. JAFFE

A REFLECTION OF FEAR Columbia, 1971
MAN ON A SWING Paramount, 1974
TAPS 20th Century-Fox, 1981, w/Stanley R. Jaffe

MICHAEL JAFFE

Business: Spectacor Films, 1145 N. McCadden Place, Los Angeles, CA, 90038, 213/871-2777

BETTER OFF DEAD Warner Bros., 1985
BAD MEDICINE 20th Century-Fox, 1985, EP w/Sam Manners & Myles Osterneck
ONE CRAZY SUMMER Warner Bros., 1986
DISORDERLIES Warner Bros., 1987, w/George A. Jackson & Michael Schultz
18 AGAIN New World, 1988, EP w/Irving Fein

ROBERT JAFFE

Business: Columbia Pictures, 3400 Riverside Dr., Burbank, CA, 91505
Agent: Camden Artists, Ltd. - Los Angeles, 213/556-2022

MOTEL HELL United Artists, 1980, w/Steven Charles Jaffe
NIGHTFLYERS New Century/Vista, 1987

STANLEY R. JAFFE

Business: Jaffe-Lansing Productions, 660 Madison Ave., New York, NY, 10021, 212/421-4410

GOODBYE, COLUMBUS Paramount, 1969
I STARTED COUNTING United Artists, 1969
BAD COMPANY Paramount, 1972
MAN ON A SWING Paramount, 1974, EP
THE BAD NEWS BEARS Paramount, 1976
KRAMER VS. KRAMER ★★ Columbia, 1979
TAPS 20th Century-Fox, 1981, w/Howard B. Jaffe
WITHOUT A TRACE 20th Century-Fox, 1983
RACING WITH THE MOON Paramount, 1984, EP w/Sherry Lansing
FIRSTBORN Paramount, 1984, EP w/Sherry Lansing
FATAL ATTRACTION ★ Paramount, 1987, w/Sherry Lansing
THE ACCUSED Paramount, 1988, w/Sherry Lansing
BLACK RAIN Paramount, 1989, w/Sherry Lansing

STEVEN-CHARLES JAFFE

Business: Pari Passu Productions, Paramount Pictures, 5555 Melrose Ave., Los Angeles, CA, 90038, 213/468-5601
Business Manager: Laurence Rose, Esq., Gang, Tyre, Ramer & Brown, 6400 Sunset Blvd., Los Angeles, CA, 90028
Agent: Camden Artists, Ltd. - Los Angeles, 213/556-2022

DEMON SEED MGM, 1977, AP
MOTEL HELL United Artists, 1980, w/Robert Jaffe
THOSE LIPS, THOSE EYES United Artists, 1980, w/Michael Pressman
NEAR DARK DEG, 1987
PLAIN CLOTHES Paramount, 1988, EP
THE FLY II 20th Century-Fox, 1989
GHOST Paramount, 1990, EP

TOMMASO JANDELLI

Business: Gold Screen Films, 6/28 Draycott Place, London SW3 2SB, England, 01/584-9466
Attorney: Nigel Bennet, Simkins Partnership, 51 Whitfield St., London W1 P5R, England, 01/631-1050

WE THINK THE WORLD OF YOU Cinecom, 1989

PETAR JANKOVIC

HEY BABU RIBA Orion Classics, 1987, EP w/George Zecevic

JOSEPH JANNI

A KIND OF LOVING Continental, 1962
BILLY LIAR Continental, 1963
DARLING ★ Embassy, 1965
FAR FROM THE MADDING CROWD MGM, 1967
SUNDAY BLOODY SUNDAY United Artists, 1971
POOR COW National General, 1967
YANKS Universal, 1979, w/Lester Persky

MELINDA JASON

Business: Melinda Jason Productions, c/o Columbia Pictures, Studio Plaza, 3400 Riverside Dr., Burbank, CA, 91505

THE FIRST POWER Orion, 1990, EP

HELMUT JEDELE

DEEP END Paramount, 1971
TWILIGHT'S LAST GLEAMING Allied Artists, 1977, EP

GRAHAME JENNINGS

HOWLING II...YOUR SISTER IS A WEREWOLF Thorn EMI, 1986, EP

MARGARET JENNINGS SOUTH

(see Margaret Jennings SOUTH)

ANDERS P. JENSEN

ANGEL TOWN Taurus, 1990, EP w/Sundip R. Shah & Sunil R. Shah

SUE JETT

(credit w/Tony Mark)
Agent: CAA - Beverly Hills, 213/288-4545

BILLY GALVIN Vestron, 1986

ZELLY AND ME Columbia, 1988
ROOFTOPS New Visions, 1989, CP w/Allan Goldstein

NORMAN JEWISON

Business: Yorktown Productions Ltd.,10202 W. Washington Blvd., Culver City, CA, 90232, 213/280-2288
Agent: Larry Auerbach, William Morris Agency - Beverly Hills, 213/274-7451

THE RUSSIANS ARE COMING, THE RUSSIANS ARE COMING ★ United Artists, 1966
GAILY, GAILY United Artists, 1969
THE LANDLORD United Artists, 1970
FIDDLER ON THE ROOF ★ United Artists, 1971
BILLY TWO HATS United Artists, 1972, w/Patrick Palmer
JESUS CHRIST SUPERSTAR Universal, 1973, w/Robert Stigwood
ROLLERBALL United Artists, 1975
F.I.S.T. United Artists, 1978
...AND JUSTICE FOR ALL Columbia, 1979, w/Patrick Palmer
THE DOGS OF WAR United Artists, 1981, EP w/Patrick Palmer
BEST FRIENDS Warner Bros., 1982, w/Patrick Palmer
ICEMAN Universal, 1984, w/Patrick Palmer
A SOLDIER'S STORY ★ Columbia, 1984, w/Patrick Palmer & Ronald L. Schwary
AGNES OF GOD Columbia, 1985, w/Patrick Palmer
MOONSTRUCK ★ MGM, 1987, w/Patrick Palmer
THE JANUARY MAN MGM/UA, 1989, w/Ezra Swerdlow
IN COUNTRY Warner Bros., 1989, w/Richard Roth

CHARLES H. JOFFE

Business: Rollins-Joffe Productions, 130 W. 57th Street, New York, NY, 10019, 212/582-9062

TAKE THE MONEY AND RUN Cinerama Releasing Corporation, 1969
DON'T DRINK THE WATER Avco Embassy, 1969
BANANAS United Artists, 1971, EP w/Jack Rollins
PLAY IT AGAIN, SAM Paramount, 1972, EP
EVERYTHING YOU ALWAYS WANTED TO KNOW ABOUT SEX* (*BUT WERE AFRAID TO ASK) United Artists, 1972
SLEEPER United Artists, 1973, EP w/Jack Rollins
LOVE AND DEATH United Artists, 1975
THE FRONT Columbia, 1976, EP
ANNIE HALL ★★ United Artists, 1977
INTERIORS United Artists, 1978
MANHATTAN United Artists, 1979
STARDUST MEMORIES United Artists, 1980, EP w/Jack Rollins
ARTHUR Orion/Warner Bros., 1981, EP
A MIDSUMMER NIGHT'S SEX COMEDY Orion/ Warner Bros., 1982
ZELIG Orion/Warner Bros., 1983, EP w/Jack Rollins
BROADWAY DANNY ROSE Orion, 1984, EP
THE HOUSE OF GOD United Artists, 1984, w/Harold Schneider
THE PURPLE ROSE OF CAIRO Orion, 1985, EP
HANNAH AND HER SISTERS ★ Orion, 1986, EP w/Jack Rollins
RADIO DAYS Orion, 1987, EP w/Jack Rollins
SEPTEMBER Orion, 1987, EP w/Jack Rollins
ANOTHER WOMAN Orion, 1988, EP w/Jack Rollins
NEW YORK STORIES Buena Vista, 1989, EP w/Jack Rollins
CRIMES & MISDEMEANORS Orion, 1989, EP w/Jack Rollins

KRISTINE JOHNSON

THROW MOMMA FROM THE TRAIN Orion, 1987, CP

MARK JOHNSON

Business: Baltimore Pictures, c/o Tri-Star Pictures, Studio Plaza, 3400 Riverside Dr., Burbank, CA, 91505, 818/954-3710
Agent: CAA - Beverly Hills, 213/288-4545

DINER MGM/UA, 1982, EP
THE NATURAL Tri-Star, 1984
YOUNG SHERLOCK HOLMES Paramount, 1985
TIN MEN Buena Vista, 1987
GOOD MORNING, VIETNAM Buena Vista, 1987, w/Larry Brezner
RAIN MAN ★★ MGM/UA, 1988
THE FAMILY Tri-Star, 1990

RICHARD JOHNSON

TURTLE DIARY Samuel Goldwyn Company, 1985
CASTAWAY Cannon, 1987, EP w/Peter Shaw
THE LONELY PASSION OF JUDITH HEARNE Island Pictures, 1987, w/Peter Nelson

ANTHONY JONES

BLUE CITY Paramount, 1986, EP w/Robert Kenner

DENNIS JONES

Contact: Directors Guild of America - Los Angeles, 213/289-2000

MRS. SOFFEL MGM/UA, 1984, AP
SHORT CIRCUIT Tri-Star, 1986, CP

ISAAC L. JONES

THE RIVER NIGER Cine Artists, 1976, w/Sidney Beckerman

LORETHA C. JONES

SCHOOL DAZE Columbia, 1988, CP w/Monty Ross

QUINCY JONES

Business: Qwest Records, 7250 Beverly Blvd., Los Angeles, CA, 90036, 213/934-4711

THE COLOR PURPLE ★ Warner Bros., 1985, w/Kathleen Kennedy, Frank Marshall & Steven Spielberg

RICHARD JORDAN

A FLASH OF GREEN Spectrafilm, 1985

JAMES JORGENSEN

THE TEXAS CHAINSAW MASSACRE PART 2 Cannon, 1986, EP w/Henry Holmes

KIM JORGENSEN

OUT OF AFRICA ★★ Universal, 1985, EP

DAVID JOSEPH

FLIGHT OF THE NAVIGATOR Buena Vista, 1986, CP

BARRY JOSSEN
IN A SHALLOW GRAVE Skouras Pictures, 1988, w/Kenneth Bowser

WALTER JOSTEN
Business: Paragon Arts International, 6777 Hollywood Blvd., Suite 700, Hollywood, CA, 90028, 213/465-5355

WITCHBOARD Cinema Group, 1987, EP
NIGHT OF THE DEMONS International Film Marketing, 1988, EP

TOM JOYNER
Contact: Directors Guild of America - Los Angeles, 213/289-2000

WORTH WINNING 20th Century-Fox, 1989, EP

EBERHARD JUNKERSDORF
SISTERS, OR THE BALANCE OF HAPPINESS Cinema 5, 1982
MARIANNE & JULIANE New Yorker, 1982
CIRCLE OF DECEIT United Artists Classics, 1982
SHEER MADNESS R5/S8, 1985
ROSA LUXEMBURG New Yorker Films, 1987
BURNING SECRET Vestron, 1988, w/Carol Lynn Greene & Norma Heyman

MARTIN JUROW
Business: 3505 Rankin St., Dallas, TX, 75205

THE HANGING TREE Warner Bros., 1959, w/Richard Shepherd
THE FUGITIVE KIND United Artists, 1960, w/Richard Shepherd
BREAKFAST AT TIFFANY'S Paramount, 1961, w/Richard Shepherd
SOLDIER IN THE RAIN Allied Artists, 1963
THE PINK PANTHER United Artists, 1964
THE GREAT RACE Warner Bros., 1965
WALTZ ACROSS TEXAS Atlantic Entertainment, 1983
TERMS OF ENDEARMENT Paramount, 1983, CP w/Penny Finkelman Cox
SYLVESTER Columbia, 1985

MILTON JUSTICE
STAYING TOGETHER Hemdale, 1989, CP

GEORGE JUSTIN
Contact: Directors Guild of America - Los Angeles, 213/289-2000

NO SMALL AFFAIR Columbia, 1984, EP

K

MICHAEL J. KAGAN
DEJA VU Cannon, 1984, AP
SWORD OF THE VALIANT Cannon, 1984, EP w/Philip M. Breen
ORDEAL BY INNOCENCE Cannon, 1985, AP
LIFEFORCE Tri-Star, 1985, AP
DEATH WISH 3 Cannon, 1985, AP
THREE KINDS OF HEAT Cannon, 1987
DUET FOR ONE Cannon, 1987, AP
SUPERMAN IV: THE QUEST FOR PEACE Warner Bros., 1987, EP

MARCEL KAHN
POWAQQATSI (FD) Cannon, 1988, LP w/ Tom Luddy

SHELDON KAHN
Business: Ivan Reitman Productions, 4000 Warner Blvd., Burbank, CA, 91522, 213/954-1771

LEGAL EAGLES Universal, 1986, AP w/Arnold Glimcher
CASUAL SEX? Universal, 1988, w/Ilona Herzberg
GHOSTBUSTERS II Columbia, 1989, AP w/Gordon A. Webb

CONNIE KAISERMAN
Business: Merchant Ivory Productions, 250 West 57th St., Suite 1913-A, New York, NY, 10023, 212/582-8049

HEAT AND DUST Universal Classics, 1983, AP
THE BOSTONIANS Almi, 1984, AP
MY LITTLE GIRL Hemdale, 1987

MISHAAL KAMAL ADHAM
(see Mishaal Kamal ADHAM)

DENNIS D. KANE
MISSING LINK Universal, 1989

MARY KANE
Contact: Directors Guild of America - New York, 212/581-0370

CALL ME Vestron, 1988, LP w/Richard Gelfand

MICHAEL KANE
Contact: Directors Guild of America - Los Angeles, 213/289-2000

STEWARDESS SCHOOL Columbia, 1987, CP w/Jerry A. Baerwitz

JOSEPH H. KANTER
IRONWEED Tri-Star, 1987, EP w/Denis Blouin & Rob Cohen
THE BIG BANG (FD) Triton, 1990

J. STEIN KAPLAN
THE FINAL TERROR Aquarius, 1984, CP

MIKE KAPLAN
THE WHALES OF AUGUST Alive Films, 1987, w/Carolyn Pfeiffer

PAUL A. KAPLAN
PARTING GLANCES Cinecom, 1986, EP

ROBERT O. KAPLAN
KRUSH GROOVE Warner Bros., 1985, EP w/George A. Jackson

TOM KARNOWSKI
RADIOACTIVE DREAMS DEG, 1986, w/Moctesuma Esparza
DOWN TWISTED Cannon, 1987, AP
CYBORG Cannon, 1989, LP

CONSTANTINE P. KAROS
THE TROUBLE WITH SPIES DEG, 1987, EP

BEVERLY KARP
MY DINNER WITH ANDRE New Yorker, 1981, w/George W. George

ANDREW S. KARSCH
Business: 10000 W. Washington Blvd., Suite 3024, Culver City, CA, 90232, 213/280-6522

THE RACHEL PAPERS MGM/UA, 1989

ERIC KARSON
Agent: Shapiro-Lichtman Talent Agency - Los Angeles, 213/859-8877
Contact: Directors Guild of America - Los Angeles, 213/289-2000

ANGEL TOWN Taurus, 1990, w/Ash R. Shah

KEES KASANDER
THE COOK, THE THIEF, HIS WIFE & HER LOVER Miramax, 1990

LAWRENCE KASANOFF
BLOOD DINER Lightning/Vestron, 1987, EP w/Ellen Steloff
THE BEAT Vestron, 1988, EP w/Ruth Vitale
YOU CAN'T HURRY LOVE Vestron, 1988, w/Jonathan D. Krane & Ellen Steloff
DREAM A LITTLE DREAM Vestron, 1989, EP w/Ellen Steloff
FAR FROM HOME Vestron, 1989, EP w/Ellen Steloff
SHE'S BACK Vestron, 1989, EP w/Richard Kestinge
BLUE STEEL MGM/UA, 1990, EP
CLASS OF 1999 Taurus, 1990, EP w/Ellen Steloff

LAWRENCE KASDAN
Agent: Bauer Benedek Agency - Los Angeles, 213/275-2421

THE BIG CHILL ★ Columbia, 1983, EP w/Marcia Nasatir
SILVERADO Columbia, 1985
CROSS MY HEART Universal, 1987
THE ACCIDENTAL TOURIST ★ Warner Bros., 1988, w/Michael Grillo & Charles Okun
IMMEDIATE FAMILY Columbia, 1989, EP

DARYL KASS
Contact: Directors Guild of America - Los Angeles, 213/289-2000

DARKMAN Universal, 1990, w/Robert G. Tapert

MARIO KASSAR
(credit w/Andrew Vajna)
Business: Carolco Pictures, 9255 Sunset Blvd., Suite 910, Los Angeles, CA, 90069, 213/850-8800

THE AMATEUR 20th Century-Fox, 1981, EP
FIRST BLOOD Orion, 1982
SUPERSTITION Almi Pictures, 1985
RAMBO: FIRST BLOOD PART II Tri-Star, 1985, EP
EXTREME PREJUDICE Tri-Star, 1987, EP
ANGEL HEART Tri-Star, 1987, EP
RAMBO III Tri-Star, 1988
RED HEAT Tri-Star, 1988, EP
DEEPSTAR SIX Tri-Star, 1989, EP
JOHNNY HANDSOME Tri-Star, 1989, EP
MOUNTAINS OF THE MOON Tri-Star, 1990, EP
NARROW MARGIN Tri-Star, 1990, EP
TOTAL RECALL Tri-Star, 1990, EP
JACOB'S LADDER Tri-Star, 1990, EP

ELLIOTT KASTNER
Business: Cinema Seven Productions, 154 West 57th St., #112, New York, NY, 10019, 212/315-1060

HARPER Warner Bros., 1966, w/Jerry Gershwin
WHERE EAGLES DARE MGM, 1968
WHEN EIGHT BELLS TOLL Cinerama Releasing, 1970
VILLAIN MGM, 1971, EP
X, Y, & ZEE Columbia, 1971, EP
FEAR IS THE KEY EMI, 1972, EP
THE LONG GOODBYE United Artists, 1973, EP
JEREMY United Artists, 1973, EP
COPS & ROBBERS United Artists, 1973
RANCHO DELUXE United Artists, 1974
11 HARROW HOUSE 20th Century-Fox, 1974
92 IN THE SHADE United Artists, 1974, EP
FAREWELL, MY LOVELY Avco Embassy, 1975, EP w/Jerry Bick
BREAKHEART PASS United Artists, 1976, EP
RUSSIAN ROULETTE Avco Embassy, 1975, EP
THE MISSOURI BREAKS United Artists, 1976, w/Robert M. Sherman
SWASHBUCKLER Universal, 1976, EP
EQUUS United Artists, 1977, w/Lester Persky
BLACK JOY Hemdale, 1977, w/Arnon Milchan
THE BIG SLEEP United Artists, 1978, w/Michael Winner
A LITTLE NIGHT MUSIC New World, 1978
THE MEDUSA TOUCH Warner Bros., 1978, w/Lew Grade & Arnon Milchan
YESTERDAY'S HERO EMI, 1979, EP
GOLDENGIRL Avco Embassy, 1979, EP
THE FIRST DEADLY SIN Filmways, 1980, EP w/Frank Sinatra
ffolkes Universal, 1980
DEATH VALLEY Universal, 1982
MAN, WOMAN & CHILD Paramount, 1983, w/Elmo Williams
GARBO TALKS MGM/UA, 1984, w/Burtt Harris
OXFORD BLUES MGM/UA, 1984, w/Cassian Elwes
ANGEL HEART Tri-Star, 1987, w/Alan Marshall
ABSOLUTION Trans World Entertainment, 1988, w/Danny O'Donovan
JACK'S BACK Palisades Entertainment, 1988
THE BLOB Tri-Star, 1988, w/Jack H. Harris
A CHORUS OF DISAPPROVAL South Gate Entertainment, 1989, EP w/Andre Blay
HOMEBOY Homeboy Productions, 1990, w/Alan Marshall

GLORIA KATZ
Agent: CAA - Beverly Hills, 213/288-4545
Contact: Writers Guild of America - Los Angeles, 213/550-1000

FRENCH POSTCARDS Paramount, 1979
BEST DEFENSE Paramount, 1984
HOWARD THE DUCK Universal, 1986

JAMES C. KATZ
NOBODY'S FOOL Island Pictures, 1986, w/Jon S. Denny
SCENES FROM THE CLASS STRUGGLE IN BEVERLY HILLS Cinecom, 1989

MARTY KATZ
Business: Walt Disney Pictures, 500 S. Buena Vista St., Burbank, CA, 91521, 818/560-1307
Contact: Directors Guild of America - Los Angeles, 213/289-2000

LOST IN AMERICA Warner Bros., 1985

PETER KATZ
DON'T LOOK NOW Paramount, 1974

RAYMOND KATZ
Business: Raymond Katz Enterprises, 9255 Sunset Blvd., #115, Los Angeles, CA, 90069, 213/273-4211

I'M GONNA GIT YOU SUCKA MGM/UA, 1989, EP w/Eric L. Gold

ROBERT KATZ
THE TELEPHONE New World, 1988, w/Moctesuma Esparza

ROBERT KAUFMAN
Contact: Writers Guild of America - Los Angeles, 213/550-1000

I LOVE MY WIFE Universal, 1970, AP
LOVE AT FIRST BITE American International, 1979, EP w/George Hamilton
HOW TO BEAT THE HIGH COST OF LIVING American International, 1980, w/Jerome M. Zeitman
THE CHECK IS IN THE MAIL Ascot Entertainment, 1986, w/Robert Krause
SHE'S OUT OF CONTROL WEG/Columbia, 1989, EP

DEREK KAVANAGH
DANCES WITH WOLVES Orion, 1990, w/Jim Wilson

RICHARD KAYE
THE TOMB Trans World Entertainment, 1986, EP w/Paul Hertzberg
THE WIZARD OF SPEED AND TIME Shapiro-Glickenhaus Entertainment, 1989, w/Deven Chierighino

ELIA KAZAN
Business: 174 East 95th St., New York, NY10128
Contact: Directors Guild of America - Los Angeles, 213/289-2000
Contact: Writers Guild of America - New York, 212/245-6180

AMERICA, AMERICA ★ Warner Bros., 1963
THE ARRANGEMENT Warner Bros./7 Arts, 1969

HOWARD KAZANJIAN
Business: Tricor Entertainment, 3855 Lankershim Blvd., North Hollywood, CA, 91604, 818/763-3157
Contact: Directors Guild of America - Los Angeles, 213/289-2000

MORE AMERICAN GRAFFITI Universal, 1979
RAIDERS OF THE LOST ARK ★ Parmount, 1981, EP w/George Lucas
RETURN OF THE JEDI 20th Century-Fox, 1983

JAMES KEACH
Contact: Writers Guild of America - Los Angeles, 213/550-1000

THE LONG RIDERS United Artists, 1980, EP w/Stacy Keach
ARMED & DANGEROUS Columbia, 1986, w/Brian Grazer
THE EXPERTS Paramount, 1989

STACY KEACH
Agent: William Morris Agency - Beverly Hills, 213/274-7451
Contact: Directors Guild of America - Los Angeles, 213/289-2000

THE LONG RIDERS United Artists, 1980, EP w/James Keach

JOHN KEARNEY
GROUND ZERO Avenue, 1988, EP w/Kent Lovell & Dennis Wright

DIANE KEATON
Agent: John Burnham, William Morris Agency - Beverly Hills, 213/274-7451

THE LEMON SISTERS Miramax, 1990, w/Joe Kelly

PAT KEHOE
Contact: Directors Guild of America - Los Angeles, 213/289-2000

FANDANGO Warner Bros., 1985, AP w/Barrie M. Osborne
TUFF TURF New World, 1985, CP

JOHN KELLEHER
Business: Liberty Films, The Forum, 74-80 Camden St., London NW1 0JL, England, 01/387-5733

EAT THE PEACH Skouras Pictures, 1987
WAR REQUIEM Anglo International, 1988, EP

LAURIE KELLER
RIDERS OF THE STORM *THE AMERICAN WAY* Miramax, 1987, w/Paul Cowan

PATRICK KELLEY
Business: Pan Arts Productions, 4000 Warner Blvd., Burbank, CA, 91522, 818/954-3631

A LITTLE ROMANCE Orion/Warner Bros., 1979, EP
DEADLY FRIEND Warner Bros., 1986, EP
THE WORLD ACCORDING TO GARP Warner Bros., 1982, EP
THE LITTLE DRUMMER GIRL Warner Bros., 1984, EP
FUNNY FARM Warner Bros., 1988, EP w/Bruce Bodner

BRIAN KELLY
BLADE RUNNER The Ladd Company/Warner Bros., 1982, EP w/Hampton Fancher

GABRIELLE KELLY
Business: Mason-Shaw Productions, 10100 Santa Monica Blvd., #496, Los Angeles, CA, 90067, 213/286-0736

D.A.R.Y.L. Paramount, 1985, CP w/Burtt Harris

GENE KELLY
Agent: ICM - Los Angeles, 213/550-4000

THAT'S DANCING! (FD) MGM, 1985, EP

JOE KELLY
HEAVEN (FD) Island Pictures, 1987
THE LEMON SISTERS Miramax, 1990, w/Diane Keaton

JOHN KEMENY
Business: Alliance Entertainment Corporation, 8439 Sunset Blvd., #404, Los Angeles, CA, 90069, 213/654-9488; 920 Yonge Street, Suite 400, Toronto, Ontario, M4W 3C7, Canada, 416/967-1174

THE APPRENTICESHIP OF DUDDY KRAVITZ Paramount, 1974
WHITE LINE FEVER Columbia, 1975
SHADOW OF THE HAWK Columbia, 1976
ICE CASTLES Columbia, 1979
QUEST FOR FIRE 20th Century-Fox, 1982, w/Denis Héroux
THE BAY BOY Orion, 1985, w/Denis Héroux
THE BOY IN BLUE 20th Century-Fox, 1986
THE WRAITH New Century, 1986
THE GATE New Century/Vista, 1987
NOWHERE TO HIDE New Century/Vista, 1987, EP
IRON EAGLE II Tri-Star, 1988, w/Sharon Harel & Jacob Kotzky

BURT KENNEDY
Business: 13138 Magnolia Blvd., Sherman Oaks, CA, 91403, 818/986-8759
Agent: Sanford-Beckett/Tobias-Skouras - Los Angeles, 213/277-6211

THE TROUBLE WITH SPIES DEG, 1987

KATHLEEN KENNEDY
Business: Amblin Entertainment, Universal Studios, 100 Universal Plaza, Bungalow 477, Universal City, CA, 91608, 818/777-4600

POLTERGEIST MGM/UA, 1982, AP
E.T. THE EXTRA-TERRESTRIAL ★ Universal, 1982, w/Steven Spielberg
TWILIGHT ZONE — THE MOVIE Warner Bros., 1983, AP
GREMLINS Warner Bros., 1984, EP w/Frank Marshall & Steven Spielberg
INDIANA JONES & THE TEMPLE OF DOOM Paramount, 1984, AP
FANDANGO Warner Bros., 1985, EP w/Frank Marshall
THE GOONIES Warner Bros., 1985, EP w/Frank Marshall & Steven Spielberg
BACK TO THE FUTURE Universal, 1985, EP w/Frank Marshall & Steven Spielberg
YOUNG SHERLOCK HOLMES Paramount, 1985, EP w/Frank Marshall & Steven Spielberg
THE COLOR PURPLE ★ Warner Bros., 1985, w/Quincy Jones, Frank Marshall & Steven Spielberg
THE MONEY PIT Universal, 1986, w/Art Levinson & Frank Marshall
AN AMERICAN TAIL (AF) Universal, 1986, EP w/David Kirschner, Frank Marshall & Steven Spielberg
INNERSPACE Warner Bros., 1987, EP w/Peter Guber, Frank Marshall, Jon Peters & Steven Spielberg
BATTERIES NOT INCLUDED Universal, 1987, EP w/Frank Marshall & Steven Spielberg
EMPIRE OF THE SUN Warner Bros., 1987, w/Frank Marshall & Steven Spielberg
WHO FRAMED ROGER RABBIT Buena Vista, 1988, EP w/Steven Spielberg
THE LAND BEFORE TIME (AF) Universal, 1988, EP w/George Lucas, Frank Marshall & Steven Spielberg
INDIANA JONES & THE LAST CRUSADE Paramount, 1989, EP w/George Lucas & Frank Marshall
DAD Universal, 1989, EP w/Frank Marshall & Steven Spielberg
BACK TO THE FUTURE PART II Universal, 1989, EP w/Frank Marshall & Steven Spielberg
ALWAYS Universal, 1989, w/Frank Marshall & Steven Spielberg
BACK TO THE FUTURE PART III Universal, 1990, EP w/Frank Marshall & Steven Spielberg
GREMLINS 2: THE NEW BATCH Warner Bros., 1990, EP w/Frank Marshall & Steven Spielberg
JOE VERSUS THE VOLCANO Warner Bros., 1990, EP w/Frank Marshall & Steven Spielberg

ROBERT KENNER
BLUE CITY Paramount, 1986, EP w/Anthony Jones

CHRIS KENNY
THE BRIDE Columbia, 1985, CP
EMPIRE OF THE SUN Warner Bros., 1987, AP
BATMAN Warner Bros., 1989, CP

JORDAN KERNER
Business: Avnet-Kerner Company, 505 N. Robertson Blvd., Los Angeles, CA, 90048, 213/271-7408

LESS THAN ZERO 20th Century-Fox, 1987, w/Jon Avnet

WILLIAM B. KERR
Contact: Directors Guild of America - Los Angeles, 213/289-2000

MAC & ME Orion, 1988, EP w/Mark Damon

IRVIN KERSHNER
Business: 9229 Sunset Blvd., Suite 818, Los Angeles, CA, 90069
Agent: CAA - Beverly Hills, 213/288-4545

WILDFIRE Cinema Group, 1988, EP w/Stanley R. Zupnik

JUDY KESSLER
GORILLAS IN THE MIST Universal, 1988, CP w/Robert Nixon

STEPHEN F. KESTEN
Contact: Directors Guild of America - New York, 212/581-0370

THE TAKING OF PELHAM 1-2-3 United Artists, 1974, AP
FOUR FRIENDS Filmways, 1981, AP
A LITTLE SEX Universal, 1982, AP
CONAN THE DESTROYER Universal, 1984, EP
MILLION DOLLAR MYSTERY DEG, 1987

RICHARD KESTINGE
SHE'S BACK Vestron, 1989, EP w/Lawrence Kasanoff

FATHER ELLWOOD E. KIESER

Business: Paulist Productions, 17575 Pacific Coast Highway, Pacific Palisades, CA, 90272, 213/454-0688
Contact: The Howard Brandy Company, Inc. - Los Angeles, 213/657-8320;

ROMERO Four Seasons Entertainment, 1989

JON KILIK

Business: Avenue of the Americas, 6th Floor, New York, NY,10019, 212/888-9115

THE BEAT Vestron, 1988, w/Julia Phillips & Nick Wechsler
DO THE RIGHT THING Universal, 1989, LP
MO' BETTER BLUES Universal, 1990, w/Spike Lee & Monty Ross

ANNE KIMMEL

Business: Kimmel-Lucas Productions, 932 N. La Brea Ave., Hollywood, CA, 90038, 213/874-0436

EATING RAOUL 20th Century-Fox International Classics, 1982
NOT FOR PUBLICATION Samuel Goldwyn Company, 1984
PAINT IT BLACK Vestron, 1989, w/Mark Forstater

SIDNEY KIMMEL

THE CLAN OF THE CAVE BEAR Warner Bros., 1986, EP w/Mark Damon, Peter Guber, John Hyde & Jon Peters

TIM KINCAID

(credit w/Cynthia DePaula)

ENEMY TERRITORY Empire, 1987
NECROPOLIS Empire, 1987

ALAN KING

Business: Odyssey Film Partners, Ltd., 6500 Wilshire Blvd., Suite 400, Los Angeles, CA, 90048, 213/655-9335

HAPPY BIRTHDAY GEMINI United Artists, 1980, EP
CATTLE ANNIE & LITTLE BRITCHES Universal, 1981, w/Rupert Hitzig
WOLFEN Orion/Warner Bros., 1981, EP
MEMORIES OF ME MGM/UA, 1988, w/Billy Crystal & Michael Hertzberg

ZALMAN KING

Agent: Arnold Rifkin, Triad Artists, Inc. - Los Angeles, 213/556-2727
Contact: Directors Guild of America - Los Angeles, 213/289-2000

ROADIE United Artists, 1980, EP
ENDANGERED SPECIES MGM/UA, 1982
9 1/2 WEEKS MGM/UA, 1986, w/Lord Anthony Rufus Isaacs
SIESTA Lorimar, 1987, EP w/Julio Caro & Nik Powell

TERRENCE KIRBY

CHILDREN OF THE CORN New World, 1984, w/Donald P. Borchers

JULIE KIRKHAM

BLACK RAIN Paramount, 1989, EP w/Craig Bolotin

GENE KIRKWOOD

Business: Cinecorp, 4000 Warner Blvd., Producers Bldg. 1, Suite 103, Burbank, CA, 91522, 818/954-1677
Contact: The Howard Brandy Company, Inc. - Los Angeles, 213/657-8320

ROCKY ★★ United Artists, 1976, EP
NEW YORK, NEW YORK United Artists, 1977, AP
COMES A HORSEMAN United Artists, 1978, w/Dan Paulson
UNCLE JOE SHANNON United Artists, 1978, EP
THE IDOLMAKER United Artists, 1980, w/Howard W. Koch Jr.
THE KEEP Paramount, 1983, w/Howard W. Koch Jr.
GORKY PARK Orion, 1983, w/Howard W. Koch Jr.
A NIGHT IN HEAVEN 20th Century-Fox, 1983, w/Howard W. Koch Jr.
THE POPE OF GREENWICH VILLAGE MGM/UA, 1984, w/Howard W. Koch Jr.
IRONWEED Tri-Star, 1987, CP w/C. O. Erickson
UHF Orion, 1989, w/John Hyde

DAVID KIRSCHNER

Business: Hanna-Barbera Productions, Inc., 3400 Cahuenga Blvd. West, Los Angeles, CA, 90068, 213/851-5000
Contact: Writers Guild of America - Los Angeles, 213/550-1000

AN AMERICAN TAIL (AF) Universal, 1986, EP w/Kathleen Kennedy, Frank Marshall & Steven Spielberg
CHILD'S PLAY MGM/UA, 1988

LAWRENCE KIRSTEIN

WITHNAIL & I Cineplex Odeon, 1987, w/Paul Heller

ROBERT KLANE

Agent: ICM - Los Angeles, 213/550-4000
Contact: Writers Guild of America - Los Angeles, 213/550-1000

WALK LIKE A MAN MGM/UA, 1987, EP
WEEKEND AT BERNIE'S 20th Century-Fox, 1989, EP w/Malcolm R. Harding

ALLEN KLEIN

Business: Abkco Records, Inc., 1700 Broadway, New York, NY, 212/399-0300

MRS. BROWN, YOU'VE GOT A LOVELY DAUGHTER MGM, 1968
THE GREEK TYCOON Universal, 1978, w/Ely Landau

JEFFREY KLEIN

Business: Jaguar Distribution Corp., 3415 S. Sepulveda Blvd., Los Angeles, CA, 90034, 213/391-6666

THE HIDDEN New Line Cinema, 1987, EP w/Stephen Diener, Dennis Harris & Lee Muhl

MEL KLEIN

A NIGHT IN THE LIFE OF JIMMY REARDON 20th Century-Fox, 1988, EP w/Noel Marshall

PAUL KLEIN

BASIC TRAINING Moviestore, 1985, EP w/Lawrence Vanger

ALAN KLEINBERG

DOWN BY LAW Island Pictures, 1986

RANDAL KLEISER

Business: Randal Kleiser Productions, 2400 Broadway, #100, Santa Monica, CA, 90404, 213/851-5224
Agent: ICM - Los Angeles, 213/550-4000

THE BLUE LAGOON Columbia, 1980
NORTH SHORE Universal, 1987, EP
GETTING IT RIGHT MCEG, 1989, w/Jonathan D. Krane

MICHAEL KLINGER

PULP United Artists, 1972

DONALD C. KLUNE

Contact: Directors Guild of America - Los Angeles, 213/289-2000

MADHOUSE Orion, 1990, CP

CHRISTOPHER W. KNIGHT

Business: Knight-Tyson Productions, 127 Broadway, Suite 220, Santa Monica, CA, 90401, 213/395-7100

HOT DOG...THE MOVIE MGM/UA, 1984, EP
WINNERS TAKE ALL Apollo, 1987, w/Tom Tatum
THE DREAM TEAM Universal, 1989

RICHARD KOBRITZ

Contact: Directors Guild of America - Los Angeles, 213/289-2000

CHRISTINE Columbia, 1983
ALIEN NATION 20th Century-Fox, 1988, w/Gale Anne Hurd

HOWARD W. KOCH

Business: Aries Films, Inc., Paramount Pictures, 5555 Melrose Ave., Los Angeles, CA, 90038, 213/468-5996
Contact: Directors Guild of America - Los Angeles, 213/289-2000

COME BLOW YOUR HORN Paramount, 1963, EP
THE MANCHURIAN CANDIDATE United Artists, 1962, EP
THE PRESIDENT'S ANALYST Paramount, 1967, EP
THE ODD COUPLE Paramount, 1968
ON A CLEAR DAY YOU CAN SEE FOREVER Paramount, 1970
PLAZA SUITE Paramount, 1971
STAR SPANGLED GIRL Paramount, 1971
LAST OF THE RED HOT LOVERS Paramount, 1972
BADGE 373 Paramount, 1973
JACQUELINE SUSANN'S ONCE IS NOT ENOUGH Paramount, 1975
AIRPLANE! Paramount, 1980, EP
DRAGONSLAYER Paramount, 1981, EP
SOME KIND OF HERO Paramount, 1982
AIRPLANE II: THE SEQUEL Paramount, 1983

HOWARD W. KOCH, JR.

Business: The Koch Company, Paramount Pictures, 5555 Melrose Ave., Los Angeles, CA, 90038, 213/960-4977

THE OTHER SIDE OF MIDNIGHT 20th Century- Fox, 1977, EP
THE IDOLMAKER United Artists, 1980, w/Gene Kirkwood
HEAVEN CAN WAIT Paramount, 1978, EP w/Charles H. Maguire
THE FRISCO KID Warner Bros., 1979, EP
HONKY TONK FREEWAY Universal/AFD, 1981, w/Don Boyd
THE KEEP Paramount, 1983, w/Gene Kirkwood
GORKY PARK Orion, 1983, w/Gene Kirkwood
A NIGHT IN HEAVEN 20th Century-Fox, 1983, w/Gene Kirkwood
THE POPE OF GREENWICH VILLAGE MGM/UA, 1984, w/Gene Kirkwood
ROOFTOPS New Visions, 1989
THE LONG WALK HOME New Visions, 1990

DAVID KOEPP

Agent: Bauer-Benedek Agency - Los Angeles, 213/275-2421
Contact: Writers Guild of America - Los Angeles, 213/550-1000

APARTMENT ZERO Skouras Pictures, 1989, w/Martin Donovan

JOHN KOHN

Contact: Writers Guild of America - Los Angeles, 213/550-1000

RACING WITH THE MOON Paramount, 1984, w/Alain Bernheim
SHANGHAI SURPRISE MGM/UA, 1986

PANCHO KOHNER

Business: Capricorn Productions, Inc., 1527 Tigertail Rd., Los Angeles, CA, 90049
Agent: Paul Kohner, Inc. - Los Angeles, CA, 90069, 213/550-1060

ST. IVES Warner Bros., 1976, w/Stanley S. Canter
THE WHITE BUFFALO United Artists, 1977
LOVE AND BULLETS ITC, 1979
WHY WOULD I LIE? MGM/UA, 1980
10 TO MIDNIGHT Cannon, 1983, w/Lance Hool
THE EVIL THAT MEN DO Tri-Star, 1984
MURPHY'S LAW Cannon, 1986
ASSASSINATION Cannon, 1987
DEATH WISH 4: THE CRACKDOWN Cannon, 1987
MESSENGER OF DEATH Cannon, 1988
KINJITE (FORBIDDEN SUBJECTS) Cannon, 1989

ITZIK KOL

THE AMBASSADOR Cannon, 1985, AP
BEAUTY AND THE BEAST Cannon, 1987, EP
RUMPLESTILTSKIN Cannon, 1987, EP

EVZEN W. KOLAR

STREET SMART Cannon, 1987, AP
MASTERS OF THE UNIVERSE Cannon, 1987, AP
BAT 21 Tri-Star, 1988, LP

DAN KOLSRUD
Contact: Directors Guild of America - Los Angeles, 213/289-2000

IMPULSE Warner Bros., 1990, EP

DANIEL P. KONDOS
(credit w/George Kondos)
STAND ALONE New World, 1985, EP

GEORGE KONDOS
(credit w/Daniel P. Kondos)
STAND ALONE New World, 1985, EP

JACKIE KONG
Attorney: Bob Brenner, Esq., 213/553-2525

NIGHT PATROL New World, 1984, CP
BLOOD DINER Lightning/Vestron, 1987, CP

FRANK KONIGSBERG
Business: The Konigsberg-Sanitsky Company, 1930 Century Park West, #400, Los Angeles, CA, 90067, 213/277-6850

JOY OF SEX Paramount, 1984
9 1/2 WEEKS MGM/UA, 1986, EP w/Keith Barish & F. Richard Northcott

LAWRENCE KONNER
Business: Konner-Rosenthal Productions, Paramount Pictures, 5555 Melrose Ave., Los Angeles, LA, 90038, 213/468-5909
Agent: InterTalent Agency, Inc. - Los Angeles, 213/271-0600

THE LEGEND OF BILLIE JEAN Tri-Star, 1985, CP w/Mark Rosenthal
THE IN CROWD Orion, 1988, w/Keith Rubinstein

JOSI W. KONSKI
Business: Laguna Productions, Inc., 6854 NW 77 Court, Miami, FL, 33166, 305/594-5674
Contact: Directors Guild of America - Los Angeles, 213/289-2000

TRADING HEARTS New Century/Vista, 1988

DAVID KOONTZ
MOMMIE DEAREST Paramount, 1981, EP w/Terence O'Neill

ARNOLD KOPELSON
Business: Inter-Ocean Film Sales, Ltd., 6100 Wilshire Blvd., Suite 1500, Los Angeles, CA, 90048, 213/932-0500

LOST AND FOUND Columbia, 1979, EP
THE LEGACY Universal, 1979, EP
FOOLIN' AROUND Columbia, 1980
NIGHT OF THE JUGGLER Columbia, 1980, EP
DIRTY TRICKS Avco Embassy, 1981, EP w/Pierre David & Victor Solnicki
PLATOON ★★ Orion, 1986
WARLOCK New World, 1989, EP
TRIUMPH OF THE SPIRIT Triumph, 1989, w/Shimon Arama

DAVID KORDA
Business: Filmaccord Productions, 3619 Motor Ave., Suite 300, Los Angeles, CA, 90034, 213/204-6270

CATTLE ANNIE & LITTLE BRITCHES Universal, 1981, AP
HALF MOON STREET 20th Century-Fox, 1986, EP w/Edward R. Pressman
LOOPHOLE Almi Pictures, 1986, w/Julian Holloway
HAMBURGER HILL Paramount, 1987, EP w/Jerry Offsay

BENNI KORZEN
RENT CONTROL Group 5 Films, 1984
THE MISFIT BRIGADE *WHEELS OF TERROR* Trans World Entertainment, 1987, w/Just Betzer
THE GIRL IN A SWING Millimeter Films, 1989, CP

ROBERT KOSBERG
Business: Guber-Peters Entertainment, Studio Plaza, 3400 Riverside Dr., Burbank, CA, 91505, 818/954-3083

COMMANDO 20th Century-Fox, 1985, AP
ONE MORE SATURDAY NIGHT Columbia, 1986, w/Jonathan Bernstein & Tova Laiter

RON KOSLOW
Agent: Jack Rapke, CAA - Beverly Hills, 213/288-4545
Contact: Writers Guild of America - Los Angeles, 213/550-1000

FIRSTBORN Paramount, 1984, CP
INTO THE NIGHT Universal, 1985, w/George Folsey Jr.

TED KOTCHEFF
Agent: CAA - Beverly Hills, 213/288-4545
Contact: Directors Guild of America - Los Angeles, 213/289-2000

SPLIT IMAGE Orion, 1982

JACOB KOTZKY
(credit w/Sharon Harel)
Business: Capitol Films, Ltd., 24 Upper Brook St., London W1Y 1PD, 01/872-0017

EVERY TIME WE SAY GOODBYE Tri-Star, 1986
IRON EAGLE II Tri-Star, 1988, w/John Kemeny

JIM KOUF
Business: Kouf-Bigelow Productions, Walt Disney Pictures, 500 S. Buena Vista St., Burbank, CA, 91521, 818/560-5103
Agent: ICM - Los Angeles, 213/550-4000

CLASS Orion, 1983, AP
SECRET ADMIRER Orion, 1985, CP
STAKEOUT Buena Vista, 1987, w/Cathleen Summers

STEVEN KOVACS
ON THE LINE Miramax, 1987, w/Jose Luis Borau
'68 New World, 1988, w/Dale Djerassi & Isabel Maxwell

GENE KRAFT
Business: Gene Kraft Productions, 7556 Woodrow Wilson Dr., Los Angeles, CA, 90046, 213/851-5322
Contact: Directors Guild of America - Los Angeles, 213/289-2000

THE BIG TOWN Columbia, 1987, EP

LARRY KRAMER

WOMEN IN LOVE United Artists, 1969

LEE KRAMER

XANADU Universal, 1980, EP
THE MAN WHO SAW TOMORROW (FD) Warner Bros., 1981, w/Paul Drane & Robert Guenette

STANLEY KRAMER

Business: Stanley Kramer Productions, 12386 Ridge Circle, Los Angeles, CA, 90049, 213/472-0065
Agent: Paul Kohner, Inc. - Los Angeles, 213/550-1060

CHAMPION United Artists, 1949
HOME OF THE BRAVE United Artists, 1949
THE MEN Columbia, 1950
CYRANO DE BERGERAC United Artists, 1950
DEATH OF A SALESMAN Columbia, 1951
HIGH NOON ★ United Artists, 1952
MY SIX CONVICTS Universal, 1952
THE SNIPER Columbia, 1952
THE HAPPY TIME Columbia, 1952
EIGHT IRON MEN Columbia, 1952
THE FOUR POSTER Columbia, 1953
THE 5000 FINGERS OF DR. T Columbia, 1953
THE JUGGLER Columbia, 1953
THE WILD ONE Columbia, 1954
THE CAINE MUTINY ★ Columbia, 1954
NOT AS A STRANGER United Artists, 1955
THE PRIDE AND THE PASSION United Artists, 1957
THE DEFIANT ONES ★ United Artists, 1958
ON THE BEACH United Artists, 1959
INHERIT THE WIND United Artists, 1960
JUDGMENT AT NUREMBERG ★ United Artists, 1961
A CHILD IS WAITING United Artists, 1962
IT'S A MAD, MAD, MAD, MAD WORLD United Artists, 1963
SHIP OF FOOLS ★ Columbia, 1965
GUESS WHO'S COMING TO DINNER ★ Columbia, 1967
THE SECRET OF SANTA VITTORIA United Artists, 1969
R.P.M. Columbia, 1970
BLESS THE BEASTS AND CHILDREN Columbia, 1971
OKLAHOMA CRUDE Columbia, 1973
THE DOMINO PRINCIPLE Avco Embassy, 1977
THE RUNNER STUMBLES 20th Century-Fox, 1979

JONATHAN D. KRANE

Business: M.C.E.G. International, 2400 Broadway, Suite 100, Santa Monica, CA, 90404, 213/315-7800

TRAIL OF THE PINK PANTHER MGM/UA, 1982, EP
CURSE OF THE PINK PANTHER MGM/UA, 1983, EP
THE MAN WHO LOVED WOMEN Columbia, 1983, EP
MICKI AND MAUDE Columbia, 1984, EP w/Lou Antonio
A FINE MESS Columbia, 1986, EP
THAT'S LIFE! Columbia, 1986, EP
BLIND DATE Tri-Star, 1987, EP w/Gary Hendler & David Permut
SLIPPING INTO DARKNESS MCEG, 1988
THE CHOCOLATE WAR MCEG, 1988
YOU CAN'T HURRY LOVE MCEG, 1988, w/Lawrence Kasanoff & Ellen Steloff
C.H.U.D. II Vestron, 1988
GETTING IT RIGHT MCEG, 1989, w/Randal Kleiser
THE EXPERTS Paramount, 1989, EP w/Jack Grossberg
LOOK WHO'S TALKING Tri-Star, 1989

STEVE KRANTZ

FRITZ THE CAT (AF) American International, 1972
HEAVY TRAFFIC (AF) American International, 1973
THE NINE LIVES OF FRITZ THE CAT (AF) American International, 1974

DONALD KRANZE

Contact: Directors Guild of America - Los Angeles, 213/289-2000

THE PURSUIT OF D. B. COOPER Universal, 1981, EP w/William Tennant
NIGHT SHIFT The Ladd Company/Warner Bros., 1982, EP

ROBERT KRAUSE

THE CHECK IS IN THE MAIL Ascot Entertainment, 1986, w/Robert Kaufman

DAVID KREBS

BEATLEMANIA American Cinema, 1981, w/Edie Landau, Ely Landau & Steven Leber

HOWARD B. KREITSEK

Contact: Writers Guild of America - Los Angeles, 213/550-1000

THE ILLUSTRATED MAN Warner Bros., 1969, w/Ted Mann

BRAD KREVOY

(credit w/Steven Stabler)

Business: Motion Picture Corporation of America, 3000 Olympic Blvd., Suite 2407, Santa Monica, CA, 90404, 213/315-4705

SWEET REVENGE Concorde, 1987
DANGEROUS LOVE Concorde, 1988
PURPLE PEOPLE EATER Concorde, 1988
MEMORIAL VALLEY MASSACRE Nelson Entertainment, 1989
MINISTRY OF VENGEANCE Motion Picture Corp. of America, 1989

MARTY KROFFT

Business: Sid and Marty Krofft Picture Corporation, 1040 N. Las Palmas Ave., Hollywood, CA, 90038, 213/467-3125

HARRY TRACY Quartet/Films, 1983, EP w/Sid Krofft & Albert J. Tenser

SID KROFFT

Business: Sid and Marty Krofft Picture Corporation, 1040 N. Las Palmas Ave., Hollywood, CA, 90038, 213/467-3125

HARRY TRACY Quartet/Films, 1983, EP w/Marty Krofft & Albert J. Tenser

LEONARD KROLL

Contact: Directors Guild of America - Los Angeles, 213/289-2000

POLICE ACADEMY 2: THEIR FIRST ASSIGNMENT Warner Bros., 1985, CP
WALK LIKE A MAN MGM/UA, 1987
FATAL BEAUTY MGM, 1987

SCOTT KROOPF
Business: Interscope Communications,10900 Wilshire Blvd., Suite 1400, Los Angeles, CA, 90024, 213/208-8525

OUTRAGEOUS FORTUNE Buena Vista, 1987, CP w/Peter V. Herald & Martin Mickelson
NO MAN'S LAND Orion, 1987, AP
BILL & TED'S EXCELLENT ADVENTURE Orion, 1989, w/Michael S. Murphey & Joel Soisson
AN INNOCENT MAN Buena Vista, 1989, EP

BARRY KROST
Business: Krost/Chapin Productions, 4000 Warner Blvd., Burbank, CA, 91522, 818/954-6526

WHEN A STRANGER CALLS Columbia, 1979, EP w/Melvin Simon
PANDEMONIUM MGM/UA, 1982, EP
AMERICAN DREAMER Warner Bros., 1984, EP
UFORIA Universal, 1985, EP w/Melvin Simon

ROY KROST
MARTIN'S DAY MGM/UA, 1985, w/Richard Dalton
TOO OUTRAGEOUS! Spectrafilm, 1987

LAWRENCE KUBIK
Business: The Kubik Company - Los Angeles, 213/859-9777
Contact: Writers Guild of America - Los Angeles, 213/550-1000

ZACHARIAH Cinerama, 1970, CP
DEATH BEFORE DISHONOR New World, 1987

STANLEY KUBRICK
Attorney: Louis C. Blau, Loeb & Loeb, 10100 Santa Monica Blvd., Los Angeles, CA, 90067, 213/552-7774
Contact: Directors Guild of America - Los Angeles, 213/656-1220

DR. STRANGELOVE OR: HOW I LEARNED TO STOP WORRYING & LOVE THE BOMB ★ Columbia, 1964
2001: A SPACE ODYSSEY MGM, 1968
A CLOCKWORK ORANGE ★ Warner Bros., 1971
BARRY LYNDON ★ Warner Bros., 1975
THE SHINING Warner Bros., 1980
FULL METAL JACKET Warner Bros., 1987

ANDREW J. KUEHN
Business: Kaleidoscope Films Ltd., 844 N. Seward St., Hollywood, CA, 90038, 213/465-1151
Contact: Directors Guild of America - Los Angeles, 213/289-2000

TERROR IN THE AISLES Universal, 1984, w/Stephen J. Netburn
D.O.A. Buena Vista, 1988, CP w/Cathleen Summers

MICHAEL KUHN
(credit w/Nigel Sinclair)
Business: Propaganda Films, 940 N. Mansfield Ave., Los Angeles, CA, 213/462-6400

THE BLUE IGUANA Paramount, 1988
FEAR, ANXIETY, AND DEPRESSION Samuel Goldwyn Company, 1989, EP
KILL ME AGAIN MGM/UA, 1989, EP

TOM KUHN
(credit w/Charles Mitchell)
Business: Lightyear Entertainment, 350 5th Ave., Suite 5101, New York, NY, 10118,

HEAVEN (FD) Island Pictures, 1987, EP w/Arlyne Rothberg
ARIA Miramax, 1988, EP
THE RETURN OF SWAMP THING Miramax, 1989, EP
THE LEMON SISTERS Miramax, 1990, EP, w/Arnold J. Holland

DARRYL J. KUNTZ
(credit w/Frank J. Kuntz)

DAKOTA Miramax, 1988

FRANK J. KUNTZ
(credit w/Darryl J. Kuntz)

DAKOTA Miramax, 1988

GARY KURFIRST
Business: 1775 Broadway, 7th Floor, New York, NY, 10019, 212/957-0900

STOP MAKING SENSE (FD) Cinecom, 1984, EP
TRUE STORIES Warner Bros., 1986
SIESTA Lorimar, 1987

JOHN A. KURI
Business: Sheffield Entertainment Corporation, 16133 Ventura Blvd., Suite 700, Encino, CA, 91436, 818/501-8471
Contact: Directors Guild of America - Los Angeles, 213/289-2000

CAPTIVE HEARTS MGM/UA, 1987

PAUL KURTA
Contact: Directors Guild of America - New York, 212/581-0370

Q UFD, 1982, AP
PERFECT STRANGERS New Line Cinema, 1984
SPECIAL EFFECTS New Line Cinema, 1984
THE STUFF New World, 1985
KEY EXCHANGE 20th Century-Fox, 1985
RETURN TO SALEM'S LOT Warner Bros., 1987
MILES FROM HOME Cinecom, 1988, w/Frederick Zollo
HEART OF DIXIE Orion, 1989, CP

GARY KURTZ
Business: Winmill Entertainment, 9336 W. Washington Blvd., Culver City, CA, 90232, 213/202-3308

AMERICAN GRAFFITI ★ Universal, 1973, CP
STAR WARS ★ 20th Century-Fox, 1977
THE EMPIRE STRIKES BACK 20th Century- Fox, 1980
THE DARK CRYSTAL Universal/AFD, 1982, w/Jim Henson
RETURN TO OZ Buena Vista, 1985, EP
SLIPSTREAM Entertainment Films, 1989

KIM KURUMADA

Contact: Directors Guild of America - Los Angeles, 213/289-2000

MIKE'S MURDER Warner Bros., 1984, EP
PERFECT Columbia, 1985, EP
MOVING Warner Bros., 1988, AP

DONALD KUSHNER

(credit w/Peter Locke)

Business: The Kushner-Locke Company, 10850 Wilshire Blvd., 9th Floor, Los Angeles, CA; 90024, 213/470-0400

TRON Buena Vista, 1982*
NUTCRACKER Atlantic Entertainment, 1986, w/Willard Carroll & Thomas L. Wilhite
POUND PUPPIES & THE LEGEND OF BIG PAW (AF) Tri-Star, 1988

KAZ KUZUI

Business: Kuzui Enterprises, 220 Fifth Ave., New York, NY, 10001, 212/683-9198

TOKYO POP Spectrafilm, 1988, w/Joel Tuber

L

ALAN LADD, JR.

Business: Pathe International, 8670 Wilshire Blvd., Beverly Hills, CA, 90211, 213/967-2225

THE WALKING STICK MGM, 1969
VILLAIN MGM, 1971, w/Jay Kanter
X, Y, & ZEE Columbia, 1971, w/Jay Kanter
FEAR IS THE KEY Paramount, 1972, w/Jay Kanter
VICE VERSA Columbia, 1988, EP

DAVID LADD

Business: Pathe International, 8670 Wilshire Blvd., Beverly Hills, CA, 90211, 213/967-2225

THE SERPENT AND THE RAINBOW Universal, 1988, w/Doug Claybourne

IAN LaFRENAIS

Agent: Elliot Webb, Broder-Kurland-Webb-Uffner Agency - Los Angeles, 213/656-9262
Contact: Writers Guild of America - Los Angeles, 213/550-1000

BULLSHOT Island Alive, 1985
WATER Atlantic Entertainment, 1986
VICE VERSA Columbia, 1988, w/Dick Clement

TOVA LAITER

Business: Imagine Entertainment, 1925 Century Park East, 23rd Floor, Los Angeles, CA, 90067, 213/277-1665

ONE MORE SATURDAY NIGHT Columbia, 1986, w/Jonathan Bernstein & Robert Kosberg
FIRE WITH FIRE Paramount, 1986, EP

CHARLES M. LaLOGGIA

Business: LaLoggia Productions - Los Angeles, 213/462-3055

FEAR NO EVIL Avco Embassy, 1981, w/Frank LaLoggia
THE LADY IN WHITE New Century/Vista, 1988, EP w/Cliff Payne

FRANK LaLOGGIA

Business: LaLoggia Productions - Los Angeles, 213/462-3055

FEAR NO EVIL Avco Embassy, 1981, w/Charles M. LaLoggia
THE LADY IN WHITE New Century/Vista, 1988, w/Andrew G. La Marca

ANDREW G. LaMARCA

THE LADY IN WHITE New Century/Vista, 1988, w/Frank LaLoggia

VERITY LAMBERT

Agent: ICM - Los Angeles, 213/550-4000

DREAMCHILD Universal, 1985, EP w/Dennis Potter
MORONS FROM OUTER SPACE Universal, 1985, EP
CLOCKWISE Universal, 1986, EP w/Nat Cohen
LINK Cannon, 1986, EP
A CRY IN THE DARK Warner Bros., 1988

ALANA H. LAMBROS

TEEN WITCH Trans World Entertainment, 1989, w/Rafael Eisenman

HUGO LAMONICA

THE STRANGER Columbia, 1987

CAROL LAMPMAN

STEPFATHER II Millimeter Films, 1989, EP

DAVID LANCASTER

Business: 3356 Bennett Dr., Los Angeles, CA, 90068, 213/874-1415

'NIGHT, MOTHER Universal, 1986, EP w/Dann Byck

JOANNA LANCASTER

(credit w/Richard Wagner)

LITTLE TREASURE Tri-Star, 1985, EP
RUTHLESS PEOPLE Buena Vista, 1986, EP w/Walter Yetnikoff

EDIE LANDAU

(credit w/Ely Landau)

Business: Edie & Ely Landau, Inc., 8863 Alcott St., #1, Los Angeles, CA, 90035, 213/274-9993

HOPSCOTCH Avco Embassy, 1980
BEATLEMANIA American Cinema, 1981, w/David Krebs & Steven Leber
THE CHOSEN 20th Century-Fox International Classics, 1982
THE HOLCROFT COVENANT Universal, 1985

ELY LANDAU

Business: Edie & Ely Landau, Inc., 8863 Alcott St., #1, Los Angeles, CA, 90035, 213/274-9993

LONG DAY'S JOURNEY INTO NIGHT Embassy, 1962, EP
THE PAWNBROKER Allied Artists, 1965, w/Herbert R. Steinman
THE MADWOMAN OF CHAILLOT Warner Bros., 1969
KING: A FILMED RECORD...MONTGOMERY TO MEMPHIS (FD) Maron, 1969
A DELICATE BALANCE American Film Theatre, 1973
THE ICEMAN COMETH American Film Theatre, 1973
THE HOMECOMING American Film Theatre, 1973
BUTLEY American Film Theatre, 1974
LUTHER American Film Theatre, 1974
RHINOCEROS American Film Theatre, 1974
LOST IN THE STARS American Film Theatre, 1974
IN CELEBRATION American Film Theatre, 1975
GALILEO American Film Theatre, 1975
THE MAN IN THE GLASS BOOTH American Film Theatre, 1975
THE GREEK TYCOON Universal, 1978, w/Allen Klein
HOPSCOTCH Avco Embassy, 1980, w/Edie Landau
BEATLEMANIA American Cinema, 1981, w/David Krebs, Edie Landau & Steven Leber
THE CHOSEN 20th Century-Fox International Classics, 1982, w/Edie Landau
THE HOLCROFT COVENANT Universal, 1985, w/Edie Landau

JON LANDAU

Contact: Directors Guild of America - Los Angeles, 213/289-2000

CAMPUS MAN Paramount, 1987, w/Peggy Fowler

HAL LANDERS

(credit w/Bobby Roberts)

THE GYPSY MOTHS MGM, 1969
THE BANK SHOT United Artists, 1974
DEATH WISH Paramount, 1974
DEATH WISH II Filmways, 1982, EP

MICHAEL S. LANDES

(credit w/Albert Schwartz)

Business: The Almi Group, 1900 Broadway, New York, NY, 10023, 212/769-6400

THE BIG SCORE Almi, 1983
I AM THE CHEESE Almi, 1983, EP w/Jack Schwartzman
THE BOSTONIANS Almi, 1984, EP

JOHN LANDIS

Agent: CAA - Beverly Hills, 213/288-4545
Contact: Directors Guild of America - Los Angeles, 213/289-2000

TWILIGHT ZONE — THE MOVIE Warner Bros., 1983, w/Steven Spielberg
CLUE Paramount, 1985, EP w/George Folsey Jr., Peter Guber & Jon Peters
AMAZON WOMEN ON THE MOON Universal, 1987, EP w/George Folsey Jr.

ALAN LANDSBURG

Business: The Landsburg Company, 11811 W. Olympic Blvd., Los Angeles, CA, 90064, 213/478-7878
Contact: Directors Guild of America - Los Angeles, 213/289-2000

JAWS 3-D Universal, 1983, EP w/Howard Lipstone
PORKY'S II: THE NEXT DAY 20th Century-Fox, 1983, EP w/Harold Greenberg & Melvin Simon

ANDREW LANE

(credit w/Wayne Crawford)

Business: Crawford-Lane Productions, 14101 Valleyheart Dr., #205, Sherman Oaks, CA, 91423, 818/501-2076
Agent: The Richland-Wunsch Agency - Los Angeles, 213/278-1955

VALLEY GIRL Atlantic Entertainment, 1983
NIGHT OF THE COMET Atlantic Entertainment, 1984
JAKE SPEED New World, 1986, w/William Fay
MORTAL PASSIONS MGM/UA, 1990, EP w/Joel Levine

CHARLES LANE

SIDEWALK STORIES Island Pictures, 1989

STEVEN LANE

THE HOWLING Avco Embassy, 1980, EP w/Daniel H. Blatt
HOWLING II...YOUR SISTER IS A WEREWOLF Thorn EMI, 1986
HOWLING III: THE MARSUPIALS Square Pictures, 1987, EP w/Robert Pringle & Edward Simons
HOWLING IV...THE ORIGINAL NIGHTMARE Allied Entertainment, 1988, EP w/Avi Lerner, Robert Pringle & Edward Simons

JENNINGS LANG

SLAUGHTERHOUSE-FIVE Universal, 1972, EP
PETE 'N' TILLIE Universal, 1972, EP
HIGH PLAINS DRIFTER Universal, 1973, EP
THE GREAT NORTHFIELD, MINNESOTA RAID Universal, 1972
CHARLEY VARRICK Universal, 1973, EP
BREEZY Universal, 1973, EP
AIRPORT '75 Universal, 1974, EP
THE FRONT PAGE Universal, 1974, EP
SWASHBUCKLER Universal, 1976
ROLLERCOASTER Universal, 1977
AIRPORT '77 Universal, 1977, EP
NUNZIO Universal, 1978
HOUSE CALLS Universal, 1978, EP
THE CONCORDE — AIRPORT '79 Universal, 1979, EP
LITTLE MISS MARKER Universal, 1980
THE STING II Universal, 1983
STICK Universal, 1985

DAVID LANGE

I AM THE CHEESE Almi, 1983

JESSICA LANGE

Business: Prairie Films, Orion Pictures, 1888 Century Park East, Los Angeles, CA, 90067, 213/282-2975
Agent: CAA - Beverly Hills, 213/288-4545

COUNTRY Buena Vista, 1984, w/William D. Wittliff

STEVE LANNING

SLIPSTREAM Entertainment Films, 1989, CP

SHERRY LANSING

(credit w/Stanley R. Jaffe)

Business: Jaffe-Lansing Productions, 5555 Melrose Avenue, Los Angeles, CA, 90038, 213/468-4575

RACING WITH THE MOON Paramount, 1984, EP
FIRSTBORN Paramount, 1984, EP
FATAL ATTRACTION ★ Paramount, 1987
THE ACCUSED Paramount, 1988
BLACK RAIN Paramount, 1989

ROBERT LANTOS

(credit w/Stephen J. Roth)

Business: Alliance Entertainment Corporation, 8439 Sunset Blvd., #404, Los Angeles, CA, 90069, 213/654-9488; 920 Yonge Street, Suite 400, Toronto, Ontario, M4W 3C7, Canada, 416/967-1174

IN PRAISE OF OLDER WOMEN Avco Embassy, 1979, w/Claude Héroux*
SUZANNE RSL/Ambassador, 1980*
AGENCY Jensen Farley, 1981
PARADISE Embassy, 1982
HEAVENLY BODIES MGM/UA, 1985
JOSHUA THEN & NOW 20th Century-Fox, 1985
SEPARATE VACATIONS RSK Entertainment, 1986
BEDROOM EYES Aquarius Releasing, 1986

ROGER LaPAGE

Contact: Directors Guild of America - Los Angeles, 213/289-2000

HAMBONE & HILLIE New World, 1984, CP

ARTHUR LAPPIN

MY LEFT FOOT ★ Miramax, 1989, LP

JACK LARSON

MIKE'S MURDER Warner Bros., 1984, AP
PERFECT Columbia, 1985, CP

ROBERT LARSON

Business: Bob Larson Productions, Universal Studios, 100 Universal City Plaza, Universal City, CA, 91608, 818/777-6360

PLAY MISTY FOR ME Universal, 1971, AP
FM Universal, 1978, CP
COAL MINER'S DAUGHTER Universal, 1980, EP
CONTINENTAL DIVIDE Universal, 1981
GORKY PARK Orion, 1983, EP
THE RIVER RAT Paramount, 1984
CRITICAL CONDITION Paramount, 1987, EP
FLETCH LIVES Universal, 1989, EP w/Bruce Bodner

LAWRENCE LASKER

(credit w/Walter F. Parkes)

Business: Paramount Pictures, 5555 Melrose Ave., Los Angeles, CA, 90038, 213/468-5000
Agent: InterTalent Agency, Inc. - Los Angeles, 213/271-0600

PROJECT X 20th Century-Fox, 1987
TRUE BELIEVER Columbia, 1989
AWAKENINGS Columbia, 1990

GENE LASKO

Contact: Directors Guild of America - New York, 212/581-0370

FOUR FRIENDS Filmways, 1981, w/Arthur Penn

MICHAEL S. LAUGHLIN

THE WHISPERERS United Artists, 1967, w/Ronald Shedlo
TWO-LANE BLACKTOP Universal, 1971
DUSTY AND SWEETS McGEE Warner Bros., 1971

DALE LAUNER

Business: 20th Century Fox, 10201 W. Pico Blvd., Bldg. 1, Suite 146, Los Angeles, CA, 90035, 213/203-2081
Contact: Writers Guild of America - Los Angeles, 213/550-1000

DIRTY ROTTEN SCOUNDRELS Orion, 1988, EP w/Charles Hirschhorn

ROBERT G. LAUREL

THE ROSARY MURDERS New Line Cinema, 1987

ARTHUR LAURENTS

Contact: Writers Guild of America - Los Angeles, 213/550-1000

THE TURNING POINT ★ 20th Century-Fox, 1977, w/Herbert Ross

SCOTT LAVIN

RETRIBUTION Taurus Entertainment, 1988, EP w/Brian Christian

LINDSAY LAW

Business: American Playhouse, 1776 Broadway, 9th Floor, New York, NY, 10019, 212/757-4300

SMOOTH TALK Spectrafilm, 1985, EP
BILLY GALVIN Vestron, 1986, EP w/Howard L. Baldwin, Stuart Benjamin & William Minot
NATIVE SON Cinecom, 1986, EP
ON VALENTINE'S DAY Angelika, 1986, EP w/Lewis Allen, Ross E. Milloy, & Peter Newman
STACKING Spectrafilm, 1987, EP
WAITING FOR THE MOON Skouras Pictures, 1987, EP
IN A SHALLOW GRAVE Skouras Pictures, 1988, EP w/Marilyn G. Haft
STAND & DELIVER Warner Bros., 1988, EP
THE WIZARD OF LONELINESS Skouras Pictures, 1988, EP
THE THIN BLUE LINE (FD) Miramax, 1988, EP
THE WASH Skouras Pictures, 1988, EP
RACHEL RIVER Taurus, 1989, EP
EAT A BOWL OF TEA Columbia, 1989, EP w/John K. Chan
SIGNS OF LIFE Avenue, 1989, EP w/Cary Brokaw
BLOODHOUNDS OF BROADWAY Columbia, 1989, EP
LONGTIME COMPANION Samuel Goldwyn Company, 1990, EP

MEL LAWRENCE

POWAQQATSI (FD) Cannon, 1988, w/Godfrey Reggio & Lawrence Taub

ROBERT LAWRENCE
Business: Imagine Entertainment, 1925 Century Park East, 23rd Floor, Los Angeles, CA, 90067, 213/277-1665

IT TAKES TWO United Artists, 1988

JOE LAYTON
Business: Radio City Music Hall Productions, 1260 Avenue of the Americas, New York, NY,10020, 212/632-4000
Personal Manager: Roy Gerber Associates, 9200 Sunset Blvd., Suite 620, Los Angeles, CA, 90069, 213/550-0100

ANNIE Columba, 1982, EP

IRVING PAUL LAZAR
Business: 211 S. Beverly Dr., Beverly Hills, CA, 90212, 213/275-6153; One East 66th St., New York, NY, 10021, 212/355-1177

NEIGHBORS Columbia, 1981, EP w/Bernie Brillstein

PAUL N. LAZARUS III
HANOVER STREET Columbia, 1979
BARBAROSA Universal/AFD, 1982

DAVID LAZER
Business: Henson Associates, c/o Walt Disney Studios, 500 S. Buena Vista St., Burbank, CA, 91521, 818/560-1000

THE GREAT MUPPET CAPER Universal/AFD, 1981, w/Frank Oz
THE DARK CRYSTAL Universal/AFD, 1982, EP
THE MUPPETS TAKE MANHATTAN Tri-Star, 1984
LABYRINTH Tri-Star, 1986, SP

LARRY LEAHY
THE LAWLESS LAND Concorde, 1988, w/ Tony Cinciripini

NORMAN LEAR
Business: Act III Communications, 1800 Century Park East, Suite 200, Los Angeles, CA, 90067, 213/553-3636

COME BLOW YOUR HORN Paramount, 1963, w/Bud Yorkin
NEVER TOO LATE Warner Bros., 1965
DIVORCE AMERICAN STYLE Columbia, 1967
THE NIGHT THEY RAIDED MINSKY'S United Artists, 1968
START THE REVOLUTION WITHOUT ME Warner Bros., 1970, EP
COLD TURKEY United Artists, 1971
THE PRINCESS BRIDE 20th Century-Fox, 1987, EP

VICKI LEBENBAUM
SIDEWALK STORIES Island Pictures, 1989, EP w/Howard M. Brickner

STEVEN LEBER
BEATLEMANIA American Cinema, 1981, w/David Krebs, Edie Landau & Ely Landau

LARRY J. LEBOW
CAGE New Century/Vista, 1989, EP

ROBERT S. LECKY
TAPEHEADS Avenue, 1988, CP
KEYS TO FREEDOM RPB Pictures/Queens Cross Productions, 1989, w/Stuart Rose

RICHARD LEDERER
EXORCIST II: THE HERETIC Warner Bros., 1977, w/John Boorman

PATRICE LEDOUX
THE BIG BLUE WEG/Columbia, 1988, EP

DAMIAN LEE
(credit w/David Mitchell)
Business: Rose & Ruby Productions, Inc., 33 Howard St., Toronto, Ontario M4X 1J6, Canada, 416/961-0555

BUSTED UP Shapiro Entertainment, 1987
WATCHERS Tri-Star, 1988
FOOD OF THE GODS II Concorde, 1989

SPIKE LEE
Business: 40 Acres & A Mule Filmworks, 124 DeKalb Ave., Brooklyn, NY, 11217, 718/624-3703

JOE'S BED-STUY BARBERSHOP: WE CUT HEADS First Run Features, 1983
SHE'S GOTTA HAVE IT Island Pictures, 1986
SCHOOL DAZE Columbia, 1988
DO THE RIGHT THING Universal, 1989
MO' BETTER BLUES Universal, 1990, w/Jon Kilik & Monty Ross

VIVIENNE LEEBOSH
TICKET TO HEAVEN United Artists Classics, 1981
SPEED ZONE Orion, 1989, CP

TOM LEETCH
Contact: Directors Guild of America - Los Angeles, 213/289-2000

THE NORTH AVENUE IRREGULARS Buena Vista, 1979, CP
THE APPLE DUMPLING GANG RIDES AGAIN Buena Vista, 1979, CP
THE WATCHER IN THE WOODS Buena Vista, 1980, CP
NIGHT CROSSING Buena Vista, 1982

ERNEST LEHMAN
Business Manager: Henry J. Bamberger, 2049 Century Park East, Los Angeles, CA, 90067, 213/553-0581
Agent: The Gersh Agency - Beverly Hills, 213/274-6611

WHO'S AFRAID OF VIRGINIA WOOLF? ★ Warner Bros., 1966
HELLO, DOLLY! ★ 20th Century-Fox, 1969
PORTNOY'S COMPLAINT Warner Bros., 1972

ARNOLD LEIBOVIT
Business: Talking Rings Entertainment, P.O. Box 2019, Beverly Hills, CA, 90213, 213/306-1909

THE PUPPETOON MOVIE Expanded Entertainment, 1987

LEO LEICHTER

THE BIKINI SHOP *THE MALIBU BIKINI SHOP* International Film Marketing, 1987, CP

JERRY LEIDER

Business: Fred Silverman Company, 12400 Wilshire Blvd., Suite 920, Los Angeles, CA, 90025, 213/826-6050

TRENCHCOAT Buena Vista, 1983

MATT LEIPZIG

Business: Columbia Pictures, Studio Plaza, 3400 Riverside Dr., Burbank, CA, 91505, 818/954-4212

BIG BAD MAMA II Concorde, 1987, AP
STRIPPED TO KILL Concorde, 1987, w/Mark Byers & Andy Ruben
THE DRIFTER Concorde, 1988, CP

DOUGLAS LEITERMAN

MILLENNIUM 20th Century-Fox, 1989

RUSTY LEMORANDE

Contact: Directors Guild of America - Los Angeles, 213/289-2000

YENTL MGM/UA, 1983, CP
ELECTRIC DREAMS MGM/UA, 1984, w/Larry De Waay
GETTING IT RIGHT MCEG, 1989, EP

JOHN THOMAS LENOX

Agent: The Agency - Los Angeles, 213/551-3000
Contact: Directors Guild of America - Los Angeles, 213/289-2000

SPLASH Buena Vista, 1984, EP

MALCOLM LEO

Business: Malcolm Leo Productions, 6536 Sunset Blvd., Hollywood, CA, 90028, 213/464-4448
Agent: Michael Peretzian, William Morris Agency - Beverly Hills, 213/274-7451

THIS IS ELVIS (FD) Warner Bros., 1981, w/Andrew Solt

MICHAEL C. LEONE

THE GREAT SMOKEY ROADBLOCK *THE LAST OF THE COWBOYS* Dimension, 1978, EP
A DIFFERENT STORY Avco Embassy, 1978, EP
GO TELL THE SPARTANS Avco Embassy, 1978, EP
GOOD GUYS WEAR BLACK American Cinema, 1978, EP
THE LATE GREAT PLANET EARTH Amram, 1979, EP
A FORCE OF ONE American Cinema, 1980, EP
THE OCTAGON American Cinema, 1980, EP w/Alan Belkin
CHARLIE CHAN AND THE CURSE OF THE DRAGON QUEEN American Cinema, 1981, EP w/Alan Belkin
I, THE JURY 20th Century-Fox, 1982, EP w/Andrew D.T. Pfeffer
THE ENTITY 20th Century-Fox, 1983, EP w/Andrew D.T. Pfeffer
TOUGH ENOUGH 20th Century-Fox, 1983, w/Andrew D.T. Pfeffer

STRATTON LEOPOLD

Contact: Directors Guild of America - Los Angeles, 213/289-2000

THE ADVENTURES OF BARON MUNCHAUSEN Columbia, 1989, SP

JEAN FRANCOIS LEPETIT

THREE MEN AND A CRADLE Samuel Goldwyn Company, 1986
THREE MEN AND A BABY Buena Vista, 1987, EP

OSCAR S. LERMAN

YESTERDAY'S HERO EMI, 1979, w/Ken Regan

AVI LERNER

AMERICAN NINJA 2 Cannon, 1987, EP
DRAGONARD Cannon, 1987, EP
ALLAN QUATERMAIN AND THE LOST CITY OF GOLD Cannon, 1987, EP
OUTLAW OF GOR Cannon, 1988, w/Harry Alan Towers
HOWLING IV...THE ORIGINAL NIGHTMARE Allied Entertainment, 1988, EP w/Steven Lane, Robert Pringle & Edward Simons
ALIEN FROM L.A. Cannon, 1988, EP
AMERICAN NINJA 3: BLOOD HUNT Cannon, 1989, EP
RIVER OF DEATH Cannon, 1989, w/Harry Alan Towers
TEN LITTLE INDIANS Cannon, 1989, EP
JOURNEY TO THE CENTER OF THE EARTH Cannon, 1989, EP w/Adam Fields & Tom Udell

DAVID V. LESTER

Contact: Directors Guild of America - Los Angeles, 213/289-2000

BULL DURHAM Orion, 1988, EP
BLAZE Buena Vista, 1989, EP w/Don Miller
LORD OF THE FLIES Columbia, 1990, CP

MARK LESTER

Agent: The Chasin Agency - Beverly Hills, 213/278-7805
Contact: Directors Guild of America - Los Angeles, 213/289-2000

THE FUNHOUSE Universal, 1981, EP w/Mace Neufeld
CLASS OFF 1999 Taurus, 1990

RICHARD LESTER

Business: Twickenham Film Studios, St. Margarets, Middlesex, England
Agent: CAA - Beverly Hills, 213/288-4545

HOW I WON THE WAR United Artists, 1967
THE BED-SITTING ROOM United Artists, 1969, w/ Oscar Lewenstein
FINDERS KEEPERS Warner Bros., 1984, EP

ROBERT LeTET

DOGS IN SPACE Skouras Pictures, 1987, EP w/Dennis Wright

MICHAEL LEVEE

CASEY'S SHADOW Columbia, 1978, EP

HAROLD LEVENTHAL

BOUND FOR GLORY ★ United Artists, 1976, w/Robert F. Blumofe

JAMES B. LEVERT, JR.
BELIZAIRE THE CAJUN Skouras Pictures, 1986, EP

DON LEVIN
(credit w/Mel Pearl)

LOVE LETTERS New World, 1983, EP
HAMBONE AND HILLIE New World, 1984, EP
THE BOYS NEXT DOOR New World, 1985, EP
MAXIMUM OVERDRIVE DEG, 1986, EP
THE SUPERNATURALS Republic Entertainment, 1987, EP
TWO MOON JUNCTION Lorimar, 1988, EP
ANGEL III: THE FINAL CHAPTER New World, 1988, EP

IRVING H. LEVIN
TO LIVE AND DIE IN L.A. New Century, 1985

LLOYD LEVIN
Business: Largo Entertainment, c/o 20th Century- Fox, 10201 W. Pico Blvd., Los Angeles, CA, 90035, 213/203-1715

DIE HARD 2 20th Century-Fox, 1990, EP w/Michael Levy

STEPHEN J. LEVIN
ALMOST YOU 20th Century-Fox, 1984, EP w/Sandy Climan & Charles C. Thieriot

SY LEVIN
FLOWERS IN THE ATTIC New World, 1987, w/Thomas Fries

JOEL LEVINE
HEADHUNTER Academy Entertainment, 1989, EP
MORTAL PASSIONS MGM/UA, 1990, EP w/Wayne Crawford & Andrew Lane

RICHARD P. LEVINE
Business: Joseph E. Levine Presents, Inc., 375 Park Ave., New York, NY, 10152, 212/826-0370

MAGIC 20th Century-Fox, 1978, w/Joseph E. Levine
TATTOO 20th Century-Fox, 1981, w/Joseph E. Levine

ROBERT F. LEVINE
THAT CHAMPIONSHIP SEASON Cannon, 1982, EP

ART LEVINSON
Agent: The Gersh Agency - Beverly Hills, 213/274-6611
Contact: Directors Guild of America - Los Angeles, 213/289-2000

MY FAVORITE YEAR MGM/UA, 1982, AP
MR. MOM 20th Century-Fox, 1983, AP
RACING WITH THE MOON Paramount, 1984, AP
THE MONEY PIT Universal, 1986, w/Kathleen Kennedy & Frank Marshall
MANNEQUIN 20th Century-Fox, 1987
LITTLE NIKITA Columbia, 1988, CP
MY STEPMOTHER IS AN ALIEN WEG/Columbia, 1988, EP w/Laurence Mark

MARK LEVINSON
(credit w/Scott Rosenfelt)
Business: Levinson-Rosenfelt Productions, 10203 Santa Monica Blvd., Los Angeles, CA, 90067, 213/284-9296
Agent: Lawrence A. Mirisch, Triad Artists, Inc. - Los Angeles, 213/556-2727

WALTZ ACROSS TEXAS Atlantic Entertainment, 1983, AP*
ROADHOUSE 66 Atlantic Entertainment, 1984
TEEN WOLF Atlantic Entertainment, 1985
REMOTE CONTROL New Century/Vista, 1988
STRANDED New Line Cinema, 1987
RUSSKIES New Century/Vista, 1987
MYSTIC PIZZA Samuel Goldwyn Company, 1988
BIG MAN ON CAMPUS Vestron, 1989, CP

ZANE W. LEVITT
Business: Zeta Entertainment, Ltd., 6565 Sunset Blvd., #321, Hollywood, CA, 90028, 213/461-7332

OUT OF THE DARK CineTel Films, 1989

ARIEL LEVY
Agent: The Agency - Los Angeles, 213/551-3000
Contact: Directors Guild of America - Los Angeles, 213/289-2000

HYPER SAPIEN Tri-Star, 1986, CP

FRANKLIN R. LEVY
Business: Catalina Production Group, 3500 W. Olive, Suite 500, Burbank, CA, 91505, 818/953-4140

NIGHTHAWKS Universal, 1981, EP w/Michael Wise
MY STEPMOTHER IS AN ALIEN WEG/Columbia, 1988, w/Ronald Parker

GENE LEVY
Contact: Directors Guild of America - Los Angeles, 213/289-2000

HYSTERICAL Embassy, 1983
STREETS OF FIRE Universal, 1984, EP
BREWSTER'S MILLIONS Universal, 1985, EP

MICHAEL LEVY
Business: Silver Pictures, 4000 Warner Blvd., Burbank, CA, 91522, 818/954-4490

FORD FAIRLANE 20th Century-Fox, 1990, EP
DIE HARD 2 20th Century-Fox, 1990, EP w/ Lloyd Levin

MICHAEL I. LEVY
Business: The Gruskoff-Levy Company, 8737 Clifton Way, Beverly Hills, CA, 90211, 213/550-7302

GOTCHA! Universal, 1985, EP
GARDENS OF STONE Tri-Star, 1987, w/Francis Ford Coppola
MASQUERADE MGM/UA, 1988

ROBERT L. LEVY
SMOKEY & THE BANDIT Universal, 1977, EP
RAD Tri-Star, 1986
THE KILLING TIME New World, 1987, w/Peter Abrams

SANDRA LEVY
HIGH TIDE Tri-Star, 1987

OSCAR LEWENSTEIN
THE KNACK - AND HOW TO GET IT United Artists, 1965
THE BED-SITTING ROOM United Artists, 1969, w/Richard Lester
RITA, SUE & BOB TOO! Orion Classics, 1987, EP

EDWARD LEWIS
SPARTACUS Universal, 1960
THE LAST SUNSET Universal, 1961, w/Eugene Frenke
THE LIST OF ADRIAN MESSENGER Universal, 1963
SECONDS Paramount, 1966
THE EXTRAORDINARY SEAMAN MGM, 1968
THE GYPSY MOTHS MGM, 1969, EP
I WALK THE LINE Columbia, 1970, EP
THE HORSEMAN Columbia, 1971
THE ICEMAN COMETH American Film Theatre, 1973, EP
EXECUTIVE ACTION National General, 1973
LOST IN THE STARS American Film Theatre, 1974, EP
RHINOCEROS American Film Theatre, 1974, EP
THE BLUE BIRD 20th Century-Fox, 1976, EP
BROTHERS Warner Bros., 1977, w/Mildred Lewis
MISSING ★ Universal, 1982, w/Mildred Lewis
CRACKERS Universal, 1984, w/Robert Cortes
THE RIVER Universal, 1984, w/Robert Cortes

MILDRED LEWIS
(credit w/Edward Lewis)

HAROLD & MAUDE Paramount, 1971, EP*
BROTHERS Warner Bros., 1977
MISSING ★ Universal, 1982

PAUL LEWIS
Contact: Directors Guild of America - Los Angeles, 213/289-2000

GETTING STRAIGHT Columbia, 1970, AP
THE LAST MOVIE Universal, 1971
OUT OF THE BLUE Discovery, 1982
THE HITCHER Tri-Star, 1986, CP
THE HOT SPOT Orion, 1990

RICHARD B. LEWIS
Business: Trilogy Entertainment Group, 1875 Century Park East, #1090, Los Angeles, CA, 90067, 213/277-5662
Agent: William Morris Agency - Beverly Hills, 213/274-7451

THE ZOO GANG New World, 1985, CP
THE KISS Tri-Star, 1988, EP

ROBERT LLOYD LEWIS
Agent: Jack Dytman, ICM - Los Angeles, 213/550-4461

SUPERSTITION Almi Releasing, 1983
HAMBURGER: THE MOTION PICTURE FM Entertainment, 1986, CP w/Donald Ross

SIMON R. LEWIS
SLIPPING INTO DARKNESS MCEG, 1988, CP w/Don Schain
THE CHOCOLATE WAR MCEG, 1988, CP

ELLIOTT LEWITT
AT CLOSE RANGE Orion, 1986, w/Don Guest
ZELLY AND ME Columbia, 1988, EP w/Tina Rathborne

ANDREW LICHT
(credit w/Jeffrey Mueller)
Business: Licht-Mueller Film Corporation, 2121 Avenue of the Stars, #2800, Los Angeles, CA, 90067, 213/551-2262

LICENSE TO DRIVE 20th Century-Fox, 1988
LITTLE MONSTERS MGM/UA, 1989, w/John A. Davis

PAUL LICHTMAN
(credit w/Arnold Fishman)

TRANSYLVANIA 6-5000 New World, 1985, EP
OUT OF CONTROL New World, 1985, EP

J. MICHAEL LIDDLE
GETTING EVEN American Distribution Group, 1986

A. MICHAEL LIEBERMAN
RED SONJA MGM/UA, 1985, EP

SANFORD LIEBERSON
Business: Pathe Entertainment, 76 Hammersmith Rd., London, W14 8YR, England, 01/603-4555

PERFORMANCE Warner Bros., 1970
THE PIED PIPER Paramount, 1972, w/David Puttnam
THAT'LL BE THE DAY EMI, 1974, w/David Puttnam
THE LAST DAYS OF MAN ON EARTH *THE FINAL PROGRAMME* New World, 1974, w/John Goldstone
MAHLER Mayfair, 1974, EP w/David Puttnam
STARDUST Columbia, 1975, w/David Puttnam
LISZTOMANIA Warner Bros., 1975, EP
RITA, SUE & BOB TOO! Orion Classics, 1987
STARS & BARS Columbia, 1988
THE MIGHTY QUINN MGM/UA, 1989, w/Ed Elbert & Marion Hunt

GARY R. LINDBERG
THAT WAS THEN...THIS IS NOW Paramount, 1985, w/John M. Ondov

GEORGE LINDER
THE RUNNING MAN Tri-Star, 1987, w/Tim Zinnemann

LESLIE LINDER
(credit w/Martin Ransohoff)

HAMLET Columbia, 1969, EP
10 RILLINGTON PLACE Columbia, 1971
SEE NO EVIL Columbia, 1971

ANDRE LINK
(credit w/John Dunning)
Business: Cinepix Inc., 8275 Mayrand St., Montreal, Quebec H4P 2C8, Canada, 514/342-2340

THEY CAME FROM WITHIN Trans-America, 1976, w/Alfred Pariser
THE HOUSE BY THE LAKE American International, 1977, EP
RABID New World, 1977, EP w/Ivan Reitman*
MEATBALLS Paramount, 1979, EP

MY BLOODY VALENTINE Paramount, 1981, w/Stephen Miller
HAPPY BIRTHDAY TO ME Columbia, 1981
SPACEHUNTER: ADVENTURES IN THE FORBIDDEN ZONE Columbia, 1983, w/Don Carmody
MEATBALLS III Moviestore, 1986, EP w/Lawrence Nesis*

ART LINSON

Business: Art Linson Productions,Paramount Pictures, 5555 Melrose Ave., Los Angeles, CA, 90038, 213/468-5763

RAFFERTY AND THE GOLD DUST TWINS Warner Bros., 1975, w/Michael Gruskoff
CAR WASH Universal, 1976, w/Gary Stromberg
AMERICAN HOT WAX Paramount, 1978
WHERE THE BUFFALO ROAM Universal, 1980
MELVIN AND HOWARD Universal, 1980, w/Don Phillips
FAST TIMES AT RIDGEMONT HIGH Universal, 1982, w/Irving Azoff
THE WILD LIFE Universal, 1984, w/Cameron Crowe
THE UNTOUCHABLES Paramount, 1987
SCROOGED Paramount, 1988, w/Richard Donner
CASUALTIES OF WAR Columbia, 1989
WE'RE NO ANGELS Paramount, 1989
DICK TRACY Buena Vista, 1990, EP w/Floyd Mutrux

MARK LIPSKY

Business: Paramount Pictures, 5555 Melrose Ave., Los Angeles, CA, 90038, 213/468-4545

COMING TO AMERICA Paramount, 1988, EP w/Leslie Belzberg
HARLEM NIGHTS Paramount, 1989, w/Robert D. Wachs
ANOTHER 48 HOURS Paramount, 1990, EP w/Ralph S. Singleton

MARK LIPSON

Business: 350 Bleecker St., #4E, New York, NY, 10014, 212/691-4305

CHILDREN OF THE CORN New World, 1984, AP
ALMOST YOU 20th Century-Fox, 1985
THE THIN BLUE LINE (FD) Miramax, 1988

HOWARD LIPSTONE

Business: The Landsburg Company, 11811 W. Olympic Blvd., Los Angeles, CA, 90064, 213/478-7878

JAWS 3-D Universal, 1983, EP w/Alan Landsburg

LYNNE LITTMAN

Agent: Joan Hyler, William Morris Agency - Beverly Hills, 213/274-7451
Contact: Directors Guild of America - Los Angeles, 213/289-2000

TESTAMENT Paramount, 1983, w/Jonathan Bernstein

ROBERT LITTMAN

Business: The Robert Littman Company, 409 N. Camden Dr., Suite 105, Beverly Hills, CA,90210, 213/278-1572

SALOME'S LAST DANCE Vestron, 1988, CP
WICKED STEPMOTHER MGM/UA, 1989

GEORGE LITTO

Business: George Litto Productions, 315 South Beverly Dr., Suite 202, Beverly Hills, CA, 90212, 213/277-8450

THIEVES LIKE US United Artists, 1974, w/Jerry Bick
OBSESSION Columbia, 1976, w/Harry N. Blum
DRIVE-IN Columbia, 1976, EP
OVER THE EDGE Orion/Warner Bros., 1979
DRESSED TO KILL Filmways, 1980
BLOW OUT Filmways, 1981
KANSAS Trans World Entertainment, 1988
NIGHT GAME Trans World Entertainment, 1989

SI LITVINOFF

WALKABOUT 20th Century-Fox, 1971
THE MAN WHO FELL TO EARTH Cinema 5, 1976, EP

LUIS LLOSA

Agent: Michael Wimer, CAA - Beverly Hills, 213/288-4545

HOUR OF THE ASSASSIN Concorde, 1987
CRIME ZONE Concorde, 1988

LAUREN LLOYD

(credit w/Wallis Nicita)

Business: Nicita-Lloyd Productions, Paramount Pictures, 5555 Melrose Ave., Los Angeles, CA, 90035, 213/468-8514

MERMAIDS Orion, 1990, w/Patrick Palmer
FIRES WITHIN Pathe, 1990

MICHAEL LLOYD

LOVELINES Tri-Star, 1984, w/Hal Taines
THE GARBAGE PAIL KIDS MOVIE Atlantic Entertainment, 1987, CP w/Melinda Palmer

MICHAEL LOBELL

Business: Lobell-Bergman Productions, 9336 W. Washington Blvd., Culver City, CA, 90230, 213/202-3362

DREAMER 20th Century-Fox, 1979
WINDOWS United Artists, 1980
SO FINE Warner Bros., 1981
THE JOURNEY OF NATTY GANN Buena Vista, 1985
CHANCES ARE Tri-Star, 1989
THE FRESHMAN Tri-Star, 1990

PETER LOCKE

(credit w/Donald Kushner)

Business: The Kushner-Locke Company, 10850 Wilshire Blvd., 9th Floor, Los Angeles, CA, 90024, 213/470-0400

THE HILLS HAVE EYES II Castle Hill, 1985, w/Barry Cahn*
NUTCRACKER Atlantic Entertainment, 1986, w/Willard Carroll & Thomas L. Wilhite
POUND PUPPIES & THE LEGEND OF BIG PAW (AF) Tri-Star, 1988

HAROLD LOEB

SOLDIER BLUE Avco Embassy, 1970, w/Gabriel Katzka

JOSEPH LOEB III

(credit w/Matthew Weisman)

Agent: CAA - Beverly Hills, 213/288-4545

BURGLAR Warner Bros., 1987, CP

VICTOR LOEWY

Business: Alliance Entertainment Corporation, 8439 Sunset Blvd., #404, Los Angeles, CA, 90069, 213/654-9488; 920 Yonge Street, Suite 400, Toronto, Ontario, M4W 3C7, Canada, 416/967-1174

EDDIE & THE CRUISERS II: EDDIE LIVES Scotti Bros., 1989, EP w/Denis Héroux, James L. Stewart & William Stuart

LOU LOMBARDO

Contact: Directors Guild of America - Los Angeles, 213/289-2000

UP IN SMOKE Paramount, 1978, w/Lou Adler
LADIES AND GENTLEMEN...THE FABULOUS STAINS Paramount, 1982, EP

MARK LOMBARDO

MISUNDERSTOOD MGM/UA, 1984, AP
PIRATES Cannon, 1986, EP w/Thom Mount

LYNN LORING

Business: MGM Television, 10202 W. Washington Blvd., Culver City, CA, 90232, 213/280-6161

MR. MOM 20th Century-Fox, 1983, w/Lauren Shuler-Donner

PATRICK LOUBERT

(credit w/Michael Hirsh & Clive A. Smith)

Business: Nelvana Ltd., 32 Atlantic Ave., Toronto, Ontario M6K 1X8, Canada, 416/588-5571; 9000 Sunset Blvd., #911, Los Angeles, CA, 90069, 213/278-8466

THE CARE BEARS MOVIE (AF) Samuel Goldwyn Company, 1985
ROCK & RULE (AF) MGM/UA, 1985, w/Michael Hirsh*
CARE BEARS MOVIE II: A NEW GENERATION (AF) Columbia, 1986
THE CARE BEARS ADVENTURE IN WONDERLAND (AF) Cineplex Odeon, 1987
BABAR: THE MOVIE (AF) New Line Cinema, 1989

DAVID LOUCKA

Agent: Bauer-Benedek Agency - Los Angeles, 213/275-2421
Contact: Writers Guild of America - Los Angeles, 213/550-1000

THE DREAM TEAM Universal, 1989, CP w/Jon Connolly

DAVID LOUGHERY

Business: Paramount Pictures, 5555 Melrose Ave., Los Angeles, CA, 90035, 213/468-5701
Agent: Bauer Benedek Agency - Los Angeles, CA, 90069, 213/275-2421

FLASHBACK Paramount, 1990, CP

R. J. LOUIS

Contact: Directors Guild of America - Los Angeles, 213/289-2000

THE KARATE KID Columbia, 1984, EP
THE KARATE KID PART II Columbia, 1986, EP
MAC AND ME Orion, 1988

DYSON LOVELL

THE CHAMP MGM/UA, 1979
ENDLESS LOVE Universal, 1981
THE COTTON CLUB Orion, 1984, EP

KENT C. LOVELL

(credit w/Dennis Wright)

BACKSTAGE Hoyts, 1988, EP
GROUND ZERO Avenue Pictures, 1988, EP w/John Kearney

PATRICIA LOVELL

PICNIC AT HANGING ROCK Atlantic Entertainment, 1975, EP
GALLIPOLI Paramount, 1981, w/Robert Stigwood

LAWRENCE LOVENTHAL

THE FIRST TIME New Line Cinema, 1982, EP w/Robert Shaye

DAVID LOWE

FIGHTING BACK Paramount, 1982, CP w/Alex DeBenedetti

HUNT LOWRY

Contact: Directors Guild of America - Los Angeles, 213/289-2000

AIRPLANE! Paramount, 1980, AP
HUMANOIDS FROM THE DEEP New World, 1980, w/Martin B. Cohen
GET CRAZY Embassy, 1983
TOP SECRET! Paramount, 1984, w/Jon Davison
BAJA OKLAHOMA HBO Pictures, 1988, EP
WILDFIRE Cinema Group, 1988, CP
REVENGE Columbia, 1990, w/Stanley Rubin

GEORGE LUCAS

Business: Lucasfilm, Ltd., P.O. Box 2009, San Rafael, CA, 94912, 415/662-1800

MORE AMERICAN GRAFFITI Universal, 1979, EP
THE EMPIRE STRIKES BACK 20th Century-Fox, 1980, EP
RAIDERS OF THE LOST ARK ★ Paramount, 1981, EP w/Howard Kazanjian
TWICE UPON A TIME Warner Bros., 1983, EP
RETURN OF THE JEDI 20th Century-Fox, 1983, EP
INDIANA JONES AND THE TEMPLE OF DOOM Paramount, 1984, EP w/Frank Marshall
MISHIMA: A LIFE IN FOUR CHAPTERS Warner Bros., 1985, EP w/Francis Ford Coppola
LABYRINTH Tri-Star, 1986, EP
HOWARD THE DUCK Universal, 1986, EP
WILLOW MGM/UA, 1988, EP
TUCKER: THE MAN AND HIS DREAM Paramount, 1988, EP
THE LAND BEFORE TIME (AF) Universal, 1988, EP w/Kathleen Kennedy, Frank Marshall & Steven Spielberg
INDIANA JONES AND THE LAST CRUSADE Paramount, 1989, EP w/Kathleen Kennedy & Frank Marshall

TOM LUDDY

Business: Zoetrope Studios, Sentinel Bldg., 916 Kearny St., San Francisco, CA, 94133, 415/789-7500

MISHIMA: A LIFE IN FOUR CHAPTERS Warner Bros., 1985, w/Mata Yamamoto

BARFLY Cannon, 1987, w/Fred Roos & Barbet Schroeder
TOUGH GUYS DON'T DANCE Cannon, 1987, EP w/Francis Coppola
KING LEAR Cannon, 1988, AP
POWAQQATSI (FD) Cannon, 1988, LP w/Marcel Kahn
WAIT UNTIL SPRING, BANDINI Orion, 1990, w/Erwin Provoost & Fred Roos

SIDNEY LUMET
Agent: CAA - Beverly Hills, 213/288-4545
Contact: Directors Guild of America - New York, 212/581-0370

THE DEADLY AFFAIR Columbia, 1967
BYE BYE BRAVERMAN Warner Bros./7 Arts, 1968
THE SEA GULL Warner Bros./7 Arts, 1968
LAST OF THE MOBILE HOT-SHOTS Warner Bros., 1970
JUST TELL ME WHAT YOU WANT Warner Bros., 1980, w/Jay Presson Allen
DANIEL Paramount, 1983, EP w/E. L. Doctorow

JAN ERIK LUNDE
BROTHERS IN ARMS Ablo, 1988, EP w/Andre Boissier

NEIL C. LUNDELL
BULLETPROOF CineTel Films, 1987, CP

MARTIN LUPEZ
MUTANT ON THE BOUNTY Skouras Pictures, 1989, w/Robert Torrance

JEFFREY LURIE
Business: Chestnut Hill Productions, c/o Tri-Star Pictures, 3400 Riverside Dr., 11th Floor, Burbank, CA, 91505, 818/972-7788

SWEET HEARTS DANCE Tri-Star, 1988
I LOVE YOU TO DEATH Tri-Star, 1990, w/Ron Moler

NELSON LYON
Contact: Writers Guild of America - New York, 213/245-6180

SPIKE OF BENSONHURST FilmDallas, 1989, w/David Weisman

SHEL LYTTON
BODY SLAM DEG, 1987, w/Mike Curb

M

COLIN MacCABE
CARAVAGGIO Cinevista, 1986, EP

SIMON MacCORKINDALE
Agent: APA - Los Angeles, 213/273-0744
Contact: Directors Guild of America - Los Angeles, 213/289-2000

STEALING HEAVEN Scotti Bros., 1989, w/Andros Epaminondas

MICHAEL MacDONALD
ONE MAGIC CHRISTMAS Buena Vista, 1985, AP
SHORT CIRCUIT II Tri-Star, 1988, EP

PETER MacDONALD
Contact: Directors Guild of America - Los Angeles, 213/289-2000

TANGO AND CASH Warner Bros., 1989, EP

PETER MacGREGOR-SCOTT
Contact: Directors Guild of America - Los Angeles, 213/289-2000

THE JERK Universal, 1979, AP
THE PRISONER OF ZENDA Universal, 1979, AP
CHEECH AND CHONG'S NEXT MOVIE Universal, 1980, AP
THE BEST LITTLE WHOREHOUSE IN TEXAS Universal, 1982, CP
CHEECH AND CHONG'S STILL SMOKIN' Paramount, 1983
CHEECH AND CHONG'S THE CORSICAN BROTHERS Orion, 1984
REVENGE OF THE NERDS 20th Century-Fox, 1984, CP
GOTCHA! Universal, 1985, SP
THE WHOOPEE BOYS Paramount, 1986, w/Adam Fields
BORN IN EAST L.A. Universal, 1987
TROOP BEVERLY HILLS WEG/Columbia, 1989, CP w/Martin Mickelson

NEIL A. MACHLIS
Contact: Directors Guild of America - Los Angeles, 213/289-2000

CAN'T STOP THE MUSIC AFD, 1980, AP
MOMMIE DEAREST Paramount, 1981, AP
GREASE 2 Paramount, 1982, AP
JOHNNY DANGEROUSLY 20th Century-Fox, 1984, AP
2010 MGM/UA, 1984, AP w/Jonathan A. Zimbert
THE MONSTER SQUAD Tri-Star, 1987, CP
PLAINS, TRAINS AND AUTOMOBILES Paramount, 1987, EP w/Michael Chinich
CHANCES ARE Tri-Star, 1989, EP w/Andrew Bergman
AN INNOCENT MAN Buena Vista, 1989, CP
POSTCARDS FROM THE EDGE Columbia, 1990, EP w/Robert Greenhut

EARLE MACK
Business: Mack-Taylor Productions, 110 E. 59th St., Suite 1405, New York, NY, 10022, 212/319-3030

THE CHILDREN OF THEATER STREET (FD) Peppercorn-Wormser, 1977
SHE DANCES ALONE Continental, 1982, w/Federico De Laurentiis

KAREN MACK
Business: Republic Pictures,12636 Beatrice St., Los Angeles, CA, 90066, 213/306-4040

IN THE MOOD Lorimar, 1987, w/Gary Adelson

WILLIAM MacKINNON
SWEETIE Avenue Pictures, 1990, w/John Maynard

ROBERT MacLEAN
CRIMINAL LAW Hemdale, 1989, w/Hilary Heath

DAVID L. MacLEOD
REDS ★ Paramount, 1981, AP
ISHTAR Columbia, 1987, AP w/Nigel Wooll
THE PICK-UP ARTIST 20th Century-Fox, 1987

MARIANNE MADDALENA
Business: Wes Craven Productions, 8271 Melrose Ave., Los Angeles, CA, 90046, 213/852-1100

SHOCKER Universal, 1989, w/Barin Kumar

DAVID MADDEN
Business: Interscope Communications, 10900 Wilshire Blvd., Suite 1400, Los Angeles, CA, 90024, 213/208-8525

RELENTLESS Universal, 1989
BLIND FURY Tri-Star, 1990, EP w/Robert W. Cort
THE FIRST POWER Orion, 1990, w/Robert W. Cort & Ted Field

BRENT MADDOCK
Agent: Nancy Roberts, Gorfaine/Schwartz/ Roberts - Beverly Hills, 213/275-9384
Contact: Writers Guild of America - Los Angeles, 213/550-1000

TREMORS Universal, 1990, w/S.S. Wilson

BEN MADDOW
THE BALCONY Continental, 1963, w/Joseph Strick

GUY MAGAR
Business: Renegade Films, 8033 Sunset Blvd., Suite 1102, Los Angeles, CA, 90046, 213/466-0786
Contact: Directors Guild of America - Los Angeles, 213/289-2000

RETRIBUTION Taurus Entertainment, 1988

CHARLES H. MAGUIRE
Business: Lucasfilm, Ltd., P.O. Box 2009, San Rafael, CA, 94912, 415/662-1800
Contact: Directors Guild of America - Los Angeles, 213/289-2000

FAIL SAFE Columbia, 1964, AP
I LOVE YOU, ALICE B. TOKLAS Warner Bros., 1968
THE ARRANGEMENT Warner Bros./7 Arts, 1969, AP
HEAVEN CAN WAIT Paramount, 1978, EP w/Howard W. Koch, Jr.
DOWNTOWN 20th Century-Fox, 1990

DEZSO MAGYAR
Agent: Paul Kohner, Inc. - Los Angeles, 213/550-1060
Contact: Directors Guild of America - Los Angeles, 213/289-2000

STREETS OF GOLD 20th Century-Fox, 1986, CP w/Patrick McCormick

ROBERT MAIER
Contact: Directors Guild of America - Los Angeles, 213/289-2000

POLYESTER New Line Cinema, 1981, LP
HAIRSPRAY New Line Cinema, 1988, LP

LEE MAJORS
Personal Manager: 818/783-3713
Contact: Directors Guild of America - Los Angeles, 213/289-2000

STEEL World Northal, 1980, EP

BORIS MALDEN
FRATERNITY VACATION New World, 1985, w/Christopher Nelson & Robert C. Peters

AMIR J. MALIN
Business: Cinecom Entertainment, 1250 Broadway, 33rd Floor, New York, NY, 10001, 212/239-8360

SWIMMING TO CAMBODIA Cinecom, 1987, EP w/Lewis Allen, Ira Deutchman & Peter Newman
MATEWAN Cinecom, 1987, EP w/Mark Balsam & Jerry Silva
MILES FROM HOME Cinecom, 1988, EP
SCENES FROM THE CLASS STRUGGLE IN BEVERLY HILLS Cinecom, 1989, EP w/Ira Deutchman

JOHN MALKOVICH
Agent: Leonard Hirshan, William Morris Agency - Los Angeles, 213/274-7451

THE ACCIDENTAL TOURIST ★ Warner Bros., 1988, EP w/Phyllis Carlyle

LOUIS MALLE
Business Manager: Gelfand, Rennert, Feldman, 212/682-0234
Agent: Sam Cohn, ICM - New York, 212/556-5600

PRETTY BABY Paramount, 1978
ALAMO BAY Tri-Star, 1985, w/Vincent Malle

VINCENT MALLE
ALAMO BAY Tri-Star, 1985, w/Louis Malle

RENÉ MALO
Business: Lance Entertainment, 9000 Sunset Blvd., Suite 915, Los Angeles, CA, 90069, 213/278-8751

INTERNAL AFFAIRS Paramount, 1990, EP w/Pierre David & David Streit

CLAUDIO MANCINI
ONCE UPON A TIME IN AMERICA The Ladd Company/ Warner Bros., 1984, EP

FRANK MANCUSO, JR.
Business: Hometown Films, Paramount Pictures, 5555 Melrose Ave., Los Angeles, CA, 90038, 213/468-8654

FRIDAY THE 13TH PART 2 Paramount, 1981, AP
FRIDAY THE 13TH PART 3 Paramount, 1982
OFF THE WALL Jensen Farley Pictures, 1983
THE MAN WHO WASN'T THERE Paramount, 1983
FRIDAY THE 13TH - THE FINAL CHAPTER Paramount, 1984
FRIDAY THE 13TH PART V - A NEW BEGINNING Paramount, 1985, EP
APRIL FOOL'S DAY Paramount, 1986
BACK TO THE BEACH Paramount, 1987
PERMANENT RECORD Paramount, 1988
INTERNAL AFFAIRS Paramount, 1990

YORAM MANDEL
PARTING GLANCES Cinecom, 1986, w/Arthur Silverman

GABRIELLE MANDELIK
Business: Robert Greenwald Productions, 10510 Culver Blvd., Culver City, CA, 90232, 213/204-0404

SWEET HEARTS DANCE Tri-Star, 1988, EP w/Robert Greenwald & Lauren Weissman

LUIS MANDOKI
Agent: Steve Rabineau, ICM - Los Angeles, 213/550-4000

GABY — A TRUE STORY Tri-Star, 1987, CP

FRITZ MANES
Agent: APA - Los Angeles, 213/273-0744
Contact: Directors Guild of America - Los Angeles, 213/289-2000

THE ENFORCER Warner Bros., 1976, AP
THE OUTLAW JOSEY WALES Warner Bros., 1976, AP
THE GAUNTLET Warner Bros., 1977, AP
EVERY WHICH WAY BUT LOOSE Warner Bros., 1978, AP
ESCAPE FROM ALCATRAZ Paramount, 1979, AP
BRONCO BILLY Warner Bros., 1980, AP
ANY WHICH WAY YOU CAN Warner Bros., 1980, EP
HONKY TONK MAN Warner Bros., 1982, EP
FIREFOX Warner Bros., 1982, EP
SUDDEN IMPACT Warner Bros., 1983, EP
TIGHTROPE Warner Bros., 1984, w/Clint Eastwood
CITY HEAT Warner Bros., 1984
PALE RIDER Warner Bros., 1985, EP
RATBOY Warner Bros., 1986
HEARTBREAK RIDGE Warner Bros., 1986, EP

MICHAEL MANHEIM
Business: The Manheim Company, c/o NBC Productions, 330 Bob Hope Dr., Burbank, CA, 91523, 818/509-7546
Agent: Bauer Benedek Agency - Los Angeles, 213/275-2421

PLAIN CLOTHES Paramount, 1988, w/Richard Wechsler

WOLF MANKOWITZ
THE HERO Avco Embassy, 1970, w/John Heyman

MICHAEL MANLEY
AMERICAN GOTHIC Vidmark Entertainment, 1988, EP w/Ray Homer & George Walker

MICHAEL MANN
Business: Michael Mann Productions, 8439 Sunset Blvd., Suite 200, Los Angeles, CA, 90069, 213/656-9755
Agent: Jeff Berg, ICM - Los Angeles, 213/550-4000

BAND OF THE HAND Tri-Star, 1986, EP

RON MANN
Business: Sphinx Productions, Ltd., 41 Riderwood Dr., Willowdale, Ontario M2L 2E7, 416/445-7492
Agent: The Colbert Agency - Toronto, 416/964-3302

COMIC BOOK CONFIDENTIAL (FD) Cinecom, 1989, w/Don Haig & Martin Harbury

TED MANN
Business: Mann Theatres Corporation of California, 9200 Sunset Blvd., Suite 200, Los Angeles, CA, 90069, 213/273-3336

THE ILLUSTRATED MAN Warner Bros., 1969, w/Howard B. Kreitsek
BUSTER & BILLIE Columbia, 1974, EP
LIFEGUARD Paramount, 1976
BRUBAKER 20th Century-Fox, 1980, EP
KRULL Columbia, 1983, EP

SAM MANNERS
Contact: Directors Guild of America - Los Angeles, 213/289-2000

MISCHIEF 20th Century-Fox, 1985, w/Michael Nolin
BAD MEDICINE 20th Century-Fox, 1985, EP w/Michael Jaffe & Myles Osterneck

MICHELLE MANNING
Contact: Directors Guild of America - Los Angeles, 213/289-2000

SIXTEEN CANDLES Universal, 1984, AP
THE BREAKFAST CLUB Universal, 1985, CP

BRIAN C. MANOOGIAN
MOONTRAP Shapiro-Glickenhaus Entertainment, 1989, EP w/ James A. Courtney & Alan M. Solomon

PETER MANOOGIAN
DEADLY WEAPON Empire, 1988

DAVID MANSON
Business: Sarabande Productions, 10000 W. Washington Blvd., Suite 3012, Culver City, CA, 90232, 213/280-6462

BIRDY Tri-Star, 1984, EP
BRING ON THE NIGHT (FD) Samuel Goldwyn Company, 1985

ALLAN MARCIL
Business: Stonehenge Productions, 10202 W. Washington Blvd., Culver City, CA, 90232, 213/280-7350

FRESH HORSES WEG/Columbia, 1988, EP

ROBERT P. MARCUCCI
THE RAZOR'S EDGE Columbia, 1984, w/Harry Benn

JAMES MARGELLOS
Contact: Directors Guild of America - Los Angeles, 213/289-2000

STRIKING BACK Film Ventures International, 1981

STAN MARGULIES
Business: The Stan Margulies Company, 6500 Wilshire Blvd., #1180, Los Angeles, CA, 90048, 213/658-4525

40 POUNDS OF TROUBLE Universal, 1962
THOSE MAGNIFICENT MEN IN THEIR FLYING MACHINES 20th Century Fox, 1965
THE PINK JUNGLE Universal, 1968
IF IT'S TUESDAY, THIS MUST BE BELGIUM United Artists, 1969
I LOVE MY WIFE Universal, 1970

WILLY WONKA & THE CHOCOLATE FACTORY
Paramount, 1971, w/David L. Wolper
ONE IS A LONELY NUMBER MGM, 1972
VISIONS OF EIGHT (FD) Cinema 5, 1973

PETER MARIS

VIPER Fries Entertainment, 1988
TRUE BLOOD Fries Entertainment, 1989

LAURENCE MARK

Business: Walt Disney Pictures, 500 S. Buena Vista St., Burbank, CA, 91521, 818/560-1000

BLACK WIDOW 20th Century-Fox, 1987, EP
MY STEPMOTHER IS AN ALIEN WEG/Columbia, 1988, EP w/Art Levinson
WORKING GIRL ★ 20th Century-Fox, 1988, EP w/Robert Greenhut
COOKIE Warner Bros., 1989

TONY MARK

(credit w/Sue Jett)

Contact: Directors Guild of America - Los Angeles, 213/289-2000

BILLY GALVIN Vestron, 1986
ZELLY & ME Columbia, 1988
ROOFTOPS New Visions, 1989, CP w/Allan Goldstein

PATRICK MARKEY

Contact: Directors Guild of America - Los Angeles, 213/289-2000

HOUSE New World, 1986, AP
STACKING Spectrafilm, 1987, CP w/Peter Burrell
DEEPSTAR SIX Tri-Star, 1989, w/Sean S. Cunningham

RUSSELL D. MARKOWITZ

Business: A Cut Above Productions, Inc., 11816 Chandler Blvd., Suite 8, North Hollywood, CA, 91606, 818/985-2105

TIME OF THE BEAST Liberty Films, 1989

J. DAVID MARKS

(credit w/Gabe Sumner)

Business: Odyssey Film Partners, Ltd., 6500 Wilshire Blvd., Suite 400, Los Angeles, CA, 90048, 213/655-9335

TAKE THIS JOB AND SHOVE IT Embassy, 1981, EP w/William J. Immerman*
SISTER SISTER New World, 1988, EP
MEMORIES OF ME MGM/UA, 1988, EP

RICHARD MARKS

JUMPIN' JACK FLASH 20th Century-Fox, 1986, AP
SAY ANYTHING 20th Century-Fox, 1989, CP

NEAL MARLENS

Business: The Black/Marlens Company, 1440 S. Sepulveda Blvd., Los Angeles, CA, 90025, 213/444-8100
Agent: Leading Artists, Inc. - Beverly Hills, 213/858-1999

SOUL MAN New World, 1986, CP w/Carol Black

SANDRA MARSH

(credit w/Terence Marsh)

Business: Sandra Marsh Management, 14930 Ventura Blvd., Suite 200, Sherman Oaks, CA, 91403, 818/905-6961

FINDERS KEEPERS Warner Bros., 1984

TERENCE MARSH

(credit w/Sandra Marsh)

Agent: Sandra Marsh Management, 14930 Ventura Blvd., Suite 200, Sherman Oaks, CA, 91403, 818/905-6961

FINDERS KEEPERS Warner Bros., 1984

ALAN MARSHALL

Business: Lowe Howard Spink - London, 01/225-3434

BUGSY MALONE Paramount, 1976
MIDNIGHT EXPRESS ★ Columbia, 1978, w/David Puttnam
FAME MGM/UA, 1980, w/David De Silva
SHOOT THE MOON MGM, 1982
PINK FLOYD - THE WALL MGM/UA, 1982
ANOTHER COUNTRY Orion Classics, 1984
BIRDY Tri-Star, 1984
ANGEL HEART Tri-Star, 1987, w/Elliott Kastner
LEONARD PART 6 Columbia, 1987, EP w/Steve Sohmer
HOMEBOY Homeboy Productions, 1990, w/Elliott Kastner
JACOB'S LADDER Tri-Star, 1990

FRANK MARSHALL

Business: Amblin Entertainment, Universal Studios, 100 Universal Plaza, Bungalow 477, Universal City, CA, 91608, 818/777-4600
Contact: Directors Guild of America - Los Angeles, 213/289-2000

PAPER MOON Paramount, 1973, AP
DAISY MILLER Paramount, 1984, AP
AT LONG LAST LOVE 20th Century-Fox, 1975, AP
NICKELODEON Columbia, 1976, AP
THE LAST WALTZ (FD) United Artists, 1978, LP
THE DRIVER 20th Century-Fox, 1978, AP
THE WARRIORS Paramount, 1979, EP
RAIDERS OF THE LOST ARK ★ Paramount, 1981
POLTERGEIST MGM, 1982, w/Steven Spielberg
TWILIGHT ZONE — THE MOVIE Warner Bros., 1983, EP
INDIANA JONES & THE TEMPLE OF DOOM Paramount, 1984, EP w/George Lucas
GREMLINS Warner Bros., 1984, EP w/Kathleen Kennedy & Steven Spielberg
FANDANGO Warner Bros., 1985, EP w/Kathleen Kennedy
THE GOONIES Warner Bros., 1985, EP w/Kathleen Kennedy & Steven Spielberg
BACK TO THE FUTURE Universal, 1985, EP w/Kathleen Kennedy & Steven Spielberg
YOUNG SHERLOCK HOLMES Paramount, 1985, EP w/Kathleen Kennedy & Steven Spielberg
THE COLOR PURPLE ★ Warner Bros., 1985, w/Quincy Jones, Kathleen Kennedy & Steven Spielberg
AN AMERICAN TAIL (AF) Universal, 1986, EP w/Kathleen Kennedy, David Kirschner & Steven Spielberg
THE MONEY PIT Universal, 1986, EP w/Kathleen Kennedy & Art Levinson
INNERSPACE Warner Bros., 1987, EP w/Peter Guber, Kathleen Kennedy, Jon Peters & Steven Spielberg

BATTERIES NOT INCLUDED Universal, 1987, EP w/Kathleen Kennedy & Steven Spielberg
EMPIRE OF THE SUN Warner Bros., 1987, w/Kathleen Kennedy & Steven Spielberg
WHO FRAMED ROGER RABBIT Buena Vista, 1988, w/Robert Watts
THE LAND BEFORE TIME (AF) Universal, 1988, EP w/Kathleen Kennedy, George Lucas & Steven Spielberg
INDIANA JONES & THE LAST CRUSADE Paramount, 1989, EP w/Kathleen Kennedy & George Lucas
DAD Universal, 1989, EP w/Kathleen Kennedy & Steven Spielberg
BACK TO THE FUTURE PART II Universal, 1989, EP w/Kathleen Kennedy & Steven Spielberg
ALWAYS Universal, 1989, w/Kathleen Kennedy & Steven Spielberg
BACK TO THE FUTURE PART III Universal, 1990, EP w/Kathleen Kennedy & Steven Spielberg
GREMLINS II Warner Bros., 1990, EP w/Kathleen Kennedy & Steven Spielberg
JOE VERSUS THE VOLCANO Warner Bros., 1990, EP w/Kathleen Kennedy & Steven Spielberg

GARRY MARSHALL
Business: Diane Frazen, Henderson Productions, 10067 Riverside Dr., North Hollywood, CA, 91602, 818/985-6417
Contact: Directors Guild of America - Los Angeles, 213/289-2000

HOW SWEET IT IS! National General, 1968, w/Jerry Belson
YOUNG DOCTORS IN LOVE 20th Century-Fox, 1982, EP

NOEL MARSHALL
THE EXORCIST ★ Warner Bros., 1973, EP
ROAR 1981
A NIGHT IN THE LIFE OF JIMMY REARDON 20th Century-Fox, 1988, EP w/Mel Klein

KENNETH MARTEL
CALL ME Vestron, 1988, w/John Quill

BONNIE BRUCKHEIMER-MARTELL
(see Bonnie BRUCKHEIMER-Martell)

PETER MARTHESHEIMER
DESPAIR New Line Cinema, 1979

ERNEST MARTIN
(credit w/Cy Feuer)

A CHORUS LINE Columbia, 1985

STEVE MARTIN
Agent: John Gaines, APA - Los Angeles, 213/273-0744
Contact: Writers Guild of America - Los Angeles, 213/550-1000

THREE AMIGOS Orion, 1986, EP
ROXANNE Columbia, 1987, EP

GABRIELLA MARTINELLI
NIGHTBREED 20th Century-Fox, 1990

MIKE MARVIN
Agent: The Irv Schechter Company - Beverly Hills, 213/278-8070

HOT DOG...THE MOVIE MGM/UA, 1984, CP

JOZSEF MARX
BRADY'S ESCAPE Satori, 1984, EP

TIMOTHY MARX
SMOOTH TALK Spectrafilm, 1985, AP
RACHEL RIVER Taurus, 1989
PENN AND TELLER GET KILLED Warner Bros., 1989, CP

ARTHUR H. MASLANSKY
Business: Bima Entertainment, Ltd., 2049 Century Park East, Suite 4050, Los Angeles, CA, 90067, 213/203-8488

GHOST WARRIOR Empire, 1986, EP w/Albert Band, Efrem Harkham & Uri Harkham
SLIPSTREAM Entertainment Films, 1989, EP w/ William Braunstein & Nigel Green

PAUL MASLANSKY
Business: Paul Maslansky Productions, 4000 Warner Blvd., Bldg. 81, Rm. 203, Burbank, CA, 91522, 818/954-3811
Contact: The Howard Brandy Company, Inc. - Los Angeles, 213/657-8320

SUDDEN TERROR National General, 1971
RAW MEAT American International, 1973
HARD TIMES Columbia, 1975, EP
RACE WITH THE DEVIL 20th Century-Fox, 1975, EP
THE BLUE BIRD 20th Century-Fox, 1976
DAMNATION ALLEY 20th Century-Fox, 1977, w/Jerome M. Zeitman
HOT STUFF Columbia, 1979, EP
CIRCLE OF IRON Avco Embassy, 1979, w/Sandy Howard
WHEN YOU COMIN' BACK, RED RYDER Columbia, 1979, CP
SCAVENGER HUNT 20th Century-Fox, 1979, CP
THE VILLAIN Columbia, 1979, EP
LOVE CHILD The Ladd Company/Warner Bros., 1982
THE SALAMANDER ITC, 1983
POLICE ACADEMY The Ladd Company/Warner Bros., 1984
RETURN TO OZ Buena Vista, 1985
POLICE ACADEMY 2: THEIR FIRST ASSIGNMENT Warner Bros., 1985
POLICE ACADEMY 3: BACK IN TRAINING Warner Bros., 1986
POLICE ACADEMY 4: CITIZENS ON PATROL Warner Bros., 1987
POLICE ACADEMY 5: ASSIGNMENT MIAMI BEACH Warner Bros., 1988
POLICE ACADEMY 6: CITY UNDER SIEGE Warner Bros., 1989
SKI PATROL Triumph Releasing, 1990, EP
THE RUSSIA HOUSE Pathe/Warner Bros., 1990, w/Fred Schepisi

JIMMY MASLON
BLOOD DINER Lightning/Vestron, 1987

MORGAN MASON
sex, lies & videotape Miramax, 1989, EP w/Nancy Tenenbaum & Nick Wechsler

PAUL MASON
Business: Trans World Entertainment, 3330 W. Cahuenga Blvd., Suite 500, Los Angeles, CA, 90068, 213/969-2800

THE LADIES CLUB New Line Cinema, 1986, w/Nick J. Mileti
THE WILD PAIR Trans World Entertainment, 1987, w/Randall Torno
SEVEN HOURS TO JUDGMENT Trans World Entertainment, 1988, EP w/Helen Sarlui-Tucker
I, MADMAN Trans World Entertainment, 1989, EP w/Helen Sarlui-Tucker

NICO MASTORAKIS
Business: Omega Entertainment, Ltd., 8760 Shoreham Dr., Suite 501, Los Angeles, CA, 90069, 213/855-0516

THE GREEK TYCOON Universal, 1978, CP w/Lawrence Myers
BLIND DATE New Line Cinema, 1984

TIM MATHESON
Business: National Lampoon Films, 242 N. Canon Dr., Beverly Hills, CA, 90212, 213/445-5400
Agent: CAA - Beverly Hills, 213/288-4545

BLIND FURY Tri-Star, 1990, w/Daniel Grodnik

WALTER MATTHAU
Agent: William Morris Agency - Beverly Hills, 213/274-7451

LITTLE MISS MARKER Universal, 1980, EP

BURNY MATTINSON
Business: Walt Disney Studios, 500 S. Buena Vista St., Burbank, CA, 91521, 818/560-1000

THE GREAT MOUSE DETECTIVE (AF) Buena Vista, 1986

ISABEL MAXWELL
'68 New World, 1988, w/Dale Djerassi & Steven Kovacs

MITCHELL MAXWELL
KEY EXCHANGE 20th Century-Fox, 1985, w/Paul Kurta

GAY MAYER
TIGER WARSAW Sony Pictures, 1988, EP w/Navin Desai & Watson Warriner

JOHN MAYNARD
THE NAVIGATOR: AN ODYSSEY ACROSS TIME Circle Releasing, 1989
SWEETIE Avenue Pictures, 1990, w/William MacKinnon

GEOFFREY MAYO
Business: UMP & Associates, Raleigh Studios, 5300 Melrose Ave., Suite 411-E, Hollywood, CA, 90038, 213/960-4580

ROCKET GIBRALTAR Columbia, 1988, EP w/Robert Fisher & Michael Ulick

MELANIE MAYRON
Agent: Triad Artists, Inc. - 213/556-2727

STICKY FINGERS Spectrafilm, 1988, w/Catlin Adams

PAULA MAZUR
Contact: Directors Guild of America - Los Angeles, 213/289-2000

HOME OF THE BRAVE (FD) Cinecom, 1986

PAUL MAZURSKY
Agent: Jeff Berg, ICM - Los Angeles, 213/550-4000
Contact: Directors Guild of America - Los Angeles, 213/289-2000

I LOVE YOU, ALICE B. TOKLAS Warner Bros., 1968, EP w/Larry Tucker
BLUME IN LOVE Warner Bros., 1973
HARRY & TONTO 20th Century-Fox, 1974
NEXT STOP, GREENWICH VILLAGE 20th Century- Fox, 1976, w/Tony Ray
AN UNMARRIED WOMAN ★ 20th Century-Fox, 1978, w/Tony Ray
WILLIE & PHIL 20th Century-Fox, 1980, w/Tony Ray
TEMPEST Columbia, 1982
MOSCOW ON THE HUDSON Columbia, 1984
DOWN AND OUT IN BEVERLY HILLS Buena Vista, 1986
MOON OVER PARADOR Universal, 1988
ENEMIES, A LOVE STORY 20th Century-Fox, 1989

EUGENE MAZZOLA
Contact: Directors Guild of America - Los Angeles, 213/289-2000

JOYRIDE American International, 1977
ALOHA SUMMER Spectrafilm, 1987
CLASS OF 1999 Taurus, 1990, CP

CHERYL McCALL
STREETWISE Angelika, 1985

RICK McCALLUM
Contact: Directors Guild of America - Los Angeles, 213/289-2000

PENNIES FROM HEAVEN MGM, 1981, EP
I OUGHT TO BE IN PICTURES 20th Century-Fox, 1982, AP
DREAMCHILD Universal, 1985, w/Kenith Trodd
LINK Cannon, 1986, CP
CASTAWAY Cannon, 1987
TRACK 29 Island Pictures, 1988
STRAPLESS Miramax, 1990

PETER McCARTHY
REPO MAN Universal, 1984, w/Jonathan Wacks
SID & NANCY Samuel Goldwyn Company, 1986, CP
TAPEHEADS Avenue, 1988
I'M GONNA GIT YOU SUCKA MGM/UA, 1989, w/Carl Craig

RICKY McCARTNEY
ICE HOUSE Upfront Films, 1989, EP

KIRBY McCAULEY

Business: 432 Park Ave. South, Suite 1509, New York, NY,10016, 212/683-7561

CHRISTINE Columbia, 1983, EP w/Mark Tarlov

KEVIN McCLORY

THUNDERBALL United Artists, 1965
NEVER SAY NEVER AGAIN Warner Bros., 1983, EP

KEVIN McCORMICK

Business: Fogwood Films, Columbia Plaza West, Burbank, CA, 91505, 818/954-1780

SATURDAY NIGHT FEVER Paramount, 1977, EP
MOMENT BY MOMENT Universal, 1978, EP
TIMES SQUARE AFD, 1980, EP w/John Nicolella
THE FAN Paramount, 1981, EP
BURGLAR Warner Bros., 1987, w/Michael Hirsh

PATRICK McCORMICK

Business: Corsair Pictures, 1740 Broadway, 23rd Floor, New York, NY, 10019, 212/603-0652 or 1640 S. Sepulveda Blvd., #216, Los Angeles, CA, 90025, 213/479-8200
Contact: Directors Guild of America - New York, 212/581-0370

WISE GUYS MGM/UA, 1986, AP
STREETS OF GOLD 20th Century-Fox, 1986, CP w/Dezso Magyar
MORGAN STEWART'S COMING HOME New Century/ Vista, 1987, AP
LAST RITES MGM/UA, 1988, w/Donald Bellisario
AND GOD CREATED WOMAN Vestron, 1988, SP
A SHOCK TO THE SYSTEM Corsair, 1990

RODDY McDOWALL

Agent: Badgley-Conner - Los Angeles, 213/278-9313

OVERBOARD MGM/UA, 1987, EP

HAL McELROY

(credit w/James McElroy)
Contact: Australian Film Commission, 9229 Sunset Blvd., Los Angeles, CA, 90069, 213/275-7074

THE CARS THAT EAT PEOPLE *THE CARS THAT ATE PARIS* New Line Cinema, 1974
PICNIC AT HANGING ROCK Atlantic Entertainment 1975
THE LAST WAVE World Northal, 1979
RAZORBACK Warner Bros., 1985*

JAMES McELROY

(credit w/Hal McElroy)
Contact: Australian Film Commission, 9229 Sunset Blvd., Los Angeles, CA, 90069, 213/275-7074

THE CARS THAT EAT PEOPLE *THE CARS THAT ATE PARIS* New Line Cinema, 1974
PICNIC AT HANGING ROCK Atlantic Entertainment, 1975
THE LAST WAVE World Northal, 1979
THE YEAR OF LIVING DANGEROUSLY MGM/UA, 1983*

WILLIAM E. McEUEN

THE JERK Universal, 1979, w/David V. Picker
DEAD MEN DON'T WEAR PLAID Universal, 1979, w/David V. Picker
THE MAN WITH TWO BRAINS Warner Bros., 1983, w/David V. Picker
THE LONELY GUY Universal, 1984, EP w/C. O. Erickson
PEE-WEE'S BIG ADVENTURE Warner Bros., 1985, EP
PULSE Columbia, 1988, EP
BIG TOP PEE-WEE Paramount, 1988, EP w/Richard Gilbert Abramson
THE BIG PICTURE Columbia, 1989, EP w/Richard Gilbert Abramson

PAUL McGUINNESS

U2: RATTLE & HUM Paramount, 1988, EP

DOUG McHENRY

KRUSH GROOVE Warner Bros., 1985, w/Michael Schultz

MARY McLAGLEN

COLD FEET Avenue, 1989, CP

VINCE McMAHON

Business: World Wrestling Federation, P.O. Box 3857, Stamford, CT, 06905

NO HOLDS BARRED New Line Cinema, 1989, EP w/Richard Glover & Hulk Hogan

JOHN McNAUGHTON

HENRY: PORTRAIT OF A SERIAL KILLER Greycat Films, 1990, w/Lisa Dedmond

PETER A. McRAE

EDGE OF SANITY Millimeter Films, 1989, EP

JOHN McTIERNAN

Agent: Ron Mardigian, William Morris Agency - Beverly Hills, 213/274-7451
Contact: Directors Guild of America - Los Angeles, 213/289-2000

FLIGHT OF THE INTRUDER Paramount, 1990, EP w/Brian Frankish

JOSEPH MEDAWAR

PRETTY SMART New World, 1987, EP
CHAMPIONS FOREVER (FD) Ion, 1989, w/Nabeel Zahid

JOE MEDJUCK

(credit w/Michael C. Gross)
Business: Ivan Reitman Productions, 4000 Warner Blvd., Burbank, CA, 91522, 213/954-1771

STRIPES Columbia, 1981, AP*
GHOSTBUSTERS Columbia, 1984, AP
LEGAL EAGLES Universal, 1986, EP
BIG SHOTS 20th Century-Fox, 1987
TWINS Universal, 1988, EP
GHOSTBUSTERS II Columbia, 1989, EP w/Bernie Brillstein

CHARLES R. MEEKER

(credit w/Edward S. Feldman)
Business: F/M Entertainment, 9454 Wilshire Blvd., #701, Beverly Hills, CA, 90212, 213/859-7050

THE HITCHER Tri-Star, 1986, EP
HAMBURGER: THE MOTION PICTURE FM Entertainment, 1986

THE GOLDEN CHILD Paramount, 1986, EP
w/Richard Tienken*
NEAR DARK DEG, 1987, EP
WIRED Taurus, 1989

GARY MEHLMAN

CIRCLE OF POWER Televicine International, 1984
THE BIKINI SHOP *THE MALIBU BIKINI SHOP*
International Film Marketing, 1987,
w/J. Kenneth Rotcop
THE NEW ADVENTURES OF PIPPI LONGSTOCKING
Columbia, 1988, w/Walter Moshay

CHRIS MELEDANDRI

(credit w/Mark R. Gordon)
Business: Paramount Pictures, 5555 Melrose Ave.,
Los Angeles, CA, 90038, 213/468-5919

QUICKSILVER Columbia, 1986, AP*
BROTHERS IN ARMS Ablo, 1988
OPPORTUNITY KNOCKS Universal, 1990

DANIEL MELNICK

Business: IndieProd, c/o Carolco, 8800 Sunset Blvd.,
5th Floor, Los Angeles, CA, 90069, 213/289-7100

STRAW DOGS Cinerama, 1971
THAT'S ENTERTAINMENT (FD) MGM, 1974, EP
THAT'S ENTERTAINMENT, PART 2 (FD) MGM/UA,
1976, w/Saul Chaplin
ALL THAT JAZZ 20th Century-Fox, 1979, EP
ALTERED STATES Warner Bros., 1980, EP
FIRST FAMILY Warner Bros., 1980
MAKING LOVE 20th Century-Fox, 1982, w/Allen Adler
UNFAITHFULLY YOURS 20th Century-Fox, 1984, EP
FOOTLOOSE Paramount, 1984, EP
QUICKSILVER Columbia, 1986, w/Michael Rachmil
ROXANNE Columbia, 1987, w/Michael Rachmil
PUNCHLINE Columbia, 1988, w/Michael Rachmil
MOUNTAINS OF THE MOON Tri-Star, 1990

BENJAMIN MELNIKER

(credit w/Michael Uslan)
Business: Bat Film Productions, 123 W. 44th St., Suite
10-K, New York, NY, 10036, 212/302-2688

SWAMP THING Embassy, 1982
BATMAN Warner Bros., 1989, EP
THE RETURN OF SWAMP THING Miramax, 1989

MICHAEL MELTZER

UP THE CREEK Orion, 1984
THE HIDDEN New Line Cinema, 1987, w/Gerald T.
Olson & Robert Shaye
DEAD HEAT New World, 1988, w/David Helpern

JULIAN MELZACK

THE HAUNTING OF JULIA Discovery, 1981, EP
ANGELA Embassy, 1984, w/Claude Héroux

JANA SUE MEMEL

Business: Chanticleer Films, 6525 Sunset Blvd., 6th Floor,
Los Angeles, CA, 90028, 213/462-4705

TOUGH GUYS Buena Vista, 1986, CP
w/Richard Hashimoto

FRANK MENKE

MARVIN & TIGE Castle Hill, 1985, EP

BRYCE MENZIES

MALCOLM Vestron, 1986, EP
RIKKY AND PETE MGM/UA, 1988, EP

BOB MERCER

SLAYGROUND Universal, 1984, EP

ISMAIL MERCHANT

Business: Merchant Ivory Productions, 250 West 57th St.,
Suite 1913-A, New York, NY, 10023, 212/582-8049

THE HOUSEHOLDER Royal Films International, 1963
SHAKESPEARE WALLAH Continental, 1966
THE GURU 20th Century-Fox, 1969
BOMBAY TALKIE Dia Films, 1970
SAVAGES Angelika, 1972
THE WILD PARTY American International, 1975
ROSELAND Cinema Shares International, 1977
HULLABALOO OVER GEORGIA & BONNIE'S PICTURES
Corinth, 1979
THE EUROPEANS Levitt-Pickman, 1979
JANE AUSTEN IN MANHATTAN Contemporary, 1980
QUARTET New World, 1981
HEAT AND DUST Universal Classics, 1983
THE BOSTONIANS Almi Pictures, 1984
A ROOM WITH A VIEW ★ Cinecom, 1986
MAURICE Cinecom, 1987
MY LITTLE GIRL Hemdale, 1987, EP
THE DECEIVERS Cinecom, 1988
SLAVES OF NEW YORK Tri-Star, 1989,
w/Gary J. Hendler

NEIL MERON

Business: Storyline Productions, Warner Bros., 4000
Warner Blvd., Burbank, CA, 91522, 818/954-6000

SING Tri-Star, 1989, CP

DAVID MERRICK

CHILD'S PLAY Paramount, 1973
THE GREAT GATSBY Paramount, 1974
SEMI-TOUGH United Artists, 1977
ROUGH CUT Paramount, 1980

KEITH MERRILL

Contact: Directors Guild of America - Los Angeles,
213/289-2000

TAKE DOWN Buena Vista, 1979

MARK METCALF

CHILLY SCENES OF WINTER *HEAD OVER HEELS*
United Artists, 1979, w/Griffin Dunne & Amy Robinson

ANDREW MEYER

Business: Act III Communications, 1800 Century Park
East, Suite 200, Los Angeles, CA, 90067,
213/553-3636

THE BREAKFAST CLUB Universal, 1985, EP
w/Gil Friesen
BETTER OFF DEAD Warner Bros., 1985, EP
w/Gil Friesen
BRING ON THE NIGHT Samuel Goldwyn Company,
1985, EP w/Gil Friesen

ONE CRAZY SUMMER Warner Bros., 1986, EP w/Gil Friesen
PROMISED LAND Vestron, 1988, EP w/Robert Redford
BREAKING IN Samuel Goldwyn Company, 1989, EP w/Sarah Ryan Black

IRWIN MEYER
Business: Ventura Entertainment Group, 4705 Laurel Canyon, Penthouse, North Hollywood, CA, 91607, 818/762-8700

DEADLY ILLUSION CineTel Films, 1987

NANCY MEYERS
Agent: ICM - Los Angeles, 213/550-4000

PRIVATE BENJAMIN Warner Bros., 1980, w/Harvey Miller & Charles Shyer
BABY BOOM MGM/UA, 1987

JOEL B. MICHAELS
Business: Cineplex Odeon Films, 1925 Century Park East, Suite 300, Los Angeles, CA, 90067, 213/553-5307

BITTERSWEET LOVE Avco Embassy, 1976, w/Gene Scott & Joseph Zappala
THE SILENT PARTNER EMC Film/Aurora, 1979
THE CHANGELING AFD, 1980, w/Garth Drabinsky
TRIBUTE 20th Century-Fox, 1980, w/Garth Drabinsky
THE AMATEUR 20th Century-Fox, 1981, w/Garth Drabinsky
LOSIN' IT Embassy, 1983, EP w/Garth Drabinsky
THE PHILADELPHIA EXPERIMENT New World, 1984, w/Douglas Curtis
BLACK MOON RISING New World, 1986, w/Douglas Curtis

LORNE MICHAELS
Business: Broadway Video, 1619 Broadway, 9th Floor, New York, NY, 10019, 212/265-7621

MR. MIKE'S MONDO VIDEO New Line Cinema, 1979, EP
GILDA LIVE (FD) Warner Bros., 1980
NOTHING LASTS FOREVER MGM/UA, 1984
THREE AMIGOS Orion, 1986, w/George Folsey Jr.

MARTIN MICKELSON
Business: Itsbinso Long, Inc., c/o Walt Disney Pictures, 500 S. Buena Vista St., Burbank, CA, 91521, 818/972-3455

HELLO AGAIN Buena Vista, 1987, CP w/G. Mac Brown, Thomas Folino & Susan Isaacs
OUTRAGEOUS FORTUNE Buena Vista, 1987, CP w/Peter V. Herald & Scott Kroopf
TROOP BEVERLY HILLS WEG/Columbia, 1989, CP w/Peter MacGregor-Scott

ROBERT MICKELSON
HARD CHOICES Lorimar, 1986

BETTE MIDLER
Business: All-Girl Pictures, Walt Disney Pictures, 500 S. Buena Vista St., Burbank, CA, 91521, 818/560-5000

BEACHES Buena Vista, 1988, w/Bonnie Bruckheimer Martell & Margaret Jennings South

MICHAEL R. MIHALICH
THE ROSARY MURDERS New Line Cinema, 1987, EP

ARNON MILCHAN
Business: New Regency Films, 9608 Wilshire Blvd., #201, Beverly Hills, CA, 90212, 213/859-8817

BLACK JOY Hemdale, 1977, w/Elliott Kastner
THE MEDUSA TOUCH Warner Bros., 1978, w/Lew Grade & Elliott Kastner
THE KING OF COMEDY 20th Century-Fox, 1983
ONCE UPON A TIME IN AMERICA The Ladd Co./ Warner Bros., 1984
BRAZIL Universal, 1985
LEGEND Universal, 1986
STRIPPER (FD) 20th Century-Fox, 1986, EP
MAN ON FIRE Tri-Star, 1987
WHO'S HARRY CRUMB? Tri-Star, 1989
BIG MAN ON CAMPUS Vestron, 1989
THEWAR OF THE ROSES 20th Century-Fox, 1989, w/James L. Brooks
Q&A Tri-Star, 1990, w/Burtt Harris
PRETTY WOMAN Buena Vista, 1990, w/Steven Reuther

JULIA MILES
FOUR FRIENDS Filmways, 1981, EP w/Michael Tolan

NICK J. MILETI
STREAMERS United Artists Classics, 1983, w/Robert Altman
THE LADIES CLUB New Line Cinema, 1986, w/Paul Mason

JOHN MILIUS
Business: Paramount Pictures, 5555 Melrose Ave., Los Angeles, CA, 90038, 213/468-5738
Agent: ICM - Los Angeles, 213/550-4000

1941 Universal, 1979, EP
HARDCORE Columbia, 1979, EP
USED CARS Columbia, 1980, EP w/Steven Spielberg
UNCOMMON VALOR Paramount, 1983, w/Buzz Feitshans

EDWARD K. MILKIS
(credit w/Thomas L. Miller)
Contact: Directors Guild of America - Los Angeles, 213/289-2000

SILVER STREAK 20th Century-Fox, 1976
FOUL PLAY Paramount, 1978
THE BEST LITTLE WHOREHOUSE IN TEXAS Universal, 1982, w/Robert L. Boyett

SCOTT MILLANEY
STRAIGHT TO HELL Island Pictures, 1988, EP w/Cary Brokaw

STUART MILLAR
Contact: Directors Guild of America - New York, 212/581-0370

THE YOUNG DOCTORS United Artists, 1961, w/Lawrence Turman
I COULD GO ON SINGING United Artists, 1963, w/Lawrence Turman
THE BEST MAN United Artists, 1964, w/Lawrence Turman
PAPER LION United Artists, 1968
SHOOT THE MOON MGM/UA, 1982, EP w/Edgar J. Scherick

DON MILLER
BLAZE Buena Vista, 1989, EP w/David V. Lester

GEORGE MILLER
Business Manager: Gang, Tyre & Brown, 6400 Sunset Blvd., Los Angeles, CA, 90028
Business: Kennedy Miller Productions, 30 Orwell St., Kings Cross, Sydney, Australia

MAD MAX BEYOND THUNDERDOME Warner Bros., 1985
DEAD CALM Warner Bros., 1989, w/Terry Hayes & Doug Mitchell

HARVEY MILLER
Business: 5538 Calhoun Ave., Van Nuys, CA, 91401, 818/997-6760
Agent: ICM - Los Angeles, 213/550-4000

PRIVATE BENJAMIN Warner Bros., 1980, w/Nancy Meyers & Charles Shyer
STUDENT BODIES Paramount, 1981, EP w/Jerry Belson

JENNIFER MILLER
Contact: Directors Guild of America - Los Angeles, 213/289-2000

HEARTS OF FIRE Lorimar, 1988, w/Jennifer Alward & Richard Marquand

RON MILLER
MOON PILOT Buena Vista, 1962, AP
BON VOYAGE! Buena Vista, 1962, AP w/Bill Walsh
SON OF FLUBBER Buena Vista, 1963, AP w/Bill Walsh
SUMMER MAGIC Buena Vista, 1963, AP
THE MISADVENTURES OF MERLIN JONES Buena Vista, 1964, AP
THE MONKEY'S UNCLE Buena Vista, 1965, CP
THAT DARN CAT! Buena Vista, 1965, CP w/Bill Walsh
LT. ROBIN CRUSOE, USN Buena Vista, 1966, CP w/Bill Walsh
MONKEYS, GO HOME! Buena Vista, 1967, CP
NEVER A DULL MOMENT Buena Vista, 1968
THE BOATNIKS Buena Vista, 1970
THE WILD COUNTRY Buena Vista, 1971
NOW YOU SEE HIM, NOW YOU DON'T Buena Vista, 1972
SNOWBALL EXPRESS Buena Vista, 1972
THE CASTAWAY COWBOY Buena Vista, 1974, w/Winston Hibler
ESCAPE TO WITCH MOUNTAIN Buena Vista, 1975, EP
NO DEPOSIT, NO RETURN Buena Vista, 1976
RIDE A WILD PONY Buena Vista, 1975
GUS Buena Vista, 1976
TREASURE OF MATECUMBE Buena Vista, 1976, EP
THE SHAGGY D.A. Buena Vista, 1976, EP
FREAKY FRIDAY Buena Vista, 1977
THE LITTLEST HORSE THIEVES *ESCAPE FROM THE DARK* Buena Vista, 1977
THE RESCUERS (AF) Buena Vista, 1977, EP
HERBIE GOES TO MONTE CARLO Buena Vista, 1977
PETE'S DRAGON Buena Vista, 1977, w/Jerome Courtland
THE CAT FROM OUTER SPACE Buena Vista, 1978
HOT LEAD AND COLD FEET Buena Vista, 1978
THE NORTH AVENUE IRREGULARS Buena Vista, 1979
THE APPLE DUMPLING GANG RIDES AGAIN Buena Vista, 1979
UNIDENTIFIED FLYING ODDBALL Buena Vista, 1979
THE BLACK HOLE Buena Vista, 1979
MIDNIGHT MADNESS Buena Vista, 1980
THE LAST FLIGHT OF NOAH'S ARK Buena Vista, 1980
HERBIE GOES BANANAS Buena Vista, 1980
THE DEVIL AND MAX DEVLIN Buena Vista, 1981, EP
THE WATCHER IN THE WOODS Buena Vista, 1981
CONDORMAN Buena Vista, 1981, EP
THE FOX AND THE HOUND (AF) Buena Vista, 1981, EP
NIGHT CROSSING Buena Vista, 1982, EP
TRON Buena Vista, 1982, EP
TEX Buena Vista, 1982, EP
NEVER CRY WOLF Buena Vista, 1983, EP
THE BLACK CAULDRON (AF) Buena Vista, 1985, EP

STEPHEN MILLER
HOG WILD Avco Embassy, 1980, EP w/Pierre David & Victor Solnicki
MY BLOODY VALENTINE Paramount, 1981, w/John Dunning & Andre Link

THOMAS L. MILLER
(credit w/Edward K. Milkis)
Business: Miller-Boyett Productions, 10202 W. Washington Blvd., Culver City, CA, 90232, 213/558-6555

SILVER STREAK 20th Century-Fox, 1976
FOUL PLAY Paramount, 1978
THE BEST LITTLE WHOREHOUSE IN TEXAS Universal, 1982, w/Robert L. Boyett

ROSS E. MILLOY
ALAMO BAY Tri-Star, 1985, EP
1918 Cinecom, 1985, w/Lillian V. Foote
ON VALENTINE'S DAY Angelika, 1986, EP w/Lewis Allen, Lindsay Law & Peter Newman
MISS FIRECRACKER Corsair, 1989, EP w/Lewis Allen
LORD OF THE FLIES Castle Rock/Columbia, 1990

STEVE MINER
Business: 1137 Second St., Suite 103, Santa Monica, CA, 90403, 213/393-0291
Agent: David Gersh, The Gersh Agency - Los Angeles, 213/274-6611

HERE COME THE TIGERS American International, 1978, w/Sean S. Cunningham
FRIDAY THE 13TH PART 2 Paramount, 1981
WARLOCK New World, 1990

MARVIN MINOFF

Business: Farrell-Minoff Productions, 14755 Ventura Blvd., #203, Sherman Oaks, CA, 91403, 818/789-5766

DOMINICK AND EUGENE Orion, 1988, w/Mike Farrell

WILLIAM MINOT

(credit w/Howard L. Baldwin)

BILLY GALVIN Vestron, 1986, EP w/Stuart Benjamin & Lindsay Law
FROM THE HIP DEG, 1987, EP w/Brian Russell

HOWARD G. MINSKY

LOVE STORY ★ Paramount, 1970

MARVIN MIRISCH

Business: The Mirisch Corporation, 100 Universal City Plaza, Universal City, CA, 91608, 818/777-1271

DRACULA Universal, 1979, EP
ROMANTIC COMEDY MGM/UA, 1983, EP

WALTER MIRISCH

Business: The Mirisch Corporation, 100 Universal City Plaza, Universal City, CA, 91608, 818/77-1271

FLAT TOP Allied Artists, 1952
THE ROSE BOWL STORY Monogram, 1952
WICHITA Allied Artists, 1955
AN ANNAPOLIS STORY Allied Artists, 1956
THE FIRST TEXAN Allied Artists, 1956
MAN OF THE WEST United Artists, 1958
THE MAGNIFICENT SEVEN United Artists, 1960
BY LOVE POSSESSED United Artists, 1961
TOYS IN THE ATTIC United Artists, 1962
TWO FOR THE SEESAW United Artists, 1962
HAWAII United Artists, 1966
IN THE HEAT OF THE NIGHT ★★ United Artists, 1967
FITZWILLY United Artists, 1968
SOME KIND OF NUT United Artists, 1969
SINFUL DAVEY United Artists, 1969, EP
HALLS OF ANGER United Artists, 1970, EP
THE HAWAIIANS United Artists, 1970
THEY CALL ME MISTER TIBBS! United Artists, 1970
THE ORGANIZATION United Artists, 1971
SCORPIO United Artists, 1972
MR. MAJESTYK United Artists, 1974
THE SPIKES GANG United Artists, 1974
MIDWAY Universal, 1976
GRAY LADY DOWN Universal, 1978
SAME TIME, NEXT YEAR Universal, 1978, w/Morton Gottlieb
DRACULA Universal, 1979
THE PRISONER OF ZENDA Universal, 1979
ROMANTIC COMEDY MGM/UA, 1983, w/Morton Gottlieb

ROBERT MISIOROWSKI

Business: Cinergi Productions, 414 N. Camden Dr., 10th Floor, Beverly Hills, CA, 90210, 213/859-0331

FOOD OF THE GODS II Concorde, 1989, EP w/Andras Hamori

RENEE MISSEL

(credit w/Howard Rosenman)

Business: The Samuel Goldwyn Company, 10203 Santa Monica Blvd., Suite 500, Los Angeles, CA, 90067, 213/552-2255

THE MAIN EVENT Warner Bros., 1979, EP
RESURRECTION Universal, 1980

CHARLES MITCHELL

(credit w/Tom Kuhn)

Business: Lightyear Entertainment, 350 5th Ave., Suite 5101, New York, NY, 10118

HEAVEN (FD) Island Pictures, 1987, EP w/Arlyne Rothberg
ARIA Miramax, 1988, EP
THE RETURN OF SWAMP THING Miramax, 1989, EP
THE LEMON SISTERS Miramax, 1990, EP w/Arnold J. Holland

DAVID MITCHELL

(credit w/Damian Lee)

Business: Rose & Ruby Productions, Inc., 33 Howard St., Toronto, Ontario M4X 1J6, Canada, 416/961-0555

BUSTED UP Shapiro Entertainment, 1987
WATCHERS Universal, 1988
FOOD OF THE GODS II Concorde, 1989

DOUG MITCHELL

(credit w/Terry Hayes)

Business: Kennedy Miller Productions, 30 Orwell St., Kings Cross, Sydney, Australia

MAD MAX BEYOND THUNDERDOME Warner Bros., 1985, CP
DEAD CALM Warner Bros., 1989, w/George Miller

J. TERRANCE MITCHELL

Agent: David List, The Agency - Los Angeles, 213/551-3000

GET ROLLIN' Aquarius, 1981

RON MITCHELL

Contact: Directors Guild of America - Los Angeles, 213/289-2000

WITCHBOARD Cinema Group, 1987, SP

YOSUKE MIZUNO

TOO MUCH Cannon, 1987, LP

ALEXANDRE MNOUCHKINE

(credit w/Georges Dancigers)

THAT MAN FROM RIO Lopert, 1964
DEAR DETECTIVE *DEAR INSPECTOR* Cinema 5, 1978
JUPITER'S THIGH Quartet, 1981
LA BALANCE Spectrafilm, 1983
THE NAME OF THE ROSE 20th Century-Fox, 1986, CP w/Franco Cristaldi*

MICHAEL MODER

Business: Viacom Productions, 10 Universal City Plaza, Universal City, CA, 91608, 818/505-7500
Contact: Directors Guild of America - Los Angeles, 213/289-2000

THEY ALL LAUGHED United Artists Classics, 1982, EP
SUMMER LOVERS Filmways, 1982
SONGWRITER Tri-Star, 1984, EP
BEVERLY HILLS COP Paramount, 1984, EP

LEONARD MOGEL

HEAVY METAL (AF) Columbia, 1981, EP

GERALD R. MOLEN

Contact: Directors Guild of America - Los Angeles, 213/289-2000

BATTERIES NOT INCLUDED Universal, 1987, AP
RAIN MAN ★★ MGM/UA, 1988, CP
BRIGHT LIGHTS, BIG CITY MGM/UA, 1988, EP

RON MOLER

Business: UMP & Associates, Raleigh Studios, 5300 Melrose Ave., Suite 411-E, Hollywood, CA, 90038 213/960-4580

BACHELOR PARTY 20th Century-Fox, 1984, w/Robert Israel
I LOVE YOU TO DEATH Tri-Star, 1990, w/Jeffrey Lurie

MARIANNE MOLONEY

Business: MTM Enterprises, 4024 Radford Ave., Studio City, CA, 91604, 818/760-5942

CLARA'S HEART Warner Bros., 1988, EP

PAUL MONASH

Business: Red Bank Films, Inc., 415 N. Crescent Dr., Suite 300, Beverly Hills, CA, 90210, 213/859-3374
Contact: Directors Guild of America - Los Angeles, 213/289-2000

BUTCH CASSIDY AND THE SUNDANCE KID ★ 20th Century-Fox, 1969, EP
SLAUGHTERHOUSE FIVE Universal, 1972
THE FRIENDS OF EDDIE COYLE Paramount, 1973
THE FRONT PAGE Universal, 1974
CARRIE United Artists, 1976
BIG TROUBLE IN LITTLE CHINA 20th Century-Fox, 1986, EP w/Keith Barish

E. C. MONELL

HIGHLANDER 20th Century-Fox, 1986, EP

MONTY MONTGOMERY

(credit w/Steven Golin & Sigurjon Sighvatsson)
Business: Propaganda Films, 940 N. Mansfield Ave., Los Angeles, CA, 213/462-6400

DADDY'S DYIN' MGM/UA, 1990
WILD AT HEART Samuel Goldwyn Company, 1990

PATRICK MONTGOMERY

Business: Archive Film Productions, 530 W. 25th St., New York, NY, 10001, 212/620-3955

THE COMPLEAT BEATLES (FD) TeleCulture, 1984, w/Stephanie Bennett

HANK MOONJEAN

Contact: Directors Guild of America - Los Angeles, 213/289-2000

THE SECRET LIFE OF AN AMERICAN WIFE 20th Century-Fox, 1968, AP
WUSA Paramount, 1970, AP
CHILD'S PLAY Paramount, 1972, AP
THE GREAT GATSBY Paramount, 1974, AP
THE FORTUNE Columbia, 1975, EP
THE END United Artists, 1978, EP
HOOPER Warner Bros., 1978
SMOKEY AND THE BANDIT PART II Universal, 1980
THE INCREDIBLE SHRINKING WOMAN Universal, 1981
PATERNITY Paramount, 1981, w/Lawrence Gordon
SHARKEY'S MACHINE Orion/Warner Bros., 1981
STROKER ACE Universal, 1983
STEALING HOME Warner Bros., 1988, w/ Thom Mount
DANGEROUS LIAISONS ★ Warner Bros., 1988, w/Norma Heyman

MICHAEL MOORCOCK

THE LAST DAYS OF MAN ON EARTH *THE FINAL PROGRAMME* New World, 1974, EP w/Roy Baird & David Puttnam

DEBORAH MOORE

LUCKY STIFF New Line Cinema, 1988, LP

DUDLEY MOORE

Agent: ICM - Los Angeles, 213/550-4000

ARTHUR 2 ON THE ROCKS Warner Bros., 1988, EP

MICHAEL MOORE

ROGER & ME (FD) Warner Bros., 1989

TERRY MOORE

Contact: Screen Actors Guild - Los Angeles, 213/465-4600

BEVERLY HILLS BRATS Taurus, 1989, w/Jerry Rivers

TIM MOORE

ROADHOUSE United Artists, 1989, EP w/StevePerry

PHILIPPE MORA

Agent: Marion Rosenberg, The Marion Rosenberg Office - Los Angeles, 213/653-7383
Contact: Directors Guild of America - Los Angeles, 213/289-2000

HOWLING III: THE MARSUPIALS Square Pictures, 1987, w/Charles Waterstreet
COMMUNION New Line Cinema, 1989, w/Dan Allingham & Whitley Strieber

JACQUES MORALI
CAN'T STOP THE MUSIC AFD, 1980, w/Henri Belolo & Allan Carr

GEORGE MORFOGEN
THEY ALL LAUGHED United Artists Classics, 1982, w/Blaine Novak
ILLEGALLY YOURS DEG, 1988

ANDRE MORGAN
(credit w/Al Ruddy)
Business: Ruddy-Morgan Productions, 120 El Camino Dr., Beverly Hills, CA, 90212, 213/271-7698

LASSITER Warner Bros., 1984, EP w/Raymond Chow
FAREWELL TO THE KING Orion, 1989
SPEED ZONE Orion, 1989, EP
IMPULSE Warner Bros., 1990

LESLIE MORGAN
Business: Corsair Pictures, 1740 Broadway, 23rd Floor, New York, NY, 10019, 212/603-0652 or 1640 S. Sepulveda Blvd., #216, Los Angeles, CA, 90025, 213/479-8200

A SHOCK TO THE SYSTEM Corsair, 1990, EP

ERROL MORRIS
Agent: CAA - Beverly Hills, 213/288-4545

THE GATES OF HEAVEN (FD) 1978
VERNON, FLORIDA (FD) 1981

GLORIA J. MORRISON
Business: Unistar International Pictures, 1119 N. McCadden Pl., Hollywood, CA, 90038, 213/462-7991

MIDNIGHT SVS Films, 1989, w/Norman Thaddeus Vane

STEVE MORRISON
WONDERLAND Vestron, 1988
MY LEFT FOOT ★ Miramax, 1989, EP w/Paul Heller

GARY MORTON
Contact: Screen Actors Guild - Los Angeles, 213/465-4600

ALL THE RIGHT MOVES 20th Century-Fox, 1983, EP

LAWRENCE MORTORFF
(formerly Lawrence Taylor-Mortorff)
Business: International Sales Organization, 10880 Wilshire Blvd., #1000, Los Angeles, CA, 90024, 213/470-0804

MARIA'S LOVERS Cannon, 1984, w/Bosko Djordjevic
HE'S MY GIRL Scotti Bros., 1987, w/Angela P. Schapiro
LADY BEWARE Scotti Bros., 1987, w/Tony Scotti
ROMERO Four Seasons Entertainment, 1989, EP w/John Sacret Young

SANDRA MOSBACHER
IN A SHALLOW GRAVE Skouras Pictures, 1988, CP

BEN MOSES
Agent: Writers & Artists Agency - Los Angeles, 213/820-2240
Contact: Directors Guild of America - Los Angeles, 213/289-2000

GOOD MORNING, VIETNAM Buena Vista, 1987, CP w/Harry Benn

WALTER MOSHAY
THE NEW ADVENTURES OF PIPPI LONGSTOCKING Columbia, 1988, w/Gary Mehlman

THOM MOUNT
Business: The Mount Co., 3723 W. Olive Ave., Burbank, CA, 91505, 818/846-1500

PIRATES Cannon, 1986, EP w/Mark Lombardo
CAN'T BUY ME LOVE Buena Vista, 1987
STEALING HOME Warner Bros., 1988, w/Hank Moonjean
BULL DURHAM Orion, 1988, w/Mark Burg
TEQUILA SUNRISE Warner Bros., 1988
FRANTIC Warner Bros., 1988, w/Tim Hampton
FRANKENSTEIN UNBOUND 20th Century-Fox, 1990, w/Roger Corman & Kobi Jaeger

P. GAEL MOURANT
MILLENNIUM 20th Century-Fox, 1989, EP w/Freddie Fields, John Foreman & Louis M. Silverstein

CAROLINE MOURIS
BEGINNERS LUCK New World, 1986

JEFFREY A. MUELLER
(credit w/Andrew Licht)
Business: Licht-Mueller Film Corporation, 2121 Avenue of the Stars, #2800, Los Angeles, CA, 90067, 213/551-2262

LICENSE TO DRIVE 20th Century-Fox, 1988
LITTLE MONSTERS MGM/UA, 1989, w/John A. Davis

EDWARD MUHL
THE LOST MAN Universal, 1969, w/Melville Tucker

LEE MUHL
HEARTBREAKERS Orion, 1985, EP w/Harry Cooper & Joseph Franck
THE HIDDEN New Line Cinema, 1987, EP w/Stephen Diener, Dennis Harris & Jeffrey Klein

MARTIN MULL
Agent: APA - Los Angeles, CA, 90069, 213/273-0744
Contact: Writers Guild of America - Los Angeles, 213/550-1000

RENTED LIPS Cine World Enterprises, 1988, w/Mort Engleberg

ROBERT MULLIGAN
Business: Boardwalk Productions, 5150 WilshireBlvd., Suite 505, Los Angeles, CA, 90036, 213/938-0109
Agent: Robert Stein, Leading Artists, Inc. - Beverly Hills, 213/858-1999

THE NICKEL RIDE 20th Century-Fox, 1974
KISS ME GOODBYE 20th Century-Fox, 1982

CHARLES B. MULVEHILL
Contact: Directors Guild of America - Los Angeles, 213/289-2000

HAROLD AND MAUDE Paramount, 1971, w/Colin Higgins
THE LAST DETAIL Columbia, 1973, AP
BOUND FOR GLORY United Artists, 1976, AP
THE POSTMAN ALWAYS RINGS TWICE Paramount, 1981, w/Bob Rafelson
FRANCES Universal, 1982, AP
SWING SHIFT Warner Bros., 1984, AP
SWEET DREAMS Tri-Star, 1985, CP
CREATOR Universal, 1985, AP
EIGHT MILLION WAYS TO DIE Tri-Star, 1986, CP
THE MILAGRO BEANFIELD WAR Universal, 1988, CP
IN COUNTRY Warner Bros., 1989, EP

ROBERT L. MUNGER
BORN AGAIN Avco Embassy, 1978, EP

MICHAEL S. MURPHEY
(credit w/Joel Soisson)
Business: Soisson Murphey Productions, 9060 Santa Monica Blvd., Suite 210, Los Angeles, CA, 90069, 213/273-3157

HAMBONE & HILLIE New World, 1984, AP
THE BOYS NEXT DOOR New World, 1985, AP
AVENGING ANGEL New World, 1985, AP
A NIGHTMARE ON ELM STREET, PART 2: FREDDY'S REVENGE New Line Cinema, 1985, LP
KGB: THE SECRET WAR Cinema Group, 1986, AP
TRICK OR TREAT DEG, 1986
THE SUPERNATURALS Republic Entertainment, 1987
BILL & TED'S EXCELLENT ADVENTURE Orion, 1989, w/Scott Kroopf

DENNIS MURPHY
Agent: Shapiro/Lichtman Talent Agency - Los Angeles, 213/859-8877
Contact: Directors Guild of America - Los Angeles, 213/289-2000

FRIDAY THE 13TH PART 2 Paramount, 1981, CP
MY BEST FRIEND IS A VAMPIRE Kings Road, 1988
BLIND FURY Tri-Star, 1990, AP

EDDIE MURPHY
Business: Paramount Pictures, 5555 Melrose Ave., Los Angeles, CA, 90038, 213/468-4545
Contact: Writers Guild of America - Los Angeles, 213/550-1000

EDDIE MURPHY RAW Paramount, 1987, EP w/Richard Tienken
HARLEM NIGHTS Paramount, 1989, EP

KAREN MURPHY
Business: 3224 Arizona, Santa Monica, CA, 90404, 213/828-2240

THIS IS SPINAL TAP Embassy, 1984
TRUE STORIES Warner Bros., 1986, CP
DRUGSTORE COWBOY Avenue Pictures, 1989, w/Nick Wechsler

MICHAEL TIMOTHY MURPHY
Business: Davis-Panzer Productions, 1438 N. Gower St., Suite 401, Los Angeles, CA, 90028, 213/463-2343

ST. HELENS Parnell, 1981
O'HARA'S WIFE Enfield, 1984, EP

BILL MURRAY
Agent: Michael Ovitz, CAA - Beverly Hills, 213/288-4545
Contact: Writers Guild of America - New York, 212/245-6180

QUICK CHANGE Warner Bros., 1990, w/Robert Greenhut

DON MURRAY
Agenr: Camden Artists - Los Angeles, 213/556-2022

ANNIE'S COMING OUT Film Australia, 1984
A TEST OF LOVE Universal, 1985

FORREST MURRAY
Contact: Directors Guild of America - New York, 212/581-0370

FIVE CORNERS Cineplex Odeon, 1988, w/Tony Bill

TOM MUSCA
Agent: Peter Rawley, ICM - Los Angeles, 213/550-4000
Contact: Writers Guild of America - Los Angeles, 213/550-1000

STAND AND DELIVER Warner Bros., 1988

JOHN MUSKER
THE LITTLE MERMAID (AF) Buena Vista, 1989, w/Howard Ashman

FLOYD MUTRUX
Agent: William Morris Agency - Beverly Hills, 213/274-7451
Contact: Directors Guild of America - Los Angeles, 213/289-2000

DICK TRACY Buena Vista, 1990, EP w/Art Linson

LAWRENCE MYERS
THE GREEK TYCOON Universal, 1978, CP w/Nico Mastorakis

LYNDA MYLES
DEFENSE OF THE REALM Hemdale, 1987, w/Robin Douet

BEN MYRON
Business: Lightmotive Ltd., Warner Brothers, 4000 Warner Blvd., Burbank, CA, 91522, 818/954-2976

SIGNAL 7 One Pass Pictures, 1986, w/Don Taylor
CHECKING OUT Warner Bros., 1989

N

DIANE NABATOFF
Business: Winkler/Daniel Productions, 5555 Melrose Ave., Los Angeles, CA, 90038, 213/468-5700

HIDER IN THE HOUSE Vestron, 1989, EP w/Steven Reuther

MIRA NAIR
Business: Mirabai Films, 6 Rivington St., New York, NY, 10002, 212/254-7826

SALAAM BOMBAY! Cinecom, 1988

STEVEN NALEVANSKY
Business: Paramount Television, 5555 Melrose Ave., Los Angeles, CA, 90038, 213/468-5519

BLOOD BEACH Jerry Gross Organization, 1981

FRANK DARIUS NAMEI
(credit w/Robert Resnikoff)

Business: Paramount Pictures, 5555 Melrose Ave., Los Angeles, CA, 90038, 213/468-4302
Agent: BBMW - Los Angeles, 213/277-4998

COLLISION COURSE DEG, 1988, CP

HERB NANAS
Business: Moress-Nanas-Golden Entertainment, 12424 Wilshire Blvd., #840, Los Angeles, CA, 90025, 213/820-9897

ROCKY III MGM/UA, 1982, EP
FIRST BLOOD Orion, 1982, CP
LOST IN AMERICA Warner Bros., 1985, EP
EYE OF THE TIGER Scotti Bros., 1986, EP w/Ben Scotti

MICHAEL NANKIN
Agent: ICM - Los Angeles, 213/550-4000
Contact: Writers Guild of America - Los Angeles, 213/550-1000

MIDNIGHT MADNESS Buena Vista, 1980, CP w/David Wechter

GARY NARDINO
Business: Orion Television, 1888 Century Park East, Los Angeles, CA, 90057, 213/282-0550

STAR TREK III: THE SEARCH FOR SPOCK Paramount, 1984, EP
FIRE WITH FIRE Paramount, 1986

JOHN NARTMANN
HARD COUNTRY AFD, 1981, CP

MARCIA NASATIR
THE BIG CHILL ★ Columbia, 1983, EP w/ Lawrence Kasdan
IRONWEED Tri-Star, 1987, w/Keith Barish
HAMBURGER HILL Paramount, 1987, w/Jim Carabatsos

RICK NATHANSON
THE ARROGANT Cannon, 1987, LP
HALLOWEEN 5: THE REVENGE OF MICHAEL MYERS Galaxy, 1989, LP

CHRISTOPHER NEAME
BELLMAN AND TRUE Island Pictures, 1987, w/ Michael Wearing

CHRIS D. NEBE
THE NAKED CAGE Cannon, 1986

GARY A. NEILL
BAT 21 Tri-Star, 1988, w/Michael Balson & David Fisher

CHRISTOPHER NELSON
Contact: Directors Guild of America - Los Angeles, 213/289-2000

FRATERNITY VACATION New World, 1985, w/Boris Malden & Robert C. Peters

JAMES NELSON
Contact: Directors Guild of America - Los Angeles, 213/289-2000

BORDERLINE AFD, 1980

JEFFREY NELSON
LIANNA United Artists Classics, 1983, w/Maggie Renzi

PETER NELSON
SMORGASBORD Warner Bros., 1985, w/Arnold Orgolini

PETER NELSON
Contact: Writers Guild of America - Los Angeles, 213/550-1000

THE LONELY PASSION OF JUDITH HEARNE Island Pictures, 1987, w/Richard Johnson

TERRY NELSON
Business: Universal Pictures, 100 Universal City Plaza, Bldg. 507, #2E, Universal City, CA, 91608, 818/777-1128
Contact: Directors Guild of America - Los Angeles, 213/289-2000

PART 2, SOUNDER Gamma III, 1976
MELVIN AND HOWARD Universal, 1980, AP
RAGGEDY MAN Universal, 1981, AP
MISSING ★ Universal, 1982, AP
CROSS CREEK Universal, 1983, CP
GHOST DAD Universal, 1990

WILLIE NELSON
Agent: ICM - Los Angeles, 213/550-4000

RED HEADED STRANGER Alive FIlms, 1986, w/William D. Wittliff

LAWRENCE NESIS
MEATBALLS Paramount, 1979, AP
HEAVY METAL (AF) Columbia, 1981, AP w/Michael Gross
MY BLOODY VALENTINE Paramount, 1981, AP
ATLANTIC CITY ★ Paramount, 1981, AP
HAPPY BIRTHDAY TO ME Columbia, 1981, AP

VIDEODROME Universal, 1983, AP
COVERGIRL Paramount, 1979, AP
MEATBALLS III Moviestore, 1986, EP w/Andre Link
BUSTED UP Shapiro Entertainment, 1987, EP

MICHAEL NESMITH

Business: Pacific Arts, 50 N. La Cienega Blvd., Suite 210, Beverly Hills, CA, 90211, 213/657-2233
Agent: William Morris Agency - Beverly Hills, 213/274-7451

TIMERIDER: THE ADVENTURE OF LYLE SWANN Jensen Farley, 1983, EP
REPO MAN Universal, 1984, EP
TAPEHEADS Avenue Pictures, 1988, EP

AMY NESS

STATIC MCEG, 1988

STEPHEN J. NETBURN

Contact: Directors Guild of America - Los Angeles, 213/289-2000

TERROR IN THE AISLES Universal, 1984, w/Andrew J. Kuehn

GEOFFREY NETHERCOTT

MERRY CHRISTMAS, MR. LAWRENCE Universal, 1983, EP w/Terry Glinwood, Masato Hara & Eiko Oshima

MACE NEUFELD

Business: Neufeld/Rehme Productions, Paramount Pictures, 5555 Melrose Ave., Hart 304, Los Angeles, CA, 90038, 213/468-4816

THE OMEN 20th Century-Fox, 1976, EP
THE FRISCO KID Warner Bros., 1979
THE FUNHOUSE Universal, 1981, EP w/Mark Lester
THE FINAL CONFLICT 20th Century-Fox, 1981, AP
THE AVIATOR MGM/UA, 1985, w/Thomas H. Brodek
TRANSYLVANIA 6-5000 New World, 1985, w/Thomas H. Brodek
NO WAY OUT Orion, 1987, EP
THE HUNT FOR RED OCTOBER Paramount, 1990
FLIGHT OF THE INTRUDER Paramount, 1990

EDWARD NEUMEIER

Agent: Bauer Benedek Agency - Los Angeles, 213/275-2421
Contact: Writers Guild of America - Los Angeles, 213/550-1000

ROBOCOP Orion, 1987, CP

PAUL NEWMAN

Agent: Michael Ovitz, CAA - Beverly Hills, 213/288-4545
Contact: Directors Guild of America - Los Angeles, 213/289-2000

RACHEL, RACHEL ★ Warner Bros., 1968
WUSA Paramount, 1970, w/John Foreman
THEY MIGHT BE GIANTS Universal, 1972, w/John Foreman
THE EFFECT OF GAMMA RAYS ON MAN-IN-THE-MOON MARIGOLDS 20th Century-Fox, 1972
HARRY AND SON Orion, 1984, w/Ronald L. Buck

PETER NEWMAN

Business: Lewis Allen Productions, 1500 Broadway, New York, NY, 10036, 212/221-2400

COME BACK TO THE 5 & DIME JIMMY DEAN, JIMMY DEAN Cinecom, 1982, AP
1918 Cinecom, 1985, EP w/Lewis Allen
ON VALENTINE'S DAY Angelika, 1986, EP w/Lewis Allen, Lindsay Law & Ross E. Milloy
SWIMMING TO CAMBODIA Cinecom, 1987, EP w/Lewis Allen, Ira Deutchman & Amir J. Malin
END OF THE LINE Orion Classics, 1987, w/Lewis Allen
O. C. AND STIGGS MGM, 1987, w/Robert Altman
LORD OF THE FLIES Castle Rock/Columbia, 1990, w/Lewis Allen

ROBERT NEWMYER

Business: Outlaw Productions, 12103 Maxwellton Rd., Studio City, CA, 91604, 818/509-7953

sex, lies & videotape Miramax, 1989, w/John Hardy

MIKE NICHOLS

Attorney: Marvin B. Meyer, Rosenfeld, Meyer & Susman, Beverly Hills, CA, 213/858-7700
Agent: Sam Cohn, ICM - New York, 212/556-5600

CARNAL KNOWLEDGE Avco Embassy, 1971
THE FORTUNE Columbia, 1975, w/Don Devlin
SILKWOOD 20th Century-Fox, 1983, w/Michael Hausman
HEARTBURN Paramount, 1986, w/Robert Greenhut
THE LONGSHOT Orion, 1986, EP
POSTCARDS FROM THE EDGE Columbia, 1990, w/John Calley

JACK NICHOLSON

Business Manager: Guild Management Corporation, Los Angeles, 213/277-9711
Agent: Sandy Bresler, Bresler, Kelly & Kipperman - Encino, 818/905-3210

RIDE IN THE WHIRLWIND Favorite/Jack H. Harris, 1966, w/Monte Hellman
THE SHOOTING Favorite/Jack H. Harris, 1966, w/Monte Hellman
HEAD Columbia, 1968, w/Bob Rafelson
DRIVE, HE SAID Columbia, 1971, w/Steve Blauner

WALLIS NICITA

(credit w/Lauren Lloyd)

Business: Nicita-Lloyd Productions, Paramount Pictures, 5555 Melrose Ave., Los Angeles, CA, 90035, 213/468-8514

MERMAIDS Orion, 1990, w/Patrick Palmer
FIRES WITHIN Pathe, 1990

DAVID A. NICKSAY

Business: Morgan Creek Productions, 1875 Century Park East, Suite 200, Los Angeles, CA, 90067, 213/284-8884

I'M DANCING AS FAST AS I CAN Paramount, 1982, AP
MRS. SOFFEL MGM/UA, 1984, w/Scott Rudin & Edgar G. Scherick
LUCAS 20th Century-Fox, 1986

STEVE NICOLAIDES
(credit w/Jeffrey Stott)
Business: Castle Rock Entertainment, 335 N. Maple Dr., Suite 135, Beverly Hills, CA, 90210, 213/285-2300
Contact: Directors Guild of America - Los Angeles, 213/289-2000

THE PRINCESS BRIDE 20th Century-Fox, 1987, AP
IT TAKES TWO United Artists, 1988, EP*
WHEN HARRY MET SALLY... Castle Rock/Columbia, 1989, CP

JOHN NICOLELLA
Agent: William Morris Agency - Beverly Hills, 213/274-7451
Contact: Directors Guild of America - Los Angeles, 213/289-2000

WINDOWS United Artists, 1980, AP
TIMES SQUARE AFD, 1980, EP w/Kevin McCormick
THE FAN Paramount, 1981, AP w/Bill Oakes
EASY MONEY Orion, 1983

ROB NILSSON
Business: Snowball Productions, 415/567-4404
Agent: Brenda Beckett, Sanford-Beckett Agency - Los Angeles, 213/208-2100

ON THE EDGE Skouras Pictures, 1986, w/Jeffrey Hayes

DAVID NIVEN, JR.
THE EAGLE HAS LANDED Columbia, 1977, w/Jack Winer
ESCAPE TO ATHENA AFD, 1979, w/Jack Winer
MONSIGNOR 20th Century-Fox, 1982, w/ Frank Yablans
BETTER LATE THAN NEVER Warner Bros., 1983, w/Jack Haley, Jr.
KIDCO 20th Century-Fox, 1984, w/Frank Yablans
THAT'S DANCING (FD) MGM, 1985, w/Jack Haley Jr.

ROBERT NIXON
Agent: William Morris Agency - Beverly Hills, 213/274-7451
Contact: Directors Guild of America - Los Angeles, 213/289-2000

GORILLAS IN THE MIST Universal, 1988, CP w/Judy Kessler

MICHAEL NOLIN
Business: Alliance Entertainment Corporation, 8439 Sunset Blvd., #404, Los Angeles, CA, 90069, 213/654-9488 or 920 Yonge Street, Suite 400, Toronto, Ontario, M4W 3C7, Canada, 416/967-1174

MISCHIEF 20th Century-Fox, 1985, w/Sam Manners
STRIPPER (FD) 20th Century-Fox, 1986, CP w/Thom Tyson
THE STRANGER Columbia, 1987, EP
84 CHARLIE MOPIC New Century/Vista, 1989

RON NORMAN
Business: Horizons Productions, 1134 N. Ogden Dr., West Hollywood, CA, 90046, 213/654-6911

LOVERS Horizons Productions, 1984
STRANGERS IN PARADISE New West, 1985

DON NORMANN
GRUNT! THE WRESTLING MOVIE New World, 1985, w/Anthony Randell

STEVEN NORTH
Business: 100 Blvd. Sebastopol, Paris, 75003, 40/279660
Contact: Writers Guild of America - Los Angeles, 213/289-2000

HOMER National General, 1970
SHANKS Paramount, 1974
WELCOME TO ARROW BEACH Warner Bros., 1974
THE BOY IN BLUE 20th Century-Fox, 1986, EP

F. RICHARD NORTHCOTT
Business: Nelson Entertainment, Inc., 335 N. Maple Dr., Suite 350, Beverly Hills, CA, 90210, 213/285-6000

9 1/2 WEEKS MGM/UA, 1986, EP w/Keith Barish & Frank Konigsberg

BLAINE NOVAK
Agent: Laurie Apelian, The Chasin Agency - Beverly Hills, 213/278-7505
Contact: Writers Guild of America - New York, 212/245-6180

THEY ALL LAUGHED United Artists Classics, 1982, w/George Morfogen

MICHAEL NOZIK
Contact: Directors Guild of America - New York, 212/581-0370

CHINA GIRL Vestron, 1987
CROSSING DELANCEY Warner Bros., 1988
SALAAM BOMBAY! Cinecom, 1988, EP w/Gabriel Auer, Cherie Rodgers & Anil Tejani

GINNY NUGENT
MUNCHIES Concorde, 1987, CP
BAD DREAMS 20th Century-Fox, 1988, AP
TREMORS Universal, 1990, LP

GRAFTON NUNES
THE LOVELESS Atlantic Entertainment, 1984, w/A. Kitman Ho

BILL OAKES
Business: RSO Films, 1041 N. Formosa Ave., Los Angeles, CA, 90046, 213/850-2601

THE FAN Paramount, 1981, AP w/John Nicolella
GREASE 2 Paramount, 1982, EP
STAYING ALIVE Paramount, 1983, EP

HERBERT L. OAKES
EDUCATING RITA Columbia, 1983, EP
NOT QUITE PARADISE New World, 1986, EP

PETER O'BRIAN
Business: Independent Pictures Inc., 151 John St., Suite 410, Toronto, Ontario M5V 2T2, Canada, 416/960-6468

THE GREY FOX United Artists Classics, 1983
ONE MAGIC CHRISTMAS Buena Vista, 1985
MY AMERICAN COUSIN Spectrafilm, 1986
JOHN AN D THE MISSUS Cinema Group, 1987, EP w/S. Howard Rosen

DENIS O'BRIEN
(credit w/George Harrison)
Business: HandMade Films, Ltd., 26 Cadogan Square, London SW1X 0JP, England, 01/584-8345; 7400 Beverly Blvd., #210, Los Angeles, CA, 90036, 213/936-8050

MONTY PYTHON'S LIFE OF BRIAN Orion/Warner Bros., 1979, EP
TIME BANDITS Avco Embassy, 1981, EP
THE MISSIONARY Columbia, 1982, EP
PRIVATES ON PARADE Orion Classics, 1984, EP
SCRUBBERS Orion Classics, 1984, EP
BULLSHOT Island Alive, 1985, EP
A PRIVATE FUNCTION Island Alive, 1985, EP
MONA LISA Island Pictures, 1986, EP
SHANGHAI SURPRISE MGM, 1986, EP
WATER Atlantic Entertainment, 1986, EP
WITHNAIL & I Cineplex Odeon, 1987, EP
THE LONELY PASSION OF JUDITH HEARNE Island Pictures, 1987, EP
BELLMAN & TRUE Island Pictures, 1987, EP w/Johnny Goodman & John Hambley
FIVE CORNERS Cineplex Odeon, 1988, EP
TRACK 29 Island Pictures, 1988, EP
THE RAGGEDY RAWNEY Four Seasons Entertainment, 1989, EP
POWWOW HIGHWAY Warner Bros., 1989, EP
CHECKING OUT Warner Bros., 1989, EP
HOW TO GET AHEAD IN ADVERTISING Warner Bros., 1989, EP
NUNS ON THE RUN 20th Century-Fox, 1990, EP

FRANCIS O'BRIEN
GALLIPOLI Paramount, 1981, EP

LORENZO O'BRIEN
WALKER Universal, 1987, w/Angel Flores-Marini

JEFFREY OBROW
Agent: Triad Artists, Inc. - Los Angeles, 213/556-2727

THE POWER Film Ventures International, 1982
PRANKS *THE DORM THAT DRIPPED BLOOD* New Image, 1983
THE KINDRED FM Entertainment, 1987

DAVID OBST
(credit w/Jeff Buhai & Steve Zacharias)
Agent: Bauer Benedek Agency - Los Angeles, 213/275-2421

REVENGE OF THE NERDS 20th Century-Fox, 1984, EP w/Peter Bart*
THE WHOOPEE BOYS Paramount, 1986, EP
JOHNNY BE GOOD Orion, 1988, EP

LYNDA OBST
(credit w/Debra Hill)
Business: Lynda Obst Productions, Columbia Pictures, Studio Plaza, 3400 Riverside Dr., Producers 8, Rm. 236, Burbank, CA, 91505, 818/954-3133

FLASHDANCE Paramount, 1983, AP w/TomJacobson*
ADVENTURES IN BABYSITTING Buena Vista, 1987
HEARTBREAK HOTEL Buena Vista, 1988

RICHARD L. O'CONNOR
Contact: Directors Guild of America - Los Angeles, 213/289-2000

DISTANT THUNDER Paramount, 1988, EP

DENIS O'DELL
A HARD DAY'S NIGHT United Artists, 1964, AP
HOW I WON THE WAR United Artists, 1967, AP
THE DEADLY AFFAIR Columbia, 1967, AP
PETULIA United Artists, 1968, AP
THE MAGIC CHRISTIAN Commonwealth United, 1970
THE OFFENCE United Artists, 1973
JUGGERNAUT United Artists, 1974, AP
ROYAL FLASH 20th Century-Fox, 1975, w/David V. Picker
ROBIN AND MARIAN Columbia, 1976, w/Richard Shepherd
THE RITZ Warner Bros., 1976
CUBA United Artists, 1979, EP

LYNN O'DONNELL
LIVING ON TOKYO TIME Skouras Pictures, 1987, w/Dennis Hayashi

MICHAEL O'DONOGHUE
Agent: William Morris Agency - New York, 212/586-5100
Contact: Writers Guild of America - New York, 212/245-6180

MR. MIKE'S MONDO VIDEO New Line Cinema, 1979

DANNY O'DONOVAN
GOLDENGIRL Avco Embassy, 1979
ABSOLUTION Trans World Entertainment, 1988, w/Elliott Kastner

CHRISTINE OESTRICHER
STRIKE IT RICH Millimeter, 1990, w/Graham Easton

JERRY OFFSAY
Business: ABC Productions, 2040 Avenue of the Stars, Los Angeles, CA, 90067, 213/557-7777

HAMBURGER HILL Paramount, 1987, EP w/David Korda
EIGHT MEN OUT Orion, 1988, EP w/Barbara Boyle

JENNIFER OGDEN
Contact: Directors Guild of America - New York, 212/581-0370

GARBO TALKS MGM/UA, 1984, AP
THE MANHATTAN PROJECT 20th Century-Fox, 1986, w/Marshall Brickman
SUSPECT Tri-Star, 1987, AP
COOKIE Warner Bros., 1989, CP
FAMILY BUSINESS Tri-Star, 1989, EP w/Burtt Harris

BERTIL OHLSSON
Business: Sandrews, Floragatan 4, Box 5612, S-114 86 Stockholm, Sweden, 08/23-47-00

AMADEUS Orion, 1984, EP w/Michael Hausman
THE UNBEARABLE LIGHTNESS OF BEING Orion, 1988, EP

KIP OHMAN
THE FLY 20th Century-Fox, 1986, CP w/Marc Boyman
THE HITCHER Tri-Star, 1986, w/David Bombyk

STUART OKEN
Business: New Visions Pictures, 5750 Wilshire Blvd., #600, Los Angeles, CA, 90036, 213/965-2500

ABOUT LAST NIGHT... Tri-Star, 1986, wJason Brett

CHARLES OKUN
(credit w/Michael Grillo)
Business: 650 N. Bronson Ave., Room 306, Hollywood, CA, 90004

LOVESICK Warner Bros., 1983*
SILVERADO Columbia, 1985, EP
CROSS MY HEART Universal, 1987, CP
THE ACCIDENTAL TOURIST ★ Warner Bros., 1988, w/Lawrence Kasdan
I LOVE YOU TO DEATH Tri-Star, 1990, EP

JONATHAN OLSBERG
Business: Glinwood Films Ltd., Swan House, 52 Poland St., London W1V 3DF, England, 01/437-1181

STICKY FINGERS Spectrafilm, 1988, EP
TOKYO POP Spectrafilm, 1988, EP

DANA OLSEN
Agent: InterTalent Agency - Los Angeles, 213/271-0600

THE 'BURBS Universal, 1989, CP

GERALD T. OLSON
Business: New Line Cinema, 116 N. Robertson Blvd., Suite 808, Los Angeles, CA, 90048, 213/854-5811
Contact: Directors Guild of America - Los Angeles, 213/289-2000

REPO MAN Universal, 1984, AP
QUIET COOL New Line Cinema, 1986, w/Robert Shaye
BLOODY BIRTHDAY Judica Productions, 1986
THE HIDDEN New Line Cinema, 1987, w/Michael Meltzer & Robert Shaye
LUCKY STIFF New Line Cinema, 1988
HOUSE PARTY New Line Cinema, 1990, EP

JOHN M. ONDOV
THAT WAS THEN...THIS IS NOW Paramount, 1985, w/Gary R. Lindberg

TERENCE O'NEILL
MOMMIE DEAREST Paramount, 1981, EP w/David Koontz

IRVING ONG
SALVATION! Circle Releasing, 1987, EP w/Michel Duval & Ned Richardson

PEER J. OPPENHEIMER
KEY EXCHANGE 20th Century-Fox, 1985, EP w/Michael Pochna & Ronald Winston

BARRY OPPER
(credit w/Rupert Harvey)
Business: Sho Films, 2300 Duane St., #9, Los Angeles, CA, 90039, 213/665-9088

ANDROID Island Alive, 1984, EP
CITY LIMITS Atlantic Entertainment, 1985
SLAMDANCE Island Pictures, 1987

KERRY ORENT
THE PRINCE OF PENNSYLVANIA New Line Cinema, 1988, CP

ARNOLD ORGOLINI
Business: Go Entertainment, Raleigh Studios, 650 N. Bronson, Suite 134, Los Angeles, CA, 90004, 213/465-4650

SMORGASBORD Warner Bros., 1985, w/Peter Nelson
HOLLYWOOD VICE SQUAD Cinema Group, 1986, w/Sandy Howard
ANGEL III: THE FINAL CHAPTER New World, 1988

BARRIE M. OSBORNE
Contact: Directors Guild of America - Los Angeles, 213/289-2000

THE BIG CHILL ★ Columbia, 1983, AP
THE COTTON CLUB Orion, 1984, LP w/Joseph Cusumano
FANDANGO Warner Bros., 1985, AP w/Pat Kehoe
PEGGY SUE GOT MARRIED Tri-Star, 1986, EP
CHILD'S PLAY MGM/UA, 1988, EP w/Elliott Geisinger

WILLIAM OSCO
NIGHT PATROL New World, 1984

EIKO OSHIMA
MERRY CHRISTMAS, MR. LAWRENCE Universal, 1983, EP w/Terry Glinwood, Masato Hara & Geoffrey Nethercott

IRVING OSHMAN
PRIVATE LESSONS Jensen Farley, 1981, CP

MYLES OSTERNECK
BAD MEDICINE 20th Century-Fox, 1985, EP w/Michael Jaffe & Sam Manners

RANDY OSTROW
(credit w/Ned Dowd)
LET IT RIDE Paramount, 1989, CP
STATE OF GRACE Orion, 1990

STANLEY O'TOOLE
THE SEVEN PERCENT SOLUTION Universal, 1976, AP
THE SQUEEZE Warner Bros., 1977
THE BOYS FROM BRAZIL 20th Century-Fox, 1978, w/Martin Richards
NIJINSKY Paramount, 1980, w/Nora Kaye
OUTLAND The Ladd Company/Warner Bros., 1981, EP

SPHINX Orion/Warner Bros., 1981
ENEMY MINE 20th Century-Fox, 1985, EP
LIONHEART Orion, 1987, w/Talia Shire
QUIGLEY DOWN UNDER Pathe, 1990, w/Alex Rose

JEAN-PAUL OUELLETTE

THE UNNAMEABLE Vidmark Entertainment, 1988, w/Dean Ramser

FRANK OZ

Agent: Mike Marcus, CAA - Beverly Hills, 213/288-4545
Contact: Directors Guild of America - Los Angeles, 213/289-2000

THE GREAT MUPPET CAPER Universal/AFD, 1981, w/David Lazer

P

AMADEO PAGANI

WAIT UNTIL SPRING, BANDINI Orion, 1990, EP w/Christian Charret, Cyril de Rouvre & Giorgio Silvago

ALAN J. PAKULA

Business: Pakula Productions, Inc., 330 West 58th St., New York, NY, 10019, 212/664-0640
Agent: William Morris Agency - Beverly Hills, 213/274-7451

FEAR STRIKES OUT Paramount, [illegible]7
TO KILL A MOCKINGBIRD ★ Unive[illegible]al, 1962
LOVE WITH THE PROPER STRANGE[illegible] Paramount, 1963
BABY, THE RAIN MUST FALL Colum[illegible], 1965
INSIDE DAISY CLOVER Warner Bros., 1965
UP THE DOWN STAIRCASE Warner B[illegible]s., 1967
THE STALKING MOON National Gener[illegible] 1968
THE STERILE CUCKOO Paramount, 1[illegible]9
KLUTE Warner Bros., 1971
LOVE & PAIN & the whole damn thing Columbia, 1973
THE PARALLAX VIEW Paramount, 1974
STARTING OVER Paramount, 1979, w/James L. Brooks
SOPHIE'S CHOICE Universal, 1982, w/Keith Barish
DREAM LOVER MGM/UA, 1986, w/Jon Boorstin
ORPHANS Lorimar, 1987
SEE YOU IN THE MORNING Warner Bros., 1989, w/Susan Solt

JULIA PALAU

Business: J & M Entertainment, 1289 Sunset Plaza Dr., Los Angeles, CA, 90069, 213/652-7733

PLAYING FOR KEEPS Universal, 1986, EP w/Michael Ryan & Patrick Wachsberger

BONNIE PALEF

Business: Snapdragon Productions, 7135 Hollywood Blvd., #1203, Los Angeles, CA, 90046, 213/850-5946

AGNES OF GOD Columbia, 1985, AP
MOONSTRUCK ★ MGM, 1987, AP
PARENTS Vestron, 1989

MAX PALEVSKY

ISLANDS IN THE STREAM Paramount, 1977, w/Peter Bart

MICHAEL PALIN

Business: Prominent Features Ltd., 68A Delancey St., London NW1 7RY, England, 01/284-1004

THE MISSIONARY Columbia, 1982, w/Neville C. Thompson

MELINDA PALMER

Contact: Writers Guild of America - Los Angeles, 213/550-1000

THE GARBAGE PAIL KIDS MOVIE Atlantic Entertainment, 1987, CP w/Michael Lloyd

PATRICK PALMER

Business: PatrickPalmer Productions, Raleigh Studios, 5254 Melrose Ave., Suite 405-D, Los Angeles, CA, 90038, 213/960-4960
Contact: Directors Guild of America - Los Angeles, 213/289-2000

THE LANDLORD United Artists, 1970, AP
FIDDLER ON THE ROOF United Artists, 1971, AP
JESUS CHRIST SUPERSTAR Universal, 1973, AP
BILLY TWO HATS United Artists, 1972, w/Norman Jewison
ROLLERBALL United Artists, 1985, AP
F.I.S.T. United Artists, 1978, AP
...AND JUSTICE FOR ALL Columbia, 1979, w/Norman Jewison
THE DOGS OF WAR United Artists, 1981, EP w/Norman Jewison
BEST FRIENDS Warner Bros., 1982, w/Norman Jewison
ICEMAN Universal, 1984, w/Norman Jewison
A SOLDIER'S STORY ★ Columbia, 1984, w/Norman Jewison & Ronald L. Schwary
AGNES OF GOD Columbia, 1985, w/Norman Jewison
CHILDREN OF A LESSER GOD ★ Paramount, 1986, w/Burt Sugarman
MOONSTRUCK ★ MGM /UA, 1987, w/Norman Jewison
STANLEY & IRIS MGM/UA, 1990, EP
MERMAIDS Orion, 1990, w/Lauren Lloyd & Wallis Nicita

BRUCE PALTROW

Attorney: Ken Meyer, Rosenfeld, Meyer & Susman, 9601 Wilshire Blvd., Beverly Hills, CA, 213/858-7700
Business: MTM Enterprises, 4024 Radford Ave., Studio City, CA, 91604, 818/760-5000

A LITTLE SEX Universal, 1982, w/Robert DeLaurentis

WILLIAM N. PANZER

(credit w/Peter Davis)
Business: Davis-Panzer Productions, 1438 N. Gower St., Suite 573, Los Angeles, CA, 90028, 213/463-2343

STUNTS New Line Cinema, 1977, EP w/Robert Shaye
STEEL World Northal, 1980
ST. HELENS Parnell, 1981, AP
THE OSTERMAN WEEKEND 20th Century-Fox, 1983
O'HARA'S WIFE Enfield, 1984
HIGHLANDER 20th Century-Fox, 1986
FREEWAY New World, 1988

GERALD S. PAONESSA
MONKEY SHINES Orion, 1988, EP w/Peter Grunwald

JOSEPH PAPP
Business: New York Shakespeare Festival, 425 Lafayette St., New York, NY, 212/598-7100
Contact: Directors Guild of America - Los Angeles 213/289-2000

THE PIRATES OF PENZANCE Universal, 1983
PLENTY 20th Century-Fox, 1985, w/Edward R. Pressman

GEORGE PAPPAS
Business: Cinema Seven Productions,154 West 57th St., #112, New York, NY, 10019, 212/315-1060

COPS & ROBBERS United Artists, 1973, AP
JEREMY United Artists, 1973
92 IN THE SHADE United Artists, 1974
FAREWELL, MY LOVELY Avco Embassy, 1975, w/Jerry Bruckheimer
THE FIRST DEADLY SIN Filmways, 1980, w/Mark Shanker
NOMADS Atlantic Entertainment, 1986, w/Cassian Elwes
HEAT New Century/Vista, 1987, w/Keith Rotman

ALFRED PARISER
Business: Edward R. Pressman Film Corporation, 4000 Warner Blvd., Prod. 5, Room 114, Burbank, CA, 91522, 818/954-3315

THEY CAME FROM WITHIN Trans-America, 1977, EP w/John Dunning & Andre Link
THE HAUNTING OF JULIA Discovery, 1981, w/Peter Fetterman
IMPROPER CHANNELS Crown International, 1981, w/Morrie Ruvinsky

MICHAEL PARISER
MARTIANS GO HOME Taurus, 1990

DAVID PARKER
(credit w/Nadia Tass)
Agent: CAA - Beverly Hills, 213/288-4545

MALCOLM Vestron, 1986
RIKKY & PETE MGM/UA, 1988

RONALD PARKER
Contact: Writers Guild of America - Los Angeles, 213/550-1000

MY STEPMOTHER IS AN ALIEN WEG/Columbia, 1988, w/Franklin R. Levy

WALTER F. PARKES
(credit w/Lawrence Lasker)
Business: Paramount Pictures, 5555 Melrose Ave., Los Angeles, CA, 90038, 213/468-5000
Agent: InterTalent Agency - Los Angeles, 213/271-0600

VOLUNTEERS Tri-Star, 1985, w/Richard Shepherd*
PROJECT X 20th Century-Fox, 1987
TRUE BELIEVER Columbia, 1989
AWAKENINGS Columbia, 1990

CLIVE PARSONS
(credit w/Davina Belling)
Business: Film & General Productions, Ltd., 10 Pembridge Place, London W2 4XB, England, 01/221-1141

INSERTS United Artists, 1975
THAT SUMMER Columbia, 1979
SCUM Berwick Street Films, 1979
BREAKING GLASS Paramount, 1980
BRITANNIA HOSPITAL United Artists Classics, 1982
GREGORY'S GIRL Samuel Goldwyn Company, 1982
COMFORT AND JOY Universal, 1984

LINDSLEY PARSONS, JR.
Contact: Directors Guild of America - Los Angeles, 213/289-2000

THE WIZARD Universal, 1989, EP

THEODORE R. PARVIN
Agent: The Artists Agency - Los Angeles, 213/828-1003
Contact: Directors Guild of America - Los Angeles, 213/289-2000

VOLUNTEERS Tri-Star, 1985, AP
HOT PURSUIT Paramount, 1987, w/Pierre David

ANDY PATERSON
RESTLESS NATIVES Orion Classics, 1986, CP

IAIN PATERSON
SWEET LORRAINE Angelika Films, 1987, LP
FRIDAY THE 13TH, PART VII — THE NEW BLOOD Paramount, 1988

MICHAEL PATTINSON
Contact: Australian Film Commission, 9229 Sunset Blvd., Los Angeles, CA, 90069, 213/275-7074

GROUND ZERO Avenue, 1988

BART PATTON
Contact: Directors Guild of America - Los Angeles, 213/289-2000

THE RAIN PEOPLE Warner Bros., 1969, w/Ronald Colby

WILLIAM PAUL
THE NINTH CONFIGURATION *TWINKLE, TWINKLE, "KILLER" KANE* Warner Bros., 1979, EP

DAN PAULSON
Business: Cinecorp, 8125 N. Lankershim Blvd., North Hollywood, CA, 91605, 818/768-8888

COMES A HORSEMAN United Artists, 1978, w/Gene Kirkwood

CLIFF PAYNE
THE LADY IN WHITE New Century/Vista, 1988, EP w/Charles M. LaLoggia

GREG PEAD
(see Yahoo SERIOUS)

CHRISTOPHER PEARCE
(credit w/Yoram Globus)
Business: Cannon Productions, 5757 Wilshire Blvd., Suite 721, Los Angeles, CA, 90036, 213/965-0901
Contact: Directors Guild of America - Los Angeles, 213/289-2000

THE ROSE GARDEN Cannon, 1989, EP
A MAN CALLED SARGE Cannon, 1990, EP

MEL PEARL
(credit w/Don Levin)

LOVE LETTERS New World, 1983, EP
HAMBONE & HILLIE New World, 1984, EP
THE BOYS NEXT DOOR New World, 1985, EP
MAXIMUM OVERDRIVE DEG, 1986, EP
THE SUPERNATURALS Republic Entertainment, 1987, EP
WEEDS DEG, 1987, EP w/Billy Cross*
TWO MOON JUNCTION Lorimar, 1988, EP
ANGEL III: THE FINAL CHAPTER New World, 1988, EP

NOEL PEARSON
MY LEFT FOOT ★ Miramax, 1989

M. J. PECKOS
BURNING SECRET Vestron, 1988, EP w/William J. Quigley
PAPERHOUSE Vestron, 1989, EP w/Dan Ireland

BILL PEIFFER
TEXASVILLE Columbia, 1990, EP w/Jake Eberts

YORAM PELMAN
COMMANDO SQUAD Trans World Entertainment, 1987, EP

ARTHUR PENN
Business: Florin Productions, 1860 Broadway, New York, NY,10023, 213/585-1470
Agent: Sam Cohn, ICM - New York, 212/556-5600

FOUR FRIENDS Filmways, 1981, w/Gene Lasko
PENN AND TELLER GET KILLED Warner Bros., 1989

EAGLE PENNELL
Attorney: Tom Garvin, Ervin, Cohen & Jessup, 9401 Wilshire Blvd., Beverly Hills, CA, 90212, 213/273-6333

LAST NIGHT AT THE ALAMO Cinecom, 1984, w/Kim Henkel

JON PENNINGTON
THE MOUSE THAT ROARED Columbia, 1959, w/Walter Shenson

LAURENCE P. PEREIRA
PREDATOR 20th Century-Fox, 1987, EP w/JimThomas

JOSEPH PEREZ
PERSONAL CHOICE Moviestore Entertainment, 1989

ANDRE PERGAMENT
ENIGMA Embassy, 1983, w/Ben Arbeid & Peter Shaw

GEORGE W. PERKINS
EXTREMITIES Atlantic Entertainment, 1986, LP w/Scott Rosenfelt

LAURIE PERLMAN
Business: Perlman Productions, 20th Century-Fox, 10201 W. Pico Blvd., Los Angeles, CA, 90035, 213/203-3482

LUCKY STIFF New Line Cinema, 1988, EP w/Miles Copeland, Derek Power & Pat Proft
VITAL SIGNS 20th Century-Fox, 1990, w/Cathleen Summers

SAM PERLMUTTER
THE FOURTH WAR Warner Bros., 1990, EP w/William Stuart

DAVID PERMUT
Business: Permut Presentations, Inc., 415 N. Crescent Dr., Suite 300, Beverly Hills, CA, 90210, 213/859-3326

FIGHTING BACK Paramount, 1982, EP w/Mark Travis
BLIND DATE Tri-Star, 1987, EP w/Gary Hendler & Jonathan D. Krane
DRAGNET Universal, 1987, w/Robert K. Weiss

RUPERT A. L. PERRIN
BEVERLY HILLS BRATS Taurus, 1989, EP

E. LEE PERRY
MEAN STREETS Warner Bros., 1973, EP

FRANK PERRY
Business: Corsair Pictures, 1740 Broadway, 23rd Floor, New York, NY, 10019, 212/603-0652; 1640 S. Sepulveda Blvd., #216, Los Angeles, CA, 90025, 213/479-8200
Agent: ICM - New York, 212/556-5600

COMPROMISING POSITIONS Paramount, 1985
HELLO AGAIN Buena Vista, 1987

PINCHAS PERRY
Business: Pinchas Perry Productions, 8200 Wilshire Blvd., Beverly Hills, CA, 90211, 213/658-658-3028

GABY — A TRUE STORY Tri-Star, 1987, EP

SIMON PERRY
ANOTHER TIME, ANOTHER PLACE Samuel Goldwyn Company, 1984
1984 Atlantic Entertainment, 1985
NANOU Umbrella/Arion, 1986
WHITE MISCHIEF Columbia, 1988

STEVE PERRY
Business: Silver Pictures, 4000 Warner Blvd., Burbank, CA, 91522, 818/954-4490
Contact: Directors Guild of America - Los Angeles, 213/289-2000

ACTION JACKSON Lorimar, 1988, AP
LETHAL WEAPON 2 Warner Bros., 1989, CP w/Jennie Lew Tugend
ROADHOUSE MGM/UA, 1989, EP w/Tim Moore
FORD FAIRLANE 20th Century-Fox, 1990, w/Joel Silver
DIE HARD 2 20th Century-Fox, 1990, CP

LESTER PERSKY

Business: Lester Persky Productions, Inc., 935 Bel Air Rd., Los Angeles, CA, 90077, 213/476-9697; 150 Central Park South, New York, NY, 10019, 212/246-7700

FORTUNE & MEN'S EYES MGM, 1971, w/Lewis Allen
EQUUS United Artists, 1977, w/Elliott Kastner
HAIR United Artists, 1979, w/Michael Butler
YANKS Universal, 1979, w/Joseph Janni

JON PETERS

(credit w/Peter Guber)

Business: Columbia Pictures, Studio Plaza, 3400 Riverside Dr., Burbank, CA, 91505, 818/972-7300

A STAR IS BORN Warner Bros., 1976*
EYES OF LAURA MARS Columbia, 1978*
THE MAIN EVENT Warner Bros., 1979, w/Barbra Streisand*
CADDYSHACK Orion/Warner Bros., 1980, EP*
DIE LAUGHING Orion/Warner Bros., 1980, EP*
AN AMERICAN WEREWOLF IN LONDON Universal, 1981, EP
SIX WEEKS Universal, 1982, EP
MISSING ★ Universal, 1982, EP
FLASHDANCE Paramount, 1983, EP
D.C. CAB Universal, 1983, EP
VISION QUEST Warner Bros., 1985
THE LEGEND OF BILLIE JEAN Tri-Star, 1985, EP
HEAD OFFICE Tri-Star, 1985, EP
THE COLOR PURPLE ★ Warner Bros., 1985, EP
CLUE Paramount, 1985, EP w/George Folsey Jr. & John Landis
THE CLAN OF THE CAVE BEAR Warner Bros., 1986, EP w/Mark Damon, John Hyde & Sidney Kimmel
YOUNGBLOOD MGM/UA, 1986, EP
THE WITCHES OF EASTWICK Warner Bros., 1987, w/Neil Canton
INNERSPACE Warner Bros., 1987, EP w/Kathleen Kennedy, Frank Marshall & Steven Spielberg
WHO'S THAT GIRL Warner Bros., 1987, EP w/Roger Birnbaum
GORILLAS IN THE MIST Universal, 1988, EP
RAIN MAN ★★ MGM/UA, 1988, EP
CADDYSHACK II Warner Bros., 1988, w/Neil Canton
BATMAN Warner Bros., 1989
TANGO & CASH Warner Bros., 1989
MISSING LINK Universal, 1989, EP

ROBERT C. PETERS

Business: New World Pictures, 1440 S. Sepulveda Blvd., Los Angeles, CA, 90025, 213/444-8100

FRATERNITY VACATION New World, 1985, w/Boris Malden & Christopher Nelson
WANTED DEAD OR ALIVE New World, 1987

JO PETERSON

FROM HOLLYWOOD TO DEADWOOD Island Pictures, 1989

DANIEL PETRIE

Agent: CAA - Beverly Hills, 213/288-4545
Contact: Directors Guild of America - Los Angeles, 213/289-2000

SQUARE DANCE *HOME IS WHERE THE HEART IS* Island Pictures, 1987

DANIEL PETRIE, JR.

Business: Walt Disney Pictures, 500 S. Buena Vista St., Burbank, CA, 91521, 818/560-6450
Agent: The Richland/Wunsch Agency - Los Angeles, 213/278-1955

SHOOT TO KILL Buena Vista, 1988, w/Ron Silverman
TURNER & HOOCH Buena Vista, 1989, EP w/Michael Hertzberg

MIKE PETZOLD

Business: Rafaella Productions, Universal Pictures, 100 Universal City Plaza, Bungalow 121-C, Universal City, CA, 91608, 818/777-2655

PRANCER Orion, 1989, CP w/Greg Taylor

JOHN PEVERALL

THE DEER HUNTER ★★ Universal, 1978, w/Michael Cimino, Michael Deeley & Barry Spikings
McVICAR Crown International, 1982, AP

MICHAEL PEYSER

Business: Hollywood Pictures, 500 S. Buena Vista St., Burbank, CA, 91521, 818/560-6677
Contact: Directors Guild of America - Los Angeles, 213/289-2000

A MIDSUMMER NIGHT'S SEX COMEDY Warner Bros./ Orion, 1982, AP
BROADWAY DANNY ROSE Orion, 1984, AP
THE PURPLE ROSE OF CAIRO Orion, 1985, AP
DESPERATELY SEEKING SUSAN Orion, 1985, EP
F/X Orion, 1986, EP
RUTHLESS PEOPLE Buena Vista, 1986
BIG BUSINESS Buena Vista, 1988, w/Steve Tisch

ANDREW D. T. PFEFFER

(credit w/Michael C. Leone)

Business: Trans World Entertainment, 3330 W. Cahuenga Blvd., Suite 500, Los Angeles, CA, 90068, 213/969-2800

I, THE JURY 20th Century-Fox, 1982, EP
TOUGH ENOUGH 20th Century-Fox, 1983, EP
THE ENTITY 20th Century-Fox, 1983, EP

CAROLYN PFEIFFER

Business: Alive Films, 8271 Melrose Ave., Los Angeles, CA, 90046, 213/852-1100

ROADIE United Artists, 1980
ENDANGERED SPECIES MGM/UA, 1982
RETURN ENGAGEMENT Island Alive, 1983
CHOOSE ME Island Alive, 1984, w/David Blocker
TROUBLE IN MIND Alive Films, 1985, w/David Blocker
THE WHALES OF AUGUST Alive Films, 1987, w/Mike Kaplan
FAR NORTH Alive Films, 1988, w/Malcolm R. Harding
THE MODERNS Alive Films, 1988, w/David Blocker
A TIME OF DESTINY Columbia, 1988, EP w/Shep Gordon

BRANDON K. PHILLIPS

THAT WAS THEN...THIS IS NOW Paramount, 1985, EP w/Alan Belkin

DON PHILLIPS

MELVIN & HOWARD Universal, 1980, w/Art Linson
THE WILD LIFE Universal, 1984, CP

JULIA PHILLIPS

STEELYARD BLUES Warner Bros., 1973, w/Tony Bill & Michael Phillips
THE STING ★★ Universal, 1973, w/Tony Bill & Michael Phillips
THE BIG BUS Paramount, 1976, EP w/Michael Phillips
TAXI DRIVER ★ Columbia, 1976, w/Michael Phillips
CLOSE ENCOUNTERS OF THE THIRD KIND Columbia, 1977, w/Michael Phillips
THE BEAT Vestron, 1988, w/Jon Kilik & Nick Wechsler

LLOYD PHILLIPS

(credit w/Robert Whitehouse)

WARLORDS OF THE 21ST CENTURY *BATTLE TRUCK* New World, 1982
NATE & HAYES Paramount, 1983

MICHAEL PHILLIPS

Business: Mercury Entertainment,10960 Wilshire Blvd., Suite 2222, Beverly Hills, CA, 90024, 213/477-4880

STEELYARD BLUES Warner Bros., 1973, w/Tony Bill & Julia Phillips
THE STING ★★ Universal, 1973, w/Tony Bill & Julia Phillips
TAXI DRIVER ★ Columbia, 1976, w/Julia Phillips
THE BIG BUS Paramount, 1976, EP w/Julia Phillips
CLOSE ENCOUNTERS OF THE THIRD KIND Columbia, 1977, w/Julia Phillips
HEARTBEEPS Universal, 1981
CANNERY ROW MGM/UA, 1982
THE FLAMINGO KID 20th Century-Fox, 1984

MARK PICK

ELENI Warner Bros., 1985, w/Nicholas Gage & Nick Vanoff

DAVID V. PICKER

Business: Two Roads Productions, 711 5th Ave., Suite 401, New York, NY, 10022, 213/702-6480

LENNY ★ United Artists, 1974, EP
JUGGERNAUT United Artists, 1974, EP
SMILE United Artists, 1975, EP w/Marion Dougherty
ROYAL FLASH 20th Century-Fox, 1975, w/ Denis O'Dell
WON TON TON, THE DOG WHO SAVED HOLLYWOOD Paramount, 1976, w/Arnold Schulman & Michael Winner
OLIVER'S STORY Paramount, 1978
THE ONE & ONLY Paramount, 1978, w/Steve Gordon
SIDNEY SHELDON'S BLOODLINE Paramount, 1979, w/Sidney Beckerman
THE JERK Universal, 1979, w/William E. McEuen
DEAD MEN DON'T WEAR PLAID Universal, 1982, w/William E. McEuen
THE MAN WITH TWO BRAINS Warner Bros., 1983, w/William E. McEuen
BEAT STREET Orion, 1984, w/Harry Belafonte
THE GOODBYE PEOPLE Embassy, 1984
LEADER OF THE BAND New Century/Vista, 1988
STELLA Samuel Goldwyn Company/Buena Vista, 1990, EP

MARK PIERSON

ELVIRA, MISTRESS OF THE DARK New World, 1988, w/Eric Gardner

LYDIA DEAN PILCHER

Business: 61 Eastern Parkway, Suite 4-G, Brooklyn, NY, 11238, 718/230-9489

SLIPPING INTO DARKNESS MCEG, 1988, LP
THE KILL-OFF Films Around the World, 1989
LONGTIME COMPANION Samuel Goldwyn Company, 1990, CP

SARAH PILLSBURY

(credit w/Midge Sanford)

Business: Sanford-Pillsbury Productions, 20th Century-Fox, 10201 W. Pico Blvd., Los Angeles, CA, 90035, 213/203-1847

DESPERATELY SEEKING SUSAN Orion, 1985
RIVER'S EDGE Island Pictures, 1987
EIGHT MEN OUT Orion, 1988
IMMEDIATE FAMILY Columbia, 1989

HOWARD PINE

STRAIGHT TIME Warner Bros., 1978, EP
THE COMPETITION Columbia, 1980, EP
THE SURVIVORS Columbia, 1983, EP

GLEN PITRE

Agent: William Morris Agency - Beverly Hills, 213/274-7451

BELIZAIRE THE CAJUN Skouras Pictures, 1986, w/Allan L. Durand

ANGELO PIZZO

Agent: ICM - Los Angeles, 213/550-4000
Contact: Writers Guild of America - Los Angeles, 213/550-1000

HOOSIERS Orion, 1986, w/Carter De Haven

GRAHAM PLACE

Contact: Directors Guild of America - Los Angeles, 213/289-2000

MILLER'S CROSSING 20th Century-Fox, 1990, w/Ethan Coen & Mark Silverman

OTTO PLASCHKES

THE HOMECOMING American Film Theatre, 1973, EP
BUTLEY American Film Theatre, 1974, EP
GALILEO American Film Theatre, 1975, EP
IN CELEBRATION American Film Theatre, 1975, EP
HOPSCOTCH Avco Embassy, 1980, EP
THE HOLCROFT COVENANT Universal, 1985, CP
SHADEY Skouras Pictures, 1987

MARC E. PLATT

Business: Orion Pictures, 1888 Century Park East, Los Angeles, CA, 90057, 213/282-0550

CAMPUS MAN Paramount, 1987, EP w/Barbara Boyle

POLLY PLATT

Business: Gracie Films, 20th Century-Fox, 10201 W. Pico Blvd., Los Angeles, CA, 90035, 213/203-3770
Contact: Writers Guild of America - Los Angeles, 213/550-1000

BROADCAST NEWS 20th Century-Fox, 1987, EP

SAY ANYTHING 20th Century-Fox, 1989
THE WAR OF THE ROSES 20th Century-Fox, 1989, EP w/Doug Claybourne

MIKE PLOTKIN

PERSONAL CHOICE Moviestore Entertainment, 1989, EP

STAN PLOTNICK

GET ROLLIN' Aquarius, 1981, EP w/Irwin Young

MICHAEL POCHNA

KEY EXCHANGE 20th Century-Fox, 1985, EP w/Peer J. Oppenheimer & Ronald Winston

STEPHEN POE

MEATBALLS PART II Tri-Star, 1984, w/Tony Bishop

HAL W. POLAIRE

(credit w/Joe Eszterhas)

Business: The Polaire Production Company, 13437 Ventura Blvd., Suite 102, Sherman Oaks, CA, 91423, 818/501-8871
Contact: Directors Guild of America - Los Angeles, 213/289-2000

BETRAYED MGM/UA, 1988, EP
MUSIC BOX Tri-Star, 1989, EP

MICHAEL POLAIRE

Contact: Directors Guild of America - Los Angeles, 213/289-2000
YOU TALKIN' TO ME? MGM/UA, 1987

MARTIN POLL

Business: Martin Poll Productions, 919 Third Ave., New York, NY, 10019, 212/371-7175; 8961 Sunset Blvd., Suite E, Los Angeles, CA, 90069, 213/285-9808

LOVE IS A BALL United Artists, 1963
SYLVIA Paramount, 1964
THE LION IN WINTER ★ Avco Embassy, 1968
THE APPOINTMENT MGM, 1968
NIGHT WATCH Avco Embassy, 1973, w/George W. George
THE MAN WHO LOVED CAT DANCING MGM, 1973, w/Eleanor Perry
LOVE & DEATH United Artists, 1975, EP
THE SAILOR WHO FELL FROM GRACE WITH THE SEA Avco Embassy, 1976
SOMEBODY KILLED HER HUSBAND Columbia, 1978
NIGHTHAWKS Universal, 1981
GIMME AN F 20th Century-Fox, 1984
HAUNTED SUMMER Cannon, 1988

SYDNEY POLLACK

Business: Mirage Enterprises, Universal Studios, 100 Universal City Plaza, Universal City, CA, 91608, 818/777-1000
Agent: CAA - Beverly Hills, 213/288-4545

THEY SHOOT HORSES, DON'T THEY? Cinerama Releasing Corporation, 1969, w/Robert Chartoff & Irwin Winkler
THE YAKUZA Warner Bros., 1975
BOBBY DEERFIELD Columbia, 1977
HONEYSUCKLE ROSE Warner Bros., 1980, EP
ABSENCE OF MALICE Columbia, 1981
TOOTSIE ★ Columbia, 1982, w/Dick Richards
SONGWRITER Tri-Star, 1984
OUT OF AFRICA ★★ Universal, 1985
BRIGHT LIGHTS, BIG CITY MGM/UA, 1988, w/Mark Rosenberg
THE FABULOUS BAKER BOYS 20th Century-Fox, 1989, EP
PRESUMED INNOCENT Warner Bros., 1990, w/Mark Rosenberg
HAVANA Universal, 1990, w/Richard Roth

DALE POLLOCK

(credit w/Gil Friesen)

Business: A & M Films, 1416 La Brea Ave., Hollywood, CA, 90028, 213/469-2411

THE BEAST Columbia, 1988, EP
THE MIGHTY QUINN MGM/UA, 1989, EP
WORTH WINNING 20th Century-Fox, 1989
BLAZE Buena Vista, 1989

PATSY POLLOCK

RITA, SUE & BOB TOO! Orion Classics, 1987, CP

JOHN POMEROY

(credit w/Don Bluth & Gary Goldman)

Business: Sullivan/Bluth Studios, 3800 W. Alameda Ave., Suite 1120, Burbank, CA, 91505, 818/840-9446

THE SECRET OF N.I.M.H. (AF) MGM/UA, 1982
AN AMERICAN TAIL (AF) Universal, 1986
THE LAND BEFORE TIME (AF) Universal, 1988
ALL DOGS GO TO HEAVEN (AF) Universal, 1989

LYLE S. PONCHER

Business: Great River Productions, 11611 San Vicente Blvd., Suite 800, Los Angeles, CA, 90049, 213/820-4680

THE CHALLENGE Embassy, 1982, EP

CARLO PONTI

THE TENTH VICTIM Avco Embassy, 1965
DR. ZHIVAGO MGM, 1966
WHAT? Avco Embassy, 1973
ANDY WARHOL'S DRACULA Bryanston, 1974, w/Andrew Braunsberg & Jean Pierre Rassam
ANDY WARHOL'S FRANKENSTEIN Bryanston, 1974, w/Andrew Braunsberg & Jean Pierre Rassam
THE PASSENGER United Artists, 1975
THE CASSANDRA CROSSING Avco Embassy, 1977
A SPECIAL DAY Cinema 5, 1977

NIKOLA POPOVIC

HEY BABU RIBA Orion Classics, 1987, w/Dragoljub Popovich

DRAGOLJUB POPOVICH

HEY BABU RIBA Orion Classics, 1987, w/Nikola Popovic

PHILIP PORCELLA

THE WIZARD OF LONELINESS Skouras Pictures, 1988, w/Thom Tyson

DENNIS POTTER

Contact: Writers Guild of America - Los Angeles, 213/550-1000

DREAMCHILD Universal, 1985, EP w/Verity Lambert

MARYKAY POWELL

VIOLETS ARE BLUE Columbia, 1986
BAJA OKLAHOMA HBO Pictures, 1988
BILOXI BLUES Universal, 1988, EP w/Joseph M. Carraciolo
LISTEN TO ME WEG/Columbia, 1989

NIK POWELL

Business: Palace Pictures, 16/17 Wardour Mews, London W1, England, 01/734-7060; 8170 Beverly Blvd., Suite 203, Los Angeles, CA, 90048, 213/655-1114

THE COMPANY OF WOLVES Cannon, 1985, EP
ABSOLUTE BEGINNERS Orion, 1986, EP w/Al Clark & Robert Devereux
SIESTA Lorimar, 1987, EP w/Julio Caro & Zalman King
HIGH SPIRITS Tri-Star, 1988, CP w/Selwyn Roberts
SHAG: THE MOVIE Hemdale, 1989, EP w/John Daly & Derek Gibson
SCANDAL Miramax, 1989, EP w/Joe Boyd, Bob Weinstein & Harvey Weinstein

DEREK POWER

THE FUNHOUSE Universal, 1981, w/Steven Bernhardt
LUCKY STIFF New Line Cinema, 1988, EP w/Miles Copeland, Laurie Perlman & Pat Proft
THE HOT SPOT Orion, 1990, EP w/Steve Ujlaki & Bill Gavin

RON PREISSMAN

THE FURY 20th Century-Fox, 1978, EP

EDWARD R. PRESSMAN

Business: Edward R. Pressman Film Corporation, 4000 Warner Blvd., Prod. 5, Room 114, Burbank, CA, 91522, 818/954-3315

OUT OF IT United Artists, 1969
THE REVOLUTIONARY United Artists, 1970
DEALING Warner Bros., 1972
SISTERS American International, 1973
BADLANDS Warner Bros., 1974, EP
PHANTOM OF THE PARADISE 20th Century-Fox, 1974
PARADISE ALLEY Universal, 1978, EP
DESPAIR New Line Cinema, 1979, EP w/Lutz Hengst
OLD BOYFRIENDS Avco Embassy, 1979, w/Michele Rappaport
HEART BEAT Orion/Warner Bros., 1980, EP w/William Tepper
THE HAND Orion/Warner Bros., 1981
DAS BOOT Columbia, 1982, EP w/Mark Damon & John Hyde
CONAN THE BARBARIAN Universal, 1982, EP w/D. Constantine Conte
THE PIRATES OF PENZANCE Universal, 1983, EP
PLENTY 20th Century-Fox, 1985, w/Joseph Papp
CRIMEWAVE Embassy, 1986, EP w/Irvin Shapiro
HALF MOON STREET 20th Century-Fox, 1986, EP w/David Korda
TRUE STORIES Warner Bros., 1986, EP
GOOD MORNING BABYLON Vestron, 1987, EP
WALKER Universal, 1987, EP
WALL STREET 20th Century-Fox, 1987
MASTERS OF THE UNIVERSE Cannon, 1987, EP
CHERRY 2000 Orion, 1988, w/Caldecott Chubb
TALK RADIO Universal, 1988, w/A. Kitman Ho
PARIS BY NIGHT Cineplex Odeon, 1990, EP
WAITING FOR THE LIGHT Triumph Releasing, 1990, EP
TO SLEEP WITH ANGER SVS Films, 1990, EP w/Danny Glover & Harris E. Tulchin
REVERSAL OF FORTUNE Warner Bros., 1990, w/Oliver Stone
MARTIANS GO HOME Taurus, 1990, EP
BLUE STEEL MGM/UA, 1990, w/Oliver Stone

MICHAEL PRESSMAN

Agent: Broder-Kurland-Webb-Uffner Agency - Los Angeles, CA, 90069, 213/656-9262
Contact: Directors Guild of America - Los Angeles, 213/289-2000

THOSE LIPS, THOSE EYES United Artists, 1980, w/Steven Charles Jaffe

NORMAN PRIGGEN

SECRET CEREMONY Universal, 1968, AP
THE GO-BETWEEN Columbia, 1971, w/John Heyman

RICHARD PRINCE

THE LEMON SISTERS Miramax, 1990, CP

ROBERT PRINGLE

HOWLING II...YOUR SISTER IS A WEREWOLF Thorn EMI, 1986, AP
HOWLING III: THE MARSUPIALS Square Pictures, 1987, EP w/Steven Lane & Edward Simons
HOWLING IV...THE ORIGINAL NIGHTMARE Allied Entertainment, 1988, EP w/Steven Lane, Avi Lerner & Edward Simons

PAT PROFT

Agent: InterTalent Agency - Los Angeles, 213/271-0600
Contact: Writers Guild of America - Los Angeles, 213/550-1000

MOVING VIOLATIONS 20th Century-Fox, 1985, EP w/Doug Draizin
LUCKY STIFF New Line Cinema, 1988, EP w/Miles Copeland, Laurie Perlman & Derek Power

CHIP PROSER

Attorney: Samantha Shad, 9465 Wilshire Blvd., Suite 920, Beverly Hills, CA, 90212, 213/276-7017
Contact: Writers Guild of America - Los Angeles, 213/550-1000

INNERSPACE Warner Bros., 1987, CP

ERWIN PROVOOST

WAIT UNTIL SPRING, BANDINI Orion, 1990, w/Tom Luddy & Fred Roos

RICHARD PRYOR

Attorney: Bloom & Dekom, Los Angeles, 213/278-8622
Agent: ICM - Los Angeles, 213/550-4000

BUSTIN' LOOSE Universal, 1981, w/Michael S. Glick
RICHARD PRYOR LIVE ON THE SUNSET STRIP Columbia, 1982
JO JO DANCER, YOUR LIFE IS CALLING Columbia, 1986

EVELYN PURCELL

Business Manager:Barbara Carswell Management, 321 S. Beverly Dr., Suite M, Beverly Hills, CA, 90212, 213/556-0563
Agent: William Morris Agency - Beverly Hills, 213/274-7451

CAGED HEAT New World, 1974
FIGHTING MAD 20th Century-Fox, 1976, CP

DAVID PUTTNAM

Business: Enigma Productions, Ltd., 15 Queen's Gate Place Mews, London SW7 5BG, England, 01/581-0238

MELODY Levitt-Pickman, 1971
THE PIED PIPER Paramount, 1972, w/Sandy Lieberson
THAT'LL BE THE DAY EMI, 1974, w/Sandy Lieberson
MAHLER Mayfair, 1974, EP w/Sandy Lieberson
THE LAST DAYS OF MAN ON EARTH *THE FINAL PROGRAMME* New World, 1974, EP w/Roy Baird & Michael Moorcock
STARDUST Columbia, 1975, w/Sandy Lieberson
LISZTOMANIA Warner Bros., 1975, w/Roy Baird
BUGSY MALONE Paramount, 1976, EP
THE DUELLISTS Paramount, 1978
MIDNIGHT EXPRESS ★ Columbia, 1978, w/Alan Marshall
FOXES United Artists, 1980, w/Gerald Ayres
CHARIOTS OF FIRE ★★ The Ladd Company/Warner Bros., 1981
LOCAL HERO Warner Bros., 1983
EXPERIENCE PREFERRED...BUT NOT ESSENTIAL Samuel Goldwyn Company, 1983
SECRETS Samuel Goldwyn Company, 1984
KIPPERBANG *P'TANG YANG, KIPPERBANG* MGM/ United Artists Classics, 1984, EP
THE KILLING FIELDS ★ Warner Bros., 1984
CAL Warner Bros., 1984, w/Stuart Craig
THE FROG PRINCE Warner Bros., 1985, EP
KNIGHTS & EMERALDS Warner Bros., 1986, EP
MR. LOVE Warner Bros., 1986, EP
SHARMA & BEYOND Cinecom, 1986, EP
FOREVER YOUNG Cinecom, 1986, EP
THOSE GLORY, GLORY DAYS Cinecom, 1986, EP
WINTER FLIGHT Cinecom, 1986, EP
ARTHUR'S HALLOWED GROUND Cinecom, 1986, EP
THE MISSION ★ Warner Bros., 1986, w/Fernando Ghia
DEFENSE OF THE REALM Hemdale, 1987, EP
MEMPHIS BELLE Warner Bros., 1990, w/Catherine Wyler

Q

JOHN QUESTED

Business: Goldcrest Films & Television Ltd., 36-44 Brewer St., London W1R 3HP, England, 01/437-8696

SUNBURN Paramount, 1979, EP w/Jay Bernstein
THE RETURN OF THE SOLDIER European Classics, 1985, EP w/J. Gordon Arnold & Edward Simons
AMERICAN GOTHIC Vidmark Entertainment, 1988

ROBERTO A. QUEZADA

PHANTASM II Universal, 1988
SURVIVAL QUEST MGM/UA, 1990

WILLIAM J. QUIGLEY

Business: Vestron Pictures, 2029 Century Park East, Suite 200, Los Angeles, CA, 90067, 213/551-1723

THE DEAD Vestron, 1987, EP
STEEL DAWN Vestron, 1987, EP w/Larry Sugar
SALOME'S LAST DANCE Vestron, 1987
THE UNHOLY Vestron, 1988
THE LAIR OF THE WHITE WORM Vestron, 1988, EP w/Dan Ireland
WAXWORK Vestron, 1988, EP w/Gregory Cascante, Dan Ireland & Mario Sotela
BURNING SECRET Vestron, 1988, EP w/MJ Peckos
THE RAINBOW Vestron, 1989, EP w/Dan Ireland
TWISTER Vestron, 1990, EP w/Dan Ireland

JOHN QUILL

CALL ME Vestron, 1988, w/Kenneth Martel

ANTHONY QUINN

Agent: BBMW - 213/277-4998

ACROSS 110th STREET United Artists, 1972, EP w/Barry Shear

GENE QUINTANO

Business: Trans World Entertainment, 3330 W. Cahuenga Blvd., Suite 500, Los Angeles, CA, 90068, 213/969-2800
Agent: ICM - Los Angeles, 213/550-4000

MAKING THE GRADE MGM/UA/Cannon, 1984

R

DAVID RABE

Agent: Bauer Benedek Agency - Los Angeles, 213/275-2421
Contact: Writers Guild of America - New York, 212/245-6180

I'M DANCING AS FAST AS I CAN Paramount, 1982, EP

HERB RABINOWITZ

PERMANENT RECORD Paramount, 1988, CP

MICHAEL RACHMIL

Contact: Directors Guild of America - Los Angeles, 213/289-2000

TOM HORN Warner Bros., 1980, AP w/Sandra Weintraub
DEAD & BURIED Avco Embassy, 1981, AP
RUNAWAY Tri-Star, 1984
QUICKSILVER Columbia, 1986, w/Daniel Melnick
ROXANNE Columbia, 1987, w/Daniel Melnick
ELVIRA, MISTRESS OF THE DARK New World, 1988, EP
PUNCHLINE Columbia, 1988, w/Daniel Melnick
NO HOLDS BARRED New Line Cinema, 1989
HARD TO KILL Warner Bros., 1990, EP w/Lee RIch
THE FLATLINERS Columbia, 1990, EP w/Peter Filardi & Scott Rudin

SARAH RADCLYFFE

Business: Working Title Ltd., 10 Livonia St., London W1V 3PH, 01/439-2424

MY BEAUTIFUL LAUNDRETTE Orion Classics, 1986, w/Tim Bevan
CARAVAGGIO Cinevista, 1986
WISH YOU WERE HERE Atlantic Entertainment, 1987
SAMMY & ROSIE GET LAID Cinecom, 1987, w/ Tim Bevan
A WORLD APART Atlantic Entertainment, 1988
PAPERHOUSE Vestron, 1989, w/Tim Bevan

ROBERT B. RADNITZ

Business: Robert Radnitz Productions, 10182 1/2 Culver Blvd., Culver City, CA, 90230, 213/837-0422

A DOG OF FLANDERS 20th Century-Fox, 1959
MISTY 20th Century-Fox, 1961
ISLAND OF BLUE DOLPHINS Universal, 1964
MY SIDE OF THE MOUNTAIN Paramount, 1968
THE LITTLE ARK National General, 1972
SOUNDER ★ 20th Century-Fox, 1972
WHERE THE LILIES BLOOM United Artists, 1974
PART 2, SOUNDER Gamma III, 1976, EP
BIRCH INTERVAL Gamma III, 1976
A HERO AIN'T NOTHIN' BUT A SANDWICH New World, 1977
CROSS CREEK Universal, 1983

BOB RAFELSON

Business: Marmont Productions, c/o Carolco, 8800 Sunset Blvd., 2nd Floor, Los Angeles, CA, 90069, 213/855-7261
Contact: Directors Guild of America - 213/289-2000

HEAD Columbia, 1968, w/Jack Nicholson
FIVE EASY PIECES ★ Columbia, 1970, w/Richard Wechsler
THE KING OF MARVIN GARDENS Columbia, 1972
STAY HUNGRY United Artists, 1976, w/Harold Schneider
THE POSTMAN ALWAYS RINGS TWICE Paramount, 1981, w/Charles Mulvehill

ALEXANDRA RAFFE

Business: Vos Productions Inc., 785 Queen Street E., #1, Toronto, Ontario M4M 1H5, Canada, 416/461-8874

I'VE HEARD THE MERMAIDS SINGING Miramax, 1987, w/Patricia Rozema

SAMUEL M. RAIMI

Business: Renaissance Motion Pictures, Inc., 28 East 10th St., New York, NY, 10003, 212/477-0432; 6381 Hollywood Blvd., Los Angeles, CA, 90028, 213/463-9936
Agent: InterTalent Agency - Los Angeles, 213/271-0600

THE EVIL DEAD New Line Cinema, 1983, EP w/Bruce Campbell

PEGGY RAJSKI

THE BROTHER FROM ANOTHER PLANET Cinecom, 1984, w/Maggie Renzi
MATEWAN Cinecom, 1987, w/Maggie Renzi
EIGHT MEN OUT Orion, 1988, CP

FRANCISCO RAMALHO, JR.

KISS OF THE SPIDER WOMAN ★ Island Alive, 1985, EP

HAROLD RAMIS

Business: Ocean Pictures, 2821 Main St., Santa Monica, CA, 90405, 213/399-9271
Agent: Jack Rapke, CAA - Beverly Hills, 213/288-4545

BACK TO SCHOOL Orion, 1986, EP w/Estelle Endler & Michael Endler

PHIL RAMONE

BODY ROCK New World, 1984, EP w/Jon Feltheimer & Charles J. Weber

DEAN RAMSER

THE UNNAMEABLE Vidmark Entertainment, 1988, w/Jean Paul Ouellette

ROGER RANDALL-CUTLER

DANCE WITH A STRANGER Samuel Goldwyn Company, 1985

ANTHONY RANDELL

GRUNT! THE WRESTLING MOVIE New World, 1985, w/Don Normann

PAUL RANNAM

VALMONT Orion, 1989, w/Michael Hausman

MARTIN RANSOHOFF

Business: Martin Ransohoff Productions, Columbia Plaza West, #24, Burbank, CA, 91505, 818/954-3491

THE AMERICANIZATION OF EMILY MGM, 1964
THE SANDPIPER MGM, 1965
THE CINCINNATI KID MGM, 1965
ICE STATION ZEBRA MGM, 1968, w/John Calley
CASTLE KEEP Columbia, 1969, w/John Calley
HAMLET Columbia, 1969, EP w/Leslie Linder
CATCH 22 Paramount, 1970, w/John Calley
THE MOONSHINE WAR MGM, 1970
10 RILLINGTON PLACE Columbia, 1971, w/Leslie Linder
SEE NO EVIL Columbia, 1971, w/Leslie Linder
THE WHITE DAWN Paramount, 1974
SILVER STREAK 20th Century-Fox, 1976, EP w/Frank Yablans
THE WANDERERS Orion/Warner Bros., 1979
NIGHTWING Columbia, 1979
THE MOUNTAIN MEN Columbia, 1980, w/Andrew Scheinman & Martin Shafer
A CHANGE OF SEASONS 20th Century-Fox, 1980
AMERICAN POP (AF) Paramount, 1981, w/Ralph Bakshi
HANKY PANKY Columbia, 1982
CLASS Orion, 1983
JAGGED EDGE Columbia, 1985
THE BIG TOWN Columbia, 1987
SWITCHING CHANNELS Tri-Star, 1988
PHYSICAL EVIDENCE Columbia, 1989
WELCOME HOME Columbia, 1989

PAUL RAPHAEL

PASCALI'S ISLAND Avenue Entertainment, 1988, CP
THE RACHEL PAPERS MGM/UA, 1989, CP

NEIL RAPP
Contact: Directors Guild of America - Los Angeles, 213/289-2000

INDEPENDENCE DAY Unifilm, 1977, w/Bobby Roth

MICHELE RAPPAPORT
Business: Carliner-Rappaport Productions, 11700 Laurelwood Dr., Studio City, CA, 91604, 818/763-4783

OLD BOYFRIENDS Avco Embassy, 1979, w/Edward R. Pressman

DANIEL RASKOV
Business: I.R.S. World Media, 8335 Sunset Blvd., Los Angeles, CA, 90069, 213/650-8010

A SINFUL LIFE New Line Cinema, 1989

TINA RATHBORNE
ZELLY AND ME Columbia, 1988, EP w/Elliott Lewitt

ERIC RATTRAY
DRAGONSLAYER Paramount, 1981, AP
BETRAYAL 20th Century-Fox International Classics, 1983
LABYRINTH Tri-Star, 1986

MICHAEL JAY RAUCH
Contact: Directors Guild of America - Los Angeles, 213/289-2000

BAND OF THE HAND Tri-Star, 1986
APPRENTICE TO MURDER New World, 1988, EP
BLUE STEEL MGM/UA, 1990, CP
REVERSAL OF FORTUNE Warner Bros., 1990, EP

TAMARA RAWITT
I'M GONNA GIT YOU SUCKA MGM/UA, 1989, CP w/Eric Barrett

FRED OLEN RAY
BIOHAZARD 21st Century, 1985
THE TOMB Trans World Entertainment, 1986, w/Ronnie Hadar
ARMED RESPONSE Cinetel, 1986, CP
COMMANDO SQUAD Trans World Entertainment, 1987, CP

TONY RAY
Contact: Directors Guild of America - Los Angeles, 213/289-2000

ALEX IN WONDERLAND MGM, 1970, AP
BLUME IN LOVE Warner Bros., 1973, AP
NEXT STOP, GREENWICH VILLAGE 20th Century-Fox, 1976, w/Paul Mazursky
AN UNMARRIED WOMAN ★ 20th Century-Fox, 1978, w/Paul Mazursky
THE ROSE 20th Century-Fox, 1979, EP
WILLIE & PHIL 20th Century-Fox, 1980, w/Paul Mazursky

MICHELE RAY-GAVRAS
HANNA K. Universal, 1983, EP

WANDA S. RAYLE
MIDNIGHT CROSSING Vestron, 1988, EP w/Gary Barber, Gregory Cascante & Doug Ireland

PETER W. REA
GRANDVIEW, U.S.A. Warner Bros., 1984, w/William Warren Blaylock

ERIC RED
Agent: Jeremy Zimmer, Bauer Benedek Agency - Los Angeles, 213/275-2421

NEAR DARK DEG, 1987, CP

ROBERT REDFORD
Business: Wildwood Enterprises, 1223 Wilshire Blvd., Suite 412, Santa Monica, CA, 90403, 213/395-5155
Agent: CAA - Beverly Hills, 213/288-4545

PROMISED LAND Vestron, 1988, EP w/Andrew Meyer
SOME GIRLS MGM/UA, 1988, EP
THE MILAGRO BEANFIELD WAR Universal, 1988, w/Moctesuma Esparza

PAUL REDSHAW
COMMUNION New Line Cinema, 1989, EP w/Gary Barber

JERRY REED
Business: Jerry Reed Enterprises - Nashville, 615/256-4770
Contact: Directors Guild of America - Los Angeles, 213/289-2000

WHAT COMES AROUND W.O. Associates, 1986, EP
BAT 21 Tri-Star, 1988, EP

GEOFFREY REEVE
Business: Geoffrey Reeve Pictures Ltd., 45 St. James Place, London SW1A 1PG, England, 01/499-0662

THE SHOOTING PARTY European Classics, 1985
HALF MOON STREET 20th Century-Fox, 1986
THE WHISTLE BLOWER Hemdale, 1987

JAMES REEVE
Business: Geoffrey Reeve Pictures Ltd., 45 St. James Place, London SW1A 1PG, England, 01/499-0662

THE WHISTLE BLOWER Hemdale, 1987, EP

KEN REGAN
YESTERDAY'S HERO EMI, 1979, w/Oscar S. Lerman

GODFREY REGGIO
POWAQQATSI (FD) Cannon, 1988, w/Mel Lawrence & Lawrence Taub

BOB REHME
Business: Neufeld/Rehme Productions, Paramount Pictures, 5555 Melrose Ave., Hart 205, Los Angeles, CA, 90038, 213/468-5736

AN EYE FOR AN EYE Avco Embassy, 1981, EP
VICE SQUAD Avco Embassy, 1982, EP w/Frank Capra Jr. & Sandy Howard

STEPHANE REICHEL
EDDIE & THE CRUISERS II: EDDIE LIVES Scotti Bros., 1989

ANDREW REICHSMAN
SIGNS OF LIFE Avenue, 1989, w/Marcus Viscidi

SHELLEY E. REID
NIGHT VISITOR MGM/UA, 1989, EP w/TomBroadbridge

CARL REINER
Business Manager: George Shapiro, Shapiro-West, 141 El Camino Dr., Beverly Hills, CA, 90212, 213/278-8896
Agent: William Morris Agency - Beverly Hills, 213/274-7451

THE COMIC Columbia, 1969, w/Aaron Ruben

ROB REINER
(credit w/Andrew Scheinman)
Business: Castle Rock Entertainment, 335 N. Maple Dr., Suite 135, Beverly Hills, CA, 90210, 213/285-2300
Agent: CAA - Beverly Hills, 213/288-4545

THE PRINCESS BRIDE 20th Century-Fox, 1987
WHEN HARRY MET SALLY... Castle Rock/Columbia, 1989

IVAN REITMAN
Business: Ivan Reitman Productions, 4000 Warner Blvd., Burbank, CA, 91522, 213/954-1771
Agent: CAA - Beverly Hills, 213/288-4545

FOXY LADY Cinepix, 1971
CANNIBAL GIRLS American International, 1973, EP
THEY CAME FROM WITHIN Trans-America, 1976
THE HOUSE BY THE LAKE American International, 1977
RABID New World, 1977, EP w/Andre Link
NATIONAL LAMPOON'S ANIMAL HOUSE Universal, 1978, w/Matty Simmons
STRIPES Columbia, 1981, w/Dan Goldberg
HEAVY METAL (AF) Columbia, 1981
SPACEHUNTER: ADVENTURES IN THE FORBIDDEN ZONE Columbia, 1983, EP
GHOSTBUSTERS Columbia, 1984
LEGAL EAGLES Universal, 1986
BIG SHOTS 20th Century-Fox, 1987, EP
CASUAL SEX? Universal, 1988, EP
FEDS Warner Bros., 1988, EP
TWINS Universal, 1988
GHOSTBUSTERS II Columbia, 1989

SIMON RELPH
Business: British Screen, 37-39 Oxford St., London W1R 1RE, England, 01/434-0291

REDS ★ Paramount, 1981, EP w/Dede Allen
PRIVATES ON PARADE Orion Classics, 1984
THE PLOUGHMAN'S LUNCH Samuel Goldwyn Company, 1984, w/Ann Scott
WETHERBY MGM/UA Classics, 1985
SECRET PLACES 20th Century-Fox, 1985, w/Ann Skinner
THE RETURN OF THE SOLDIER European Classics, 1985, w/Ann Skinner

ROBERT E. RELYEA
Business: Paramount Pictures, 5555 Melrose Ave., Hollywood, CA, 90038, 213/468-5512
Contact: Directors Guild of America - Los Angeles, 213/289-2000

BULLITT Warner Bros., 1968, EP
THE REIVERS National General, 1969, EP
ADAM AT SIX A.M. National General, 1970, EP
LE MANS National General, 1971, EP
THE DAY OF THE DOLPHIN Avco Embassy, 1973
THE SAVAGE IS LOOSE Campbell Devon, 1974, EP
BLAME IT ON RIO 20th Century-Fox, 1984, AP

MAGGIE RENZI
(credit w/Peggy Rajski)

LIANNA United Artists Classics, 1983, w/Jeffrey Nelson*
THE BROTHER FROM ANOTHER PLANET Cinecom, 1984
MATEWAN Cinecom, 1987

ROBERT D. RESNIKOFF
(credit w/ Frank Darius Namei)
Business: Paramount Pictures, 5555 Melrose Ave., Los Angeles, CA, 90038, 213/468-4302
Agent: Bauer Benedek Agency - Los Angeles, 213/275-2421

COLLISION COURSE DEG, 1988, CP

PAUL REUBENS
(Pee-Wee Herman)
Business: Paramount Pictures, 5555 Melrose Ave., Los Angeles, CA, 90038, 213/468-4504
Contact: Michael McLean - 818/505-0945

BIG TOP PEE-WEE Paramount, 1988, w/Debra Hill

STEVEN REUTHER
(credit w/Mitchell Cannold)
Business: New Regency Films, 9608 Wilshire Blvd., Suite 201, Beverly Hills, CA, 90212, 213/859-8817

DIRTY DANCING Vestron, 1987, EP
CHINA GIRL Vestron, 1987, EP
AND GOD CREATED WOMAN Vestron, 1988, EP w/Ruth Vitale
CALL ME Vestron, 1988, EP w/Ruth Vitale
BIG MAN ON CAMPUS Vestron, 1989, EP
PARENTS Vestron, 1989, EP
HIDER IN THE HOUSE Vestron, 1989, EP w/Diane Nabatoff*
PRETTY WOMAN Buena Vista, 1990, w/Arnon Milchan*

PHILLIP RHEE
BEST OF THE BEST Taurus, 1989, w/Peter E. Strauss

MIKE RHODES
Contact: Directors Guild of America - Los Angeles, 213/289-2000

ROMERO Four Seasons Entertainment, 1989, SP

LEE RICH
(credit w/Merv Adelson)
Business: Lee Rich Productions, 4000 Warner Blvd., Burbank, CA, 91522, 818/954-3556

THE MAN Paramount, 1972*
WHO IS KILLING THE GREAT CHEFS OF EUROPE? Warner Bros., 1972, EP
THE CHOIRBOYS Universal, 1977
THE BIG RED ONE United Artists, 1980, EP
HARD TO KILL Warner Bros., 1990, EP w/Michael Rachmil*

RON RICH
GHOST FEVER Miramax, 1987, w/Edward Coe

JEF RICHARD
HIT LIST New Line Cinema, 1989, CP

DICK RICHARDS
Agent: Rick Ray, Triad Artists, Inc. - Los Angeles, 213/556-2727
Contact: Directors Guild of America - Los Angeles, 213/289-2000

MARCH OR DIE Columbia, 1977, w/Jerry Bruckheimer
TOOTSIE ★ Columbia, 1982, w/Sydney Pollack

MARTIN RICHARDS
Business: Producers Circle, 1350 Avenue of the Americas, New York, NY, 10019, 212/765-6760

THE BOYS FROM BRAZIL 20th Century-Fox, 1978, w/Stanley O'Toole
FORT APACHE, THE BRONX 20th Century-Fox, 1981, w/Tom Fiorello

SUSAN RICHARDS
WINTER FLIGHT Cinecom, 1986, w/Robin Douet
MR. LOVE Warner Bros., 1986, w/Robin Douet
KNIGHTS AND EMERALDS Warner Bros., 1986, w/Raymond Day
STARS AND BARS Columbia, 1988, CP

NED RICHARDSON
SALVATION! Circle Releasing, 1987, EP w/Michel Duval & Irving Ong

TONY RICHARDSON
Business: Woodfall Ltd., Hill House,1 Little New St., London EC4A 3TR, England; 1478 N. Kings Rd., Los Angeles, CA, 90069, 213/656-5314
Contact: Directors Guild of America - Los Angeles, 213/289-2000

TOM JONES ★★ United Artists, 1963

W. D. RICHTER
Business: Granite Pictures, c/o Castle Rock Entertainment, 335 N. Maple Dr., #135, Beverly Hills, CA, 90210, 213/285-2310
Agent: Shapiro-Lichtman, Inc. - Los Angeles, 213/859-8877

THE ADVENTURES OF BUCKAROO BANZAI ACROSS THE EIGHTH DIMENSION 20th Century-Fox, 1984, w/Neil Canton

BRUCE RICKER
THELONIOUS MONK: STRAIGHT, NO CHASER (FD) Warner Bros., 1988, w/Charlotte Zwerin

JEFF RINGLER
BEST OF THE BEST Taurus, 1989, EP w/Frank Giustra & Michael Holzman

SARA RISHER
Business: New Line Cinema, 116 N. Robertson Blvd., Suite 808, Los Angeles, CA, 90048, 213/854-5811

POLYESTER New Line Cinema, 1981, AP
THE FIRST TIME New Line Cinema, 1982, AP
A NIGHTMARE ON ELM STREET New Line Cinema, 1984, CP
A NIGHTMARE ON ELM STREET 2: FREDDY'S REVENGE New Line Cinema, 1985, CP
QUIET COOL New Line Cinema, 1986, AP
A NIGHTMARE ON ELM STREET 3: DREAM WARRIORS New Line Cinema, 1987, CP
MY DEMON LOVER New Line Cinema, 1987, CP
THE PRINCE OF PENNSYLVANIA New Line Cinema, 1988, EP w/Robert Shaye
HAIRSPRAY New Line Cinema, 1988, EP w/Robert Shaye
A NIGHTMARE ON ELM STREET 4: THE DREAM MASTER New Line Cinema, 1988, EP w/Stephen Diener
A NIGHTMARE ON ELM STREET PART 5: THE DREAM CHILD New Line Cinema, 1989, EP w/Jon Turtle

EDWARD L. RISSIEN
CASTLE KEEP Columbia, 1969, AP
SNOW JOB Warner Bros., 1972
THE CRAZY WORLD OF JULIUS VROODER 20th Century-Fox, 1974, w/Arthur Hiller
SAINT JACK New World, 1979, EP w/Hugh Hefner

DANTON RISSNER
A SUMMER STORY Atlantic Entertainment, 1988

MICHAEL RITCHIE
Business: Miracle Pictures, 22 Miller Ave., Mill Valley, CA, 94941, 415/383-2564
Agent: Sam Cohn, ICM - New York, 212/556-5600

SMILE United Artists, 1975
DIVINE MADNESS (FD) The Ladd Company/Warner Brothers, 1980

MARTIN RITT
Business Manager: Larry Martindale, Morgan & Martindale, 10780 Santa Monica Blvd., Los Angeles, CA, 90025, 213/474-0810
Agent: ICM - Los Angeles, 213/550-4000

THE FRONT Columbia, 1976
NORMA RAE ★ 20th Century-Fox, 1979, w/Tamara Asseyev & Alex Rose

JERRY RIVERS
BEVERLY HILLS BRATS Taurus Entertainment, 1989, w/Terry Moore

DAVID ROACH
YOUNG EINSTEIN Warner Bros., 1989, w/Warwick Ross & Yahoo Serious

JOHN F. ROACH
Business: Force Ten Productions, 587 Perugia Way, Bel Air, CA, 90077, 213/471-0257

PARADISE ALLEY Universal, 1978, w/Ronald A. Suppa
JAKE SPEED New World, 1986, EP
THE IN CROWD Orion, 1988, EP w/Jeff Franklin

JILL ROBB
CAREFUL, HE MIGHT HEAR YOU 20th Century-Fox, 1984

LANCE H. ROBBINS
Business: 12210 Nebraska Ave., Los Angeles, CA, 90025, 213/820-3046

BACKSTREET STRAYS Vidmark Entertainment, 1990

MATTHEW ROBBINS
Agent: Jeff Berg, ICM - Los Angeles, 213/550-4000
Contact: Directors Guild of America - Los Angeles, 213/289-2000

WARNING SIGN 20th Century-Fox, 1985, EP

BOBBY ROBERTS
(credit w/Hal Landers)

THE GYPSY MOTHS MGM, 1969
THE BANK SHOT United Artists, 1974
DEATH WISH Paramount, 1974
DEATH WISH II Filmways, 1982, EP

SELWYN ROBERTS
HIGH SPIRITS Tri-Star, 1988, CP w/Nik Powell

ROBBIE ROBERTSON
Personal Manager: Nick Wechsler, Addis-Wechsler & Associates, 8444 Wilshire Blvd., 5th Floor, Beverly Hills, CA, 90211, 213/653-8867

THE LAST WALTZ (FD) United Artists, 1978
CARNY United Artists, 1980

STANLEY ROBERTSON
Business: JillChris Productions, Columbia Pictures, Columbia Plaza, Producers 8, #220, Burbank, CA, 91505, 818/954-2446

GHOST DAD Universal, 1990, EP

AMY ROBINSON
(credit w/Griffin Dunne)
Business: Double Play Productions, 1250 Broadway, New York, NY, 10019, 212/643-1077

CHILLY SCENES OF WINTER *HEAD OVER HEELS* United Artists, 1979, w/Mark Metcalf
BABY IT'S YOU Paramount, 1983
AFTER HOURS The Geffen Company/Warner Bros., 1985, w/Robert F. Colesberry
RUNNING ON EMPTY Warner Bros., 1988

DON ROBINSON
Business: Paragon Arts International, 6777 Hollywood Blvd., Suite 700, Hollywood, CA, 90028, 213/465-5355

NIGHT OF THE DEMONS IFM, 1988, LP

JAMES G. ROBINSON
Business: Morgan Creek Productions, 1875 Century Park East, Suite 200, Los Angeles, CA, 90067, 213/284-8884

THE STONE BOY 20th Century-Fox, 1984, EP
GRUNT! THE WRESTLING MOVIE New World, 1985, EP
WHERE THE RIVER RUNS BLACK MGM, 1986, EP
YOUNG GUNS 20th Century-Fox, 1988, EP w/John Fusco
SKIN DEEP 20th Century-Fox, 1989, EP w/Joe Roth
RENEGADES Universal, 1989, EP w/Robert W. Cort, Ted Field & Joe Roth
ENEMIES, A LOVE STORY 20th Century-Fox, 1989, EP w/Joe Roth
NIGHTBREED 20th Century-Fox, 1990, EP w/Joe Roth
THE EXORCIST: 1990 20th Century-Fox, 1990, EP w/Joe Roth
COUPE DE VILLE Universal, 1990, EP

PHIL ALDEN ROBINSON
Agent: Peter Turner, William Morris Agency - Beverly Hills, 213/274-7451
Contact: Directors Guild of America - Los Angeles, 213/289-2000

ALL OF ME Universal, 1984, AP

MARC ROCCO
DREAM A LITTLE DREAM Vestron, 1989, w/D. E. Eisenberg

DON ROCHAMBEAU
THE WIZARD OF SPEED AND TIME Shapiro-Glickenhaus Entertainment, 1989, EP

FRANC RODDAM
Agent: Hildy Gottlieb, ICM - Los Angeles, 213/550-4000
Contact: Directors Guild of America - Los Angeles, 213/289-2000

WAR PARTY Hemdale, 1989, EP w/Chris Chesser

CHERIE RODGERS
SALAAM BOMBAY! Cinecom, 1988, EP w/Gabriel Auer, Michael Nozik & Anil Tejani

JAMES T. ROE III
THE RACHEL PAPERS United Artists, 1989, EP w/Eric Fellner

LUC ROEG
BIG TIME (FD) Island Pictures, 1988

MICHAEL ROEMER
Business: Yale School of Art, Box 1605-A Yale Station, New Haven, CT, 06520, 203/432-2600

THE PLOT AGAINST HARRY New Yorker Films, 1990, w/Robert M. Young

GEORGE J. ROEWE III
KILL ME AGAIN MGM/UA, 1989, LP

OTHON ROFFIEL
THE BLUE IGUANA Paramount, 1988, CP w/Angel Flores-Marini

PHILLIP ROGERS
SHOOT TO KILL Buena Vista, 1988, EP

STAN ROGOW
Business: NBC Productions, 330 Bob Hope Dr., Burbank, CA, 91523, 818/840-7558

THE CLAN OF THE CAVE BEAR Warner Bros., 1986, CP

GUNTER ROHRBACH
DAS BOOT Columbia, 1982
THE NEVERENDING STORY Warner Bros., 1984, CP

SANDRA WEINTRAUB ROLAND
(formerly Sandra Weintraub)
Business: Fred Weintraub Productions, 1923 1/2 Westwood Blvd., #2, Los Angeles, CA, 90025, 213/470-8787
Agent: J. Michael Bloom & Associates - Los Angeles, 213/275-6800

TOM HORN Warner Bros., 1980, AP w/Michael Rachmil
THE PRINCESS ACADEMY Empire, 1987

JACK ROLLINS
(credit w/Charles H. Joffe)
Business: Rollins-Morra-Brezner, 801 Westmount Dr., Los Angeles, CA, 90069, 213/657-5384

BANANAS United Artists, 1971, EP
SLEEPER United Artists, 1973, EP
STARDUST MEMORIES United Artists, 1980, EP
ZELIG Orion/Warner Bros., 1983, EP
HANNAH AND HER SISTERS ★ Orion, 1986, EP
RADIO DAYS Orion, 1987, EP
SEPTEMBER Orion, 1987, EP
ANOTHER WOMAN Orion, 1988, EP
NEW YORK STORIES Buena Vista, 1989, EP
CRIMES AND MISDEMEANORS Orion, 1989, EP

RIC R. ROMAN
SENIORS Cinema Shares Inernational, 1978, EP

FRED ROOS
Business: F.R. Productions, 2980 Beverly Glen Circle, Suite 203, Los Angeles, CA, 90077, 213/470-9212

DRIVE, HE SAID Columbia, 1971, AP
THE CONVERSATION Paramount, 1974, w/Francis Ford Coppola
THE GODFATHER - PART II ★★ Paramount, 1974, CP w/Gray Frederickson
THE BLACK STALLION United Artists, 1979, w/ Tom Sternberg
APOCALYPSE NOW ★ United Artists, 1979, w/ Gray Frederickson & Tom Sternberg
ONE FROM THE HEART Columbia, 1982, w/Gray Frederickson
THE ESCAPE ARTIST Orion/Warner Bros., 1982, EP w/Francis Ford Coppola
HAMMETT Orion/Warner Bros., 1982, w/Ronald Colby & Don Guest
THE BLACK STALLION RETURNS MGM/UA, 1983, w/Doug Claybourne & Tom Sternberg
THE OUTSIDERS Warner Bros., 1983, w/Gray Frederickson
RUMBLE FISH Universal, 1983, w/Doug Claybourne
THE COTTON CLUB Orion, 1984, CP w/Sylvio Tabet
SEVEN MINUTES IN HEAVEN Warner Bros., 1986
GARDENS OF STONE Tri-Star, 1987, EP w/Jay Emmett, David Valdes & Stan Weston
BARFLY Cannon, 1987, w/Tom Luddy & Barbet Schroeder
TUCKER — THE MAN & HIS DREAM Paramount, 1988, w/Fred Fuchs
NEW YORK STORIES "Life Without Zoe" Buena Vista, 1989, w/Fred Fuchs
WAIT UNTIL SPRING, BANDINI Orion, 1990, w/Tom Luddy & Erwin Provoost

TOM ROPELEWSKI
Agent: ICM - Los Angeles, 213/550-4000

LOVERBOY Tri-Star, 1989, EP w/Leslie Dixon

ALEXANDRA (ALEX) ROSE
Business: Alex Rose Productions, 6507 West 5th St., Los Angeles, CA, 90048, 213/936-4847

DRIVE-IN Columbia, 1976, w/Tamara Asseyev
BIG WEDNESDAY Warner Bros., 1978, EP w/Tamara Asseyev
I WANNA HOLD YOUR HAND Universal, 1978, w/Tamara Asseyev
NORMA RAE ★ 20th Century-Fox, 1979, w/Tamara Asseyev & Martin Ritt
NOTHING IN COMMON Tri-Star, 1986
OVERBOARD MGM/UA, 1987, w/Anthea Sylbert
QUIGLEY DOWN UNDER Pathe, 1990, w/Stanley O'Toole

MEGAN ROSE
Business: Alex Rose Productions, 1630 S. Greenfield Ave., Los Angeles, CA, 90025

QUIGLEY DOWN UNDER Pathe, 1990, CP

REGINALD ROSE
Agent: Sy Fischer, Preferred Artists,- Encino, 818/990-0305
Contact: Writers Guild of America - Los Angeles, 213/550-1000

TWELVE ANGRY MEN ★ United Artists, 1957, w/Henry Fonda

SEYMOUR ROSE
KEYS TO FREEDOM RPB Pictures/Queens Cross Productions, 1989, EP

STUART ROSE
KEYS TO FREEDOM RPB Pictures/Queens Cross Productions, 1989, w/Robert S. Lecky

EDWARD ROSEN
AMERICATHON United Artists, 1979, EP

MARTIN ROSEN
Business: 305 San Anselmo Ave., San Anselmo, CA, 94960, 415/456-1414

WOMEN IN LOVE United Artists, 1969, w/Larry Kramer
WATERSHIP DOWN (AF) Avco Embassy, 1978
SMOOTH TALK Spectrafilm, 1985
THE PLAGUE DOGS (AF) Nepenth Productions, 1985
STACKING Spectrafilm, 1987

ROBERT L. ROSEN

Attorney: Marty Weiss, 12301 Wilshire Blvd., Suite 203, Los Angeles, CA, 90025, 213/820-8872
Contact: Directors Guild of America - Los Angeles, 213/289-2000

TOGETHER BROTHERS 20th Century-Fox, 1974
THE FRENCH CONNECTION II 20th Century-Fox, 1975
BLACK SUNDAY Paramount, 1976, EP
PROPHECY Paramount, 1979
GOING APE! Paramount, 1981
THE CHALLENGE Embassy, 1982, w/Ron Beckman
RAW COURAGE *COURAGE* New World, 1984, w/Ronny Cox
PORKY'S REVENGE 20th Century-Fox, 1985
WORLD GONE WILD Lorimar, 1988
DEAD BANG Warner Bros., 1989, EP
THE FOURTH WAR Warner Bros., 1990, LP

S. HOWARD ROSEN

Business: Nova Motion Pictures Ltd., 1200 Bay St., Suite 703, Toronto, Ontario M5R 2A5, Canada, 416/923-9230

JOHN AND THE MISSUS Cinema Group, 1987, EP w/Peter O'Brian

JEFFREY M. ROSENBAUM

FIREWALKER Cannon, 1986, EP w/Norman Aladjem

MARK ROSENBERG

Business: Mirage Enterprises, Universal Studios, 100 Universal City Plaza, Universal City, CA, 91608, 818/777-1000

BRIGHT LIGHTS, BIG CITY MGM/UA, 1988, w/Sydney Pollack
MAJOR LEAGUE Paramount, 1989, EP
THE FABULOUS BAKER BOYS 20th Century-Fox, 1989, w/Paula Weinstein
PRESUMED INNOCENT Warner Bros., 1990, w/Sydney Pollack

MAX ROSENBERG

SCREAM AND SCREAM AGAIN American International, 1969, w/Milton Subotsky

RICK ROSENBERG

(credit w/Robert Christiansen)

Business: Chris-Rose Productions, 4000 Warner Blvd., Producers 2, #1104-A, Burbank, CA, 91522, 818/954-1748

ADAM AT SIX A.M. National General, 1970
HIDE IN PLAIN SIGHT MGM/UA, 1980

MICHAEL ROSENBLATT

(credit w/Thomas Coleman)

VALLEY GIRL Atlantic Entertainment, 1983, EP
ROADHOUSE 66 Atlantic Entertainment, 1984, EP
ALPHABET CITY Atlantic Entertainment, 1984, EP
TEEN WOLF Atlantic Entertainment, 1985, EP
THE MEN'S CLUB Atlantic Entertainment, 1986, EP w/John Harada
EXTREMITIES Atlantic Entertainment, 1986, EP
NUTCRACKER Atlantic Entertainment, 1986, EP
SUMMER HEAT Atlantic Entertainment, 1987, EP
STEEL JUSTICE Atlantic Entertainment, 1987, EP
WILD THING Atlantic Entertainment, 1987, EP
THE GARBAGE PAIL KIDS MOVIE Atlantic Entertainment, 1987, EP
TEEN WOLF TOO Atlantic Entertainment, 1987, EP
COP Atlantic Entertainment, 1988, EP
PATTY HEARST Atlantic Entertainment, 1988, EP

MARVIN J. ROSENBLUM

1984 Atlantic Entertainment, 1985, EP

MIKE ROSENFELD

(credit w/Charles Fries)

Business: Kenwood Productions, 6922 Hollywood Blvd., Los Angeles, CA, 90028, 213/468-8318

THRASHIN' Fries Entertainment, 1986
OUT OF BOUNDS Columbia, 1986

SCOTT M. ROSENFELT

(credit w/Mark Levinson)

Business: Levinson-Rosenfelt Productions, 10203 Santa Monica Blvd., Los Angeles, CA, 90067, 213/284-9296
Agent: Lawrence A. Mirisch, Triad Artists, Inc. - Los Angeles, CA, 90067, 213/556-2727

WALTZ ACROSS TEXAS Atlantic Entertainment, 1983, CP*
ROADHOUSE 66 Atlantic Entertainment, 1984
TEEN WOLF Atlantic Entertainment, 1985
EXTREMITIES Atlantic Entertainment, 1986, LP w/George W. Perkins*
REMOTE CONTROL New Century/Vista, 1988
STRANDED New Line Cinema, 1987
RUSSKIES New Century/Vista, 1987
MYSTIC PIZZA Samuel Goldwyn Company, 1988
BIG MAN ON CAMPUS Vestron, 1989, CP

JAMES ROSENFIELD

WAVELENGTH New World, 1983

LOIS ROSENFIELD

BANG THE DRUM SLOWLY Paramount, 1973, w/Maurice Rosenfield

MAURICE ROSENFIELD

BANG THE DRUM SLOWLY Paramount, 1973, w/Lois Rosenfield
WAVELENGTH New World, 1983, EP

HOWARD ROSENMAN

Business: Sandollar Productions, 8730 Sunset Blvd., Penthouse, Los Angeles, CA, 90069, 213/659-5933

SPARKLE Warner Bros., 1976
THE MAIN EVENT Warner Bros., 1979, EP w/Rene Missel
RESURRECTION Universal, 1980, w/Rene Missel
LOST ANGELS Orion, 1989, w/Thomas Baer
GROSS ANATOMY Buena Vista, 1989, w/Debra Hill

MARK D. ROSENTHAL

Business: Konner-Rosenthal Productions, Paramount Pictures, 5555 Melrose Ave., Los Angeles, CA, 90038, 213/468-5909
Agent: InterTalent Agency - Los Angeles, 213/271-0600

THE LEGEND OF BILLIE JEAN Tri-Star, 1985, CP w/Lawrence Konner

DONALD H. ROSS
Agent: The Cooper Agency - Los Angeles, 213/277-8422

HAMBURGER: THE MOTION PICTURE FM Entertainment, 1986, CP w/Robert Lloyd Lewis

GARY A. ROSS
Agent: CAA - Beverly Hills, 213/288-4545
Contact: Writers Guild of America - Los Angeles, 213/550-1000

BIG 20th Century-Fox, 1988, CP w/Anne Spielberg

HERBERT ROSS
Business: Warner Bros. Pictures, c/o Burbank Studios, Ranch 1 #41, 3701 Oak St., Burbank, CA, 91505, 818/954-6536
Agent: CAA - Beverly Hills, 213/288-4545

THE SEVEN-PERCENT SOLUTION Universal, 1976
THE TURNING POINT ★ 20th Century-Fox, 1977, w/Arthur Laurents
PENNIES FROM HEAVEN MGM, 1981, w/Nora Kaye
I OUGHT TO BE IN PICTURES 20th Century-Fox, 1982, w/Neil Simon
MAX DUGAN RETURNS 20th Century-Fox, 1983, w/Neil Simon
THE SECRET OF MY SUCCESS Universal, 1987

MONTY ROSS
Business: 40 Acres & A Mule Filmworks, 124 DeKalb Ave., Brooklyn, NY, 11217, 718/624-3703

SCHOOL DAZE Columbia, 1988, CP w/Loretha C. Jones
DO THE RIGHT THING Universal, 1989, CP
MO' BETTER BLUES Universal, 1990, w/Jon Kilik & Spike Lee

WARWICK ROSS
YOUNG EINSTEIN Warner Bros., 1989, w/David Roach & Yahoo Serious

PETER ROSTEN
TRUE BELIEVER Columbia, 1989, EP

J. KENNETH ROTCOP
Agent: Barry Perelman Agency - Los Angeles, 213/274-5999
Contact: Writers Guild of America - Los Angeles, 213/550-1000

THE BIKINI SHOP *THE MALIBU BIKINI SHOP* International Film Marketing, 1987, w/Gary Mehlman

ANNA ROTH
Business: 2255 Beverly Glen Pl., Los Angeles, CA, 90077, 213/475-8673

UNDER FIRE Orion, 1983, AP
THE EXPENDABLES Concorde, 1988, w/Christopher Santiago
DADDY'S BOYS Concorde, 1988, AP
DANCE OF THE DAMNED Concorde, 1989, CP w/Reid Shane

BOBBY ROTH
Business: 7469 Melrose Ave., Suite 35, Los Angeles, CA, 90046, 213/651-0288
Contact: Directors Guild of America - Los Angeles, 213/289-2000

INDEPENDENCE DAY Unifilm, 1977, w/Neil Rapp
HEARTBREAKERS Orion, 1985, w/Bob Weis

JOE ROTH
Business: 20th Century-Fox, 10201 W. Pico Blvd., Los Angeles, CA, 90035, 213/277-2211
Contact: Directors Guild of America - Los Angeles, 213/289-2000

TUNNELVISION World Wide, 1976
CRACKING UP American International, 1977, EP
OUR WINNING SEASON American International, 1978
AMERICATHON United Artists, 1979
LADIES AND GENTLEMEN...THE FABULOUS STAINS Paramount, 1982
THE FINAL TERROR Aquarius, 1984
THE STONE BOY 20th Century-Fox, 1984, w/Ivan Bloch
BACHELOR PARTY 20th Century-Fox, 1984, EP
MOVING VIOLATIONS 20th Century-Fox, 1985, w/Harry Ufland
STREETS OF GOLD 20th Century-Fox, 1986, w/Harry Ufland
OFF BEAT Buena Vista, 1986, w/Harry Ufland
WHERE THE RIVER RUNS BLACK MGM, 1986, w/Harry Ufland
P.K. & THE KID Castle Hill, 1987
REVENGE OF THE NERDS II: NERDS IN PARADISE 20th Century-Fox, 1987, EP
YOUNG GUNS 20th Century-Fox, 1988, w/Christopher Cain
DEAD RINGERS 20th Century-Fox, 1988
RENEGADES Universal, 1989, EP w/Robert W. Cort, Ted Field & James G. Robinson
SKIN DEEP 20th Century-Fox, 1989, EP w/James G. Robinson
ENEMIES, A LOVE STORY 20th Century-Fox, 1989, EP w/James G. Robinson
NIGHTBREED 20th Century-Fox, 1990, EP w/James G. Robinson
THE EXORCIST: 1990 20th Century-Fox, 1990, EP w/James G. Robinson

RICHARD ROTH
Business: 1017 N. LaCienega Blvd., Los Angeles, CA, 90069, 213/658-7070

THE WAY WE WERE Columbia, 1973, AP
JULIA ★ 20th Century-Fox, 1977
BLUE VELVET DEG, 1986, EP
MANHUNTER DEG, 1986
IN COUNTRY Warner Bros., 1989, w/Norman Jewison
HAVANA Universal, 1990, w/Sydney Pollack

RICHARD A. ROTH
SUMMER OF '42 Warner Bros., 1971
OUR TIME Warner Bros., 1974
THE ADVENTURE OF SHERLOCK HOLMES' SMARTER BROTHER 20th Century-Fox, 1975
OUTLAND The Ladd Company/Warner Bros., 1981

STEPHEN J. ROTH
(credit w/Robert Lantos)
Business: Alliance Entertainment Corporation, 8439 Sunset Blvd., #404, Los Angeles, CA, 90069, 213/654-9488; 920 Yonge Street, Suite 400, Toronto, Ontario, M4W 3C7, Canada, 416/967-1174

IN PRAISE OF OLDER WOMEN Avco Embassy, 1979, EP w/Harold Greenberg*
SUZANNE RSL/Ambassador, 1980, EP*
AGENCY Jensen Farley, 1981
PARADISE Embassy, 1982
HEAVENLY BODIES MGM/UA, 1985
JOSHUA THEN & NOW 20th Century-Fox, 1985
SEPARATE VACATIONS RSK Entertainmet, 1986
BEDROOM EYES Aquarius Releasing, 1986

STEVE ROTH
SECRET ADMIRER Orion, 1985
EIGHT MILLION WAYS TO DIE Tri-Star, 1986
SCROOGED Paramount, 1988, EP
DEAD BANG Warner Bros., 1989

ARLYNE ROTHBERG
Business: 213/276-2214

CRIMES OF THE HEART DEG, 1986, CP w/Bill Gerber
HEAVEN (FD) Island Pictures, 1987, EP w/Tom Kuhn & Charles Mitchell

JEFFREY ROTHBERG
Contact: Writers Guild of America - Los Angeles, 213/550-1000

HIDING OUT DEG, 1987

KEITH ROTHMAN
BROKEN ENGLISH Lorimar, 1981, w/Bert Schneider
HEAT New Century/Vista, 1987, w/George Pappas

MOSES ROTHMAN
ffolkes Universal, 1980, EP

TOM ROTHMAN
Business: The Samuel Goldwyn Company, 10203 Santa Monica Blvd., Suite 500, Los Angeles, CA, 90067, 213/552-2255

DOWN BY LAW Island Pictures, 1986, CP w/Jim Stark

RON ROTHOLZ
Business: Cinehaus, 745 W. 55th St., Suite 1011, New York, NY, 10019, 212/245-9060

STATE OF GRACE Orion, 1990, EP w/Michael Hausman

RICHARD ROTHSTEIN
Agent: ICM - Los Angeles, 213/550-4000
Contact: Directors Guild of America - Los Angeles, 213/289-2000

DEATH VALLEY Universal, 1982, CP w/Stanley Beck

WILLIAM J. ROUHANA, JR.
Business: M.C.E.G. International, 2400 Broadway, Suite 100, Santa Monica, CA, 90404, 213/315-7800

SLIPPING INTO DARKNESS MCEG, 1988, EP

YVES ROUSSET-ROUARD
A LITTLE ROMANCE Orion/Warner Bros., 1979, w/Robert L. Crawford

CHARLES ROVEN
Business: Roven-Cavallo Entertainment, Raleigh Studios, 650 Bronson Ave., Suite 218 West, Los Angeles, CA, 90038, 213/960-4921

HEART LIKE A WHEEL 20th Century-Fox, 1983
MADE IN U.S.A. Tri-Star, 1988
JOHNNY HANDSOME Tri-Star, 1989
THE BLOOD OF HEROES New Line Cinema, 1990
CADILLAC MAN Orion, 1990

GLENYS ROWE
DOGS IN SPACE Skouras Pictures, 1987

PATRICIA ROZEMA
Business: Vos Productions Inc., 785 Queen Street E., #1, Toronto, Ontario M4M 1H5, Canada, 416/461-8874

I'VE HEARD THE MERMAIDS SINGING Miramax, 1987, w/Alexandra Raffe

AL RUBAN
Contact: Directors Guild of America - New York, 212/581-0370

FACES Continental, 1968, AP
HUSBANDS Columbia, 1970
MINNIE & MOSKOWITZ Universal, 1971
THE KILLING OF A CHINESE BOOKIE Faces Distribution, 1976
OPENING NIGHT Faces Distribution, 1977
LOVE STREAMS Cannon, 1984, EP
HAPPY NEW YEAR Columbia, 1987, EP

JANINE RUBEIZ
DEATHWATCH Quartet, 1982, w/Gabriel Boustani

AARON RUBEN
Agent: Robinson, Weintraub, Gross, Inc. - Los Angeles, 213/653-5802
Contact: Writers Guild of America - Los Angeles, 213/550-1000

THE COMIC Columbia, 1969, w/Carl Reiner

ANDY RUBEN
Business: Concorde Films, 11600 San Vicente Blvd., Los Angeles, CA, 90049, 213/820-6733

STRIPPED TO KILL Concorde, 1987, w/Mark Byers & Matt Leipzig
DANCE OF THE DAMNED Concorde, 1989
STRIPPED TO KILL 2 Concorde, 1989
STREETS Concorde, 1990

RICK RUBIN
TOUGHER THAN LEATHER New Line Cinema, 1988, EP w/Russell Simmons

STANLEY RUBIN

Agent: Triad Artists, Inc. - Los Angeles, 213/556-2727
Contact: Writers Guild of America - Los Angeles, 213/550-1000

THE PRESIDENT'S ANALYST Paramount, 1967
REVENGE Columbia, 1990, w/Hunt Lowry

KEITH RUBINSTEIN

THE BOYS NEXT DOOR New World, 1985, w/Sandy Howard
AVENGING ANGEL New World, 1985, w/Sandy Howard
KGB: THE SECRET WAR Cinema Group, 1986, w/Sandy Howard
ODD JOBS Tri-Star, 1986
THE IN CROWD Orion, 1988, w/Lawrence Konner

RICHARD P. RUBINSTEIN

Business: Laurel Entertainment, Inc., 928 Broadway, New York, NY, 10010, 212/674-3800

MARTIN Libra, 1978
DAWN OF THE DEAD United Film Distribution, 1979
KNIGHTRIDERS United Film Distribution, 1981
CREEPSHOW Warner Bros., 1982
DAY OF THE DEAD United Film Distribution, 1985
PET SEMATARY Paramount, 1989
TALES FROM THE DARKSIDE — THE MOVIE Paramount, 1990

ALBERT S. RUDDY

Business: Ruddy-Morgan Productions, 120 El Camino Dr., Beverly Hills, CA, 90212, 213/271-7698

THE WILD SEED Universal, 1965
LITTLE FAUSS & BIG HALSEY Paramount, 1970
MAKING IT 20th Century-Fox, 1971
THE GODFATHER ★★ Paramount, 1972
THE LONGEST YARD Paramount, 1974
MATILDA American International, 1978
THE CANNONBALL RUN 20th Century-Fox, 1981
DEATH HUNT 20th Century-Fox, 1981, EP w/Raymond Chow
MEGAFORCE 20th Century-Fox, 1982
LASSITER Warner Bros., 1984
THE CANNONBALL RUN II Warner Bros., 1984
FAREWELL TO THE KING Orion, 1989, w/Andre Morgan
SPEED ZONE Orion, 1989, EP w/Andre Morgan
IMPULSE Warner Bros., 1990, w/Andre Morgan

SCOTT RUDIN

Business: Paramount Pictures, 5555 Melrose Ave., Los Angeles, CA, 90038, 213/468-4600

I'M DANCING AS FAST AS I CAN Paramount, 1982, w/Edgar G. Scherick
MRS. SOFFEL MGM/UA, 1984, w/David A. Nicksay & Edgar G. Scherick
RECKLESS MGM/UA, 1984, w/Edgar G. Scherick
THE FLATLINERS Columbia, 1990, EP w/Peter Filardi & Michael Rachmil

JOSEPH RUFFALO

(credit w/Robert Cavallo & Steven Fargnoli)

PURPLE RAIN Warner Bros., 1984
UNDER THE CHERRY MOON Warner Bros., 1986
SIGN O' THE TIMES Cineplex Odeon, 1987

LORD ANTHONY RUFUS ISAACS

Business: New Galactic Films, 8737 Clifton Way, Beverly Hills, CA, 90211, 213/273-5642

9 1/2 WEEKS MGM/UA, 1986, w/Zalman King
COHEN & TATE Hemdale, 1989, w/Jeff Young

ED RUGOFF

Agent: William Morris Agency - Beverly Hills, 213/274-7451
Contact: Writers Guild of America - Los Angeles, 213/550-1000

MANNEQUIN 20th Century-Fox, 1987, EP w/Joseph Farrell

RICHARD RUSH

Agent: CAA - Beverly Hills, 213/288-4545
Contact: Directors Guild of America - Los Angeles, 213/289-2000

TOO SOON TO LOVE Universal, 1959
GETTING STRAIGHT Columbia, 1970
FREEBIE & THE BEAN Warner Bros., 1974
THE STUNT MAN 20th Century-Fox, 1980

SUSAN RUSKIN

Business: Pal-Mel Productions, 9350 Wilshire Blvd., Suite 316, Beverly Hills, CA, 90212, 213/859-0497

HAUNTED HONEYMOON Orion, 1986

BRIAN RUSSELL

FROM THE HIP DEG, 1987, EP w/Howard L. Baldwin & William Minot
SPELLBINDER MGM/UA, 1988, w/Joe Wizan

CHUCK RUSSELL

Agent: Robert Stein, Leading Artists, Inc. - Beverly Hills, CA, 90210, 213/858-1999
Contact: Writers Guild of America - Los Angeles, 213/550-1000

HELL NIGHT Aquarius, 1981, EP w/Joseph Wolf
THE SEDUCTION Avco Embassy, 1982, EP w/Frank Capra Jr. & Joseph Wolf
BODY ROCK New World, 1984, AP
DREAMSCAPE 20th Century-Fox, 1984, AP
GIRLS JUST WANT TO HAVE FUN New World, 1985
BACK TO SCHOOL Orion, 1986

KEN RUSSELL

Agent: The Robert Littman Company - Beverly Hills, 213/278-1572
Contact: Directors Guild of America - Los Angeles, 213/289-2000

THE MUSIC LOVERS United Artists, 1971
THE DEVILS Warner Bros., 1971
THE BOY FRIEND MGM, 1971
SAVAGE MESSIAH MGM, 1972
TOMMY Columbia, 1975, w/Robert Stigwood
THE LAIR OF THE WHITE WORM Vestron, 1988
THE RAINBOW Vestron, 1989

AARON RUSSO
Business: Aaron Russo Productions, 451 West 54th St., New York, NY, 10019, 212/974-8540; 1309 Valleyheart Dr., Studio City, 91604, 818/501-8794

THE ROSE 20th Century-Fox, 1979, w/Marvin Worth
PARTNERS Paramount, 1982
TRADING PLACES Paramount, 1983
TEACHERS MGM/UA, 1984
WISE GUYS MGM/UA, 1986
RUDE AWAKENING Orion, 1989

IRWIN RUSSO
WISE GUYS MGM/UA, 1986, EP

MORRIE RUVINSKY
Contact: Writers Guild of America - Los Angeles, 213/550-1000

IMPROPER CHANNELS Crown International, 1981, w/Alfred Pariser

JOHN RYAN
STICKY FINGERS Spectrafilm, 1988, LP

MICHAEL RYAN
Business: J & M Entertainment, 1289 Sunset Plaza Dr., Los Angeles, CA, 90069, 213/652-7733

PLAYING FOR KEEPS Universal, 1986, EP w/Julia Palau & Patrick Wachsberger

S

ALEXANDER SACHS
GINGER ALE AFTERNOON Skouras Pictures, 1989, EP

WILLIAM SACKHEIM
Business: Universal Studios, 100 Universal City Plaza, Universal City, CA, 91608, 818/777-1000
Contact: Writers Guild of America - Los Angeles, 213/550-1000

THE IN-LAWS Warner Bros., 1979, w/Arthur Hiller
THE COMPETITION Columbia, 1980
THE SURVIVORS Columbia, 1983
NO SMALL AFFAIR Columbia, 1984

ALAN SACKS
Business: Heritage Entertainment, 7920 Sunset Blvd., Suite 200, Los Angeles, CA, 90046, 213/850-5858

THRASHIN' Fries Entertainment, 1986

FOUAD SAID
ACROSS 110th STREET United Artists, 1972, w/Ralph Serpe

WAFIC SAID
THE FOURTH PROTOCOL Lorimar, 1987, EP w/ Michael Caine & Frederick Forsyth

OTTO SALAMON
Contact: Directors Guild of America - New York, 212/581-0370

BASIC TRAINING Moviestore, 1985, w/Gilbert Adler

ANGELIKA SALEH
Business: Angelika Films, 1974 Broadway, New York, NY, 10023, 212/769-1400

SWEET LORRAINE Angelika Films, 1987, EP w/Joseph Saleh

JOSEPH SALEH
Business: Angelika Films, 1974 Broadway, New York, NY, 10023, 212/769-1400

SWEET LORRAINE Angelika Films, 1987, EP w/Angelika Saleh

ALEXANDER SALKIND
BLUEBEARD Cinerama Releasing Corporation, 1972
THE THREE MUSKETEERS 20th Century-Fox, 1974
THE FOUR MUSKETEERS 20th Century-Fox, 1975, w/Michael Salkind

ILYA SALKIND
BLUEBEARD Cinerama Releasing Corporation, 1972, EP
THE THREE MUSKETEERS 20th Century-Fox, 1974, EP w/Pierre Spengler
THE FOUR MUSKETEERS 20th Century-Fox, 1975, EP w/Pierre Spengler
CROSSED SWORDS 20th Century-Fox, 1978, EP
SUPERMAN Warner Bros., 1978, EP
SUPERMAN II Warner Bros., 1981, EP
SUPERMAN III Warner Bros., 1983, EP
SUPERGIRL Warner Bros., 1984, EP
SANTA CLAUS - THE MOVIE Tri-Star, 1985, w/Pierre Spengler

MICHAEL SALKIND
THE FOUR MUSKETEERS 20th Century-Fox, 1975, w/Alexander Salkind

ROBERT SALLIN
Contact: Directors Guild of America - Los Angeles, 213/289-2000

STAR TREK II: THE WRATH OF KHAN Paramount, 1982

HARRY SALTZMAN
THE IRON PETTICOAT MGM, 1956
LOOK BACK IN ANGER Warner Bros., 1958
THE ENTERTAINER Continental, 1960, EP
SATURDAY NIGHT & SUNDAY MORNING Continental, 1961, EP
DR. NO United Artists, 1962, w/Albert R. Broccoli
CALL ME BWANA United Artists, 1963, w/Albert R. Broccoli
FROM RUSSIA WITH LOVE United Artists, 1963, w/Albert R. Broccoli
GOLDFINGER United Artists, 1964, w/Albert R. Broccoli
THE IPCRESS FILE Universal, 1965
FUNERAL IN BERLIN Paramount, 1966
YOU ONLY LIVE TWICE United Artists, 1967, w/Albert R. Broccoli
BILLION DOLLAR BRAIN United Artists, 1967

BATTLE OF BRITAIN United Artists, 1969, w/S. Benjamin Fisz
PLAY DIRTY United Artists, 1969
ON HER MAJESTY'S SECRET SERVICE United Artists, 1969, w/Albert R. Broccoli
DIAMONDS ARE FOREVER United Artists, 1971, w/Albert R. Broccoli
LIVE & LET DIE United Artists, 1973, w/Albert R. Broccoli
THE MAN WITH THE GOLDEN GUN United Artists, 1974, w/Albert R. Broccoli
NIJINSKY Paramount, 1980, EP

DAVID SALVEN

Contact: Directors Guild of America - Los Angeles, 213/289-2000
Agent: Smith Gosnell Agency - Pacific Palisades, 213/459-0307

DEAL OF THE CENTURY Warner Bros., 1983, AP
TWICE IN A LIFETIME Bud Yorkin Company, 1985, EP
SPACECAMP 20th Century-Fox, 1986, AP
RAMPAGE DEG, 1988
THE GUARDIAN Universal, 1990, EP

COKE SAMS

ERNEST SAVES CHRISTMAS Buena Vista, 1988, CP w/Justis Greene
ERNEST GOES TO JAIL Buena Vista, 1990, CP

RON SAMUELS

Business: Ron Samuels Productions, Inc., 120 El Camino Dr., Beverly Hills, CA, 90212, 213/273-8964

IRON EAGLE Tri-Star, 1986, w/Joe Wizan

PETER SAMUELSON

(credit w/Ted Field)

Business: Westwood Pictures, 1130 Westwood Blvd., Los Angeles, CA, 90024, 213/208-1000

REVENGE OF THE NERDS 20th Century-Fox, 1984
TURK 182 20th Century-Fox, 1985, EP w/Robert Cort

DAN SANDBURG

Q UFD, 1982, EP

IAN SANDER

D.O.A. Buena Vista, 1988, w/Laura Ziskin
EVERYBODY'S ALL-AMERICAN Warner Bros., 1988, w/Taylor Hackford & Laura Ziskin

JACK FROST SANDERS

Contact: Directors Guild of America - Los Angeles, 213/289-2000

KING OF THE MOUNTAIN Universal, 1981
THE WOMAN IN RED Orion, 1984, EP
THE MAN WITH ONE RED SHOE 20th Century-Fox, 1985, AP
SOLARBABIES MGM/UA, 1986, w/Irene Walzer

BARRY SANDLER

Agent: Harris & Goldberg - Los Angeles, 213/553-5200
Contact: Writers Guild of America - Los Angeles, 213/550-1000

MAKING LOVE 20th Century-Fox, 1982, AP
CRIMES OF PASSION New World, 1984

EDWARD SANDS

A PASSAGE TO INDIA Columbia, 1984, CP

MIDGE SANFORD

(credit w/Sarah Pillsbury)

Business: Sanford-Pillsbury Productions, 20th Century-Fox, 10201 W. Pico Blvd., Los Angeles, CA, 90035, 213/203-1847

DESPERATELY SEEKING SUSAN Orion, 1985
RIVER'S EDGE Island Pictures, 1987
EIGHT MEN OUT Orion, 1988
IMMEDIATE FAMILY Columbia, 1989

JONATHAN SANGER

Business: Chanticleer Films, 6525 Sunset Blvd., 6th Floor, Los Angeles, CA, 90028, 213/462-4705
Contact: Directors Guild of America - Los Angeles, 213/289-2000

FATSO 20th Century-Fox, 1980, AP
THE ELEPHANT MAN ★ Paramount, 1980
FRANCES Universal, 1982
THE DOCTOR & THE DEVILS 20th Century- Fox, 1985
CODE NAME: EMERALD MGM/UA, 1985, CP w/Howard Alston
FLIGHT OF THE NAVIGATOR Buena Vista, 1986, EP w/Mark Damon, Malcolm R. Harding & John Hyde

CHRISTOPHER SANTIAGO

THE EXPENDABLES Concorde, 1988, w/Anna Roth

HENRY G. SAPERSTEIN

Business: 14101 Valleyheart Dr., Suite 200, Sherman Oaks, CA, 91423, 818/990-3800

GAY PURR-EE (AF) Warner Bros., 1962, EP
WHAT'S UP TIGER LILY? American International, 1966, EP

PETER SAPHIER

Business: Paramount Pictures, 5555 Melrose Ave., Los Angeles, CA, 90038, 213/468-4506

EDDIE MACON'S RUN Universal, 1983, EP
SCARFACE Universal, 1983, CP

DERAN SARAFIAN

Agent: Triad Artists, Inc. - Los Angeles, 213/556-2727

ALIEN PREDATOR Trans World Entertainment, 1987, w/Carlos Aured

JOSEPH SARGENT

Agent: Martin Shapiro, Shapiro-Lichtman, Inc. - Los Angeles, 213/859-8877
Contact: Directors Guild of America - Los Angeles, 213/289-2000

JAWS THE REVENGE Universal, 1987

ARTHUR M. SARKISSIAN

QUIET COOL New Line Cinema, 1986, EP w/Pierre David & Larry Thompson
WANTED DEAD OR ALIVE New World, 1988, EP

EDUARD SARLUI

(credit w/Moshe Diamant)

Business: Trans World Entertainment, 3330 W. Cahuenga Blvd., Suite 500, Los Angeles, CA, 90068, 213/969-2800

ALIEN PREDATOR Trans World Entertainment, 1987, EP w/Helen Sarlui-Tucker
HIGH SPIRITS Tri-Star, 1988, EP
FULL MOON IN BLUE WATER Trans World Entertainment, 1988, EP
TEEN WITCH Trans World Entertainment, 1989, EP
NIGHT GAME Trans World Entertainment, 1989, EP

HELEN SARLUI-TUCKER

Business: Trans World Entertainment, 3330 W. Cahuenga Blvd., Suite 500, Los Angeles, CA, 90068, 213/969-2800

ALIEN PREDATOR Trans World Entertainment, 1987, EP w/Eduard Sarlui
THE WILD PAIR Trans World Entertainment, 1987, EP
SEVEN HOURS TO JUDGMENT Trans World Entertainment, 1988, EP w/Paul Mason
I, MADMAN Trans World Entertainment, 1989, EP w/Paul Mason

DAVID SAUNDERS

Business: Vision International, 3330 W. Cahuenga Blvd., Suite 500, Los Angeles, CA, 90068, 213/969-2900

HELLRAISER New World, 1987, EP w/Mark Armstrong & Christopher Webster
HIGH SPIRITS Tri-Star, 1988, w/Stephen Woolley
BAT 21 Tri-Star, 1988, CP w/Mark Damon
UNDER THE BOARDWALK New World, 1989, EP
WILD ORCHID Triumph Releasing, 1990, EP w/James Dyer

JEREMY SAUNDERS

THE SHOOTING PARTY European Classics, 1985, EP

LEE SAVIN

BROTHERS Warner Bros., 1977, EP

EDWARD SAXON

Business: Clinica Estetico Ltd., 1600 Broadway, #503, New York, NY, 10019, 212/262-2777

SWIMMING TO CAMBODIA Cinecom, 1987, AP
SOMETHING WILD Orion, 1987, EP
MARRIED TO THE MOB Orion, 1988, w/Kenneth Utt
MIAMI BLUES Orion, 1990, EP w/Fred Ward

GUILIO SBARIGIA

A MATTER OF TIME American International, 1976, EP w/Samuel Z. Arkoff
SALON KITTY American International, 1976, w/Ermanno Donati

ROBERT L. SCHAFFEL

Business: Paramount Pictures, 5555 Melrose Ave., Los Angeles, CA, 90038, 213/468-5000

GORDON'S WAR 20th Century-Fox, 1973
SUNNYSIDE American International, 1979
LOOKIN' TO GET OUT Paramount, 1982
TABLE FOR FIVE Warner Bros., 1983
AMERICAN ANTHEM Columbia, 1986, w/Doug Chapin
DISTANT THUNDER Paramount, 1988
JACKNIFE Cineplex Odeon, 1989, w/Carol Baum

DON SCHAIN

Contact: Directors Guild of America - Los Angeles, 213/289-2000

SLIPPING INTO DARKNESS MCEG, 1988, CP w/Simon R. Lewis

ANGELA P. SCHAPIRO

Business: 9600 Kirkside Rd., Los Angeles, CA, 90035, 213/558-0531

HE'S MY GIRL Scotti Bros., 1987, w/Lawrence Mortorff
THE IRON TRIANGLE Scotti Bros., 1989, w/Tony Scotti

JEFF SCHECHTMAN

PIRANHA New World, 1978, EP w/Roger Corman
PIRANHA II *THE SPAWNING* Saturn International, 1983, w/Chako van Leuwen
BODY ROCK New World, 1984

ANDREW SCHEINMAN

Business: Castle Rock Entertainment, 335 N. Maple Dr., Suite 135, Beverly Hills, CA, 90210, 213/285-2300

THE MOUNTAIN MEN Columbia, 1980, w/Martin Shafer & Martin Ransohoff
THE AWAKENING Orion/Warner Bros., 1980, w/Robert H. Solo & Martin Shafer
MODERN ROMANCE Columbia, 1981, w/Martin Shafer
THE SURE THING Embassy, 1985, CP
STAND BY ME Columbia, 1986, w/Bruce A. Evans & Raynold Gideon
THE PRINCESS BRIDE 20th Century-Fox, 1987, w/Rob Reiner
WHEN HARRY MET SALLY... Castle Rock/Columbia, 1989, w/Rob Reiner

FRED SCHEPISI

Contact: Directors Guild of America - Los Angeles, 213/289-2000

THE CHANT OF JIMMIE BLACKSMITH New Yorker Films, 1980
THE RUSSIA HOUSE Pathe/Warner Bros., 1990, w/Paul Maslansky

EDGAR J. SCHERICK

Business: Saban-Scherick Productions, 4000 W. Alameda Blvd., Burbank, CA, 91505, 818/972-4870

THE BIRTHDAY PARTY Continental, 1968, EP
FOR LOVE OF IVY Cinerama Releasing Corporation, 1968, w/Jay Weston
THANK YOU ALL VERY MUCH Columbia, 1969, EP
RING OF BRIGHT WATER Cinerama Releasing Corporation, 1969, EP
JENNY Cinerama Releasing Corporation, 1970
THE HEARTBREAK KID 20th Century-Fox, 1972
THE TAKING OF PELHAM 1-2-3 United Artists, 1974, w/Gabriel Katzka
THE STEPFORD WIVES Columbia, 1975
I NEVER PROMISED YOU A ROSE GARDEN New World, 1977, EP w/Roger Corman
SUCCESS *THE AMERICAN SUCCESS COMPANY* Columbia, 1979, w/Daniel H. Blatt

SHOOT THE MOON MGM/UA, 1982, EP w/Stuart Millar
I'M DANCING AS FAST AS I CAN Paramount, 1982, w/Scott Rudin
RECKLESS MGM/UA, 1984, w/Scott Rudin
MRS. SOFFEL MGM/UA, 1984, w/David A. Nicksay & Scott Rudin

ELLIOT SCHICK
Agent: The Gersh Agency - Beverly Hills, 213/274-6611
Contact: Directors Guild of America - Los Angeles, 213/289-2000

MARIE MGM/UA, 1985, EP
MASTERS OF THE UNIVERSE Cannon, 1987, CP
CHERRY 2000 Orion, 1988, CP

REENE SCHISGAL
POWER 20th Century-Fox, 1986, w/Mark Tarlov

PAUL SCHIFF
Business: Morgan Creek Productions, 1875 Century Park East, Suite 200, Los Angeles, CA, 90067, 213/284-8884

REVENGE OF THE NERDS II: NERDS IN PARADISE 20th Century-Fox, 1987, AP
YOUNG GUNS 20th Century-Fox, 1988, CP w/Irby Smith
RENEGADES Universal, 1989, CP
COUPE DE VILLE Universal, 1990, w/Larry Brezner

JOHN SCHLESINGER
Agent: Jeff Berg, ICM - Los Angeles, 213/550-4000
Contact: Directors Guild of America - Los Angeles, 213/289-2000

THE FALCON & THE SNOWMAN Orion, 1985, w/Gabriel Katzka
THE BELIEVERS Orion, 1987, w/Beverly J. Camhe & Michael Childers

JULIAN SCHLOSSBERG
Business: Castle Hill Productions, 1414 Avenue of the Americas, New York, NY, 10019, 212/888-0080

TEN FROM YOUR SHOW OF SHOWS Continental, 1973, EP
NO NUKES (FD) Warner Bros., 1980, w/Danny Goldberg
IN THE SPIRIT Castle Hill, 1990, w/Beverly Irby

ARNE L. SCHMIDT
Business: 2501 Banyon Dr., Los Angeles, CA, 90049
Contact: Directors Guild of America - Los Angeles, 213/289-2000

HEART LIKE A WHEEL 20th Century-Fox, 1983, AP
ROBOCOP Orion, 1987
THROW MOMMA FROM THE TRAIN Orion, 1987, EP
THE GREAT OUTDOORS Universal, 1988
THE PACKAGE Orion, 1989, EP
AWAKENINGS Columbia, 1990, EP w/Elliot Abbott

WOLF SCHMIDT
Business: Kodiak Films, Inc., 11075 Santa Monica Blvd., Los Angeles, CA, 90025, 213/479-8575

THE PASSOVER PLOT Atlas, 1977
RIDING THE EDGE Trans World Entertainment, 1989
THE FOURTH WAR Warner Bros., 1990

RICHARD SCHMIECHEN
Business: 213/657-9131

THE TIMES OF HARVEY MILK (FD) Teleculture, 1984

BERT SCHNEIDER
EASY RIDER Columbia, 1969, EP
FIVE EASY PIECES ★ Columbia, 1970, EP
THE LAST PICTURE SHOW Columbia, 1971, EP
DRIVE, HE SAID Columbia, 1970, EP
A SAFE PLACE Columbia, 1971, EP
HEARTS & MINDS (FD) Warner Bros., 1975, EP
TRACKS Castle Hill Productions, 1976, EP
DAYS OF HEAVEN Paramount, 1978, w/Harold Schneider
BROKEN ENGLISH Lorimar, 1981, w/Keith Rothman

HAROLD SCHNEIDER
Business: Paramount Pictures, 5555 Melrose Ave., Los Angeles, CA, 90038, 213/468-5825
Contact: Directors Guild of America - Los Angeles, 213/289-2000

FIVE EASY PIECES ★ Columbia, 1970, AP
THE LAST PICTURE SHOW Columbia, 1971, AP
STAY HUNGRY United Artists, 1976, w/Bob Rafelson
DAYS OF HEAVEN Paramount, 1978, w/Bert Schneider
GOIN' SOUTH Paramount, 1978, w/Harry Gittes
THE ENTITY 20th Century-Fox, 1983
WARGAMES MGM/UA, 1983
THE HOUSE OF GOD United Artists, 1984, w/Charles H. Joffe
BLACK WIDOW 20th Century-Fox, 1987
SOMEONE TO WATCH OVER ME Columbia, 1987, w/Thierry De Ganay
THE TWO JAKES Paramount, 1990, w/Robert Evans

PAUL SCHRADER
Agent: ICM - Los Angeles, 213/550-4000
Contact: Directors Guild of America - New York, 212/581-0370

OLD BOYFRIENDS Avco Embassy, 1989, EP

SHELDON SCHRAGER
Business: Columbia Pictures, Studio Plaza, 3400 Riverside Dr., Burbank, CA, 91505, 818/954-2701
Contact: Directors Guild of America - Los Angeles, 213/289-2000

THE DAY OF THE LOCUST Paramount, 1975, EP
PROMISES IN THE DARK Orion/Warner Bros., 1979, EP
STARS AND BARS Columbia, 1988, EP
THE KARATE KID PART III Columbia, 1989, EP

BARBET SCHROEDER
Business: Les Films du Losange, 26 Avenue Pierre de Serbie, Paris 75116, France, 04/472-5412
Contact: Directors Guild of America - Los Angeles, 213/289-2000

CELINE & JULIE GO BOATING New Yorker Films, 1978
BARFLY Cannon, 1987, w/Tom Luddy & Fred Roos

THOMAS SCHUEHLY
VERONIKA VOSS United Artists Classics, 1982

OUT OF ORDER Sandstar Releasing, 1985, w/Matthias Deyle
THE NAME OF THE ROSE 20th Century-Fox, 1986, EP w/Jake Eberts
THE ADVENTURES OF BARON MUNCHAUSEN Columbia, 1989

SANDRA SCHULBERG
WILDROSE Troma, 1985
BELIZAIRE THE CAJUN Skouras Pictures, 1986, LP
WAITING FOR THE MOON Skouras Pictures, 1987

ARNOLD SCHULMAN
Agent: Martin Baum, Creative Artists Agency - Beverly Hills, 213/288-4545
Business Manager: Starr & Co., 350 Park Ave., New York, NY, 10022, 212/759-6556

WON TON TON, THE DOG WHO SAVED HOLLYWOOD Paramount, 1976, w/David V. Picker & Michael Winner
PLAYERS Paramount, 1979, EP

SAMUEL SCHULMAN
TO LIVE & DIE IN L.A. New Century, 1985, EP

CHIZ SCHULTZ
Business: Fireside Entertainment Corporation, 1650 Broadway, Suite 1001, New York, NY, 10019, 212/489-8160

THE ANGEL LEVINE United Artists, 1970
GANJA & HESS *BLOOD COUPLE* Kelly- Jordan, 1973

MICHAEL SCHULTZ
Business: Crystalite Productions, P.O. Box 1940, Santa Monica, CA, 90406
Agent: Lou Pitt, ICM - Los Angeles, 213/550-4000

KRUSH GROOVE Warner Bros., 1985, w/Doug McHenry
DISORDERLIES Warner Bros., 1987, w/George A. Jackson & Michael Jaffe

WIELAND SCHULZ-KEIL
UNDER THE VOLCANO Universal, 1984, w/Moritz Borman
THE DEAD Vestron, 1987, w/Chris Sievernich
TWISTER Vestron, 1990

MARTHA SCHUMACHER
Business: 8670 WIlshire Blvd., 3rd Floor, Beverly Hills, CA, 90211, 213/289-6100

FIRESTARTER Universal, 1984, AP
STEPHEN KING'S SILVER BULLET Paramount, 1985
STEPHEN KING'S CAT'S EYE *CAT'S EYE* MGM/UA, 1985
RAW DEAL DEG, 1986
MAXIMUM OVERDRIVE DEG, 1986
KING KONG LIVES DEG, 1986
THE BEDROOM WINDOW DEG, 1987
DATE WITH AN ANGEL DEG, 1987

MARTIN C. SCHUTE
WHOSE LIFE IS IT ANYWAY? MGM, 1981, EP w/Ray Cooney
SCANDALOUS Orion, 1984, CP

AARON SCHWAB
Business: MMA Inc., 8484 Wilshire Blvd., Suite 235, Beverly Hills, CA, 90211, 213/852-1956

CHATTAHOOCHEE Hemdale, 1990, EP

FAYE SCHWAB
Business: MMA Inc., 8484 Wilshire Blvd., Suite 235, Beverly Hills, CA, 90211, 213/852-1956

THE MORNING AFTER 20th Century-Fox, 1986, EP
CHATTAHOOCHEE Hemdale, 1990

ALBERT SCHWARTZ
(credit w/Michael S. Landes)
Business: The Almi Group, 1900 Broadway, New York, NY, 10023, 212/769-6400

THE BIG SCORE Almi, 1983
I AM THE CHEESE Almi, 1983, EP w/Jack Schwartzman
THE BOSTONIANS Almi, 1984, EP

BERNARD SCHWARTZ
Business: Bernard Schwartz Productions, 2029 Century Park East, Suite 320, Los Angeles, CA, 90067, 213/277-3700

EYE OF THE CAT Universal, 1969, w/Phillip Hazelton
JENNIFER ON MY MIND United Artists, 1971
THAT MAN BOLT Universal, 1973
BUCKTOWN American International, 1975
TRACKDOWN United Artists, 1976
COAL MINER'S DAUGHTER ★ Universal, 1980
ROAD GAMES Avco Embassy, 1981, EP
PSYCHO II Universal, 1983, EP
ST. ELMO'S FIRE Columbia, 1985, EP w/Ned Tanen
SWEET DREAMS Tri-Star, 1985

IRVING SCHWARTZ
(credit w/Harry Hurwitz)
THE ROSEBUD BEACH HOTEL *THE BIG LOBBY* Almi, 1984
THAT'S ADEQUATE That's Adequate Company, 1986

RUSSELL SCHWARTZ
Business: Miramax Films, 18 East 48th St., New York, NY, 10017, 212/888-2662

THEY ALL LAUGHED United Artists Classics, 1982, AP
A NIGHT IN THE LIFE OF JIMMY REARDON 20th Century-Fox, 1988

TERI SCHWARTZ
Agent: ICM - Los Angeles, 213/550-4000
Contact: Directors Guild of America - Los Angeles, 213/289-2000

NUTS Warner Bros., 1987, EP w/Cis Corman
BEACHES Buena Vista, 1988, EP
JOE VERSUS THE VOLCANO Warner Bros., 1990

JACK SCHWARTZMAN
Business: Schwartzman Pictures, Inc., 11340 W. Olympic Blvd., Suite 165, Los Angeles, CA, 90064, 213/312-0828

BEING THERE United Artists, 1979, EP
NEVER SAY NEVER AGAIN Warner Bros., 1983
I AM THE CHEESE Almi, 1983, EP w/Michael S. Landes & Albert Schwartz

RAD Tri-Star, 1986, EP
HYPER SAPIEN Tri-Star, 1986
LIONHEART Orion, 1987, EP w/Francis Ford Coppola

RONALD L. SCHWARY
Business: Schwary Enterprises, Inc., c/o Stan Karp, 10350 Santa Monica Blvd., Suite 200, Los Angeles, CA, 90025, 213/277-0711
Contact: Directors Guild of America - Los Angeles, 213/289-2000

ORDINARY PEOPLE ★★ Paramount, 1980
ABSENCE OF MALICE Columbia, 1981, EP
TOOTSIE ★ Columbia, 1982, EP
LET'S SPEND THE NIGHT TOGETHER Embassy, 1983
A SOLDIER'S STORY ★ Columbia, 1984, w/Norman Jewison & Patrick Palmer
BATTERIES NOT INCLUDED Universal, 1987

KENNETH SCHWENKER
ICE HOUSE Upfront Films, 1989, CP

RALPH SCOBIE
HOME IS WHERE THE HART IS Atlantic Entertainment, 1987, EP w/Richard Strafehl

ALLAN SCOTT
Agent: Littman & Brown, 409 N. Camden Dr., Suite 105, Beverly Hills, CA, 90210, 213/278-1572
Contact: Writers Guild of America - Los Angeles, 213/550-1000

TAFFIN MGM/UA, 1988, EP

ANN SCOTT
(see Ann SKINNER)

DARIN SCOTT
Agent: Irene Robinson Group - Los Angeles, 213/274-5101

STEPFATHER II Millimeter, 1989, w/William Burr
TO SLEEP WITH ANGER SVS Films, 1990, w/Thomas S. Byrnes & Caldecott Chubb

GENE SCOTT
BITTERSWEET LOVE Avco Embassy, 1976, w/Joel B. Michaels & Joseph Zappala

JANE SCOTT
Business: Paramount Pictures, 5555 Melrose Ave., Hollywood, CA, 90067, 213/468-5796

CROCODILE DUNDEE Paramount, 1986, LP
CROCODILE DUNDEE II Paramount, 1988, w/John Cornell

MARTHA SCOTT
Agent: The Barry Freed Company - Los Angeles, 213/274-6898

FIRST MONDAY IN OCTOBER Paramount, 1981, w/Paul Heller

PIPPA SCOTT
Business: Linden Productions, 10850 Wilshire Blvd., #250, Los Angeles, CA, 90024, 213/474-2234

MEET THE HOLLOWHEADS Moviestore, 1989, EP

RIDLEY SCOTT
Business: Too Magic, Columbia Pictures, Producers 8, #226, Columbia Plaza, Burbank, CA, 91505, 818/954-1878
Agent: Jeff Berg, ICM - Los Angeles, 213/550-4000

SOMEONE TO WATCH OVER ME Columbia, 1987, EP

BEN SCOTTI
(credit w/Fred Scotti)
Business: Scotti Brothers Pictures, Inc., 2114 Pico Blvd., Santa Monica, CA, 90405, 213/452-4040

EYE OF THE TIGER Scotti Bros., 1986, EP w/Herb Nanas
LADY BEWARE Scotti Bros., 1987, EP
THE IRON TRIANGLE Scotti Bros., 1989, EP

FRED SCOTTI
(credit w/Ben Scotti)
Business: Scotti Brothers Pictures, Inc., 2114 Pico Blvd., Santa Monica, CA, 90405, 213/452-4040

LADY BEWARE Scotti Bros., 1987, EP
THE IRON TRIANGLE Scotti Bros., 1989, EP

TONY SCOTTI
Business: Scotti/Vinnedge TV, 6277 Selma Ave., Hollywood, CA, 90028, 213/466-1006

EYE OF THE TIGER Scotti Bros., 1986
LADY BEWARE Scotti Bros., 1987, w/Lawrence Mortorff
THE IRON TRIANGLE Scotti Bros., 1989, w/Angela P. Schapiro

STEVEN SEAGAL
Business: Seagal-Feder-Nasso Productions, Warner Brothers, 4000 Warner Blvd., Burbank, CA, 91522, 818/954-4267
Agent: Michael Ovitz, CAA - Beverly Hills, 213/288-4545

ABOVE THE LAW Warner Bros., 1988, w/Andrew Davis

SUSAN SEIDELMAN
Business Manager: Shedler & Shedler, 225 W. 34th St., New York, NY, 10122, 212/564-6656
Agent: Sam Cohn, ICM - New York, 212/556-5600

SMITHEREENS New Line Cinema, 1982
MAKING MR. RIGHT Orion, 1987, EP w/Dan Enright
COOKIE Warner Bros., 1989, EP w/Alice Arlen & Nora Ephron
SHE-DEVIL Orion, 1989, w/Jonathan Brett

MARK SEILER
PLENTY 20th Century-Fox, 1985, EP

ARLENE SELLERS
(credit w/Alex Winitsky)
Business: Lantana Productions, 3000 Olympic Blvd., Suite 1300, Santa Monica, CA, 90404, 213/315-4777

THE SEVEN-PERCENT SOLUTION Universal, 1976, EP
CROSS OF IRON Avco Embassy, 1977
SILVER BEARS Columbia, 1977
BREAKTHROUGH *SERGEANT STEINER* Maverick Pictures International, 1978
HOUSE CALLS Universal, 1978

THE LADY VANISHES Rank, 1979, EP w/Michael Carreras
CUBA United Artists, 1979
BLUE SKIES AGAIN Warner Bros., 1983
SWING SHIFT Warner Bros., 1984, EP
SCANDALOUS Orion, 1984
IRRECONCILABLE DIFFERENCES Warner Bros., 1984
BAD MEDICINE 20th Century-Fox, 1985
STANLEY & IRIS MGM/UA, 1990

CHARLES E. SELLIER, JR.
Agent: The Schallert Agency - Beverly Hills, 213/276-2044

THE MYSTERIOUS MONSTERS (FD) Sunn Classic, 1976, w/Robert Guenette & David L. Wolper
THE BERMUDA TRIANGLE (FD) Sunn Classic, 1978
BEYOND & BACK (FD) Sunn Classic, 1978
LEGEND OF THE WILD Jensen Farley, 1981
THE BOOGENS Jensen Farley, 1982

YAHOO SERIOUS
(Greg Pead)
Contact: Australian Film Commission, 9229 Sunset Blvd., Los Angeles, CA, 90069, 213/275-7074

YOUNG EINSTEIN Warner Bros., 1989, w/David Roach & Warwick Ross

JOHN SERONG
THE GARBAGE PAIL KIDS MOVIE Atlantic Entertainment, 1987, SP

RALPH SERPE
LOLA American International, 1971, AP w/Norman Thaddeus Vane
ACROSS 110th STREET United Artists, 1972, w/Fouad Said
DRUM United Artists, 1976
MANDINGO Paramount, 1975, EP

ALEX SESSA
Business: Arles International, S.A., Lavalle 1710-60-11, 1048 Buenos Aires, Argentina, 54-1-814-3859

WIZARDS OF THE LOST KINGDOM Concorde, 1985, w/Frank Isaac
BARBARIAN QUEEN Concorde, 1985, w/Frank Isaac
COCAINE WARS Concorde, 1985, w/Roger Corman

JOHN SEXTON
PHAR LAP 20th Century-Fox, 1984
BURKE AND WILLS Hemdale, 1987, w/Graeme Clifford

JULIAN SEYMOUR
ANOTHER COUNTRY Orion Classics, 1984, EP w/Robert Fox

SUSAN SHADBURNE
Business: Millennium Pictures,Inc., 2580 N.W. Upshur, Portland, OR, 97210, 503/227-7041

THE ADVENTURES OF MARK TWAIN Atlantic Entertainment, 1986, AP
SHADOW PLAY New World, 1986, w/Dan Biggs & Will Vinton

MARTIN SHAFER
(credit w/Andrew Scheinman)
Business: Castle Rock Entertainment, 335 N. Maple Dr., Suite 135, Beverly Hills, CA, 90210, 213/285-2300

THE MOUNTAIN MEN Columbia, 1980, w/Martin Ransohoff
THE AWAKENING Orion/Warner Bros., 1980, w/Robert H. Solo
MODERN ROMANCE Columbia, 1981

RENEE A. SHAFRANSKY
Agent: ICM - Los Angeles, 213/550-4000
Contact: Writers Guild of America - New York, 212/245-6180

VARIETY Horizon Films, 1985
SWIMMING TO CAMBODIA Cinecom, 1987

ROBERT SHAFTER
TIME WALKER New World, 1982, EP

STEVE SHAGAN
Agent: William Morris Agency - Beverly Hills, 213/274-7451
Contact: Writers Guild of America - Los Angeles, 213/550-1000

SAVE THE TIGER Paramount, 1973
THE FORMULA MGM/UA, 1980

ASH R. SHAH
Business: Imperial Entertainment Corp., 6430 Sunset Blvd., Suite 1500, Hollywood, CA, 90028, 213/463-4003

ANGEL TOWN Taurus, 1990, w/Eric Karson

SUNDIP R. SHAH
Business: Imperial Entertainment Corp., 6430 Sunset Blvd., Suite 1500, Hollywood, CA, 90028, 213/463-4003

ANGEL TOWN Taurus, 1990, EP w/Anders P. Jensen & Sunil R. Shah

SUNIL R. SHAH
(credit w/Moshe Barkat & Moshe Diamant)
Business: Imperial Entertainment Corp., 6430 Sunset Blvd., Suite 1500, Hollywood, CA, 90028, 213/463-4003

PRAY FOR DEATH American Distribution Group, 1986, EP
RAGE OF HONOR Trans World Entertainment, 1987, EP
ANGEL TOWN Taurus, 1990, EP w/Anders P. Jensen & Sundip R. Shah

MICHAEL SHAMBERG
Business: Ocean Pictures, 2821 Main St., Santa Monica, CA, 90405, 213/399-9271

HEART BEAT Orion/Warner Bros., 1980, w/Alan Greisman
MODERN PROBLEMS 20th Century-Fox, 1981, w/Alan Greisman
THE BIG CHILL ★ Columbia, 1983
CLUB PARADISE Warner Bros., 1986
SALVATION! Circle Releasing, 1987, w/Beth B
A FISH CALLED WANDA MGM/UA, 1988
HOW I GOT INTO COLLEGE 20th Century- Fox, 1989

REID SHANE

Business: Concorde Films, 11600 San Vicente Blvd., Los Angeles, CA, 90049, 213/820-6733

THE TERROR WITHIN Concorde, 1989, CP w/Rodman Flender
DANCE OF THE DAMNED Concorde, 1989, CP w/Anna Roth

JOHN HERMAN SHANER

Agent: Robinson, Weintraub, Gross, Inc. - Los Angeles, 213/653-5802
Contact: Writers Guild of America - Los Angeles, 213/550-1000

THE LAST MARRIED COUPLE IN AMERICA Universal, 1980, w/Edward S. Feldman

MARK SHANKER

THE FIRST DEADLY SIN Filmways, 1980, w/George Pappas

GEORGE SHAPIRO

Business: Shapiro/West, 151 El Camino Dr., Beverly Hills, CA, 90210

THE LAST REMAKE OF BEAU GESTE Universal, 1977, EP w/Howard West
IN GOD WE TRUST Universal, 1980, w/Howard West
SUMMER RENTAL Paramount, 1985
SUMMER SCHOOL Paramount, 1987, w/Howard West
BERT RIGBY, YOU'RE A FOOL Warner Bros., 1989

IRVIN SHAPIRO

CRIMEWAVE Embassy, 1986, EP w/Edward R. Pressman

LEONARD SHAPIRO

Business: Shapiro Glickenhaus Entertainment, 12001 Ventura Place, 4th Floor, Studio City, CA, 91604 818/766-8500

SHAKEDOWN Universal, 1988, EP w/Alan M. Solomon

MICHAEL SHAPIRO

DEADLY ILLUSION CineTel Films, 1987, EP w/Rodney Sheldon

ROBERT SHAPIRO

Business: Robert Shapiro Productions, 329 N. Wetherly Dr., #205, Beverly Hills, CA, 90211, 213/271-0779

PEE-WEE'S BIG ADVENTURE Warner Bros., 1985, w/Richard Gilbert Abramson
EMPIRE OF THE SUN Warner Bros., 1987, EP
ARTHUR 2 ON THE ROCKS Warner Bros., 1988

STANLEY SHAPIRO

Contact: Writers Guild of America - Los Angeles, 213/550-1000

FOR PETE'S SAKE Columbia, 1974, w/Martin Erlichman
SENIORS Cinema Shares Inernational, 1978, w/Carter De Haven
CARBON COPY Avco Embassy, 1981, w/Carter De Haven

STUART S. SHAPIRO

MONDO NEW YORK 4th & Broadway, 1988
COMEDY'S DIRTIEST DOZEN 4th & Broadway, 1989

SUSAN HILLARY SHAPIRO

GINGER ALE AFTERNOON Skouras Pictures, 1989, w/Rafal Zielinski

TED SHAPIRO

TRACKS Castle Hill Productions, 1976, w/Norman I. Cohen & Howard Zucker

BRUCE SHARMAN

HENRY V Samuel Goldwyn Company, 1989

HARVE SHARMAN

SHOOT Avco Embassy, 1976

CLIVE SHARP

LOLA *TWINKY* American International, 1971

JAN SHARP

THE GOOD WIFE Atlantic Entertainment, 1987

PETER SHAW

ENIGMA Embassy, 1983, w/Ben Arbeid & Andre Pergament
CHAMPIONS Embassy, 1984
CASTAWAY Cannon, 1987, EP w/Richard Johnson
TAFFIN MGM/UA, 1988

SAM SHAW

A WOMAN UNDER THE INFLUENCE Faces International, 1974
OPENING NIGHT Faces International, 1977, EP
GLORIA Columbia, 1980, EP

TOM SHAW

THE NINTH CONFIGURATION *TWINKLE, TWINKLE, "KILLER" KANE* Warner Bros., 1979, AP
MR. NORTH Samuel Goldwyn Company, 1988, CP
TEQUILA SUNRISE Warner Bros., 1988, EP

ROBERT SHAYE

Business: New Line Cinema, 116 N. Robertson Blvd., Suite 808, Los Angeles, CA, 90048, 213/854-5811

STUNTS New Line Cinema, 1977, EP w/Peter S. Davis
POLYESTER New Line Cinema, 1981, EP
ALONE IN THE DARK New Line Cinema, 1982
THE FIRST TIME New Line Cinema, 1982, EP w/Lawrence Loventhal
XTRO New Line Cinema, 1983, EP
A NIGHTMARE ON ELM STREET New Line Cinema, 1984, EP
A NIGHTMARE ON ELM STREET 2: FREDDY'S REVENGE New Line Cinema, 1985
CRITTERS New Line Cinema, 1986, EP
QUIET COOL New Line Cinema, 1986, w/Gerald T. Olson
A NIGHTMARE ON ELM STREET 3: DREAM WARRIORS New Line Cinema, 1987
MY DEMON LOVER New Line Cinema, 1987
STRANDED New Line Cinema, 1987, EP
THE HIDDEN New Line Cinema, 1987, w/Michael Meltzer & Gerald T. Olson
THE PRINCE OF PENNSYLVANIA New Line Cinema, 1988, EP w/Sara Risher

CRITTERS 2: THE MAIN COURSE New Line Cinema, 1988
HAIRSPRAY New Line Cinema, 1988, EP w/Sara Risher
A NIGHTMARE ON ELM STREET 4: THE DREAM MASTER New Line Cinema, 1988, w/Rachel Talalay
A NIGHTMARE ON ELM STREET 5: THE DREAM CHILD New Line Cinema, 1989, w/Rupert Harvey
LEATHERFACE: THE TEXAS CHAINSAW MASSACRE III New Line Cinema, 1990, EP
HEART CONDITION New Line Cinema, 1990, EP

RONALD SHEDLO

Contact: Weissmann, Wolff, Bergman, Coleman & Silverman, 9665 Wilshire Blvd., Suite 900, Beverly Hills, CA, 90209, 213/858-7888

THE WHISPERERS United Artists, 1967, w/Michael S. Laughlin
THE RECKONING Columbia, 1971
BACK ROADS Warner Bros., 1981
THE DRESSMAKER Euro-American Classics, 1988

MARTIN SHEEN

(credit w/William R. Greenblatt)

Business: Symphony Pictures, 5711 W. Slauson Blvd., #226, Culver City, CA, 90230, 213/649-3668
Agent: Glennis Liberty, The Liberty Agency - Los Angeles, 213/824-7937

JUDGMENT IN BERLIN New Line Cinema, 1988, EP w/Jeffrey Auerbach
DA FilmDallas, 1988, EP w/Sam Grogg

JON SHEINBERG

Business: Lee Rich Productions, 4000 Warner Blvd., Burbank, CA, 91522, 818/954-3556

HARD TO KILL Warner Brothers, 1990, CP

RODNEY SHELDON

DEADLY ILLUSION CineTel Films, 1987, EP w/Michael Shapiro

WALTER SHENSON

Business: Shenson Films, 120 El Camino Dr., Suite 200, Beverly Hills, CA, 90212, 213/275-6886

THE MOUSE THAT ROARED Columbia, 1959, w/Jon Pennington
A MATTER OF WHO MGM, 1962, w/Milton Holmes
THE MOUSE ON THE MOON United Artists, 1963
A HARD DAY'S NIGHT United Artists, 1964
HELP! United Artists, 1965
30 IS A DANGEROUS AGE, CYNTHIA Columbia, 1968
DIGBY, THE BIGGEST DOG IN THE WORLD Cinerama Releasing, 1974
THE CHICKEN CHRONICLES Avco Embassy, 1977
REUBEN, REUBEN 20th Century-Fox International Classics, 1983
ECHO PARK Atlantic Entertainment, 1986

PETER SHEPHERD

Business: Cannon Productions, 5757 Wilshire Blvd., Suite 721, Los Angeles, CA, 90036, 213/965-0901

LAMBADA Warner Bros., 1990

RICHARD SHEPHERD

Agent: The Artists Agency, 10000 Santa Monica Blvd., Suite 305, Los Angeles, CA, 90067, 213/277-7779

THE HANGING TREE Warner Bros., 1959, w/Martin Jurow
THE FUGITIVE KIND United Artists, 1960, w/Martin Jurow
BREAKFAST AT TIFFANY'S Paramount, 1961, w/Martin Jurow
ROBIN AND MARIAN Columbia, 1976, w/Denis O'Dell
ALEX AND THE GYPSY 20th Century-Fox, 1976
THE HUNGER MGM/UA, 1983
VOLUNTEERS Tri-Star, 1985, w/Walter F. Parkes

VICTOR SHER

POSITIVE I.D. Universal, 1987, EP

DANIEL A. SHERKOW

SUSPECT Tri-Star, 1987
RACE TO GLORY New Century/Vista, 1989, w/Jon Gordon

JERRY SHERLOCK

CHARLIE CHAN & THE CURSE OF THE DRAGON QUEEN American Cinema, 1981
THE HUNT FOR RED OCTOBER Paramount, 1990, EP w/Larry De Waay

GARY A. SHERMAN

Agent: Camden Artists, Ltd. - Los Angeles, 213/556-2022
Contact: Directors Guild of America - Los Angeles, 213/289-2000

POLTERGEIST III MGM/UA, 1988, EP

ROBERT M. SHERMAN

SCARECROW Warner Bros., 1973
NIGHT MOVES Warner Bros., 1975
THE MISSOURI BREAKS United Artists, 1976, w/Elliott Kastner
OH, GOD! YOU DEVIL Warner Bros., 1984
DEADLY FRIEND Warner Bros., 1986

TERI SHIELDS

SAHARA MGM/UA, 1984, EP

BARRY SHILS

THE STUFF New World, 1985, AP
VAMPIRE'S KISS Hemdale, 1989, w/Barbara Zitwer

TALIA SHIRE

Business: Schwartzman Pictures,Inc., 11340 W. Olympic Blvd., Suite 165, Los Angeles, CA, 90064, 213/312-0828

HYPER SAPIEN Tri-Star, 1986, EP
LIONHEART Orion, 1987, w/Stanley O'Toole

MARK SHIVAS

Business: British Broadcasting Corporation, Woodlands, 80 Wood Lane, London W12, England

RICHARD'S THINGS New World, 1981
MOONLIGHTING Universal, 1982, w/Jerzy Skolimowski
A PRIVATE FUNCTION Island Alive, 1985
THE WITCHES Warner Bros., 1989

MARC SHMUGER
Contact: Writers Guild of America - Los Angeles, 213/550-1000

DEAD OF WINTER MGM/UA, 1987, w/John Bloomgarden

DEL SHORES
Business: Warner Bros. TV, 4000 Warner Blvd., Burbank, CA, 91522, 818/954-3135
Agent: Artists Circle Entertainment - Los Angeles, 213/275-6330

DADDY'S DYIN' MGM/UA, 1990, EP w/Bobbie Edrick

SKIP SHORT
FLASHPOINT Tri-Star, 1984

MURRAY SHOSTAK
Agent: Camden Artists, Ltd. - Los Angeles, 213/556-2022

DEATH HUNT 20th Century-Fox, 1981
SILENCE OF THE NORTH Universal, 1982
MARIA CHAPDELAINE Moviestore, 1986, w/Robert Baylis
LOVE SONGS Spectrafilm, 1986, EP w/Marie-Christine Chouraqui
SPEED ZONE Orion, 1989

LAUREN SHULER-DONNER
(formerly Lauren Shuler)
Business: Shuler-Donner Productions, Warner Brothers, 4000 Warner Blvd., Burbank, CA, 91521, 818/954-3611

MR. MOM 20th Century-Fox, 1983, w/Lynn Loring
LADYHAWKE Warner Bros., 1985, w/Richard Donner
ST. ELMO'S FIRE Columbia, 1985
PRETTY IN PINK Paramount, 1986
THREE FUGITIVES Buena Vista, 1989

RONALD SHUSETT
Agent: Triad Artists, Inc. - Los Angeles, 213/556-2727
Contact: Writers Guild of America - Los Angeles, 213/550-1000

ALIEN 20th Century-Fox, 1979, EP
DEAD AND BURIED Avco Embassy, 1981, w/Robert Fentress
KING KONG LIVES DEG, 1986, EP
TOTAL RECALL Tri-Star, 1990, w/Buzz Feitshans

CHARLES SHYER
Agent: ICM - Los Angeles, 213/550-4000
Contact: Directors Guild of America - Los Angeles, 213/289-2000

PRIVATE BENJAMIN Warner Bros., 1980, w/Nancy Meyers & Harvey Miller

ARLENE SIDARIS
Business: Malibu Bay Films, 8560 Sunset Blvd., 2nd Floor, Los Angeles, CA, 90069, 213/278-5056

MALIBU EXPRESS Malibu Bay Films, 1984
HARD TICKET TO HAWAII Malibu Bay Films, 1987
PICASSO TRIGGER Malibu Bay Films, 1988
SAVAGE BEACH Malibu Bay Films, 1989

STEVEN JAY SIEGEL
Agent: Bauer Benedek Agency - Los Angeles, 213/275-2421
Contact: Writers Guild of America - Los Angeles, 213/550-1000

K-9 Universal, 1989, CP

CHRIS SIEVERNICH
Business: Delta Films, 853 Broadway, Suite 1711, New York, NY, 10003, 212/473-3600

LIGHTNING OVER WATER Gray City, 1981
THE STATE OF THINGS Gray City, 1983
PARIS, TEXAS 20th Century-Fox, 1984, EP
THE DEAD Vestron, 1987, w/Wieland Schulz-Keil

SIGURJON SIGHVATSSON
(credit w/Steven Golin)
Business: Propaganda Films, 940 N. Mansfield Ave., Los Angeles, CA, 213/462-6400

PRIVATE INVESTIGATIONS MGM, 1987
THE BLUE IGUANA Paramount, 1988
FEAR, ANXIETY AND DEPRESSION Samuel Goldwyn Company, 1989, w/Stanley Wlodkowski
KILL ME AGAIN MGM/UA, 1989, w/David W. Warfield
DADDY'S DYIN' MGM/UA, 1990, w/Monty Montgomery
WILD AT HEART Samuel Goldwyn Company, 1990, w/Monty Montgomery

SERGE SILBERMAN
EXPOSED MGM/UA, 1983, EP
RAN Orion Classics, 1985, w/Masato Hara

STIRLING SILLIPHANT
Agent: CAA - Beverly Hills, 213/288-4545
Contact: Writers Guild of America - Los Angeles, 213/550-1000

CATCH THE HEAT Trans World Entertainment, 1987, EP w/Moshe Diamant

JERRY SILVA
Business: Double Helix Films, Inc., 275 Seventh Ave., #2003, New York, NY, 10001

FUNLAND Double Helix, 1987, EP w/Kirk Smith & Stan Wakefield
MATEWAN Cinecom, 1987, EP w/Mark Balsam & Amir J. Malin
FAST FOOD Fries Entertainment, 1989, EP

GIORGIO SILVAGO
WAIT UNTIL SPRING, BANDINI Orion, 1990, EP w/Christian Charret, Cyril de Rouvre & Amadeo Pagani

ALAIN SILVER
Business: Pendragon Film Ltd., 9336 Washington Blvd., Culver City, CA, 90230, 213/559-0346
Contact: Directors Guild of America - Los Angeles, 213/289-2000

NIGHT VISITOR MGM/UA, 1989

DIANE SILVER
Contact: Writers Guild of America - Los Angeles, 213.550-1000

NATIVE SON Cinecom, 1986

DINA SILVER
Business: Midwest Film Productions, 600 Madison Avenue, New York, NY, 10022, 213/355-0282

OLD ENOUGH Orion Classics, 1984
A WALK ON THE MOON Skouras Pictures, 1987

JEFFREY SILVER
Contact: Directors Guild of America - Los Angeles, 213/289-2000

RAPPIN' Cannon, 1985, AP
SHAG: THE MOVIE Hemdale, 1989, LP

JOAN MICKLIN SILVER
Business: Midwest Film Productions, 600 Madison Avenue, New York, NY, 10022, 212/355-0282
Agent: Broder/Kurland/Webb/Uffner - Los Angeles, 213/656-9262

ON THE YARD Midwest Film Productions, 1979

JOEL SILVER
Business: Silver Pictures, 4000 Warner Blvd., Burbank, CA, 91522, 818/954-4490

THE WARRIORS Paramount, 1979, AP
XANADU Universal, 1980, CP
48 HOURS Paramount, 1982, w/Lawrence Gordon
JEKYLL & HYDE...TOGETHER AGAIN Paramount, 1982, EP
STREETS OF FIRE Universal, 1984, w/Lawrence Gordon
BREWSTER'S MILLIONS Universal, 1985, w/Lawrence Gordon
WEIRD SCIENCE Universal, 1985
COMMANDO 20th Century-Fox, 1985
JUMPIN' JACK FLASH 20th Century-Fox, 1986, w/Lawrence Gordon
LETHAL WEAPON Warner Bros., 1987, w/Richard Donner
PREDATOR 20th Century-Fox, 1987, w/John Davis & Lawrence Gordon
ACTION JACKSON Lorimar, 1988
DIE HARD 20th Century-Fox, 1988, w/Lawrence Gordon
LETHAL WEAPON 2 Warner Bros., 1989, w/Richard Donner
ROADHOUSE MGM/UA, 1989
FORD FAIRLANE 20th Century-Fox, 1990, w/Steve Perry
DIE HARD 2 20th Century-Fox, 1990, w/Lawrence Gordon

RAPHAEL D. SILVER
Business: Midwest Film Productions, 600 Madison Avenue, New York, NY, 10022, 212/355-0282
Contact: Directors Guild of America - New York, 2132/581-0370

HESTER STREET Midwest Film Productions, 1975
BETWEEN THE LINES Midwest Film Productions, 1977
CROSSING DELANCEY Warner Bros., 1988, EP

TIMOTHY SILVER
Contact: Directors Guild of America - Los Angeles, 213/289-2000

FRIDAY THE 13TH PART V - A NEW BEGINNING Paramount, 1985

ARTHUR SILVERMAN
PARTING GLANCES Cinecom, 1986, w/Yoram Mandel

JACK SILVERMAN
CRACK HOUSE Cannon, 1989, EP

JIM SILVERMAN
CRACK HOUSE Cannon, 1989

RON SILVERMAN
BUSTER AND BILLIE Columbia, 1974
LIFEGUARD Paramount, 1976, EP
BRUBAKER 20th Century-Fox, 1980
KRULL Columbia, 1983
SHOOT TO KILL Buena Vista, 1988, w/Daniel Petrie Jr.

LOUIS M. SILVERSTEIN
STRANGE BREW MGM/UA, 1983
MILLENNIUM 20th Century-Fox, 1989, EP w/Freddie Fields, John Foreman & P. Gael Mourant

ALAN SIMMONDS
TICKET TO HEAVEN United Artists Classics, 1981, CP

MATTY SIMMONS
Business: National Lampoon Films, 3619 Motor Ave., #300, Los Angeles, CA, 90034, 213/204-6270
Contact: Writers Guild of America - Los Angeles, 213/550-1000

NATIONAL LAMPOON'S ANIMAL HOUSE Universal, 1978, w/Ivan Reitman
NATIONAL LAMPOON'S MOVIE MADNESS United Artists, 1981
NATIONAL LAMPOON'S CLASS REUNION 20th Century-Fox, 1982
NATIONAL LAMPOON'S VACATION Warner Bros., 1983
NATIONAL LAMPOON'S EUROPEAN VACATION Warner Bros., 1985
NATIONAL LAMPOON'S CHRISTMAS VACATION Warner Bros., 1989, EP

RUDD SIMMONS
LASERMAN Peter Wang Films/Hong Kong Film Workshop, 1988, AP
MYSTERY TRAIN Orion Classics, 1989, LP

RUSSELL SIMMONS
Business: Def Jam Records, 652 Broadway, 3rd Floor, New York, NY, 10012, 212/979-2610

KRUSH GROOVE Warner Bros., 1985, CP
TOUGHER THAN LEATHER New Line Cinema, 1988, EP w/Rick Rubin

JOEL SIMON
(credit w/Bill Todman Jr.)
Business: Todman-Simon Productions, 10202 W. Washington Blvd., #204, Culver City, CA, 90232, 213/280-7673

MARRIED TO THE MOB Orion, 1988, EP
HARD TO KILL Warner Bros., 1990, w/Gary Adelson

MELVIN SIMON
WHEN A STRANGER CALLS Columbia, 1979, EP w/Barry Krost
TILT Warner Bros., 1979, EP
MY BODYGUARD 20th Century-Fox, 1980, EP
THE STUNT MAN 20th Century-Fox, 1980, EP
THE MAN WITH BOGART'S FACE *SAM MARLOW, PRIVATE EYE* 20th Century-Fox, 1980, EP
CHU CHU & THE PHILLY FLASH 20th Century-Fox, 1981, EP
PORKY'S 20th Century-Fox, 1982, EP w/Harold Greenberg
PORKY'S II: THE NEXT DAY 20th Century-Fox, 1983, EP w/Harold Greenberg & Alan Landsburg
PORKY'S REVENGE 20th Century-Fox, 1985, EP w/Milton Goldstein
UFORIA Universal, 1985, EP w/Barry Krost

NEIL SIMON
Personal Manager: Albert DaSilva - Los Angeles, 213/752-9323
Contact: Writers Guild of America - Los Angeles, 213/550-1000

ONLY WHEN I LAUGH Columbia, 1981, w/Roger M. Rothstein
I OUGHT TO BE IN PICTURES 20th Century-Fox, 1982, w/Herbert Ross
MAX DUGAN RETURNS 20th Century-Fox, 1983, w/Herbert Ross

EDWARD SIMONS
THE RETURN OF THE SOLDIER European Classics, 1985, EP w/J. Gordon Arnold & John Quested
HOWLING III: THE MARSUPIALS Square Pictures, 1987, EP w/Steven Lane & Robert Pringle
HOWLING IV...THE ORIGINAL NIGHTMARE Allied Entertainment, 1988, EP w/Steven Lane, Avi Lerner & Robert Pringle
EDGE OF SANITY Millimeter Films, 1989, w/Harry Alan Towers
COMMUNION New Line Cinema, 1989, CP

M. H. SIMONSONS
Business: International Rainbow Pictures, 9165 Sunset Blvd., Penthouse, Los Angeles, CA, 90069, 213/271-0202

SOMEONE TO LOVE International Rainbow/ Castle Hill, 1987

DON SIMPSON
(credit w/Jerry Bruckheimer)
Business: Simpson-Bruckheimer Productions, Paramount Pictures, 5555 Melrose Ave., Los Angeles, CA, 90038,213/468-4518

FLASHDANCE Paramount, 1983
BEVERLY HILLS COP Paramount, 1984
THIEF OF HEARTS Paramount, 1984
TOP GUN Paramount, 1986
BEVERLY HILLS COP II Paramount, 1987
DAYS OF THUNDER Paramount, 1990

MICHAEL A. SIMPSON
Business: Double Helix Films, Inc., 303 W. 76th St., Suite B, New York, NY, 10023, 212/769-0202

FUNLAND Double Helix, 1987, w/William VanDerKloot
FAST FOOD Fries Entertainment, 1989, w/Stan Wakefield

PETER R. SIMPSON
Business: Simcom International, Inc., 9570 Wilshire Blvd., Penthouse, Beverly Hills, CA, 90212, 213/274-5830

BULLIES Universal, 1986
HELLO MARY LOU: PROM NIGHT II Samuel Goldwyn Company, 1987

GREG H. SIMS
Business: Arrowhead Entertainment, 20th Century-Fox, 10201 W. Pico Blvd., Los Angeles, CA, 90035, 213/203-2790

TO DIE FOR Skouras Pictures, 1989, EP w/Lee Caplin

FRANK SINATRA
Business Manager: Nathan Golden, 8501 Wilshire Blvd., Suite 250, Beverly Hills, CA, 90211, 213/855-0850
Contact: Directors Guild of America - Los Angeles, 213/289-2000

THE FIRST DEADLY SIN Filmways, 1980, EP w/Elliott Kastner

JOSHUA SINCLAIR
JUDGMENT IN BERLIN New Line Cinema, 1988, w/Ingrid Windlisch

NIGEL SINCLAIR
(credit w/Michael Kuhn)
Business: Propaganda Films, 940 N. Mansfield Ave., Los Angeles, CA, 213/462-6400

THE BLUE IGUANA Paramount, 1988, EP
FEAR, ANXIETY & DEPRESSION Samuel Goldwyn Company, 1989, EP
KILL ME AGAIN MGM/UA, 1990, EP

ROBERT SINGER
(credit w/Daniel H. Blatt)
Business: Daniel H. Blatt Productions, 10202 W. Washington Blvd., Culver City, CA, 90230, 213/280-5170

BURNT OFFERINGS United Artists, 1976, AP*
INDEPENDENCE DAY Warner Bros., 1983
CUJO Warner Bros., 1983
LET'S GET HARRY Tri-Star, 1986

RALPH S. SINGLETON
Business: R. S. Singleton Productions, c/o Perry & Neidorf, 315 S. Beverly Dr., #412, Beverly Hills, CA, 90212, 213/553-0171
Agent: Harold Cohen, Associated Management - Los Angeles, 213/550-0570

PET SEMATARY Paramount, 1989, AP
HARLEM NIGHTS Paramount, 1989, CP
ANOTHER 48 HOURS Paramount, 1990, EP w/Mark Lipsky

CALVIN SKAGGS
ON VALENTINE'S DAY Angelika, 1986, w/Lillian V. Foote
THE WASH Skouras Pictures, 1988

ANN SKINNER
(formerly Ann Scott)
(credit w/Simon Relph)

THE PLOUGHMAN'S LUNCH Samuel Goldwyn Company, 1984
SECRET PLACES 20th Century-Fox, 1985
THE RETURN OF THE SOLDIER European Classics, 1985
THE GOOD FATHER Skouras Pictures, 1987*

DANIEL SKLAR
RED SCORPION Shapiro Glickenhaus, 1989, EP w/Robert Abramoff & Paul Erickson

JERZY SKOLIMOWSKI
Agent: ICM - Los Angeles, 213/550-4000
Contact: Directors Guild of America - Los Angeles, 213/289-2000

MOONLIGHTING Universal, 1982, w/Mark Shivas

DIMITRI T. SKOURAS
BLIND DATE New Line Cinema, 1984, EP

JOSEPH SKRZYNSKI
HIGH TIDE Tri-Star, 1987, EP w/Antony I. Ginnane

JON SLAN
Business: Paragon Motion Pictures Inc., 260 Richmond Street W., Suite 405, Toronto, Ontario M5V 1W5, Canada, 416/977-2929; 2211 Corinth Ave., #305, Los Angeles, CA, 90064, 213/478-7272

FISH HAWK Avco Embassy, 1981
THRESHOLD 20th Century-Fox International Classics, 1983, w/Michael Burns

BUD SMITH
Agent: Bauer Benedek Agency - Los Angeles, 213/275-2421
Contact: Directors Guild of America - Los Angeles, 213/289-2000

THE KARATE KID Columbia, 1984, AP
TO LIVE AND DIE IN L.A. New Century, 1985, CP

CLIVE A. SMITH
(credit w/Michael Hirsh & Patrick Loubert)
Business: Nelvana Ltd., 32 Atlantic Ave., Toronto, Ontario M6K 1X8, Canada,416/588-5571; 9000 Sunset Blvd., #911, Los Angeles, CA, 90069, 213/278-8466

THE CARE BEARS MOVIE (AF) Samuel Goldwyn Company, 1985
CARE BEARS MOVIE II: A NEW GENERATION (AF) Columbia, 1986
THE CARE BEARS ADVENTURE IN WONDER-LAND (AF) Cineplex Odeon, 1987
BABAR: THE MOVIE (AF) New Line Cinema, 1989

DONNA SMITH
Contact: Universal City Studios, 100 Universal Plaza, Bldg. 500, 11th Floor, Universal City, CA, 91608 818/777-4272

SOUL MAN New World, 1986, LP
NIGHT OF THE CREEPS Tri-Star, 1986, AP
K-9 Universal, 1989, EP

HOWARD SMITH
RHINESTONE 20th Century-Fox, 1984, w/Marvin Worth
PUMPKINHEAD United Artists, 1988, w/Richard C. Weinman
RELENTLESS New Line Cinema, 1989

IAIN SMITH
Business: Enigma Productions, Ltd., 15 Queen's Gate Place Mews, London SW7 5BG, England, 01/581-0238

LOCAL HERO Warner Bros., 1983, AP
THE KILLING FIELDS ★ Warner Bros., 1984, AP
THE FROG PRINCE Warner Bros., 1985
THE MISSION ★ Warner Bros., 1986, AP
HEARTS OF FIRE Lorimar, 1988, CP

IRA N. SMITH
AMITYVILLE II: THE POSSESSION Orion, 1982, w/Stephen R. Greenwald

IRBY SMITH
Business: Morgan Creek Productions, 1801 Century Park East, Suite 1910, Los Angeles, CA, 90067, 213/284-8884
Contact: Directors Guild of America - Los Angeles, 213/289-2000

YOUNG GUNS 20th Century-Fox, 1988, CP w/Paul Schiff
MAJOR LEAGUE Paramount, 1989, w/Chris Chesser
ENEMIES, A LOVE STORY 20th Century-Fox, 1989, CP w/Pato Guzman

KIRK SMITH
FUNLAND Double Helix, 1987, EP w/Jerry Silva & Stan Wakefield

P. MICHAEL SMITH
WIRED Taurus, 1989, EP w/Paul Carran

THOMAS G. SMITH
Business: Walt Disney Pictures, 500 S. Buena Vista St., Olive Bldg. #912, Burbank, CA, 91521, 818/972-3577

HONEY, I SHRUNK THE KIDS Buena Vista, 1989, EP

PETER SNELL
Business: British Lion Screen Entertainment, Pinewood Studios, Pinewood Rd., Iver, Bucks., SL0 0NH, England, 01/0753-651-700

THE WICKER MAN Warner Bros., 1974
TURTLE DIARY Samuel Goldwyn Company, 1986, EP
LADY JANE Paramount, 1986
A PRAYER FOR THE DYING Samuel Goldwyn Company, 1987

HAROLD SOBEL
DANGEROUSLY CLOSE Cannon, 1986

RAINER SOEHNLEIN
Agent: Peter Rawley, ICM - Los Angeles, 213/550-4000

THE LIGHTSHIP Castle Hill, 1986, EP

STEVE SOHMER
Contact: Directors Guild of America - Los Angeles, 213/289-2000

LEONARD PART 6 Columbia, 1987, EP w/Alan Marshall

JOEL SOISSON
(credit w/Michael S. Murphey)

Business: Soisson Murphey Productions, 9060 Santa Monica Blvd., Suite 210, Los Angeles, CA, 90069, 213/273-3157

HAMBONE & HILLIE New World, 1984, AP
THE BOYS NEXT DOOR New World, 1985, AP
AVENGING ANGEL New World, 1985, AP
A NIGHTMARE ON ELM STREET, PART 2: FREDDY'S REVENGE New Line Cinema, 1985, LP
KGB: THE SECRET WAR Cinema Group, 1986, AP
TRICK OR TREAT DEG, 1986
THE SUPERNATURALS Republic Entertainment, 1987
BILL & TED'S EXCELLENT ADVENTURE Orion, 1989, w/Scott Kroopf

VICTOR SOLNICKI
(credit w/Pierre David)

Business: Jillian Film & Investment Corp., 142-144 Davenport Rd., Toronto, Ontario M5R 1J2, Canada, 416/922-3168

THE BROOD New World, 1979, EP
HOG WILD Avco Embassy, 1980, EP w/Stephen Miller
SCANNERS Avco Embassy, 1981, EP
GAS Paramount, 1981, EP
DIRTY TRICKS Avco Embassy, 1981, EP w/Arnold Kopelson
VISITING HOURS 20th Century-Fox, 1982, EP
VIDEODROME Universal, 1983, EP
COVERGIRL New World, 1984, EP

ROBERT H. SOLO
Business: The SoloFilm Company, 9507 Santa Monica Blvd., Beverly Hills, CA, 90210, 213/282-2795

SCROOGE National General, 1970
THE DEVILS Warner Bros., 1971, w/Ken Russell
INVASION OF THE BODY SNATCHERS United Artists, 1978
THE AWAKENING Orion/Warner Bros., 1980, w/Andrew Scheinman & Martin Shafer
I, THE JURY 20th Century-Fox, 1982
BAD BOYS Universal, 1983
COLORS Orion, 1988
ABOVE THE LAW Warner Bros., 1988, EP
WINTER PEOPLE Columbia, 1989

ALAN M. SOLOMON
Business: Shapiro Glickenhaus Entertainment, 12001 Ventura Place, 4th Floor, Studio City, CA, 91604, 818/766-8500

SHAKEDOWN Universal, 1988, EP w/Leonard Shapiro
MOONTRAP Shapiro-Glickenhaus Entertainment, 1989, EP w/James A. Courtney & Brian C. Manoogian

KEN SOLOMON
PRETTY SMART New World, 1987, w/Jeff Begun

HERBERT F. SOLOW
Contact: Directors Guild of America - Los Angeles, 213/289-2000

GET CRAZY Embassy, 1983, EP
SAVING GRACE Embassy, 1986

ANDREW SOLT
Business: Andrew Solt Productions, 9121 Sunset Blvd., Beverly Hills, CA, 90069, 213/276-9522
Agent: William Morris Agency - Beverly Hills, 213/274-7451

THIS IS ELVIS (FD) Warner Bros., 1981, w/Malcolm Leo
IMAGINE: JOHN LENNON (FD) Warner Bros., 1988, w/David L. Wolper

SUSAN SOLT
Business: Pakula Productions, Inc., 330 West 58th St., New York, NY, 10019, 212/664-0640

DREAM LOVER MGM/UA, 1986, AP
ORPHANS Lorimar, 1987, CP
SEE YOU IN THE MORNING Warner Bros., 1989, w/Alan J. Pakula
PRESUMED INNOCENT Warner Bros., 1990, EP

MARY ROSE SOLTI
BILLY JACK Warner Bros., 1973

MARIO SOTELA
Business: Sotela Pictures, Ltd., 9000 Sunset Blvd., #1000, Los Angeles, CA, 90069, 213/271-5858

WAXWORK Vestron, 1988, EP w/Gregory Cascante, Dan Ireland & William J. Quigley

MICHAEL SOURAPAS
Business: SPI Entertainment, 279 South Beverly Dr., Penthouse, Beverly Hills, CA, 90212, 213/827-4229

ALIEN PREDATOR Trans World Entertainment, 1987, CP

MARGARET JENNINGS SOUTH
Business: All-Girl Pictures, Walt Disney Pictures, 500 S. Buena Vista St., Burbank, CA, 91521, 818/560-5000

BEACHES Buena Vista, 1988, w/Bonnie Bruckheimer-Martell & Bette Midler

CAROLINE SPACK
LETTER TO BREZHNEV Circle Releasing, 1986, CP

TERRY SPAZEK
THE DREAM TEAM Universal, 1989, SP

ARMAND SPECA
LOVE AT STAKE Tri-Star, 1988, CP

AARON SPELLING

Business: Aaron Spelling Productions, 1041 N. Formosa Ave., Los Angeles, CA, 90046, 213/850-2413

CALIFORNIA SPLIT Columbia, 1974, EP w/Leonard J. Goldberg
BABY BLUE MARINE Columbia, 1976, w/Leonard J. Goldberg
MR. MOM 20th Century-Fox, 1983, EP
'NIGHT, MOTHER Universal, 1986, w/Alan Greisman
CROSS MY HEART Universal, 1987, EP w/Alan Greisman
SURRENDER Warner Bros., 1987, w/Alan Greisman
THREE O'CLOCK HIGH Universal, 1987, EP w/Alan Greisman
SATISFACTION 20th Century-Fox, 1988, w/Alan Greisman
LOOSE CANNONS Tri-Star, 1990, w/Alan Greisman

NORMAN SPENCER

CRY FREEDOM Universal, 1987, CP w/John Briley

PIERRE SPENGLER

THE THREE MUSKETEERS 20th Century-Fox, 1974, EP w/Ilya Salkind
THE FOUR MUSKETEERS 20th Century-Fox, 1975, EP w/Ilya Salkind
CROSSED SWORDS Warner Bros., 1978
SUPERMAN Warner Bros., 1978
SUPERMAN II Warner Bros., 1981
SUPERMAN III Warner Bros., 1983
SANTA CLAUS - THE MOVIE Tri-Star, 1985, w/Ilya Salkind
THE RETURN OF THE MUSKETEERS Universal, 1990

ELAINE SPERBER

BLUE HEAVEN Vestron/Shapiro Entertainment, 1985

STEPHANE SPERRY

BABAR: THE MOVIE (AF) New Line Cinema, 1989, EP w/Yannick Bernard & Pierre Bertrand-Jaume

LARRY SPIEGEL

Business: Appledown Films, Inc., 9687 Olympic Blvd., Beverly Hills, CA, 90291, 213/552-1833

DEATH GAME Levitt-Pickman, 1977
PHOBIA Paramount, 1979
REMO WILLIAMS: THE ADVENTURE BEGINS... Orion, 1985
FIELDS OF HONOR Pathe, 1990

ANNE SPIELBERG

Agent: CAA - Beverly Hills, 213/288-4545
Contact: Writers Guild of America - Los Angeles, 213/550-1000

BIG 20th Century-Fox, 1988, CP w/Gary Ross

STEVEN SPIELBERG

Business: Amblin Entertainment, Universal Studios, 100 Universal Plaza, Bungalow 477, Universal City, CA, 91608, 818/777-4600
Contact: Directors Guild of America - Los Angeles, 213/289-2000

I WANNA HOLD YOUR HAND Universal, 1978, EP
USED CARS Columbia, 1980, EP w/John Milius
CONTINENTAL DIVIDE Universal, 1981, EP w/Bernie Brillstein
POLTERGEIST MGM, 1982, w/Frank Marshall
E.T. THE EXTRA-TERRESTRIAL ★ Universal, 1982, w/Kathleen Kennedy
TWILIGHT ZONE - THE MOVIE Warner Bros., 1983, w/John Landis
GREMLINS Warner Bros., 1984, EP w/Kathleen Kennedy & Frank Marshall
THE GOONIES Warner Bros., 1985, EP w/Kathleen Kennedy & Frank Marshall
BACK TO THE FUTURE Universal, 1985, EP w/Kathleen Kennedy & Frank Marshall
YOUNG SHERLOCK HOLMES Paramount, 1985, EP w/Kathleen Kennedy & Frank Marshall
THE COLOR PURPLE ★ Warner Bros., 1985, w/Quincy Jones, Kathleen Kennedy & Frank Marshall
AN AMERICAN TAIL (AF) Universal, 1986, EP w/Kathleen Kennedy, David Kirschner & Frank Marshall
THE MONEY PIT Universal, 1986, EP w/David Giler
INNERSPACE Warner Bros., 1987, EP w/Peter Guber, Kathleen Kennedy, Frank Marshall & Jon Peters
BATTERIES NOT INCLUDED Universal, 1987, EP w/Kathleen Kennedy & Frank Marshall
EMPIRE OF THE SUN Warner Bros., 1987, w/Kathleen Kennedy & Frank Marshall
WHO FRAMED ROGER RABBIT Buena Vista, 1988, EP w/Kathleen Kennedy
THE LAND BEFORE TIME (AF) Universal, 1988, EP w/Kathleen Kennedy, George Lucas & Frank Marshall
DAD Universal, 1989, EP w/Kathleen Kennedy & Frank Marshall
BACK TO THE FUTURE II Universal, 1989, EP w/Kathleen Kennedy & Frank Marshall
ALWAYS Paramount, 1989, w/Kathleen Kennedy & Frank Marshall
BACK TO THE FUTURE III Universal, 1990, EP w/Kathleen Kennedy & Frank Marshall
JOE VERSUS THE VOLCANO Warner Bros., 1990, EP w/Kathleen Kennedy & Frank Marshall

BARRY SPIKINGS

(credit w/Michael Deeley)

Business: Nelson Entertainment, Inc., 335 N. Maple Dr., Suite 350, Beverly Hills, CA, 90210, 213/285-6000

CONDUCT UNBECOMING Allied Artists, 1975
THE MAN WHO FELL TO EARTH Cinema 5, 1976
THE DEER HUNTER ★★ Universal, 1978, w/Michael Cimino & John Peverall
CONVOY United Artists, 1978, EP

SUSAN SPINKS

UFORIA Universal, 1985, CP

RICHARD M. SPITALNY

RHINESTONE 20th Century-Fox, 1984, CP w/Bill Blake

ROGER SPOTTISWOODE

Agent: InterTalent Agency - Los Angeles, 213/271-0600
Contact: Directors Guild of America - Los Angeles, 213/289-2000

BABY...SECRET OF THE LOST LEGEND Buena Vista, 1985, EP

STEVEN STABLER
(credit w/Brad Krevoy)
Business: Motion Picture Corporation of America, 3000 Olympic Blvd., Suite 2407, Santa Monica, CA, 90404, 213/315-4705

SWEET REVENGE Concorde, 1987
DANGEROUS LOVE Motion Picture Corp. of America, 1988
PURPLE PEOPLE EATER Concorde, 1988
MEMORIAL VALLEY MASSACRE Nelson Entertainment, 1989
MINISTRY OF VENGEANCE Motion Picture Corp. of America, 1989

PAUL STADER
Contact: Directors Guild of America - Los Angeles, 213/289-2000

IT'S ALIVE III: ISLAND OF THE ALIVE Warner Bros., 1987

NIGEL STAFFORD-CLARK
STORMY MONDAY Atlantic Entertainment, 1988

PATRICIA STALLONE
SUMMER HEAT Atlantic Entertainment, 1987, LP
PULSE Columbia, 1988

SYLVESTER STALLONE
Business: White Eagle Enterprises, 2308 Broadway, Santa Monica, CA, 90404, 213/828-8988
Agent: CAA - Beverly Hills, 213/288-4545

STAYING ALIVE Paramount, 1983, w/Robert Stigwood

CHRISTOPHER STAMP
TOMMY Columbia, 1975, EP w/Beryl Vertue

MICHAEL STANLEY-EVANS
GANDHI ★★ Columbia, 1982, EP

MARTIN STARGER
Business: Marstar Productions, 20th Century-Fox, 10201 W. Pico Blvd., Los Angeles, CA, 90035, 213/203-3970

NASHVILLE ★ Paramount, 1975, EP w/Jerry Weintraub
THE DOMINO PRINCIPLE Avco Embassy, 1977, EP
MOVIE, MOVIE Warner Bros., 1978, EP
AUTUMN SONATA New World, 1978
THE MUPPET MOVIE AFD, 1979, EP
RAISE THE TITANIC AFD, 1980, EP
FROM THE LIFE OF THE MARIONETTES Universal/ AFD, 1980, EP w/Lew Grade
BORDERLINE AFD, 1980, EP
SATURN 3 AFD, 1980, EP
HARD COUNTRY AFD, 1981, EP
THE LEGEND OF THE LONE RANGER Universal/ AFD, 1981, EP
THE GREAT MUPPET CAPER Universal/AFD, 1981, EP
BARBAROSA Universal/AFD, 1982, EP
SOPHIE'S CHOICE Universal, 1982, EP
CODE NAME: EMERALD MGM/UA, 1985
MASK Universal, 1985

JIM STARK
DOWN BY LAW Island Pictures, 1986, CP w/Tom Rothman
CANDY MOUNTAIN International Film Exchange, 1987
MYSTERY TRAIN Orion Classics, 1989

RAY STARK
Business: Rastar Productions, Inc., Columbia Plaza West, #18, Burbank, CA, 91505, 818/954-2400

THE WORLD OF SUZIE WONG Paramount, 1960
FUNNY GIRL ★ Columbia, 1968
THE OWL & THE PUSSYCAT Columbia, 1970
FAT CITY Columbia, 1972
THE WAY WE WERE Columbia, 1973
FUNNY LADY Columbia, 1975
THE SUNSHINE BOYS United Artists, 1975
MURDER BY DEATH Columbia, 1976
ROBIN AND MARIAN Columbia, 1976, EP
THE GOODBYE GIRL ★ Warner Bros., 1977
CASEY'S SHADOW Columbia, 1978
THE CHEAP DETECTIVE Columbia, 1978
CALIFORNIA SUITE Columbia, 1978
CHAPTER TWO Columbia, 1979
THE ELECTRIC HORSEMAN Columbia, 1979
SEEMS LIKE OLD TIMES Columbia, 1980
ANNIE Columbia, 1982
THE SLUGGER'S WIFE Columbia, 1985
BRIGHTON BEACH MEMOIRS Universal, 1986
NOTHING IN COMMON Tri-Star, 1986, EP
PEGGY SUE GOT MARRIED Tri-Star, 1986, EP
BILOXI BLUES Universal, 1988
STEEL MAGNOLIAS Tri-Star, 1989

WILBUR STARK
Business: 3712 Barham Blvd., C-203, Los Angeles, CA, 90068, 213/851-0572

THE THING Universal, 1982, EP

MARY STEENBURGEN
Agent: ICM - Los Angeles, 213/550-4000

END OF THE LINE Orion Classics, 1987, EP

KEN STEIN
THE DRIFTER Concorde, 1988

HERBERT R. STEINMANN
THE PAWNBROKER Allied Artists, 1965, w/Ely Landau

ELLEN STELOFF
(credit w/Lawrence Kasanoff)
Business: Steven Haft Productions, 20th Century- Fox, 10201 W. Pico Blvd., Los Angeles, CA, 90035, 213/203-2974

BLOOD DINER Lightning/Vestron, 1987, EP
YOU CAN'T HURRY LOVE Vestron, 1988, w/Jonathan D. Krane
DREAM A LITTLE DREAM Vestron, 1989, EP
FAR FROM HOME Vestron, 1989, EP
CLASS OF 1999 Taurus, 1990, EP

SKIP STELOFF
Business: Heritage Entertainment, 11500 W. Olympic Blvd., Suite 300, Los Angeles, CA, 90064, 213/477-8100

MR. NORTH Samuel Goldwyn Company, 1988, w/Steven Haft

RICHARD STENTA
Contact: Directors Guild of America - Los Angeles, 213/289-2000

LET IT RIDE Paramount, 1989, EP
FLASHBACK Paramount, 1990, EP

ROBERT STERLING
WINTER KILLS Avco Embassy, 1979, EP w/Leonard J. Goldberg

DAVID G. STERN
RACE TO GLORY New Century/Vista, 1989, EP
ALL'S FAIR Moviestore Entertainment, 1989, EP

JOSEPH STERN
NO MAN'S LAND Orion, 1987, w/Dick Wolf
DAD Universal, 1989, w/Gary David Goldberg

TOM STERNBERG
THE BLACK STALLION United Artists, 1979, w/Fred Roos
APOCALYPSE NOW ★ United Artists, 1979, CP w/Gray Frederickson & Fred Roos
THE BLACK STALLION RETURNS MGM/UA, 1983, w/Doug Claybourne & Fred Roos
DIM SUM: A LITTLE BIT OF HEART Orion Classics, 1985, w/Wayne Wang & Danny Yung
EAT A BOWL OF TEA Columbia, 1989

CHARLES STETTLER
DISORDERLIES Warner Bros., 1987, EP w/Joseph E. Zynczak

ROY STEVENS
Agent: Sandra Marsh Management - Sherman Oaks, 818/905-6961

THE BED SITTING ROOM United Artists, 1969, AP
RYAN'S DAUGHTER MGM, 1970, AP
LION OF THE DESERT UFD, 1981, AP
PLENTY 20th Century-Fox, 1985, AP
A CRY IN THE DARK Warner Bros., 1988, LP

RICK STEVENSON
Agent: William Morris Agency - Beverly Hills, 213/274-7451

PRIVILEGED New Yorker, 1983
RESTLESS NATIVES Orion Classics, 1986
PROMISED LAND Vestron, 1988
SOME GIRLS MGM/UA, 1988

JAMES L. STEWART
Business: Aurora Productions, Inc., 8642 Melrose Ave., Suite 200, Los Angeles, CA, 90069, 213/854-5742

WHY WOULD I LIE? MGM/UA, 1980, EP w/Rich Irvine
HEART LIKE A WHEEL 20th Century-Fox, 1983, EP w/Rich Irvine
MAXIE Orion, 1985, EP w/Rich Irvine
THE ALLNIGHTER Universal, 1987, EP
EDDIE & THE CRUISERS II: EDDIE LIVES Scotti Bros., 1989, EP w/Denis Héroux, Victor Loewy & William Stewart

ARNOLD STIEFEL
Business: Arnold Stiefel Company, 9200 Sunset Blvd., Suite 415, Los Angeles, CA, 90069, 213/274-7510

ABOUT LAST NIGHT... Tri-Star, 1986, EP

ROBERT STIGWOOD
Business: RSO Films, 1041 N. Formosa Ave., Los Angeles, CA, 90046, 213/850-2601; The Robert Stigwood Organization, Ltd., 118-120 Wardour St., London, England, 01/437-2512

JESUS CHRIST SUPERSTAR Universal, 1973, w/Norman Jewison
TOMMY Columbia, 1975, w/Ken Russell
SATURDAY NIGHT FEVER Paramount, 1977, EP
SGT. PEPPER'S LONELY HEARTS CLUB BAND Universal, 1978
GREASE Paramount, 1978, w/Allan Carr
MOMENT BY MOMENT Universal, 1978
TIMES SQUARE AFD, 1980, w/Jacob Brackman
THE FAN Paramount, 1981
GALLIPOLI Paramount, 1981, w/Patricia Lovell
GREASE 2 Paramount, 1982, w/Allan Carr
STAYING ALIVE Paramount, 1983, w/Sylvester Stallone

NICOLAS STILLADIS
FRIENDS, LOVERS, AND LUNATICS Fries Entertainment, 1989

MARC STIRDIVANT
Agent: Daniel Ostroff, Daniel Ostroff Agency - Los Angeles, 213/278-2020
Contact: Writers Guild of America - Los Angeles, 213/550-1000

NIGHT CROSSING Buena Vista, 1982, AP
WITHOUT A CLUE Orion, 1988

RICHARD R. ST. JOHNS
Business: Cinevent Corporation, 5200 Longridge Ave., Sherman Oaks, CA, 91401, 818/788-1133

MATILDA American International, 1978, EP
THE WANDERERS Orion/Warner Bros., 1979, EP
NIGHTWING Columbia, 1979, EP
A CHANGE OF SEASONS 20th Century-Fox, 1980, EP
THE FINAL COUNTDOWN United Artists, 1980, EP
THE MOUNTAIN MEN Columbia, 1980, EP
AMERICAN POP (AF) Paramount, 1981, EP
DEAD & BURIED Avco Embassy, 1981, EP
VENOM Paramount, 1982, EP w/Louis A. Stroller
FIRE & ICE (AF) 20th Century-Fox, 1983, EP w/John Hyde

OLIVER STONE
Business: Ixtlan, Inc., 321 Hampton, Suite 105, Venice, CA, 90291, 213/399-2550
Agent: CAA - Beverly Hills, 213/288-4545

SALVADOR Hemdale, 1986, w/Gerald Green
BORN ON THE FOURTH OF JULY ★ Universal, 1989, w/A. Kitman Ho
BLUE STEEL MGM/UA, 1990, w/Edward R. Pressman
REVERSAL OF FORTUNE Warner Bros., 1990, w/Edward R. Pressman

JEFFREY STOTT
(credit w/Steve Nicolaides)
Business: Castle Rock Entertainment, 335 N. Maple Dr., Suite 135, Beverly Hills, CA, 90210, 213/285-2300

THE PRINCESS BRIDE 20th Century-Fox, 1987, AP
WHEN HARRY MET SALLY... Castle Rock/Columbia, 1989, CP

RICHARD STRAFEHL
HOME IS WHERE THE HART IS Atlantic Entertainment, 1987, EP w/Ralph Scobie

GREG STRANGIS
(credit w/Sam Strangis)
Business: Ten Four Productions, 11300 W. Olympic Blvd., #870, Los Angeles, CA, 90064, 213/473-4747

TALK RADIO Universal, 1988, EP

SAM STRANGIS
(credit w/Greg Strangis)
Business: Ten Four Productions, 11300 W. Olympic Blvd., #870, Los Angeles, CA, 90064, 213/473-4747
Contact: Directors Guild of America - Los Angeles, 213/289-2000

TALK RADIO Universal, 1988, EP

PETER STRAUSS
BUSTER Tri-Star, 1988, EP w/Frank Giustra
BEST OF THE BEST Taurus, 1989, w/Phillip Rhee

BARBRA STREISAND
Business: Barwood Films, 75 Rockefeller Plaza, Suite 1709, New York, NY, 10019, 212/484-7300
Agent: CAA - Beverly Hills, 213/288-4545

A STAR IS BORN Warner Bros., 1976, EP
THE MAIN EVENT Warner Bros., 1979, w/Jon Peters
YENTL MGM/UA, 1983
NUTS Warner Bros., 1987

DAVID STREIT
Contact: Directors Guild of America - Los Angeles, 213/289-2000

DEEP IN THE HEART *HANDGUN* Warner Bros., 1984, CP
RIVER'S EDGE Island Pictures, 1987, CP
PASS THE AMMO New Century/Vista, 1988, LP
INTERNAL AFFAIRS Paramount, 1990, EP w/Pierre David & René Malo

JOSEPH STRICK
Agent: David Dworski & Associates - Los Angeles, 213/273-6173
Contact: Directors Guild of America - Los Angeles, 213/289-2000

THE BALCONY Continental, 1963, w/Ben Maddow
NEVER CRY WOLF Buena Vista, 1983, w/Lewis Allen & Jack Couffer

WHITLEY STRIEBER
Agent: CAA - Beverly HIlls, 213/288-4545
Contact: Writers Guild of America - New York, 212/245-6180

COMMUNION New Line Cinema, 1989, w/Dan Allingham & Philippe Mora

LOUIS A. STROLLER
Business: Martin Bregman Productions, 100 Universal City Plaza, Universal City, CA, 91608, 818/777-4950
Contact: Directors Guild of America - Los Angeles, 213/289-2000

CARRIE United Artists, 1976, AP
THE SEDUCTION OF JOE TYNAN Universal, 1979, EP
SIMON Orion/Warner Bros., 1980, EP
THE FOUR SEASONS Universal, 1981, EP
VENOM Paramount, 1982, EP w/Richard R. St. Johns
EDDIE MACON'S RUN Universal, 1983
SCARFACE Universal, 1983, EP
SWEET LIBERTY Universal, 1986, EP
REAL MEN MGM/UA, 1987, EP
A NEW LIFE Paramount, 1988, EP
SEA OF LOVE Universal, 1989, w/Martin Bregman

JOHN STRONG
STEEL JUSTICE Atlantic Entertainment, 1987

ALEXANDER STUART
INSIGNIFICANCE Island Alive, 1985, EP

WALKER STUART
Business: Lewis Allen Productions, 1500 Broadway, New York, NY, 10036, 212/221-2400
Contact: Directors Guild of America - Los Angeles, 213/289-2000

NEVER CRY WOLF Buena Vista, 1983, AP
1918 Cinecom, 1985, CP
END OF THE LINE Orion Classics, 1987, CP

WILLIAM STUART
Business: Aurora Productions, Inc., 8642 Melrose Ave., Suite 200, Los Angeles, CA, 90069, 213/854-5742

EDDIE & THE CRUISERS II: EDDIE LIVES Scotti Bros., 1989, EP w/Denis Héroux, Victor Loewy & James L. Stewart
THE FOURTH WAR Warner Bros., 1990, EP w/Sam Perlmutter

GORDON STULBERG
A CHORUS LINE Columbia, 1985, EP

PEGGY ANN STULBERG
GET ROLLIN' Aquarius, 1981, CP

LAWRENCE STURHAHN
Contact: Directors Guild of America - Los Angeles, 213/289-2000

THX 1138 Warner Bros., 1970

MILTON SUBOTSKY
Business: Amicus Productions, Ltd., 20 Stradella Rd., London SE24 9HA, England, 01/274-3205

IT'S TRAD, DAD RING-A-DING RHYTHM Columbia, 1962, EP

SCREAM AND SCREAM AGAIN American International, 1969, w/Max Rosenberg
STEPHEN KING'S CAT'S EYE *CAT'S EYE* MGM/UA, 1985, CP
MAXIMUM OVERDRIVE DEG, 1986, CP

HIDEAKI SUDA
MYSTERY TRAIN Orion Classics, 1989, EP w/Kunjiro Hirata

LARRY SUGAR
Business: Sugar Entertainment Inc., 15821 Ventura Blvd., Suite 290, Encino, CA, 91436, 818/789-6555

STEEL DAWN Vestron, 1987, EP w/William J. Quigley

BURT SUGARMAN
Business: 150 El Camino Dr., #303, Beverly Hills, CA, 90212, 213/273-0900

EXTREMITIES Atlantic Entertainment, 1986
CRIMES OF THE HEART DEG, 1986, EP
CHILDREN OF A LESSER GOD ★ Paramount, 1986, w/Patrick Palmer

MORRIS F. SULLIVAN
Business: Sullivan/Bluth Studios, 3800 W. Alameda Ave., Suite 1120, Burbank, CA, 91505, 818/840-9446

ALL DOGS GO TO HEAVEN (AF) Universal, 1989, EP w/George A. Walker

CATHLEEN SUMMERS
Business: Summers-Quaid Productions, c/o Orion Pictures, 1888 Century Park East, Los Angeles, CA, 90057, 213/282-2679

CLASS Orion, 1983, EP
STAKEOUT Buena Vista, 1987, w/Jim Kouf
D.O.A. Buena Vista, 1988, CP w/Andrew J. Kuehn
VITAL SIGNS 20th Century-Fox, 1990, w/Laurie Perlman

GABE SUMNER
Business: Odyssey Film Partners, Ltd., 6500 Wilshire Blvd., Suite 400, Los Angeles, CA, 90048, 213/655-9335

THE HEAVENLY KID Orion, 1985, EP w/Stephen G. Cheikes
MEMORIES OF ME MGM/UA, 1988, EP w/J. David Marks

SHIRLEY SUN
A GREAT WALL Orion Classics, 1986

RONALD A. SUPPA
PARADISE ALLEY Universal, 1978, w/John F. Roach

DONALD SUTHERLAND
Agent: CAA - Beverly Hills, 213/288-4545

STEELYARD BLUES Warner Bros., 1973, EP

TED SWANSON
Contact: Directors Guild of America - Los Angeles, 213/289-2000

NOBODY'S PERFEKT Columbia, 1981, EP

EZRA SWERDLOW
Contact: Directors Guild of America - New York, 212/581-0370

SPACEBALLS MGM/UA, 1987, CP
RADIO DAYS Orion, 1987, AP
THE JANUARY MAN MGM/UA, 1989, w/Norman Jewison
EVERYBODY WINS Orion, 1990, CP

ANTHEA SYLBERT
Business: Hawn/Sylbert Productions, Hollywood Pictures, 500 S. Buena Vista St., Animation Bldg. 1-D-6, Burbank, CA, 91521, 818/560-6101

PROTOCOL Warner Bros., 1984
WILDCATS Warner Bros., 1986
OVERBOARD MGM/UA, 1987, w/Alexandra Rose

DUSTY SYMONDS
Agent: Sandra Marsh Management - Sherman Oaks, 818/905-6961

FINDERS KEEPERS Warner Bros., 1984, AP
WITCHES Warner Bros., 1989, LP

T

SYLVIO TABET
FADE TO BLACK American Cinema, 1980, EP w/Irwin Yablans
THE COTTON CLUB Orion, 1984, CP w/ Fred Roos
DEAD RINGERS 20th Century-Fox, 1988, EP w/Carol Baum

VINCENT TAI
DIM SUM: A LITTLE BIT OF HEART Orion Classics, 1985, EP

HAL TAINES
LOVELINES Tri-Star, 1984, w/Michael Lloyd

RACHEL TALALAY
Business: New Line Cinema,116 N. Robertson Blvd., Suite 808, Los Angeles, CA, 90048, 213/854-5811

A NIGHTMARE ON ELM STREET 3: DREAM WARRIORS New Line Cinema, 1987, LP
HAIRSPRAY New Line Cinema, 1988
A NIGHTMARE ON ELM STREET 4: THE DREAM MASTER New Line Cinema, 1988, w/Robert Shaye
CRY-BABY Universal, 1990

FLAVIO R. TAMBELLINI
WHERE THE RIVER RUNS BLACK MGM, 1986, LP w/Bruno Barreto

NED TANEN
Business: Paramount Pictures, 5555 Melrose Ave., Los Angeles, CA, 90038, 213/468-5000

SIXTEEN CANDLES Universal, 1984, EP
THE BREAKFAST CLUB Universal, 1985, w/John Hughes
ST. ELMO'S FIRE Columbia, 1985, EP w/Bernard Schwartz

MICHAEL TANNEN
ONE-TRICK PONY Warner Bros., 1980
THE SQUEEZE Tri-Star, 1987, w/Rupert Hitzig

MARK M. TANZ
INSIDE MOVES AFD, 1980, w/Richard W. Goodwin

ROBERT G. TAPERT
Business: Renaissance Motion Pictures, Inc., 28 East 10th St., New York, NY, 10003, 213/477-0432; 6381 Hollywood Blvd., Los Angeles, CA, 90028, 213/463-9936

THE EVIL DEAD New Line Cinema, 1983
CRIMEWAVE Embassy, 1986
EVIL DEAD 2: DEAD BY DAWN DEG, 1987
EASY WHEELS Fries Entertainment, 1989, EP w/Bruce Campbell
DARKMAN Universal, 1990, w/Daryl Kass

JONATHAN T. TAPLIN
Business: Trans Pacific Films, 3000 W. Olympic Blvd., #1410, Santa Monica, CA, 90404, 213/315-4701

MEAN STREETS Warner Bros., 1973
GRAVY TRAIN Columbia, 1974
THE LAST WALTZ United Artists, 1978, EP
CARNY United Artists, 1980, EP
UNDER FIRE Orion, 1983
GRANDVIEW, U.S.A. Warner Bros., 1984, EP w/Andrew Gellis
BABY...SECRET OF THE LOST LEGEND Buena Vista, 1985
MY SCIENCE PROJECT Buena Vista, 1985

MARK TARLOV
Business: Polar Entertainment, 9100 Sunset Blvd., Suite 260, Los Angeles, CA, 90069, 213/278-4752; 357 W. 19th St., Room 3-W, New York, NY, 10011, 212/633-1766

CHRISTINE Columbia, 1983, EP w/Kirby McCauley
POWER 20th Century-Fox, 1986, w/Reene Schisgal
WHITE WATER SUMMER Columbia, 1987
SECOND SIGHT Warner Bros., 1989
AUNT JULIA & THE SCRIPTWRITER Cinecom, 1990, w/John Fiedler

JOHN TARNOFF
Business: Village Roadshow Pictures, 2121 Avenue of the Stars, 22nd Floor, Los Angeles, CA, 90067, 213/282-8964

OUT OF BOUNDS Columbia, 1986, EP w/Ray Hartwick

NADIA TASS
(credit w/David Parker)
Agent: CAA - Beverly Hills, 213/288-4545

MALCOLM Vestron, 1986
RIKKY & PETE MGM/UA, 1988

TOM TATUM
WINNERS TAKE ALL Apollo, 1987, w/Christopher W. Knight

LAWRENCE TAUB
POWAQQATSI (FD) Cannon, 1988, w/Mel Lawrence & Godfrey Reggio

BARBI TAYLOR
ROAD GAMES Avco Embassy, 1981, CP

DON TAYLOR
SIGNAL 7 One Pass Pictures, 1986, w/Ben Myron

GEOFFREY TAYLOR
MOSCOW ON THE HUDSON Columbia, 1984, AP
DOWN AND OUT IN BEVERLY HILLS Buena Vista, 1986, AP
MOON OVER PARADOR Universal, 1988, CP w/Pato Guzman

GREG TAYLOR
PRANCER Orion, 1989, CP w/Mike Petzold

JEFFREY TAYLOR
A HANDFUL OF DUST New Line Cinema, 1988, EP w/Kent Walwin

LAWRENCE TAYLOR-MORTORFF
(see Lawrence MORTORFF)

MICHAEL TAYLOR
Business: Mack-Taylor Productions, 110 East 59th St., Suite 1405, New York, NY, 10022, 212/319-3030

LAST EMBRACE United Artists, 1979, w/Dan Wigutow
THE PURSUIT OF D. B. COOPER Universal, 1981, w/Dan Wigutow
HIDER IN THE HOUSE Vestron, 1989, w/Edward Teets

EDWARD TEETS
Contact: Directors Guild of America - Los Angeles, 213/289-2000

SHARKEY'S MACHINE Orion/Warner Bros., 1981, AP
LOOKIN' TO GET OUT Paramount, 1982, AP
UNDER FIRE Orion, 1983, EP
THE FALCON AND THE SNOWMAN Orion, 1985, CP
JUST BETWEEN FRIENDS Orion, 1986, w/Allan Burns
THE BELIEVERS Orion, 1987, EP
THREE MEN AND A BABY Buena Vista, 1987, CP
HIDER IN THE HOUSE Vestron, 1989, w/Michael Taylor

MIGUEL TEJADA-FLORES
Agent: Harris & Goldberg - Los Angeles, 213/553-5200
Contact: Writers Guild of America - Los Angeles, 213/550-1000

DUDES New Century/Vista, 1988, w/Herb Jaffe

ANIL TEJANI
SALAAM BOMBAY! Cinecom, 1988, EP w/Gabriel Auer, Michael Nozik & Cherie Rodgers

NANCY TENENBAUM
sex, lies & videotape Miramax, 1989, EP w/Morgan Mason & Nick Wechsler

TIM TENNANT
Agent: Gorfaine/Schwartz/Roberts - Beverly Hills, 213/275-9384
Contact: Directors Guild of America - Los Angeles, 213/289-2000

HOT DOG...THE MOVIE MGM/UA, 1984, AP
GHOST TOWN Trans World Entertainment, 1988

WILLIAM TENNANT
Business: M.C.E.G. International, 2400 Broadway, Suite 100, Santa Monica, CA, 90404, 213/315-7800

THE PURSUIT OF D. B. COOPER Universal, 1981, EP w/Donald Kranze
KING OF THE MOUNTAIN Universal, 1981, EP
SUMMER HEAT Atlantic Entertainment, 1987

ALBERT J. TENSER
HARRY TRACY Quartet/Films, 1983, EP w/Marty Krofft & Sid Krofft

WILLIAM TEPPER
Contact: Writers Guild of America - Los Angeles, 213/550-1000

HEART BEAT Orion/Warner Bros., 1980, EP w/Edward R. Pressman

CHARLES C. THIERIOT
(credit w/Sandy Climan)

ALMOST YOU 20th Century-Fox, 1984, EP w/Stephen J. Levin
3:15 THE MOMENT OF TRUTH Dakota Entertainment, 1986, EP w/Andrew Bullians & Jean Bullians
THE BIKINI SHOP *THE MALIBU BIKINI SHOP* International Film Marketing, 1987, EP w/Andrew Bullians & Jean Bullians

ANNA THOMAS
Agent: Jeff Berg, ICM - Los Angeles, 213/550-4000
Contact: Writers Guild of America - Los Angeles, 213/550-1000

THE HAUNTING OF M Nu-Image, 1981
EL NORTE Cinecom/Island Alive, 1984
A TIME OF DESTINY Columbia, 1988

DAVID C. THOMAS
Business: Zeta Entertainment, Ltd., 6565 Sunset Blvd., #321, Hollywood, CA, 90028, 213/461-7332
Contact: Directors Guild of America - Los Angeles, 213/289-2000

STAND ALONE New World, 1985, CP
WELCOME TO 18 American Distribution Group, 1986
OUT OF THE DARK Cinetel, 1989, CP

GARTH THOMAS
CHECKING OUT Warner Bros., 1989, CP

JEREMY THOMAS
Business: World Film Services Ltd., Pinewood Studios, Iver Heath, Bucks., SL0 0NH, England, 0753-651700

EUREKA UA Classics, 1984
MERRY CHRISTMAS, MR. LAWRENCE Universal, 1983
INSIGNIFICANCE Island Alive, 1985
THE HIT Island Alive, 1985
GOOD TO GO Island Pictures, 1986, EP w/Chris Blackwell
THE LAST EMPEROR ★★ Columbia, 1987
EVERYBODY WINS Orion, 1990
THE SHELTERING SKY Warner Bros., 1990

JIM THOMAS
Agent: InterTalent Agency, Inc. - Los Angeles, 213/271-0600
Contact: Writers Guild of America - Los Angeles, 213/550-1000

PREDATOR 20th Century-Fox, 1987, EP w/Laurence P. Pereira
THE RESCUE Buena Vista, 1988, CP w/John Thomas

JOHN THOMAS
Agent: InterTalent Agency, Inc. - Los Angeles, 213/271-0600
Contact: Writers Guild of America - Los Angeles, 213/550-1000

THE RESCUE Buena Vista, 1988, CP w/Jim Thomas

PETER THOMAS
FROGS American International, 1972, w/George Edwards

RAMSEY THOMAS
Agent: Stone-Manners - Los Angeles, 213/275-9599
Contact: Directors Guild of America - Los Angeles, 213/289-2000

A MAN CALLED DAGGER MGM, 1968, AP
THE AROUSERS *SWEET KILL* New World, 1970, AP
SOME CALL IT LOVING Cine Globe, 1973, AP
BLUE SUNSHINE Cinema Shares International, 1979, AP
HALLOWEEN 5: THE REVENGE OF MICHAEL MYERS Galaxy, 1989

TONY THOMAS
(credit w/Paul Junger Witt)
Business: Witt-Thomas Productions, 846 N. Cahuenga Blvd., Los Angeles, CA, 90038, 213/464-1333

FIRSTBORN Paramount, 1984
DEAD POETS SOCIETY ★ Buena Vista, 1989, w/Steven Haft

JOHN THOMPSON
HERCULES Cannon, 1983, EP
THE ASSISI UNDERGROUND Cannon, 1985, AP
DETECTIVE SCHOOL DROPOUTS *DUMB DICKS* Cannon, 1986, AP
OTELLO Cannon, 1986, EP
DANCERS Cannon, 1987, AP
THE BARBARIANS Cannon, 1987
HAUNTED SUMMER Cannon, 1988, AP

LARRY THOMPSON
Business: The Larry A. Thompson Organization, 345 N. Maple Dr., Suite 183, Beverly Hills, CA, 90210, 213/288-0700

QUIET COOL New Line Cinema, 1986, EP w/Pierre David & Arthur Sarkissian
MY DEMON LOVER New Line Cinema, 1987, EP w/Pierre David

NEVILLE C. THOMPSON

THE MISSIONARY Columbia, 1982, w/Michael Palin

TOMMY THOMPSON

Contact: Directors Guild of America - Los Angeles, 213/289-2000

IMAGES Columbia, 1972
A WEDDING 20th Century-Fox, 1978, EP
A PERFECT COUPLE 20th Century-Fox, 1979, EP
HEALTH 20th Century-Fox, 1980, EP

JOEL THURM

Business: NBC Entertainment, 3000 W. Alameda Ave., Burbank, CA, 91523, 818/840-4444

ELVIRA, MISTRESS OF THE DARK New World, 1988, SP

RICHARD TIENKEN

Business: Paramount Pictures, 5555 Melrose Ave., Los Angeles, CA, 90038, 213/468-4545

THE GOLDEN CHILD Paramount, 1986, EP w/Charles R. Meeker
BEVERLY HILLS COP II Paramount, 1987, w/Robert D. Wachs
EDDIE MURPHY RAW Paramount, 1987, EP w/Eddie Murphy

ERIC TILL

Contact: Directors Guild of America - Los Angeles, 213/289-2000

IF YOU COULD SEE WHAT I HEAR Jensen Farley Pictures, 1982

HUGH TIRRELL

THE ADVENTURES OF MARK TWAIN (AF) Atlantic Entertainment, 1986, EP

STEVE TISCH

Business: The Steve Tisch Company, 515 N. Robertson Blvd., Los Angeles, CA, 90048, 213/278-7680

OUTLAW BLUES Warner Bros., 1977
ALMOST SUMMER Universal, 1978, EP
COAST TO COAST Paramount, 1980, w/Jon Avnet
RISKY BUSINESS The Geffen Company/Warner Bros., 1983, w/Jon Avnet
DEAL OF THE CENTURY Warner Bros., 1983, EP w/Jon Avnet & Paul Brickman
SOUL MAN New World, 1976
HOT TO TROT Warner Bros., 1988
BIG BUSINESS Buena Vista, 1988, w/Michael Peyser
HEART OF DIXIE Orion, 1989
HEART CONDITION New Line Cinema, 1990
BAD INFLUENCE Triumph, 1990

JAMES TOBACK

Business Manager: David Kaufman, Kaufman & Nachbar, 100 Merrick Rd., Rockville Centre, NY, 516/536-5760
Agent: Jeff Berg, ICM - Los Angeles, 213/550-4000

LOVE AND MONEY Paramount, 1982
EXPOSED MGM/UA, 1983

MARC TOBEROFF

ZOMBIE HIGH Cinema Group, 1987, w/Aziz Ghazal

BILL TODMAN, JR.

(credit w/Joel Simon)

Business: Todman-Simon Productions, 10202 W. Washington Blvd., #204, Culver City, CA, 90232, 213/280-7673

MARRIED TO THE MOB Orion, 1988, EP
HARD TO KILL Warner Bros., 1990, w/Gary Adelson

JERRY TOKOFSKY

Business: Zupnik Enterprises, Inc., 9229 Sunset Blvd., Suite 818, Los Angeles, CA, 90069, 213/273-9125

WHERE'S POPPA United Artists, 1970
BORN TO WIN United Artists, 1971, EP
PATERNITY Paramount, 1981, EP
DREAMSCAPE 20th Century-Fox, 1984, CP
FEAR CITY Chevy Chase Distribution, 1985, CP
WILDFIRE Cinema Group, 1988

MICHAEL TOLAN

FOUR FRIENDS Filmways, 1981, EP w/Julia Miles

FRANK D. TOLIN

SURF II International Films, 1984, EP w/Lou George

DAVID TOMBLIN

THE ADVENTURES OF BARON MUNCHAUSEN Columbia, 1989, LP

KEN TOPOLSKY

THE WIZARD Universal, 1989, w/David Chisholm

BURT TOPPER

Contact: Directors Guild of America - Los Angeles, 213/289-2000

C.H.O.M.P.S. Orion, 1979, CP

RANDALL TORNO

THE WILD PAIR Trans World Entertainment, 1987, w/Paul Mason

ROBERT TORRANCE

MUTANT ON THE BOUNTY Skouras Pictures, 1989, w/Martin Lupez

HARRY ALAN TOWERS

Business: 21st Century Film Corporation, 8200 Wilshire Blvd., Beverly Hills, CA, 90211, 213/658-3000

LIGHTNING — THE WHITE STALLION Cannon, 1986
WARRIOR QUEEN *POMPEII* Seymour Borde & Associates, 1987
DRAGONARD Cannon, 1987
OUTLAW OF GOR Cannon, 1988, w/Avi Lerner
AMERICAN NINJA 3: BLOOD HUNT Cannon, 1989
RIVER OF DEATH Cannon, 1989, w/Avi Lerner
TEN LITTLE INDIANS Cannon, 1989
EDGE OF SANITY Millimeter Films, 1989, w/Edward Simons
THE PHANTOM OF THE OPERA 21st Century Film Corporation, 1989

ROBERT TOWNE

Agent: ICM - Los Angeles, 213/550-4000
Contact: Directors Guild of America - Los Angeles, 213/289-2000

PERSONAL BEST Warner Bros., 1982
THE BEDROOM WINDOW DEG, 1987, EP

ROGER TOWNE

Business: Rolling Hills Productions, 204 South Beverly Dr., #166, Beverly Hills, CA, 90212, 213/275-0872
Agent: ICM - Los Angeles, 213/550-4000

THE NATURAL Tri-Star, 1984, EP w/Philip M. Breen

ROBERT TOWNSEND

Agent: Leading Artists, Inc. - Beverly Hills, 213/858-1999
Contact: Directors Guild of America - Los Angeles, 213/289-2000

HOLLYWOOD SHUFFLE Samuel Goldwyn Company, 1987

MARC TRABULUS

Business: GMS, 7025 Santa Monica Blvd., Hollywood, CA, 90038, 213/856-4848

SUMMER SCHOOL Paramount, 1987, EP

MARK TRAVIS

FIGHTING BACK Paramount, 1982, EP w/David Permut

MICHAEL TRIKILIS

SIX PACK 20th Century-Fox, 1982

KENITH TRODD

BRIMSTONE AND TREACLE United Artists Classics, 1982
DREAMCHILD Universal, 1985, w/Rick McCallum

BOET TROSKIE

THE GODS MUST BE CRAZY II WEG/Columbia, 1990

DOUGLAS TRUMBULL

Business: Showscan Film Corporation, 3939 Landmark St., Culver City, CA, 90230, 213/558-0150
Business Manager: Larry Goldberg, Nagler & Schneider, 9460 Wilshire Blvd., Suite 410, Beverly Hills, CA, 90212, 213/274-8201

BRAINSTORM MGM/UA, 1983

JOEL TUBER

Contact: Directors Guild of America - New York, 212/581-0370

SILKWOOD 20th Century-Fox, 1983, AP
MAKING MR. RIGHT Orion, 1987, w/Michael Wise
TOKYO POP Spectrafilm, 1988, w/Kaz Kuzui

HELEN SARLUI-TUCKER

(see Helen SARLUI-Tucker)

LARRY TUCKER

Contact: Writers Guild of America - Los Angeles, 213/550-1000

I LOVE YOU, ALICE B. TOKLAS Warner Bros., 1968, EP w/Paul Mazursky
BOB & CAROL & TED & ALICE Columbia, 1969
ALEX IN WONDERLAND MGM, 1970

MELVILLE TUCKER

THE LOST MAN Universal, 1969, w/Edward Muhl
A WARM DECEMBER National General, 1973
UPTOWN SATURDAY NIGHT Warner Bros., 1974
LET'S DO IT AGAIN Warner Bros., 1975
A PIECE OF THE ACTION Warner Bros., 1977
STIR CRAZY Columbia, 1980, EP
HANKY PANKY Columbia, 1982, EP
FAST FORWARD Columbia, 1985, EP

MARTIN TUDOR

HIDING OUT DEG, 1987, EP

CHRIS TUFTY

BLOODY BIRTHDAY Judica Productions, 1986, EP

JENNIE LEW TUGEND

SCROOGED Paramount, 1988, AP
LETHAL WEAPON 2 Warner Bros., 1989, CP w/Steve Perry

HARRIS E. TULCHIN

TO SLEEP WITH ANGER SVS Films, 1990, EP w/Danny Glover & Edward R. Pressman

JOHN TURMAN

Business: The Turman-Foster Company, 3400 Riverside Dr., 11th Floor, Burbank, CA, 91505, 818/972-7774

FULL MOON IN BLUE WATER Trans World Entertainment, 1988, w/David Foster & Lawrence Turman

LAWRENCE TURMAN

Business: The Turman-Foster Company, 3400 Riverside Dr., 11th Floor, Burbank, CA, 91505, 818/972-7774
Contact: Directors Guild of America - Los Angeles, 213/289-2000

THE YOUNG DOCTORS United Artists, 1961, w/Stuart Millar*
I COULD GO ON SINGING United Artists, 1963, w/Stuart Millar*
THE BEST MAN United Artists, 1964, w/Stuart Millar*
THE GRADUATE ★ Embassy, 1967*
THE FLIM-FLAM MAN 20th Century-Fox, 1967*
PRETTY POISON 20th Century-Fox, 1968, EP*
THE NICKEL RIDE 20th Century-Fox, 1974, EP
THE DROWNING POOL Warner Bros., 1975
FIRST LOVE Paramount, 1977
HEROES Universal, 1977
THE LEGACY Columbia, 1978
TRIBUTE 20th Century-Fox, 1980, EP w/Richard S. Bright
CAVEMAN United Artists, 1981
THE THING Universal, 1982
SECOND THOUGHTS Universal, 1983

MASS APPEAL Universal, 1984
THE MEAN SEASON Orion, 1985
SHORT CIRCUIT Tri-Star, 1986
RUNNING SCARED MGM/UA, 1986
FULL MOON IN BLUE WATER Trans World Entertainment, 1988, w/John Turman
SHORT CIRCUIT II Tri-Star, 1988, w/Gary Foster
GLEAMING THE CUBE 20th Century-Fox, 1989

JON TURTLE
A NIGHTMARE ON ELM STREET 5: THE DREAM CHILD New Line Cinema, 1989, EP w/Sara Risher

NORMAN TWAIN
LEAN ON ME Warner Bros., 1989

THOM TYSON
Business: Knight-Tyson Productions, 127 Broadway, Suite 220, Santa Monica, CA, 90401, 213/395-7100
Contact: Directors Guild of America - Los Angeles, 213/289-2000

STRIPPER 20th Century-Fox, 1986, CP w/Michael Nolin
THE WIZARD OF LONELINESS Skouras Pictures, 1988, w/Philip Porcella

U

TOM UDELL
JOURNEY TO THE CENTER OF THE EARTH Cannon, 1989, EP w/Adam Fields & Avi Lerner

HARRY UFLAND
Business: Ufland Productions, 10000 W. Washington Blvd., #3020, Culver City, CA, 90232, 213/280-6499

MOVING VIOLATIONS 20th Century-Fox, 1985, w/Joe Roth
STREETS OF GOLD 20th Century-Fox, 1986, w/Joe Roth
OFF BEAT Buena Vista, 1986, w/Joe Roth
WHERE THE RIVER RUNS BLACK MGM, 1986, w/Joe Roth
THE LAST TEMPTATION OF CHRIST Universal, 1988, EP

STEVE UJLAKI
Contact: Writers Guild of America - Los Angeles, 213/550-1000

COURAGE MOUNTAIN Triumph, 1990
THE HOT SPOT Orion, 1990, EP w/Bill Gavin & Derek Power

MICHAEL ULICK
Business: UMP & Associates, Raleigh Studios, 5300 Melrose Ave., Suite 411-E, Hollywood, CA, 90038, 213/960-4580
Contact: Directors Guild of America - New York, 212/581-0370

ROCKET GIBRALTAR Columbia, 1988, EP w/Robert Fisher & Geoffrey Mayo

ANTHONY B. UNGER
DON'T LOOK NOW Paramount, 1974, EP

MICHAEL USLAN
(credit w/Benjamin Melniker)

SWAMP THING Embassy, 1982
THE RETURN OF SWAMP THING Miramax, 1989
BATMAN Warner Bros., 1989, EP

KENNETH UTT
Contact: Directors Guild of America - New York, 212/581-0370

THE SUBJECT WAS ROSES MGM, 1968, AP
MIDNIGHT COWBOY United Artists, 1969, AP
THE BOYS IN THE BAND National General, 1970, AP
THE PEOPLE NEXT DOOR Avco Embassy, 1970, AP
THE FRENCH CONNECTION 20th Century-Fox, 1971, AP
GODSPELL Columbia, 1973, AP
THE SEVEN-UPS 20th Century-Fox, 1973, EP
ALL THAT JAZZ 20th Century-Fox, 1979, AP w/Wolfgang Glattes
EYEWITNESS 20th Century-Fox, 1981, AP
STILL OF THE NIGHT MGM/UA, 1982, AP w/Wolfgang Glattes
STAR 80 The Ladd Company/Warner Bros., 1983, w/Wolfgang Glattes
HEAVEN HELP US Tri-Star, 1985, AP
POWER 20th Century-Fox, 1986, AP w/Wolfgang Glattes
SOMETHING WILD Orion, 1987, w/Jonathan Demme
MARRIED TO THE MOB Orion, 1988, w/Edward Saxon
MIAMI BLUES Orion, 1990, CP w/Ron Bozman

ANDREW VAJNA
(credit w/Mario Kassar)
Business: Cinergi Productions, 414 N. Camden Dr.,10th Floor, Beverly Hills, CA, 90210, 213/859-0331

THE AMATEUR 20th Century-Fox, 1981, EP
FIRST BLOOD Orion, 1982
SUPERSTITION Almi Pictures, 1985
RAMBO: FIRST BLOOD PART II Tri-Star, 1985, EP
EXTREME PREJUDICE Tri-Star, 1987, EP
ANGEL HEART Tri-Star, 1987, EP
RAMBO III Tri-Star, 1988
RED HEAT Tri-Star, 1988, EP
DEEPSTAR SIX Tri-Star, 1989, EP
JOHNNY HANDSOME Tri-Star, 1989, EP
NARROW MARGIN Tri-Star, 1990, EP
TOTAL RECALL Tri-Star, 1990, EP
JACOB'S LADDER Tri-Star, 1990, EP
MOUNTAINS OF THE MOON Tri-Star, 1990, EP

DAVID VALDES
Business: Malpaso Productions, 4000 Warner Blvd., Burbank, CA, 91522, 818/954-2567
Agent: Bauer Benedek Agency - Los Angeles, 213/275-2421

PALE RIDER Warner Bros., 1985, AP
RATBOY Warner Bros., 1986, AP
LIKE FATHER, LIKE SON Tri-Star, 1987, w/Brian Grazer

GARDENS OF STONE Tri-Star, 1987, EP w/Jay Emmett, Fred Roos & Stan Weston
BIRD Warner Bros., 1988, EP
THE DEAD POOL Warner Bros., 1988
PINK CADILLAC Warner Bros., 1989
WHITE HUNTER, BLACK HEART Warner Bros., 1990, EP

RENEE VALENTE
Business: 13601 Ventura Blvd., #195, Sherman Oaks, CA, 91423, 818/501-5250

LOVING COUPLES 20th Century-Fox, 1980

DON Van ATTA
Agent: Broder/Kurland/Webb/Uffner - Los Angeles, 213/656-9262
Contact: Directors Guild of America - Los Angeles, 213/289-2000

PRAY FOR DEATH American Distribution Group, 1986
CATCH THE HEAT Trans World Entertainment, 1987
RAGE OF HONOR Trans World Entertainment, 1987

WILLIAM VANDERKLOOT
Business: Double Helix Films, Inc., 303 W. 76th St., Suite B, New York, NY, 10023, 212/769-0202

FUNLAND Double Helix, 1987, w/Michael A. Simpson

NORMAN THADDEUS VANE
Business: Screen Writers Productions, 1411 N. Harper Ave., Los Angeles, CA, 90046, 213/656-9260

LOLA American International, 1971, AP w/Ralph Serpe
CLUB LIFE *KING OF THE CITY* Troma, 1986
MIDNIGHT SVS Films, 1989, w/Gloria J. Morrison

RICHARD VANE
THE BOY WHO COULD FLY Lorimar, 1986, CP
HARRY & THE HENDERSONS Universal, 1987, w/William Dear
TAP Tri-Star, 1989, w/Gary Adelson
ALWAYS Universal, 1989, CP

LAWRENCE VANGER
BASIC TRAINING Moviestore, 1985, EP w/Paul Klein
CERTAIN FURY New World, 1985, EP

CHAKO Van LEUWEN
PIRANHA II *THE SPAWNING* Saturn International, 1983, w/Jeff Schechtman

NICK VANOFF
Business: 1438 N. Gower St., Box 21, Hollywood, CA, 90028, 213/467-1001
Agent: William Morris Agency - Beverly Hills, 213/274-7451

ELENI Warner Bros., 1985, w/Nicholas Gage & Mark Pick

TIM Van RELLIM
EAT THE RICH New Line Cinema, 1987
THE DECEIVERS Cinecom, 1988, CP

ED VANSTON
BENJI THE HUNTED Buena Vista, 1987, EP

STERLING Van WAGENEN
THE TRIP TO BOUNTIFUL Island Pictures, 1985, w/Horton Foote

MICHAEL VARHOL
Agent: ICM - Los Angeles, 213/550-4000
Contact: Directors Guild of America - Los Angeles, 213/289-2000

THE BIG PICTURE Columbia, 1989

CARLOS VASALLO
CRYSTAL HEART New World, 1987
FISTFIGHTER Taurus, 1989

RONALDO VASCONCELLOS
THE LAIR OF THE WHITE WORM Vestron, 1988, LP
THE RAINBOW Vestron, 1989, LP

BEN VAUGHN
BENJI THE HUNTED Buena Vista, 1987

FRANCIS VEBER
Agent: CAA - Beverly Hills, 213/288-4545
Contact: Directors Guild of America - Los Angeles, 213/289-2000

PARTNERS Paramount, 1982, EP
THREE FUGITIVES Buena Vista, 1989, EP

JOHN VEITCH
Business: Tri-Star Pictures, 1875 Century Park East, Los Angeles, CA, 90067, 213/282-0870

FAST FORWARD Columbia, 1985
SUSPECT Tri-Star, 1987, EP

ROBERT VELAISE
THE GO-BETWEEN Columbia, 1971, EP

BERYL VERTUE
TOMMY Columbia, 1975, EP w/Christopher Stamp
SPARKLE Warner Bros., 1976, EP w/Peter Brown

MARK VICTOR
(credit w/Michael Grais)
Agent: APA - Los Angeles, 213/273-0744
Contact: Writers Guild of America - Los Angeles, 213/550-1000

POLTERGEIST II: THE OTHER SIDE MGM, 1986
GREAT BALLS OF FIRE! Orion, 1989, EP

JOSE VICUNA
RUSTLER'S RHAPSODY Paramount, 1985, EP

DIMITRI VILLARD
(credit w/Robby Wald)
Business: New Star Entertainment, 260 S. Beverly Dr., #200, Beverly Hills, CA, 90212, 213/205-0666

TIME WALKER New World, 1982, w/Jason Williams*
ONCE BITTEN Samuel Goldwyn Company, 1985, w/Frank E. Hildebrand

FLIGHT OF THE NAVIGATOR Buena Vista, 1986
DEATH OF AN ANGEL 20th Century-Fox, 1986, EP w/Charles J. Weber
PURGATORY New Star Entertainment, 1989, EP
EASY WHEELS Fries Entertainment, 1989

ROBERT VINCE
MILLENNIUM 20th Century-Fox, 1989, CP

LUCIANO VINCENZONI
ORCA Paramount, 1976, w/Dino De Laurentiis

WILL VINTON
Business: Will Vinton Productions, Inc., 1400 NW 22nd St., Portland, OR, 97210, 503/225-1130

THE ADVENTURES OF MARK TWAIN (AF) Atlantic Entertainment, 1986
SHADOW PLAY New World, 1986, w/Dan Biggs & Susan Shadburne
WILL VINTON'S FESTIVAL OF CLAYMATION (AF) Expanded Entertainment, 1987

JOE VIOLA
Contact: Directors Guild of America - Los Angeles, 213/289-2000

ANGELS HARD AS THEY COME New World, 1972, w/Jonathan Demme

MARCUS VISCIDI
Contact: Directors Guild of America - New York, 212/581-0370

ROCKET GIBRALTAR Columbia, 1988, CP
SIGNS OF LIFE Avenue, 1989, w/Andrew Reichsman

RUTH VITALE
Business: UBU Productions, 5555 Melrose Ave., Los Angeles, CA, 90038, 213/468-8625

THE BEAT Vestron, 1988, EP w/Lawrence Kasanoff
CALL ME Vestron, 1988, EP w/Mitchell Cannold & Steven Reuther
AND GOD CREATED WOMAN Vestron, 1988, EP w/Mitchell Cannold & Steven Reuther

DAVID E. VOGEL
THREE O'CLOCK HIGH Universal, 1987

SUSAN VOGELFANG
BIG MAN ON CAMPUS Vestron, 1989, LP

RAY VOLPE
POUND PUPPIES & THE LEGEND OF BIG PAW (AF) Tri-Star, 1988, EP w/Edd Griles

ROBERT D. WACHS
Business: Paramount Pictures, 5555 Melrose Ave., Los Angeles, CA, 90038, 213/468-4545
Contact: Writers Guild of America - Los Angeles, 213/550-1000

THE GOLDEN CHILD Paramount, 1986, w/ Edward S. Feldman
BEVERLY HILLS COP II Paramount, 1987, EP w/Richard Tienken
EDDIE MURPHY RAW Paramount, 1987, w/Keenen Ivory Wayans
COMING TO AMERICA Paramount, 1988, w/George Folsey Jr.
HARLEM NIGHTS Paramount, 1989, w/Mark Lipsky

PATRICK WACHSBERGER
Business: Odyssey/Cinecom International, 6500 Wilshire Blvd., Suite 400, Los Angeles, CA, 90048, 213/655-9335

PLAYING FOR KEEPS Universal, 1986, EP w/Julia Palau & Michael Ryan
Q & A Tri-Star, 1990, EP

JONATHAN WACKS
Agent: Jeremy Zimmer, Bauer Benedek Agency - Los Angeles, 213/275-2421

REPO MAN Universal, 1984, w/Peter McCarthy

JANE WAGNER
Agent: ICM - Los Angeles, 213/550-4000
Contact: Writers Guild of America - Los Angeles, 213/550-1000

THE INCREDIBLE SHRINKING WOMAN Universal, 1981, EP

RAYMOND WAGNER
PETULIA Warner Bros./7Arts, 1968
LOVING Columbia, 1970, EP
CODE OF SILENCE Orion, 1985
HERO AND THE TERROR Cannon, 1988
RENT-A-COP Kings Road, 1988
TURNER & HOOCH Buena Vista, 1989

RICHARD WAGNER
(credit w/Joanna Lancaster)

LITTLE TREASURE Tri-Star, 1985, EP
RUTHLESS PEOPLE Buena Vista, 1986, EP w/Walter Yetnikoff

STAN WAKEFIELD
Business: Double Helix Films, Inc., 275 Seventh Ave., #2003, New York, NY, 10001

FUNLAND Double Helix, 1987, EP w/Jerry Silva & Kirk Smith
FAST FOOD Fries Entertainment, 1989, w/Michael A. Simpson

ROBBY WALD
(credit w/Dimitri Villard)
Business: New Star Entertainment, 260 S. Beverly Dr., #200, Beverly Hills, CA, 90212, 213/205-0666

ONCE BITTEN Samuel Goldwyn Company, 1985, w/Frank E. Hildebrand
FLIGHT OF THE NAVIGATOR Buena Vista, 1986
DEATH OF AN ANGEL 20th Century-Fox, 1986, EP w/Charles J. Weber
PURGATORY New Star Entertainment, 1989, EP
EASY WHEELS Fries Entertainment, 1989

RUTH WALDBURGER
CANDY MOUNTAIN International Film Exchange, 1988

KEN WALES
Business: Ken Wales Productions, 856 Yale St., Santa Monica, CA, 90403, 213/828-0405
Contact: Directors Guild of America - Los Angeles, 213/289-2000

THE PARTY United Artists, 1967, AP
WATERHOLE #3 Paramount, 1968, AP
PETER GUNN Paramount, 1968, AP
DARLING LILI Paramount, 1970, AP
THE WILD ROVERS MGM, 1971, w/Blake Edwards
THE TAMARIND SEED Avco Embassy, 1974
ISLANDS IN THE STREAM Paramount, 1977, AP
REVENGE OF THE PINK PANTHER MGM/UA, 1978, AP
THE PRODIGAL World Wide Pictures, 1984
DOOR TO DOOR Castle Hill Productions, 1984

GEORGE WALKER
AMERICAN GOTHIC Vidmark Entertainment, 1988, EP w/Ray Homer & Michael Manley

GEORGE A. WALKER
ALL DOGS GO TO HEAVEN (AF) Universal, 1989, EP w/Morris F. Sullivan

GARY WALKOW
Agent: The Chasin Agency - Beverly Hills, 213/278-7505
Attorney: Frank Gruber - Los Angeles, 213/274-5638

THE TROUBLE WITH DICK Fever Dream Production Company, 1989, w/Bob Augur

JOSEPHINE WALLACE
BAIL JUMPER Angelika Films, 1990, EP

JOSEPH WALSH
Contact: Writers Guild of America - Los Angeles, 213/550-1000

CALIFORNIA SPLIT Columbia, 1974, w/Robert Altman

MARTIN WALTERS
NIGHTSTICK Production Distribution Company, 1987
BLUE MONKEY Spectrafilm, 1987
PRETTYKILL Spectrafilm, 1987, w/John R. Bowey

KENT WALWIN
A HANDFUL OF DUST New Line Cinema, 1988, EP w/Jeffrey Taylor

IRENE WALZER
TO BE OR NOT TO BE 20th Century-Fox, 1983, AP
SOLARBABIES MGM/UA, 1986, w/Jack Frost Sanders

WAYNE WANG
Business: C.I.M. Productions, 665 Bush St., San Francisco, CA, 94108, 415/433-2342
Agent: William Morris Agency - Beverly Hills, 213/274-7451

CHAN IS MISSING New Yorker, 1982
DIM SUM: A LITTLE BIT OF HEART Orion Classics, 1985, w/Tom Sternberg & Danny Yung
LIFE IS CHEAP Far East Stars, 1990, EP w/John Koonchung Chan

GEOFFREY WANSELL
WHEN THE WHALES CAME 20th Century-Fox, 1989, EP

FRED WARD
Agent: STE Representation, Ltd. - Beverly Hills, 213/550-3982

MIAMI BLUES Orion, 1990, EP w/Edward Saxon

DAVID W. WARFIELD
KILL ME AGAIN MGM/UA, 1989, w/Steven Golin & Sigurjon Sighvatsson

WATSON WARRINER
TIGER WARSAW Sony Pictures, 1988, EP w/Navin Desai & Gay Mayer

DORI B. WASSERMAN
LITTLE MONSTERS United Artists, 1989, EP w/Mitchell Cannold

JOHN WATERS
Agent: InterTalent Agency - Los Angeles, CA, 90069, 213/271-0600

MONDO TRASHO Dreamland/Film Makers, 1970
PINK FLAMINGOS Saliva Films, 1974
FEMALE TROUBLE New Line Cinema, 1975
DESPERATE LIVING New Line Cinema, 1977
POLYESTER New Line Cinema, 1981
HAIRSPRAY New Line Cinema, 1988, CP w/Stanley F. Buchthal

CHARLES WATERSTREET
HOWLING III: THE MARSUPIALS Square Pictures, 1987, w/Philippe Mora

JOHN WATSON
(credit w/Pen Densham)
Business: Trilogy Entertainment Group, 1875 Century Park East, #1090, Los Angeles, CA, 90067, 213/277-5662
Agent: William Morris Agency - Beverly Hills, 213/274-7451

THE ZOO GANG New World, 1985
THE KISS Tri-Star, 1988

MIKE WATTS
Business: Virgin Vision Ltd., 328 Kensal Rd., London W10 5XJ, England, 01/968-8888

ARIA Miramax, 1988, CP w/Al Clark & Robert Devereux

ROBERT WATTS
Agent: Duncan Heath Associates, Paramount House, 162/170 Wardour St., London W1V 4AB, England

THE EMPIRE STRIKES BACK 20th Century-Fox, 1980, AP w/Jim Bloom
RAIDERS OF THE LOST ARK ★ Paramount, 1981, AP
RETURN OF THE JEDI 20th Century-Fox, 1983, CP w/Jim Bloom
INDIANA JONES AND THE TEMPLE OF DOOM Paramount, 1984
WHO FRAMED ROGER RABBIT Buena Vista, 1988, w/Frank Marshall
INDIANA JONES AND THE LAST CRUSADE Paramount, 1989

ROY WATTS
ANGEL New World, 1984, w/Donald P. Borchers

KEENEN IVORY WAYANS
Business: Ivory Way Productions, 10000 W. Washington Blvd., Culver City, CA, 90232, 213/280-6512
Agent: InterTalent Agency - Los Angeles, CA, 90069, 213/271-0600

EDDIE MURPHY RAW Paramount, 1987, w/Robert D. Wachs

MICHAEL WEARING
BELLMAN AND TRUE Island Pictures, 1987, w/Christopher Neame

CASSIUS VERNON WEATHERSBY
D.C. CAB Universal, 1983, CP

GORDON A. WEBB
Contact: Directors Guild of America - Los Angeles, 213/289-2000

BRUBAKER 20th Century-Fox, 1980, AP
FLETCH Universal, 1985, AP
WILDCATS Warner Bros., 1986, AP
THE GOLDEN CHILD Paramount, 1986, AP
THE COUCH TRIP Orion, 1988, CP
GHOSTBUSTERS II Columbia, 1989, AP w/Sheldon Kahn

MONICA WEBB
PARTY LINE SVS Films, 1988, CP

WILLIAM WEBB
PARTY LINE SVS Films, 1988, w/Kurt Anderson & Thomas S. Byrnes

BRUCE WEBER
Contact: Directors Guild of America - New York, 212/581-0370

LET'S GET LOST (FD) Zeitgeist, 1989

CHARLES J. WEBER
Business: M.C.E.G. International, 2400 Broadway, Suite 100, Santa Monica, CA, 90404, 213/315-7800

BODY ROCK New World, 1984, EP w/Jon Feltheimer & Phil Ramone
CHILDREN OF THE CORN New World, 1984, EP w/Earl Glick
DEATH OF AN ANGEL 20th Century-Fox, 1986, EP w/Dimitri Villard & Robby Wald

CHRISTOPHER WEBSTER
HELLRAISER New World, 1987, EP w/Mark Armstrong & David Saunders
HELLBOUND: HELLRAISER II New World, 1988, EP w/Clive Barker
HEATHERS New World, 1989, EP
MEET THE APPLEGATES New World, 1989, EP w/Steve White

PAUL WEBSTER
THE TALL GUY Miramax, 1990

NICK WECHSLER
Business: Addis-Wechsler & Associates, 8444 Wilshire Blvd.,5th Floor, Beverly Hills,CA, 90211, 213/653-8867

THE BEAT Vestron, 1988, w/Jon Kilik & Julia Phillips
sex, lies & videotape Miramax, 1989, EP w/Morgan Mason & Nancy Tenenbaum
DRUGSTORE COWBOY Avenue, 1989, w/Karen Murphy

RICHARD WECHSLER
FIVE EASY PIECES ★ Columbia, 1970, w/Bob Rafelson
PLAIN CLOTHES Paramount, 1988, w/Michael Manheim

DAVID WECHTER
Agent: William Morris Agency - Beverly Hills, 213/274-7451

MIDNIGHT MADNESS Buena Vista, 1980, CP w/MichaelNankin

JOAN WEIDMAN
CRACK HOUSE Cannon, 1989, CP

HERMAN WEIGEL
Business: Neue Constantin Film, GmbH & Co Verleih KG, Kaiserstraße 39, D-8000 München 40, West Germany, 38-60-90

LAST EXIT TO BROOKLYN Cinecom, 1990, CP

RICHARD C. WEINMAN
Contact: Directors Guild of America - Los Angeles, 213/289-2000

PUMPKINHEAD United Artists, 1988, w/Howard Smith

BOB WEINSTEIN
(credit w/Harvey Weinstein)
Business: Miramax Films, 18 East 48th St., New York, NY, 10017, 212/888-2662

PLAYING FOR KEEPS Universal, 1986, w/Alan Brewer
SCANDAL Miramax, 1989, EP w/Joe Boyd & Nik Powell
STRIKE IT RICH Milliimeter, 1990, EP

HARVEY WEINSTEIN
(credit w/Bob Weinstein)

Business: Miramax Films, 18 East 48th St., New York, NY, 10017, 212/888-2662
Contact: Directors Guild of America - New York, 212/581-0370

PLAYING FOR KEEPS Universal, 1986, w/Alan Brewer
SCANDAL Miramax, 1989, EP w/Joe Boyd & Nik Powell
STRIKE IT RICH Milliimeter, 1990, EP

HENRY T. WEINSTEIN

Business: Cannon Productions, 640 N. San Vicente Blvd., Los Angeles, CA, 90048, 213/658-2100
Contact: The Howard Brandy Company, Inc. - Los Angeles, CA, 90069, 213/657-8320; 75 Rockfeller Plaza,Suite 1706, New York, NY, 10019

CERVANTES *THE YOUNG REBEL* American International, 1969, EP
THE MADWOMAN OF CHAILLOT Warner Bros., 1969, EP
THE MAGIC CHRISTIAN Commonwealth United, 1970, EP
A DELICATE BALANCE American Film Theatre, 1973, AP
THE ICEMAN COMETH American Film Theatre, 1973, AP
THE HOMECOMING American Film Theatre, 1973, AP
BUTLEY American Film Theatre, 1974, AP
LUTHER American Film Theatre, 1974, AP
RHINOCEROS American Film Theatre, 1974, AP
LOST IN THE STARS American Film Theatre, 1974, AP
IN CELEBRATION American Film Theatre, 1975, AP
GALILEO American Film Theatre, 1975, AP
THE MAN IN THE GLASS BOOTH American Film Theatre, 1975, AP
RUNAWAY TRAIN Cannon, 1985, EP w/Robert A. Goldston & Robert Whitmore
52 PICK-UP Cannon, 1986, EP
TEXASVILLE Columbia, 1990, w/Peter Bogdanovich & Robert Whitmore

LISA WEINSTEIN

Business: Paramount Pictures, 5555 Melrose Ave., Los Angeles, CA, 90038, 213/468-5608

GHOST Paramount, 1990

PAULA WEINSTEIN

Business: Paula Weinstein Productions, 10000 W. Washington Blvd., #3022, Culver City, CA, 90232, 213/280-6187

AMERICAN FLYERS Warner Bros., 1985, w/Gareth Wigan
A DRY WHITE SEASON MGM/UA, 1989
THE FABULOUS BAKER BOYS 20th Century-Fox, 1989, w/Mark Rosenberg

FRED WEINTRAUB

Business: Fred Weintraub Productions, 1923 1/2 Westwood Blvd., #2, Los Angeles, CA, 90025, 213/470-8787

ENTER THE DRAGON Warner Bros., 1973, w/Paul Heller
BLACK BELT JONES Warner Bros., 1974, w/Paul Heller
INVASION OF THE BEE GIRLS Centaur, 1974
TRUCK TURNER American International, 1974, w/Paul Heller
GOLDEN NEEDLES American International, 1974, w/Paul Heller
IT'S SHOWTIME United Artists, 1976, w/Paul Heller
HOT POTATO Warner Bros., 1976, w/Paul Heller
OUTLAW BLUES Warner Bros., 1977, EP w/Paul Heller
THE PACK Warner Bros., 1977, w/Paul Heller
CHECKERED FLAG OR CRASH Universal, 1978, w/Paul Heller
THE PROMISE Universal, 1979, w/Paul Heller
TOM HORN Warner Bros., 1980, EP
FORCE: FIVE American Cinema, 1981
HIGH ROAD TO CHINA Warner Bros., 1983
GYMKATA MGM/UA, 1985
OUT OF CONTROL New World, 1985, w/Daniel Grodnik
THE WOMEN'S CLUB Lightning, 1987
THE PRINCESS ACADEMY Empire, 1987, EP
SHOW OF FORCE Paramount, 1990

JERRY WEINTRAUB

Business: Weintraub Entertainment Group, 11111 Santa Monica Blvd., 20th Floor, Los Angeles, CA, 90025, 213/477-8900

NASHVILLE ★ Paramount, 1975, EP w/Martin Starger
9/30/55 Universal, 1977
OH, GOD! Warner Bros., 1978
CRUISING United Artists, 1980
ALL NIGHT LONG Universal, 1981, w/Leonard Goldberg
DINER MGM/UA, 1982
THE KARATE KID Columbia, 1984
HAPPY NEW YEAR Columbia, 1987
THE KARATE KID PART II Columbia, 1986
THE KARATE KID PART III Columbia, 1989

SANDRA WEINTRAUB ROLAND
(see Sandra Weintraub ROLAND)

BOB WEIS

HEARTBREAKERS Orion, 1985, w/Bobby Roth
THE RAGGEDY RAWNEY Four Seasons Entertainment, 1989

DOUGLAS J. WEISER

Contact: Writers Guild of America - Los Angeles, 213/550-1000

MIDNIGHT CROSSING Vestron, 1988, CP

DAVID WEISMAN

KISS OF THE SPIDER WOMAN ★ Island Alive, 1985
SPIKE OF BENSONHURST FilmDallas, 1989, w/Nelson Lyon

MATTHEW WEISMAN
(credit w/Joseph Loeb III)

Agent: CAA - Beverly Hills, 213/288-4545
Contact: Writers Guild of America - Los Angeles, 213/550-1000

BURGLAR Warner Bros., 1987, CP

JEFF WEISS

ROCKET GIBRALTAR Columbia, 1988

ROBERT K. WEISS
Business: Universal Studios, Bldg. 157, Rm. 209, 100 Universal City Plaza, Universal City, CA, 91608, 818/777-1281
Contact: Directors Guild of America - Los Angeles, 213/289-2000

THE KENTUCKY FRIED MOVIE United Film Distribution, 1977
THE BLUES BROTHERS Universal, 1980
DOCTOR DETROIT Universal, 1983
AMAZON WOMEN ON THE MOON Universal, 1987
DRAGNET Universal, 1987, w/David Permut
THE NAKED GUN: FROM THE FILES OF POLICE SQUAD Paramount, 1988
CRAZY PEOPLE Paramount, 1990, EP

BURT WEISSBOURD
GHOST STORY Universal, 1981
RAGGEDY MAN Universal, 1981, w/William D. Wittliff

LAUREN WEISSMAN
SWEET HEARTS DANCE Tri-Star, 1988, EP w/Robert Greenwald & Gabrielle Mandelik
I LOVE YOU TO DEATH Tri-Star, 1990, CP w/Patrick C. Wells

BO WELCH
THE ACCIDENTAL TOURIST Warner Bros., 1988, EP

JOHN WELLS
NICE GIRLS DON'T EXPLODE New World, 1987, w/Douglas Curtis

PATRICK C. WELLS
Business: Patrick C. Wells Associates, Inc., 2415 Vado Drive, Los Angeles, CA, 90046, 213/650-8544

THE PERSONALS New World, 1982
SPACE RAGE Vestron, 1985, AP
YOUNGBLOOD MGM/UA, 1986, w/Peter Bart
I LOVE YOU TO DEATH Tri-Star, 1990, CP w/ Lauren Weissman
HONOR BOUND MGM/UA, 1990, AP
THE CELLAR Moviestore, 1990, w/Steven E. Burman & John Woodward

CHARLES WESSLER
COLD FEET Cinecom, 1984

DONALD WEST
Business: Paul Maslansky Productions, 4000 Warner Blvd., Burbank, CA, 91522, 818/954-3811

POLICE ACADEMY 3: BACK IN TRAINING Warner Bros., 1986, AP
POLICE ACADEMY 4: CITIZENS ON PATROL Warner Bros., 1987, AP
POLICE ACADEMY 5: ASSIGNMENT MIAMI BEACH Warner Bros., 1988, CP
POLICE ACADEMY 6: CITY UNDER SIEGE Warner Bros., 1989, CP
SKI PATROL Triumph Releasing, 1990, w/Phillip B. Goldfine

HOWARD WEST
(credit w/George Shapiro)
Business: Shapiro/West, 151 El Camino Dr., Beverly Hills, CA, 90210

THE LAST REMAKE OF BEAU GESTE Universal, 1977, EP
IN GOD WE TRUST Universal, 1980
SUMMER SCHOOL Paramount, 1987

JAY WESTON
Business: Jay Weston Productions, 141 El Camino Dr., Suite 104, Beverly Hills, CA, 90212, 213/278-2900

FOR LOVE OF IVY Cinerama, 1968, w/Edgar J. Scherick
LADY SINGS THE BLUES Paramount, 1972, w/James S. White
W.C. FIELDS & ME Universal, 1976
NIGHT OF THE JUGGLER Columbia, 1980
CHU CHU & THE PHILLY FLASH 20th Century-Fox, 1981
BUDDY BUDDY MGM/UA, 1981
UNDERGROUND ACES Filmways, 1981
SIDEOUT Tri-Star, 1990, EP

STAN WESTON
VISION QUEST Warner Bros., 1985, EP w/Adam Fields
GARDENS OF STONE Tri-Star, 1987, EP w/Jay Emmett, Fred Roos & David Valdes

HANS WETH
CHRISTIANE F. New World, 1982, w/Bernd Eichinger

JIM WHEAT
Agent: The Gersh Agency - Beverly Hills, 213/274-6611
Contact: Writers Guild of America - Los Angeles, 213/550-1000

AFTER MIDNIGHT MGM/UA, 1989, w/Richard Arlook, Peter Greene & Ken Wheat

KEN WHEAT
Agent: The Gersh Agency - Beverly Hills, 213/274-6611
Contact: Writers Guild of America - Los Angeles, 213/550-1000

AFTER MIDNIGHT MGM/UA, 1989, w/Richard Arlook, Peter Greene & Jim Wheat

MICHAEL WHITE
THE ROCKY HORROR PICTURE SHOW 20th Century-Fox, 1976
THE HOUND OF THE BASKERVILLES Atlantic Entertainment, 1979, EP w/Andrew Braunsberg
SHOCK TREATMENT 20th Century-Fox, 1981, EP w/Lou Adler
URGH! A MUSIC WAR (FD) Lorimar, 1982
STRANGERS KISS Orion Classics, 1984, EP
WHITE MISCHIEF Columbia, 1988, EP
THE DECEIVERS Cinecom, 1988, EP
NUNS ON THE RUN 20th Century-Fox, 1990

PAUL WHITE
Business: Wild Street Pictures, 6525 Sunset Blvd., 8th Floor, Hollywood, CA, 90028, 213/466-1230

THE UNNAMEABLE Vidmark Entertainment, 1988, EP

STEVE WHITE

Business: Steve White Productions, 1145 McCadden Pl., Los Angeles, CA, 90038, 213/962-1923

MEET THE APPLEGATES New World, 1989, EP w/Christopher Webster

VICTORIA WHITE

STEEL MAGNOLIAS Tri-Star, 1989, EP

ROB WHITEHOUSE

(credit w/Lloyd Phillips)

WARLORDS OF THE 21ST CENTURY *BATTLE TRUCK* New World, 1982
NATE & HAYES Paramount, 1983

ROBERT WHITMORE

Contact: The Howard Brandy Company, Inc. - Los Angeles, 213/657-8320; 75 Rockfeller Plaza, Suite 1706, New York, NY, 10019

RUNAWAY TRAIN Cannon, 1985, EP w/Robert A. Goldston & Henry T. Weinstein
TEXASVILLE Columbia, 1990, w/Peter Bogdanovich & Henry T. Weinstein

HOLLISTER WHITWORTH

CHAMPIONS FOREVER (FD) Ion, 1989, EP w/Tom Bellagio

DOUGLAS WICK

Business: Red Wagon Productions, Columbia Pictures, Producers 8, #239, Burbank, CA, 91505, 818/954-3067

WORKING GIRL ★ 20th Century-Fox, 1988

JAN WIERINGA

POWWOW HIGHWAY Warner Bros., 1989

SAM WIESENTHAL

THE KREMLIN LETTER 20th Century-Fox, 1970, w/Carter De Haven

GARETH WIGAN

Business: Columbia Pictures, Studio Plaza, 3400 Riverside Dr., Burbank, CA, 91505

AMERICAN FLYERS Warner Bros., 1985, w/Paula Weinstein

DENIS WIGMAN

THE COOK, THE THIEF, HIS WIFE & HER LOVER Miramax, 1990, CP w/Pascale Dauman & Daniel Toscan duPlantier

LIONEL WIGRAM

Business: Alive Films, 8271 Melrose Blvd., Los Angeles, CA, 90046, 213/852-1100

NEVER ON TUESDAY Palisades Entertainment, 1987, w/Brad Wyman
WARM SUMMER RAIN Trans World Entertainment, 1990, w/Cassian Elwes

DAN WIGUTOW

LAST EMBRACE United Artists, 1979, w/Michael Taylor
THE PURSUIT OF D. B. COOPER Universal, 1981, w/Michael Taylor
HEAVEN HELP US Tri-Star, 1985, w/Mark Carliner

BILLY WILDER

Agent: Gary Salt, Paul Kohner, Inc. - Los Angeles, 213/550-1060
Contact: Directors Guild of America - Los Angeles, 213/289-2000

ACE IN THE HOLE *THE BIG CARNIVAL* Paramount, 1951
STALAG 17 Paramount, 1953
SABRINA Paramount, 1954
THE SEVEN YEAR ITCH Twentieth Century-Fox, 1955, w/Charles K. Feldman
LOVE IN THE AFTERNOON Allied Artists, 1957
SOME LIKE IT HOT United Artists, 1959
THE APARTMENT ★★ United Artists, 1960
ONE, TWO, THREE United Artists, 1961
IRMA LA DOUCE United Artists, 1963
KISS ME, STUPID United Artists, 1964
THE FORTUNE COOKIE United Artists, 1966
THE PRIVATE LIFE OF SHERLOCK HOLMES United Artists, 1970
AVANTI! United Artists, 1972
FEDORA United Artists, 1979

THOMAS L. WILHITE

Business: Hyperion Entertainment, 837 Traction Ave., #402, Los Angeles, CA, 90013, 213/625-2921

NUTCRACKER Atlantic Entertainment, 1986, w/Willard Carroll, Donald Kushner & Peter Locke

BERNARD WILLIAMS

Contact: Peter Grossman, 9665 Wilshire Blvd., Suite 900, Beverly Hills, CA, 90212, 213/858-7888

A CLOCKWORK ORANGE ★ Warner Bros., 1971, AP
LADY CAROLINE LAMB United Artists, 1973, AP
BARRY LYNDON Warner Bros., 1975, AP
THE LAST REMAKE OF BEAU GESTE 20th Century- Fox, 1977, AP
THE BIG SLEEP United Artists, 1978, AP
FLASH GORDON Universal, 1980, EP
RAGTIME Paramount, 1981, EP w/Michael Hausman
AMITYVILLE II: THE POSSESSION Orion, 1982, EP
THE BOUNTY Orion, 1984
MIRACLES Orion, 1986
MANHUNTER DEG, 1986, EP
WISDOM 20th Century-Fox, 1986
WHO'S THAT GIRL Warner Bros., 1987, w/Rosilyn Heller
DIRTY ROTTEN SCOUNDRELS Orion, 1988
WAR PARTY Hemdale, 1989, w/John Daly & Derek Gibson

DWIGHT WILLIAMS

Contact: Directors Guild of America - New York, 212/581-0370

THE WHITE GIRL Tony Brown Productions, 1990, LP

ELMO WILLIAMS
Contact: Directors Guild of America - Los Angeles, 213/289-2000

THE LONGEST DAY 20th Century-Fox, 1962, AP
THE BLUE MAX 20th Century-Fox, 1966, EP
TORA! TORA! TORA! 20th Century-Fox, 1970
SIDEWINDER ONE Avco Embassy, 1977
CARAVANS Universal, 1978
SOGGY BOTTOM U.S.A. Gaylord, 1982
MAN, WOMAN & CHILD Paramount, 1983, w/Elliott Kastner
ERNEST GOES TO CAMP Buena Vista, 1987, EP w/Martin Erlichman

JAN WILLIAMS
THE LAST FLIGHT OF NOAH'S ARK Buena Vista, 1980, CP
CONDORMAN Buena Vista, 1981

JASON WILLIAMS
TIME WALKER New World, 1982, w/Dimitri Villard

LEON WILLIAMS
STAND ALONE New World, 1985

STACY WILLIAMS
Contact: Directors Guild of America - Los Angeles, 213/289-2000

ERNEST GOES TO CAMP Buena Vista, 1987
ERNEST SAVES CHRISTMAS Buena Vista, 1988, w/Doug Claybourne
ERNEST GOES TO JAIL Buena Vista, 1990

DANIEL WILSON
THE HANDMAID'S TALE Cinecom, 1989

JIM WILSON
Business: Tig Productions, Raleigh Studios, 650 N. Bronson, #211, Los Angeles, CA, 90004, 213/871-4401

DANCES WITH WOLVES Orion, 1990, w/Derek Kavanagh

JOHN G. WILSON
Business: 818/501-0771
Contact: Directors Guild of America - Los Angeles, 213/289-2000

JO JO DANCER, YOUR LIFE IS CALLING Columbia, 1986, AP
ABOVE THE LAW Warner Bros., 1988, CP
FRESH HORSES WEG/Columbia, 1988, AP
SHE'S OUT OF CONTROL WEG/Columbia, 1989, CP

LARRY WILSON
Agent: CAA - Beverly Hills, 213/288-4545
Contact: Writers Guild of America - Los Angeles, 213/550-1000

BEETLEJUICE Warner Bros., 1988, w/Michael Bender & Richard Hashimoto

MICHAEL G. WILSON
Business: Warfield Productions, 10000 W. Washington Blvd., Culver City, CA, 90232, 213/280-6565
Contact: Writers Guild of America - Los Angeles, 213/550-1000

MOONRAKER United Artists, 1979, EP
FOR YOUR EYES ONLY United Artists, 1981
OCTOPUSSY MGM/UA, 1983, EP
A VIEW TO A KILL MGM/UA, 1985, w/Albert R. Broccoli
THE LIVING DAYLIGHTS MGM/UA, 1987, w/ Albert R. Broccoli
LICENCE TO KILL MGM/UA, 1989, w/Albert R. Broccoli

SANDY WILSON
Agent: Writers & Artists Agency - Los Angeles, 213/820-2240

MY AMERICAN COUSIN Spectrafilm, 1986, CP

S. S. WILSON
Agent: Nancy Roberts, Gorfaine/Schwartz/Roberts - Beverly Hills, 213/275-9384
Contact: Writers Guild of America - Los Angeles, 213/550-1000

TREMORS Universal, 1990, w/Brent Maddock

DAVID WIMBURY
Business: HandMade Films, Ltd., 26 Cadogan Square, London SW1X 0JP, England, 01/584-8345; 7400 Beverly Blvd., #210, Los Angeles, CA, 90036, 213/936-8050

BULLSHOT Island Alive, 1985, AP
ABSOLUTE BEGINNERS Orion, 1986, AP
WATER Atlantic Entertainment, 1986, CP
WITHNAIL AND I Cineplex Odeon, 1987, CP
A HANDFUL OF DUST New Line Cinema, 1988, AP
HOW TO GET AHEAD IN ADVERTISING Warner Bros., 1989

SIMON WINCER
Agent: Jane Sindell, CAA - Beverly Hills, 213/288-4545
Contact: Directors Guild of America - Los Angeles, 213/289-2000

THE MAN FROM SNOWY RIVER 20th Century- Fox, 1983, EP w/Michael Edgley

INGRID WINDLISCH
JUDGMENT IN BERLIN New Line Cinema, 1988, w/Joshua Sinclair

JACK WINER
(credit w/David Niven Jr.)

THE EAGLE HAS LANDED Columbia, 1977
ESCAPE TO ATHENA AFD, 1979
F/X Orion, 1986, w/Dodi Fayed*

ALEX WINITSKY
(credit w/Arlene Sellers)
Business: Lantana Productions, 3000 Olympic Blvd., Suite 1300, Santa Monica, CA, 90404, 213/315-4777

THE SEVEN-PERCENT SOLUTION Universal, 1976, EP
CROSS OF IRON Avco Embassy, 1977
SILVER BEARS Columbia, 1977

BREAKTHROUGH *SERGEANT STEINER* Maverick Pictures International, 1978
HOUSE CALLS Universal, 1978
THE LADY VANISHES Rank, 1979, EP w/Michael Carreras
CUBA United Artists, 1979
BLUE SKIES AGAIN Warner Bros., 1983
SWING SHIFT Warner Bros., 1984, EP
SCANDALOUS Orion, 1984
IRRECONCILABLE DIFFERENCES Warner Bros., 1984
BAD MEDICINE 20th Century-Fox, 1985
STANLEY & IRIS MGM, 1990

HENRY WINKLER

Business: Winkler/Daniel Productions, 5555 Melrose Ave., Los Angeles, CA, 90038, 213/468-5700
Agent: ICM - Los Angeles, 213/550-4000

THE SURE THING Embassy, 1985, EP

IRWIN WINKLER

(credit w/Robert Chartoff)

Business: Winkler Films, 10125 W. Washington Blvd., Culver City, CA, 90230, 213/204-0474
Contact: Directors Guild of America - Los Angeles, 213/289-2000

DOUBLE TROUBLE MGM, 1967, w/Judd Bernard*
BLUE Paramount, 1968, w/Judd Bernard*
THE SPLIT MGM, 1968
THEY SHOOT HORSES, DON'T THEY? Cinerama Releasing Corporation, 1969, w/Sydney Pollack
LEO THE LAST United Artists, 1970
THE STRAWBERRY STATEMENT MGM, 1970
BELIEVE IN ME MGM, 1971
THE GANG THAT COULDN'T SHOOT STRAIGHT MGM, 1971
THE MECHANIC United Artists, 1972
THE NEW CENTURIONS Columbia, 1972
THUMB TRIPPING Avco Embassy, 1972
UP THE SANDBOX National General, 1972
BUSTING United Artists, 1974
S*P*Y*S 20th Century-Fox, 1974
BREAKOUT Columbia, 1975
THE GAMBLER Paramount, 1974
PEEPER 20th Century-Fox, 1976
NICKELODEON Columbia, 1976
ROCKY ★★ United Artists, 1976
NEW YORK, NEW YORK United Artists, 1977
VALENTINO United Artists, 1977
COMES A HORSEMAN United Artists, 1978, EP
UNCLE JOE SHANNON United Artists, 1978
ROCKY II United Artists, 1979
RAGING BULL ★ United Artists, 1980
TRUE CONFESSIONS United Artists, 1981
ROCKY III MGM/UA, 1982
AUTHOR! AUTHOR! 20th Century-Fox, 1982*
THE RIGHT STUFF ★ The Ladd Company/Warner Bros., 1983
ROCKY IV MGM/UA, 1985
REVOLUTION Warner Bros., 1985*
ROUND MIDNIGHT Warner Bros., 1986*
BETRAYED MGM/UA, 1988*
MUSIC BOX Tri-Star, 1989*
GOOD FELLAS Warner Bros., 1990*

MICHAEL WINNER

Business: Scimitar Films, Ltd., 6-8 Sackville St., London W1X 1DD, England, 01/734-8385
Contact: Directors Guild of America - Los Angeles, 213/289-2000

DEATH WISH Paramount, 1974, CP
WON TON TON, THE DOG WHO SAVED HOLLYWOOD Paramount, 1976, w/David V. Picker & Arnold Schulman
THE BIG SLEEP United Artists, 1978, w/Elliott Kastner
SCREAM FOR HELP Lorimar, 1984
DEATH WISH 3 Cannon, 1985, CP
A CHORUS OF DISAPPROVAL South Gate Entertainment, 1989

RONALD WINSTON

KEY EXCHANGE 20th Century-Fox, 1985, EP w/Peer J. Oppenheimer & Michael Pochna

RALPH WINTER

Business: Paramount Pictures, 5555 Melrose Ave., Los Angeles, CA, 90038, 213/468-5797

STAR TREK IV: THE VOYAGE HOME Paramount, 1986, EP
STAR TREK V: THE FINAL FRONTIER Paramount, 1989, EP

LOREN WINTERS

(credit w/Paul Winters)

THE FREEWAY MANIAC Cannon, 1988

PAUL WINTERS

(credit w/Loren Winters)

THE FREEWAY MANIAC Cannon, 1988

MICHAEL WISE

NIGHTHAWKS Universal, 1981, EP w/Franklin R. Levy
MAKING MR. RIGHT Orion, 1987, w/Joel Tuber

ROBERT WISE

Business: Robert Wise Productions, 315 S. Beverly Dr., Suite 214, Beverly Hills, CA, 90212, 213/284-7932
Agent: Phil Gersh, The Gersh Agency - Beverly Hills, 213/274-6611

WEST SIDE STORY ★★ United Artists, 1961
THE SOUND OF MUSIC ★★ 20th Century-Fox, 1965
THE SAND PEBBLES ★ 20th Century-Fox, 1966
WISDOM 20th Century-Fox, 1986, EP

DAVID WISNIEVITZ

Contact: Directors Guild of America - Los Angeles, 213/289-2000

THE BALLAD OF GREGORIO CORTEZ Embassy, 1983, AP
VALENTINO RETURNS Skouras Pictures, 1989, w/Peter Hoffman
OLD GRINGO Columbia, 1989, EP
GHOST DAD Universal, 1989, AP

PAUL JUNGER WITT

(credit w/Tony Thomas)

Business: Witt-Thomas Productions, 846 N. Cahuenga Blvd., Los Angeles, CA, 90038, 213/464-1333
Agent: CAA - Beverly Hills, 213/288-4545

FIRSTBORN Paramount, 1984
DEAD POETS SOCIETY ★ Buena Vista, 1989, w/Steven Haft

WILLIAM D. WITTLIFF

Business: 510 Baylor, Austin, TX, 78703, 512/476-6821
Agent: ICM - Los Angeles, 213/550-4000

RAGGEDY MAN Universal, 1981, w/Burt Weissbourd
BARBAROSA Universal/AFD, 1982, CP
COUNTRY Buena Vista, 1984, w/Jessica Lange
RED HEADED STRANGER Alive FIlms, 1986, w/Willie Nelson

TED WITZER

SIX PACK 20th Century-Fox, 1982, EP w/Edward S. Feldman

JOE WIZAN

Business: Wizan/Black Films, 11999 San Vicente Blvd., Suite 450, Los Angeles, CA, 90049, 213/472-6133

JEREMIAH JOHNSON Warner Bros., 1972
JUNIOR BONNER ABC/Cinerama, 1972
PRIME CUT National General, 1972
99 & 44/100 PERCENT DEAD 20th Century- Fox, 1974
AUDREY ROSE United Artists, 1977, w/Frank De Felitta
VOICES MGM/UA, 1979
...AND JUSTICE FOR ALL Columbia, 1979, EP
BEST FRIENDS Warner Bros., 1982, EP
TWO OF A KIND 20th Century-Fox, 1983, w/Roger M. Rothstein
UNFAITHFULLY YOURS 20th Century-Fox, 1984, w/Marvin Worth
IRON EAGLE Tri-Star, 1986, w/Ron Samuels
TOUGH GUYS Buena Vista, 1986
SPELLBINDER MGM/UA, 1988, w/Brian Russell
SPLIT DECISION New Century/Vista, 1988
THE GUARDIAN Universal, 1990
SHORT TIME 20th Century-Fox, 1990, EP w/Mickey Borofsky

STANLEY WLODKOWSKI

Business: 24 W. 96th St., #2F, New York, NY, 10025, 212/749-1676

FEAR, ANXIETY & DEPRESSION Samuel Goldwyn Company, 1989, w/Steve Golin & Sigurjon Sighvatsson
LONGTIME COMPANION Samuel Goldwyn Company, 1990

DICK WOLF

Contact: Writers Guild of America - Los Angeles, 213/550-1000

NO MAN'S LAND Orion, 1987, w/Joseph Stern

GORDON WOLF

Contact: Directors Guild of America - Los Angeles, 213/289-2000

UFORIA Universal, 1985
DUDES New Century/Vista, 1987, LP

JOSEPH WOLF

Business: Ascot Entertainment Group, 9000 Sunset Blvd., Suite 1010, Los Angeles, CA, 90069, 213/273-9501

HELL NIGHT Aquarius, 1981, EP w/Chuck Russell
HALLOWEEN II Universal, 1981, EP w/Irwin Yablans
HALLOWEEN III: SEASON OF THE WITCH Universal, 1982, EP w/Irwin Yablans
PARASITE Embassy, 1982, EP w/Irwin Yablans
THE SEDUCTION Avco Embassy, 1982, EP w/Frank Capra Jr. & Chuck Russell
A NIGHTMARE ON ELM STREET New Line Cinema, 1984, EP w/Stanley Dudelson

MICHAEL B. WOLF

S.O.B. Lorimar/Paramount, 1981, EP

JUDITH WOLINSKY

Business: International Rainbow Pictures, 9165 Sunset Blvd., Penthouse 300, Los Angeles, CA, 90069, 213/271-0202

ALWAYS Samuel Goldwyn Company, 1985, AP
SOMEONE TO LOVE International Rainbow/Castle Hill, 1987, AP
NEW YEAR'S DAY International Rainbow, 1989

RON WOLOTZKY

IN A SHALLOW GRAVE Skouras Pictures, 1988, LP

DAVID L. WOLPER

Business: David L. Wolper Productions, Inc., Warner Bros., 4000 Warner Blvd., Burbank, CA, 91522, 818/954-1707

THE BRIDGE AT REMAGEN United Artists, 1969
IF IT'S TUESDAY, THIS MUST BE BELGIUM United Artists, 1969, EP
I LOVE MY WIFE Universal, 1970, EP
WILLY WONKA AND THE CHOCOLATE FACTORY Paramount, 1971, w/Stan Margulies
THE HELLSTROM CHRONICLE Cinema 5, 1971
ONE IS A LONELY NUMBER MGM, 1972, EP
KING, QUEEN, KNAVE Avco Embassy, 1972, w/Lutz Hengst
VISIONS OF EIGHT (FD) Cinema 5, 1973, EP
WATTSTAX (FD) Columbia, 1973, EP
THE MYSTERIOUS MONSTERS (FD) Sunn Classic, 1976, w/Robert Guenette & Charles E. Sellier Jr.
THE MAN WHO SAW TOMORROW (FD) Warner Bros., 1981, EP
THIS IS ELVIS (FD) Warner Bros., 1981, EP
IMAGINE: JOHN LENNON (FD) Warner Bros., 1988, w/Andrew Solt

JAMES WOODS

Agent: CAA - Beverly Hills, 213/288-4545

COP Atlantic Entertainment, 1988, w/James B. Harris

JOHN WOODWARD

THE CELLAR Moviestore, 1990, w/Patrick C. Wells & Steven E. Burman

DENNIS WOOLF

RETURN TO WATERLOO New Line Cinema, 1985

JAMES WOOLF
Business: Romulus Films, Ltd., Suite 14, The Chambers, Chelsea Harbour, London S.W.10, England

ROOM AT THE TOP ★ Continental, 1959, w/Sir John Woolf

SIR JOHN WOOLF
Business: Romulus Films, Ltd., Suite 14, The Chambers, Chelsea Harbour, London S.W.10, England

ROOM AT THE TOP ★ Continental, 1959, w/James Woolf
THE L-SHAPED ROOM Columbia, 1963, w/Richard Attenborough
LIFE AT THE TOP Columbia, 1965
OLIVER! ★★ Columbia, 1968
THE DAY OF THE JACKAL Universal, 1973, w/Julien Derode & David Deutsch
THE ODESSA FILE Columbia, 1974

NIGEL WOOLL
Agent: Sandra Marsh Management - Sherman Oaks, 818/905-6961

THE DRESSER ★ Columbia, 1983, AP
ELENI Warner Bros., 1985, AP
ISHTAR Columbia, 1987, AP w/David L. MacLeod
WILLOW MGM/UA, 1988

STEPHEN WOOLLEY
Business: Palace Pictures, 16/17 Wardour Mews, London W1, England, 01/734-7060; 8170 Beverly Blvd., Suite 203, Los Angeles, CA, 90048, 213/655-1114

THE COMPANY OF WOLVES Cannon, 1985, w/Chris Brown
ABSOLUTE BEGINNERS Orion, 1986, w/Chris Brown
MONA LISA Island Pictures, 1986, w/Patrick Cassavetti
HIGH SPIRITS Tri-Star, 1988, w/David Saunders
SCANDAL Miramax, 1989
SHAG: THE MOVIE Hemdale, 1989, w/Julia Chasman

CHUCK WORKMAN
Business: Calliope Films, 195 S. Beverly Dr., Suite 414, Beverly Hills, CA, 90212, 213/271-0964
Agent: APA - Los Angeles, 213/273-0744

THE MONEY Coliseum, 1977

HOWARD WORTH
Contact: Directors Guild of America - Los Angeles, 213/289-2000

WILD ORCHID Triumph Releasing, 1990, CP

MARVIN WORTH
Business: Paramount Pictures, 5555 Melrose Ave., Los Angeles, CA, 90038, 213/468-5788

WHERE'S POPPA? United Artists, 1970, w/Jerry Tokofsky
LENNY ★ United Artists, 1974
FIRE SALE 20th Century-Fox, 1977
THE ROSE 20th Century-Fox, 1979, w/Aaron Russo
MAD MAGAZINE PRESENTS UP THE ACADEMY Warner Bros., 1980, w/Danton Rissner
SOUP FOR ONE Warner Bros., 1982
UNFAITHFULLY YOURS 20th Century-Fox, 1984, w/Joe Wizan
RHINESTONE 20th Century-Fox, 1984, w/Howard Smith
FALLING IN LOVE Paramount, 1984
PATTY HEARST Atlantic Entertainment, 1988
SEE NO EVIL, HEAR NO EVIL Tri-Star, 1989
FLASHBACK Paramount, 1990, w/David Loughery

DENNIS WRIGHT
(credit w/Kent C. Lovell)

DOGS IN SPACE Skouras Pictures, 1987, EP w/Robert Le Tet*
BACKSTAGE Hoyts, 1988, EP
GROUND ZERO Avenue, 1988, EP w/John Kearney

ROBERT S. WUNSCH
Business: Richland/Wunsch Agency, 9220 Sunset Blvd., Los Angeles, CA, 90069, 213/278-1955

SLAP SHOT Universal, 1977, w/Stephen J. Friedman
DEFIANCE American International, 1980, EP

CATHERINE WYLER
Business: 213/271-8681

MEMPHIS BELLE Warner Bros., 1990, w/David Puttnam

BRAD WYMAN
Business: Palisades Pictures, 1875 Century Park East, 3rd Floor, Los Angeles, CA, 90067, 213/785-3100

WHITE OF THE EYE Palisades Entertainment, 1987, w/Cassian Elwes
NEVER ON TUESDAY Palisades Entertainment, 1987, w/Lionel Wigram

FRANK YABLANS
Business: Frank Yablans Productions, Columbia Pictures, Columbia Plaza, Burbank, CA, 91505, 818/954-3142

SILVER STREAK 20th Century-Fox, 1976, EP w/Martin Ransohoff
THE OTHER SIDE OF MIDNIGHT 20th Century- Fox, 1977
THE FURY 20th Century-Fox, 1978
NORTH DALLAS FORTY Paramount, 1979
MOMMIE DEAREST Paramount, 1981
MONSIGNOR 20th Century-Fox, 1982, w/David Niven Jr.
THE STAR CHAMBER 20th Century-Fox, 1983
KIDCO 20th Century-Fox, 1984, w/David Niven Jr.
BUY AND CELL Empire, 1989
LISA MGM/UA, 1990

IRWIN YABLANS
ROLLER BOOGIE United Artists, 1979, EP
FADE TO BLACK American Cinema, 1980, EP w/Sylvio Tabet
HALLOWEEN II Universal, 1981, EP w/Joseph Wolf
HELL NIGHT Aquarius, 1981, w/Bruce Cohn Curtis
PARASITE Embassy, 1982, EP w/Joseph Wolf
HALLOWEEN III: SEASON OF THE WITCH Universal, 1982, EP w/Joseph Wolf

THE SEDUCTION Avco Embassy, 1982, w/Bruce Cohn Curtis
TANK Universal, 1984
SCREAM FOR HELP Lorimar, 1984, EP
PRISON Empire, 1988
WHY ME? Triumph, 1990, EP

MATA YAMAMOTO
MISHIMA: A LIFE IN FOUR CHAPTERS Warner Bros., 1985, w/Tom Luddy

GEORGE YANEFF
THE TRIP TO BOUNTIFUL Island Pictures, 1985, EP w/Sam Grogg

MARIE YATES
FRANCES Universal, 1982, CP

PETER YATES
Agent: CAA - Beverly Hills, 213/288-4545
Contact: Directors Guild of America - New York, 212/581-0370

BREAKING AWAY ★ 20th Century-Fox, 1979
EYEWITNESS 20th Century-Fox, 1981
THE DRESSER ★ Columbia, 1983
THE HOUSE ON CARROLL STREET Orion, 1988, w/Robert F. Colesberry

WILLIAM ROBERT YATES
AMY Buena Vista, 1981, EP

LINDA YELLEN
Agent: Lennie Hirshan, William Morris Agency - Beverly Hills, 213/274-7451
Contact: Directors Guild of America - New York, 212/581-0370

EVERYBODY WINS Orion, 1990, EP w/Terry Glinwood

WALTER YETNIKOFF
Business: CBS Records, 1801 Century Park West, Los Angeles, CA, 90067, 213/556-4700

RUTHLESS PEOPLE Buena Vista, 1986, EP w/JoAnna Lancaster & Richard Wagner

BUD YORKIN
Business: Bud Yorkin Productions, 132 South Rodeo Dr., Suite 300, Beverly Hills, CA, 90212, 213/274-8111
Agent: CAA - Beverly Hills, 213/288-4545

COME BLOW YOUR HORN Paramount, 1963, w/Norman Lear
THE NIGHT THEY RAIDED MINSKY'S United Artists, 1968, EP
START THE REVOLUTION WITHOUT ME Warner Bros., 1970
COLD TURKEY United Artists, 1971, EP
THE THIEF WHO CAME TO DINNER Warner Bros., 1973
DEAL OF THE CENTURY Warner Bros., 1983
TWICE IN A LIFETIME Bud Yorkin Company, 1985

IRWIN YOUNG
Business: DuArt Film Laboratories, 245 W. 55th St., New York, NY, 10019, 212/757-4580

ALAMBRISTA! Bobwin/Film Haus, 1977, w/Michael Hausman
GET ROLLIN' EP w/Stan Plotnick

JEFF YOUNG
Contact: Directors Guild of America - Los Angeles, 213/289-2000

SPLIT IMAGE Orion, 1982, EP
COHEN & TATE Hemdale, 1989, w/Lord Anthony Rufus Isaacs

JOHN SACRET YOUNG
Business: "China Beach," Warner Bros. TV, 4000 Warner Blvd., Burbank, CA, 91522, 818/954-6000
Agent: ICM - Los Angeles, 213/550-4000

ROMERO Four Seasons Entertainment, 1989, EP w/Lawrence Mortorff

ROBERT M. YOUNG
Agent: John Gaines, APA - Los Angeles, 213/273-0744
Contact: Directors Guild of America - Los Angeles, 213/289-2000

THE PLOT AGAINST HARRY New Yorker Films, 1990, w/Michael Roemer

NG SEE YUEN
NO RETREAT, NO SURRENDER II Shapiro Glickenhaus, 1989, EP

BRIAN YUZNA
RE-ANIMATOR Empire, 1985
FROM BEYOND Empire, 1986
DOLLS Empire, 1987

Z

STEVE ZACHARIAS
(credit w/Jeff Buhai & David Obst)
Agent: Bauer Benedek Agency - Los Angeles, 213/275-2421
Contact: Writers Guild of America - Los Angeles, 213/550-1000

THE WHOOPEE BOYS Paramount, 1986, EP
JOHNNY BE GOOD Orion, 1988, EP

CRAIG ZADAN
Business: Storyline Productions, Warner Bros., 4000 Warner Blvd., Burbank, CA, 91522, 818/954-6000

FOOTLOOSE Paramount, 1984, w/Michael Rachmil
SING Tri-Star, 1989

SAUL ZAENTZ

Business: The Saul Zaentz Company, 2600 Tenth St., Berkeley, CA, 94710, 415/549-1528

ONE FLEW OVER THE CUCKOO'S NEST ★★ United Artists, 1975, w/Michael Douglas
THREE WARRIORS Fantasy Films, 1977, w/Sy Gomberg
LORD OF THE RINGS United Artists, 1978
AMADEUS ★★ Orion, 1984
THE MOSQUITO COAST Warner Bros., 1986, EP
THE UNBEARABLE LIGHTNESS OF BEING Orion, 1988

NABEEL ZAHID

CHAMPIONS FOREVER (FD) Ion, 1989, w/Joseph Medawar

JOHN ZANE

Contact: Directors Guild of America - Los Angeles, 213/289-2000

SIDEOUT Tri-Star, 1990, CP

LILI FINI ZANUCK

(credit w/David Brown & Richard D. Zanuck)

Business: The Zanuck Company, 202 N. Canon Dr., Beverly Hills, CA, 90210, 213/274-0261

COCOON 20th Century-Fox, 1985
COCOON: THE RETURN 20th Century-Fox, 1988
DRIVING MISS DAISY ★★ Warner Bros., 1989

RICHARD D. ZANUCK

(credit w/David Brown)

Business: The Zanuck Company, 202 N. Canon Dr., Beverly Hills, CA, 90210, 213/274-0261

Sssssss Universal, 1973, EP
WILLIE DYNAMITE Universal, 1974
THE SUGARLAND EXPRESS Universal, 1974
THE GIRL FROM PETROVKA Universal, 1974
THE BLACK WINDMILL Universal, 1974
THE EIGER SANCTION Universal, 1974, EP
JAWS ★ Universal, 1975
MACARTHUR Universal, 1977, EP
JAWS II Universal, 1978
THE ISLAND Universal, 1980
NEIGHBORS Columbia, 1981
THE VERDICT ★ 20th Century-Fox, 1982
COCOON 20th Century-Fox, 1985, w/Lili Fini Zanuck
TARGET Warner Bros., 1985
COCOON: THE RETURN 20th Century-Fox, 1988, w/Lili Fini Zanuck
DRIVING MISS DAISY ★★ Warner Bros., 1989, w/Lili Fini Zanuck*

GEORGE ZECEVIC

Business: Smart Egg Pictures, 7080 Hollywood Blvd., Suite 518, Hollywood, CA, 90028, 213/463-8937

HEY BABU RIBA Orion Classics, 1987, EP w/Petar Jankovic
OMEGA SYNDROME New World, 1987, EP
DOUBLE REVENGE Smart Egg Releasing, 1988, EP w/Luigi Cingolani
CAMERON'S CLOSET SVS Films, 1989, EP
SPACED INVADERS Buena Vista, 1990

JEROME M. ZEITMAN

HOW TO BEAT THE HIGH COST OF LIVING American International, 1980, w/Robert Kaufman

RAFAL ZIELINSKI

Business: Vision Pictures, 3170 Ramezay Place, Montreal, Quebec H3Y 2B5, Canada, 514/932-0396

GINGER ALE AFTERNOON Skouras Pictures, 1989, w/Susan Hillary Shapiro

JONATHAN A. ZIMBERT

Business: Paramount Pictures, 5555 Melrose Ave., Los Angeles, CA, 90038, 213/468-5923

THE STAR CHAMBER 20th Century-Fox, 1983, AP
2010 MGM/UA, 1984, AP w/Neil A. Machlis
RUNNING SCARED MGM, 1986, AP
THE MONSTER SQUAD Tri-Star, 1987
THE PRESIDIO Paramount, 1988, EP
NARROW MARGIN Tri-Star, 1990

VERNON ZIMMERMAN

Business: P.O. Box 900, Beverly Hills, CA, 90213, 213/203-3394
Business Manager: Eric Weissmann, Weissmann, Wolff, Bergman, Coleman & Schulman, 9665 Wilshire Blvd., Suite 900, Beverly Hills, CA, 90212, 213/858-7888

DEADHEAD MILES Paramount, 1982, w/Tony Bill

FRED ZINNEMANN

Business: 128 Mount St., London W1, England, 01/499-8810
Agent: Lennie Hirshan, William Morris Agency - Beverly Hills, 213/274-7451

THE SUNDOWNERS ★ Warner Bros., 1960
A MAN FOR ALL SEASONS ★★ Columbia, 1966
FIVE DAYS ONE SUMMER The Ladd Company/Warner Bros., 1982

TIM ZINNEMANN

Agent: ICM - Los Angeles, 213/550-4000
Contact: Directors Guild of America - Los Angeles, 213/289-2000

SMILE United Artists, 1975, AP
STRAIGHT TIME Warner Bros., 1978, w/Stanley Back
A SMALL CIRCLE OF FRIENDS United Artists, 1980
THE LONG RIDERS United Artists, 1980
TEX Buena Vista, 1982
IMPULSE 20th Century-Fox, 1984
FANDANGO Warner Bros., 1985
CROSS ROADS Columbia, 1986, EP
THE RUNNING MAN Tri-Star, 1987, w/George Linder
PET SEMATARY Paramount, 1989, EP

LAURA ZISKIN

Business: Walt Disney Pictures, 500 S. Buena Vista St., Burbank, CA, 91521, 818/560-5976

EYES OF LAURA MARS Columbia, 1978, AP
MURPHY'S ROMANCE Columbia, 1985
NO WAY OUT Orion, 1987, w/Robert Garland
D.O.A. Buena Vista, 1988, w/Ian Sander
EVERYBODY'S ALL-AMERICAN Warner Bros., 1988, w/Taylor Hackford & Ian Sander

THE RESCUE Buena Vista, 1988
PRETTY WOMAN Buena Vista, 1990

DAVID ZITO
BREAKIN' Cannon, 1984, w/Allen DeBevoise

BARBARA ZITWER
VAMPIRE'S KISS Hemdale, 1989, w/Barry Shils

FREDERICK ZOLLO
MILES FROM HOME Cinecom, 1988, w/Paul Kurta
MISSISSIPPI BURNING ★ Orion, 1988, w/Robert F. Colesberry

DAVID ZUCKER
(credit w/Jim Abrahams & Jerry Zucker)
Business: 11777 San Vicente Blvd., Suite 640, Los Angeles, CA, 90049, 213/826-1333
Agent: CAA - Beverly Hills, 213/288-4545

AIRPLANE! Paramount, 1980, EP
THE NAKED GUN: FROM THE FILES OF POLICE SQUAD Paramount, 1988, EP

HOWARD ZUCKER
TRACKS Castle Hill Productions, 1976, w/Norman I. Cohen & Ted Shapiro

JERRY ZUCKER
(credit w/Jim Abrahams & David Zucker)
Business: 11777 San Vicente Blvd., Suite 640, Los Angeles, CA, 90049, 213/826-1333
Agent: CAA - Beverly Hills, 213/288-4545

AIRPLANE! Paramount, 1980, EP
THE NAKED GUN: FROM THE FILES OF POLICE SQUAD Paramount, 1988, EP

STANLEY R. ZUPNIK
Business: Zupnik Enterprises, 9229 Sunset Blvd., Los Angeles, CA, 90069, 213/273-9125

DREAMSCAPE 20th Century-Fox, 1984, EP w/Tom Curtis
WILDFIRE Jody Ann Productions, 1989, EP w/Irvin Kershner

A. MARTIN ZWEIBACK
(credit w/Adrienne Zweibach)
Agent: APA - Los Angeles, 213/273-0744
Contact: Writers Guild of America - Los Angeles, 213/550-1000

GRACE QUIGLEY *THE ULTIMATE SOLUTION OF GRACE QUIGLEY* MGM/UA/Cannon, 1984, EP

ADRIENNE ZWEIBACK
(credit w/A. Martin Zweibach)

GRACE QUIGLEY *THE ULTIMATE SOLUTION OF GRACE QUIGLEY* MGM/UA/Cannon, 1984, EP

CHARLOTTE ZWERIN
Contact: Directors Guild of America - New York, 212/581-0370

THELONIOUS MONK: STRAIGHT, NO CHASER (FD) Warner Bros., 1988, w/Bruce Ricker

JOSEPH E. ZYNCZAK
DISORDERLIES Warner Bros., 1987, EP w/Charles Stettler

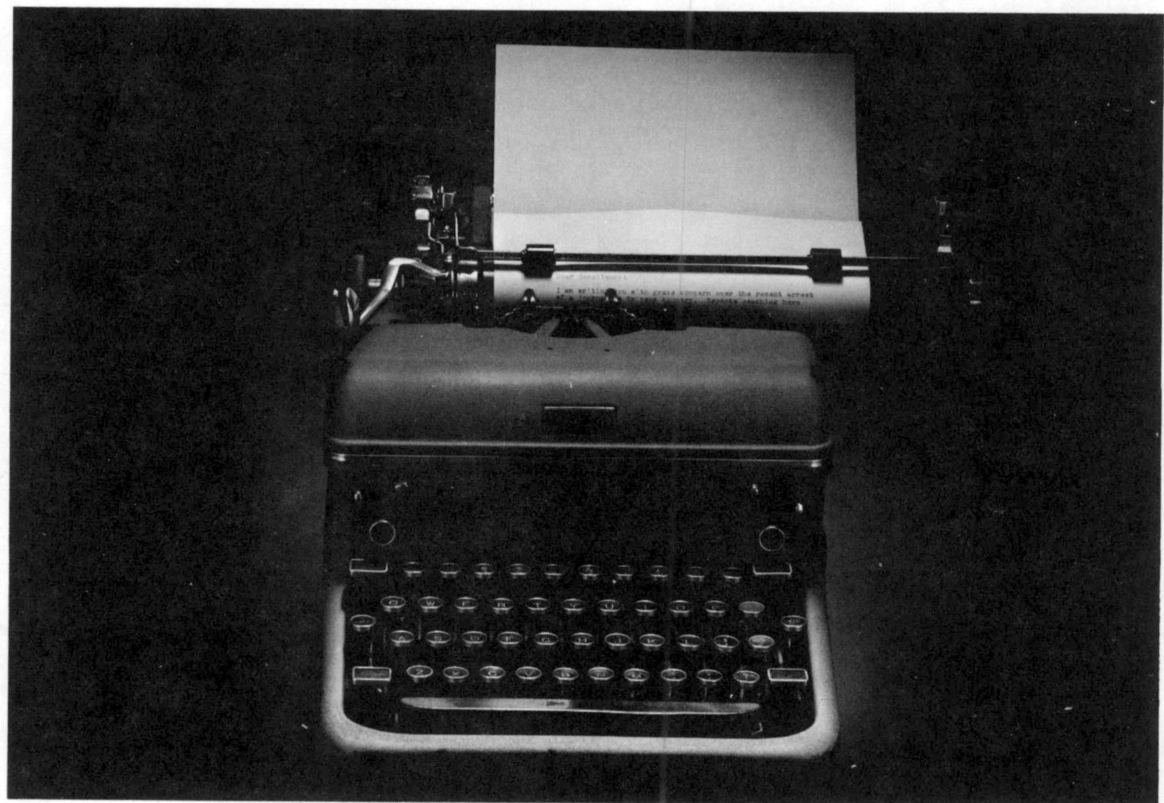

This is one of the most powerful weapons in the fight for human rights.

It can help more innocent people get out of prison and free from torture than all the guns in the world. It's a guarantee to human rights everywhere on the globe. Everyday.

Amnesty International uses this weapon very effectively. Since 1961, A.I. has helped more than 25,000 women, men and children win their freedom from prison and torture. With simple, yet effective letters. Write today. It may be the most powerful letter you've ever written.

Write a letter, save a life.

Yes, I want to become a member of Amnesty International and make a difference.
Enclosed is my tax-deductible contribution for: ☐$25 ☐$35 ☐$50 ☐$75 ☐$100 ☐ Other $ ______
Minimum annual contribution is $25. $15 for students, senior citizens and limited income.

Name ____________________

Address ____________________

City ____________________ State ______ Zip Code ______

LE89

Amnesty International USA
322 Eighth Avenue, New York, New York 10001

INDEX

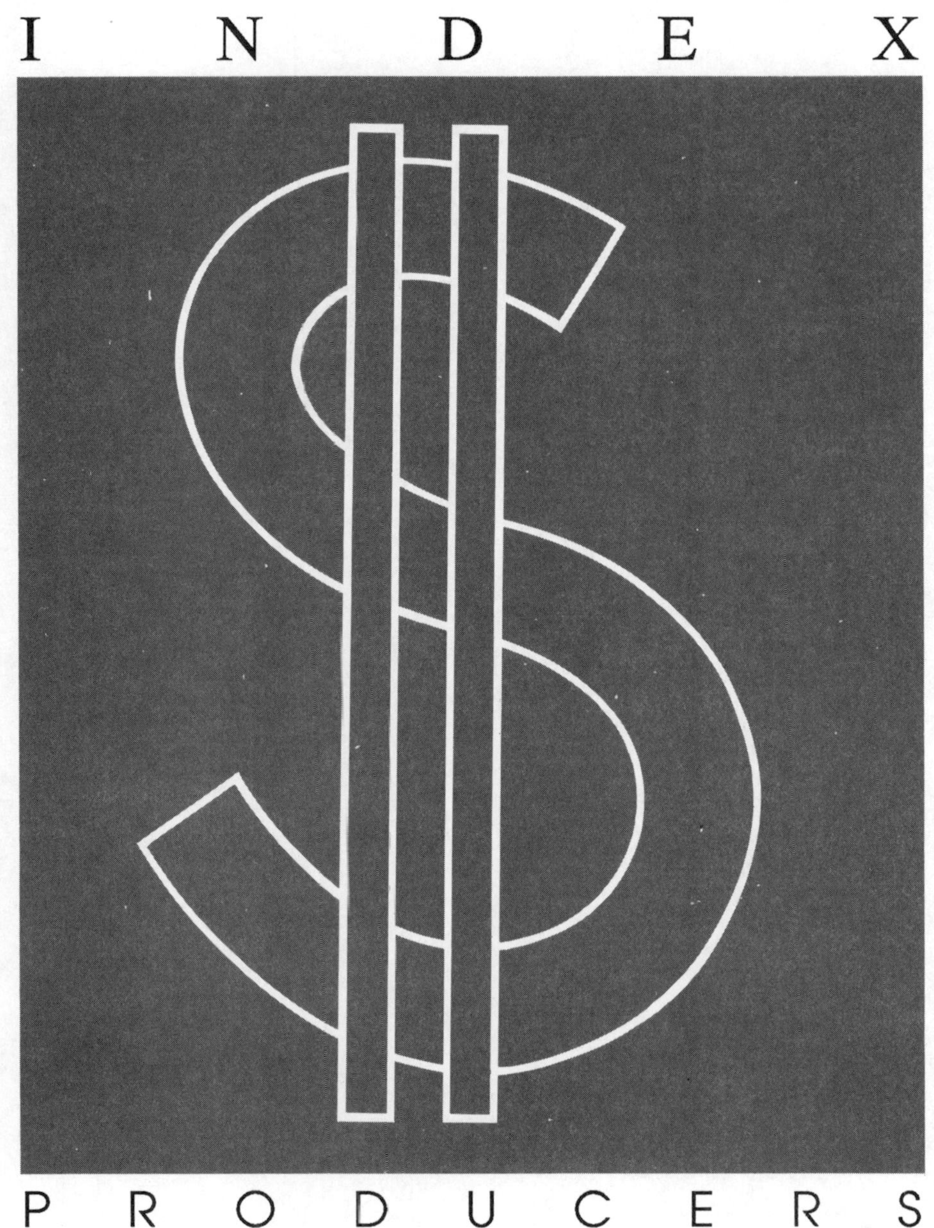

PRODUCERS

INDEX OF FILM TITLES --- FILM PRODUCERS

NOTE: This is not an index of every film ever made, only those listed in this directory.

† = deceased

3 WOMEN ..... ROBERT ALTMAN
3 WOMEN ..... SCOTT BUSHNELL
3:15 THE MOMENT OF TRUTH ..... ANDREW BULLIANS
3:15 THE MOMENT OF TRUTH ..... CHARLES C. THIERIOT
3:15 THE MOMENT OF TRUTH ..... DENNIS BRODY
3:15 THE MOMENT OF TRUTH ..... JEAN BULLIANS
3:15 THE MOMENT OF TRUTH ..... ROBERT KENNER
3:15 THE MOMENT OF TRUTH ..... SANDY CLIMAN
9 1/2 WEEKS ..... FRANK KONIGSBERG
9 1/2 WEEKS ..... KEITH BARISH
9/30/55 ..... JERRY WEINTRAUB
10 ..... BLAKE EDWARDS
10 RILLINGTON PLACE ..... LESLIE LINDER
10 RILLINGTON PLACE ..... MARTIN RANSOHOFF
10 ..... TONY ADAMS
11 HARROW HOUSE ..... ELLIOTT KASTNER
18 AGAIN ..... IRVING FEIN
18 AGAIN ..... MICHAEL JAFFE
18 AGAIN ..... WALTER COBLENZ
30 IS A DANGEROUS AGE, CYNTHIA ..... WALTER SHENSON
40 POUNDS OF TROUBLE ..... TED MANN
48 HOURS ..... D. CONSTANTINE CONTE
48 HOURS ..... JOEL SILVER
48 HOURS ..... LAWRENCE GORDON
52 PICK-UP ..... HENRY T. WEINSTEIN
52 PICK-UP ..... MENAHEM GOLAN
52 PICK-UP ..... YORAM GLOBUS
'68 ..... DALE DJERASSI
'68 ..... ISABEL MAXWELL
'68 ..... STEVEN KOVACS
84 CHARING CROSS ROAD ..... GEOFFREY HELMAN
84 CHARLIE MOPIC ..... JILL GRIFFITH
84 CHARLIE MOPIC ..... MICHAEL NOLIN
92 IN THE SHADE ..... ELLIOTT KASTNER
92 IN THE SHADE ..... GEORGE PAPPAS
99 AND 44/100 PERCENT DEAD ..... JOE WIZAN
1900 ..... ALBERTO GRIMALDI
1918 ..... LEWIS ALLEN
1941 ..... BUZZ FEITSHANS
1969 ..... BILL BADALATO
1969 ..... DANIEL GRODNIK
1969 ..... THOMAS COLEMAN
1984 ..... AL CLARK
1984 ..... MARVIN J. ROSENBLUM
1984 ..... ROBERT DEVEREUX
1984 ..... SIMON PERRY
2001: A SPACE ODYSSEY ..... STANLEY KUBRICK
2010 ..... JONATHAN A. ZIMBERT
2010 ..... JULIA PHILLIPS
2010 ..... NEIL A. MACHLIS
5000 FINGERS OF DR. T, THE ..... STANLEY KRAMER
41,000,000 DUCK, THE ..... BILL ANDERSON

A

ABOUT LAST NIGHT ..... JASON BRETT
ABOUT LAST NIGHT ..... STUART OKEN
ABOUT LAST NIGHT... ..... ARNOLD STIEFEL
ABOVE THE LAW ..... ANDREW DAVIS
ABOVE THE LAW ..... JOHN G. WILSON
ABOVE THE LAW ..... ROBERT H. SOLO
ABOVE THE LAW ..... STEVEN SEAGAL
ABSENCE OF MALICE ..... SYDNEY POLLACK
ABSENCE OF MALICE ..... RONALD L. SCHWARY
ABSOLUTE BEGINNERS ..... AL CLARK
ABSOLUTE BEGINNERS ..... CHRIS BROWN
ABSOLUTE BEGINNERS ..... DAVID WIMBURY
ABSOLUTE BEGINNERS ..... NIK POWELL
ABSOLUTE BEGINNERS ..... ROBERT DEVEREUX
ABSOLUTE BEGINNERS ..... STEPHEN WOOLLEY
ABSOLUTION ..... DANNY O'DONOVAN
ABSOLUTION ..... ELLIOTT KASTNER
ABYSS, THE ..... GALE ANNE HURD
ACCIDENTAL TOURIST, THE ..... BO WELCH
ACCIDENTAL TOURIST, THE ..... CHARLES OKUN
ACCIDENTAL TOURIST, THE ..... JOHN MALKOVICH
ACCIDENTAL TOURIST, THE ..... LAWRENCE KASDAN
ACCIDENTAL TOURIST, THE ..... MICHAEL GRILLO
ACCIDENTAL TOURIST, THE ..... PHYLLIS CARLYLE
ACCUSED, THE ..... JACK ROE
ACCUSED, THE ..... SHERRY LANSING
ACCUSED, THE ..... STANLEY R. JAFFE
ACE IN THE HOLE ..... BILLY WILDER
ACROSS 110TH STREET ..... ANTHONY QUINN
ACROSS 110TH STREET ..... BARRY SHEAR
ACROSS 110TH STREET ..... FOUAD SAID
ACROSS 110TH STREET ..... RALPH SERPE
ACT OF THE HEART ..... JENNINGS LANG
ACTION JACKSON ..... JOEL SILVER
ACTION JACKSON ..... STEVE PERRY
ADAM AT SIX A.M. ..... ROBERT CHRISTIANSEN
ADAM AT SIX A.M. ..... ROBERT E. RELYEA
ADAM AT SIX A.M. ..... RICK ROSENBERG
ADVENTURES IN BABYSITTING ..... DEBRA HILL
ADVENTURES IN BABYSITTING ..... LYNDA OBST
ADVENTURES OF BARON MUNCHAUSEN, THE ..... DAVID TOMBLIN
ADVENTURES OF BARON MUNCHAUSEN, THE ..... RAY COOPER
ADVENTURES OF BARON MUNCHAUSEN, THE ..... THOMAS SCHUEHLY
ADVENTURES OF BARON MUNCHAUSEN, THE ..... STRATTON LEOPOLD
ADVENTURES OF BARON MUNCHAUSEN,THE ..... JAKE EBERTS
ADVENTURES OF BULLWHIP GRIFFIN,THE ..... BILL ANDERSON
ADVENTURES OF MARK TWAIN, THE ..... HUGH TIRRELL
ADVENTURES OF MARK TWAIN, THE ..... SUSAN SHADBURNE
ADVENTURES OF MARK TWAIN, THE ..... WILL VINTON
ADVENTURES OF SHERLOCK HOLMES' SMARTER BROTHER, THE ..... RICHARD A. ROTH
AFRICAN QUEEN, THE ..... SIR JOHN WOOLF
AFTER HOURS ..... GRIFFIN DUNNE
AFTER HOURS ..... ROBERT F. COLESBERRY
AFTER HOURS ..... AMY ROBINSON
AFTER MIDNIGHT ..... ALLAN DENNIS
AFTER MIDNIGHT ..... BARRY J. HIRSCH
AFTER MIDNIGHT ..... JIM WHEAT
AFTER MIDNIGHT ..... KEN WHEAT
AFTER MIDNIGHT ..... PETER GREENE
AFTER MIDNIGHT ..... RICHARD ARLOOK
AFTER THE FOX ..... JOHN BRYAN
AGAINST ALL ODDS ..... BILL BORDEN
AGAINST ALL ODDS ..... JERRY BICK
AGAINST ALL ODDS ..... TAYLOR HACKFORD
AGAINST ALL ODDS ..... WILLIAM S. GILMORE
AGENCY ..... ROBERT BAYLIS
AGENCY ..... ROBERT LANTOS
AGENCY ..... STEPHEN J. ROTH
AGNES OF GOD ..... BONNIE PALEF
AGNES OF GOD ..... CHARLES MILHAUPT
AGNES OF GOD ..... NORMAN JEWISON
AGNES OF GOD ..... PATRICK PALMER
AIRPLANE! ..... HUNT LOWRY
AIRPLANE! ..... HOWARD W. KOCH
AIRPLANE! ..... JON DAVISON
AIRPLANE! ..... JERRY ZUCKER
AIRPLANE! ..... DAVID ZUCKER
AIRPLANE! ..... JIM ABRAHAMS
AIRPLANE II: THE SEQUEL ..... HOWARD W. KOCH
AIRPORT '75 ..... JENNINGS LANG
AIRPORT '77 ..... WILLIAM FRYE
AIRPORT '77 ..... JENNINGS LANG
ALAMBRISTA! ..... MICHAEL HAUSMAN
ALAMO BAY ..... LOUIS MALLE
ALAMO BAY ..... ROSS E. MILLOY
ALAMO BAY ..... VINCENT MALLE
ALAN QUATERMAIN AND THE LOST CITY OF GOLD ..... AVI LERNER
ALAN QUATERMAIN AND THE LOST CITY OF GOLD ..... MENAHEM GOLAN
ALAN QUATERMAIN AND THE LOST CITY OF GOLD ..... MICHAEL GREENBURG
ALAN QUATERMAIN AND THE LOST CITY OF GOLD ..... YORAM GLOBUS
ALEX & THE GYPSY ..... RICHARD SHEPHERD
ALEX IN WONDERLAND ..... LARRY TUCKER
ALEX IN WONDERLAND ..... TONY RAY
ALFIE ..... LEWIS GILBERT
ALIEN ..... RONALD SHUSETT
ALIEN ..... WALTER HILL
ALIEN ..... DAVID GILER
ALIEN ..... GORDON CARROLL
ALIENS ..... DAVID GILER
ALIENS ..... GORDON CARROLL
ALIENS ..... WALTER HILL
ALIENS ..... GALE ANNE HURD
ALIEN FROM L.A. ..... AVI LERNER
ALIEN FROM L.A. ..... MENAHEM GOLAN
ALIEN FROM L.A. ..... YORAM GLOBUS
ALIEN NATION ..... GALE ANNE HURD
ALIEN NATION ..... RICHARD KOBRITZ
ALIEN PREDATOR ..... CARLOS AURED
ALIEN PREDATOR ..... DERAN SARAFIAN
ALIEN PREDATOR ..... MICHAEL SOURAPAS
ALL DOGS GO TO HEAVEN ..... DON BLUTH
ALL DOGS GO TO HEAVEN ..... GARY GOLDMAN
ALL DOGS GO TO HEAVEN ..... GEORGE A. WALKER
ALL DOGS GO TO HEAVEN ..... JOHN POMEROY
ALL DOGS GO TO HEAVEN ..... MORRIS F. SULLIVAN
ALL NEAT IN BLACK STOCKINGS ..... LEON CLORE
ALL NIGHT LONG ..... LEONARD J. GOLDBERG
ALL NIGHT LONG ..... JERRY WEINTRAUB
ALL OF ME ..... STEPHEN J. FRIEDMAN
ALL OF ME ..... PHIL ALDEN ROBINSON
ALL THAT JAZZ ..... KENNETH UTT
ALL THAT JAZZ ..... WOLFGANG GLATTES
ALL THAT JAZZ ..... DANIEL MELNICK
...ALL THE MARBLES ..... WILLIAM ALDRICH
ALL THE PRESIDENT'S MEN ..... WALTER COBLENZ
ALL THE RIGHT MOVES ..... GARY MORTON
ALL THE RIGHT MOVES ..... PHILLIP GOLDFARB
ALL THE RIGHT MOVES ..... STEPHEN DEUTSCH
ALL'S FAIR ..... DAVID G. STERN
ALL'S FAIR ..... JON GORDON
ALLNIGHTER, THE ..... JAMES L. STEWART
ALLNIGHTER, THE ..... NANCY ISRAEL
ALLNIGHTER, THE ..... TAMAR SIMON HOFFS
ALMOST PERFECT AFFAIR, AN ..... TERRY CARR
ALMOST SUMMER ..... ROB COHEN
ALMOST SUMMER ..... STEVE TISCH
ALMOST YOU ..... CHARLES C. THIERIOT
ALMOST YOU ..... MARK LIPSON
ALMOST YOU ..... SANDY CLIMAN
ALMOST YOU ..... STEPHEN J. LEVIN
ALOHA SUMMER ..... EUGENE MAZZOLA
ALOHA SUMMER ..... MIKE GRECO
ALOHA SUMMER ..... WARREN CHANEY
ALONE IN THE DARK ..... ROBERT SHAYE
ALPHA BETA ..... TIMOTHY BURRILL
ALPHABET CITY ..... ANDREW BRAUNSBERG
ALPHABET CITY ..... MICHAEL ROSENBLATT
ALPHABET CITY ..... THOMAS COLEMAN
ALTERED STATES ..... HOWARD GOTTFRIED
ALTERED STATES ..... DANIEL MELNICK
ALWAYS ..... FRANK MARSHALL
ALWAYS ..... JUDITH WOLINSKY
ALWAYS ..... KATHLEEN KENNEDY
ALWAYS ..... RICHARD VANE
ALWAYS ..... STEVEN SPIELBERG
AMADEUS ..... SAUL ZAENTZ
AMADEUS ..... MICHAEL HAUSMAN
AMARCORD ..... FRANCO CRISTALDI
AMATEUR, THE ..... GARTH DRABINSKY
AMATEUR, THE ..... JOEL B. MICHAELS
AMAZING GRACE AND CHUCK ..... DAVID FIELD
AMAZING GRACE AND CHUCK ..... ROGER M. ROTHSTEIN†
AMAZON WOMEN ON THE MOON ..... GEORGE FOLSEY JR.
AMAZON WOMEN ON THE MOON ..... ROBERT K. WEISS
AMBASSADOR, THE ..... ITZIK KOL
AMBASSADOR, THE ..... MENAHEM GOLAN
AMBASSADOR, THE ..... YORAM GLOBUS
AMERICA 3000 ..... MENAHEM GOLAN
AMERICA 3000 ..... YORAM GLOBUS
AMERICA, AMERICA ..... ELIA KAZAN
AMERICAN ANTHEM ..... DOUG CHAPIN
AMERICAN ANTHEM ..... FREDDIE FIELDS
AMERICAN ANTHEM ..... ROBERT L. SCHAFFEL
AMERICAN DREAMER ..... BARRY KROST
AMERICAN DREAMER ..... DOUG CHAPIN
AMERICAN FLYERS ..... GARETH WIGAN
AMERICAN FLYERS ..... GREGG CHAMPION

AMERICAN FLYERS ... PAULA WEINSTEIN
AMERICAN GIGOLO ... FREDDIE FIELDS
AMERICAN GIGOLO ... JERRY BRUCKHEIMER
AMERICAN GOTHIC ... GEORGE WALKER
AMERICAN GOTHIC ... JOHN QUESTED
AMERICAN GOTHIC ... MICHAEL MANLEY
AMERICAN GOTHIC ... RAY HOMER
AMERICAN GRAFFITI ... FRANCIS FORD COPPOLA
AMERICAN GRAFFITI ... GARY KURTZ
AMERICAN HOT WAX ... ART LINSON
AMERICAN NINJA ... MENAHEM GOLAN
AMERICAN NINJA ... YORAM GLOBUS
AMERICAN NINJA 2 ... AVI LERNER
AMERICAN NINJA 2 ... MENAHEM GOLAN
AMERICAN NINJA 2 ... YORAM GLOBUS
AMERICAN NINJA 3: BLOOD HUNT ... AVI LERNER
AMERICAN NINJA 3: BLOOD HUNT ... HARRY ALAN TOWERS
AMERICAN POP ... RICHARD R. ST. JOHNS
AMERICAN POP ... ROY BAIRD
AMERICAN POP ... MARTIN RANSOHOFF
AMERICAN SUCCESS COMPANY, THE ... DANIEL H. BLATT
AMERICAN SUCCESS COMPANY, THE ... EDGAR J. SCHERICK
AMERICAN TAIL, AN ... DAVID KIRSCHNER
AMERICAN TAIL, AN ... DON BLUTH
AMERICAN TAIL, AN ... FRANK MARSHALL
AMERICAN TAIL, AN ... GARY GOLDMAN
AMERICAN TAIL, AN ... JOHN POMEROY
AMERICAN TAIL, AN ... KATHLEEN KENNEDY
AMERICAN TAIL, AN ... STEVEN SPIELBERG
AMERICAN WEREWOLF IN LONDON, AN ... GEORGE FOLSEY JR.
AMERICAN WEREWOLF IN LONDON, AN ... JON PETERS
AMERICAN WEREWOLF IN LONDON, AN ... PETER GUBER
AMERICANIZATION OF EMILY, THE ... MARTIN RANSOHOFF
AMERICATHON ... EDWARD ROSEN
AMERICATHON ... JOE ROTH
AMITYVILLE HORROR , THE ... SAMUEL Z. ARKOFF
AMITYVILLE II: THE POSSESSION ... BERNARD WILLIAMS
AMITYVILLE II: THE POSSESSION ... STEPHEN R. GREENWALD
AMITYVILLE II:THE POSSESSION ... IRA N. SMITH
AMY ... JEROME COURTLAND
AMY ... WILLIAM ROBERT YATES
AND GOD CREATED WOMAN ... EMILIA CROW
AND GOD CREATED WOMAN ... GEORGE BRAUNSTEIN
AND GOD CREATED WOMAN ... MITCHELL CANNOLD
AND GOD CREATED WOMAN ... PATRICK MCCORMICK
AND GOD CREATED WOMAN ... ROBERT CROW
AND GOD CREATED WOMAN ... RON HAMADY
AND GOD CREATED WOMAN ... RUTH VITALE
AND GOD CREATED WOMAN ... STEVEN REUTHER
AND JUSTICE FOR ALL ... NORMAN JEWISON
AND JUSTICE FOR ALL ... PATRICK PALMER
AND JUSTICE FOR ALL ... JOE WIZAN
ANDROID ... BARRY OPPER
ANDROID ... MARY ANN FISHER
ANDROID ... RUPERT HARVEY
ANDY & THE AIRWAVE RANGERS ... ROGER CORMAN
ANDY & THE AIRWAVE RANGERS ... TED HOROVITZ
ANDY WARHOL'S DRACULA ... ANDREW BRAUNSBERG
ANDY WARHOL'S DRACULA ... CARLO PONTI
ANDY WARHOL'S FRANKENSTEIN ... ANDREW BRAUNSBERG
ANDY WARHOL'S FRANKENSTEIN ... CARLO PONTI
ANGEL ... DONALD P. BORCHERS
ANGEL ... ROY WATTS
ANGEL HEART ... ALAN MARSHALL
ANGEL HEART ... ANDREW VAJNA
ANGEL HEART ... MARIO KASSAR
ANGEL HEART ... ELLIOTT KASTNER
ANGEL III: THE FINAL CHAPTER ... ARNOLD ORGOLINI
ANGEL III: THE FINAL CHAPTER ... DON LEVIN
ANGEL III: THE FINAL CHAPTER ... MEL PEARL
ANGEL LEVINE, THE ... CHIZ SCHULTZ
ANGEL LEVINE, THE ... KENNETH UTT
ANGEL TOWN ... ANDERS P. JENSEN
ANGEL TOWN ... ASH R. SHAH
ANGEL TOWN ... ERIC KARSON
ANGEL TOWN ... SUNDIP R. SHAH
ANGEL TOWN ... SUNIL R. SHAH
ANGELA ... CLAUDE HEROUX
ANGELA ... JULIAN MELZACK
ANGELA ... ZEV BRAUN
ANGELO MY LOVE ... ROBERT DUVALL
ANGELS HARD AS THEY COME ... JOE VIOLA
ANGELS HARD AS THEY COME ... JONATHAN DEMME
ANIMAL WORLD, THE ... IRWIN ALLEN
ANNA ... DEIRDRE GAINOR
ANNA ... JULIANNE GILLIAM
ANNA ... YUREK BOGAYEVICZ
ANNA ... ZANNE DEVINE
ANNAPOLIS STORY, AN ... WALTER MIRISCH
ANNIE ... JOE LAYTON
ANNIE ... RAY STARK
ANNIE HALL ... CHARLES H. JOFFE
ANNIE HALL ... ROBERT GREENHUT
ANNIE'S COMING OUT ... DON MURRAY
ANOTHER 48 HOURS ... D. CONSTANTINE CONTE
ANOTHER 48 HOURS ... LAWRENCE GORDON
ANOTHER 48 HOURS ... MARK LIPSKY
ANOTHER 48 HOURS ... RALPH S. SINGLETON
ANOTHER 48 HOURS ... ROBERT D. WACHS
ANOTHER COUNTRY ... ALAN MARSHALL
ANOTHER COUNTRY ... ROBERT FOX
ANOTHER COUNTRY ... JULIAN SEYMOUR
ANOTHER TIME, ANOTHER PLACE ... PAUL COWAN
ANOTHER TIME, ANOTHER PLACE ... SIMON PERRY
ANOTHER TIME, ANOTHER PLACE ... TIMOTHY BURRILL
ANY WEDNESDAY ... JULIUS J. EPSTEIN
ANY WHICH WAY YOU CAN ... FRITZ MANES
ANY WHICH WAY YOU CAN ... ROBERT DALEY
APARTMENT ZERO ... BRIAN ALLMAN
APARTMENT ZERO ... DAVID KOEPP
APARTMENT ZERO ... MARTIN DONOVAN
APARTMENT ZERO ... STEPHEN J. COLE
APARTMENT, THE ... BILLY WILDER
APOCALYPSE NOW ... FRANCIS FORD COPPOLA
APOCALYPSE NOW ... GRAY FREDERICKSON
APOCALYPSE NOW ... FRED ROOS
APOCALYPSE NOW ... TOM STERNBERG
APPLE DUMPLING GANG, THE ... BILL ANDERSON
APPLE DUMPLING GANG RIDES AGAIN, THE ... RON MILLER
APPLE DUMPLING GANG RIDES AGAIN, THE ... TOM LEETCH
APPOINTMENT WITH DEATH ... MENAHEM GOLAN
APPOINTMENT WITH DEATH ... MOUSTAPHA AKKAD
APPOINTMENT WITH DEATH ... TOM BOUTROSS
APPOINTMENT WITH DEATH ... YORAM GLOBUS
APPOINTMENT, THE ... MARTIN POLL
APPRENTICE TO MURDER ... HOWARD K. GROSSMAN
APPRENTICE TO MURDER ... MICHAEL JAY RAUCH
APPRENTICESHIP OF DUDDY KRAVITZ, THE ... JOHN KEMENY
APRIL FOOL'S DAY ... FRANK MANCUSO JR.
APRIL FOOLS, THE ... GORDON CARROLL
ARABESQUE ... STANLEY DONEN
ARABIAN NIGHTS ... ALBERTO GRIMALDI
ARIA ... AL CLARK
ARIA ... CHARLES MITCHELL
ARIA ... DON BOYD
ARIA ... MIKE WATTS
ARIA ... ROBERT DEVEREUX
ARIA ... TOM KUHN
ARMED AND DANGEROUS ... BRIAN GRAZER
ARMED AND DANGEROUS ... JAMES KEACH
ARMED RESPONSE ... FRED OLEN RAY
ARMED RESPONSE ... LISA M. HANSEN
ARMED RESPONSE ... PAUL HERTZBERG
AROUSERS, THE ... TAMARA ASSEYEV
AROUSERS, THE ... RAMSEY THOMAS
ARRANGEMENT, THE ... ELIA KAZAN
ARRANGEMENT, THE ... SIDNEY LUMET
ARROGANT, THE ... PHILIPPE BLOT
ARROGANT, THE ... RICK NATHANSON
ARTHUR ... CHARLES H. JOFFE
ARTHUR ... ROBERT GREENHUT
ARTHUR 2 ON THE ROCKS ... DUDLEY MOORE
ARTHUR 2 ON THE ROCKS ... ROBERT SHAPIRO
ARTHUR'S HALLOWED GROUND ... CHRIS GRIFFIN
ASSASSINATION ... MENAHEM GOLAN
ASSASSINATION ... PANCHO KOHNER
ASSASSINATION ... YORAM GLOBUS
ASSISI UNDERGROUND, THE ... JOHN THOMPSON
ASSISI UNDERGROUND, THE ... MENAHEM GOLAN
ASSISI UNDERGROUND, THE ... YORAM GLOBUS
AT CLOSE RANGE ... DON GUEST
AT CLOSE RANGE ... ELLIOTT LEWITT
AT CLOSE RANGE ... DEREK GIBSON
AT CLOSE RANGE ... JOHN DALY
AT LONG LAST LOVE ... FRANK MARSHALL
AT LONG LAST LOVE ... PETER BOGDANOVICH
ATLANTIC CITY ... DENIS HEROUX
ATLANTIC CITY ... GABRIEL BOUSTANI
ATLANTIC CITY ... JOSEPH BEAUBIEN
ATLANTIC CITY ... LAWRENCE NESIS
AUDREY ROSE ... JOE WIZAN
AUNT JULIA AND THE SCRIPTWRITER ... JOHN FIEDLER
AUNT JULIA AND THE SCRIPTWRITER ... JOSEPH M. CARACCIOLO
AUNT JULIA AND THE SCRIPTWRITER ... MARK TARLOV
AUTHOR! AUTHOR! ... ROBERT CHARTOFF
AUTHOR! AUTHOR! ... IRWIN WINKLER
AUTUMN SONATA ... MARTIN STARGER
AVALANCHE ... ROGER CORMAN
AVALANCHE EXPRESS ... MERV ADELSON
AVANTI! ... ALBERTO GRIMALDI
AVANTI! ... BILLY WILDER
AVENGING ANGEL ... JOEL SOISSON
AVENGING ANGEL ... KEITH RUBINSTEIN
AVENGING ANGEL ... MICHAEL S. MURPHEY
AVENGING ANGEL ... SANDY HOWARD
AVENGING FORCE ... MENAHEM GOLAN
AVENGING FORCE ... YORAM GLOBUS
AVIATOR, THE ... MACE NEUFELD
AVIATOR, THE ... THOMAS H. BRODEK
AWAKENING, THE ... ANDREW SCHEINMAN
AWAKENING, THE ... MARTIN SHAFER
AWAKENING, THE ... ROBERT H. SOLO
AWAKENINGS ... ARNE L. SCHMIDT
AWAKENINGS ... ELLIOT ABBOTT
AWAKENINGS ... LAWRENCE LASKER
AWAKENINGS ... WALTER F. PARKES

B

BABAR: THE MOVIE ... CLIVE A. SMITH
BABAR: THE MOVIE ... MICHAEL HIRSH
BABAR: THE MOVIE ... PATRICK LOUBERT
BABAR: THE MOVIE ... PIERRE BERTRAND-JAUME
BABAR: THE MOVIE ... STEPHANE SPERRY
BABAR: THE MOVIE ... YANNICK BERNARD
BABETTE'S FEAST ... BO CHRISTENSEN
BABETTE'S FEAST ... JUST BETZER
BABY BLUE MARINE ... LEONARD J. GOLDBERG
BABY BLUE MARINE ... AARON SPELLING
BABY BOOM ... NANCY MEYERS
BABY IT'S YOU ... GRIFFIN DUNNE
BABY IT'S YOU ... AMY ROBINSON
BABY IT'S YOU ... ROBERT F. COLESBERRY
BABY, THE RAIN MUST FALL ... ALAN J. PAKULA
BABY...SECRET OF THE LOST LEGEND ... JONATHAN T. TAPLIN
BABY...SECRET OF THE LOST LEGEND ... ROGER SPOTTISWOODE
BACHELOR PARTY ... JOE ROTH
BACHELOR PARTY ... ROBERT ISRAEL
BACHELOR PARTY ... RON MOLER
BACK ROADS ... RONALD SHEDLO
BACK TO SCHOOL ... CHUCK RUSSELL
BACK TO SCHOOL ... ESTELLE ENDLER†
BACK TO SCHOOL ... HAROLD RAMIS
BACK TO SCHOOL ... MICHAEL ENDLER
BACK TO THE BEACH ... ANNETTE FUNICELLO
BACK TO THE BEACH ... FRANK MANCUSO JR.
BACK TO THE BEACH ... FRANKIE AVALON
BACK TO THE FUTURE ... BOB GALE
BACK TO THE FUTURE ... KATHLEEN KENNEDY
BACK TO THE FUTURE ... NEIL CANTON
BACK TO THE FUTURE ... FRANK MARSHALL
BACK TO THE FUTURE ... STEVEN SPIELBERG
BACK TO THE FUTURE II ... BOB GALE
BACK TO THE FUTURE II ... FRANK MARSHALL
BACK TO THE FUTURE II ... KATHLEEN KENNEDY
BACK TO THE FUTURE II ... NEIL CANTON
BACK TO THE FUTURE II ... STEVEN SPIELBERG
BACK TO THE FUTURE III ... BOB GALE
BACK TO THE FUTURE III ... FRANK MARSHALL
BACK TO THE FUTURE III ... KATHLEEN KENNEDY
BACK TO THE FUTURE III ... NEIL CANTON
BACK TO THE FUTURE III ... STEVEN SPIELBERG
BACKLASH ... BILL BENNETT
BACKSTAGE ... DENNIS WRIGHT
BACKSTAGE ... GEOFF BURROWES
BACKSTAGE ... KENT C. LOVELL
BACKSTREET STRAYS ... LANCE H. ROBBINS
BAD BOYS ... MARTIN HORNSTEIN
BAD BOYS ... ROBERT H. SOLO
BAD COMPANY ... STANLEY R. JAFFE
BAD DREAMS ... GALE ANNE HURD
BAD DREAMS ... GINNY NUGENT
BAD INFLUENCE ... BERNIE GOLDMANN
BAD INFLUENCE ... MORRIE EISENMANN

BAD INFLUENCE ... RICHARD BECKER
BAD INFLUENCE ... STEVE TISCH
BAD MEDICINE ... JEFFREY GANZ
BAD MEDICINE ... MICHAEL JAFFE
BAD MEDICINE ... MYLES OSTERNECK
BAD MEDICINE ... SAM MANNERS
BAD MEDICINE ... ALEX WINITSKY
BAD MEDICINE ... ARLENE SELLERS
BAD NEWS BEARS GO TO JAPAN, THE ... TERRY CARR
BAD NEWS BEARS IN BREAKING TRAINING, THE ... LEONARD J. GOLDBERG
BAD NEWS BEARS, THE ... STANLEY R. JAFFE
BADGE 373 ... HOWARD W. KOCH
BADLANDS ... EDWARD R. PRESSMAN
BAGDAD CAFE ... ELEONORE ADLON
BAGDAD CAFE ... PERCY ADLON
BAIL JUMPER ... JESSICA SALEH HUNT
BAIL JUMPER ... JOSEPHINE WALLACE
BAJA OKLAHOMA ... HUNT LOWRY
BAJA OKLAHOMA ... MARYKAY POWELL
BALCONY, THE ... BEN MADDOW
BALCONY, THE ... JOSEPH STRICK
BALLAD OF CABLE HOGUE, THE ... PHIL FELDMAN
BALLAD OF CABLE HOGUE, THE ... WILLIAM FARALLA
BALLAD OF GREGORIO CORTEZ, THE ... DAVID WISNIEVITZ
BALLAD OF GREGORIO CORTEZ, THE ... MOCTESUMA ESPARZA
BALLAD OF GREGORIO CORTEZ, THE ... MICHAEL HAUSMAN
BANANAS ... CHARLES H. JOFFE
BANANAS ... JACK GROSSBERG
BAND OF THE HAND ... MICHAEL JAY RAUCH
BAND OF THE HAND ... MICHAEL MANN
BANDIT OF ZHOBE, THE ... ALBERT R. BROCCOLI
BANDIT OF ZHOBE, THE ... IRVING ALLEN†
BANG THE DRUM SLOWLY ... BILL BADALATO
BANG THE DRUM SLOWLY ... LOIS ROSENFIELD
BANG THE DRUM SLOWLY ... MAURICE ROSENFIELD
BANK SHOT, THE ... BOBBY ROBERTS
BANK SHOT, THE ... HAL LANDERS
BARBARELLA ... DINO DE LAURENTIIS
BARBARIAN QUEEN ... ALEX SESSA
BARBARIAN QUEEN ... FRANK ISAAC
BARBARIAN QUEEN ... ROGER CORMAN
BARBARIANS, THE ... JOHN THOMPSON
BARBAROSA ... PAUL N. LAZARUS III
BARBAROSA ... WILLIAM D. WITTLIFF
BARBAROSA ... MARTIN STARGER
BAREFOOT EXECUTIVE, THE ... BILL ANDERSON
BARFLY ... BARBET SCHROEDER
BARFLY ... JACK BARAN
BARFLY ... MENAHEM GOLAN
BARFLY ... YORAM GLOBUS
BARFLY ... TOM LUDDY
BARFLY ... FRED ROOS
BARRY LYNDON ... JAN HARLAN
BARRY LYNDON ... BERNARD WILLIAMS
BARRY LYNDON ... STANLEY KUBRICK
BASIC TRAINING ... GILBERT ADLER
BASIC TRAINING ... OTTO SALAMON
BASKET CASE ... EDGAR IEVINS
BASKET CASE 2 ... EDGAR IEVINS
BASKET CASE 2 ... JAMES GLICKENHAUS
BAT 21 ... DAVID FISHER
BAT 21 ... DAVID SAUNDERS
BAT 21 ... EVZEN W. KOLAR
BAT 21 ... GARY A. NEILL
BAT 21 ... JERRY REED
BAT 21 ... MARK DAMON
BAT 21 ... MICHAEL BALSON
BATMAN ... BENJAMIN MELNIKER
BATMAN ... CHRIS KENNY
BATMAN ... JON PETERS
BATMAN ... MICHAEL USLAN
BATMAN ... PETER GUBER
BATTERIES NOT INCLUDED ... GERALD R. MOLEN
BATTERIES NOT INCLUDED ... KATHLEEN KENNEDY
BATTERIES NOT INCLUDED ... RONALD L. SCHWARY
BATTERIES NOT INCLUDED ... FRANK MARSHALL
BATTERIES NOT INCLUDED ... STEVEN SPIELBERG
BATTLE BEYOND THE STARS ... ROGER CORMAN
BATTLE BEYOND THE STARS ... ED CARLIN
BATTLE BEYOND THE SUN ... ROGER CORMAN
BATTLE FOR THE PLANET OF THE APES ... FRANK CAPRA JR.
BATTLE OF BRITAIN, THE ... HARRY SALTZMAN
BATTLE OF BRITAIN, THE ... S. BENJAMIN FISZ†
BATTLE TRUCK ... LLOYD PHILLIPS
BAY BOY, THE ... DENIS HEROUX
BAY BOY, THE ... FRANK JACOBS
BAY BOY, THE ... JOHN KEMENY
BAY BOY, THE ... RENE CLEITMAN
BAY BOY, THE ... SUSAN CAVAN
BEACH BALL ... ROGER CORMAN
BEACH BLANKET BINGO ... SAMUEL Z. ARKOFF
BEACH BLANKET BINGO ... JAMES H. NICHOLSON†
BEACH PARTY ... SAMUEL Z. ARKOFF
BEACHES ... BETTE MIDLER
BEACHES ... BONNIE BRUCKHEIMER-MARTELL
BEACHES ... MARGARET JENNINGS SOUTH
BEACHES ... TERI SCHWARTZ
BEACHES ... NICK ABDO
BEAST WITHIN, THE ... GABRIEL KATZKA†
BEAST WITHIN, THE ... HARVEY BERNHARD
BEAST, THE ... DALE POLLOCK
BEAST, THE ... GIL FRIESEN
BEAST, THE ... JOHN FIEDLER
BEAT STREET ... DAVID V. PICKER
BEAT STREET ... HARRY BELAFONTE
BEAT THE DEVIL ... SIR JOHN WOOLF
BEAT, THE ... JON KILIK
BEAT, THE ... JULIA PHILLIPS
BEAT, THE ... LAWRENCE KASANOFF
BEAT, THE ... NICK WECHSLER
BEAT, THE ... RUTH VITALE
BEATLEMANIA ... DAVID KREBS
BEATLEMANIA ... EDIE LANDAU
BEATLEMANIA ... STEVEN LEBER
BEATLEMANIA ... ELY LANDAU
BEAUTY AND THE BEAST ... ITZIK KOL
BEAUTY AND THE BEAST ... MENAHEM GOLAN
BEAUTY AND THE BEAST ... YORAM GLOBUS
BEAUTY AND THE BEAST ... HANK MOONJEAN
BED-SITTING ROOM, THE ... OSCAR LEWENSTEIN
BED-SITTING ROOM, THE ... RICHARD LESTER
BED-SITTING ROOM, THE ... ROY STEVENS
BEDAZZLED ... STANLEY DONEN
BEDFORD INCIDENT, THE ... JAMES B. HARRIS
BEDROOM EYES ... ROBERT LANTOS
BEDROOM EYES ... STEPHEN J. ROTH
BEDROOM WINDOW, THE ... MARTHA SCHUMACHER
BEDROOM WINDOW, THE ... ROBERT TOWNE
BEER ... JAMES D. BRUBAKER
BEER ... ROBERT CHARTOFF
BEETLEJUICE ... LARRY WILSON
BEETLEJUICE ... MICHAEL BENDER
BEETLEJUICE ... RICHARD HASHIMOTO
BEGINNERS LUCK ... CAROLINE MOURIS
BEGUILED, THE ... JENNINGS LANG
BEING THERE ... ANDREW BRAUNSBERG
BEING THERE ... JACK SCHWARTZMAN
BELIEVE IN ME ... ROBERT CHARTOFF
BELIEVE IN ME ... IRWIN WINKLER
BELIEVERS, THE ... BEVERLY J. CAMHE
BELIEVERS, THE ... EDWARD TEETS
BELIEVERS, THE ... JOHN SCHLESINGER
BELIEVERS, THE ... MICHAEL CHILDERS
BELIZAIRE THE CAJUN ... ALLAN L. DURAND
BELIZAIRE THE CAJUN ... GLEN PITRE
BELIZAIRE THE CAJUN ... JAMES B. LEVERT JR.
BELIZAIRE THE CAJUN ... SANDRA SCHULBERG
BELLMAN AND TRUE ... CHRISTOPHER NEAME
BELLMAN AND TRUE ... DENIS O'BRIEN
BELLMAN AND TRUE ... GEORGE HARRISON
BELLMAN AND TRUE ... JOHN HAMBLEY
BELLMAN AND TRUE ... JOHNNY GOODMAN
BELLMAN AND TRUE ... MICHAEL WEARING
BENEATH THE PLANET OF THE APES ... MORT ABRAHAMS
BENJI THE HUNTED ... BEN VAUGHN
BENJI THE HUNTED ... CAROLYN CAMP
BENJI THE HUNTED ... ED VANSTON
BERMUDA TRIANGLE, THE ... CHARLES E. SELLIER JR.
BERT RIGBY, YOU'RE A FOOL ... GEORGE SHAPIRO
BEST DEFENSE ... GLORIA KATZ
BEST FRIENDS ... JOE WIZAN
BEST FRIENDS ... NORMAN JEWISON
BEST LITTLE WHOREHOUSE IN TEXAS, THE ... ROBERT BOYETT
BEST LITTLE WHOREHOUSE IN TEXAS, THE ... EDWARD K. MILKIS
BEST LITTLE WHOREHOUSE IN TEXAS, THE ... PETER MACGREGOR-SCOTT
BEST MAN, THE ... STUART MILLAR
BEST OF THE BEST ... FRANK GIUSTRA
BEST OF THE BEST ... JEFF RINGLER
BEST OF THE BEST ... MARLON STAGGS
BEST OF THE BEST ... MICHAEL HOLZMAN
BEST OF THE BEST ... PETER E. STRAUSS
BEST OF THE BEST ... PHILLIP RHEE
BEST OF TIMES, THE ... GORDON CARROLL
BEST SELLER ... DEREK GIBSON
BEST SELLER ... CARTER DE HAVEN
BEST SELLER ... JOHN DALY
BETRAYAL ... ERIC RATTRAY
BETRAYAL ... STEVEN HAFT
BETRAYED ... HAL W. POLAIRE
BETRAYED ... IRWIN WINKLER
BETRAYED ... JOE ESZTERHAS
BETSY, THE ... JACK GROSSBERG
BETTER LATE THAN NEVER ... JACK HALEY JR.
BETTER LATE THAN NEVER ... RAYMOND CHOW
BETTER LATE THAN NEVER ... DAVID NIVEN, JR.
BETTER OFF DEAD ... ANDREW MEYER
BETTER OFF DEAD ... GIL FRIESEN
BETTER OFF DEAD ... MICHAEL JAFFE
BETTER WATCH OUT ... PATRICIA FOULKROD
BETWEEN THE LINES ... RAPHAEL D. SILVER
BEVERLY HILLS BRATS ... JERRY RIVERS
BEVERLY HILLS BRATS ... RUPERT A. L. PERRIN
BEVERLY HILLS BRATS ... TERRY MOORE
BEVERLY HILLS COP ... DON SIMPSON
BEVERLY HILLS COP ... MICHAEL MODER
BEVERLY HILLS COP ... JERRY BRUCKHEIMER
BEVERLY HILLS COP II ... RICHARD TIENKEN
BEVERLY HILLS COP II ... ROBERT D. WACHS
BEVERLY HILLS COP II ... DON SIMPSON
BEVERLY HILLS COP II ... JERRY BRUCKHEIMER
BEYOND & BACK ... CHARLES E. SELLIER JR.
BEYOND REASON ... HOWARD W. KOCH
BEYOND THE DOOR ... OBIDIO G. ASSONITIS
BEYOND THE LIMIT ... JOHN HEYMAN
BEYOND THE LIMIT ... NORMA HEYMAN
BEYOND THE POSEIDON ADVENTURE ... IRWIN ALLEN
BEYOND THE REEF ... RAFFAELLA DE LAURENTIIS
BEYOND THERAPY ... ROGER BERLIND
BEYOND THERAPY ... SCOTT BUSHNELL
BEYOND THERAPY ... STEVEN HAFT
BIBLE, THE ... DINO DE LAURENTIIS
BIDDY ... RICHARD GOODWIN
BIG ... ANNE SPIELBERG
BIG ... GARY ROSS
BIG ... JAMES L. BROOKS
BIG ... ROBERT GREENHUT
BIG BAD MAMA ... ROGER CORMAN
BIG BAD MAMA II ... MATT LEIPZIG
BIG BAD MAMA II ... ROGER CORMAN
BIG BANG, THE ... JOSEPH H. KANTER
BIG BLUE, THE ... PATRICE LEDOUX
BIG BUS, THE ... FRED FREEMAN
BIG BUS, THE ... JULIA PHILLIPS
BIG BUS, THE ... LAWRENCE J. COHEN
BIG BUS, THE ... MICHAEL PHILLIPS
BIG BUSINESS ... STEVE TISCH
BIG BUSINESS ... MICHAEL PEYSER
BIG CHILL, THE ... BARRIE M. OSBORNE
BIG CHILL, THE ... LAWRENCE KASDAN
BIG CHILL, THE ... MARCIA NASATIR
BIG CHILL, THE ... MICHAEL SHAMBERG
BIG COUNTRY ... ARNE L. SCHMIDT
BIG EASY, THE ... MORT ENGELBERG
BIG MAN ON CAMPUS ... ARNON MILCHAN
BIG MAN ON CAMPUS ... MARK LEVINSON
BIG MAN ON CAMPUS ... MITCHELL CANNOLD
BIG MAN ON CAMPUS ... STEVEN REUTHER
BIG MAN ON CAMPUS ... SUSAN VOGELFANG
BIG MAN ON CAMPUS ... SCOTT ROSENFELT
BIG PICTURE, THE ... MICHAEL VARHOL
BIG PICTURE, THE ... RICHARD GILBERT ABRAMSON
BIG RED ONE, THE ... GENE CORMAN
BIG RED ONE, THE ... LEE RICH
BIG RED ONE, THE ... MERV ADELSON
BIG SCORE, THE ... ALBERT SCHWARTZ
BIG SCORE, THE ... DAVID FORBES
BIG SCORE, THE ... HARRY HURWITZ
BIG SCORE, THE ... MICHAEL S. LANDES
BIG SHOTS ... IVAN REITMAN
BIG SHOTS ... JOE MEDJUCK
BIG SHOTS ... MICHAEL C. GROSS
BIG SLEEP, THE ... BERNARD WILLIAMS
BIG SLEEP, THE ... ELLIOTT KASTNER
BIG SLEEP, THE ... MICHAEL WINNER
BIG TIME ... CHRIS BLACKWELL
BIG TIME ... LUC ROEG
BIG TOP PEE-WEE ... DEBRA HILL
BIG TOP PEE-WEE ... PAUL REUBENS
BIG TOP PEE-WEE ... RICHARD GILBERT ABRAMSON
BIG TOWN, THE ... GENE KRAFT
BIG TOWN, THE ... DON CARMODY
BIG TOWN, THE ... MARTIN RANSOHOFF
BIG TROUBLE ... MICHAEL LOBELL

BIG TROUBLE IN LITTLE CHINA ... LARRY J. FRANCO
BIG TROUBLE IN LITTLE CHINA ... PAUL MONASH
BIG WEDNESDAY ... TAMARA ASSEYEV
BIG WEDNESDAY ... ALEXANDRA ROSE
BIG WEDNESDAY ... BUZZ FEITSHANS
BIKINI BEACH ... SAMUEL Z. ARKOFF
BIKINI BEACH ... JAMES H. NICHOLSON†
BIKINI SHOP, THE ... ANDREW BULLIANS
BIKINI SHOP, THE ... CHARLES C. THIERIOT
BIKINI SHOP, THE ... GARY MEHLMAN
BIKINI SHOP, THE ... J. KENNETH ROTCOP
BIKINI SHOP, THE ... JEAN BULLIANS
BIKINI SHOP, THE ... LEO LEICHTER
BIKINI SHOP, THE ... SANDY CLIMAN
BILL AND TED'S EXCELLENT ADVENTURE ... JOEL SOISSON
BILL AND TED'S EXCELLENT ADVENTURE ... MICHAEL S. MURPHEY
BILL AND TED'S EXCELLENT ADVENTURE ... ROBERT W. CORT
BILL AND TED'S EXCELLENT ADVENTURE ... SCOTT KROOPF
BILL AND TED'S EXCELLENT ADVENTURE ... STEPHEN DEUTSCH
BILL AND TED'S EXCELLENT ADVENTURE ... TED FIELD
BILLY GALVIN ... HOWARD L. BALDWIN
BILLY GALVIN ... LINDSAY LAW
BILLY GALVIN ... STUART BENJAMIN
BILLY GALVIN ... SUE JETT
BILLY GALVIN ... TONY MARK
BILLY GALVIN ... WILLIAM MINOT
BILLY JACK ... MARY ROSE SOLTI
BILLY JACK ... TOM LAUGHLIN
BILLY JACK GOES TO WASHINGTON ... FRANK CAPRA JR.
BILLY JACK GOES TO WASHINGTON ... TOM LAUGHLIN
BILLY LIAR ... JOSEPH JANNI
BILLY TWO HATS ... PATRICK PALMER
BILLY TWO HATS ... NORMAN JEWISON
BILOXI BLUES ... JOSEPH M. CARACCIOLO
BILOXI BLUES ... MARYKAY POWELL
BILOXI BLUES ... RAY STARK
BINGO LONG TRAVELING ALL-STARS AND MOTOR KINGS, THE ... BERRY GORDY
BINGO LONG TRAVELING ALL-STARS AND MOTOR KINGS, THE ... MICHAEL CHINICH
BINGO LONG TRAVELING ALL-STARS AND MOTOR KINGS, THE ... ROB COHEN
BIOHAZARD ... FRED OLEN RAY
BIRCH INTERVAL ... ROBERT B. RADNITZ
BIRD ... CLINT EASTWOOD
BIRD ... DAVID VALDES
BIRD ON A WIRE ... JOHN BADHAM
BIRD ON A WIRE ... ROB COHEN
BIRD ON A WIRE ... ROBERT W. CORT
BIRD ON A WIRE ... TED FIELD
BIRDY ... DAVID MANSON
BIRDY ... GIL FRIESEN
BIRDY ... ALAN MARSHALL
BIRTHDAY PARTY, THE ... EDGAR J. SCHERICK
BISCUIT EATER, THE ... BILL ANDERSON
BITTERSWEET LOVE ... GENE SCOTT
BITTERSWEET LOVE ... JOSEPH ZAPPALA
BITTERSWEET LOVE ... JOEL B. MICHAELS
BLACK BELT JONES ... FRED WEINTRAUB
BLACK BELT JONES ... PAUL HELLER
BLACK CAULDRON, THE ... JOE HALE
BLACK CAULDRON, THE ... RON MILLER
BLACK HOLE, THE ... RON MILLER
BLACK JOY ... ELLIOTT KASTNER
BLACK JOY ... ARNON MILCHAN
BLACK KNIGHT, THE ... ALBERT R. BROCCOLI
BLACK KNIGHT, THE ... IRVING ALLEN†
BLACK KNIGHT, THE ... PHIL C. SAMUEL
BLACK MARBLE, THE ... FRANK CAPRA JR.
BLACK MOON RISING ... DOUGLAS CURTISS
BLACK MOON RISING ... JOEL B. MICHAELS
BLACK RAIN ... CRAIG BOLOTIN
BLACK RAIN ... JULIE KIRKHAM
BLACK RAIN ... SHERRY LANSING
BLACK RAIN ... STANLEY R. JAFFE
BLACK STALLION, THE ... FRANCIS FORD COPPOLA
BLACK STALLION, THE ... FRED ROOS
BLACK STALLION, THE ... TOM STERNBERG
BLACK STALLION RETURNS, THE ... FRED ROOS
BLACK STALLION RETURNS, THE ... FRANCIS FORD COPPOLA
BLACK STALLION RETURNS, THE ... DOUG CLAYBOURNE
BLACK STALLION RETURNS, THE ... TOM STERNBERG
BLACK SUNDAY ... ROBERT EVANS
BLACK SUNDAY ... ROBERT L. ROSEN
BLACK WIDOW ... BOB RAFELSON
BLACK WIDOW ... HAROLD SCHNEIDER
BLACK WIDOW ... LAURENCE MARK
BLACK WINDMILL, THE ... DAVID BROWN
BLACK WINDMILL, THE ... RICHARD D. ZANUCK
BLACKJACK ... TONY GARNETT
BLACKOUT ... IVAN REITMAN
BLACKOUT ... JOHN DUNNING
BLADE RUNNER ... BRIAN KELLY
BLADE RUNNER ... HAMPTON FANCHER
BLADE RUNNER ... MICHAEL DEELEY
BLAME IT ON RIO ... LARRY GELBART
BLAME IT ON RIO ... ROBERT E. RELYEA
BLAME IT ON RIO ... STANLEY DONEN
BLAZE ... DALE POLLOCK
BLAZE ... DAVID V. LESTER
BLAZE ... DON MILLER
BLAZE ... GIL FRIESEN
BLAZING SADDLES ... MICHAEL HERTZBERG
BLESS THE BEASTS AND CHILDREN ... STANLEY KRAMER
BLIND DATE ... BLAKE EDWARDS
BLIND DATE ... DAVID PERMUT
BLIND DATE ... DEMETRI T. SKOURAS
BLIND DATE ... GARY J. HENDLER†
BLIND DATE ... JONATHAN D. KRANE
BLIND DATE ... NICO MASTORAKIS
BLIND DATE ... TONY ADAMS
BLIND FURY ... DANIEL GRODNIK
BLIND FURY ... DAVID MADDEN
BLIND FURY ... DENNIS MURPHY
BLIND FURY ... ROBERT W. CORT
BLIND FURY ... TIM MATHESON
BLISS ... ANTHONY BUCKLEY
BLOB, THE ... ANDRE BLAY
BLOB, THE ... ELLIOTT KASTNER
BLOB, THE ... JACK H. HARRIS
BLOB, THE ... RUPERT HARVEY
BLOOD BEACH ... NEIL CANTON
BLOOD BEACH ... STEVEN NALEVANSKY
BLOOD BEACH ... SIDNEY BECKERMAN
BLOOD DINER ... ELLEN STELOFF
BLOOD DINER ... JACKIE KONG
BLOOD DINER ... JIMMY MASLON
BLOOD DINER ... LAWRENCE KASANOFF
BLOOD OF OTHERS, THE ... JOHN KEMENY
BLOOD OF HEROES, THE ... CHARLES ROVEN
BLOOD SIMPLE ... DANIEL F. BACANER
BLOOD SIMPLE ... ETHAN COEN
BLOODBROTHERS ... STEPHEN J. FRIEDMAN
BLOODFIST ... ROGER CORMAN
BLOODHOUNDS OF BROADWAY ... LINDSAY LAW
BLOODY BIRTHDAY ... CHRIS TUFTY
BLOODY BIRTHDAY ... GERALD T. OLSON
BLOODY MAMA ... ROGER CORMAN
BLOODY MAMA ... JAMES H. NICHOLSON†
BLOODY MAMA ... SAMUEL Z. ARKOFF
BLOODY MAMA ... NORMAN T. HERMAN
BLOW OUT ... FRED CARUSO
BLOW OUT ... GEORGE LITTO
BLUE ... IRWIN WINKLER
BLUE ... JUDD BERNARD
BLUE BIRD, THE ... PAUL MASLANSKY
BLUE BIRD, THE ... EDWARD LEWIS
BLUE CITY ... ANTHONY JONES
BLUE CITY ... ROBERT KENNER
BLUE CITY ... WALTER HILL
BLUE CITY ... WILLIAM HAYWARD
BLUE COLLAR ... DON GUEST
BLUE COLLAR ... ROBIN FRENCH
BLUE HEAVEN ... ELAINE SPERBER
BLUE HEAVEN ... JEFF DANNENBAUM
BLUE HEAVEN ... KATHLEEN DOWDEY
BLUE IGUANA, THE ... ANGEL FLORES-MARINI
BLUE IGUANA, THE ... MICHAEL KUHN
BLUE IGUANA, THE ... NIGEL SINCLAIR
BLUE IGUANA, THE ... OTHON ROFFIEL
BLUE IGUANA, THE ... STEVEN GOLIN
BLUE IGUANA, THE ... SIGURJON SIGHVATSSON
BLUE LAGOON, THE ... RANDAL KLEISER
BLUE LAGOON, THE ... RICHARD FRANKLIN
BLUE MAX, THE ... ELMO WILLIAMS
BLUE MONKEY ... MARTIN WALTERS
BLUE MONKEY ... TOM FOX
BLUE SKIES AGAIN ... ALEX WINITSKY
BLUE SKIES AGAIN ... ARLENE SELLERS
BLUE STEEL ... EDWARD R. PRESSMAN
BLUE STEEL ... LAWRENCE KASANOFF
BLUE STEEL ... MICHAEL JAY RAUCH
BLUE STEEL ... OLIVER STONE
BLUE SUNSHINE ... RAMSEY THOMAS
BLUE THUNDER ... ANDREW FOGELSON
BLUE THUNDER ... GORDON CARROLL
BLUE THUNDER ... GREGG CHAMPION
BLUE THUNDER ... PHIL FELDMAN
BLUE VELVET ... FRED CARUSO
BLUE VELVET ... RICHARD ROTH
BLUEBEARD ... ALEXANDER SALKIND
BLUEBEARD ... ILYA SALKIND
BLUES BROTHERS, THE ... BERNIE BRILLSTEIN
BLUES BROTHERS, THE ... GEORGE FOLSEY JR.
BLUES BROTHERS, THE ... ROBERT K. WEISS
BLUME IN LOVE ... PAUL MAZURSKY
BLUME IN LOVE ... TONY RAY
BOATNIKS, THE ... RON MILLER
BOB & CAROL & TED & ALICE ... LARRY TUCKER
BOBBY DEERFIELD ... SYDNEY POLLACK
BOBBY DEERFIELD ... JOHN FOREMAN
BODY AND SOUL ... MENAHEM GOLAN
BODY AND SOUL ... YORAM GLOBUS
BODY CHEMISTRY ... ALIDA CAMP
BODY CHEMISTRY ... RODMAN FLENDER
BODY DOUBLE ... BRIAN DE PALMA
BODY DOUBLE ... HOWARD GOTTFRIED
BODY HEAT ... FRED T. GALLO
BODY ROCK ... CHARLES J. WEBER
BODY ROCK ... CHUCK RUSSELL
BODY ROCK ... JEFF SCHECHTMAN
BODY ROCK ... JON FELTHEIMER
BODY ROCK ... PHIL RAMONE
BODY SLAM ... GRAHAM HENDERSON
BODY SLAM ... MIKE CURB
BODY SLAM ... SHEL LYTTON
BODY, THE ... TONY GARNETT
BOLERO ... BO DEREK
BOLERO ... MENAHEM GOLAN
BOLERO ... YORAM GLOBUS
BOMBAY TALKIE ... ISMAIL MERCHANT
BON VOYAGE! ... BILL WALSH†
BON VOYAGE! ... RON MILLER
BONNIE AND CLYDE ... WARREN BEATTY
BOOGENS, THE ... CHARLES E. SELLIER JR.
BOOST, THE ... DANIEL H. BLATT
BOOST, THE ... DEREK GIBSON
BOOST, THE ... JOHN DALY
BORDER RADIO ... MARCUS DE LEON
BORDER, THE ... EDGAR BRONFMAN JR.
BORDER, THE ... NEIL HARTLEY
BORDERLINE ... JAMES NELSON
BORDERLINE ... MARTIN STARGER
BORN AGAIN ... FRANK CAPRA JR.
BORN AGAIN ... ROBERT L. MUNGER
BORN IN EAST L.A. ... STAN COLEMAN
BORN IN EAST L.A. ... PETER MACGREGOR-SCOTT
BORN IN FLAMES ... LIZZIE BORDEN
BORN LOSERS ... TOM LAUGHLIN
BORN ON THE FOURTH OF JULY ... A. KITMAN HO
BORN ON THE FOURTH OF JULY ... OLIVER STONE
BORN TO KILL ... ROGER CORMAN
BORN TO RACE ... ANDREW BULLIANS
BORN TO RACE ... JEAN BULLIANS
BORN TO WIN ... JERRY TOKOFSKY
BOSS' WIFE, THE ... THOMAS H. BRODEK
BOSTONIANS, THE ... ALBERT SCHWARTZ
BOSTONIANS, THE ... CONNIE KAISERMAN
BOSTONIANS, THE ... ISMAIL MERCHANT
BOSTONIANS, THE ... MICHAEL S. LANDES
BOULEVARD NIGHTS ... BILL BENENSON
BOULEVARD NIGHTS ... TONY BILL
BOUND FOR GLORY ... CHARLES B. MULVEHILL
BOUND FOR GLORY ... HAROLD LEVENTHAL
BOUND FOR GLORY ... ROBERT F. BLUMOFE
BOUNTY, THE ... BERNARD WILLIAMS
BOXCAR BERTHA ... ROGER CORMAN
BOY FRIEND, THE ... HARRY BENN
BOY FRIEND, THE ... KEN RUSSELL
BOY IN BLUE, THE ... DENIS HEROUX
BOY IN BLUE, THE ... JOHN KEMENY
BOY IN BLUE, THE ... STEVEN NORTH
BOY NEXT DOOR/SEX AND THE TEENAGER , THE ... MORT ABRAHAMS
BOY WHO COULD FLY, THE ... BRIAN FRANKISH
BOY WHO COULD FLY, THE ... RICHARD VANE
BOYFRIEND SCHOOL, THE ... DEREK GIBSON
BOYFRIEND SCHOOL, THE ... GEORGE BRAUNSTEIN
BOYFRIEND SCHOOL, THE ... JOHN DALY
BOYFRIEND SCHOOL, THE ... RON HAMADY
BOYS FROM BRAZIL, THE ... MARTIN RICHARDS
BOYS FROM BRAZIL, THE ... ROBERT FRYER
BOYS FROM BRAZIL, THE ... STANLEY O'TOOLE
BOYS IN THE BAND, THE ... KENNETH UTT
BOYS NEXT DOOR, THE ... JOEL SOISSON
BOYS NEXT DOOR, THE ... KEITH RUBINSTEIN
BOYS NEXT DOOR, THE ... MEL PEARL
BOYS NEXT DOOR, THE ... MICHAEL S. MURPHEY

BOYS NEXT DOOR, THE .... SANDY HOWARD
BOYS NEXT DOOR, THE .... DON LEVIN
BRADDOCK: MISSING IN ACTION III .... MENAHEM GOLAN
BRADDOCK: MISSING IN ACTION III .... YORAM GLOBUS
BRADY'S ESCAPE .... JOZSEF MARX
BRADY'S ESCAPE .... ROBERT HALMI JR.
BRADY'S ESCAPE .... ROBERT HALMI SR.
BRAIN DAMAGE .... AL EICHER
BRAIN DAMAGE .... ANDRE BLAY
BRAIN DAMAGE .... EDGAR IEVINS
BRAIN DEAD .... JULIE CORMAN
BRAINSTORM .... DOUGLAS TRUMBULL
BRAINSTORM .... JOEL L. FREEDMAN
BRAINSTORM .... JACK GROSSBERG
BRAINSTORM .... JOHN FOREMAN
BRAZIL .... ARNON MILCHAN
BRAZIL .... PATRICK CASSAVETTI
BREAKFAST AT TIFFANY'S .... MARTIN JUROW
BREAKFAST AT TIFFANY'S .... RICHARD SHEPHERD
BREAKFAST CLUB, THE .... NED TANEN
BREAKFAST CLUB, THE .... ANDREW MEYER
BREAKFAST CLUB, THE .... GIL FRIESEN
BREAKFAST CLUB, THE .... MICHELLE MANNING
BREAKHEART PASS .... JERRY GERSHWIN
BREAKHEART PASS .... ELLIOTT KASTNER
BREAKIN' .... ALLEN DEBEVOISE
BREAKIN' .... DAVID ZITO
BREAKIN' .... MENAHEM GOLAN
BREAKIN' .... YORAM GLOBUS
BREAKIN' 2: ELECTRIC BOOGALOO .... MENAHEM GOLAN
BREAKIN' 2: ELECTRIC BOOGALOO .... YORAM GLOBUS
BREAKING AWAY .... PETER YATES
BREAKING GLASS .... DAVINA BELLING
BREAKING GLASS .... DODI FAYED
BREAKING GLASS .... CLIVE PARSONS
BREAKING IN .... ANDREW MEYER
BREAKING IN .... HARRY GITTES
BREAKING IN .... SARAH RYAN BLACK
BREAKING POINT .... BOB CLARK
BREAKING POINT .... CLAUDE HEROUX
BREAKOUT .... ROBERT CHARTOFF
BREAKOUT .... RONALD L. BUCK
BREAKOUT .... IRWIN WINKLER
BREATHLESS .... KEITH ADDIS
BREATHLESS .... MARTIN ERLICHMAN
BREED APART, A .... DAN ALLINGHAM
BREED APART, A .... DEREK GIBSON
BREED APART, A .... JOHN DALY
BREEZY .... ROBERT DALEY
BREEZY .... JENNINGS LANG
BRENDA STARR .... MYRON A. HYMAN
BRENDA STARR .... JOHN D. BACKE
BREWSTER MCCLOUD .... LOU ADLER
BREWSTER'S MILLIONS .... GENE LEVY
BREWSTER'S MILLIONS .... JOEL SILVER
BREWSTER'S MILLIONS .... LAWRENCE GORDON
BRIDE, THE .... CHRIS KENNY
BRIDE, THE .... KEITH ADDIS
BRIDE, THE .... LLOYD FONVIELLE
BRIDE, THE .... VICTOR DRAI
BRIDGE AT REMAGEN, THE .... DAVID L. WOLPER
BRIGHT LIGHTS, BIG CITY .... GERALD R. MOLEN
BRIGHT LIGHTS, BIG CITY .... MARK ROSENBERG
BRIGHT LIGHTS, BIG CITY .... SYDNEY POLLACK
BRIGHTON BEACH MEMOIRS .... DAVID CHASMAN
BRIGHTON BEACH MEMOIRS .... JOSEPH M. CARACCIOLO
BRIGHTON BEACH MEMOIRS .... RAY STARK
BRIMSTONE & TREACLE .... KENITH TRODD
BRIMSTONE & TREACLE .... NAIM ATTALLAH
BRING ON THE NIGHT .... ANDREW MEYER
BRING ON THE NIGHT .... DAVID MANSON
BRING ON THE NIGHT .... GIL FRIESEN
BRITANNIA HOSPITAL .... CLIVE PARSONS
BRITTANIA HOSPITAL .... DAVINA BELLING
BROADCAST NEWS .... PENNY FINKELMAN COX
BROADCAST NEWS .... POLLY PLATT
BROADCAST NEWS .... JAMES L. BROOKS
BROADWAY DANNY ROSE .... MICHAEL PEYSER
BROADWAY DANNY ROSE .... CHARLES H. JOFFE
BROADWAY DANNY ROSE .... ROBERT GREENHUT
BROKEN ENGLISH .... KEITH ROTHMAN
BROKEN ENGLISH .... BERT SCHNEIDER
BRONCO BILLY .... FRITZ MANES
BRONCO BILLY .... NEAL DOBROFSKY
BRONCO BILLY .... ROBERT DALEY
BROOD, THE .... VICTOR SOLNICKI
BROOD, THE .... CLAUDE HEROUX
BROOD, THE .... PIERRE DAVID
BROTHER FROM ANOTHER PLANET, THE .... MAGGIE RENZI
BROTHER FROM ANOTHER PLANET, THE .... PEGGY RAJSKI
BROTHERS .... EDWARD LEWIS
BROTHERS .... LEE SAVIN
BROTHERS .... MILDRED LEWIS
BROTHERS IN ARMS .... ANDRE BOISSIER
BROTHERS IN ARMS .... JAN ERIK LUNDE
BROTHERS IN ARMS .... MARK R. GORDON
BROTHERS IN ARMS .... CHRIS MELEDANDRI
BRUBAKER .... GORDON A. WEBB
BRUBAKER .... RON SILVERMAN
BRUBAKER .... TED MANN
BUCKAROO BANZAI .... NEIL CANTON
BUCKAROO BANZAI .... W. D. RICHTER
BUCKAROO BANZAI .... SIDNEY BECKERMAN
BUCKTOWN .... BERNARD SCHWARTZ
BUDDY BUDDY .... ALAIN BERNHEIM
BUDDY BUDDY .... JAY WESTON
BUDDY SYSTEM, THE .... ALAIN CHAMMAS
BUFFALO BILL AND THE INDIANS .... ROBERT ALTMAN
BUFFALO BILL AND THE INDIANS .... SCOTT BUSHNELL
BUGSY MALONE .... ALAN MARSHALL
BUGSY MALONE .... DAVID PUTTNAM
BUGSY MALONE .... ROBERT STIGWOOD
BULL DURHAM .... DAVID V. LESTER
BULL DURHAM .... MARK BURG
BULL DURHAM .... THOM MOUNT
BULLET FOR PRETTY BOY, A .... ROGER CORMAN
BULLETPROOF .... LISA M. HANSEN
BULLETPROOF .... NEIL C. LUNDELL
BULLETPROOF .... PAUL HERTZBERG
BULLIES .... PETER HALEY
BULLIES .... PETER SIMPSON
BULLITT .... ROBERT E. RELYEA
BULLITT .... PHILIP D'ANTONI
BULLSHOT .... DAVID WIMBURY
BULLSHOT .... DENIS O'BRIEN
BULLSHOT .... GEORGE HARRISON
BULLSHOT .... IAN LAFRENAIS
BUONA SERA, MRS. CAMPBELL .... C.O. ERICKSON
'BURBS, THE .... LARRY BREZNER
'BURBS, THE .... DANA OLSEN
'BURBS, THE .... MICHAEL FINNELL
BURGLAR .... JOSEPH LOEB III
BURGLAR .... KEVIN MCCORMICK
BURGLAR .... MATTHEW WEISMAN
BURGLAR .... MICHAEL HIRSH
BURGLAR .... TOM JACOBSON
BURKE AND WILLS .... GRAEME CLIFFORD
BURKE AND WILLS .... JOHN SEXTON
BURNI .... ALBERTO GRIMALDI
BURNING SECRET .... CAROL LYNN GREENE
BURNING SECRET .... EBERHARD JUNKERSDORF
BURNING SECRET .... MJ PECKOS
BURNING SECRET .... NORMA HEYMAN
BURNING SECRET .... RON CARR
BURNING SECRET .... WILLIAM J. QUIGLEY
BURNT OFFERINGS .... ROBERT SINGER
BURNT OFFERINGS .... DAN CURTIS
BUSINESS AS USUAL .... MENAHEM GOLAN
BUSINESS AS USUAL .... SARA GEATER
BUSINESS AS USUAL .... YORAM GLOBUS
BUSTED UP .... DAMIAN LEE
BUSTED UP .... DAVID MITCHELL
BUSTED UP .... LAWRENCE NESIS
BUSTER .... DEREK GIBSON
BUSTER .... FRANK GIUSTRA
BUSTER .... JOHN DALY
BUSTER .... NORMA HEYMAN
BUSTER .... PETER STRAUSS
BUSTER .... REDMOND MORRIS
BUSTER AND BILLIE .... RON SILVERMAN
BUSTER AND BILLIE .... TED MANN
BUSTIN' LOOSE .... MICHAEL S. GLICK
BUSTIN' LOOSE .... RICHARD PRYOR
BUSTIN' LOOSE .... WILLIAM GREAVES
BUSTING .... ROBERT CHARTOFF
BUSTING .... IRWIN WINKLER
BUTCH AND SUNDANCE: THE EARLY DAYS .... GABRIEL KATZKA†
BUTCH AND SUNDANCE: THE EARLY DAYS .... STEVEN BACH
BUTCH CASSIDY AND THE SUNDANCE KID .... PAUL MONASH
BUTCH CASSIDY AND THE SUNDANCE KID .... JOHN FOREMAN
BUTLEY .... ELY LANDAU
BUTLEY .... OTTO PLASCHKES
BUTLEY .... HENRY T. WEINSTEIN
BUY AND CELL .... FRANK YABLANS
BUY AND CELL .... CHARLES BAND
BY LOVE POSSESSED .... WALTER MIRISCH
BYE BYE BRAVERMAN .... SIDNEY LUMET

C

C.C. AND COMPANY .... ALLAN CARR
C.C. AND COMPANY .... ROGER SMITH
C.H.O.M.P.S. .... SAMUEL Z. ARKOFF
C.H.O.M.P.S. .... BURT TOPPER
C.H.O.M.P.S. .... JOSEPH BARBERA
C.H.U.D. II .... JONATHAN D. KRANE
CABARET .... CY FEUER
CABARET .... ERNEST MARTIN
CADDYSHACK .... MICHAEL SHAMBERG
CADDYSHACK .... JON PETERS
CADDYSHACK II .... JON PETERS
CADDYSHACK II .... NEIL CANTON
CADDYSHACK II .... PETER GUBER
CADILLAC MAN .... CHARLES ROVEN
CADILLAC MAN .... ROGER DONALDSON
CAGE .... LANG ELLIOTT
CAGE .... LARRY J. LEBOW
CAGED HEAT .... EVELYN PURCELL
CAINE MUTINY, THE .... STANLEY KRAMER
CAL .... STUART CRAIG
CAL .... TERENCE CLEGG
CAL .... DAVID PUTTNAM
CALIFORNIA DREAMING .... SAMUEL Z. ARKOFF
CALIFORNIA SPLIT .... JOSEPH WALSH
CALIFORNIA SPLIT .... LEONARD J. GOLDBERG
CALIFORNIA SPLIT .... ROBERT ALTMAN
CALIFORNIA SPLIT .... AARON SPELLING
CALIFORNIA SUITE .... RAY STARK
CALL ME .... JOHN QUILL
CALL ME .... KENNETH MARTEL
CALL ME .... MARY KANE
CALL ME .... MITCHELL CANNOLD
CALL ME .... RICHARD GELFAND
CALL ME .... RUTH VITALE
CALL ME .... STEVEN REUTHER
CALL ME BWANA .... HARRY SALTZMAN
CALL ME BWANA .... ALBERT R. BROCCOLI
CAMELOT .... JOEL FREEMAN
CAMERON'S CLOSET .... GEORGE ZECEVIC
CAMERON'S CLOSET .... JOHN S. CURRAN
CAMERON'S CLOSET .... LUIGI CINGOLANI
CAMPUS MAN .... BARBARA BOYLE
CAMPUS MAN .... JON LANDAU
CAMPUS MAN .... MARC E. PLATT
CAMPUS MAN .... PEGGY FOWLER
CANDLESHOE .... RON MILLER
CAN'T BUY ME LOVE .... JERE HENSHAW
CAN'T BUY ME LOVE .... MARK BURG
CAN'T BUY ME LOVE .... RON BECKMAN
CAN'T BUY ME LOVE .... THOM MOUNT
CAN'T STOP THE MUSIC .... ALLAN CARR
CAN'T STOP THE MUSIC .... HENRI BELOLO
CAN'T STOP THE MUSIC .... JACQUES MORALI
CANDIDATE, THE .... WALTER COBLENZ
CANDY MOUNTAIN .... ELLIOTT LEWITT
CANDY MOUNTAIN .... GERALD B. DEARING
CANDY MOUNTAIN .... JIM STARK
CANDY MOUNTAIN .... RUTH WALDBURGER
CANNERY ROW .... MICHAEL PHILLIPS
CANNIBAL GIRLS .... DAN GOLDBERG
CANNONBALL RUN, THE .... DAVID SHAMROY HAMBURGER
CANNONBALL RUN, THE .... RAYMOND CHOW
CANNONBALL RUN, THE .... ALBERT S. RUDDY
CANNONBALL RUN II, THE .... ALBERT S. RUDDY
CANTERBURY TALES, THE .... ALBERTO GRIMALDI
CAPONE .... ROGER CORMAN
CAPTIVE HEARTS .... MILTON GOLDSTEIN
CAPTIVE HEARTS .... JOHN A. KURI
CAR WASH .... GARY STROMBERG
CAR WASH .... ART LINSON
CARAVAGGIO .... COLIN MACCABE
CARAVAGGIO .... SARAH RADCLYFFE
CARAVANS .... ELMO WILLIAMS
CARBON COPY .... STANLEY SHAPIRO
CARBON COPY .... CARTER DE HAVEN
CARBON COPY .... JOHN DALY
CARE BEARS ADVENTURE IN WONDERLAND .... LENORA HUME
CARE BEARS ADVENTURE IN WONDERLAND, THE .... CLIVE A. SMITH
CARE BEARS ADVENTURE IN WONDERLAND, THE .... MICHAEL HIRSH
CARE BEARS ADVENTURE IN WONDERLAND, THE .... PATRICK LOUBERT
CARE BEARS MOVIE II: A NEW GENERATION, THE .... CLIVE A. SMITH
CARE BEARS MOVIE II: A NEW GENERATION, THE .... LENORA HUME
CARE BEARS MOVIE II: A NEW GENERATION, THE .... MICHAEL HIRSH

CARE BEARS MOVIE II: A NEW GENERATION, THE ..... PATRICK LOUBERT
CARE BEARS MOVIE, THE ..... CLIVE A. SMITH
CARE BEARS MOVIE, THE ..... MICHAEL HIRSH
CARE BEARS MOVIE, THE ..... PATRICK LOUBERT
CAREFUL, HE MIGHT HEAR YOU ..... JILL ROBB
CARNAL KNOWLEDGE ..... MIKE NICHOLS
CARNY ..... JONATHAN T. TAPLIN
CARNY ..... ROBBIE ROBERTSON
CARRIE ..... LOUIS A. STROLLER
CARRIE ..... PAUL MONASH
CARS THAT EAT PEOPLE, THE ..... HAL MCELROY
CARS THAT EAT PEOPLE, THE ..... JAMES MCELROY
CASANOVA ..... ALBERTO GRIMALDI
CASEY'S SHADOW ..... MICHAEL LEVEE
CASEY'S SHADOW ..... RAY STARK
CASSANDRA CROSSING, THE ..... LORD LEW GRADE
CASSANDRA CROSSING, THE ..... CARLO PONTI
CASTAWAY ..... PETER SHAW
CASTAWAY ..... RICHARD JOHNSON
CASTAWAY ..... RICK MCCALLUM
CASTAWAY COWBOY, THE ..... RON MILLER
CASTAWAY COWBOY, THE ..... WINSTON HIBLER†
CASTLE KEEP ..... EDWARD L. RISSIEN
CASTLE KEEP ..... JOHN CALLEY
CASTLE KEEP ..... MARTIN RANSOHOFF
CASUAL SEX? ..... ILONA HERZBERG
CASUAL SEX? ..... IVAN REITMAN
CASUAL SEX? ..... SHELDON KAHN
CASUALTIES OF WAR ..... ART LINSON
CASUALTIES OF WAR ..... FRED CARUSO
CAT FROM OUTER SPACE, THE ..... RON MILLER
CAT PEOPLE ..... CHARLES FRIES
CAT PEOPLE ..... JERRY BRUCKHEIMER
CATCH 22 ..... JOHN CALLEY
CATCH 22 ..... MARTIN RANSOHOFF
CATCH THE HEAT ..... DON VAN ATTA
CATCH THE HEAT ..... MOSHE DIAMANT
CATCH THE HEAT ..... STIRLING SILLIPHANT
CATTLE ANNIE AND LITTLE BRITCHES ..... DEREK GIBSON
CATTLE ANNIE AND LITTLE BRITCHES ..... JOHN DALY
CATTLE ANNIE AND LITTLE BRITCHES ..... ALAN KING
CATTLE ANNIE AND LITTLE BRITCHES ..... RUPERT HITZIG
CAVEMAN ..... LAWRENCE TURMAN
CELINE AND JULIE GO BOATING ..... BARBET SCHROEDER
CELLAR, THE ..... PATRICK C. WELLS
CELLAR, THE ..... JOHN WOODWARD
CELLAR, THE ..... STEVEN E. BURMAN
CERTAIN FURY ..... GILBERT ADLER
CERTAIN FURY ..... LAWRENCE VANGER
CERVANTES ..... HENRY T. WEINSTEIN
CHAIRMAN, THE ..... MORT ABRAHAMS
CHALLENGE, THE ..... LYLE PONCHER
CHALLENGE, THE ..... RON BECKMAN
CHALLENGE, THE ..... ROBERT L. ROSEN
CHAMP, THE ..... DYSON LOVELL
CHAMPION ..... STANLEY KRAMER
CHAMPIONS ..... PETER SHAW
CHAMPIONS FOREVER ..... HOLLISTER WHITWORTH
CHAMPIONS FOREVER ..... JOSEPH MEDAWAR
CHAMPIONS FOREVER ..... NABEEL ZAHID
CHAMPIONS FOREVER ..... TOM BELLAGIO
CHAN IS MISSING ..... WAYNE WANG
CHANCES ARE ..... ANDREW BERGMAN
CHANCES ARE ..... MICHAEL LOBELL
CHANCES ARE ..... NEIL A. MACHLIS
CHANGE OF SEASONS, A ..... MARTIN RANSOHOFF
CHANGE OF SEASONS, A ..... RICHARD R. ST. JOHNS
CHANGELING, THE ..... JOEL B. MICHAELS
CHANGELING, THE ..... GARTH DRABINSKY
CHANGES ..... HALL BARTLETT
CHANT OF JIMMIE BLACKSMITH, THE ..... FRED SCHEPISI
CHANT OF JIMMIE BLACKSMITH, THE ..... ROY STEVENS
CHAPLINESQUE, MY LIFE AND HARD TIMES ..... HARRY HURWITZ
CHAPTER TWO ..... RAY STARK
CHAPTER TWO ..... ROGER M. ROTHSTEIN†
CHARADE ..... STANLEY DONEN
CHARIOTS OF FIRE ..... DODI FAYED
CHARIOTS OF FIRE ..... DAVID PUTTNAM
CHARLEY AND THE ANGEL ..... BILL ANDERSON
CHARLEY VARRICK ..... JENNINGS LANG
CHARLIE CHAN AND THE CURSE OF THE DRAGON QUEEN ..... ALAN BELKIN
CHARLIE CHAN AND THE CURSE OF THE DRAGON QUEEN ..... JERRY SHERLOCK
CHARLIE CHAN AND THE CURSE OF THE DRAGON QUEEN ..... MICHAEL C. LEONE
CHATTAHOOCHEE ..... AARON SCHWAB
CHATTAHOOCHEE ..... FAYE SCHWAB
CHATTAHOOCHEE ..... SUE BADEN-POWELL
CHATTANOOGA CHOO CHOO ..... GEORGE EDWARDS
CHATTANOOGA CHOO CHOO ..... JILL GRIFFITH
CHATTANOOGA CHOO CHOO ..... PHIL BORACK
CHATTERBOX ..... BRUCE COHN CURTIS
CHEAP DETECTIVE, THE ..... RAY STARK
CHECK IS IN THE MAIL, THE ..... ROBERT KAUFMAN
CHECK IS IN THE MAIL, THE ..... ROBERT KRAUSE
CHECKERED FLAG OR CRASH ..... FRED WEINTRAUB
CHECKERED FLAG OR CRASH ..... PAUL HELLER
CHECKING OUT ..... BEN MYRON
CHECKING OUT ..... DENIS O'BRIEN
CHECKING OUT ..... GARTH THOMAS
CHECKING OUT ..... GEORGE HARRISON
CHEECH & CHONG'S NEXT MOVIE ..... PETER MACGREGOR-SCOTT
CHEECH AND CHONG'S NEXT MOVIE ..... HOWARD BROWN
CHEECH AND CHONG'S NICE DREAMS ..... HOWARD BROWN
CHEECH & CHONG'S STILL SMOKIN' ..... PETER MACGREGOR-SCOTT
CHEECH & CHONG'S THE CORSICAN BROTHERS ..... PETER MACGREGOR-SCOTT
CHEETAH ..... ROBERT HALMI SR.
CHEETAH ..... ROY EDWARD DISNEY
CHERRY 2000 ..... CALDECOTT CHUBB
CHERRY 2000 ..... ELLIOT SCHICK
CHERRY 2000 ..... LLOYD FONVIELLE
CHERRY 2000 ..... EDWARD R. PRESSMAN
CHICAGO JOE AND THE SHOWGIRL ..... TIM BEVAN
CHICKEN CHRONICLES, THE ..... WALTER SHENSON
CHICKEN CHRONICLES, THE ..... DAN ALLINGHAM
CHILD IS WAITING, A ..... STANLEY KRAMER
CHILD'S PLAY ..... BARRIE M. OSBORNE
CHILD'S PLAY ..... DAVID KIRSCHNER
CHILD'S PLAY ..... ELLIOTT GEISINGER
CHILD'S PLAY ..... HANK MOONJEAN
CHILDREN OF A LESSER GOD ..... BURT SUGARMAN
CHILDREN OF A LESSER GOD ..... PATRICK PALMER
CHILDREN OF SANCHEZ, THE ..... HALL BARTLETT
CHILDREN OF THE CORN ..... CHARLES J. WEBER
CHILDREN OF THE CORN ..... DONALD P. BORCHERS
CHILDREN OF THE CORN ..... EARL GLICK
CHILDREN OF THE CORN ..... MARK LIPSON
CHILDREN OF THE CORN ..... TERRENCE KIRBY
CHILDREN OF THEATER STREET, THE ..... EARLE MACK
CHILLY SCENES OF WINTER ..... GRIFFIN DUNNE
CHILLY SCENES OF WINTER ..... MARK METCALF
CHILLY SCENES OF WINTER ..... AMY ROBINSON
CHINA GIRL ..... MICHAEL NOZIK
CHINA GIRL ..... MITCHELL CANNOLD
CHINA GIRL ..... STEVEN REUTHER
CHINA SYNDROME, THE ..... BRUCE GILBERT
CHINA SYNDROME, THE ..... MICHAEL DOUGLAS
CHINATOWN ..... ROBERT EVANS
CHITTY CHITTY BANG BANG ..... ALBERT R. BROCCOLI
CHOCOLATE WAR, THE ..... JONATHAN D. KRANE
CHOCOLATE WAR, THE ..... SIMON R. LEWIS
CHOIRBOYS, THE ..... LEE RICH
CHOIRBOYS, THE ..... MARIO BREGNI
CHOIRBOYS, THE ..... MARK DAMON
CHOIRBOYS, THE ..... PIETRO BREGNI
CHOIRBOYS, THE ..... MERV ADELSON
CHOKE CANYON ..... OBIDIO G. ASSONITIS
CHOOSE ME ..... CAROLYN PFEIFFER
CHOOSE ME ..... DAVID BLOCKER
CHOPPING MALL ..... JULIE CORMAN
CHORUS LINE, A ..... CY FEUER
CHORUS LINE, A ..... ERNEST MARTIN
CHORUS LINE, A ..... GORDON STULBERG
CHORUS LINE, A ..... JOSEPH M. CARACCIOLO
CHORUS OF DISAPPROVAL, A ..... ANDRE BLAY
CHORUS OF DISAPPROVAL, A ..... ELLIOTT KASTNER
CHORUS OF DISAPPROVAL, A ..... MICHAEL WINNER
CHOSEN , THE ..... ELY LANDAU
CHOSEN, THE ..... EDIE LANDAU
CHOSEN, THE ..... JONATHAN BERNSTEIN
CHRISTIANE F. ..... BERND EICHINGER
CHRISTIANE F. ..... HANS WETH
CHRISTINE ..... BARRY BERNARDI
CHRISTINE ..... KIRBY MCCAULEY
CHRISTINE ..... LARRY J. FRANCO
CHRISTINE ..... MARK TARLOV
CHRISTINE ..... RICHARD KOBRITZ
CHRISTMAS STORY, A ..... BOB CLARK
CHRISTMAS STORY, A ..... RENE DUPONT
CHU CHU AND THE PHILLY FLASH ..... MELVIN SIMON
CHU CHU AND THE PHILLY FLASH ..... JAY WESTON
CHUCK BERRY: HAIL! HAIL! ROCK 'N' ROLL! ..... CHUCK BERRY
CHUCK BERRY: HAIL! HAIL! ROCK 'N' ROLL! ..... STEPHANIE BENNETT
CINCINNATI KID, THE ..... JOHN CALLEY
CINCINNATI KID, THE ..... MARTIN RANSOHOFF
CIRCLE OF DECEIT ..... EBERHARD JUNKERSDORF
CIRCLE OF IRON ..... SANDY HOWARD
CIRCLE OF IRON ..... PAUL MASLANSKY
CIRCLE OF POWER ..... GARY MEHLMAN
CISCO PIKE ..... GERALD AYRES
CITIZENS BAND ..... PAUL BRICKMAN
CITIZENS BAND ..... SHEP FIELDS
CITIZENS BAND ..... FREDDIE FIELDS
CITY HEAT ..... FRITZ MANES
CITY LIMITS ..... BARRY OPPER
CITY LIMITS ..... RUPERT HARVEY
CITY LIMITS ..... WARREN GOLDBERG
CITY ON FIRE ..... CLAUDE HEROUX
CLAN OF THE CAVE BEAR , THE ..... PETER GUBER
CLAN OF THE CAVE BEAR, THE ..... GERALD I. ISENBERG
CLAN OF THE CAVE BEAR, THE ..... MARK DAMON
CLAN OF THE CAVE BEAR, THE ..... SIDNEY KIMMEL
CLAN OF THE CAVE BEAR, THE ..... STAN ROGOW
CLAN OF THE CAVE BEAR, THE ..... JON PETERS
CLARA'S HEART ..... MARIANNE MOLONEY
CLARA'S HEART ..... MARTIN ELFAND
CLASS ..... CATHLEEN SUMMERS
CLASS ..... JIM KOUF
CLASS ..... MARTIN RANSOHOFF
CLASS OF 1999 ..... EUGENE MAZZOLA
CLASS OF 1999 ..... ELLEN STELOFF
CLASS OF 1999 ..... LAWRENCE KASANOFF
CLASS OF 1999 ..... MARK L. LESTER
CLASS OF MISS MACMICHAEL, THE ..... GEORGE BARRIE
CLASS OF MISS MACMICHAEL, THE ..... JUDD BERNARD
CLEAN AND SOBER ..... PATRICK KELLEY
CLEAN AND SOBER ..... RON HOWARD
CLEAN AND SOBER ..... TONY GANZ
CLEAN AND SOBER ..... DEBORAH BLUM
CLEAN AND SOBER ..... JAY DANIEL
CLOAK AND DAGGER ..... ALLAN CARR
CLOAK AND DAGGER ..... C.O. ERICKSON
CLOCKWISE ..... MICHAEL CODRON
CLOCKWISE ..... NAT COHEN
CLOCKWISE ..... VERITY LAMBERT
CLOCKWORK ORANGE, A ..... STANLEY KUBRICK
CLOCKWORK ORANGE, A ..... BERNARD WILLIAMS
CLOSE ENCOUNTERS OF THE THIRD KIND ..... JULIA PHILLIPS
CLOSE ENCOUNTERS OF THE THIRD KIND ..... MICHAEL PHILLIPS
CLUB LIFE ..... NORMAN THADDEUS VANE
CLUB PARADISE ..... ALAN GREISMAN
CLUB PARADISE ..... MICHAEL SHAMBERG
CLUE ..... JOHN LANDIS
CLUE ..... PETER GUBER
CLUE ..... GEORGE FOLSEY JR.
CLUE ..... JON PETERS
CLUE ..... DEBRA HILL
COAL MINER'S DAUGHTER ..... BERNARD SCHWARTZ
COAL MINER'S DAUGHTER ..... ROBERT LARSON
COAST TO COAST ..... TERRY CARR
COAST TO COAST ..... JON AVNET
COAST TO COAST ..... STEVE TISCH
COBRA ..... JAMES D. BRUBAKER
COBRA ..... MENAHEM GOLAN
COBRA ..... YORAM GLOBUS
COCAINE WARS ..... ALEX SESSA
COCAINE WARS ..... ROGER CORMAN
COCKFIGHTER ..... ROGER CORMAN
COCKLESHELL HEROES, THE ..... ALBERT R. BROCCOLI
COCKTAIL ..... ROBERT W. CORT
COCKTAIL ..... SCOTT KROOPF
COCOON ..... DAVID BROWN
COCOON ..... RICHARD D. ZANUCK
COCOON: THE RETURN ..... DAVID BROWN
COCOON: THE RETURN ..... LILI FINI ZANUCK
COCOON: THE RETURN ..... RICHARD D. ZANUCK
CODE NAME: EMERALD ..... HOWARD ALSTON
CODE NAME: EMERALD ..... JONATHAN SANGER
CODE NAME: EMERALD ..... MARTIN STARGER
CODE OF SILENCE ..... RAYMOND WAGNER
COHEN & TATE ..... JEFF YOUNG

COHEN & TATE .... ANTHONY RUFUS ISAACS
COLD FEET .... CASSIAN ELWES
COLD FEET .... CHARLES WESSLER
COLD FEET .... MARY MCLAGLEN
COLD FEET .... CARY BROKAW
COLD STEEL .... LISA M. HANSEN
COLD STEEL .... PAUL HERTZBERG
COLD TURKEY .... BUD YORKIN
COLD TURKEY .... NORMAN LEAR
COLLISION COURSE .... FRANK DARIUS NAMEI
COLLISION COURSE .... RENE DUPONT
COLLISION COURSE .... ROBERT W. CORT
COLLISION COURSE .... ROBERT RESNIKOFF
COLLISION COURSE .... TED FIELD
COLOR OF MONEY, THE .... BARBARA DE FINA
COLOR OF MONEY, THE .... IRVING AXELRAD
COLOR PURPLE, THE .... FRANK MARSHALL
COLOR PURPLE, THE .... KATHLEEN KENNEDY
COLOR PURPLE, THE .... PETER GUBER
COLOR PURPLE, THE .... QUINCY JONES
COLOR PURPLE, THE .... STEVEN SPIELBERG
COLORS .... ROBERT H. SOLO
COMA .... MARTIN ERLICHMAN
COME BACK .... HALL BARTLETT
COME BACK TO THE 5 & DIME JIMMY DEAN, JIMMY DEAN .... GIRAUD CHESTER
COME BACK TO THE 5 & DIME JIMMY DEAN, JIMMY DEAN ... ROBERT ALTMAN
COME BACK TO THE 5 & DIME JIMMY DEAN, JIMMY DEAN ..... PETER NEWMAN
COME BACK TO THE 5 & DIME, JIMMY DEAN, JIMMY DEAN .... SCOTT BUSHNELL
COME BLOW YOUR HORN .... BUD YORKIN
COME BLOW YOUR HORN .... HOWARD W. KOCH
COME BLOW YOUR HORN .... NORMAN LEAR
COME SEE THE PARADISE .... ROBERT F. COLESBERRY
COME SEPTEMBER .... ALAN J. PAKULA
COMEBACK TRAIL, THE .... HARRY HURWITZ
COMEDY'S DIRTIEST DOZEN .... STUART S. SHAPIRO
COMES A HORSEMAN .... DAN PAULSON
COMES A HORSEMAN .... GENE KIRKWOOD
COMES A HORSEMAN .... ROBERT CHARTOFF
COMES A HORSEMAN .... IRWIN WINKLER
COMFORT AND JOY .... CLIVE PARSONS
COMFORT AND JOY .... DAVINA BELLING
COMFORT AND JOY .... PADDY HIGSON
COMIC, THE .... AARON RUBEN
COMIC, THE .... CARL REINER
COMIC BOOK CONFIDENTIAL .... DON HAIG
COMIC BOOK CONFIDENTIAL ..... MARTIN HARBURY
COMIC BOOK CONFIDENTIAL .... RON MANN
COMING HOME .... JEROME HELLMAN
COMING TO AMERICA .... LESLIE BELZBERG
COMING TO AMERICA .... MARK LIPSKY
COMMANDO .... ROBERT KOSBERG
COMMANDO .... JOEL SILVER
COMMANDO SQUAD .... ALAN AMIEL
COMMANDO SQUAD .... FRED OLEN RAY
COMMANDO SQUAD .... YORAM PELMAN
COMMUNION .... DAN ALLINGHAM
COMMUNION .... EDWARD SIMONS
COMMUNION .... GARY BARBER
COMMUNION .... PAUL REDSHAW
COMMUNION .... PHILIPPE MORA
COMMUNION .... WHITLEY STRIEBER
COMPANY OF WOLVES, THE .... CHRIS BROWN
COMPANY OF WOLVES, THE .... NIK POWELL
COMPANY OF WOLVES, THE .... STEPHEN WOOLLEY
COMPETITION, THE .... HOWARD PINE
COMPETITION, THE .... WILLIAM SACKHEIM
COMPLEAT BEATLES, THE .... PATRICK MONTGOMERY
COMPLEAT BEATLES, THE .... STEPHANIE BENNETT
COMPROMISING POSITIONS .... FRANK PERRY
COMPROMISING POSITIONS .... SALAH M. HASSANEIN
COMPUTER WORE TENNIS SHOES, THE .... BILL ANDERSON
CONAN THE BARBARIAN .... D. CONSTANTINE CONTE
CONAN THE BARBARIAN .... RAFFAELLA DE LAURENTIIS
CONAN THE BARBARIAN .... BUZZ FEITSHANS
CONAN THE BARBARIAN .... EDWARD R. PRESSMAN
CONAN THE DESTROYER .... RAFFAELLA DE LAURENTIIS
CONAN THE DESTROYER .... STEPHEN F. KESTEN
CONAN THE DESTROYER .... EDWARD R. PRESSMAN
CONCORDE - AIRPORT '79, THE .... JENNINGS LANG
CONCORDE - AIRPORT '79, THE .... WILLIAM FRYE
CONDORMAN .... JAN WILLIAMS
CONDORMAN .... RON MILLER
CONDUCT UNBECOMING .... BARRY SPIKINGS
CONDUCT UNBECOMING .... MICHAEL DEELEY
CONSUMING PASSIONS ...... WILLIAM P. CARTLIDGE
CONTINENTAL DIVIDE .... BERNIE BRILLSTEIN
CONTINENTAL DIVIDE .... ROBERT LARSON
CONTINENTAL DIVIDE .... STEVEN SPIELBERG
CONVERSATION, THE ..... FRANCIS FORD COPPOLA
CONVOY .... BARRY SPIKINGS
CONVOY .... MICHAEL DEELEY
COOGAN'S BLUFF .... JENNINGS LANG
COOK, THE THIEF, HIS WIFE & HER LOVER, THE ...... DANIEL TOSCAN DUPLANTIER
COOK, THE THIEF, HIS WIFE & HER LOVER, THE .... DENIS WIGMAN
COOK, THE THIEF, HIS WIFE & HER LOVER, THE .... KEES KASANDER
COOK, THE THIEF, HIS WIFE & HER LOVER, THE .... PASCALE DAUMAN
COOKIE .... JENNIFER OGDEN
COOKIE .... LAURENCE MARK
COOL BREEZE .... GENE CORMAN
COOL HAND LUKE .... GORDON CARROLL
COP .... JAMES B. HARRIS
COP .... JAMES WOODS
COPS AND ROBBERS .... GEROGE PAPPAS
COPS AND ROBBERS .... ELLIOTT KASTNER
CORVETTE SUMMER .... HAL BARWOOD
COTTON CLUB, THE .... ROBERT EVANS
COTTON CLUB, THE .... BARRIE M. OSBORNE
COTTON CLUB, THE .... JOSEPH CUSUMANO
COTTON CLUB, THE .... MILTON FORMAN
COTTON CLUB, THE .... SYLVIO TABET
COTTON CLUB, THE .... DYSON LOVELL
COTTON CLUB, THE .... FRED ROOS
COUCH TRIP, THE .... GORDON A. WEBB
COUCH TRIP, THE .... LAWRENCE GORDON
COUNTRY .... JESSICA LANGE
COUNTRY .... WILLIAM BEAUDINE JR.
COUNTRY .... WILLIAM D. WITTLIFF
COUPE DE VILLE .... JAMES G. ROBINSON
COUPE DE VILLE .... JERRY A. BAERWITZ
COUPE DE VILLE .... LARRY BREZNER
COUPE DE VILLE .... MIKE BINDER
COUPE DE VILLE .... PAUL SCHIFF
COURAGE .... ROBERT L. ROSEN
COURAGE MOUNTAIN .... JOEL DOUGLAS
COURAGE MOUNTAIN .... STEVE ULJAKI
COURT MARTIAL .... SIR JOHN WOOLF
COUSINS .... GEORGE GOODMAN
COUSINS .... WILLIAM ALLYN
COVERGIRL .... CLAUDE HEROUX
COVERGIRL .... LAWRENCE NESIS
COVERGIRL .... VICTOR SOLNICKI
COVERGIRL .... PIERRE DAVID
CRACK HOUSE .... JACK SILVERMAN
CRACK HOUSE .... JIM SILVERMAN
CRACK HOUSE .... JOAN WEIDMAN
CRACKERS .... ROBERT CORTES
CRACKERS .... EDWARD LEWIS
CRAZY WORLD OF JULIUS VROODER, THE .... EDWARD L. RISSIEN
CRAZY WORLD OF JULIUS VROODER, THE .... ARTHUR HILLER
CRAZY WORLD OF JULIUS VROODER, THE .... HUGH M. HEFNER
CREATOR .... STEPHEN J. FRIEDMAN
CREATOR .... CHARLES B. MULVEHILL
CREEPSHOW .... SALAH M. HASSANEIN
CREEPSHOW .... RICHARD P. RUBINSTEIN
CREEPSHOW 2 .... DAVID BALL
CREEPSHOW 2 .... RICHARD P. RUBINSTEIN
CRIME ZONE .... LUIS LLOSA
CRIME ZONE .... ROGER CORMAN
CRIMES AND MISDEMEANORS .... CHARLES H. JOFFE
CRIMES AND MISDEMEANORS .... JACK ROLLINS
CRIMES AND MISDEMEANORS .... ROBERT GREENHUT
CRIMES OF PASSION .... BARRY SANDLER
CRIMES OF THE HEART .... ARLYNE ROTHBERG
CRIMES OF THE HEART .... BILL GERBER
CRIMES OF THE HEART .... BURT SUGARMAN
CRIMES OF THE HEART .... FREDDIE FIELDS
CRIMEWAVE .... IRVIN SHAPIRO
CRIMEWAVE .... ROBERT G. TAPERT
CRIMEWAVE .... EDWARD R. PRESSMAN
CRIMINAL LAW .... DEREK GIBSON
CRIMINAL LAW .... HILARY HEATH
CRIMINAL LAW .... JOHN DALY
CRIMINAL LAW .... KEN GORD
CRIMINAL LAW .... ROBERT MACLEAN
CRITICAL CONDITION .... ROBERT LARSON
CRITTERS .... ROBERT SHAYE
CRITTERS .... RUPERT HARVEY
CRITTERS 2: THE MAIN COURSE ... ROBERT SHAYE
CROCODILE DUNDEE .... JANE SCOTT
CROCODILE DUNDEE .... JOHN CORNELL
CROCODILE DUNDEE II .... JOHN CORNELL
CROCODILE DUNDEE II .... PAUL HOGAN
CROCODILE DUNDEE II .... JANE SCOTT
CROSS COUNTRY .... RONALD I. COHEN
CROSS CREEK .... ROBERT B. RADNITZ
CROSS CREEK .... TERRY NELSON
CROSS MY HEART .... ALAN GREISMAN
CROSS MY HEART .... CHARLES OKUN
CROSS MY HEART .... LAWRENCE KASDAN
CROSS MY HEART .... MICHAEL GRILLO
CROSS MY HEART .... AARON SPELLING
CROSS OF IRON .... ALEX WINITSKY
CROSS OF IRON .... ARLENE SELLERS
CROSSED SWORDS .... ILYA SALKIND
CROSSED SWORDS .... PIERRE SPENGLER
CROSSING DELANCEY .... MICHAEL NOZIK
CROSSING DELANCEY .... RAPHAEL D. SILVER
CROSSOVER DREAMS .... MANUEL ARCE
CROSSROADS .... MARK CARLINER
CROSSROADS .... TIM ZINNEMANN
CRUISING .... BURTT HARRIS
CRUISING .... JERRY WEINTRAUB
CRUSOE .... ANDREW BRAUNSBERG
CRY BABY KILLER .... ROGER CORMAN
CRY-BABY .... JIM ABRAHAMS
CRY-BABY .... RACHEL TALALAY
CRY-BABY .... BRIAN GRAZER
CRY FREEDOM .... JOHN BRILEY
CRY FREEDOM .... NORMAN SPENCER
CRY FREEDOM .... TERENCE CLEGG
CRY FREEDOM .... RICHARD ATTENBOROUGH
CRY IN THE DARK, A .... MENAHEM GOLAN
CRY IN THE DARK, A .... ROY STEVENS
CRY IN THE DARK, A .... VERITY LAMBERT
CRY IN THE DARK, A .... YORAM GLOBUS
CRY IN THE WILD, A .... JULIE CORMAN
CRY OF THE BANSHEE .... SAMUEL Z. ARKOFF
CRYSTAL HEART .... CARLOS VASALLO
CUBA .... ALEX WINITSKY
CUBA .... DENIS O'DELL
CUBA .... ARLENE SELLERS
CUJO .... DANIEL H. BLATT
CUJO .... ROBERT SINGER
CURSE OF THE PINK PANTHER .... JONATHAN D. KRANE
CURSE OF THE PINK PANTHER .... BLAKE EDWARDS
CURSE OF THE PINK PANTHER .... TONY ADAMS
CURSE, THE .... LOUIS FULCI
CURSE, THE .... MOSHE DIAMANT
CURSE, THE .... OBIDIO G. ASSONITIS
CUTTER'S WAY .... JEFFREY CHERNOV
CUTTER'S WAY .... PAUL R. GURIAN
CYBORG .... MENAHEM GOLAN
CYBORG .... TOM KARNOWSKI
CYBORG .... YORAM GLOBUS
CYCLONE .... PAUL HERTZBERG
CYRANO DE BERGERAC .... STANLEY KRAMER

D

D.A.R.Y.L. .... GABRIELLE KELLY
D.A.R.Y.L. .... JOHN HEYMAN
D.A.R.Y.L. .... BURTT HARRIS
D.C. CAB .... CASSIUS VERNON WETHERSBY
D.C. CAB .... PETER GUBER
D.C. CAB .... PETER V. HERALD
D.C. CAB .... TOPPER CAREW
D.C. CAB .... JON PETERS
D.O.A. .... ANDREW J. KUEHN
D.O.A. .... CATHLEEN SUMMERS
D.O.A. .... IAN SANDER
D.O.A. .... LAURA ZISKIN
DA .... JULIE CORMAN
DA .... MARTIN SHEEN
DA .... SAM GROGG
DA .... WILLIAM R. GREENBLATT
DAD .... FRANK MARSHALL
DAD .... GARY DAVID GOLDBERG
DAD .... KATHLEEN KENNEDY
DAD .... STEVEN SPIELBERG

DAD ..... JOSEPH STERN
DADDY'S BOYS ..... ANNA ROTH
DADDY'S BOYS ..... ROGER CORMAN
DADDY'S DYIN' ..... MONTY MONTGOMERY
DADDY'S DYIN' ..... SIGURJON SIGHVATSSON
DADDY'S DYIN' ..... STEVEN GOLIN
DADDY'S DYIN' ..... BOBBIE EDRICK
DADDY'S DYIN' ..... DEL SHORES
DAISY MILLER ..... FRANK MARSHALL
DAISY MILLER ..... PETER BOGDANOVICH
DAKOTA ..... DARRYL J. KUNTZ
DAKOTA ..... FRANK J. KUNTZ
DAMIEN - OMEN II ..... HARVEY BERNHARD
DAMNATION ALLEY ..... PAUL MASLANSKY
DAMNED RIVER ..... CONRAD HOOL
DAMNED RIVER ..... LANCE HOOL
DANCE OF DEATH, THE ..... JOHN BRABOURNE
DANCE OF DEATH, THE ..... RICHARD GOODWIN
DANCE OF THE DAMNED ..... ANDY RUBEN
DANCE OF THE DAMNED ..... ANNA ROTH
DANCE OF THE DAMNED ..... REID SHANE
DANCE WITH A STRANGER ..... PAUL COWAN
DANCE WITH A STRANGER ..... ROGER RANDALL-CUTLER
DANCERS ..... CHARLES FRANCE
DANCERS ..... JOHN THOMPSON
DANCERS ..... MENAHEM GOLAN
DANCERS ..... NORA KAYE†
DANCERS ..... YORAM GLOBUS
DANCERS ..... JACK BRODSKY
DANCES WITH WOLVES ..... DEREK KAVANAGH
DANCES WITH WOLVES ..... JIM WILSON
DANCES WITH WOLVES ..... KEVIN COSTNER
DANGEROUS LIAISONS ..... CHRISTOPHER HAMPTON
DANGEROUS LIAISONS ..... HANK MOONJEAN
DANGEROUS LIAISONS ..... NORMA HEYMAN
DANGEROUS LOVE ..... BRAD KREVOY
DANGEROUS LOVE ..... BRIAN J. O'SULLIVAN
DANGEROUS LOVE ..... ERIC BROOKS
DANGEROUS LOVE ..... STEVEN STABLER
DANGEROUSLY CLOSE ..... HAROLD SOBEL
DANGEROUSLY CLOSE ..... MENAHEM GOLAN
DANGEROUSLY CLOSE ..... YORAM GLOBUS
DANIEL ..... E.L. DOCTOROW
DANIEL ..... JOHN HEYMAN
DANIEL ..... SIDNEY LUMET
DANIEL ..... BURTT HARRIS
DANNY BOY ..... BARRY BLACKMORE
DANNY BOY ..... JOHN BOORMAN
DARK CRYSTAL, THE ..... DAVID LAZER
DARK CRYSTAL, THE ..... GARY KURTZ
DARK CRYSTAL, THE ..... JIM HENSON
DARK OF THE SUN ..... GEORGE ENGLUND
DARK STAR ..... JOHN CARPENTER
DARKMAN ..... DARYL KASS
DARKMAN ..... ROBERT G. TAPERT
DARLING ..... JOSEPH JANNI
DARLING LILI ..... BLAKE EDWARDS
DARLING LILI ..... TONY ADAMS
DARLING LILI ..... KEN WALES
DARLING LILI ..... OWEN CRUMP
DARWIN ADVENTURE , THE ..... EDGAR J. SCHERICK
DAS BOOT ..... GUNTER ROHRBACH
DAS BOOT ..... JOHN HYDE
DAS BOOT ..... MARK DAMON
DAS BOOT ..... MICHAEL BITTINS
DAS BOOT ..... EDWARD R. PRESSMAN
DATE NIGHT ..... TOVA LAITER
DATE WITH AN ANGEL ..... MARTHA SCHUMACHER
DAVID AND LISA ..... PAUL HELLER
DAWN OF THE DEAD ..... RICHARD P. RUBINSTEIN
DAY IN THE DEATH OF JOE EGG, A ..... DAVID DEUTSCH
DAY OF THE DEAD ..... SALAH M. HASSANEIN
DAY OF THE DEAD ..... RICHARD P. RUBINSTEIN
DAY OF THE DOLPHIN, THE ..... ROBERT E. RELYEA
DAY OF THE JACKAL, THE ..... DAVID DEUTSCH
DAY OF THE JACKAL, THE ..... JULIEN DERODE
DAY OF THE JACKAL, THE ..... SIR JOHN WOOLF
DAY OF THE LOCUST, THE ..... RONALD SHEDLO
DAY OF THE LOCUST, THE ... SHELDON SCHRAGER
DAY OF THE LOCUST, THE ..... JEROME HELLMAN
DAYS OF HEAVEN ..... JACOB BRACKMAN
DAYS OF HEAVEN ..... HAROLD SCHNEIDER
DAYS OF HEAVEN ..... BERT SCHNEIDER
DEAD AND BURIED ..... MICHAEL RACHMIL
DEAD AND BURIED ..... RICHARD R. ST. JOHNS
DEAD AND BURIED ..... ROBERT FENTRESS
DEAD AND BURIED ..... RONALD SHUSETT
DEAD BANG ..... ROBERT L. ROSEN
DEAD BANG ..... STEVE ROTH
DEAD CALM ..... DOUG MITCHELL
DEAD CALM ..... GEORGE MILLER
DEAD CALM ..... TERRY HAYES
DEAD HEAT ..... DAVID HELPERN
DEAD HEAT ..... MICHAEL MELTZER
DEAD MEN DON'T WEAR PLAID ..... DAVID V. PICKER
DEAD MEN DON'T WEAR PLAID ..... WILLIAM E. MCEUEN
DEAD OF WINTER ..... JOHN BLOOMGARDEN
DEAD OF WINTER ..... MARC SHMUGER
DEAD POETS SOCIETY ..... PAUL JUNGER WITT
DEAD POETS SOCIETY ..... STEVEN HAFT
DEAD POETS SOCIETY ..... TONY THOMAS
DEAD POOL, THE ..... DAVID VALDES
DEAD RINGERS ..... CAROL BAUM
DEAD RINGERS ..... DAVID CRONENBERG
DEAD RINGERS ..... JOE ROTH
DEAD RINGERS ..... JOHN BOARD
DEAD RINGERS ..... MARC BOYMAN
DEAD RINGERS ..... SYLVIO TABET
DEAD ZONE, THE ..... DEBRA HILL
DEAD, THE ..... CHRIS SIEVERNICH
DEAD, THE ..... WIELAND SCHULZ-KEIL
DEAD, THE ..... WILLIAM J. QUIGLEY
DEADHEAD MILES ..... TONY BILL
DEADHEAD MILES ..... VERNON ZIMMERMAN
DEADLY AFFAIR, THE ..... DENIS O'DELL
DEADLY AFFAIR, THE ..... SIDNEY LUMET
DEADLY BLESSING ..... WILLIAM S. GILMORE
DEADLY FORCE ..... SANDY HOWARD
DEADLY FORCE ..... DEREK GIBSON
DEADLY FORCE ..... JOHN DALY
DEADLY FRIEND ..... PATRICK KELLEY
DEADLY FRIEND ..... ROBERT L. CRAWFORD
DEADLY FRIEND ..... ROBERT M. SHERMAN
DEADLY GAME, THE ..... ELY LANDAU
DEADLY ILLUSION ..... IRWIN MEYER
DEADLY ILLUSION ..... MICHAEL SHAPIRO
DEADLY ILLUSION ..... RODNEY SHELDON
DEADLY WEAPON ..... PETER MANOOGIAN
DEADLY WEAPON ..... CHARLES BAND
DEAL OF THE CENTURY ..... BUD YORKIN
DEAL OF THE CENTURY ..... DAVID SALVEN
DEAL OF THE CENTURY ..... JON AVNET
DEAL OF THE CENTURY ..... PAUL BRICKMAN
DEAL OF THE CENTURY ..... STEVE TISCH
DEALERS ..... ANDREW BROWN
DEALERS ..... JOHN HAMBLEY
DEALERS ..... WILLIAM P. CARTLIDGE
DEALING ..... EDWARD R. PRESSMAN
DEAR AMERICA ..... BILL COUTURIE
DEAR AMERICA ..... THOMAS BIRD
DEAR DETECTIVE ..... ALEXANDRE MNOUCHKINE
DEAR DETECTIVE ..... GEORGES DANCIGERS
DEATH BEFORE DISHONOR ..... LAWRENCE KUBIK
DEATH GAME ..... LARRY SPIEGEL
DEATH HUNT ..... MURRAY SHOSTAK
DEATH HUNT ..... RAYMOND CHOW
DEATH HUNT ..... ROBERT BAYLIS
DEATH OF A SALESMAN ..... STANLEY KRAMER
DEATH OF AN ANGEL ..... CHARLES J. WEBER
DEATH OF AN ANGEL ..... DIMITRI VILLARD
DEATH OF AN ANGEL ..... PETER BURRELL
DEATH ON THE NILE ..... RICHARD GOODWIN
DEATH ON THE NILE ..... JOHN BRABOURNE
DEATH RACE 2000 ..... ROGER CORMAN
DEATH SHIP ..... HAROLD GREENBERG
DEATH SHIP ..... SANDY HOWARD
DEATH VALLEY ..... STANLEY BECK
DEATH VALLEY ..... ELLIOTT KASTNER
DEATH WISH ..... BOBBY ROBERTS
DEATH WISH ..... HAL LANDERS
DEATH WISH ..... MICHAEL WINNER
DEATH WISH II ..... BOBBY ROBERTS
DEATH WISH II ..... HAL LANDERS
DEATH WISH II ..... MENAHEM GOLAN
DEATH WISH II ..... YORAM GLOBUS
DEATH WISH 3 ..... MENAHEM GOLAN
DEATH WISH 3 ..... YORAM GLOBUS
DEATH WISH 3 ..... MICHAEL J. KAGAN
DEATH WISH 3 ..... MICHAEL WINNER
DEATH WISH 4: THE CRACKDOWN ..... MENAHEM GOLAN
DEATH WISH 4: THE CRACKDOWN ..... PANCHO KOHNER
DEATH WISH 4: THE CRACKDOWN ..... YORAM GLOBUS
DEATHSPORT ..... ROGER CORMAN
DEATHTRAP ..... BURTT HARRIS
DEATHTRAP ..... JAY PRESSON ALLEN
DEATHWATCH ..... GABRIEL BOUSTANI
DEATHWATCH ..... JANINE RUBELZ
DECAMERON, THE ..... ALBERTO GRIMALDI
DECEIVERS, THE ..... MICHAEL WHITE
DECEIVERS, THE ..... TIM VAN RELLIM
DECEIVERS, THE ..... ISMAIL MERCHANT
DECLINE OF WESTERN CIVILIZATION PART II: THE METAL YEARS, THE ..... MILES A. COPELAND III
DECLINE OF WESTERN CIVILIZATION PART II: THE METAL YEARS, THE ..... PAUL COLICHMAN
DECLINE OF WESTERN CIVILIZATION PART II: THE METAL YEARS, THE ..... JONATHAN DAYTON
DECLINE OF WESTERN CIVILIZATION PART II: THE METAL YEARS, THE ..... VALERIE FARIS
DEEP END ..... HELMUT JEDELE
DEEP IN THE HEART ..... DAVID STREIT
DEEP IN THE HEART ..... TONY GARNETT
DEEP, THE ..... PETER GUBER
DEEPSTAR SIX ..... ANDREW VAJNA
DEEPSTAR SIX ..... MARIO KASSAR
DEEPSTAR SIX ..... PATRICK MARKEY
DEEPSTAR SIX ..... SEAN S. CUNNINGHAM
DEER HUNTER, THE ..... ROBERT E. RELYEA
DEER HUNTER, THE ..... JOANN CARELLI
DEER HUNTER, THE ..... MICHAEL DEELEY
DEER HUNTER, THE ..... BARRY SPIKINGS
DEER HUNTER, THE ..... JOHN DEVERALL
DEER HUNTER, THE ..... MICHAEL CIMINO
DEFENSE OF THE REALM ..... LYNDA MYLES
DEFENSE OF THE REALM ..... ROBIN DOUET
DEFENSE OF THE REALM ..... DAVID PUTTNAM
DEFIANCE ..... ROBERT S. WUNSCH
DEFIANCE ..... WILLIAM S. GILMORE
DEFIANCE ..... JERRY BRUCKHEIMER
DEFIANT ONES, THE ..... STANLEY KRAMER
DEJA VU ..... MENAHEM GOLAN
DEJA VU ..... MICHAEL J. KAGAN
DEJA VU ..... YORAM GLOBUS
DELICATE BALANCE, A ..... ELY LANDAU
DELICATE BALANCE, A ..... NEIL HARTLEY
DELICATE BALANCE, A ..... JACK GROSSBERG
DELICATE BALANCE, A ..... HENRY T. WEINSTEIN
DELINQUENTS, THE ..... ROBERT ALTMAN
DELTA FORCE, THE ..... MENAHEM GOLAN
DELTA FORCE, THE ..... YORAM GLOBUS
DEMENTIA 13 ..... ROGER CORMAN
DEMON SEED ..... HERB JAFFE
DEMON SEED ..... STEVEN-CHARLES JAFFE
DESERT BLOOM ..... MICHAEL HAUSMAN
DESERT BLOOM ..... RICHARD FISCHOFF
DESERT HEARTS ..... DONNA DEITCH
DESPAIR ..... EDWARD R. PRESSMAN
DESPAIR ..... LUTZ HENGST
DESPAIR ..... PETER MARTHESHEIMER
DESPERATE LIVING ..... JOHN WATERS
DESPERATELY SEEKING SUSAN ..... MIDGE SANFORD
DESPERATELY SEEKING SUSAN ..... SARAH PILLSBURY
DESPERATELY SEEKING SUSAN ..... MICHAEL PEYSER
DETECTIVE SCHOOL DROPOUTS ..... JOHN THOMPSON
DETECTIVE SCHOOL DROPOUTS ..... MENAHEM GOLAN
DETECTIVE SCHOOL DROPOUTS ..... YORAM GLOBUS
DEVIL AND MAX DEVLIN, THE ..... JEROME COURTLAND
DEVIL AND MAX DEVLIN, THE ..... RON MILLER
DEVIL'S ANGELS ..... ROGER CORMAN
DEVIL'S ANGELS ..... SAMUEL Z. ARKOFF
DEVILS, THE ..... ROBERT SOLO
DEVILS, THE ..... KEN RUSSELL
DEVILS, THE ..... ROY BAIRD
DIAMOND SKULLS ..... TIM BEVAN
DIAMONDS ARE FOREVER ..... ALBERT R. BROCCOLI
DIAMONDS ARE FOREVER ..... HARRY SALTZMAN
DICK TRACY ..... WARREN BEATTY
DICK TRACY ..... ART LINSON
DICK TRACY ..... FLOYD MUTRUX
DIE HARD ..... CHARLES GORDON
DIE HARD ..... LAWRENCE GORDON
DIE HARD ..... JOEL SILVER
DIE HARD 2 ..... JOEL SILVER
DIE HARD 2 ..... LAWRENCE GORDON
DIE HARD 2 ..... LLOYD LEVIN

DIE HARD 2 .... MICHAEL LEVY
DIE HARD 2 .... STEVE PERRY
DIE LAUGHING .... JON PETERS
DIFFERENT STORY, A .... MICHAEL C. LEONE
DIGBY, THE BIGGEST DOG IN THE WORLD .... WALTER SHENSON
DILLINGER .... LAWRENCE GORDON
DILLINGER .... SAMUEL Z. ARKOFF
DILLINGER .... BUZZ FEITSHANS
DIM SUM: A LITTLE BIT OF HEART .... TOM STERNBERG
DIM SUM: A LITTLE BIT OF HEART .... DANNY YUNG
DIM SUM: A LITTLE BIT OF HEART .... VINCENT TAI
DIM SUM: A LITTLE BIT OF HEART .... WAYNE WANG
DINER .... MARK JOHNSON
DINER .... JERRY WEINTRAUB
DIRT BIKE KID, THE .... JULIE CORMAN
DIRTY DANCING .... DORO BACHRACH
DIRTY DANCING .... ELEANOR BERGSTEIN
DIRTY DANCING .... LINDA GOTTLIEB
DIRTY DANCING .... MITCHELL CANNOLD
DIRTY DANCING .... STEVEN REUTHER
DIRTY HARRY .... ROBERT DALEY
DIRTY ROTTEN SCOUNDRELS .... BERNARD WILLIAMS
DIRTY ROTTEN SCOUNDRELS .... CHARLES HIRSCHHORN
DIRTY ROTTEN SCOUNDRELS .... DALE LAUNER
DIRTY TRICKS .... ARNOLD KOPELSON
DIRTY TRICKS .... VICTOR SOLNICKI
DIRTY TRICKS .... CLAUDE HEROUX
DIRTY TRICKS .... PIERRE DAVID
DISORDERLIES .... CHARLES STETTLER
DISORDERLIES .... GEORGE A. JACKSON
DISORDERLIES .... JOSEPH ZYNCZAK
DISORDERLIES .... MICHAEL JAFFE
DISORDERLIES .... MICHAEL SCHULTZ
DISORGANIZED CRIME .... JOHN BADHAM
DISORGANIZED CRIME .... LYNN BIGELOW
DISORGANIZED CRIME .... ROB COHEN
DISTANT THUNDER .... RICHARD L. O'CONNOR
DISTANT THUNDER .... DICK O'CONNOR
DISTANT THUNDER .... ROBERT L. SCHAFFEL
DISTANT VOICES, STILL LIVES .... JENNIFER HOWARTH
DIVINE MADNESS .... HOWARD JEFFREY
DIVINE MADNESS .... MICHAEL RITCHIE
DIVORCE AMERICAN STYLE .... NORMAN LEAR
DO THE RIGHT THING .... JON KILIK
DO THE RIGHT THING .... MONTY ROSS
DO THE RIGHT THING .... SPIKE LEE
DOCTOR AND THE DEVILS, THE .... JONATHAN SANGER
DOCTOR AND THE DEVILS, THE .... MEL BROOKS
DOCTOR AND THE DEVILS, THE .... GEOFFREY HELMAN
DOCTOR DETROIT .... PETER V. HERALD
DOCTOR DETROIT .... ROBERT K. WEISS
DOG DAY AFTERNOON .... MARTIN BREGMAN
DOG DAY AFTERNOON .... MARTIN ELFAND
DOG DAY AFTERNOON .... ROBERT GREENHUT
DOG OF FLANDERS , A .... ROBERT B. RADNITZ
DOGS IN SPACE .... DENNIS WRIGHT
DOGS IN SPACE .... GLENYS ROWE
DOGS IN SPACE .... ROBERT LETET
DOGS OF WAR, THE .... NORMAN JEWISON
DOGS OF WAR, THE .... LARRY DE WAAY
DOGS OF WAR, THE .... PATRICK PALMER
DOIN' TIME ON PLANET EARTH .... MENAHEM GOLAN
DOIN' TIME ON PLANET EARTH .... YORAM GLOBUS
DOLLS .... BRIAN YUZNA
DOLLS .... CHARLES BAND
DOMINICK AND EUGENE .... MARVIN MINOFF
DOMINICK AND EUGENE .... MIKE FARRELL
DOMINO PRINCIPAL, THE .... MARTIN STARGER
DOMINO PRINCIPLE, THE .... STANLEY KRAMER
DON'T DRINK THE WATER .... CHARLES H. JOFFE
DON'T DRINK THE WATER .... JACK GROSSBERG
DON'T LOOK NOW .... ANTHONY B. UNGER
DON'T LOOK NOW .... PETER KATZ
DOOR TO DOOR .... KEN WALES
DOUBLE REVENGE .... GEORGE ZECEVIC
DOUBLE REVENGE .... JOHN S. CURRAN
DOUBLE REVENGE .... LUIGI CINGOLANI
DOUBLE REVENGE .... T.J. CASTRONOVO
DOUBLE TROUBLE .... IRWIN WINKLER
DOUBLE TROUBLE .... JUDD BERNARD
DOWN AND OUT IN BEVERLY HILLS .... GEOFFREY TAYLOR
DOWN AND OUT IN BEVERLY HILLS .... PATO GUZMAN
DOWN AND OUT IN BEVERLY HILLS .... PAUL MAZURSKY
DOWN BY LAW .... ALAN KLEINBERG
DOWN BY LAW .... CARY BROKAW
DOWN BY LAW .... JIM STARK
DOWN BY LAW .... OTTO GROKENBERGER
DOWN BY LAW .... TOM ROTHMAN
DOWN TWISTED .... MENAHEM GOLAN
DOWN TWISTED .... TOM KARNOWSKI
DOWN TWISTED .... YORAM GLOBUS
DOWNHILL RACER .... RICHARD GREGSON
DOWNTOWN .... GALE ANNE HURD
DR. DETROIT .... BERNIE BRILLSTEIN
DR. NO .... ALBERT R. BROCCOLI
DR. STRANGLOVE OR: HOW I LEARNED TO STOP WORRYING AND LOVE THE BOMB .... STANLEY KUBRICK
DR. SYN, ALIAS THE SCARECROW .... BILL ANDERSON
DR. ZHIVAGO .... CARLO PONTI
DRACULA .... MARVIN MIRISCH
DRACULA .... WALTER MIRISCH
DRAGNET .... BERNIE BRILLSTEIN
DRAGNET .... DAVID PERMUT
DRAGNET .... ROBERT K. WEISS
DRAGONARD .... AVI LERNER
DRAGONFLY .... GILBERT CATES
DRAGONFLY .... SAMUEL Z. ARKOFF
DRAGONSLAYER .... ERIC RATTRAY
DRAGONSLAYER .... HOWARD W. KOCH
DRAGONSLAYER .... HAL BARWOOD
DREAM A LITTLE DREAM .... D.E. EISENBERG
DREAM A LITTLE DREAM .... ELLEN STELOFF
DREAM A LITTLE DREAM .... LAWRENCE KASANOFF
DREAM A LITTLE DREAM .... MARC ROCCO
DREAM LOVER .... JON BOORSTIN
DREAM LOVER .... SUSAN SOLT
DREAM LOVER .... WILLIAM C. GERRITY
DREAM TEAM, THE .... CHRISTOPHER W. KNIGHT
DREAM TEAM, THE .... DAVID LOUCKA
DREAM TEAM, THE .... JON CONNOLLY
DREAM TEAM, THE .... JOSEPH M. CARACCIOLO
DREAM TEAM, THE .... TERRY SPAZEK
DREAMCHILD .... DENNIS POTTER
DREAMCHILD .... KENITH TRODD
DREAMCHILD .... RICK MCCALLUM
DREAMCHILD .... VERITY LAMBERT
DREAMER .... MICHAEL LOBELL
DREAMSCAPE .... BRUCE COHN CURTIS
DREAMSCAPE .... CHUCK RUSSELL
DREAMSCAPE .... JERRY TOKOFSKY
DREAMSCAPE .... STANLEY R. ZUPNIK
DREAMSCAPE .... TOM CURTIS
DRESSED TO KILL .... FRED CARUSO
DRESSED TO KILL .... GEORGE LITTO
DRESSED TO KILL .... SAMUEL Z. ARKOFF
DRESSER, THE .... NIGEL WOOLL
DRESSER, THE .... PETER YATES
DRESSMAKER, THE .... RONALD SHEDLO
DRIFTER, THE .... KEN STEIN
DRIFTER, THE .... MATT LEIPZIG
DRIFTER, THE .... ROGER CORMAN
DRIVE, HE SAID .... HARRY GITTES
DRIVE, HE SAID .... STEVE BLAUNER
DRIVE, HE SAID .... FRED ROOS
DRIVE, HE SAID .... JACK NICHOLSON
DRIVE, HE SAID .... BERT SCHNEIDER
DRIVE-IN .... GEORGE LITTO
DRIVE-IN .... ALEXANDRA ROSE
DRIVE-IN .... TAMARA ASSEYEV
DRIVER, THE .... FRANK MARSHALL
DRIVER, THE .... LAWRENCE GORDON
DRIVING ME CRAZY .... ANDREW BRAUNSBERG
DRIVING MISS DAISY .... DAVID BROWN
DRIVING MISS DAISY .... JAKE EBERTS
DRIVING MISS DAISY .... LILI FINI ZANUCK
DRIVING MISS DAISY .... RICHARD D. ZANUCK
DROWNING POOL, THE .... LAWRENCE TURMAN
DROWNING POOL, THE .... DAVID FOSTER
DRUGSTORE COWBOY .... CARY BROKAW
DRUGSTORE COWBOY .... KAREN MURPHY
DRUGSTORE COWBOY .... NICK WECHSLER
DRUM .... RALPH SERPE
DRUM .... DINO DE LAURENTIIS
DRY WHITE SEASON, A .... PAULA WEINSTEIN
DRY WHITE SEASON, A .... TIM HAMPTON
DUDES .... GORDON WOLF
DUDES .... HERB JAFFE
DUDES .... MIGUEL TEJADA-FLORES
DUELLISTS, THE .... DAVID PUTTNAM
DUET FOR ONE .... MENAHEM GOLAN
DUET FOR ONE .... MICHAEL J. KAGAN
DUET FOR ONE .... YORAM GLOBUS
DUNGEONMASTER, THE .... CHARLES BAND
DUNWICH HORROR, THE .... ROGER CORMAN
DUNWICH HORROR, THE .... JAMES H. NICHOLSON†
DUNWICH HORROR, THE .... SAMUEL Z. ARKOFF
DUSTY AND SWEETS MCGEE .... MICHAEL S. LAUGHLIN
DUTCH TREAT .... MENAHEM GOLAN
DUTCH TREAT .... YORAM GLOBUS

E

E.T. THE EXTRA-TERRESTRIAL .... KATHLEEN KENNEDY
E.T. THE EXTRA-TERRESTRIAL .... MELISSA MATHISON
E.T. THE EXTRA-TERRESTRIAL .... STEVEN SPIELBERG
EAGLE HAS LANDED, THE .... JACK WINER
EAGLE HAS LANDED, THE .... DAVID NIVEN, JR.
EARTH GIRLS ARE EASY .... TONY GARNETT
EASY MONEY .... ESTELLE ENDLER†
EASY MONEY .... JOHN NICOLELLA
EASY RIDER .... PETER FONDA
EASY RIDER .... WILLIAM HAYWARD
EASY RIDER .... BERT SCHNEIDER
EASY WHEELS .... BRUCE CAMPBELL
EASY WHEELS .... DIMITRI VILLARD
EASY WHEELS .... ROBBY WALD
EASY WHEELS .... ROBERT G. TAPERT
EAT A BOWL OF TEA .... JOHN K. CHAN
EAT A BOWL OF TEA .... LINDSAY LAW
EAT A BOWL OF TEA .... TOM STERNBERG
EAT AND RUN .... JACK BRIGGS
EAT MY DUST .... ROGER CORMAN
EAT THE PEACH .... DAVID COLLINS
EAT THE PEACH .... JOHN KELLEHER
EAT THE RICH .... TIM VAN RELLIM
EATING RAOUL .... ANNE KIMMEL
EAVES DROPPER, THE .... PAUL HELLER
ECHO PARK .... WALTER SHENSON
EDDIE AND THE CRUISERS II EDDIE LIVES .... JAMES L. STUART
EDDIE AND THE CRUISERS II: EDDIE LIVES .... STEPHANE REICHEL
EDDIE AND THE CRUISERS II: EDDIE LIVES .... WENDY GREAN
EDDIE AND THE CRUISERS II: EDDIE LIVES .... DENIS HEROUX
EDDIE AND THE CRUISERS II: EDDIE LIVES .... VICTOR LOEWY
EDDIE AND THE CRUISERS II: EDDIE LIVES .... WILLIAM STUART
EDDIE MACON'S RUN .... LOUIS A. STROLLER
EDDIE MACON'S RUN .... MARTIN BREGMAN
EDDIE MACON'S RUN .... PETER SAPHIER
EDDIE MURPHY RAW .... EDDIE MURPHY
EDDIE MURPHY RAW .... JEFFREY CHERNOV
EDDIE MURPHY RAW .... KEENEN IVORY WAYANS
EDDIE MURPHY RAW .... ROBERT D. WACHS
EDGE OF SANITY .... EDWARD SIMONS
EDGE OF SANITY .... HARRY ALAN TOWERS
EDGE OF SANITY .... PETER A. MCRAE
EDUCATING RITA .... HERBERT L. OAKES
EDUCATING RITA .... LEWIS GILBERT
EFFECT OF GAMMA RAYS ON MAN-ON-THE-MOON MARIGOLDS, THE .... JOHN FOREMAN
EFFECT OF GAMMA RAYS ON MAN-IN-THE-MOON MARIGOLDS, THE .... PAUL NEWMAN
EIGER SANCTION , THE .... RICHARD D. ZANUCK
EIGER SANCTION, THE .... DAVID BROWN
EIGER SANCTION, THE .... JENNINGS LANG
EIGER SANCTION, THE .... ROBERT DALEY
EIGHT IRON MEN .... STANLEY KRAMER
EIGHT MEN OUT .... BARBARA BOYLE
EIGHT MEN OUT .... JERRY OFFSAY
EIGHT MEN OUT .... PEGGY RAJSKI
EIGHT MEN OUT .... SARAH PILLSBURY
EIGHT MEN OUT .... MIDGE SANFORD
EIGHT MILLION WAYS TO DIE .... CHARLES B. MULVEHILL
EIGHT MILLION WAYS TO DIE .... STEVE ROTH
EL NORTE .... ANNA THOMAS
ELECTRA GLIDE IN BLUE .... JAMES WILLIAM GUERCIO
ELECTRA GLIDE IN BLUE .... RUPERT HITZIG
ELECTRIC DREAMS .... LARRY DE WAAY
ELECTRIC DREAMS .... RUSTY LEMORANDE
ELECTRIC HORSEMAN, THE .... RAY STARK
ELENI .... MARK PICK
ELENI .... NICHOLAS GAGE
ELENI .... NICK VANOFF
ELENI .... NIGEL WOOLL

ELEPHANT MAN, THE ... JONATHAN SANGER
ELEPHANT MAN, THE ... STUART CORNFELD
ELIMINATORS ... CHARLES BAND
ELVIRA, MISTRESS OF THE DARK ... ERIC GARDNER
ELVIRA, MISTRESS OF THE DARK ... JOEL THURM
ELVIRA, MISTRESS OF THE DARK ... MARK PIERSON
ELVIRA, MISTRESS OF THE DARK ... MICHAEL RACHMIL
ELVIS: THAT'S THE WAY IT IS ... DALE HUTCHINSON
EMERALD FOREST, THE ... EDGAR F. GROSS
EMERALD FOREST, THE ... JOHN BOORMAN
EMERALD FOREST, THE ... MICHAEL DRYHURST
EMIL AND THE DETECTIVES ... PETER V. HERALD
EMPIRE OF THE ANTS ... BERT I. GORDON
EMPIRE OF THE ANTS ... SAMUEL Z. ARKOFF
EMPIRE OF THE SUN ... CHRIS KENNY
EMPIRE OF THE SUN ... KATHLEEN KENNEDY
EMPIRE OF THE SUN ... ROBERT SHAPIRO
EMPIRE OF THE SUN ... FRANK MARSHALL
EMPIRE OF THE SUN ... STEVEN SPIELBERG
EMPIRE STRIKES BACK, THE ... GARY KURTZ
EMPIRE STRIKES BACK, THE ... GEORGE LUCAS
EMPIRE STRIKES BACK, THE ... JIM BLOOM
EMPIRE STRIKES BACK, THE ... ROBERT WATTS
END OF THE LINE ... LEWIS ALLEN
END OF THE LINE ... MARY STEENBURGEN
END OF THE LINE ... PETER NEWMAN
END OF THE LINE ... WALKER STUART
END, THE ... LAWRENCE GORDON
END, THE ... HANK MOONJEAN
ENDANGERED SPECIES ... CAROLYN PFEIFFER
ENDANGERED SPECIES ... ZALMAN KING
ENDLESS LOVE ... DYSON LOVELL
ENDLESS LOVE ... KEITH BARISH
ENEMIES, A LOVE STORY ... IRBY SMITH
ENEMIES, A LOVE STORY ... JAMES G. ROBINSON
ENEMIES, A LOVE STORY ... JOE ROTH
ENEMIES, A LOVE STORY ... PATO GUZMAN
ENEMIES, A LOVE STORY ... PAUL MAZURSKY
ENEMY MINE ... STANLEY O'TOOLE
ENEMY MINE ... STEPHEN J. FRIEDMAN
ENEMY TERRITORY ... CYNTHIA DE PAULA
ENEMY TERRITORY ... TIM KINCAID
ENEMY TERRITORY ... CHARLES BAND
ENFORCER, THE ... FRITZ MANES
ENIGMA ... ANDRE PERGAMENT
ENIGMA ... BEN ARBEID
ENIGMA ... PETER SHAW
ENORMOUS CHANGES AT THE LAST MINUTE ... MIRRA BANK
ENTER THE DRAGON ... FRED WEINTRAUB
ENTER THE DRAGON ... PAUL HELLER
ENTER THE NINJA ... JUDD BERNARD
ENTER THE NINJA ... YORAM GLOBUS
ENTERTAINER, THE ... HARRY SALTZMAN
ENTITY, THE ... ANDREW D.T. PFEFFER
ENTITY, THE ... MICHAEL C. LEONE
ENTITY, THE ... HAROLD SCHNEIDER
EQUUS ... LESTER PERSKY
EQUUS ... ELLIOTT KASTNER
ERIK THE VIKING ... JOHN GOLDSTONE
ERIK THE VIKING ... TERRY GLINWOOD
ERNEST GOES TO CAMP ... MARTIN ERLICHMAN
ERNEST GOES TO CAMP ... STACY WILLIAMS
ERNEST GOES TO CAMP ... ELMO WILLIAMS
ERNEST GOES TO JAIL ... COKE SAMS
ERNEST GOES TO JAIL ... MARTIN ERLICHMAN
ERNEST GOES TO JAIL ... STACY WILLIAMS
ERNEST SAVES CHRISTMAS ... COKE SAMS
ERNEST SAVES CHRISTMAS ... DOUG CLAYBOURNE
ERNEST SAVES CHRISTMAS ... JOSEPH L. AKERMAN
ERNEST SAVES CHRISTMAS ... JUSTIS GREENE
ERNEST SAVES CHRISTMAS ... MARTIN ERLICHMAN
ERNEST SAVES CHRISTMAS ... STACY WILLIAMS
ESCAPE ARTIST, THE ... FRED ROOS
ESCAPE ARTIST, THE ... BUCK HOUGHTON
ESCAPE ARTIST, THE ... DOUG CLAYBOURNE
ESCAPE ARTIST, THE ... FRANCIS FORD COPPOLA
ESCAPE FROM ALCATRAZ ... FRITZ MANES
ESCAPE FROM ALCATRAZ ... ROBERT DALEY
ESCAPE FROM NEW YORK ... BARRY BERNARDI
ESCAPE FROM NEW YORK ... DEBRA HILL
ESCAPE FROM NEW YORK ... LARRY J. FRANCO
ESCAPE TO ATHENA ... JACK WINER
ESCAPE TO ATHENA ... DAVID NIVEN, JR.
ESCAPE TO WITCH MOUNTAIN ... JEROME COURTLAND
ESCAPE TO WITCH MOUNTAIN ... RON MILLER

EUREKA ... JEREMY THOMAS
EUREKA ... JOHN FOREMAN
EUROPEANS, THE ... ISMAIL MERCHANT
EVERLASTING SECRET FAMILY, THE ... ANTONY I. GINNANE
EVERY TIME WE SAY GOODBYE ... JACOB KOTZKY
EVERY TIME WE SAY GOODBYE ... SHARON HAREL
EVERY WHICH WAY BUT LOOSE ... FRITZ MANES
EVERY WHICH WAY BUT LOOSE ... ROBERT DALEY
EVERYBODY WINS ... EZRA SWERDLOW
EVERYBODY WINS ... JEREMY THOMAS
EVERYBODY WINS ... TERRY GLINWOOD
EVERYBODY'S ALL-AMERICAN ... ALAN C. BLOMQUIST
EVERYBODY'S ALL-AMERICAN ... STUART BENJAMIN
EVERYBODY'S ALL-AMERICAN ... TAYLOR HACKFORD
EVERYBODY'S ALL-AMERICAN ... LAURA ZISKIN
EVERYBODY'S ALL-AMERICAN ... IAN SANDER
EVERYTHING YOU ALWAYS WANTED TO KNOW ABOUT SEX* (*BUT WERE AFRAID TO ASK) ... CHARLES H. JOFFE
EVERYTHING YOU ALWAYS WANTED TO KNOW ABOUT SEX* (*BUT WERE AFRAID TO ASK) ... JACK BRODSKY
EVERYTHING YOU ALWAYS WANTED TO KNOW ABOUT SEX* (*BUT WERE AFRAID TO ASK) ... JACK GROSSBERG
EVIL DEAD, THE ... BRUCE CAMPBELL
EVIL DEAD, THE ... ROBERT G. TAPERT
EVIL DEAD, THE ... SAMUEL M. RAIMI
EVIL DEAD 2: DEAD BY DAWN ... ROBERT G. TAPERT
EVIL THAT MEN DO, THE ... PANCHO KOHNER
EVIL UNDER THE SUN ... JOHN BRABOURNE
EVIL UNDER THE SUN ... RICHARD GOODWIN
EXCALIBUR ... JOHN BOORMAN
EXCALIBUR ... MICHAEL DRYHURST
EXECUTIVE ACTION ... DAN BESSIE
EXECUTIVE ACTION ... GARY HOROWITZ
EXECUTIVE ACTION ... EDWARD LEWIS
EXORCIST, THE ... NOEL MARSHALL
EXORCIST, THE ... WILLIAM PETER BLATTY
EXORCIST II: THE HERETIC ... JOHN BOORMAN
EXORCIST II: THE HERETIC ... RICHARD LEDERER
EXORCIST: 1990, THE ... CARTER DE HAVEN
EXORCIST: 1990, THE ... JAMES G. ROBINSON
EXORCIST: 1990, THE ... JOE ROTH
EXPENDABLES, THE ... ANNA ROTH
EXPENDABLES, THE ... CHRISTOPHER SANTIAGO
EXPERIENCE PREFERRED... BUT NOT ESSENTIAL ... DAVID PUTTNAM
EXPERIENCE PREFERRED... BUT NOT ESSENTIAL ... CHRIS GRIFFIN
EXPERTS, THE ... JACK GROSSBERG
EXPERTS, THE ... JAMES KEACH
EXPERTS, THE ... JONATHAN D. KRANE
EXPLORERS ... DAVID BOMBYK†
EXPLORERS ... MICHAEL FINNELL
EXPLORERS ... PAUL MONASH
EXPLORERS ... CHARLES R. MEEKER
EXPLORERS ... EDWARD S. FELDMAN
EXPOSED ... JAMES TOBACK
EXPOSED ... SERGE SILBERMAN
EXTERMINATOR 2 ... MARK BUNTZMAN
EXTERMINATOR 2 ... MENAHEM GOLAN
EXTERMINATOR 2 ... YORAM GLOBUS
EXTRAORDINARY SEAMAN , THE ... EDWARD LEWIS
EXTRAORDINARY SEAMAN, THE ... JOHN H. CUSHINGHAM
EXTREMITIES ... BURT SUGARMAN
EXTREMITIES ... GEORGE W. PERKINS
EXTREMITIES ... MICHAEL ROSENBLATT
EXTREMITIES ... SCOTT ROSENFELT
EXTREMITIES ... THOMAS COLEMAN
EYE FOR AN EYE, AN ... BOB REHME
EYE FOR AN EYE, AN ... FRANK CAPRA JR.
EYE OF THE CAT ... PHILLIP HAZELTON
EYE OF THE CAT ... BERNARD SCHWARTZ
EYE OF THE NEEDLE ... STEPHEN J. FRIEDMAN
EYE OF THE TIGER ... BEN SCOTTI
EYE OF THE TIGER ... HERB NANAS
EYES OF LAURA MARS ... JACK H. HARRIS
EYES OF LAURA MARS ... JON PETERS
EYES OF LAURA MARS ... LAURA ZISKIN
EYEWITNESS ... KENNETH UTT
EYEWITNESS ... PETER YATES

F

F.I.S.T. ... GENE CORMAN
F.I.S.T. ... NORMAN JEWISON
F/X ... DODI FAYED
F/X ... JACK WINER
F/X ... MICHAEL PEYSER
FABULOUS BAKER BOYS, THE ... PAULA WEINSTEIN
FABULOUS BAKER BOYS, THE ... SYDNEY POLLACK
FABULOUS BAKER BOYS, THE ... WILLIAM FINNEGAN
FACES ... AL RUBAN
FADE TO BLACK ... SYLVIO TABET
FADE TO BLACK ... IRWIN YABLANS
FAIL SAFE ... CHARLES H. MAGUIRE
FALCON AND THE SNOWMAN, THE ... JOHN DALY
FALCON AND THE SNOWMAN, THE ... DEREK GIBSON
FALCON AND THE SNOWMAN, THE ... EDWARD TEETS
FALCON AND THE SNOWMAN, THE ... GABRIEL KATZKA†
FALCON AND THE SNOWMAN, THE ... JOHN SCHLESINGER
FALLING IN LOVE ... MARVIN WORTH
FALLING IN LOVE ... ROBERT F. COLESBERRY
FAME ... DAVID DE SILVA
FAME ... ALAN MARSHALL
FAME ... DAVID PUTTNAM
FAMILY BUSINESS ... BURTT HARRIS
FAMILY BUSINESS ... JENNIFER OGDEN
FAMILY BUSINESS ... LAWRENCE GORDON
FAMILY, THE ... MARK JOHNSON
FAN , THE ... ROBERT STIGWOOD
FAN, THE ... BILL OAKES
FAN, THE ... JOHN NICOLELLA
FAN, THE ... KEVIN MCCORMICK
FANDANGO ... BARRIE M. OSBORNE
FANDANGO ... PAT KEHOE
FANDANGO ... FRANK MARSHALL
FANDANGO ... KATHLEEN KENNEDY
FANDANGO ... TIM ZINNEMANN
FANTASTIC PLANET ... ROGER CORMAN
FAR FROM HOME ... ELLEN STELOFF
FAR FROM HOME ... LAWRENCE KASANOFF
FAR FROM THE MADDING CROWD ... JOSEPH JANNI
FAR NORTH ... CAROLYN PFEIFFER
FAR NORTH ... JAMES KELLEY
FAR NORTH ... MALCOLM R. HARDING
FAR NORTH ... SHEP GORDON
FAREWELL TO THE KING ... ALBERT S. RUDDY
FAREWELL TO THE KING ... ANDRE MORGAN
FAREWELL, MY LOVELY ... ELLIOTT KASTNER
FAREWELL, MY LOVELY ... JERRY BRUCKHEIMER
FAREWELL, MY LOVELY ... JERRY BICK
FAST AND THE FURIOUS, THE ... ROGER CORMAN
FAST BREAK ... JACK GROSSBERG
FAST BREAK ... JERRY FRANKEL
FAST BREAK ... STEPHEN J. FRIEDMAN
FAST CHARLIE...THE MOONBEAM RIDER ... ROGER CORMAN
FAST CHARLIE...THE MOONBEAM RIDER ... SAUL KRUGMAN
FAST FOOD ... JERRY SILVA
FAST FOOD ... MICHAEL A. SIMPSON
FAST FOOD ... STAN WAKEFIELD
FAST FORWARD ... JOHN VEITCH
FAST FORWARD ... MELVILLE TUCKER
FAST TIMES AT RIDGEMONT HIGH ... IRVING AZOFF
FAST TIMES AT RIDGEMONT HIGH ... ART LINSON
FAST TIMES AT RIDGEMONT HIGH ... C.O. ERICKSON
FAST-WALKING ... JAMES B. HARRIS
FAT CITY ... RAY STARK
FAT MAN AND LITTLE BOY ... JOHN CALLEY
FAT MAN AND LITTLE BOY ... TONY GARNETT
FATAL ATTRACTION ... SHERRY LANSING
FATAL ATTRACTION ... STANLEY R. JAFFE
FATAL BEAUTY ... LEONARD KROLL
FATSO ... JONATHAN SANGER
FATSO ... STUART CORNFELD
FEAR CITY ... BRUCE COHN CURTIS
FEAR CITY ... JERRY TOKOFSKY
FEAR IS THE KEY ... ALAN LADD JR.
FEAR IS THE KEY ... JAY KANTER
FEAR IS THE KEY ... ELLIOTT KASTNER
FEAR NO EVIL ... CHARLES M. LALOGGIA
FEAR NO EVIL ... FRANK LALOGGIA
FEAR STRIKES OUT ... ALAN J. PAKULA
FEAR, ANXIETY, AND DEPRESSION ... MICHAEL KUHN

FEAR, ANXIETY, AND DEPRESSION ... NIGEL SINCLAIR
FEAR, ANXIETY, AND DEPRESSION ... SIGURJON SIGHVATSSON
FEAR, ANXIETY, AND DEPRESSION ... STANLEY WLODKOWSKI
FEAR, ANXIETY, AND DEPRESSION ... STEVEN GOLIN
FEDORA ... BILLY WILDER
FEDS ... DAN GOLDBERG
FEDS ... IVAN REITMAN
FEDS ... LEN BLUM
FELLINI SATYRICON ... ALBERTO GRIMALDI
FEMALE TROUBLE ... JOHN WATERS
FERRIS BUELLER'S DAY OFF ... JOHN HUGHES
FERRIS BUELLER'S DAY OFF ... MICHAEL CHINICH
FERRIS BUELLER'S DAY OFF ... TOM JACOBSON
FEVER PITCH ... FREDDIE FIELDS
FFOLKES ... MOSES ROTHMAN
FFOLKES ... ELLIOTT KASTNER
FIDDLER ON THE ROOF ... NORMAN JEWISON
FIELD OF DREAMS ... BRIAN FRANKISH
FIELD OF DREAMS ... CHARLES GORDON
FIELD OF DREAMS ... LAWRENCE GORDON
FIELDS OF HONOR ... LARRY SPIEGEL
FIGHTING BACK ... ALEX DE BENEDETTI
FIGHTING BACK ... DAVID LOWE
FIGHTING BACK ... DAVID PERMUT
FIGHTING BACK ... MARK TRAVIS
FIGHTING BACK ... D. CONSTANTINE CONTE
FIGHTING MAD ... EVELYN PURCELL
FIGHTING MAD ... ROGER CORMAN
FIGHTING PRINCE OF DONEGAL, THE ... BILL ANDERSON
FINAL CONFLICT, THE ... MACE NEUFELD
FINAL CONFLICT, THE ... RICHARD DONNER
FINAL CONFLICT, THE ... HARVEY BERNHARD
FINAL COUNTDOWN, THE ... PETER DOUGLAS
FINAL COUNTDOWN, THE ... RICHARD R. ST. JOHNS
FINAL PROGRAMME, THE ... ROY BAIRD
FINAL TERROR, THE ... JOE ROTH
FINAL TERROR, THE ... J. STEIN KAPLAN
FINDERS KEEPERS ... DUSTY SYMONDS
FINDERS KEEPERS ... RICHARD LESTER
FINDERS KEEPERS ... SANDRA MARSH
FINDERS KEEPERS ... TERENCE MARSH
FINE MADNESS, A ... JEROME HELLMAN
FINE MESS, A ... JONATHAN D. KRANE
FINE MESS, A ... BLAKE EDWARDS
FINE MESS, A ... TONY ADAMS
FINIAN'S RAINBOW ... JOEL FREEMAN
FIRE AND ICE ... FRANK FRAZETTA
FIRE AND ICE ... JOHN HYDE
FIRE AND ICE ... RICHARD R. ST. JOHNS
FIRE AND ICE ... ROY BAIRD
FIRE AND ICE ... MARTIN RANSOHOFF
FIRE DOWN BELOW ... ALBERT R. BROCCOLI
FIRE SALE ... MARVIN WORTH
FIRE WITH FIRE ... GARY NARDINO
FIRE WITH FIRE ... TOVA LAITER
FIREFOX ... CLINT EASTWOOD
FIREFOX ... FRITZ MANES
FIRES WITHIN ... JIM BLOOM
FIRES WITHIN ... LAUREN LLOYD
FIRES WITHIN ... WALLIS NICITA
FIRESTARTER ... MARTHA SCHUMACHER
FIRESTARTER ... FRANK CAPRA JR.
FIREWALKER ... JEFFREY M. ROSENBAUM
FIREWALKER ... MENAHEM GOLAN
FIREWALKER ... NORMAN ALADJEM
FIREWALKER ... YORAM GLOBUS
FIRST BLOOD ... HERB NANAS
FIRST BLOOD ... MARIO KASSAR
FIRST BLOOD ... BUZZ FEITSHANS
FIRST BLOOD ... ANDREW VAJNA
FIRST DEADLY SIN, THE ... FRANK SINATRA
FIRST DEADLY SIN, THE ... GEORGE PAPPAS
FIRST DEADLY SIN, THE ... MARK SHANKER
FIRST DEADLY SIN, THE ... ELLIOTT KASTNER
FIRST FAMILY, THE ... DANIEL MELNICK
FIRST LOVE ... DAVID FOSTER
FIRST LOVE ... LAWRENCE TURMAN
FIRST MONDAY IN OCTOBER ... MARTHA SCOTT
FIRST MONDAY IN OCTOBER ... PAUL HELLER
FIRST POWER, THE ... DAVID MADDEN
FIRST POWER, THE ... ROBERT W. CORT
FIRST POWER, THE ... TED FIELD
FIRST POWER, THE ... MELINDA JASON
FIRST TEXAN, THE ... WALTER MIRISCH
FIRST TIME, THE ... ALLAN CARR
FIRST TIME, THE ... LAWRENCE LOVENTHAL
FIRST TIME, THE ... ROBERT SHAYE
FIRST TIME, THE ... ROGER SMITH
FIRST TIME, THE ... SAM IRVIN
FIRST TIME, THE ... SARA RISHER
FIRSTBORN ... PAUL JUNGER WITT
FIRSTBORN ... RON KOSLOW
FIRSTBORN ... STANLEY R. JAFFE
FIRSTBORN ... TONY THOMAS
FIRSTBORN ... SHERRY LANSING
FISH CALLED WANDA, A ... STEVE ABBOTT
FISH CALLED WANDA, A ... JOHN CLEESE
FISH CALLED WANDA, A ... MICHAEL SHAMBERG
FISH HAWK ... JON SLAN
FISTFIGHTER ... CARLOS VASALLO
FITZWILLY ... WALTER MIRISCH
FIVE CORNERS ... DENIS O'BRIEN
FIVE CORNERS ... FORREST MURRAY
FIVE CORNERS ... GEORGE HARRISON
FIVE CORNERS ... TONY BILL
FIVE DAYS ONE SUMMER ... FRED ZINNEMANN
FIVE DAYS ONE SUMMER ... PETER BEALE
FIVE EASY PIECES ... BOB RAFELSON
FIVE EASY PIECES ... HAROLD SCHNEIDER
FIVE EASY PIECES ... RICHARD WECHSLER
FIVE EASY PIECES ... BERT SCHNEIDER
FIVE WEEKS IN A BALLOON ... IRWIN ALLEN
FLAMINGO KID, THE ... MICHAEL PHILLIPS
FLAMINGO KID, THE ... NICK ABDO
FLASH GORDON ... BERNARD WILLIAMS
FLASH GORDON ... DINO DE LAURENTIIS
FLASH OF GREEN, A ... RICHARD JORDAN
FLASH OF GREEN, A ... SAM GOWAN
FLASHBACK ... DAVID LOUGHERY
FLASHBACK ... MARVIN WORTH
FLASHBACK ... RICHARD STENTA
FLASHDANCE ... LYNDA OBST
FLASHDANCE ... PETER GUBER
FLASHDANCE ... TOM JACOBSON
FLASHDANCE ... DON SIMPSON
FLASHDANCE ... JERRY BRUCKHEIMER
FLASHDANCE ... JON PETERS
FLASHPOINT ... SKIP SHORT
FLAT TOP ... WALTER MIRISCH
FLATLINERS, THE ... MICHAEL DOUGLAS
FLATLINERS, THE ... MICHAEL RACHMIL
FLATLINERS, THE ... PETER FILARDI
FLATLINERS, THE ... RICK BIEBER
FLATLINERS, THE ... SCOTT RUDIN
FLETCH ... GORDON A. WEBB
FLETCH ... ALAN GREISMAN
FLETCH ... PETER DOUGLAS
FLETCH LIVES ... ALAN GREISMAN
FLETCH LIVES ... BRUCE BODNER
FLETCH LIVES ... PETER DOUGLAS
FLIGHT OF THE INTRUDER ... BRIAN FRANKISH
FLIGHT OF THE INTRUDER ... JOHN MCTIERNAN
FLIGHT OF THE INTRUDER ... MACE NEUFELD
FLIGHT OF THE NAVIGATOR ... DAVID JOSEPH
FLIGHT OF THE NAVIGATOR ... DIMITRI VILLARD
FLIGHT OF THE NAVIGATOR ... JOHN HYDE
FLIGHT OF THE NAVIGATOR ... JONATHAN SANGER
FLIGHT OF THE NAVIGATOR ... MALCOLM R. HARDING
FLIGHT OF THE NAVIGATOR ... MARK DAMON
FLIGHT OF THE NAVIGATOR ... ROBBY WALD
FLIGHT OF THE SPRUCE GOOSE, THE ... MICHAEL HAUSMAN
FLOWERS IN THE ATTIC ... SY LEVIN
FLOWERS IN THE ATTIC ... THOMAS FRIES
FLY, THE ... KIP OHMAN
FLY, THE ... MARC BOYMAN
FLY, THE ... STUART CORNFELD
FLY II, THE ... STEVEN-CHARLES JAFFE
FM ... ROBERT LARSON
FM ... RAND HOLSTON
FOG, THE ... DEBRA HILL
FOG, THE ... CHARLES B. BLOCH
FOOD OF THE GODS ... BERT I. GORDON
FOOD OF THE GODS ... SAMUEL Z. ARKOFF
FOOD OF THE GODS II ... ANDRAS HAMORI
FOOD OF THE GODS II ... DAMIAN LEE
FOOD OF THE GODS II ... DAVID MITCHELL
FOOD OF THE GODS II ... ROBERT MISIOROWSKI
FOOL FOR LOVE ... MENAHEM GOLAN
FOOL FOR LOVE ... SCOTT BUSHNELL
FOOL FOR LOVE ... YORAM GLOBUS
FOOLIN' AROUND ... ARNOLD KOPELSON
FOOTLOOSE ... CRAIG ZADAN
FOOTLOOSE ... LEWIS J. RACHMIL†
FOOTLOOSE ... DANIEL MELNICK
FOR A FEW DOLLARS MORE ... ALBERTO GRIMALDI
FOR KEEPS ... JERRY BELSON
FOR KEEPS ... WALTER COBLENZ
FOR LOVE OF IVY ... EDGAR J. SCHERICK
FOR LOVE OF IVY ... JAY WESTON
FOR PETE'S SAKE ... PHIL FELDMAN
FOR PETE'S SAKE ... STANLEY SHAPIRO
FOR PETE'S SAKE ... MARTIN ERLICHMAN
FOR QUEEN AND COUNTRY ... TIM BEVAN
FOR YOUR EYES ONLY ... ALBERT R. BROCCOLI
FOR YOUR EYES ONLY ... MICHAEL G. WILSON
FORBIDDEN DANCE, THE ... AMI ARTZI
FORBIDDEN DANCE, THE ... MARC S. FISCHER
FORBIDDEN DANCE, THE ... MENAHEM GOLAN
FORBIDDEN DANCE, THE ... RICHARD L. ALBERT
FORBIDDEN WORLD ... ROGER CORMAN
FORBIDDEN ZONE ... GENE CUNNINGHAM
FORBIDDEN ZONE ... RICHARD ELFMAN
FORCE 10 FROM NAVARONE ... SAMUEL Z. ARKOFF
FORCE OF ONE, A ... MICHAEL C. LEONE
FORCE: FIVE ... FRED WEINTRAUB
FORD FAIRLANE ... JOEL SILVER
FORD FAIRLANE ... MICHAEL LEVY
FORD FAIRLANE ... STEVE PERRY
FOREVER YOUNG ... CHRIS GRIFFIN
FOREVER YOUNG ... DAVID PUTTNAM
FORMULA, THE ... STEVE SHAGAN
FORT APACHE, THE BRONX ... TOM FIORELLO
FORTUNE AND MEN'S EYES ... LESTER PERSKY
FORTUNE AND MEN'S EYES ... LEWIS ALLEN
FORTUNE COOKIE, THE ... BILLY WILDER
FORTUNE, THE ... DON DEVLIN
FORTUNE, THE ... MIKE NICHOLS
FORTUNE, THE ... HANK MOONJEAN
FORTY-DEUCE ... STEVEN FIERBERG
FOUL PLAY ... EDWARD K. MILKIS
FOUL PLAY ... THOMAS L. MILLER
FOUL PLAY ... ROBERT BOYETT
FOUR FRIENDS ... JULIA MILES
FOUR FRIENDS ... MICHAEL TOLAN
FOUR FRIENDS ... ARTHUR PENN
FOUR FRIENDS ... GENE LASKO
FOUR FRIENDS ... STEPHEN F. KESTEN
FOUR MUSKETEERS, THE ... IMICHAEL SALKIND
FOUR MUSKETEERS, THE ... IPIERRE SPENGLER
FOUR MUSKETEERS, THE ... ILYA SALKIND
FOUR MUSKETEERS, THE ... ALEXANDER SALKIND
FOUR SEASONS, THE ... LOUIS A. STROLLER
FOUR SEASONS, THE ... MARTIN BREGMAN
FOURPOSTER, THE ... STANLEY KRAMER
FOURTH PROTOCOL, THE ... FREDERICK FORSYTH
FOURTH PROTOCOL, THE ... MICHAEL CAINE
FOURTH PROTOCOL, THE ... TIMOTHY BURRILL
FOURTH PROTOCOL, THE ... WAFIC SAID
FOURTH WAR, THE ... SAM PERLMUTTER
FOURTH WAR, THE ... ROBERT L. ROSEN
FOURTH WAR, THE ... WILLIAM STUART
FOURTH WAR, THE ... WOLF SCHMIDT
FOX AND THE HOUND, THE ... RON MILLER
FOXES ... GERALD AYRES
FOXES ... DAVID PUTTNAM
FOXY BROWN ... BUZZ FEITSHANS
FRANCES ... CHARLES B. MULVEHILL
FRANCES ... JONATHAN SANGER
FRANCES ... MARIE YATES
FRANCES ... MEL BROOKS
FRANKENSTEIN UNBOUND ... KOBI JAEGER
FRANKENSTEIN UNBOUND ... ROGER CORMAN
FRANKENSTEIN UNBOUND ... THOM MOUNT
FRANTIC ... THOM MOUNT
FRANTIC ... TIM HAMPTON
FRATERNITY VACATION ... BORIS MALDEN
FRATERNITY VACATION ... CHRISTOPHER NELSON
FRATERNITY VACATION ... DENISE DI NOVI
FRATERNITY VACATION ... ROBERT C. PETERS
FREAKY FRIDAY ... RON MILLER
FREEBIE AND THE BEAN ... RICHARD RUSH
FREEWAY MANIAC, THE ... LOREN WINTERS
FREEWAY MANIAC, THE ... PAUL WINTERS
FRENCH CONNECTION, THE ... KENNETH UTT
FRENCH CONNECTION, THE ... PHILIP D'ANTONI
FRENCH CONNECTION II, THE ... ROBERT L. ROSEN
FRENCH LIEUTENANT'S WOMAN, THE ... LEON CLORE
FRENCH LIEUTENANT'S WOMAN, THE ... GEOFFREY HELMAN
FRENCH POSTCARDS ... GLORIA KATZ
FRESH HORSES ... ALLAN MARCIL
FRESH HORSES ... DICK BERG
FRESH HORSES ... JOHN G. WILSON
FRESHMAN, THE ... MICHAEL LOBELL
FRIDAY THE 13TH ... FRANK MANCUSO JR.
FRIDAY THE 13TH - THE FINAL CHAPTER ... FRANK MANCUSO JR.
FRIDAY THE 13TH PART 2 ... DENNIS MURPHY
FRIDAY THE 13TH PART 2 ... LISA BARSAMIAN
FRIDAY THE 13TH PART 2 ... STEVE MINER
FRIDAY THE 13TH PART 3 ... LISA BARSAMIAN
FRIDAY THE 13TH PART 3 ... TONY BISHOP

FRIDAY THE 13TH PART V- A NEW BEGINNING ... TIMOTHY SILVER
FRIDAY THE 13TH PART V - A NEW BEGINNING ... FRANK MANCUSO JR.
FRIDAY THE 13TH, PART VII - THE NEW BLOOD ... IAIN PATERSON
FRIDAY THE 13TH PART VIII - JASON TAKES MANHATTAN ... RANDOLPH CHEVELDAVE
FRIENDS, LOVERS, & LUNATICS ... NICOLAS STILLADIS
FRIENDS, LOVERS, & LUNATICS ... SYD CAPPE
FRIENDS OF EDDIE COYLE, THE ... PAUL MONASH
FRIGHT NIGHT ... HERB JAFFE
FRIGHT NIGHT ... JERRY A. BAERWITZ
FRIGHT NIGHT PART II ... HERB JAFFE
FRIGHT NIGHT PART II ... MORT ENGELBERG
FRISCO KID, THE ... MACE NEUFELD
FRISCO KID, THE ... HOWARD W. KOCH JR.
FRITZ THE CAT ... STEVE KRANTZ
FROG PRINCE, THE ... DAVID PUTTNAM
FROGS ... GEORGE EDWARDS
FROGS ... NORMAN T. HERMAN
FROGS ... PETER THOMAS
FROM BEYOND ... BRIAN YUZNA
FROM BEYOND ... ROBERTO BESSI
FROM BEYOND ... CHARLES BAND
FROM HOLLYWOOD TO DEADWOOD ... BILL BYRNE
FROM HOLLYWOOD TO DEADWOOD ... JO PETERSON
FROM RUSSIA WITH LOVE ... HARRY SALTZMAN
FROM THE HIP ... BOB CLARK
FROM THE HIP ... BRIAN RUSSELL
FROM THE HIP ... HOWARD L. BALDWIN
FROM THE HIP ... RENE DUPONT
FROM THE HIP ... WILLIAM MINOT
FROM THE LIFE OF THE MARIONETTES ... MARTIN STARGER
FROM THE LIFE OF THE MARIONETTES ... LORD LEW GRADE
FRONT PAGE, THE ... PAUL MONASH
FRONT PAGE, THE ... JENNINGS LANG
FRONT, THE ... MARTIN RITT
FRONT, THE ... CHARLES H. JOFFE
FUGITIVE KIND, THE ... MARTIN JUROW
FUGITIVE KIND, THE ... RICHARD SHEPHERD
FULL METAL JACKET ... JAN HARLAN
FULL METAL JACKET ... PHILIP HOBBS
FULL METAL JACKET ... STANLEY KUBRICK
FULL MOON HIGH ... LARRY COHEN
FULL MOON IN BLUE WATER ... DAVID FOSTER
FULL MOON IN BLUE WATER ... EDUARD SARLUI
FULL MOON IN BLUE WATER ... JOHN TURMAN
FULL MOON IN BLUE WATER ... MOSHE DIAMANT
FULL MOON IN BLUE WATER ... LAWRENCE TURMAN
FUNERAL IN BERLIN ... HARRY SALTZMAN
FUNHOUSE, THE ... DEREK POWER
FUNHOUSE, THE ... MACE NEUFELD
FUNHOUSE, THE ... MARK LESTER
FUNHOUSE, THE ... STEVEN BERNHARDT
FUNLAND ... JERRY SILVA
FUNLAND ... KIRK SMITH
FUNLAND ... STAN WAKEFIELD
FUNLAND ... MICHAEL A. SIMPSON
FUNLAND ... WILLIAM VANDERKLOOT
FUNNY FARM ... GEORGE ROY HILL
FUNNY FARM ... PATRICK KELLEY
FUNNY FARM ... ROBERT L. CRAWFORD
FUNNY FARM ... BRUCE BODNER
FUNNY FARM ... CLAUDE HEROUX
FUNNY FARM, THE ... PIERRE DAVID
FUNNY GIRL ... RAY STARK
FUNNY LADY ... RAY STARK
FURY, THE ... FRANK YABLANS
FURY, THE ... JACK B. BERNSTEIN
FURY, THE ... RON PREISSMAN
FUTURE COP ... CHARLES BAND
FUTUREWORLD ... SAMUEL Z. ARKOFF
FUZZ ... CHARLES R. MEEKER
FUZZ ... EDWARD S. FELDMAN

G

GABY - A TRUE STORY ... LUIS MANDOKI
GABY - A TRUE STORY ... PINCHAS PERRY
GAILY, GAILY ... NORMAN JEWISON
GALAXY OF TERROR ... ROGER CORMAN
GALILEO ... OTTO PLASCHKES
GALILEO ... ELY LANDAU
GALILEO ... HENRY T. WEINSTEIN
GALLIPOLI ... FRANCIS O'BRIEN
GALLIPOLI ... PATRICIA LOVELL
GALLIPOLI ... ROBERT STIGWOOD
GAMBLER, THE ... IRWIN WINKLER
GAMBLER, THE ... ROBERT CHARTOFF
GANDHI ... MICHAEL STANLEY-EVANS
GANDHI ... RANI DUBE
GANDHI ... RICHARD ATTENBOROUGH
GANG THAT COULDN'T SHOOT STRAIGHT, THE ... ROBERT CHARTOFF
GANG THAT COULDN'T SHOOT STRAIGHT, THE ... IRWIN WINKLER
GANJA AND HESS ... CHIZ SCHULTZ
GARBAGE PAIL KIDS MOVIE, THE ... JOHN SERONG
GARBAGE PAIL KIDS MOVIE, THE ... MELINDA PALMER
GARBAGE PAIL KIDS MOVIE, THE ... MICHAEL LLOYD
GARBAGE PAIL KIDS MOVIE, THE ... MICHAEL ROSENBLATT
GARBAGE PAIL KIDS MOVIE, THE ... ROD AMATEAU
GARBAGE PAIL KIDS MOVIE, THE ... THOMAS COLEMAN
GARBO TALKS ... BURTT HARRIS
GARBO TALKS ... JENNIFER OGDEN
GARBO TALKS ... ELLIOTT KASTNER
GARDENS OF STONE ... DAVID VALDES
GARDENS OF STONE ... JAY EMMETT
GARDENS OF STONE ... STAN WESTON
GARDENS OF STONE ... FRANCIS FORD COPPOLA
GAS ... PIERRE DAVID
GAS ... VICTOR SOLNICKI
GAS ... CLAUDE HEROUX
GAS-S-S ... ROGER CORMAN
GATE, THE ... ANDRAS HAMORI
GATE, THE ... JOHN KEMENY
GATES OF HEAVEN, THE ... ERROL MORRIS
GAUNTLET, THE ... FRITZ MANES
GAUNTLET, THE ... ROBERT DALEY
GAY PURR-EE ... HENRY G. SAPERSTEIN
GET CRAZY ... HERBERT F. SOLOW
GET CRAZY ... HUNT LOWRY
GET ROLLIN' ... IRWIN YOUNG
GET ROLLIN' ... J. TERRANCE MITCHELL
GET ROLLIN' ... PEGGY ANN STULBERG
GET ROLLIN' ... STAN PLOTNICK
GET TO KNOW YOUR RABBIT ... PAUL GAER
GET TO KNOW YOUR RABBIT ... STEVEN BERNHARDT
GETAWAY, THE ... MITCHELL BROWER
GETAWAY, THE ... DAVID FOSTER
GETAWAY, THE ... LAWRENCE TURMAN
GETTING EVEN ... J. MICHAEL LIDDLE
GETTING EVEN ... JEAN HIGGINS
GETTING IT RIGHT ... JONATHAN D. KRANE
GETTING IT RIGHT ... RANDAL KLEISER
GETTING IT RIGHT ... RUSTY LEMORANDE
GETTING STRAIGHT ... PAUL LEWIS
GETTING STRAIGHT ... RICHARD RUSH
GHOST ... LISA WEINSTEIN
GHOST ... STEVEN-CHARLES JAFFE
GHOST DAD ... DAVID WISNIEVITZ
GHOST DAD ... STANLEY ROBERTSON
GHOST DAD ... TERRY NELSON
GHOST FEVER ... EDWARD COE
GHOST FEVER ... RON RICH
GHOST STORY ... BURT WEISSBOURD
GHOST STORY ... DOUGLAS GREEN
GHOST TOWN ... TIM TENNANT
GHOST TOWN ... CHARLES BAND
GHOST WARRIOR ... ARTHUR H. MASLANSKY
GHOST WARRIOR ... EFREM HARKHAM
GHOST WARRIOR ... URI HARKHAM
GHOST WARRIOR ... CHARLES BAND
GHOSTBUSTERS ... IVAN REITMAN
GHOSTBUSTERS ... JOE MEDJUCK
GHOSTBUSTERS ... MICHAEL C. GROSS
GHOSTBUSTERS ... BERNIE BRILLSTEIN
GHOSTBUSTERS II ... GORDON A. WEBB
GHOSTBUSTERS II ... IVAN REITMAN
GHOSTBUSTERS II ... SHELDON KAHN
GHOSTWARRIOR ... ALBERT BAND
GIG, THE ... NORMAN IRVING COHEN
GILDA LIVE ... LORNE MICHAELS
GIMME AN F ... MARTIN POLL
GINGER ALE AFTERNOON ... ALEXANDER SACHS
GINGER ALE AFTERNOON ... RAFAL ZIELINSKI
GINGER ALE AFTERNOON ... SUSAN HILLARY SHAPIRO
GINGER AND FRED ... ALBERTO GRIMALDI
GIRL FROM PETROVKA , THE ... DAVID BROWN
GIRL FROM PETROVKA , THE ... RICHARD D. ZANUCK
GIRL IN A SWING, THE ... BENNI KORZEN
GIRL IN A SWING, THE ... JUST BETZER
GIRL IN THE PICTURE, THE ... PADDY HIGSON
GIRL WITH THE RED HAIR, THE ... CHRIS BROUWER
GIRL WITH THE RED HAIR, THE ... HAIG BALIAN
GIRLS JUST WANT TO HAVE FUN ... CHUCK RUSSELL
GIRLS JUST WANT TO HAVE FUN ... STUART CORNFELD
GLASS HOUSES ... GEORGE FOLSEY JR.
GLASS MENAGERIE, THE ... JOSEPH M. CARACCIOLO
GLASS MENAGERIE, THE ... BURTT HARRIS
GLEAMING THE CUBE ... DAVID FOSTER
GLEAMING THE CUBE ... LAWRENCE TURMAN
GLORIA ... SAM SHAW
GLORY ... FREDDIE FIELDS
GO TELL THE SPARTANS ... ALLAN F. BODOH
GO TELL THE SPARTANS ... MICHAEL C. LEONE
GO TELL THE SPARTANS ... MITCHELL CANNOLD
GO-BETWEEN, THE ... NORMAN PRIGGEN
GO-BETWEEN, THE ... JOHN HEYMAN
GODFATHER, THE ... GRAY FREDERICKSON
GODFATHER, THE ... ALBERT S. RUDDY
GODFATHER - PART II , THE ... FRED ROOS
GODFATHER - PART II , THE ... FRANCIS FORD COPPOLA
GODFATHER - PART II , THE ... GRAY FREDERICKSON
GODS MUST BE CRAZY II, THE ... BOET TROSKIE
GODSEND, THE ... MENAHEM GOLAN
GODSEND, THE ... YORAM GLOBUS
GODSPELL ... KENNETH UTT
GOIN' ALL THE WAY ... TONY BILL
GOIN' SOUTH ... HARRY GITTES
GOIN' SOUTH ... HAROLD SCHNEIDER
GOING APE! ... DEREK GIBSON
GOING APE! ... JOHN DALY
GOING APE! ... ROBERT L. ROSEN
GOING BERSERK ... DENISE DI NOVI
GOING BERSERK ... PIERRE DAVID
GOING BERSERK ... CLAUDE HEROUX
GOING IN STYLE ... FRED T. GALLO
GOING IN STYLE ... TONY BILL
GOING IN STYLE ... LEONARD GAINES
GOLDEN CHILD, THE ... DENNIS FELDMAN
GOLDEN CHILD, THE ... GORDON A. WEBB
GOLDEN CHILD, THE ... RICHARD TIENKEN
GOLDEN CHILD, THE ... EDWARD S. FELDMAN
GOLDEN CHILD, THE ... CHARLES R. MEEKER
GOLDEN NEEDLES ... FRED WEINTRAUB
GOLDEN NEEDLES ... PAUL HELLER
GOLDEN SEAL, THE ... SAMUEL GOLDWYN JR.
GOLDENGIRL ... DANNY O'DONOVAN
GOLDENGIRL ... ELLIOTT KASTNER
GOLDFINGER ... ALBERT R. BROCCOLI
GOLDFINGER ... HARRY SALTZMAN
GOOD FATHER, THE ... ANN SCOTT
GOOD FELLAS ... BARBARA DE FINA
GOOD FELLAS ... IRWIN WINKLER
GOOD GUYS WEAR BLACK ... ALLAN F. BODOH
GOOD GUYS WEAR BLACK ... MICHAEL C. LEONE
GOOD MORNING BABYLON ... CALDECOTT CHUBB
GOOD MORNING BABYLON ... GIULIANI DE NEGRI
GOOD MORNING BABYLON ... LLOYD FONVIELLE
GOOD MORNING BABYLON ... EDWARD R. PRESSMAN
GOOD MORNING, VIETNAM ... BEN MOSES
GOOD MORNING, VIETNAM ... HARRY BENN
GOOD MORNING, VIETNAM ... LARRY BREZNER
GOOD MORNING, VIETNAM ... MARK JOHNSON
GOOD MOTHER, THE ... ARNOLD GLIMCHER
GOOD TO GO ... CHRIS BLACKWELL
GOOD TO GO ... DOUGLAS DILGE
GOOD TO GO ... JEREMY THOMAS
GOOD TO GO ... SEAN FERRER
GOOD WIFE, THE ... JAN SHARP
GOOD, THE BAD AND THE UGLY, THE ... ALBERTO GRIMALDI
GOODBYE GIRL, THE ... RAY STARK
GOODBYE PEOPLE, THE ... DAVID V. PICKER
GOODBYE, COLUMBUS ... STANLEY R. JAFFE
GOODBYE, MR. CHIPS ... MORT ABRAHAMS
GOONIES , THE ... FRANK MARSHALL
GOONIES , THE ... KATHLEEN KENNEDY
GOONIES, THE ... HARVEY BERNHARD
GOONIES, THE ... RICHARD DONNER
GOONIES, THE ... STEVEN SPIELBERG
GORDON'S WAR ... EDGAR J. SCHERICK
GORDON'S WAR ... ROBERT L. SCHAFFEL
GORILLAS IN THE MIST ... ARNOLD GLIMCHER
GORILLAS IN THE MIST ... JUDY KESSLER
GORILLAS IN THE MIST ... PETER GUBER
GORILLAS IN THE MIST ... RICK BAKER

GORILLAS IN THE MIST ... ROBERT NIXON
GORILLAS IN THE MIST ... TERENCE CLEGG
GORILLAS IN THE MIST ... JON PETERS
GORKY PARK ... EFREM HARKHAM
GORKY PARK ... GENE KIRKWOOD
GORKY PARK ... HOWARD W. KOCH JR.
GORKY PARK ... ROBERT LARSON
GORKY PARK ... URI HARKHAM
GOTCHA! ... MICHAEL I. LEVY
GOTCHA! ... PAUL G. HENSLER
GOTCHA! ... PETER MACGREGOR-SCOTT
GOTHIC ... AL CLARK
GOTHIC ... PENNY CORKE
GOTHIC ... ROBERT DEVEREUX
GRACE QUIGLEY ... A. MARTIN ZWEIBACK
GRACE QUIGLEY ... ADRIENNE ZWEIBACK
GRACE QUIGLEY ... MENAHEM GOLAN
GRACE QUIGLEY ... YORAM GLOBUS
GRAND THEFT AUTO ... JON DAVISON
GRAND THEFT AUTO ... ROGER CORMAN
GRANDVIEW, U.S.A. ... ANDREW GELLIS
GRANDVIEW, U.S.A. ... JONATHAN T. TAPLIN
GRANDVIEW, U.S.A. ... PETER W. REA
GRANDVIEW, U.S.A ... WILLIAM WARREN BLAYLOCK
GRAVY TRAIN ... JONATHAN T. TAPLIN
GRAY LADY DOWN ... WALTER MIRISCH
GREASE ... ALLAN CARR
GREASE ... ROBERT STIGWOOD
GREASE 2 ... BILL OAKES
GREASE 2 ... NEIL A. MACHLIS
GREASE 2 ... ALLAN CARR
GREASE 2 ... ROBERT STIGWOOD
GREAT AMERICAN TRAGEDY, A ... RONALD SHEDLO
GREAT BALLS OF FIRE! ... ADAM FIELDS
GREAT BALLS OF FIRE! ... MARK VICTOR
GREAT BALLS OF FIRE! ... MICHAEL GRAIS
GREAT EXPECTATIONS ... RONALD NEAME
GREAT GATSBY, THE ... DAVID MERRICK
GREAT GATSBY, THE ... ROBERT EVANS
GREAT GATSBY, THE ... HANK MOONJEAN
GREAT IMPOSTOR, THE ... ALAN J. PAKULA
GREAT MOUSE DETECTIVE, THE ... BURNY MATTINSON
GREAT MUPPET CAPER, THE ... DAVID LAZER
GREAT MUPPET CAPER, THE ... FRANK OZ
GREAT MUPPET CAPER, THE ... JIM HENSON
GREAT MUPPET CAPER, THE ... MARTIN STARGER
GREAT NORTHFIELD, MINNESOTA RAID, THE ... JENNINGS LANG
GREAT OUTDOORS, THE ... ARNE L. SCHMIDT
GREAT OUTDOORS, THE ... JOHN HUGHES
GREAT OUTDOORS, THE ... TOM JACOBSON
GREAT RACE, THE ... MARTIN JUROW
GREAT RESCUE, THE ... VICTORIA MEYERINK
GREAT SCOUT AND CATHOUSE THURSDAY, THE ... SAMUEL Z. ARKOFF
GREAT SMOKEY ROADBLOCK, THE ... MICHAEL C. LEONE
GREAT TRAIN ROBBERY, THE ... JOHN FOREMAN
GREAT WALDO PEPPER, THE ... GEORGE ROY HILL
GREAT WALDO PEPPER, THE ... ROBERT L. CRAWFORD
GREAT WALDO PEPPER, THE ... JENNINGS LANG
GREAT WALL, A ... SHIRLEY SUN
GREEK TYCOON, THE ... ALLEN KLEIN
GREEK TYCOON, THE ... LAWRENCE MYERS
GREEK TYCOON, THE ... NICO MASTORAKIS
GREEK TYCOON, THE ... ELY LANDAU
GREEK TYCOON, THE ... MORT ABRAHAMS
GREEK TYCOON, THE ... PETER HOWARTH
GREETINGS ... CHARLES HIRSCH
GREGORY'S GIRL ... DAVINA BELLING
GREGORY'S GIRL ... CLIVE PARSONS
GREMLINS ... MICHAEL FINNELL
GREMLINS ... FRANK MARSHALL
GREMLINS ... KATHLEEN KENNEDY
GREMLINS ... STEVEN SPIELBERG
GREMLINS 2: THE NEW BATCH ... FRANK MARSHALL
GREMLINS 2: THE NEW BATCH ... KATHLEEN KENNEDY
GREMLINS 2: THE NEW BATCH ... MICHAEL FINNELL
GREMLINS 2: THE NEW BATCH ... STEVEN SPIELBERG
GREY FOX, THE ... BARRY HEALEY
GREY FOX, THE ... DAVID H. BRADY
GREY FOX, THE ... PETER O'BRIAN
GREY FOX, THE ... PHILLIP BORSOS
GREYSTOKE: THE LEGEND OF TARZAN, LORD OF THE APES ... HUGH HUDSON
GROSS ANATOMY ... CAROL BAUM
GROSS ANATOMY ... DEBRA HILL
GROSS ANATOMY ... HOWARD ROSENMAN
GROSS ANATOMY ... SANDY GALLIN
GROUND ZERO ... DENNIS WRIGHT
GROUND ZERO ... JOHN KEARNEY
GROUND ZERO ... KENT C. LOVELL
GROUND ZERO ... MICHAEL PATTINSON
GRUNT! THE WRESTLING MOVIE ... ANTHONY RANDELL
GRUNT! THE WRESTLING MOVIE ... DON NORMANN
GRUNT! THE WRESTLING MOVIE ... JAMES G. ROBINSON
GUARDIAN, THE ... DAVID SALVEN
GUARDIAN, THE ... JOE WIZAN
GUARDIAN, THE ... MICKEY BOROFSKY
GUARDIAN, THE ... DAN GREENBURG
GUARDIAN, THE ... TODD BLACK
GUESS WHO'S COMING TO DINNER ... STANLEY KRAMER
GUEST, THE ... GERALD BERMAN
GUNG HO ... DEBORAH BLUM
GUNG HO ... RON HOWARD
GUNG HO ... TONY GANZ
GURU, THE ... ISMAIL MERCHANT
GUS ... RON MILLER
GYMKATA ... FRED WEINTRAUB
GYPSY MOTHS, THE ... BOBBY ROBERTS
GYPSY MOTHS, THE ... HAL LANDERS
GYPSY MOTHS, THE ... EDWARD LEWIS

H

HAIR ... MICHAEL BUTLER
HAIR ... ROBERT GREENHUT
HAIR ... LESTER PERSKY
HAIRSPRAY ... JOHN WATERS
HAIRSPRAY ... RACHEL TALALAY
HAIRSPRAY ... ROBERT MAIER
HAIRSPRAY ... ROBERT SHAYE
HAIRSPRAY ... SARA RISHER
HAIRSPRAY ... STANLEY F. BUCHTHAL
HALF A SIXPENCE ... JOHN DARK
HALF MOON STREET ... DAVID KORDA
HALF MOON STREET ... GEOFFREY REEVE
HALF MOON STREET ... EDWARD R. PRESSMAN
HALLOWEEN ... DEBRA HILL
HALLOWEEN ... FRANK YABLANS
HALLOWEEN ... KOOL LUSBY
HALLOWEEN ... IRWIN YABLANS
HALLOWEEN II ... DEBRA HILL
HALLOWEEN II ... IRWIN YABLANS
HALLOWEEN II ... JOHN CARPENTER
HALLOWEEN II ... JOSEPH WOLF
HALLOWEEN III: SEASON OF THE WITCH ... DEBRA HILL
HALLOWEEN III: SEASON OF THE WITCH ... IRWIN YABLANS
HALLOWEEN III: SEASON OF THE WITCH ... JOSEPH WOLF
HALLOWEEN III:SEASON OF THE WITCH ... JOHN CARPENTER
HALLOWEEN 4: THERETURN OF MICHAEL MYERS ... MOUSTAPHA AKKAD
HALLOWEEN 4: THE RETURN OF MICHAEL MYERS ... PAUL FREEMAN
HALLOWEEN 5: THE REVENGE OF MICHAEL MYERS ... MOUSTAPHA AKKAD
HALLOWEEN 5: THE REVENGE OF MICHAEL MYERS ... RAMSEY THOMAS
HALLOWEEN 5: THE REVENGE OF MICHAEL MYERS ... RICK NATHANSON
HALLS OF ANGER ... WALTER MIRISCH
HAMBONE AND HILLIE ... DON LEVIN
HAMBONE AND HILLIE ... GARY GILLINGHAM
HAMBONE AND HILLIE ... JOEL SOISSON
HAMBONE AND HILLIE ... MEL PEARL
HAMBONE AND HILLIE ... MICHAEL S. MURPHEY
HAMBONE AND HILLIE ... ROGER LAPAGE
HAMBONE AND HILLIE ... SANDY HOWARD
HAMBURGER HILL ... JIM CARABATSOS
HAMBURGER HILL ... LARRY DE WAAY
HAMBURGER HILL ... MARCIA NASATIR
HAMBURGER HILL ... DAVID KORDA
HAMBURGER HILL ... JERRY OFFSAY
HAMBURGER...THE MOTION PICTURE ... CHARLES R. MEEKER
HAMBURGER...THE MOTION PICTURE ... EDWARD S. FELDMAN
HAMBURGER...THE MOTION PICTURE ... DONALD ROSS
HAMBURGER...THE MOTION PICTURE ... ROBERT LLOYD LEWIS
HAMLET ... LESLIE LINDER
HAMLET ... NEIL HARTLEY
HAMLET ... MARTIN RANSOHOFF
HAMMETT ... FRANCIS FORD COPPOLA
HAMMETT ... FRED ROOS
HAMMETT ... RONALD COLBY
HAMMETT ... DON GUEST
HAND, THE ... CLARK L. PAYLOW
HAND, THE ... EDWARD R. PRESSMAN
HANDFUL OF DUST, A ... DAVID WIMBURY
HANDFUL OF DUST, A ... DEREK GRANGER
HANDFUL OF DUST, A ... JEFFREY TAYLOR
HANDFUL OF DUST, A ... KENT WALWIN
HANDGUN ... TONY GARNETT
HANDMAID'S TALE, THE ... DANIEL WILSON
HANDMAID'S TALE, THE ... WOLFGANG GLATTES
HANGING TREE, THE ... MARTIN JUROW
HANGING TREE, THE ... RICHARD SHEPHERD
HANKY PANKY ... MELVILLE TUCKER
HANKY PANKY ... MARTIN RANSOHOFF
HANNA K. ... COSTA-GAVRAS
HANNA K. ... MICHELE RAY-GAVRAS
HANNA'S WAR ... CARLOS GIL
HANNA'S WAR ... MENAHEM GOLAN
HANNA'S WAR ... YORAM GLOBUS
HANNAH AND HER SISTERS ... CHARLES H. JOFFE
HANNAH AND HER SISTERS ... JACK ROLLINS
HANNAH AND HER SISTERS ... ROBERT GREENHUT
HANNAH K. ... EDWARD LEWIS
HANOI HILTON, THE ... MENAHEM GOLAN
HANOI HILTON, THE ... STEPHEN DART
HANOI HILTON, THE ... YORAM GLOBUS
HANOVER STREET ... PAUL N. LAZARUS III
HAPPIEST MILLIONAIRE, THE ... BILL ANDERSON
HAPPY BIRTHDAY, GEMINI ... RUPERT HITZIG
HAPPY BIRTHDAY, GEMINI ... ALAN KING
HAPPY BIRTHDAY TO ME ... ANDRE LINK
HAPPY BIRTHDAY TO ME ... LAWRENCE NESIS
HAPPY BIRTHDAY TO ME ... STEWART HARDING
HAPPY BIRTHDAY TO ME ... JOHN DUNNING
HAPPY HOOKER GOES HOLLYWOOD, THE ... MENAHEM GOLAN
HAPPY HOOKER GOES HOLLYWOOD, THE ... YORAM GLOBUS
HAPPY NEW YEAR ... AL RUBAN
HAPPY NEW YEAR ... JERRY WEINTRAUB
HAPPY TIME, THE ... STANLEY KRAMER
HARD CHOICES ... EARLE MACK
HARD CHOICES ... ROBERT MICKELSON
HARD COUNTRY ... DAVID GREENE
HARD COUNTRY ... JOHN NARTMANN
HARD COUNTRY ... MACK BING
HARD COUNTRY ... MARTIN STARGER
HARD DAY'S NIGHT, A ... DENIS O'DELL
HARD DAY'S NIGHT, A ... WALTER SHENSON
HARD TICKET TO HAWAII ... ARLENE SIDARIS
HARD TIMES ... LAWRENCE GORDON
HARD TIMES ... PAUL MASLANSKY
HARD TO HOLD ... JOE GOTTFRIED
HARD TO HOLD ... D. CONSTANTINE CONTE
HARD TO KILL ... BILL TODMAN JR.
HARD TO KILL ... GARY ADELSON
HARD TO KILL ... JOEL SIMON
HARD TO KILL ... LEE RICH
HARD TO KILL ... MICHAEL RACHMIL
HARD TO KILL ... JON SHEINBERG
HARD TRAVELING ... HELEN GARVEY
HARDBODIES ... JEFF BEGUN
HARDBODIES ... KEN DALTON
HARDCORE ... JOHN MILIUS
HARDCORE ... BUZZ FEITSHANS
HARLEM NIGHTS ... EDDIE MURPHY
HARLEM NIGHTS ... MARK LIPSKY
HARLEM NIGHTS ... RALPH S. SINGLETON
HARLEM NIGHTS ... ROBERT D. WACHS
HARLEQUIN ... ANTONY I. GINNANE
HARLEQUIN ... WILLIAM FAYMAN
HAROLD AND MAUDE ... CHARLES B. MULVEHILL
HAROLD AND MAUDE ... MILDRED LEWIS
HAROLD AND MAUDE ... EDWARD LEWIS
HARPER ... ELLIOTT KASTNER
HARPER ... JERRY GERSHWIN
HARRY AND SON ... MALCOLM R. HARDING
HARRY AND SON ... PAUL NEWMAN
HARRY AND SON ... RONALD L. BUCK
HARRY AND THE HENDERSONS ... RICHARD VANE
HARRY AND THE HENDERSONS ... WILLIAM DEAR
HARRY AND TONTO ... PAUL MAZURSKY
HARRY AND WALTER GO TO NEW YORK ... TONY BILL
HARRY AND WALTER GO TO NEW YORK ... HARRY GITTES

HARRY AND WALTER GO TO NEW YORK ... DON DEVLIN
HARRY TRACY ... ALBERT J. TENSER
HARRY TRACY ... MARTY KROFFT
HARRY TRACY ... RONALD I. COHEN
HARRY TRACY ... SID KROFFT
HAUNTED HONEYMOON ... SUSAN RUSKIN
HAUNTED SUMMER ... JOHN THOMPSON
HAUNTED SUMMER ... MARTIN POLL
HAUNTED SUMMER ... MENAHEM GOLAN
HAUNTED SUMMER ... YORAM GLOBUS
HAUNTING OF JULIA, THE ... ALFRED PARISER
HAUNTING OF JULIA, THE ... PETER FETTERMAN
HAUNTING OF M, THE ... ANNA THOMAS
HAUNTING OF MORELLA, THE ... RODMAN FLENDER
HAUNTING OF MORELLA, THE ... ROGER CORMAN
HAVANA ... RICHARD ROTH
HAVANA ... SYDNEY POLLACK
HAWAII ... WALTER MIRISCH
HAWAIIANS, THE ... WALTER MIRISCH
HE'S MY GIRL ... ANGELA P. SCHAPIRO
HE'S MY GIRL ... LAWRENCE MORTORFF
HEAD ... BOB RAFELSON
HEAD ... JACK NICHOLSON
HEAD OFFICE ... DEBRA HILL
HEAD OFFICE ... JON PETERS
HEADHUNTER ... JAY DAVIDSON
HEADHUNTER ... JOEL LEVINE
HEALTH ... ROBERT ALTMAN
HEALTH ... SCOTT BUSHNELL
HEALTH ... TOMMY THOMPSON
HEART BEAT ... EDWARD R. PRESSMAN
HEART BEAT ... MICHAEL SHAMBERG
HEART CONDITION ... BERNIE GOLDMANN
HEART CONDITION ... MARIE CANTIN
HEART CONDITION ... ROBERT SHAYE
HEART CONDITION ... STEVE TISCH
HEART IS A LONELY HUNTER, THE ... JOEL FREEMAN
HEART LIKE A WHEEL ... ARNE L. SCHMIDT
HEART LIKE A WHEEL ... MARTY KATZ
HEART LIKE A WHEEL ... RICH IRVINE
HEART LIKE A WHEEL ... CHARLES ROVEN
HEART LIKE A WHEEL ... JAMES L. STEWART
HEART OF DIXIE ... MARTIN DAVIDSON
HEART OF DIXIE ... PAUL KURTA
HEART OF DIXIE ... STEVE TISCH
HEART OF MIDNIGHT ... ANDREW GATY
HEARTBEAT ... ALAN GREISMAN
HEARTBEEPS ... DOUGLAS GREEN
HEARTBEEPS ... MICHAEL PHILLIPS
HEARTBREAK HOTEL ... DEBRA HILL
HEARTBREAK HOTEL ... LYNDA OBST
HEARTBREAK KID, THE ... EDGAR J. SCHERICK
HEARTBREAK RIDGE ... CLINT EASTWOOD
HEARTBREAK RIDGE ... FRITZ MANES
HEARTBREAKERS ... BOB WEIS
HEARTBREAKERS ... BOBBY ROTH
HEARTBREAKERS ... HARRY COOPER
HEARTBREAKERS ... JOSEPH FRANCK
HEARTBREAKERS ... LEE MUHL
HEARTLAND ... BETH FERRIS
HEARTLAND ... MICHAEL HAUSMAN
HEARTS AND MINDS ... BERT SCHNEIDER
HEARTS OF FIRE ... DOUG HARRIS
HEARTS OF FIRE ... IAIN SMITH
HEARTS OF FIRE ... JENNIFER MILLER
HEARTS OF FIRE ... RICHARD MARQUAND†
HEARTS OF FIRE ... GERALD W. ABRAMS
HEARTS OF FIRE ... JENNIFER ALWARD
HEARTS OF THE WEST ... TONY BILL
HEAT ... GEORGE PAPPAS
HEAT ... KEITH ROTHMAN
HEAT AND DUST ... CONNIE KAISERMAN
HEAT AND DUST ... ISMAIL MERCHANT
HEATHERS ... CHRISTOPHER WEBSTER
HEATHERS ... DENISE DI NOVI
HEAVEN ... DIANE KEATON
HEAVEN ... JOE KELLY
HEAVEN CAN WAIT ... CHARLES H. MAGUIRE
HEAVEN CAN WAIT ... HOWARD W. KOCH JR.
HEAVEN CAN WAIT ... WARREN BEATTY
HEAVEN HELP US ... DAN WIGUTOW
HEAVEN HELP US ... KENNETH UTT
HEAVEN HELP US ... MARK CARLINER
HEAVEN'S GATE ... JOANN CARELLI
HEAVENLY BODIES ... ANDRAS HAMORI
HEAVENLY BODIES ... STEPHEN J. ROTH
HEAVENLY BODIES ... ROBERT LANTOS
HEAVENLY KID, THE ... GABE SUMNER
HEAVENLY KID, THE ... MORT ENGELBERG
HEAVENLY KID, THE ... STEPHEN G. CHEIKES
HEAVY METAL ... IVAN REITMAN
HEAVY METAL ... LAWRENCE NESIS
HEAVY METAL ... LEONARD MOGEL
HEAVY METAL ... MICHAEL C. GROSS
HEAVY PETTING ... OBIE BENZ
HEAVY TRAFFIC ... STEVE KRANTZ
HELL BELOW ZERO ... ALBERT R. BROCCOLI
HELL BELOW ZERO ... GEORGE W. WILLOUGHBY
HELL BELOW ZERO ... IRVING ALLEN†
HELL NIGHT ... BRUCE COHN CURTIS
HELL NIGHT ... CHUCK RUSSELL
HELL NIGHT ... IRWIN YABLANS
HELL NIGHT ... JOSEPH WOLF
HELL SQUAD ... KENNETH HARTFORD
HELL SQUAD ... MENAHEM GOLAN
HELL SQUAD ... YORAM GLOBUS
HELLBOUND: HELLRAISER II ... CHRISTOPHER FIGG
HELLBOUND: HELLRAISER II ... CHRISTOPHER WEBSTER
HELLBOUND: HELLRAISER II ... CLIVE BARKER
HELLO AGAIN ... FRANK PERRY
HELLO AGAIN ... G. MAC BROWN
HELLO AGAIN ... MARTIN MICKELSON
HELLO AGAIN ... SALAH M. HASSANEIN
HELLO AGAIN ... SUSAN ISAACS
HELLO AGAIN ... THOMAS FOLINO
HELLO MARY LOU: PROM NIGHT II ... PETER SIMPSON
HELLO MARY LOU: PROM NIGHT II ... PETER HALEY
HELLO, DOLLY! ... ERNEST LEHMAN
HELLRAISER ... CHRISTOPHER FIGG
HELLRAISER ... CHRISTOPHER WEBSTER
HELLRAISER ... DAVID SAUNDERS
HELLRAISER ... MARK ARMSTRONG
HELLSTROM CHRONICLE, THE ... DAVID L. WOLPER
HELP! ... WALTER SHENSON
HENRY V ... BRUCE SHARMAN
HENRY V ... STEPHEN EVANS
HENRY VIII AND HIS SIX WIVES ... ROY BAIRD
HENRY: PORTRAIT OF A SERIAL KILLER ... JOHN MCNAUGHTON
HENRY: PORTRAIT OF A SERIAL KILLER ... LISA DEDMOND
HENRY: PORTRAIT OF A SERIAL KILLER ... MALIK B. ALI
HENRY: PORTRAIT OF A SERIAL KILLER ... WALEED B. ALI
HER ALIBI ... KEITH BARISH
HER ALIBI ... MARTIN ELFAND
HERBIE GOES BANANAS ... RON MILLER
HERBIE GOES TO MONTE CARLO ... RON MILLER
HERCULES ... JOHN THOMPSON
HERCULES ... MENAHEM GOLAN
HERCULES ... YORAM GLOBUS
HERE COME THE TIGERS ... SEAN S. CUNNINGHAM
HERE COME THE TIGERS ... STEVEN MINER
HERO AIN'T NOTHIN' BUT A SANDWICH, A ... ROBERT B. RADNITZ
HERO AND THE TERROR ... RAYMOND WAGNER
HERO AND THE TERROR ... MENAHEM GOLAN
HERO AND THE TERROR ... YORAM GLOBUS
HERO AT LARGE ... ROGER M. ROTHSTEIN†
HERO AT LARGE ... STEPHEN J. FRIEDMAN
HERO, THE ... JOHN HEYMAN
HERO, THE ... WOLF MANKOWITZ
HEROES ... DAVID FOSTER
HEROES ... LAWRENCE TURMAN
HESTER STREET ... RAPHAEL D. SILVER
HEY BABU RIBA ... DRAGOLJUB POPOVICH
HEY BABU RIBA ... GEORGE ZECEVIC
HEY BABU RIBA ... NIKOLA POPOVIC
HEY BABU RIBA ... PETAR JANKOVIC
HEY GOOD LOOKIN' ... ROY BAIRD
HI, MOM! ... CHARLES HIRSCH
HIDDEN, THE ... DENNIS HARRIS
HIDDEN, THE ... GERALD T. OLSON
HIDDEN, THE ... JEFFREY KLEIN
HIDDEN, THE ... LEE MUHL
HIDDEN, THE ... MICHAEL MELTZER
HIDDEN, THE ... STEPHEN DIENER
HIDDEN, THE ... ROBERT SHAYE
HIDE IN PLAIN SIGHT ... ROBERT CHRISTIANSEN
HIDE IN PLAIN SIGHT ... RICK ROSENBERG
HIDER IN THE HOUSE ... DIANE NABATOFF
HIDER IN THE HOUSE ... EARLE MACK
HIDER IN THE HOUSE ... EDWARD TEETS
HIDER IN THE HOUSE ... LEM DOBBS
HIDER IN THE HOUSE ... MICHAEL TAYLOR
HIDER IN THE HOUSE ... STEVEN REUTHER
HIDER IN THE HOUSE ... STUART CORNFELD
HIDING OUT ... JEFFREY ROTHBERG
HIDING OUT ... MARTIN TUDOR
HIGH ANXIETY ... MEL BROOKS
HIGH FLIGHT ... ALBERT R. BROCCOLI
HIGH FLIGHT ... IRVING ALLEN†
HIGH HOPES ... SIMON CHANNING-WILLIANS
HIGH HOPES ... TOM DONALD
HIGH HOPES ... VICTOR GLYNN
HIGH NOON ... STANLEY KRAMER
HIGH PLAINS DRIFTER ... JENNINGS LANG
HIGH PLAINS DRIFTER ... ROBERT DALEY
HIGH RISK ... DEREK GIBSON
HIGH RISK ... GERALD GREEN
HIGH RISK ... JOE RAFFILL
HIGH RISK ... JOHN DALY
HIGH ROAD TO CHINA ... FRED WEINTRAUB
HIGH ROAD TO CHINA ... RAYMOND CHOW
HIGH SCHOOL BIG SHOT ... ROGER CORMAN
HIGH SPIRITS ... DAVID SAUNDERS
HIGH SPIRITS ... EDUARD SARLUI
HIGH SPIRITS ... MARK DAMON
HIGH SPIRITS ... MOSHE DIAMANT
HIGH SPIRITS ... NIK POWELL
HIGH SPIRITS ... SELWYN ROBERTS
HIGH SPIRITS ... STEPHEN WOOLLEY
HIGH TIDE ... ANTONY I. GINNANE
HIGH TIDE ... SANDRA LEVY
HIGH-BALLIN' ... STANLEY CHASE
HIGH-BALLIN' ... WILLIAM HAYWARD
HIGHLANDER ... E.C. MONELL
HIGHLANDER ... WILLIAM N. PANZER
HIGHLANDER ... PETER S. DAVIS
HIGHWAY DRAGNET ... ROGER CORMAN
HILLS HAVE EYES II, THE ... BARRY CAHN
HILLS HAVE EYES II, THE ... PETER LOCKE
HIRED HAND, THE ... WILLIAM HAYWARD
HISTORY OF THE WORLD - PART I, THE ... STUART CORNFELD
HISTORY OF THE WORLD - PART I, THE ... MEL BROOKS
HIT LIST ... JEF RICHARD
HIT LIST ... LISA M. HANSEN
HIT LIST ... PAUL HERTZBERG
HIT MAN ... GENE CORMAN
HIT, THE ... JEREMY THOMAS
HITCHER, THE ... DAVID BOMBYK†
HITCHER, THE ... KIP OHMAN
HITCHER, THE ... PAUL LEWIS
HITCHER, THE ... EDWARD S. FELDMAN
HITCHER, THE ... CHARLES R. MEEKER
HOG WILD ... CLAUDE HEROUX
HOG WILD ... STEPHEN MILLER
HOG WILD ... VICTOR SOLNICKI
HOG WILD ... PIERRE DAVID
HOLCROFT COVENANT, THE ... EDIE LANDAU
HOLCROFT COVENANT, THE ... MORT ABRAHAMS
HOLCROFT COVENANT, THE ... OTTO PLASCHKES
HOLCROFT COVENANT, THE ... ELY LANDAU
HOLLYWOOD BOULEVARD ... MICHAEL FINNELL
HOLLYWOOD BOULEVARD ... JON DAVISON
HOLLYWOOD SHUFFLE ... CARL CRAIG
HOLLYWOOD SHUFFLE ... ROBERT TOWNSEND
HOLLYWOOD VICE SQUAD ... ARNOLD ORGOLINI
HOLLYWOOD VICE SQUAD ... SANDY HOWARD
HOME IS WHERE THE HART IS ... JOHN M. ECKERT
HOME IS WHERE THE HART IS ... RALPH SCOBIE
HOME IS WHERE THE HART IS ... RICHARD STRAFEHL
HOME OF THE BRAVE ... PAULA MAZUR
HOME OF THE BRAVE ... STANLEY KRAMER
HOMEBOY ... ALAN MARSHALL
HOMEBOY ... ELLIOTT KASTNER
HOMECOMING, THE ... OTTO PLASCHKES
HOMECOMING, THE ... ELY LANDAU
HOMECOMING, THE ... HENRY T. WEINSTEIN
HOMER AND EDDIE ... JAMES CADY
HOMER AND EDDIE ... MORITZ BORMAN
HONEY, I SHRUNK THE KIDS ... PENNY FINKELMAN COX
HONEY, I SHRUNK THE KIDS ... THOMAS G. SMITH
HONEYSUCKLE ROSE ... GENE TAFT
HONEYSUCKLE ROSE ... SYDNEY POLLACK
HONKY TONK FREEWAY ... DON BOYD
HONKY TONK FREEWAY ... HOWARD W. KOCH JR.
HONKY TONK FREEWAY ... GENE KIRKWOOD
HONKY TONK MAN ... FRITZ MANES
HONKY TONK MAN ... CLINT EASTWOOD
HONOR BOUND ... PATRICK C. WELLS
HOOPER ... LAWRENCE GORDON
HOOPER ... HANK MOONJEAN
HOOSIERS ... CARTER DE HAVEN
HOOSIERS ... DEREK GIBSON
HOOSIERS ... JOHN DALY
HOPE AND GLORY ... EDGAR F. GROSS
HOPE AND GLORY ... JAKE EBERTS
HOPE AND GLORY ... JOHN BOORMAN
HOPE AND GLORY ... MICHAEL DRYHURST
HOPSCOTCH ... EDIE LANDAU
HOPSCOTCH ... OTTO PLASCHKES
HOPSCOTCH ... ELY LANDAU

HORROR SHOW, THE .... SEAN S. CUNNINGHAM
HORSEMAN, THE .... EDWARD LEWIS
HOSPITAL MASSACRE .... MENAHEM GOLAN
HOSPITAL MASSACRE .... YORAM GLOBUS
HOSPITAL, THE .... HOWARD GOTTFRIED
HOSPITAL, THE .... JACK GROSSBERG
HOT CHILI .... MENAHEM GOLAN
HOT CHILI .... YORAM GLOBUS
HOT DOG .... CHARLES R. MEEKER
HOT DOG .... EDWARD S. FELDMAN
HOT DOG... THE MOVIE .... CHRISTOPHER W. KNIGHT
HOT DOG...THE MOVIE .... MIKE MARVIN
HOT DOG...THE MOVIE .... TIM TENNANT
HOT LEAD AND COLD FEET .... RON MILLER
HOT POTATO .... FRED WEINTRAUB
HOT POTATO .... PAUL HELLER
HOT PURSUIT .... PIERRE DAVID
HOT PURSUIT .... THEODORE R. PARVIN
HOT RESORT .... MENAHEM GOLAN
HOT RESORT .... YORAM GLOBUS
HOT SPOT, THE .... BILL GAVIN
HOT SPOT, THE .... DEBORAH GOTTLIEB
HOT SPOT, THE .... DEREK POWER
HOT SPOT, THE .... PAUL LEWIS
HOT SPOT, THE .... STEVE UJLAKI
HOT STUFF .... MORT ENGELBERG
HOT STUFF .... PAUL MASLANSKY
HOT TO TROT .... STEVE TISCH
HOT TO TROT .... WENDY FINERMAN
HOTEL NEW HAMPSHIRE, THE .... NEIL HARTLEY
HOUND OF THE BASKERVILLES, THE ... ANDREW BRAUNSBERG
HOUND OF THE BASKERVILLES, THE .... JOHN GOLDSTONE
HOUR OF THE ASSASSIN .... LUIS LLOSA
HOUR OF THE ASSASSIN .... MARY ANN FISHER
HOUR OF THE ASSASSIN .... ROGER CORMAN
HOUSE .... PATRICK MARKEY
HOUSE .... SEAN S. CUNNINGHAM
HOUSE BY THE LAKE, THE .... ANDRE LINK
HOUSE BY THE LAKE, THE .... IVAN REITMAN
HOUSE BY THE LAKE, THE .... JOHN DUNNING
HOUSE CALLS .... JENNINGS LANG
HOUSE CALLS .... ARLENE SELLERS
HOUSE CALLS .... ALEX WINITSKY
HOUSE II: THE SECOND STORY .... SEAN S. CUNNINGHAM
HOUSE OF DARK SHADOWS .... DAN CURTIS
HOUSE OF GAMES .... MICHAEL HAUSMAN
HOUSE OF GOD, THE .... CHARLES H. JOFFE
HOUSE OF GOD, THE .... HAROLD SCHNEIDER
HOUSE OF THE LONG SHADOWS .... MENAHEM GOLAN
HOUSE OF THE LONG SHADOWS .... YORAM GLOBUS
HOUSE ON CARROLL STREET, THE .... ARLENE DONOVAN
HOUSE ON CARROLL STREET, THE .... ROBERT BENTON
HOUSEHOLDER, THE .... ISMAIL MERCHANT
HOW I GOT INTO COLLEGE .... ELIZABETH CANTILLON
HOW I GOT INTO COLLEGE .... MICHAEL SHAMBERG
HOW I WON THE WAR .... DENIS O'DELL
HOW I WON THE WAR .... RICHARD LESTER
HOW TO BEAT THE HIGH COST OF LIVING .... JEROME M. ZEITMAN
HOW TO BEAT THE HIGH COST OF LIVING .... ROBERT KAUFMAN
HOW TO BEAT THE HIGH COST OF LIVING .... SAMUEL Z. ARKOFF
HOW TO GET AHEAD IN ADVERTISING .... DENIS O'BRIEN
HOW TO GET AHEAD IN ADVERTISING .... GEORGE HARRISON
HOW TO GET AHEAD IN ADVERTISING .... RAY COOPER
HOW TO MURDER A RICH UNCLE .... ALBERT R. BROCCOLI
HOW TO MURDER A RICH UNCLE .... IRVING ALLEN†
HOW TO MURDER YOUR WIFE .... GORDON CARROLL
HOWARD THE DUCK .... GARY KURTZ
HOWARD THE DUCK .... GEORGE LUCAS
HOWARD THE DUCK .... GLORIA KATZ
HOWARD THE DUCK .... ROBERT LATHAM BROWN
HOWLING, THE .... JACK CONRAD
HOWLING, THE .... MICHAEL FINNELL
HOWLING, THE .... ROBERT SINGER
HOWLING II...YOUR SISTER IS A WEREWOLF .... JOHN DALY
HOWLING II...YOUR SISTER IS A WEREWOLF .... DEREK GIBSON
HOWLING II...YOUR SISTER IS A WEREWOLF .... GRAHAME JENNINGS
HOWLING II...YOUR SISTER IS A WEREWOLF .... STEVEN LANE
HOWLING III: THE MARSUPIALS .... CHARLES WATERSTREET
HOWLING III: THE MARSUPIALS .... PHILIPPE MORA
HOWLING III: THE MARSUPIALS .... ROBERT PRINGLE
HOWLING III: THE MARSUPIALS .... STEVEN LANE
HOWLING III: THE MARSUPIALS, ... EDWARD SIMONS
HOWLING IV...THE ORIGINAL NIGHTMARE .... AVI LERNER
HOWLING IV...THE ORIGINAL NIGHTMARE .... ROBERT PRINGLE
HOWLING IV...THE ORIGINAL NIGHTMARE .... STEVEN LANE
HOWLING IV...THE ORIGINAL NIGHTMARE .... EDWARD SIMONS
HULLABALOO OVER GEORGIA AND BONNIE'S PICTURES .... ISMAIL MERCHANT
HUMANOIDS FROM THE DEEP .... HUNT LOWRY
HUMANOIDS FROM THE DEEP .... MARTIN B. COHEN
HUNGER, THE .... RICHARD SHEPHERD
HUNT FOR RED OCTOBER, THE .... JERRY SHERLOCK
HUNT FOR RED OCTOBER, THE .... LARRY DE WAAY
HUNT FOR RED OCTOBER, THE ..... MACE NEUFELD
HUNTED, THE .... ROBERT L. SCHAFFEL
HUNTER, THE .... MORT ENGELBERG
HURRICANE .... DINO DE LAURENTIIS
HURRICANE ROSY .... ALBERTO GRIMALDI
HUSBANDS .... AL RUBAN
HYPER SAPIEN .... ARIEL LEVY
HYPER SAPIEN .... JACK SCHWARTZMAN
HYPER SAPIEN .... TALIA SHIRE
HYSTERICAL .... GENE LEVY

I

I AM A CAMERA .... SIR JOHN WOOLF
I AM THE CHEESE .... ALBERT SCHWARTZ
I AM THE CHEESE .... DAVID LANGE
I AM THE CHEESE .... JACK SCHWARTZMAN
I AM THE CHEESE .... MICHAEL S. LANDES
I COULD GO ON SINGING .... STUART MILLAR
I ESCAPED FROM DEVIL'S SLAND .... GENE CORMAN
I ESCAPED FROM DEVIL'S ISLAND .... ROGER CORMAN
I LOVE MY WIFE .... ROBERT KAUFMAN
I LOVE MY WIFE .... STAN MARGULIES
I LOVE MY WIFE .... DAVID L. WOLPER
I LOVE YOU TO DEATH .... CHARLES OKUN
I LOVE YOU TO DEATH .... JEFFREY LURIE
I LOVE YOU TO DEATH .... MICHAEL GRILLO
I LOVE YOU TO DEATH .... PATRICK C. WELLS
I LOVE YOU TO DEATH .... RON MOLER
I LOVE YOU TO DEATH .... LAUREN WEISSMAN
LOVE YOU ALICE B. TOKLAS .... CHARLES H. MAGUIRE
I LOVE YOU, ALICE B. TOKLAS .... LARRY TUCKER
I LOVE YOU, ALICE B. TOKLAS ...... PAUL MAZURSKY
I NEVER PROMISED YOU A ROSE GARDEN .... DANIEL H. BLATT
I NEVER PROMISED YOU A ROSE GARDEN .... EDGAR J. SCHERICK
I NEVER PROMISED YOU A ROSE GARDEN .... MICHAEL HAUSMAN
I NEVER PROMISED YOU A ROSE GARDEN .... ROGER CORMAN
I NEVER PROMISED YOU A ROSE GARDEN .... TERENCE F. DEANE
I OUGHT TO BE IN PICTURES .... HERBERT ROSS
I OUGHT TO BE IN PICTURES .... NEIL SIMON
I OUGHT TO BE IN PICTURES .... RICK MCCALLUM
I OUGHT TO BE IN PICTURES .... ROGER M. ROTHSTEIN†
I START COUNTING .... DAVID GREENE
I STARTED COUNTING .... STANLEY R. JAFFE
I WALK THE LINE .... EDWARD LEWIS
I WANNA HOLD YOUR HAND .... BOB GALE
I WANNA HOLD YOUR HAND .... STEVEN SPIELBERG
I WANNA HOLD YOUR HAND .... TAMARA ASSEYEV
I WANNA HOLD YOUR HAND ..... ALEXANDRA ROSE
I'M DANCING AS FAST AS I CAN .... DAVID A. NICKSAY
I'M DANCING AS FAST AS I CAN .... DAVID RABE
I'M DANCING AS FAST AS I CAN .... EDGAR J. SCHERICK
I'M DANCING AS FAST AS I CAN .... SCOTT RUDIN
I'M GONNA GIT YOU SUCKA .... CARL CRAIG
I'M GONNA GIT YOU SUCKA .... ERIC BARRETT
I'M GONNA GIT YOU SUCKA .... ERIC L. GOLD
I'M GONNA GIT YOU SUCKA .... PETER MCCARTHY
I'M GONNA GIT YOU SUCKA .... RAYMOND KATZ
I'M GONNA GIT YOU SUCKA .... TAMARA RAWITT
I'VE HEARD THE MERMAIDS SINGING .... ALEXANDRA RAFFE
I'VE HEARD THE MERMAIDS SINGING ...... DON HAIG
I'VE HEARD THE MERMAIDS SINGING .... PATRICIA ROZEMA
I, MADMAN .... HELEN SARLUI-TUCKER
I, MADMAN .... PAUL MASON
I, MADMAN .... RAFAEL EISENMAN
I, THE JURY .... MARTIN HORNSTEIN
I, THE JURY .... MICHAEL C. LEONE
I, THE JURY .... ROBERT H. SOLO
I, THE JURY .... ANDREW D.T. PFEFFER
ICE CASTLES .... JOHN KEMENY
ICE CASTLES .... ROSILYN HELLER
ICE HOUSE .... BO BRINKMAN
ICE HOUSE .... KENNETH SCHWENKER
ICE HOUSE .... RICKY MCCARTNEY
ICE PIRATES, THE .... JOHN FOREMAN
ICE STATION ZEBRA .... JOHN CALLEY
ICE STATION ZEBRA .... MARTIN RANSOHOFF
ICEMAN .... NORMAN JEWISON
ICEMAN .... PATRICK PALMER
ICEMAN COMETH, THE .... EDWARD LEWIS
ICEMAN COMETH, THE .... ELY LANDAU
IDAHO TRANSFER .... WILLIAM HAYWARD
IDOLMAKER, THE .... GENE KIRKWOOD
IDOLMAKER, THE .... HOWARD W. KOCH JR.
IF .... ROY BAIRD
IF IT'S TUESDAY, IT MUST BE BELGIUM .... STAN MARGULIES
IF IT'S TUESDAY, THIS MUST BE BELGIUM .... DAVID L. WOLPER
IF YOU COULD SEE WHAT I HEAR .... DALE FALCONER
IF YOU COULD SEE WHAT I HEAR .... ERIC TILL
IF YOU COULD SEE WHAT I HEAR .... GENE CORMAN
ILLEGALLY YOURS .... GEORGE MORFOGEN
ILLEGALLY YOURS .... PETER BOGDANOVICH
ILLEGALLY YOURS .... GARETH WIGAN
ILLEGALLY YOURS .... PAULA WEINSTEIN
ILLUSTRATED MAN, THE .... TED MANN
ILLUSTRATED MAN, THE ...... HOWARD B. KREITSEK
ILLUSTRIOUS CORPSES .... ALBERTO GRIMALDI
IMAGES .... TOMMY THOMPSON
IMAGINE: JOHN LENNON .... ANDREW SOLT
IMAGINE: JOHN LENNON .... DAVID L. WOLPER
IMMEDIATE FAMILY .... LAWRENCE KASDAN
IMMEDIATE FAMILY .... MIDGE SANFORD
IMMEDIATE FAMILY .... SARAH PILLSBURY
IMPROPER CHANNELS .... ALFRED PARISER
IMPROPER CHANNELS .... MORRIE RUVINSKY
IMPULSE .... ALBERT S. RUDDY
IMPULSE .... ANDRE MORGAN
IMPULSE .... TIM ZINNEMANN
IMPULSE .... DAN KOLSRUD
IN A SHALLOW GRAVE .... BARRY JOSSEN
IN A SHALLOW GRAVE .... KENNETH BOWSER
IN A SHALLOW GRAVE .... LINDSAY LAW
IN A SHALLOW GRAVE .... MARILYN G. HAFT
IN A SHALLOW GRAVE .... RON WOLOTZKY
IN A SHALLOW GRAVE .... SANDRA MOSBACHER
IN CELEBRATION .... OTTO PLASCHKES
IN CELEBRATION .... ELY LANDAU
IN CELEBRATION .... HENRY T. WEINSTEIN
IN COUNTRY .... CHARLES B. MULVEHILL
IN COUNTRY .... NORMAN JEWISON
IN COUNTRY .... RICHARD ROTH
IN CROWD, THE .... JEFFREY HORNADAY
IN CROWD, THE .... KAREN ESSEX
IN CROWD, THE .... JEFF FRANKLIN
IN CROWD, THE .... JOHN F. ROACH
IN CROWD, THE .... KEITH RUBINSTEIN
IN CROWD, THE .... LAWRENCE KONNER
IN GOD WE TRUST .... GEORGE SHAPIRO
IN GOD WE TRUST .... HOWARD WEST
IN GOD WE TRUST .... NORMAN T. HERMAN
IN PRAISE OF OLDER WOMEN .... HAROLD GREENBERG
IN PRAISE OF OLDER WOMEN ..... CLAUDE HEROUX
IN PRAISE OF OLDER WOMEN .... STEPHEN J. ROTH
IN THE HEAT OF THE NIGHT .... WALTER MIRISCH
IN THE MOOD .... BRIAN FRANKISH
IN THE MOOD .... GARY ADELSON

INDEX

FILM PRODUCERS

IN THE MOOD ... KAREN MACK
IN THE NICK ... ALBERT R. BROCCOLI
IN THE SPIRIT ... BEVERLY IRBY
IN THE SPIRIT ... JULIAN SCHLOSSBERG
IN-LAWS, THE ... ALAN ARKIN
IN-LAWS, THE ... ARTHUR HILLER
IN-LAWS, THE ... WILLIAM SACKHEIM
INCREDIBLE SHRINKING WOMAN, THE ... HANK MOONJEAN
INCREDIBLE SHRINKING WOMAN, THE ... JANE WAGNER
INCUBUS, THE ... JOHN M. ECKERT
INCUBUS, THE ... MARC BOYMAN
INCUBUS, THE ... STEPHEN J. FRIEDMAN
INDEPENDENCE DAY ... BOBBY ROTH
INDEPENDENCE DAY ... NEIL RAPP
INDEPENDENCE DAY ... ROBERT SINGER
INDIANA JONES AND THE LAST CRUSADE ... FRANK MARSHALL
INDIANA JONES AND THE LAST CRUSADE ... GEORGE LUCAS
INDIANA JONES AND THE LAST CRUSADE ... KATHLEEN KENNEDY
INDIANA JONES AND THE LAST CRUSADE ... ROBERT WATTS
INDIANA JONES AND THE TEMPLE OF DOOM ... GEORGE LUCAS
INDIANA JONES AND THE TEMPLE OF DOOM ... KATHLEEN KENNEDY
INDIANA JONES AND THE TEMPLE OF DOOM ... ROBERT WATTS
INDIANA JONES AND THE TEMPLE OF DOOM ... FRANK MARSHALL
INHERIT THE WIND ... STANLEY KRAMER
INNERSPACE ... CHIP PROSER
INNERSPACE ... MICHAEL FINNELL
INNOCENT MAN, AN ... NEIL A. MACHLIS
INNOCENT MAN, AN ... ROBERT W. CORT
INNOCENT MAN, AN ... SCOTT KROOPF
INNOCENT MAN, AN ... TED FIELD
INSERTS ... CLIVE PARSONS
INSERTS ... DAVINA BELLING
INSERTS ... HARRY BENN
INSIDE DAISY CLOVER ... ALAN J. PAKULA
INSIDE MOVES ... MARK M. TANZ
INSIDE MOVES ... R. W. GOODWIN
INSIDE OUT ... SIDNEY BECKERMAN
INSIGNIFICANCE ... ALEXANDER STUART
INSIGNIFICANCE ... JEREMY THOMAS
INTERIORS ... ROBERT GREENHUT
INTERIORS ... CHARLES H. JOFFE
INTERNAL AFFAIRS ... FRANK MANCUSO JR.
INTERNAL AFFAIRS ... PIERRE DAVID
INTERNAL AFFAIRS ... RENE MALO
INTERNAL AFFAIRS ... DAVID STREIT
INTO THE NIGHT ... DAN ALLINGHAM
INTO THE NIGHT ... LESLIE BELZBERG
INTO THE NIGHT ... RON KOSLOW
INTO THE NIGHT ... GEORGE FOLSEY JR.
INVADERS FROM MARS ... MENAHEM GOLAN
INVADERS FROM MARS ... YORAM GLOBUS
IINVASION OF THE BEE GIRLS ... FRED WEINTRAUB
INVASION OF THE BODY SNATCHERS ... ROBERT H. SOLO
INVASION U.S.A. ... MENAHEM GOLAN
INVASION U.S.A. ... YORAM GLOBUS
IPCRESS FILE, THE ... HARRY SALTZMAN
IRMA LA DOUCE ... BILLY WILDER
IRON EAGLE ... JOE WIZAN
IRON EAGLE ... KEVIN ELDERS
IRON EAGLE ... RON SAMUELS
IRON EAGLE II ... ANDRAS HAMORI
IRON EAGLE II ... JACOB KOTZKY
IRON EAGLE II ... JOHN KEMENY
IRON EAGLE II ... SHARON HAREL
IRON PETTICOAT, THE ... HARRY SALTZMAN
IRON TRIANGLE, THE ... ANGELA P. SCHAPIRO
IRON TRIANGLE, THE ... BEN SCOTTI
IRON TRIANGLE, THE ... FRED SCOTTI
IRON TRIANGLE, THE ... TONY SCOTTI
IRON WARRIOR ... OBIDIO G. ASSONITIS
IRONWEED ... DENIS BLOUIN
IRONWEED ... JOSEPH H. KANTER
IRONWEED ... KEITH BARISH
IRONWEED ... ROB COHEN
IRONWEED ... MARCIA NASATIR
IRONWEED ... GENE KIRKWOOD
IRRECONCILABLE DIFFERENCES ... ALEX WINITSKY
IRRECONCILABLE DIFFERENCES ... ARLENE SELLERS
ISHTAR ... DAVID L. MACLEOD
ISHTAR ... NIGEL WOOLL
ISHTAR ... WARREN BEATTY
ISLAND OF BLUE DOLPHINS ... ROBERT B. RADNITZ
ISLAND, THE ... DAVID BROWN
ISLAND, THE ... RICHARD D. ZANUCK
ISLANDS IN THE STREAM ... MAX PALEVSKY
ISLANDS IN THE STREAM ... PETER BART
ISLANDS IN THE STREAM ... KEN WALES
IT TAKES TWO ... ROBERT LAWRENCE
IT TAKES TWO ... STEVE NICOLAIDES
IT'S A FUNNY, FUNNY WORLD ... MENAHEM GOLAN
IT'S A FUNNY, FUNNY WORLD ... YORAM GLOBUS
IT'S A MAD, MAD, MAD, MAD WORLD ... STANLEY KRAMER
IT'S ALIVE III: ISLAND OF THE ALIVE ... LARRY COHEN
IT'S ALIVE III: ISLAND OF THE ALIVE ... PAUL STRADER
IT'S MY TURN ... JAY PRESSON ALLEN
IT'S MY TURN ... MARTIN ELFAND
IT'S SHOWTIME ... FRED WEINTRAUB
IT'S SHOWTIME ... PAUL HELLER
IT'S TRAD, DAD ... MILTON SUBOTSKY

J

JABBERWOCKY ... JOHN GOLDSTONE
JACK'S BACK ... ELLIOTT KASTNER
JACKNIFE ... CAROL BAUM
JACKNIFE ... ROBERT SCHAFFEL
JACKNIFE ... SANDY GALLIN
JACKSON COUNTY JAIL ... ROGER CORMAN
JACOB'S LADDER ... ALAN MARSHALL
JACOB'S LADDER ... MARIO KASSAR
JACOB'S LADDER ... ANDREW VAJNA
JACQUELINE SUSANN'S ONCE IS NOT ENOUGH ... HOWARD W. KOCH
JAGGED EDGE ... MARTIN RANSOHOFF
JAGUAR LIVES! ... SANDY HOWARD
JAKE SPEED ... ANDREW LANE
JAKE SPEED ... JOHN F. ROACH
JAKE SPEED ... WILLIAM FAY
JAKE SPEED ... WAYNE CRAWFORD
JAMES CLAVELL'S TAI-PAN ... RAFFAELLA DE LAURENTIIS
JAMES DEAN STORY, THE ... GEORGE W. GEORGE
JAMES DEAN STORY, THE ... ROBERT ALTMAN
JANE AUSTEN IN MANHATTAN ... ISMAIL MERCHANT
JANUARY MAN, THE ... EZRA SWERDLOW
JANUARY MAN, THE ... NORMAN JEWISON
JAWS ... DAVID BROWN
JAWS ... RICHARD D. ZANUCK
JAWS 2 ... DAVID BROWN
JAWS 2 ... RICHARD D. ZANUCK
JAWS 3-D ... ALAN LANDSBURG
JAWS 3-D ... HOWARD LIPSTONE
JAWS 3-D ... RUPERT HITZIG
JAWS - THE REVENGE ... JOSEPH SARGENT
JAZZ BOAT ... ALBERT R. BROCCOLI
JEKYLL AND HYDE... TOGETHER AGAIN ... LAWRENCE GORDON
JEKYLL AND HYDE... TOGETHER AGAIN ... JOEL SILVER
JENNIFER ON MY MIND ... BERNARD SCHWARTZ
JENNY ... EDGAR J. SCHERICK
JEREMIAH JOHNSON ... JOE WIZAN
JEREMY ... GEORGE PAPPAS
JEREMY ... ELLIOTT KASTNER
JERK, THE ... PETER MACGREGOR-SCOTT
JERK, THE ... DAVID V. PICKER
JERK, THE ... WILLIAM E. MCEUEN
JESUS ... RICHARD DALTON
JESUS ... JOHN HEYMAN
JESUS CHRIST SUPERSTAR ... NORMAN JEWISON
JESUS CHRIST SUPERSTAR ... PATRICK PALMER
JESUS CHRIST SUPERSTAR ... ROBERT STIGWOOD
JEWEL OF THE NILE, THE ... JACK BRODSKY
JEWEL OF THE NILE, THE ... MICHAEL DOUGLAS
JINXED ... HERB JAFFE
JINXED ... HOWARD JEFFREY
JO JO DANCER, YOUR LIFE IS CALLING ... JOHN G. WILSON
JO JO DANCER, YOUR LIFE IS CALLING ... MARVIN WORTH
JO JO DANCER, YOUR LIFE IS CALLING ... RICHARD PRYOR
JOE KIDD ... JENNINGS LANG
JOE KIDD ... ROBERT DALEY
JOE KIDD ... SIDNEY BECKERMAN
JOE VERSUS THE VOLCANO ... FRANK MARSHALL
JOE VERSUS THE VOLCANO ... KATHLEEN KENNEDY
JOE VERSUS THE VOLCANO ... STEVEN SPIELBERG
JOE VERSUS THE VOLCANO ... TERI SCHWARTZ
JOE'S BED-STUY BARBERSHOP: WE CUT HEADS ... SPIKE LEE
JOHN AND THE MISSUS ... JOHN HUNTER
JOHN AND THE MISSUS ... PETER O'BRIAN
JOHN AND THE MISSUS ... S. HOWARD ROSEN
JOHNNY BE GOOD ... ADAM FIELDS
JOHNNY BE GOOD ... JEFF BUHAI
JOHNNY BE GOOD ... STEVE ZACHARIAS
JOHNNY BE GOOD ... DAVID OBST
JOHNNY DANGEROUSLY ... BUD AUSTIN
JOHNNY DANGEROUSLY ... HARRY COLOMBY
JOHNNY DANGEROUSLY ... MICHAEL HERTZBERG
JOHNNY DANGEROUSLY ... NEIL A. MACHLIS
JOHNNY HANDSOME ... ANDREW VAJNA
JOHNNY HANDSOME ... CHARLES ROVEN
JOHNNY HANDSOME ... MARIO KASSAR
JONATHAN LIVINGSTON SEAGULL ... HALL BARTLETT
JOSHUA THEN AND NOW ... STEPHEN J. ROTH
JOSHUA THEN AND NOW ... ROBERT LANTOS
JOURNEY OF NATTY GANN, THE ... MICHAEL LOBELL
JOURNEY TO THE CENTER OF THE EARTH ... ADAM FIELDS
JOURNEY TO THE CENTER OF THE EARTH ... AVI LERNER
JOURNEY TO THE CENTER OF THE EARTH ... TOM UDELL
JOY OF SEX ... FRANK KONIGSBERG
JOY OF SEX ... MATTY SIMMONS
JOY OF SEX ... GARY NARDINO
JOYRIDE ... EUGENE MAZZOLA
JOYSTICKS ... GREYDON CLARK
JUDGMENT AT NUREMBERG ... STANLEY KRAMER
JUDGMENT IN BERLIN ... INGRID WINDLISCH
JUDGMENT IN BERLIN ... JEFFERY AUERBACH
JUDGMENT IN BERLIN ... JOSHUA SINCLAIR
JUDGMENT IN BERLIN ... MARTIN SHEEN
JUDGMENT IN BERLIN ... WILLIAM R. GREENBLATT
JUGGERNAUT ... DAVID V. PICKER
JUGGERNAUT ... DENIS O'DELL
JUGGERNAUT ... RICHARD DEKOKER
JUGGLER, THE ... STANLEY KRAMER
JULIA ... RICHARD ROTH
JUMPIN' JACK FLASH ... LAWRENCE GORDON
JUMPIN' JACK FLASH ... RICHARD MARKS
JUMPIN' JACK FLASH ... MARVIN WORTH
JUNIOR BONNER ... MICKEY BOROFSKY
JUNIOR BONNER ... JOE WIZAN
JUPITER'S THIGH ... ALEXANDRE MNOUCHKINE
JUPITER'S THIGH ... GEORGES DANCIGERS
JUST BETWEEN FRIENDS ... ALLAN BURNS
JUST BETWEEN FRIENDS ... EDWARD TEETS
JUST ONE OF THE GUYS ... JEFF FRANKLIN
JUST ONE OF THE GUYS ... ANDREW FOGELSON
JUST TELL ME WHAT YOU WANT ... BURTT HARRIS
JUST TELL ME WHAT YOU WANT ... JAY PRESSON ALLEN
JUST TELL ME WHAT YOU WANT ... SIDNEY LUMET
JUST THE WAY YOU ARE ... LEO L. FUCHS

K

K-9 ... CHARLES GORDON
K-9 ... DONNA SMITH
K-9 ... LAWRENCE GORDON
K-9 ... STEVEN JAY SIEGEL
KANSAS ... MOSHE DIAMANT
KANSAS ... GEORGE LITTO
KANSAS CITY BOMBER ... MARTIN ELFAND
KARATE KID, THE ... BUD SMITH
KARATE KID, THE ... R. J. LOUIS
KARATE KID, THE ... JERRY WEINTRAUB
KARATE KID PART II, THE ... JERRY WEINTRAUB
KARATE KID PART II, THE ... R. J. LOUIS
KARATE KID PART III, THE ... JERRY WEINTRAUB
KEEP, THE ... COLIN M. BREWER
KEEP, THE ... GENE KIRKWOOD
KEEP, THE ... HOWARD W. KOCH JR.
KELLY'S HEROES ... GABRIEL KATZKA†
KELLY'S HEROES ... SIDNEY BECKERMAN
KENTUCKY FRIED MOVIE, THE ... ROBERT K. WEISS
KES ... TONY GARNETT
KEY EXCHANGE ... MICHAEL POCHNA
KEY EXCHANGE ... PAUL KURTA
KEY EXCHANGE ... PEER J. OPPENHEIMER
KEY EXCHANGE ... RONALD WINSTON

KEYS TO FREEDOM ..... ROBERT S. LECKY
KEYS TO FREEDOM ..... SEYMOUR ROSE
KEYS TO FREEDOM ..... STUART ROSE
KGB: THE SECRET WAR ..... JOEL SOISSON
KGB: THE SECRET WAR ..... KEITH RUBINSTEIN
KGB: THE SECRET WAR ..... MICHAEL S. MURPHEY
KGB: THE SECRET WAR ..... SANDY HOWARD
KGB: THE SECRET WAR ..... PETER COLLISTER
KICKBOXER ..... MARK DI SALLE
KIDCO ..... FRANK YABLANS
KIDCO ..... DAVID NIVEN, JR.
KILL ME AGAIN ..... DAVID W. WARFIELD
KILL ME AGAIN ..... GEORGE J. ROEWE III
KILL ME AGAIN ..... MICHAEL KUHN
KILL ME AGAIN ..... NIGEL SINCLAIR
KILL ME AGAIN ..... SIGURJON SIGHVATSSON
KILL ME AGAIN ..... STEVEN GOLIN
KILL-OFF, THE ..... LYDIA DEAN PILCHER
KILLERS OF KILIMANJARO ..... ALBERT R. BROCCOLI
KILLERS OF KILIMANJARO ..... IRVING ALLEN†
KILLING AFFAIR, A ..... JOHN D. BACKE
KILLING AFFAIR, A ..... MYRON A. HYMAN
KILLING FIELDS, THE ..... DAVID PUTTNAM
KILLING FIELDS, THE ..... IAIN SMITH
KILLING HEAT ..... MARK FORSTATER
KILLING OF A CHINESE BOOKIE, THE ..... AL RUBAN
KILLING TIME, THE ..... J.P. GUERIN
KILLING TIME, THE ..... PETER ABRAMS
KILLING TIME, THE ..... ROBERT LEVY
KILLING, THE ..... JAMES B. HARRIS
KIND OF LOVING, A ..... JOSEPH JANNI
KINDRED, THE ..... JEFFREY OBROW
KINDRED, THE ..... JOEL FREEMAN
KINDRED, THE ..... STACEY GIACHINO
KING: A FILMED RECORD ..... ELY LANDAU
KING DAVID ..... MARTIN ELFAND
KING KONG ..... DINO DE LAURENTIIS
KING KONG ..... JACK GROSSBERG
KING KONG LIVES ..... MARTHA SCHUMACHER
KING KONG LIVES ..... RONALD SHUSETT
KING LEAR ..... MENAHEM GOLAN
KING LEAR ..... TOM LUDDY
KING LEAR ..... YORAM GLOBUS
KING OF COMEDY, THE ..... ROBERT F. COLESBERRY
KING OF COMEDY, THE ..... ROBERT GREENHUT
KING OF COMEDY, THE ..... ARNON MILCHAN
KING OF MARVIN GARDENS, THE ..... BOB RAFELSON
KING OF THE GYPSIES ..... DINO DE LAURENTIIS
KING OF THE MOUNTAIN ..... JACK FROST SANDERS
KING SOLOMON'S MINES ..... MENAHEM GOLAN
KING SOLOMON'S MINES ..... YORAM GLOBUS
KING, QUEEN, KNAVE ..... LUTZ HENGST
KING, QUEEN, KNAVE ..... DAVID L. WOLPER
KINJITE (FORBIDDEN SUBJECTS) ..... MENAHEM GOLAN
KINJITE (FORBIDDEN SUBJECTS) ..... PANCHO KOHNER
KINJITE (FORBIDDEN SUBJECTS) ..... YORAM GLOBUS
KIPPERBANG ..... CHRIS GRIFFIN
KIPPERBANG ..... DAVID PUTTNAM
KISS ME GOODBYE ..... ROBERT MULLIGAN
KISS ME, STUPID ..... BILLY WILDER
KISS OF THE SPIDER WOMAN ..... DAVID WEISMAN
KISS OF THE SPIDER WOMAN ..... FRANCISCO RAMALHO JR.
KISS, THE ..... JOHN WATSON
KISS, THE ..... PEN DENSHAM
KISS, THE ..... RICHARD B. LEWIS
KITCHEN TOTO, THE ..... MENAHEM GOLAN
KITCHEN TOTO, THE ..... YORAM GLOBUS
KLUTE ..... ALAN J. PAKULA
KNACK - AND HOW TO GET IT, THE ..... MICHAEL DEELEY
KNACK - AND HOW TO GET IT, THE ..... OSCAR LEWENSTEIN
KNIGHTRIDERS ..... SALAH M. HASSANEIN
KNIGHTRIDERS ..... RICHARD P. RUBINSTEIN
KNIGHTS AND EMERALDS ..... RAYMOND DAY
KNIGHTS AND EMERALDS ..... SUSAN RICHARDS
KNIGHTS AND EMERALDS ..... DAVID PUTTNAM
KOOL BLUE ..... PATRICIA FOULKROD
KRAMER VS. KRAMER ..... STANLEY R. JAFFE
KREMLIN LETTER, THE ..... SAM WIESENTHAL
KREMLIN LETTER, THE ..... CARTER DE HAVEN
KRULL ..... TED MANN
KRULL ..... GEOFFREY HELMAN
KRULL ..... RON SILVERMAN
KRUSH GROOVE ..... DOUG MCHENRY
KRUSH GROOVE ..... GEORGE A. JACKSON
KRUSH GROOVE ..... MICHAEL SCHULTZ
KRUSH GROOVE ..... RUSSELL SIMMONS

L

L-SHAPED ROOM, THE ..... RICHARD ATTENBOROUGH
L-SHAPED ROOM, THE ..... SIR JOHN WOOLF
LA BALANCE ..... ALEXANDRE MNOUCHKINE
LA BALANCE ..... GEORGES DANCIGERS
LA BAMBA ..... TAYLOR HACKFORD
LA TRAVIATA ..... TARAK BEN AMMAR
LABYRINTH ..... DAVID LAZER
LABYRINTH ..... ERIC RATTRAY
LABYRINTH ..... GEORGE LUCAS
LADIES AND GENTLEMEN...THE FABULOUS STAINS ..... LOU LOMBARDO
LADIES AND GENTLEMEN...THE FABULOUS STAINS ..... JOE ROTH
LADIES CLUB, THE ..... PAUL MASON
LADY BEWARE ..... BEN SCOTTI
LADY BEWARE ..... FRED SCOTTI
LADY BEWARE ..... LAWRENCE MORTORFF
LADY BEWARE ..... TONY SCOTTI
LADY CAROLINE LAMB ..... BERNARD WILLIAMS
LADY CAROLINE LAMB ..... FERNANDO GHIA
LADY IN RED, THE ..... JULIE CORMAN
LADY IN WHITE, THE ..... ANDREW G. LA MARCA
LADY IN WHITE, THE ..... CHARLES M. LALOGGIA
LADY IN WHITE, THE ..... CLIFF PAYNE
LADY IN WHITE, THE ..... FRANK LALOGGIA
LADY JANE ..... PETER SNELL
LADY SINGS THE BLUES ..... JAMES S. WHITE
LADY SINGS THE BLUES ..... BERRY GORDY
LADY SINGS THE BLUES ..... JAY WESTON
LADY VANISHES, THE ..... MICHAEL CARRERAS
LADY VANISHES, THE ..... ARLENE SELLERS
LADY VANISHES, THE ..... ALEX WINITSKY
LADYHAWKE ..... LAUREN SHULER-DONNER
LADYHAWKE ..... RICHARD DONNER
LADYHAWKE ..... HARVEY BERNHARD
LAIR OF THE WHITE WORM, THE ..... WILLIAM J. QUIGLEY
LAIR OF THE WHITE WORM, THE ..... DAN IRELAND
LAIR OF THE WHITE WORM, THE ..... KEN RUSSELL
LAIR OF THE WHITE WORM, THE ..... RONALDO VASCONCELLOS
LAMBADA ..... PETER SHEPHERD
LAND BEFORE TIME, THE ..... DON BLUTH
LAND BEFORE TIME, THE ..... FRANK MARSHALL
LAND BEFORE TIME, THE ..... GARY GOLDMAN
LAND BEFORE TIME, THE ..... GEORGE LUCAS
LAND BEFORE TIME, THE ..... JOHN POMEROY
LAND BEFORE TIME, THE ..... KATHLEEN KENNEDY
LAND BEFORE TIME, THE ..... STEVEN SPIELBERG
LANDLORD, THE ..... NORMAN JEWISON
LASERMAN ..... RUDD SIMMONS
LASSITER ..... ALBERT S. RUDDY
LASSITER ..... ANDRE MORGAN
LASSITER ..... RAYMOND CHOW
LAST AMERICAN HERO, THE ..... JOE WIZAN
LAST AMERICAN VIRGIN, THE ..... MENAHEM GOLAN
LAST AMERICAN VIRGIN, THE ..... YORAM GLOBUS
LAST DAYS OF MAN ON EARTH, THE ..... DAVID PUTTNAM
LAST DAYS OF MAN ON EARTH , THE ..... ROY BAIRD
LAST DAYS OF MAN ON EARTH, THE ..... JOHN GOLDSTONE
LAST DAYS OF MAN ON EARTH, THE ..... MICHAEL MOORCOCK
LAST DAYS OF MAN ON EARTH, THE ..... SANDY LIEBERSON
LAST DETAIL, THE ..... GERALD AYRES
LAST DETAIL, THE ..... CHARLES B. MULVEHILL
LAST DRAGON, THE ..... RUPERT HITZIG
LAST DRAGON, THE ..... BERRY GORDY
LAST EMBRACE ..... DAN WIGUTOW
LAST EMBRACE ..... MICHAEL TAYLOR
LAST EMPEROR, THE ..... JEREMY THOMAS
LAST EXIT TO BROOKLYN ..... BERND EICHINGER
LAST EXIT TO BROOKLYN ..... HERMAN WEIGEL
LAST FLIGHT OF NOAH'S ARK, THE ..... JAN WILLIAMS
LAST FLIGHT OF NOAH'S ARK, THE ..... RON MILLER
LAST MARRIED COUPLE IN AMERICA, THE ..... CHARLES R. MEEKER
LAST MARRIED COUPLE IN AMERICA, THE ..... EDWARD S. FELDMAN
LAST MARRIED COUPLE IN AMERICA, THE ..... GILBERT CATES
LAST MARRIED COUPLE IN AMERICA, THE ..... JOSEPH CATES
LAST MOVIE, THE ..... PAUL LEWIS
LAST MOVIE, THE ..... MICHAEL GRUSKOFF
LAST NIGHT AT THE ALAMO ..... EAGLE PENNELL
LAST NIGHT AT THE ALAMO ..... KIM HENKEL
LAST OF THE COWBOYS, THE ..... MICHAEL C. LEONE
LAST OF THE FINEST, THE ..... JERE CUNNINGHAM
LAST OF THE FINEST, THE ..... JOHN A. DAVIS
LAST OF THE MOBILE HOT-SHOTS ..... SIDNEY LUMET
LAST OF THE RED HOT LOVERS ..... HOWARD W. KOCH
LAST PICTURE SHOW, THE ..... HAROLD SCHNEIDER
LAST PICTURE SHOW, THE ..... STEPHEN J. FRIEDMAN
LAST PICTURE SHOW, THE ..... BERT SCHNEIDER
LAST REMAKE OF BEAU GESTE, THE ..... WILLIAM S. GILMORE
LAST REMAKE OF BEAU GESTE, THE ..... BERNARD WILLIAMS
LAST REMAKE OF BEAU GESTE, THE ..... GEORGE SHAPIRO
LAST REMAKE OF BEAU GESTE, THE ..... HOWARD WEST
LAST RESORT ..... JULIE CORMAN
LAST RESORT ..... NESSA COOPER
LAST RITES ..... DONALD BELLISARIO
LAST RITES ..... PATRICK MCCORMICK
LAST RUN, THE ..... CARTER DE HAVEN
LAST STARFIGHTER, THE ..... EDWARD O. DE NAULT
LAST STARFIGHTER, THE ..... MERV ADELSON
LAST SUMMER ..... ALFRED W. CROWN
LAST SUMMER ..... SIDNEY BECKERMAN
LAST SUNSET, THE ..... EUGENE FRENKE
LAST SUNSET, THE ..... EDWARD LEWIS
LAST TANGO IN PARIS ..... ALBERTO GRIMALDI
LAST TEMPTATION OF CHRIST, THE ..... BARBARA DE FINA
LAST TEMPTATION OF CHRIST, THE ..... HARRY UFLAND
LAST WALTZ, THE ..... FRANK MARSHALL
LAST WALTZ, THE ..... JONATHAN T. TAPLIN
LAST WALTZ, THE ..... ROBBIE ROBERTSON
LAST WAVE, THE ..... DEREK POWER
LAST WAVE, THE ..... HAL MCELROY
LAST WAVE, THE ..... JAMES MCELROY
LATE GREAT PLANET EARTH, THE ..... MICHAEL C. LEONE
LATE SHOW, THE ..... ROBERT ALTMAN
LATINO ..... BENJAMIN BERG
LAW AND DISORDER ..... EDGAR J. SCHERICK
LAWLESS LAND, THE ..... JUAN FORCH
LAWLESS LAND, THE ..... LARRY LEAHY
LAWLESS LAND, THE ..... ROGER CORMAN
LAWLESS LAND, THE ..... TONY CINCIRIPINI
LAZARO ..... JOE ROTH
LE MANS ..... ROBERT E. RELYEA
LEADBELLY ..... JACK GROSSBERG
LEADER OF THE BAND ..... DAVID V. PICKER
LEAN ON ME ..... JOHN G. AVILDSEN
LEAN ON ME ..... NORMAN TWAIN
LEATHERFACE: THE TEXAS CHAINSAW MASSACRE III ..... ROBERT ENGELMAN
LEATHERFACE: THE TEXAS CHAINSAW MASSACRE III ..... ROBERT SHAYE
LEGACY, THE ..... ARNOLD KOPELSON
LEGACY, THE ..... DAVID FOSTER
LEGACY, THE ..... LAWRENCE TURMAN
LEGAL EAGLES ..... ARNOLD GLIMCHER
LEGAL EAGLES ..... IVAN REITMAN
LEGAL EAGLES ..... JOE MEDJUCK
LEGAL EAGLES ..... MICHAEL C. GROSS
LEGAL EAGLES ..... SHELDON KAHN
LEGEND ..... TIM HAMPTON
LEGEND ..... JON PETERS
LEGEND ..... PETER GUBER
LEGEND ..... ARNON MILCHAN
LEGEND OF BILLIE JEAN, THE ..... JON PETERS
LEGEND OF BILLIE JEAN, THE ..... LAWRENCE KONNER
LEGEND OF BILLIE JEAN, THE ..... MARK ROSENTHAL
LEGEND OF BILLIE JEAN, THE ..... PETER GUBER
LEGEND OF BILLIE JEAN, THE ..... ROB COHEN
LEGEND OF THE LONE RANGER, THE ..... MARTIN STARGER
LEGEND OF THE LONE RANGER, THE ..... WALTER COBLENZ
LEGEND OF THE WILD ..... CHARLES E. SELLIER JR.
LEMON SISTERS, THE ..... JOE KELLY
LEMON SISTERS, THE ..... TOM KUHN
LEMON SISTERS, THE ..... ARNOLD J. HOLLAND
LEMON SISTERS, THE ..... CHARLES MITCHELL
LEMON SISTERS, THE ..... DIANE KEATON
LENNY ..... DAVID V. PICKER

LENNY ... MARVIN WORTH
LENNY ... ROBERT GREENHUT
LEO AND LOREE ... RON HOWARD
LEO THE LAST ... ROBERT CHARTOFF
LEO THE LAST ... IRWIN WINKLER
LEONARD PART 6 ... BILL COSBY
LESS THAN ZERO ... JON AVNET
LESS THAN ZERO ... JORDAN KERNER
LET IT RIDE ... DAVID GILER
LET IT RIDE ... NED DOWD
LET IT RIDE ... RANDY OSTROW
LET IT RIDE ... RICHARD STENTA
LET'S DO IT AGAIN ... MELVILLE TUCKER
LET'S GET HARRY ... DANIEL H. BLATT
LET'S GET HARRY ... ROBERT SINGER
LET'S GET LOST ... BRUCE WEBER
LET'S SPEND THE NIGHT TOGETHER ... RONALD L. SCHWARY
LETHAL WEAPON ... JOEL SILVER
LETHAL WEAPON ... RICHARD DONNER
LETHAL WEAPON 2 ... JENNIE LEW TUGEND
LETHAL WEAPON 2 ... JOEL SILVER
LETHAL WEAPON 2 ... RICHARD DONNER
LETHAL WEAPON 2 ... STEVE PERRY
LETTER TO BREZHNEV ... CAROLINE SPACK
LETTER TO BREZHNEV ... FRANK CLARKE
LETTER TO BREZHNEV ... JANET GODDARD
LEVIATHAN ... AURELIO DE LAURENTIIS
LEVIATHAN ... CHARLES GORDON
LEVIATHAN ... LAWRENCE GORDON
LEVIATHAN ... LUIGI DE LAURENTIIS
LIANNA ... JEFFREY NELSON
LIANNA ... MAGGIE RENZI
LICENSE TO DRIVE ... ANDREW LICHT
LICENSE TO DRIVE ... JEFFREY A. MUELLER
LICENSE TO DRIVE ... JOHN A. DAVIS
LICENSE TO DRIVE ... MACK BING
LICENSE TO KILL ... MICHAEL G. WILSON
LIFE AND TIMES OF JUDGE ROY BEAN, THE ... JOHN FOREMAN
LIFE AT THE TOP ... SIR JOHN WOOLF
LIFE IS CHEAP ... JOHN K. CHAN
LIFE IS CHEAP ... WAYNE WANG
LIFE IS CHEAP ... WINNIE FREDERIKSZ
LIFEFORCE ... MENAHEM GOLAN
LIFEFORCE ... MICHAEL J. KAGAN
LIFEFORCE ... YORAM GLOBUS
LIFEGUARD ... RON SILVERMAN
LIFEGUARD ... TED MANN
LIGHT AT THE EDGE OF THE WORLD , THE ... ILYA SALKIND
LIGHT AT THE EDGE OF THE WORLD, THE ... ALEXANDER SALKIND
LIGHT OF DAY ... DOUG CLAYBOURNE
LIGHT OF DAY ... KEITH BARISH
LIGHT OF DAY ... ROB COHEN
LIGHTNING - THE WHITE STALLION ... HARRY ALAN TOWERS
LIGHTNING OVER WATER ... CHRIS SIEVERNICH
LIGHTSHIP, THE ... BILL BENENSON
LIGHTSHIP, THE ... MORITZ BORMAN
LIGHTSHIP, THE ... RAINER SOEHNLEIN
LIKE FATHER, LIKE SON ... BRIAN GRAZER
LIKE FATHER, LIKE SON ... DAVID VALDES
LILY IN LOVE ... PETER BACSO
LILY IN LOVE ... ROBERT HALMI JR.
LILY IN LOVE ... ROBERT HALMI SR.
LINK ... RICHARD FRANKLIN
LINK ... RICK MCCALLUM
LINK ... VERITY LAMBERT
LION HEART ... FRANCIS FORD COPPOLA
LION IN WINTER, THE ... MARTIN POLL
LION OF THE DESERT ... ROY STEVENS
LIONHEART ... STANLEY O'TOOLE
LIONHEART ... TALIA SHIRE
LIPSTICK ... FREDDIE FIELDS
LIPSTICK ... DINO DE LAURENTIIS
LISA ... FRANK YABLANS
LIST OF ADRIAN MESSENGER, THE ... EDWARD LEWIS
LISTEN TO ME ... JERRY A. BAERWITZ
LISTEN TO ME ... MARYKAY POWELL
LISZTOMANIA ... SANDY LIEBERSON
LISZTOMANIA ... ROY BAIRD
LISZTOMANIA ... DAVID PUTTNAM
LITTLE ARK, THE ... ROBERT B. RADNITZ
LITTLE CIGARS ... ALBERT BAND
LITTLE CIGARS ... SAMUEL Z. ARKOFF
LITTLE DARLINGS ... STEPHEN J. FRIEDMAN
LITTLE DORRIT ... JOHN BRABOURNE
LITTLE DORRIT ... RICHARD GOODWIN
LITTLE DRAGONS, THE ... ROBERT S. BREMSON
LITTLE DRAGONS, THE ... TONY BILL
LITTLE DRUMMER GIRL, THE ... PATRICK KELLEY
LITTLE FAUSS AND BIG HALSY ... ALBERT S. RUDDY
LITTLE MALCOLM AND HIS STRUGGLE AGAINST THE EUNUCHS ... GEORGE HARRISON
LITTLE MERMAID, THE ... HOWARD ASHMAN
LITTLE MERMAID, THE ... JOHN MUSKER
LITTLE MISS MARKER ... WALTER MATTHAU
LITTLE MISS MARKER ... JENNINGS LANG
LITTLE MONSTERS ... ANDREW LICHT
LITTLE MONSTERS ... DORI B. WASSERMAN
LITTLE MONSTERS ... JACK GROSSBERG
LITTLE MONSTERS ... JEFFREY MUELLER
LITTLE MONSTERS ... JOHN A. DAVIS
LITTLE MONSTERS ... MITCHELL CANNOLD
LITTLE MURDERS ... JACK BRODSKY
LITTLE NIGHT MUSIC, A ... ELLIOTT KASTNER
LITTLE NIKITA ... ART LEVINSON
LITTLE NIKITA ... HARRY GITTES
LITTLE PRINCE, THE ... STANLEY DONEN
LITTLE ROMANCE, A ... PATRICK KELLEY
LITTLE ROMANCE, A ... ROBERT L. CRAWFORD
LITTLE ROMANCE, A ... YVES ROUSSET-ROUARD
LITTLE SEX, A ... BRUCE PALTROW
LITTLE SEX, A ... ROBERT DE LAURENTIS
LITTLE SEX, A ... STEPHEN F. KESTEN
LITTLE SHOP OF HORRORS ... DAVID GEFFEN
LITTLE SHOP OF HORRORS ... ROGER CORMAN
LITTLE SHOP OF HORRORS ... WILLIAM S. GILMORE
LITTLE TREASURE ... HERB JAFFE
LITTLE TREASURE ... JOANNA LANCASTER
LITTLE TREASURE ... RICHARD WAGNER
LITTLEST HORSE THIEVES, THE ... RON MILLER
LIVE AND LET DIE ... ALBERT R. BROCCOLI
LIVE AND LET DIE ... HARRY SALTZMAN
LIVING DAYLIGHTS, THE ... ALBERT R. BROCCOLI
LIVING DAYLIGHTS, THE ... MICHAEL G. WILSON
LIVING ON TOKYO TIME ... DENNIS HAYASHI
LIVING ON TOKYO TIME ... LYNN O'DONNELL
LOCAL HERO ... IAIN SMITH
LOCAL HERO ... DAVID PUTTNAM
LOCKUP ... CHARLES GORDON
LOCKUP ... LAWRENCE GORDON
LOCKUP ... MICHAEL S. GLICK
LOLA ... CLIVE SHARP
LOLA ... NORMAN THADDEUS VANE
LOLA ... RALPH SERPE
LOLA ... JOHN HEYMAN
LOLITA ... JAMES B. HARRIS
LONE WOLF MCQUADE ... YORAM BEN-AMI
LONELY GUY, THE ... ARTHUR HILLER
LONELY GUY, THE ... C.O. ERICKSON
LONELY GUY, THE ... WILLIAM E. MCEUEN
LONELY PASSION OF JUDITH HEARNE, THE ... DENIS O'BRIEN
LONELY PASSION OF JUDITH HEARNE, THE ... GEORGE HARRISON
LONELY PASSION OF JUDITH HEARNE, THE ... PETER NELSON
LONELY PASSION OF JUDITH HEARNE, THE ... RICHARD JOHNSON
LONG DAY'S JOURNEY INTO NIGHT ... ELY LANDAU
LONG GOOD FRIDAY, THE ... BARRY HANSON
LONG GOODBYE, THE ... ELLIOTT KASTNER
LONG GOODBYE, THE ... JERRY BICK
LONG RIDERS, THE ... STACY KEACH
LONG RIDERS, THE ... TIM ZINNEMANN
LONGEST DAY, THE ... ELMO WILLIAMS
LONGEST YARD, THE ... ALBERT S. RUDDY
LONGSHOT, THE ... LANG ELLIOTT
LONGSHOT, THE ... MIKE NICHOLS
LONGTIME COMPANION ... LYDIA DEAN PILCHER
LONGTIME COMPANION ... LINDSAY LAW
LONGTIME COMPANION ... STANLEY WLODKOWSKI
LOOK BACK IN ANGER ... HARRY SALTZMAN
LOOK WHO'S TALKING ... BOB GRAY
LOOK WHO'S TALKING ... JONATHAN D. KRANE
LOOKER ... HOWARD JEFFREY
LOOKIN' TO GET OUT ... ANDREW BRAUNSBERG
LOOKIN' TO GET OUT ... EDWARD TEETS
LOOKIN' TO GET OUT ... ROBERT L. SCHAFFEL
LOOKING FOR MR. GOODBAR ... FREDDIE FIELDS
LOOPHOLE ... DAVID KORDA
LOOPHOLE ... JULIAN HOLLOWAY
LOOSE CANNONS ... AARON SPELLING
LOOSE CANNONS ... ALAN GREISMAN
LOOSE CANNONS ... RENE DUPONT
LORD OF THE FLIES ... DAVID LESTER
LORD OF THE FLIES ... PETER NEWMAN
LORD OF THE FLIES ... ROSS MILLOY
LORD OF THE FLIES ... LEWIS ALLEN
LORD OF THE RINGS ... SAUL ZAENTZ
LORDS OF DISCIPLINE, THE ... GABRIEL KATZKA†
LORDS OF DISCIPLINE, THE ... HERB JAFFE
LORDS OF THE DEEP ... RODMAN FLENDER
LORDS OF THE DEEP ... ROGER CORMAN
LOSIN' IT ... GARTH DRABINSKY
LOSIN' IT ... JOEL B. MICHAELS
LOST AND FOUND ... ARNOLD KOPELSON
LOST ANGELS ... ANDREW Z. DAVIS
LOST ANGELS ... HOWARD ROSENMAN
LOST ANGELS ... THOMAS BAER
LOST BOYS, THE ... JOHN HYDE
LOST BOYS, THE ... MARK DAMON
LOST IN AMERICA ... HERB NANAS
LOST IN AMERICA ... MARTY KATZ
LOST IN THE STARS ... EDWARD LEWIS
LOST IN THE STARS ... ELY LANDAU
LOST IN THE STARS ... HENRY T. WEINSTEIN
LOST MAN, THE ... EDWARD MUHL
LOST MAN, THE ... MELVILLE TUCKER
LOST WORLD, THE ... IRWIN ALLEN
LOUISIANA ... JOHN KEMENY
LOVE AND BULLETS ... PANCHO KOHNER
LOVE AND DEATH ... CHARLES H. JOFFE
LOVE AND DEATH ... FRED T. GALLO
LOVE AND DEATH ... MARTIN POLL
LOVE AND MONEY ... JAMES TOBACK
LOVE AND PAIN AND THE WHOLE DAMNED THING ... ALAN J. PAKULA
LOVE AT FIRST BITE ... GEORGE HAMILTON
LOVE AT FIRST BITE ... JOEL FREEMAN
LOVE AT FIRST BITE ... ROBERT KAUFMAN
LOVE AT FIRST BITE ... DOUG CHAPIN
LOVE AT LARGE ... DAVID BLOCKER
LOVE AT STAKE ... ARMAND SPECA
LOVE AT STAKE ... DEREK GIBSON
LOVE AT STAKE ... JOHN DALY
LOVE AT STAKE ... MICHAEL GRUSKOFF
LOVE CHILD ... PAUL MASLANSKY
LOVE HURTS ... DORO BACHRACH
LOVE IN THE AFTERNOON ... BILLY WILDER
LOVE IS A BALL ... MARTIN POLL
LOVE LETTERS ... DON LEVIN
LOVE LETTERS ... MEL PEARL
LOVE LETTERS ... ROGER CORMAN
LOVE SONGS ... ELIE CHOURAQUI
LOVE SONGS ... MARIE-CHRISTINE CHOURAQUI
LOVE SONGS ... MURRAY SHOSTAK
LOVE SONGS ... ROBERT BAYLIS
LOVE STORY ... HOWARD G. MINSKY
LOVE STREAMS ... AL RUBAN
LOVE STREAMS ... MENAHEM GOLAN
LOVE STREAMS ... YORAM GLOBUS
LOVE WITH THE PROPER STRANGER ... ALAN J. PAKULA
LOVELESS, THE ... A. KITMAN HO
LOVELESS, THE ... GRAFTON NUNES
LOVELINES ... MICHAEL LLOYD
LOVERBOY ... GARY FOSTER
LOVERBOY ... LESLIE DIXON
LOVERBOY ... TOM ROPELEWSKI
LOVERBOY ... WILLIE HUNT
LOVERS ... RON NORMAN
LOVERS AND LIARS ... ALBERTO GRIMALDI
LOVIN' MOLLY ... STEPHEN J. FRIEDMAN
LOVING ... RAYMOND WAGNER
LOVING COUPLES ... RENEE VALENTE
LT. ROBIN CRUSOE, USN ... BILL WALSH†
LT. ROBIN CRUSOE, USN ... RON MILLER
LUCAS ... DAVID A. NICKSAY
LUCAS ... LAWRENCE GORDON
LUCKIEST MAN IN THE WORLD, THE ... NORMAN IRVING COHEN
LUCKY LADY ... MICHAEL GRUSKOFF
LUCKY STIFF ... DEBORAH MOORE
LUCKY STIFF ... DEREK POWER
LUCKY STIFF ... GERALD T. OLSON
LUCKY STIFF ... MILES A. COPELAND III
LUCKY STIFF ... LAURIE PERLMAN
LUCKY STIFF ... PAT PROFT
LUST IN THE DUST ... ALLAN GLASER
LUST IN THE DUST ... TAB HUNTER
LUTHER ... ELY LANDAU
LUTHER ... JACK GROSSBERG
LUTHER ... MORT ABRAHAMS
LUTHER ... HENRY T. WEINSTEIN
LUV ... GORDON CARROLL

M

MAC AND ME ... MARK DAMON
MAC AND ME ... R. J. LOUIS
MAC AND ME ... WILLIAM B. KERR
MACARONI ... AURELIO DE LAURENTIIS

MACARONI ... FRANCO COMMITTERI
MACARONI ... LUIGI DE LAURENTIIS
MACARTHUR ... RICHARD D. ZANUCK
MACARTHUR ... DAVID BROWN
MACARTHUR ... FRANK MCCARTHY
MACBETH ... ANDREW BRAUNSBERG
MACBETH ... TIMOTHY BURRILL
MACK THE KNIFE ... MENAHEM GOLAN
MACK THE KNIFE ... STANLEY CHASE
MACK THE KNIFE ... YORAM GLOBUS
MACK, THE ... HARVEY BERNHARD
MACKINTOSH MAN, THE ... JOHN FOREMAN
MAD MAGAZINE PRESENTS UP THE ACADEMY ... BERNIE BRILLSTEIN
MAD MAX BEYOND THUNDERDOME ... DOUG MITCHELL
MAD MAX BEYOND THUNDERDOME ... GEORGE MILLER
MAD MAX BEYOND THUNDERDOME ... TERRY HAYES
MADAME SOUSATZKA ... ROBIN DALTON
MADE IN HEAVEN ... BRUCE A. EVANS
MADE IN HEAVEN ... RAYNOLD GIDEON
MADE IN HEAVEN ... DAVID BLOCKER
MADE IN U.S.A. ... CHARLES ROVEN
MADE IN U.S.A. ... DEREK GIBSON
MADE IN U.S.A. ... JOHN DALY
MADHOUSE ... DONALD C. KLUNE
MAD MAGAZINE PRESENTS UP THE ACADEMY ... BERNIE BRILLSTEIN
MADWOMAN OF CHAILLOT, THE ... HENRY T. WEINSTEIN
MADWOMAN OF CHAILLOT, THE ... ELY LANDAU
MAGIC ... C.O. ERICKSON
MAGIC ... JOSEPH E. LEVINE†
MAGIC ... RICHARD P. LEVINE
MAGIC CHRISTIAN, THE ... HENRY T. WEINSTEIN
MAGIC CHRISTIAN, THE ... DENIS O'DELL
MAGIC VOYAGE OF SINBAD, THE ... ROGER CORMAN
MAGICIAN OF LUBLIN, THE ... HARRY N. BLUM
MAGICIAN OF LUBLIN, THE ... MENAHEM GOLAN
MAGICIAN OF LUBLIN, THE ... YORAM GLOBUS
MAGNUM FORCE ... ROBERT DALEY
MAHLER ... ROY BAIRD
MAHLER ... SANDY LIEBERSON
MAHLER ... DAVID PUTTNAM
MAHOGANY ... JACK BALLARD
MAHOGANY ... ROB COHEN
MAID TO ORDER ... HERB JAFFE
MAID TO ORDER ... MORT ENGELBERG
MAIN EVENT, THE ... BARBRA STREISAND
MAIN EVENT, THE ... JON PETERS
MAIN EVENT, THE ... RENEE MISSEL
MAIN EVENT, THE ... HOWARD ROSENMAN
MAJOR LEAGUE ... CHRIS CHESSER
MAJOR LEAGUE ... IRBY SMITH
MAJOR LEAGUE ... JULIE BERGMANN
MAJOR LEAGUE ... MARK ROSENBERG
MAKING IT ... ALBERT S. RUDDY
MAKING LOVE ... ALLEN ADLER
MAKING LOVE ... BARRY SANDLER
MAKING LOVE ... DANIEL MELNICK
MAKING MR. RIGHT ... DAN ENRIGHT
MAKING MR. RIGHT ... JOEL TUBER
MAKING MR. RIGHT ... MICHAEL WISE
MAKING MR. RIGHT ... SUSAN SEIDELMAN
MAKING THE GRADE ... GENE QUINTANO
MALCOLM ... BRYCE MENZIES
MALCOLM ... DAVID PARKER
MALCOLM ... NADIA TASS
MALIBU EXPRESS ... ARLENE SIDARIS
MALIBU HIGH ... LAWRENCE D. FOLDES
MALONE ... LEO L. FUCHS
MAN AND BOY ... BILL COSBY
MAN CALLED DAGGER, A ... RAMSEY THOMAS
MAN CALLED HORSE, A ... SANDY HOWARD
MAN CALLED SARGE, A ... CHRISTOPHER PEARCE
MAN CALLED SARGE, A ... GENE CORMAN
MAN CALLED SARGE, A ... YORAM GLOBUS
MAN CALLED SLEDGE, A ... DINO DE LAURENTIIS
MAN FOR ALL SEASONS, A ... FRED ZINNEMANN
MAN FROM SNOWY RIVER, THE ... GEOFF BURROWES
MAN FROM SNOWY RIVER, THE ... MICHAEL EDGLEY
MAN FROM SNOWY RIVER, THE ... SIMON WINCER
MAN IN THE GLASS BOOTH, THE ... ELY LANDAU
MAN IN THE GLASS BOOTH, THE ... HENRY T. WEINSTEIN
MAN IN THE GLASS BOOTH, THE ... MORT ABRAHAMS
MAN INSIDE, THE ... ALBERT R. BROCCOLI
MAN INSIDE, THE ... IRVING ALLEN†
MAN OF LA MANCHA ... ARTHUR HILLER
MAN OF LA MANCHA ... SAUL CHAPLIN
MAN OF LA MANCHA ... ALBERTO GRIMALDI
MAN OF THE WEST ... WALTER MIRISCH
MAN ON A SWING ... HOWARD B. JAFFE
MAN ON A SWING ... STANLEY R. JAFFE
MAN ON FIRE ... ARNON MILCHAN
MAN TO MAN ... JOEL SILVER
MAN WHO FELL TO EARTH, THE ... BARRY SPIKINGS
MAN WHO FELL TO EARTH, THE ... MICHAEL DEELEY
MAN WHO FELL TO EARTH, THE ... SI LITVINOFF
MAN WHO LOVED CAT DANCING, THE ... MARTIN POLL
MAN WHO LOVED CAT DANCING, THE ... ELEANOR PERRY
MAN WHO LOVED WOMEN , THE ... BLAKE EDWARDS
MAN WHO LOVED WOMEN, THE ... TONY ADAMS
MAN WHO LOVED WOMEN, THE ... JONATHAN D. KRANE
MAN WHO SAW TOMORROW, THE ... DAVID L. WOLPER
MAN WHO SAW TOMORROW, THE ... PAUL DRANE
MAN WHO SAW TOMORROW, THE ... J. ROBERT GUENETTE
MAN WHO SAW TOMORROW, THE ... LEE KRAMER
MAN WHO WASN'T THERE, THE ... FRANK MANCUSO JR.
MAN WHO WOULD BE KING, THE ... JOHN FOREMAN
MAN WITH BOGART'S FACE, THE ... ANDREW J. FENADY
MAN WITH BOGART'S FACE, THE ... MELVIN SIMON
MAN WITH ONE RED SHOE, THE ... JACK FROST SANDERS
MAN WITH ONE RED SHOE, THE ... VICTOR DRAI
MAN WITH THE GOLDEN GUN, THE ... ALBERT R. BROCCOLI
MAN WITH THE GOLDEN GUN, THE ... HARRY SALTZMAN
MAN WITH TWO BRAINS , THE ... DAVID V. PICKER
MAN WITH TWO BRAINS, THE ... WILLIAM E. MCEUEN
MAN, THE ... LEE RICH
MAN, THE ... MARTY KATZ
MAN, WOMAN AND CHILD ... JERRY BICK
MAN, WOMAN AND CHILD ... ELLIOTT KASTNER
MAN, WOMAN AND CHILD ... ELMO WILLIAMS
MAN, WOMAN AND CHILD ... STANLEY BECK
MANCHURIAN CANDIDATE, THE ... HOWARD W. KOCH
MANDINGO ... RALPH SERPE
MANHATTAN ... CHARLES H. JOFFE
MANHATTAN ... ROBERT GREENHUT
MANHATTAN PROJECT, THE ... JENNIFER OGDEN
MANHATTAN PROJECT, THE ... MARSHALL BRICKMAN
MANHUNTER ... BERNARD WILLIAMS
MANHUNTER ... RICHARD ROTH
MANIFESTO ... MENAHEM GOLAN
MANIFESTO ... YORAM GLOBUS
MANNEQUIN ... ART LEVINSON
MANNEQUIN ... EDWARD RUGOFF
MANNEQUIN ... JOSEPH FARRELL
MARATHON MAN ... ROBERT EVANS
MARATHON MAN ... SIDNEY BECKERMAN
MARCH OR DIE ... DICK RICHARDS
MARCH OR DIE ... JERRY BRUCKHEIMER
MARIA CHAPDELAINE ... HAROLD GREENBERG
MARIA CHAPDELAINE ... MURRAY SHOSTAK
MARIA CHAPDELAINE ... ROBERT BAYLIS
MARIA'S LOVERS ... BOSKO DJORDJEVIC
MARIA'S LOVERS ... LAWRENCE MORTORFF
MARIA'S LOVERS ... MENAHEM GOLAN
MARIA'S LOVERS ... YORAM GLOBUS
MARIANNE AND JULIANE ... EBERHARD JUNKERSDORF
MARIE ... ELLIOT SCHICK
MARIE ... FRANK CAPRA JR.
MARIGOLDS IN AUGUST ... JONATHAN COHEN
MARIGOLDS IN AUGUST ... MARK FORSTATER
MARLOWE ... SIDNEY BECKERMAN
MARLOWE ... GABRIEL KATZKA†
MAROONED ... FRANK CAPRA JR.
MARRIED TO THE MOB ... BILL TODMAN JR.
MARRIED TO THE MOB ... EDWARD SAXON
MARRIED TO THE MOB ... JOEL SIMON
MARRIED TO THE MOB ... KENNETH UTT
MARRIED TO THE MOB ... RON BOZMAN
MARTIANS GO HOME ... EDWARD R. PRESSMAN
MARTIANS GO HOME ... MICHAEL PARISER
MARTIN ... RICHARD P. RUBINSTEIN
MARTIN'S DAY ... RICHARD DALTON
MARTIN'S DAY ... ROY KROST
MARVIN AND TIGE ... FRANK MENKE
MARVIN AND TIGE ... WANDA DELL
MASK ... HOWARD ALSTON
MASK ... MARTIN STARGER
MASQUERADE ... MICHAEL I. LEVY
MASS APPEAL ... DAVID FOSTER
MASS APPEAL ... LAWRENCE TURMAN
MASTER GUNFIGHTER, THE ... TOM LAUGHLIN
MASTERS OF THE UNIVERSE ... EDWARD R. PRESSMAN
MASTERS OF THE UNIVERSE ... ELLIOT SCHICK
MASTERS OF THE UNIVERSE ... EVZEN W. KOLAR
MASTERS OF THE UNIVERSE ... MENAHEM GOLAN
MASTERS OF THE UNIVERSE ... YORAM GLOBUS
MATEWAN ... AMIR J. MALIN
MATEWAN ... IRA DEUTCHMAN
MATEWAN ... JERRY SILVA
MATEWAN ... MAGGIE RENZI
MATEWAN ... MARK BALSAM
MATEWAN ... PEGGY RAJSKI
MATILDA ... ALBERT S. RUDDY
MATILDA ... RICHARD R. ST. JOHNS
MATTER OF TIME, A ... GUILIO SBARIGIA
MATTER OF TIME, A ... SAMUEL Z. ARKOFF
MATTER OF WHO , A ... WALTER SHENSON
MAURICE ... ISMAIL MERCHANT
MAX DUGAN RETURNS ... ROGER M. ROTHSTEIN†
MAX DUGAN RETURNS ... HERBERT ROSS
MAX DUGAN RETURNS ... NEIL SIMON
MAXIE ... CARTER DE HAVEN
MAXIE ... JAMES L. STEWART
MAXIE ... RICH IRVINE
MAXIMUM OVERDRIVE ... DON LEVIN
MAXIMUM OVERDRIVE ... MARTHA SCHUMACHER
MAXIMUM OVERDRIVE ... MEL PEARL
MAXIMUM OVERDRIVE ... MILTON SUBOTSKY
MCCABE & MRS. MILLER ... DAVID FOSTER
MCCABE & MRS. MILLER ... MITCHELL BROWER
MCCABE & MRS. MILLER ... ROBERT ALTMAN
MCVICAR ... BILL CURBISHLEY
MCVICAR ... JOHN PEVERALL
MCVICAR ... ROGER DALTREY
MCVICAR ... ROY BAIRD
ME AND HIM ... BERND EICHINGER
ME AND HIM ... JAKE EBERTS
MEAN SEASON, THE ... LAWRENCE TURMAN
MEAN SEASON, THE ... DAVID FOSTER
MEAN STREETS ... E. LEE PERRY
MEAN STREETS ... JONATHAN T. TAPLIN
MEATBALLS ... DAN GOLDBERG
MEATBALLS ... JOHN DUNNING
MEATBALLS ... LAWRENCE NESIS
MEATBALLS III ... DON CARMODY
MEATBALLS III ... JOHN DUNNING
MEATBALLS PART II ... JOHN DUNNING
MEATBALLS PART II ... LISA BARSAMIAN
MEATBALLS PART II ... STEPHEN POE
MEATBALLS PART II ... TONY BISHOP
MECHANIC, THE ... IRWIN WINKLER
MECHANIC, THE ... ROBERT CHARTOFF
MEDUSA TOUCH, THE ... ARNON MILCHAN
MEDUSA TOUCH, THE ... ELLIOTT KASTNER
MEDUSA TOUCH, THE ... LORD LEW GRADE
MEET THE APPLEGATES ... DENISE DI NOVI
MEET THE HOLLOWHEADS ... JOHN CHAVEZ
MEET THE HOLLOWHEADS ... JOSEPH GRACE
MEET THE HOLLOWHEADS ... PIPPA SCOTT
MEGAFORCE ... ALBERT S. RUDDY
MEGAFORCE ... DAVID SHAMROY HAMBURGER
MEGAFORCE ... RAYMOND CHOW
MELODY ... DAVID PUTTNAM
MELVIN AND HOWARD ... ART LINSON
MELVIN AND HOWARD ... DON PHILLIPS
MELVIN AND HOWARD ... TERRY NELSON
MEMORIAL VALLEY MASSACRE ... BRAD KREVOY
MEMORIAL VALLEY MASSACRE ... STEVEN STABLER
MEMORIES OF ME ... ALAN KING
MEMORIES OF ME ... BILLY CRYSTAL
MEMORIES OF ME ... GABE SUMNER
MEMORIES OF ME ... J. DAVID MARKS
MEMORIES OF ME ... MICHAEL HERTZBERG
MEMPHIS BELLE ... CATHERINE WYLER
MEMPHIS BELLE ... DAVID PUTTNAM
MEN DON'T LEAVE ... JON AVNET
MEN DON'T LEAVE ... PAUL BRICKMAN
MEN'S CLUB, THE ... MICHAEL ROSENBLATT
MEN'S CLUB, THE ... THOMAS COLEMAN
MEN'S CLUB, THE ... HOWARD GOTTFRIED
MEN, THE ... STANLEY KRAMER
MERCENARY, THE ... ALBERTO GRIMALDI
MERMAIDS ... LAUREN LLOYD

MERMAIDS ..... PATRICK PALMER
MERMAIDS ..... WALLIS NICITA
MERRY CHRISTMAS, MR. LAWRENCE ..... EIKO OSHIMA
MERRY CHRISTMAS, MR. LAWRENCE ..... GEOFFREY NETHERCOTT
MERRY CHRISTMAS, MR. LAWRENCE ..... JEREMY THOMAS
MERRY CHRISTMAS, MR. LAWRENCE ..... MASATO HARA
MERRY CHRISTMAS, MR. LAWRENCE ..... TERRY GLINWOOD
MESSENGER OF DEATH ..... YORAM GLOBUS
MESSENGER OF DEATH ..... MENAHEM GOLAN
MESSENGER OF DEATH ..... PANCHO KOHNER
METEOR ..... GABRIEL KATZKA†
METEOR ..... SANDY HOWARD
MIAMI BLUES ..... EDWARD SAXON
MIAMI BLUES ..... FRED WARD
MIAMI BLUES ..... GARY GOETZMAN
MIAMI BLUES ..... JONATHAN DEMME
MIAMI BLUES ..... KENNETH UTT
MIAMI BLUES ..... RON BOZMAN
MICKI & MAUDE ..... JONATHAN D. KRANE
MICKI & MAUDE ..... LOU ANTONIO
MICKI & MAUDE ..... TONY ADAMS
MIDDLE AGE CRAZY ..... ROBERT COOPER
MIDDLE AGE CRAZY ..... RONALD I. COHEN
MIDNIGHT ..... GLORIA J. MORRISON
MIDNIGHT ..... NORMAN THADDEUS VANE
MIDNIGHT COWBOY ..... JEROME HELLMAN
MIDNIGHT COWBOY ..... KENNETH UTT
MIDNIGHT CROSSING ..... DAN IRELAND
MIDNIGHT CROSSING ..... DOUG WEISER
MIDNIGHT CROSSING ..... GARY BARBER
MIDNIGHT CROSSING ..... GREGORY CASCANTE
MIDNIGHT CROSSING ..... MATHEW HAYDEN
MIDNIGHT CROSSING ..... WANDA S. RAYLE
MIDNIGHT EXPRESS ..... ALAN MARSHALL
MIDNIGHT EXPRESS ..... DAVID PUTTNAM
MIDNIGHT EXPRESS ..... PETER GUBER
MIDNIGHT MADNESS ..... DAVID WECHTER
MIDNIGHT MADNESS ..... MAICHEL NANKIN
MIDNIGHT MADNESS ..... RON MILLER
MIDNIGHT RUN ..... MARTIN BREST
MIDNIGHT RUN ..... WILLIAM S. GILMORE
MIDSUMMER NIGHT'S DREAM, A ..... MARTIN RANSOHOFF
MIDSUMMER NIGHT'S SEX COMEDY, A ..... CHARLES H. JOFFE
MIDSUMMER NIGHT'S SEX COMEDY, A ..... MICHAEL PEYSER
MIDSUMMER NIGHT'S SEX COMEDY, A ..... ROBERT GREENHUT
MIDWAY ..... WALTER MIRISCH
MIGHTY QUINN, THE ..... DALE POLLOCK
MIGHTY QUINN, THE ..... ED ELBERT
MIGHTY QUINN, THE ..... GIL FRIESEN
MIGHTY QUINN, THE ..... MARION HUNT
MIGHTY QUINN, THE ..... SANDY LIEBERSON
MIKE'S MURDER ..... JACK LARSON
MIKE'S MURDER ..... KIM KURUMADA
MIKEY AND NICKY ..... BUD AUSTIN
MIKEY AND NICKY ..... MICHAEL HAUSMAN
MILAGRO BEANFIELD WAR, THE ..... CHARLES B. MULVEHILL
MILAGRO BEANFIELD WAR, THE ..... GARY J. HENDLER†
MILAGRO BEANFIELD WAR, THE ..... MOCTESUMA ESPARZA
MILAGRO BEANFIELD WAR, THE ..... ROBERT REDFORD
MILENNIUM ..... LOUIS M. SILVERSTEIN
MILENNIUM ..... P. GAEL MOURANT
MILENNIUM ..... ROBERT VINCE
MILES FROM HOME ..... AMIR J. MALIN
MILES FROM HOME ..... FREDERICK ZOLLO
MILES FROM HOME ..... PAUL KURTA
MILES FROM HOME ..... RANDY FINCH
MILES FROM HOME ..... RUSS SMITH
MILLENNIUM ..... DOUGLAS LEITERMAN
MILLENNIUM ..... FREDDIE FIELDS
MILLENNIUM ..... JOHN FOREMAN
MILLENNIUM ..... JOHN M. ECKERT
MILLER'S CROSSING ..... BEN BARENHOLTZ
MILLER'S CROSSING ..... ETHAN COEN
MILLER'S CROSSING ..... GRAHAM PLACE
MILLER'S CROSSING ..... MARK SILVERMAN†
MILLION DOLLAR MYSTERY ... STEPHEN F. KESTEN
MINISTRY OF VENGEANCE ..... BRAD KREVOY
MINISTRY OF VENGEANCE ..... STEVEN STABLER
MINNIE AND MOSKOWITZ ..... AL RUBAN
MIRACLE MILE ..... DEREK GIBSON
MIRACLE MILE ..... JOHN DALY
MIRACLE MILE ..... GRAHAM COTTLE
MIRACLE OF THE WHITE STALLIONS ..... PETER V. HERALD
MIRACLES ..... BERNARD WILLIAMS
MIRACLES ..... DAVID GREENWALT
MIRACLES ..... STEVE ROTH
MIRROR CRACK'D, THE ..... RICHARD GOODWIN
MIRROR CRACK'D, THE ..... JOHN BRABOURNE
MISADVENTURES OF MERLIN JONES, THE ..... RON MILLER
MISCHIEF ..... MICHAEL NOLIN
MISCHIEF ..... NOEL BLACK
MISCHIEF ..... SAM MANNERS
MISFIT BRIGADE, THE ..... BENNI KORZEN
MISFIT BRIGADE, THE ..... JUST BETZER
MISHIMA: A LIFE IN FOUR CHAPTERS ..... FRANCIS FORD COPPOLA
MISHIMA: A LIFE IN FOUR CHAPTERS ..... GEORGE LUCAS
MISHIMA: A LIFE IN FOUR CHAPTERS ..... MATA YAMAMOTO
MISHIMA: A LIFE IN FOUR CHAPTERS ..... TOM LUDDY
MISS FIRECRACKER ..... FRED BERNER
MISS FIRECRACKER ..... LEWIS ALLEN
MISS FIRECRACKER ..... RICHARD COLL
MISS FIRECRACKER ..... ROSS E. MILLOY
MISSING ..... EDWARD LEWIS
MISSING ..... MILDRED LEWIS
MISSING ..... TERRY NELSON
MISSING ..... JON PETERS
MISSING ..... PETER GUBER
MISSING IN ACTION ..... LANCE HOOL
MISSING IN ACTION ..... MENAHEM GOLAN
MISSING IN ACTION ..... YORAM GLOBUS
MISSING IN ACTION 2: THE BEGINNING ..... MENAHEM GOLAN
MISSING IN ACTION 2: THE BEGINNING ..... YORAM GLOBUS
MISSION, THE ..... FERNANDO GHIA
MISSION, THE ..... IAIN SMITH
MISSION, THE ..... DAVID PUTTNAM
MISSIONARY, THE ..... DENIS O'BRIEN
MISSIONARY, THE ..... GEORGE HARRISON
MISSIONARY, THE ..... MICHAEL PALIN
MISSIONARY, THE ..... NEVILLE C. THOMPSON
MISSISSIPPI BURNING ..... FREDERICK ZOLLO
MISSISSIPPI BURNING ..... ROBERT F. COLESBERRY
MISSOURI BREAKS, THE ..... ELLIOTT KASTNER
MISSOURI BREAKS, THE ..... ROBERT M. SHERMAN
MISTY ..... ROBERT B. RADNITZ
MISUNDERSTOOD ..... CRAIG BAUMGARTEN
MISUNDERSTOOD ..... KEITH BARISH
MISUNDERSTOOD ..... MARK LOMBARDO
MISUNDERSTOOD ..... TARAK BEN AMMAR
MIXED BLOOD ..... ANTOINE GANNAGE
MIXED BLOOD ..... STEVEN FIERBERG
MO' BETTER BLUES ..... JON KILIK
MO' BETTER BLUES ..... MONTY ROSS
MO' BETTER BLUES ..... SPIKE LEE
MODERN GIRLS ..... GARY GOETZMAN
MODERN PROBLEMS ..... ALAN GREISMAN
MODERN PROBLEMS ..... MICHAEL SHAMBERG
MODERN ROMANCE ..... ANDREW SCHEINMAN
MODERNS, THE ..... CAROLYN PFEIFFER
MODERNS, THE ..... DAVID BLOCKER
MODERNS, THE ..... SHEP GORDON
MOMENT BY MOMENT ..... KEVIN MCCORMICK
MOMENT BY MOMENT ..... ROBERT STIGWOOD
MOMMIE DEAREST ..... FRANK YABLANS
MOMMIE DEAREST ..... NEIL A. MACHLIS
MONA LISA ..... CHRIS BROWN
MONA LISA ..... DENIS O'BRIEN
MONA LISA ..... GEORGE HARRISON
MONA LISA ..... PATRICK CASSAVETTI
MONA LISA ..... RAY COOPER
MONA LISA ..... STEPHEN WOOLLEY
MONDO NEW YORK ..... DORIAN HENDRIX
MONDO NEW YORK ..... STUART S. SHAPIRO
MONDO TRASHO ..... JOHN WATERS
MONEY PIT, THE ..... DAVID GILER
MONEY PIT, THE ..... ART LEVINSON
MONEY PIT, THE ..... FRANK MARSHALL
MONEY PIT, THE ..... KATHLEEN KENNEDY
MONEY PIT, THE ..... STEVEN SPIELBERG
MONKEY SHINES ..... CHARLES EVANS
MONKEY SHINES ..... GERALD S. PAONESSA
MONKEY SHINES ..... PETER GRUNWALD
MONKEY SHINES ..... PETER MCINTOSH
MONKEY'S, GO HOME! ..... RON MILLER
MONKEY'S UNCLE, THE ..... RON MILLER
MONSIGNOR ..... DAVID NIVEN JR.
MONSIGNOR ..... FRANK YABLANS
MONSTER FROM THE OCEAN FLOOR ..... ROGER CORMAN
MONSTER SQUAD, THE ..... KEITH BARISH
MONSTER SQUAD, THE ..... NEIL A. MACHLIS
MONSTER SQUAD, THE ..... PETER HYAMS
MONSTER SQUAD, THE ..... ROB COHEN
MONSTER SQUAD, THE ..... JONATHAN A. ZIMBERT
MONTY PYTHON AND THE HOLY GRAIL ..... JOHN GOLDSTONE
MONTY PYTHON AND THE HOLY GRAIL ..... MARK FORSTATER
MONTY PYTHON'S LIFE OF BRIAN ..... DENIS O'BRIEN
MONTY PYTHON'S LIFE OF BRIAN ..... GEORGE HARRISON
MONTY PYTHON'S LIFE OF BRIAN ..... JOHN GOLDSTONE
MONTY PYTHON'S THE MEANING OF LIFE ..... JOHN GOLDSTONE
MOON OVER PARADOR ..... GEOFFREY TAYLOR
MOON OVER PARADOR ..... PATO GUZMAN
MOON OVER PARADOR ..... PAUL MAZURSKY
MOONLIGHTING ..... JERZY SKOLIMOWSKI
MOONLIGHTING ..... MARK SHIVAS
MOON PILOT ..... BILL ANDERSON
MOON PILOT ..... RON MILLER
MOONRAKER ..... MICHAEL G. WILSON
MOONRAKER ..... ALBERT R. BROCCOLI
MOONSHINE WAR, THE ..... MARTIN RANSOHOFF
MOON-SPINNERS, THE ..... BILL ANDERSON
MOONSTRUCK ..... BONNIE PALEF
MOONSTRUCK ..... PATRICK PALMER
MOONSTRUCK ..... NORMAN JEWISON
MOONTRAP ..... ALAN M. SOLOMON
MOONTRAP ..... BRIAN C. MANOOGIAN
MOONTRAP ..... JAMES A. COURTNEY
MOONTRAP ..... ROBERT DYKE
MORE AMERICAN GRAFFITI ..... GEORGE LUCAS
MORE AMERICAN GRAFFITI ... HOWARD KAZANJIAN
MORGAN STEWART'S COMING HOME ..... PATRICK MCCORMICK
MORGAN STEWART'S COMING HOME ..... STEPHEN J. FRIEDMAN
MORGAN: A SUITABLE CASE FOR TREATMENT ..... LEON CLORE
MORNING AFTER, THE ..... BRUCE GILBERT
MORNING AFTER, THE ..... FAYE SCHWAB
MORNING AFTER, THE ..... LOIS BONFIGLIO
MORNING AFTER, THE ..... WOLFGANG GLATTES
MORONS FROM OUTER SPACE ..... BARRY HANSON
MORONS FROM OUTER SPACE ..... VERITY LAMBERT
MORTAL PASSIONS ..... GWEN FIELD
MORTAL PASSIONS ..... ANDREW LANE
MORTAL PASSIONS ..... JOEL LEVINE
MORTAL PASSIONS ..... WAYNE CRAWFORD
MOSCOW ON THE HUDSON ..... PAUL MAZURSKY
MOSCOW ON THE HUDSON ..... GEOFFREY TAYLOR
MOSCOW ON THE HUDSON ..... PATO GUZMAN
MOSQUITO COAST, THE ..... JEROME HELLMAN
MOSQUITO COAST, THE ..... SAUL ZAENTZ
MOSQUITO SQUADRON ..... WALTER MIRISCH
MOTEL HELL ..... HERB JAFFE
MOTEL HELL ..... ROBERT JAFFE
MOTEL HELL ..... STEVEN-CHARLES JAFFE
MOUNTAIN KING ..... RON SILVERMAN
MOUNTAIN MEN, THE ..... MARTIN RANSOHOFF
MOUNTAIN MEN, THE ..... ANDREW SCHEINMAN
MOUNTAIN MEN, THE ..... MARTIN SHAFER
MOUNTAIN MEN, THE ..... RICHARD R. ST. JOHNS
MOUNTAINS OF THE MOON ..... ANDREW VAJNA
MOUNTAINS OF THE MOON ..... DANIEL MELNICK
MOUNTAINS OF THE MOON ..... MARIO KASSAR
MOUSE ON THE MOON, THE ..... WALTER SHENSON
MOUSE THAT ROARED, THE ..... WALTER SHENSON
MOVERS AND SHAKERS ..... WILLIAM ASHER
MOVIE MOVIE ..... STANLEY DONEN
MOVIE MOVIE ..... MARTIN STARGER
MOVING ..... KIM KURUMADA
MOVING ..... STUART CORNFELD
MOVING VIOLATION ..... JULIE CORMAN
MOVING VIOLATION ..... ROGER CORMAN
MOVING VIOLATIONS ..... DOUG DRAIZIN
MOVING VIOLATIONS ..... HARRY UFLAND
MOVING VIOLATIONS ..... PAT PROFT
MOVING VIOLATIONS ..... ROBERT ISRAEL
MOVING VIOLATIONS ..... JOE ROTH
MR. BILLION ..... STEVEN BACH
MR. BILLION ..... KEN FRIEDMAN
MR. LOVE ..... ROBIN DOUET
MR. LOVE ..... SUSAN RICHARDS
MR. LOVE ..... DAVID PUTTNAM
MR. MAJESTYK ..... WALTER MIRISCH
MR. MIKE'S MONDO VIDEO ..... LORNE MICHAELS

N

MR. MIKE'S MONDO VIDEO ... MICHAEL O'DONOGHUE
MR. MOM ... AARON SPELLING
MR. MOM ... ART LEVINSON
MR. MOM ... HARRY COLOMBY
MR. MOM ... LAUREN SHULER-DONNER
MR. MOM ... LYNN LORING
MR. NORTH ... DAVID R. AMES
MR. NORTH ... JOHN HUSTON†
MR. NORTH ... SKIP STELOFF
MR. NORTH ... STEVEN HAFT
MR. NORTH ... TOM SHAW
MRS. BROWN, YOU'VE GOT A LOVELY DAUGHTER ... ALLEN KLEIN
MRS. SOFFEL ... DAVID A. NICKSAY
MRS. SOFFEL ... DENNIS JONES
MRS. SOFFEL ... SCOTT RUDIN
MRS. SOFFEL ... EDGAR J. SCHERICK
MUNCHIES ... GINNY NUGENT
MUNCHIES ... ROGER CORMAN
MUPPET MOVIE, THE ... MARTIN STARGER
MUPPET MOVIE, THE ... JIM HENSON
MUPPETS TAKE MANHATTAN, THE ... DAVID LAZER
MUPPETS TAKE MANHATTAN, THE ... JIM HENSON
MURDER BY DEATH ... RAY STARK
MURDER ON THE ORIENT EXPRESS ... JOHN BRABOURNE
MURDER ON THE ORIENT EXPRESS ... RICHARD GOODWIN
MURDERS IN THE RUE MORGUE ... SAMUEL Z. ARKOFF
MURPHY'S LAW ... JILL IRELAND
MURPHY'S LAW ... MENAHEM GOLAN
MURPHY'S LAW ... PANCHO KOHNER
MURPHY'S LAW ... YORAM GLOBUS
MURPHY'S ROMANCE ... LAURA ZISKIN
MURPHY'S WAR ... MICHAEL DEELEY
MUSCLE BEACH PARTY ... JAMES H. NICHOLSON†
MUSCLE BEACH PARTY ... QROBERT DILLON
MUSCLE BEACH PARTY ... SAMUEL Z. ARKOFF
MUSIC BOX ... HAL W. POLAIRE
MUSIC BOX ... IRWIN WINKLER
MUSIC BOX ... JOE ESZTERHAS
MUSIC LOVERS, THE ... ROY BAIRD
MUTANT ON THE BOUNTY ... MARTIN LUPEZ
MUTANT ON THE BOUNTY ... ROBERT TORRANCE
MY AMERICAN COUSIN ... PETER O'BRIAN
MY AMERICAN COUSIN ... SANDY WILSON
MY BEAUTIFUL LAUNDRETTE ... SARAH RADCLYFFE
MY BEAUTIFUL LAUNDRETTE ... TIM BEVAN
MY BEST FRIEND IS A VAMPIRE ... DENNIS MURPHY
MY BLOODY VALENTINE ... ANDRE LINK
MY BLOODY VALENTINE ... JOHN DUNNING
MY BLOODY VALENTINE ... LAWRENCE NESIS
MY BLOODY VALENTINE ... STEPHEN MILLER
MY BODYGUARD ... DON DEVLIN
MY BODYGUARD ... MELVIN SIMON
MY DEMON LOVER ... LARRY THOMPSON
MY DEMON LOVER ... PIERRE DAVID
MY DEMON LOVER ... PIETER JAN BRUGGE
MY DEMON LOVER ... ROBERT SHAYE
MY DEMON LOVER ... SARA RISHER
MY DINNER WITH ANDRE ... BEVERLY KARP
MY DINNER WITH ANDRE ... GEORGE W. GEORGE
MY FAVORITE YEAR ... ART LEVINSON
MY FAVORITE YEAR ... MICHAEL GRUSKOFF
MY LEFT FOOT ... NOEL PEARSON
MY LEFT FOOT ... ARTHUR LAPPIN
MY LITTLE GIRL ... CONNIE KAISERMAN
MY LITTLE GIRL ... ISMAIL MERCHANT
MY SCIENCE PROJECT ... JONATHAN T. TAPLIN
MY SIDE OF THE MOUNTAIN ... ROBERT B. RADNITZ
MY SIX CONVICTS ... STANLEY KRAMER
MY STEPMOTHER IS AN ALIEN ... ART LEVINSON
MY STEPMOTHER IS AN ALIEN ... FRANKLIN R. LEVY
MY STEPMOTHER IS AN ALIEN ... LAURENCE MARK
MY STEPMOTHER IS AN ALIEN ... RONALD PARKER
MYSTERIOUS MONSTERS, THE ... CHARLES E. SELLIER JR.
MYSTERIOUS MONSTERS, THE ... DAVID L. WOLPER
MYSTERIOUS MONSTERS, THE ... ROBERT GUENETTE
MYSTERY TRAIN ... HIDEAKI SUDA
MYSTERY TRAIN ... JIM STARK
MYSTERY TRAIN ... KUNJIRO HIRATA
MYSTERY TRAIN ... RUDD SIMMONS
MYSTIC PIZZA ... MARK LEVINSON
MYSTIC PIZZA ... SAMUEL GOLDWYN JR.
MYSTIC PIZZA ... SCOTT ROSENFELT
NADINE ... ARLENE DONOVAN
NADINE ... WOLFGANG GLATTES
NAKED ANGELS ... ROGER CORMAN
NAKED CAGE, THE ... CHRIS D. NEBE
NAKED CAGE, THE ... MENAHEM GOLAN
NAKED CAGE, THE ... YORAM GLOBUS
NAKED FACE, THE ... MENAHEM GOLAN
NAKED FACE, THE ... YORAM GLOBUS
NAKED GUN, THE ... DAVID ZUCKER
NAKED GUN, THE ... JERRY ZUCKER
NAKED GUN, THE ... JIM ABRAHAMS
NAME OF THE ROSE, THE ... ALEXANDRE MNOUCHKINE
NAME OF THE ROSE, THE ... BERND EICHINGER
NAME OF THE ROSE, THE ... FRANCO CRISTALDI
NAME OF THE ROSE, THE ... JAKE EBERTS
NAME OF THE ROSE, THE ... THOMAS SCHUEHLY
NANOU ... SIMON PERRY
NARROW MARGIN ... ANDREW VAJNA
NARROW MARGIN ... MARIO KASSAR
NARROW MARGIN ... JONATHAN A. ZIMBERT
NASHVILLE ... ROBERT ALTMAN
NASHVILLE ... JERRY WEINTRAUB
NASHVILLE ... SCOTT BUSHNELL
NASHVILLE ... MARTIN STARGER
NATE AND HAYES ... LLOYD PHILLIPS
NATE AND HAYES ... ROBERT WHITEHOUSE
NATIONAL LAMPOON'S ANIMAL HOUSE ... MATTY SIMMONS
NATIONAL LAMPOON'S ANIMAL HOUSE ... IVAN REITMAN
NATIONAL LAMPOON'S CHRISTMAS VACATION ... JOHN HUGHES
NATIONAL LAMPOON'S CHRISTMAS VACATION ... MATTY SIMMONS
NATIONAL LAMPOON'S CHRISTMAS VACATION ... TOM JACOBSON
NATIONAL LAMPOON'S CLASS REUNION ... HARMON BERNS
NATIONAL LAMPOON'S CLASS REUNION ... MATTY SIMMONS
NATIONAL LAMPOON'S CLASS REUNION ... PETER V. HERALD
NATIONAL LAMPOON'S EUROPEAN VACATION ... MATTY SIMMONS
NATIONAL LAMPOON'S EUROPEAN VACATION ... STUART CORNFELD
NATIONAL LAMPOON'S MOVIE MADNESS ... MATTY SIMMONS
NATIONAL LAMPOON'S VACATION ... MATTY SIMMONS
NATIVE SON ... DIANE SILVER
NATIVE SON ... LINDSAY LAW
NATURAL, THE ... MARK JOHNSON
NATURAL, THE ... PHILIP M. BREEN
NATURAL, THE ... ROBERT F. COLESBERRY
NATURAL, THE ... ROGER TOWNE
NAVIGATOR, THE ... JOHN MAYNARD
NAVIGATOR: AN ODYSSEY ACROSS TIME, THE ... GARY HANNAM
NEAR DARK ... EDWARD S. FELDMAN
NEAR DARK ... ERIC RED
NEAR DARK ... STANLEY R. JAFFE
NEAR DARK ... STEVEN-CHARLES JAFFE
NEAR DARK ... CHARLES R. MEEKER
NECROPOLIS ... CYNTHIA DEPAULA
NECROPOLIS ... TIM KINCAID
NEIGHBORS ... DAVID BROWN
NEIGHBORS ... IRVING PAUL LAZAR
NEIGHBORS ... BERNIE BRILLSTEIN
NEIGHBORS ... RICHARD D. ZANUCK
NETWORK ... HOWARD GOTTFRIED
NEVER A DULL MOMENT ... RON MILLER
NEVER CRY WOLF ... JACK COUFFER
NEVER CRY WOLF ... JOSEPH STRICK
NEVER CRY WOLF ... LEWIS ALLEN
NEVER CRY WOLF ... RON MILLER
NEVER CRY WOLF ... WALKER STUART
NEVER ON TUESDAY ... BRAD WYMAN
NEVER ON TUESDAY ... CASSIAN ELWES
NEVER ON TUESDAY ... LIONEL WIGRAM
NEVER SAY NEVER AGAIN ... JACK SCHWARTZMAN
NEVER SAY NEVER AGAIN ... KEVIN MCCLORY
NEVER SAY NEVER AGAIN ... MICHAEL DRYHURST
NEVER TOO LATE ... NORMAN LEAR
NEVERENDING STORY, THE ... BERND EICHINGER
NEVERENDING STORY, THE ... DIETER GIESSLER
NEVERENDING STORY, THE ... GUNTER ROHRBACH
NEVERENDING STORY, THE ... JOHN HYDE
NEVERENDING STORY, THE ... MARK DAMON
NEVERENDING STORY II, THE ... DIETER GIESSLER
NEVERENDING STORY II, THE ... TIM HAMPTON
NEW ADVENTURES OF PIPPI LONGSTOCKING, THE ... GARY MEHLMAN
NEW ADVENTURES OF PIPPI LONGSTOCKING, THE ... KEN ANNAKIN
NEW ADVENTURES OF PIPPI LONGSTOCKING, THE ... MISHAAL KAMAL ADHAM
NEW ADVENTURES OF PIPPI LONGSTOCKING, THE ... WALTER MOSHAY
NEW CENTURIONS, THE ... ROBERT CHARTOFF
NEW CENTURIONS, THE ... IRWIN WINKLER
NEW KIDS, THE ... BARBARA DE FINA
NEW KIDS, THE ... SEAN S. CUNNINGHAM
NEW KIDS, THE ... ANDREW FOGELSON
NEW LEAF, A ... STANLEY R. JAFFE
NEW LIFE, A ... LOUIS A. STROLLER
NEW LIFE, A ... MARTIN BREGMAN
NEW YEAR'S DAY ... JUDITH WOLINSKY
NEW YORK STORIES ... BARBARA DE FINA
NEW YORK STORIES ... CHARLES H. JOFFE
NEW YORK STORIES ... FRED FUCHS
NEW YORK STORIES ... FRED ROOS
NEW YORK STORIES ... JACK ROLLINS
NEW YORK STORIES ... ROBERT GREENHUT
NEW YORK, NEW YORK ... ROBERT CHARTOFF
NEW YORK, NEW YORK ... GENE KIRKWOOD
NEW YORK, NEW YORK ... IRWIN WINKLER
NEXT MAN, THE ... MARTIN BREGMAN
NEXT OF KIN ... LARRY DE WAAY
NEXT OF KIN ... LES ALEXANDER
NEXT STOP, GREENWICH VILLAGE ... PAUL MAZURSKY
NEXT STOP, GREENWICH VILLAGE ... TONY RAY
NICE GIRLS DON'T EXPLODE ... DOUGLAS CURTIS
NICE GIRLS DON'T EXPLODE ... JOHN WELLS
NICKEL RIDE, THE ... ROBERT MULLIGAN
NICKEL RIDE, THE ... DAVID FOSTER
NICKEL RIDE, THE ... LAWRENCE TURMAN
NICKELODEON ... FRANK MARSHALL
NICKELODEON ... IRWIN WINKLER
NICKELODEON ... ROBERT CHARTOFF
NIGHT CROSSING ... MARC STIRDIVANT
NIGHT CROSSING ... RON MILLER
NIGHT CROSSING ... TOM LEETCH
NIGHT FORCE ... VICTORIA MEYERINK
NIGHT FRIEND ... DON HAIG
NIGHT FRIEND ... PATRICIA GERRETSEN
NIGHT GAME ... EDUARD SARLUI
NIGHT GAME ... GEORGE LITTO
NIGHT GAME ... MOSHE DIAMANT
NIGHT IN HEAVEN, A ... GENE KIRKWOOD
NIGHT IN HEAVEN, A ... HOWARD W. KOCH JR.
NIGHT IN THE LIFE OF JIMMY REARDON, A ... MEL KLEIN
NIGHT IN THE LIFE OF JIMMY REARDON, A ... NOEL MARSHALL
NIGHT IN THE LIFE OF JIMMY REARDON, A ... RUSSELL SCHWARTZ
NIGHT MOVES ... ROBERT M. SHERMAN
NIGHT OF DARK SHADOWS ... DAN CURTIS
NIGHT OF THE COMET ... ANDREW LANE
NIGHT OF THE COMET ... WAYNE CRAWFORD
NIGHT OF THE CREEPS ... CHARLES GORDON
NIGHT OF THE CREEPS ... DONNA SMITH
NIGHT OF THE CREEPS ... WILLIAM FINNEGAN
NIGHT OF THE DEMONS ... DON ROBINSON
NIGHT OF THE DEMONS ... JOE AUGUSTYN
NIGHT OF THE DEMONS ... WALTER JOSTEN
NIGHT OF THE FOLLOWING DAY, THE ... ELLIOTT KASTNER
NIGHT OF THE JUGGLER ... ARNOLD KOPELSON
NIGHT OF THE JUGGLER ... JAY WESTON
NIGHT PATROL ... JACKIE KONG
NIGHT PATROL ... WILLIAM OSCO
NIGHT SHIFT ... BRIAN GRAZER
NIGHT SHIFT ... DON KRANZE
NIGHT THEY RAIDEDI MINSKY'S, THE ... BUD YORKIN
NIGHT THEY RAIDED MINSKY'S, THE ... NORMAN LEAR
NIGHT VISITOR ... ALAIN SILVER
NIGHT VISITOR ... SHELLEY E. REID
NIGHT VISITOR ... TOM BROADBRIDGE
NIGHT WATCH ... MARTIN POLL
NIGHT WATCH ... GEORGE W. GEORGE
NIGHTBREED ... JAMES G. ROBINSON
NIGHTBREED ... GABRIELLA MARTINELLI
NIGHTBREED ... JOE ROTH
NIGHTBREED ... CHRISTOPHER FIGG
NIGHTFALL ... JULIE CORMAN
NIGHTFLYERS ... HERB JAFFE

NIGHTFLYERS ... ROBERT JAFFE
NIGHTHAWKS ... FRANKLIN R. LEVY
NIGHTHAWKS ... MARTIN POLL
NIGHTHAWKS ... MICHAEL WISE
NIGHTMARE IN CHICAGO ... ROBERT ALTMAN
NIGHTMARE ON ELM STREET, A ... JOSEPH WOLF
NIGHTMARE ON ELM STREET, A ... ROBERT SHAYE
NIGHTMARE ON ELM STREET, A ... SARA RISHER
NIGHTMARE ON ELM STREET, A ... STANLEY DUDELSON
NIGHTMARE ON ELM STREET 2: FREDDY'S REVENGE, A ... JOEL SOISSON
NIGHTMARE ON ELM STREET 2: FREDDY'S REVENGE, A ... ROBERT SHAYE
NIGHTMARE ON ELM STREET 2: FREDDY'S REVENGE, A ... SARA RISHER
NIGHTMARE ON ELM STREET 2: FREDDY'S REVENGE, A ... STANLEY DUDELSON
NIGHTMARE ON ELM STREET 2: FREDDY'S REVENGE, A ... STEPHEN DIENER
NIGHTMARE ON ELM STREET 2: FREDDY'S REVENGE, A ... MICHAEL S. MURPHEY
NIGHTMARE ON ELM STREET 3: DREAM WARRIORS, A ... RACHEL TALALAY
NIGHTMARE ON ELM STREET 3: DREAM WARRIORS, A ... ROBERT SHAYE
NIGHTMARE ON ELM STREET 3: DREAM WARRIORS, A ... SARA RISHER
NIGHTMARE ON ELM STREET 3: DREAM WARRIORS, A ... STEPHEN DIENER
NIGHTMARE ON ELM STREET 3: DREAM WARRIORS, A ... WES CRAVEN
NIGHTMARE ON ELM STREET 4: THE DREAM MASTER, A ... ROBERT SHAYE
NIGHTMARE ON ELM STREET 4: THE DREAM MASTER, A ... SARA RISHER
NIGHTMARE ON ELM STREET 4: THE DREAM MASTER, A ... STEPHEN DIENER
NIGHTMARE ON ELM STREET 5: THE DREAM CHILD, A ... SARA RISHER
NIGHTMARE ON ELM STREET 5: THE DREAM CHILD, A ... ROBERT SHAYE
NIGHTMARE ON ELM STREET 5: THE DREAM CHILD, A ... RUPERT HARVEY
'NIGHT, MOTHER ... AARON SPELLING
'NIGHT, MOTHER ... ALAN GREISMAN
'NIGHT, MOTHER ... CHERYL DOWNEY
'NIGHT, MOTHER ... DANN BYCK
'NIGHT, MOTHER ... DAVID LANCASTER
'NIGHT, MOTHER ... WALLACE WORSLEY
NIGHTSTICK ... MARTIN WALTERS
NIGHTWING ... RICHARD R. ST. JOHNS
NIGHTWING ... MARTIN RANSOHOFF
NIJINSKY ... NORA KAYE†
NIJINSKY ... STANLEY O'TOOLE
NIJINSKY ... HARRY SALTZMAN
NINE LIVES OF FRITZ THE CAT, THE ... STEVE KRANTZ
NINE TO FIVE ... BRUCE GILBERT
NINJA III: THE DOMINATION ... MENAHEM GOLAN
NINJA III: THE DOMINATION ... YORAM GLOBUS
NINTH CONFIGURATION, THE ... TOM SHAW
NINTH CONFIGURATION, THE ... WILLIAM PETER BLATTY
NO DEPOSIT, NO RETURN ... RON MILLER
NO HOLDS BARRED ... HULK HOGAN
NO HOLDS BARRED ... MICHAEL RACHMIL
NO HOLDS BARRED ... RICHARD GLOVER
NO HOLDS BARRED ... VINCE MCMAHON
NO MAN'S LAND ... JOSEPH STERN
NO MAN'S LAND ... RON HOWARD
NO MAN'S LAND ... SCOTT KROOPF
NO MAN'S LAND ... TONY GANZ
NO MAN'S LAND ... DICK WOLF
NO MERCY ... D. CONSTANTINE CONTE
NO MERCY ... MICHAEL HAUSMAN
NO NUKES ... DANNY GOLDBERG
NO NUKES ... JULIAN SCHLOSSBERG
NO RETREAT, NO SURRENDER II ... NG SEE YUEN
NO RETREAT, NO SURRENDER II ... ROY HORAN
NO SMALL AFFAIR ... GEORGE JUSTIN
NO SMALL AFFAIR ... WILLIAM SACKHEIM
NO TIME TO DIE ... ALBERT R. BROCCOLI
NO TIME TO DIE ... IRVING ALLEN†
NO WAY OUT ... LAURA ZISKIN
NO WAY OUT ... MACE NEUFELD
NO WAY OUT ... ROBERT GARLAND
NOBODY'S FOOL ... CARY BROKAW
NOBODY'S FOOL ... JAMES C. KATZ
NOBODY'S FOOL ... JON S. DENNY
NOBODY'S PERFEKT ... TED SWANSON
NOBODY'S PERFEKT ... MORT ENGELBERG
NOMADS ... CASSIAN ELWES
NOMADS ... GEORGE PAPPAS
NOMADS ... JERRY GERSHWIN
NOMADS ... ELLIOTT KASTNER
NORMA RAE ... MARTIN RITT
NORMA RAE ... TAMARA ASSEYEV
NORMA RAE ... ALEXANDRA ROSE
NORTH AVENUE IRREGULARS, THE ... RON MILLER
NORTH AVENUE IRREGULARS, THE ... TOM LEETCH
NORTH DALLAS FORTY ... FRANK YABLANS
NORTH DALLAS FORTY ... JACK B. BERNSTEIN
NORTH SHORE ... RANDAL KLEISER
NORTH SHORE ... WILLIAM FINNEGAN
NOT AS A STRANGER ... STANLEY KRAMER
NOT FOR PUBLICATION ... ANNE KIMMEL
NOT FOR PUBLICATION ... MARK FORSTATER
NOT QUITE PARADISE ... HERBERT L. OAKES
NOT QUITE PARADISE ... LEWIS GILBERT
NOT QUITE PARADISE ... WILLIAM P. CARTLIDGE
NOTHING IN COMMON ... ALEXANDRA ROSE
NOTHING IN COMMON ... NICK ABDO
NOTHING IN COMMON ... RAY STARK
NOTHING LASTS FOREVER ... JOHN HEAD
NOTHING LASTS FOREVER ... LORNE MICHAELS
NOTHING PERSONAL ... ALAN HAMEL
NOTHING PERSONAL ... DAVID PERLMUTTER
NOTHING PERSONAL ... JAY BERNSTEIN
NOTHING PERSONAL ... NORMAN HIRSCHFELD
NOWHERE TO HIDE ... ANDRAS HAMORI
NOWHERE TO HIDE ... JOHN KEMENY
NOWHERE TO RUN ... JULIE CORMAN
NOW YOU SEE HIM, NOW YOU DON'T ... RON MILLER
NUMBER ONE WITH A BULLET ... MENAHEM GOLAN
NUMBER ONE WITH A BULLET ... YORAM GLOBUS
NUNS ON THE RUN ... DENIS O'BRIEN
NUNS ON THE RUN ... GEORGE HARRISON
NUNS ON THE RUN ... MICHAEL WHITE
NUNS ON THE RUN ... SIMON BOSANQUET
NUNZIO ... JENNINGS LANG
NUTCRACKER ... DONALD KUSHNER
NUTCRACKER ... MICHAEL ROSENBLATT
NUTCRACKER ... PETER LOCKE
NUTCRACKER ... THOMAS COLEMAN
NUTCRACKER ... THOMAS L. WILHITE
NUTCRACKER ... WILLARD CARROLL
NUTS ... BARBRA STREISAND
NUTS ... CIS CORMAN
NUTS ... TERI SCHWARTZ

O

O'HARA'S WIFE ... MICHAEL TIMOTHY MURPHY
O'HARA'S WIFE ... PETER S. DAVIS
O'HARA'S WIFE ... WILLIAM N. PANZER
O.C. AND STIGGS ... LEWIS ALLEN
O.C. AND STIGGS ... PETER NEWMAN
O.C. AND STIGGS ... ROBERT ALTMAN
O.C. AND STIGGS ... SCOTT BUSHNELL
OBSESSION ... GEORGE LITTO
OBSESSION ... HARRY N. BLUM
OBSESSION ... ROBERT S. BREMSON
OCTAGON, THE ... ALAN BELKIN
OCTAGON, THE ... JOEL FREEMAN
OCTAGON, THE ... MICHAEL C. LEONE
OCTOPUSSY ... ALBERT R. BROCCOLI
OCTOPUSSY ... MICHAEL G. WILSON
ODD BALLS ... ROGER CORMAN
ODD COUPLE, THE ... HOWARD W. KOCH
ODD JOBS ... KEITH RUBINSTEIN
ODESSA FILE, THE ... SIR JOHN WOOLF
ODONGO ... ALBERT R. BROCCOLI
ODONGO ... IRVING ALLEN†
OF LOVE AND DESIRE ... RICHARD RUSH
OF UNKNOWN ORIGIN ... CLAUDE HEROUX
OF UNKNOWN ORIGIN ... PIERRE DAVID
OFF BEAT ... HARRY UFLAND
OFF BEAT ... JOE ROTH
OFF LIMITS ... ALAN BARNETTE
OFF THE WALL ... FRANK MANCUSO JR.
OFF THE WALL ... LISA BARSAMIAN
OFFENCE, THE ... DENIS O'DELL
OFFICER AND A GENTLEMAN, AN ... MERV ADELSON
OFFICER AND A GENTLEMAN, AN ... MARTIN ELFAND
OH, GOD! ... JERRY WEINTRAUB
OH, GOD! YOU DEVIL ... IRVING FEIN
OH, GOD! YOU DEVIL ... ROBERT M. SHERMAN
OKLAHOMA CRUDE ... STANLEY KRAMER
OLD BOYFRIENDS ... MICHELE RAPPAPORT
OLD BOYFRIENDS ... PAUL SCHRADER
OLD BOYFRIENDS ... EDWARD R. PRESSMAN
OLD ENOUGH ... DINA SILVER
OLD GRINGO ... LOIS BONFIGLIO
OLD GRINGO ... DAVID WISNIEVITZ
OLIVER! ... SIR JOHN WOOLF
OLIVER'S STORY ... DAVID V. PICKER
OMEGA SYNDROME ... GEORGE ZECEVIC
OMEGA SYNDROME ... LUIGI CINGOLANI
OMEN, THE ... HARVEY BERNHARD
OMEN, THE ... MACE NEUFELD
ON A CLEAR DAY YOU CAN SEE FOREVER ... HOWARD W. KOCH
ON GOLDEN POND ... BRUCE GILBERT
ON HER MAJESTY'S SECRET SERVICE ... ALBERT R. BROCCOLI
ON HER MAJESTY'S SECRET SERVICE ... HARRY SALTZMAN
ON THE BEACH ... STANLEY KRAMER
ON THE EDGE ... JEFFREY HAYES
ON THE EDGE ... ROB NILSSON
ON THE LINE ... JOSE LUIS BORAU
ON THE LINE ... STEVEN KOVACS
ON THE YARD ... JOAN MICKLIN SILVER
ON VALENTINE'S DAY ... CALVIN SKAGGS
ON VALENTINE'S DAY ... LEWIS ALLEN
ON VALENTINE'S DAY ... LILLIAN V. FOOTE
ON VALENTINE'S DAY ... LINDSAY LAW
ON VALENTINE'S DAY ... PETER NEWMAN
ON VALENTINE'S DAY ... ROSS E. MILLOY
ONCE BITTEN ... DIMITRI VILLARD
ONCE BITTEN ... FRANK E. HILDEBRAND
ONCE BITTEN ... ROBBY WALD
ONCE BITTEN ... SAMUEL GOLDWYN JR.
ONCE UPON A TIME IN AMERICA ... ARNON MILCHAN
ONCE UPON A TIME IN AMERICA ... CLAUDIO MANCINI
ONE AND ONLY, THE ... DAVID V. PICKER
ONE AND ONLY, THE ... ROBERT HALMI SR.
ONE & ONLY GENUINE ORIGINAL FAMILY BAND, THE ... BILL ANDERSON
ONE CRAZY SUMMER ... ANDREW MEYER
ONE CRAZY SUMMER ... GIL FRIESEN
ONE CRAZY SUMMER ... MICHAEL JAFFE
ONE FLEW OVER THE CUCKOO'S NEST ... MICHAEL DOUGLAS
ONE FLEW OVER THE CUCKOO'S NEST ... SAUL ZAENTZ
ONE FROM THE HEART ... ARMYAN BERNSTEIN
ONE FROM THE HEART ... BERNARD GERSTEN
ONE FROM THE HEART ... FRED ROOS
ONE FROM THE HEART ... GRAY FREDERICKSON
ONE IS A LONELY NUMBER ... STAN MARGULIES
ONE IS A LONELY NUMBER ... TED MANN
ONE IS A LONELY NUMBER ... DAVID L. WOLPER
ONE MAGIC CHRISTMAS ... MICHAEL MACDONALD
ONE MAGIC CHRISTMAS ... PETER O'BRIAN
ONE MAGIC CHRISTMAS ... PHILLIP BORSOS
ONE MORE SATURDAY NIGHT ... DAN AYKROYD
ONE MORE SATURDAY NIGHT ... JONATHAN BERNSTEIN
ONE MORE SATURDAY NIGHT ... ROBERT KOSBERG
ONE MORE SATURDAY NIGHT ... TOVA LAITER
ONE SUMMER LOVE ... SAMUEL Z. ARKOFF
ONE, TWO, THREE ... BILLY WILDER
ONE-TRICK PONY ... MICHAEL HAUSMAN
ONE-TRICK PONY ... MICHAEL TANNEN
ONION FIELD, THE ... WALTER COBLENZ
ONLY ONCE IN A LIFETIME ... MOCTESUMA ESPARZA
ONLY WHEN I LAUGH ... ROGER M. ROTHSTEIN†
OPEN SEASON, AN ... DAVID BROWN
OPEN SEASON, AN ... RICHARD D. ZANUCK
OPENING NIGHT ... AL RUBAN
OPENING NIGHT ... SAM SHAW
OPERATION DAYBREAK ... CARTER DE HAVEN
OPERATION THUNDERBOLT ... MENAHEM GOLAN
OPERATION THUNDERBOLT ... YORAM GLOBUS
OPPORTUNITY KNOCKS ... BRAD GREY
OPPORTUNITY KNOCKS ... BRIAN GRAZER
OPPORTUNITY KNOCKS ... CHRIS MELEDANDRI
OPPORTUNITY KNOCKS ... MARK R. GORDON
OPPORTUNITY KNOCKS ... RAY HARTWICK
OPTIONS ... CONRAD HOOL
OPTIONS ... EDGAR BOLD
ORCA ... LUCIANO VINCENZONI
ORCA ... DINO DE LAURENTIIS
ORDEAL BY INNOCENCE ... JENNY CRAVEN
ORDEAL BY INNOCENCE ... MENAHEM GOLAN
ORDEAL BY INNOCENCE ... MICHAEL J. KAGAN
ORDEAL BY INNOCENCE ... YORAM GLOBUS
ORDINARY PEOPLE ... RONALD L. SCHWARY
ORGANIZATION, THE ... WALTER MIRISCH
ORPHANS ... ALAN J. PAKULA
ORPHANS ... SUSAN SOLT

OSTERMAN WEEKEND, THE .... DON GUEST
OSTERMAN WEEKEND, THE .... PETER S. DAVIS
OSTERMAN WEEKEND, THE .... WILLIAM N. PANZER
OTELLO .... JOHN THOMPSON
OTELLO .... MENAHEM GOLAN
OTELLO .... YORAM GLOBUS
OTHER SIDE OF MIDNIGHT, THE .... MARTIN RANSOHOFF
OTHER SIDE OF MIDNIGHT, THE .... FRANK YABLANS
OTHER SIDE OF MIDNIGHT, THE .... HOWARD W. KOCH JR.
OTHER SIDE OF THE MOUNTAIN, THE .... EDWARD S. FELDMAN
OTHER SIDE OF THE MOUNTAIN - PART 2, THE .... EDWARD S. FELDMAN
OUR TIME .... RICHARD A. ROTH
OUR WINNING SEASON .... SAMUEL Z. ARKOFF
OUR WINNING SEASON .... JOE ROTH
OUT COLD .... DEREK GIBSON
OUT COLD .... GEORGE BRAUNSTEIN
OUT COLD .... JOHN DALY
OUT COLD .... RON HAMADY
OUT OF AFRICA .... KIM JORGENSEN
OUT OF AFRICA .... TERENCE CLEGG
OUT OF AFRICA .... SYDNEY POLLACK
OUT OF BOUNDS .... CHARLES FRIES
OUT OF BOUNDS .... JOHN TARNOFF
OUT OF BOUNDS .... MIKE ROSENFELD
OUT OF BOUNDS .... RAY HARTWICK
OUT OF CONTROL .... ARNOLD FISHMAN
OUT OF CONTROL .... DANIEL GRODNIK
OUT OF CONTROL .... FRED WEINTRAUB
OUT OF CONTROL .... PAUL LICHTMAN
OUT OF IT .... EDWARD R. PRESSMAN
OUT OF ORDER .... MATTHIAS DEYLE
OUT OF ORDER .... THOMAS SCHUEHLY
OUT OF THE BLUE .... PAUL LEWIS
OUT OF THE DARK .... DAVID C. THOMAS
OUT OF THE DARK .... ZANE W. LEVITT
OUTFIT, THE .... CARTER DE HAVEN
OUTLAND .... RICHARD A. ROTH
OUTLAND .... STANLEY O'TOOLE
OUTLAW BLUES .... FRED WEINTRAUB
OUTLAW BLUES .... PAUL HELLER
OUTLAW BLUES .... STEVE TISCH
OUTLAW BLUES .... JON AVNET
OUTLAW JOSEY WALES, THE .... FRITZ MANES
OUTLAW JOSEY WALES, THE .... ROBERT DALEY
OUTLAW OF GOR .... AVI LERNER
OUTLAW OF GOR .... HARRY ALAN TOWERS
OUTRAGEOUS FORTUNE .... MARTIN MICKELSON
OUTRAGEOUS FORTUNE .... PETER V. HERALD
OUTRAGEOUS FORTUNE .... ROBERT W. CORT
OUTRAGEOUS FORTUNE .... SCOTT KROOPF
OUTRAGEOUS FORTUNE .... TED FIELD
OUTSIDE CHANCE .... ROGER CORMAN
OUTSIDERS, THE .... FRANCIS FORD COPPOLA
OUTSIDERS, THE .... GRAY FREDERICKSON
OUTSIDERS, THE .... FRED ROOS
OVER THE EDGE .... GEORGE LITTO
OVER THE TOP .... JAMES D. BRUBAKER
OVER THE TOP .... MENAHEM GOLAN
OVER THE TOP .... YORAM GLOBUS
OVERBOARD .... ALEXANDRA ROSE
OVERBOARD .... NICK ABDO
OVERBOARD .... RODDY MCDOWALL
OVERBOARD .... ANTHEA SYLBERT
OWL AND THE PUSSYCAT, THE .... RAY STARK
OXFORD BLUES .... CASSIAN ELWES
OXFORD BLUES .... ELLIOTT KASTNER

P

P.K. AND THE KID .... JOE ROTH
P.O.W. THE ESCAPE .... MENAHEM GOLAN
P.O.W. THE ESCAPE .... YORAM GLOBUS
PACK, THE .... FRED WEINTRAUB
PACK, THE .... PAUL HELLER
PACKAGE, THE .... ANDREW DAVIS
PACKAGE, THE .... ARNE L. SCHMIDT
PACKAGE, THE .... BEVERLY J. CAMHE
PACKAGE, THE .... DENNIS HAGGERTY
PACKAGE, THE .... TOBIE HAGGERTY
PADDY .... TAMARA ASSEYEV
PALE RIDER .... DAVID VALDES
PALE RIDER .... CLINT EASTWOOD
PALE RIDER .... FRITZ MANES
PANDEMONIUM .... BARRY KROST
PANDEMONIUM .... DOUG CHAPIN
PAPER MOON .... FRANK MARSHALL
PAPER MOON .... PETER BOGDANOVICH
PAPERHOUSE .... DAN IRELAND
PAPERHOUSE .... M. J. PECKOS
PAPERHOUSE .... SARAH RADCLYFFE
PAPERHOUSE .... TIM BEVAN
PAPER LION .... STUART MILLAR
PARADISE .... ROBERT LANTOS
PARADISE .... STEPHEN J. ROTH
PARADISE ALLEY .... JOHN F. ROACH
PARADISE ALLEY .... RONALD A. SUPPA
PARADISE ALLEY .... EDWARD R. PRESSMAN
PARALLAX VIEW, THE .... ALAN J. PAKULA
PARASITE .... CHARLES BAND
PARASITE .... IRWIN YABLANS
PARASITE .... JOSEPH WOLF
PARATROOPER .... ALBERT R. BROCCOLI
PARENTHOOD .... BRIAN GRAZER
PARENTHOOD .... JOSEPH M. CARACCIOLO
PARENTS .... BONNIE PALEF
PARENTS .... MITCHELL CANNOLD
PARENTS .... STEVEN REUTHER
PARIS BY NIGHT .... EDWARD R. PRESSMAN
PARIS BY NIGHT .... PATRICK CASSAVETTI
PARIS, TEXAS .... CHRIS SIEVERNICH
PARIS, TEXAS .... DON GUEST
PARSIFAL .... FRANCIS FORD COPPOLA
PART 2, SOUNDER .... ROBERT B. RADNITZ
PART 2, SOUNDER .... TERRY NELSON
PARTING GLANCES .... ARTHUR SILVERMAN
PARTING GLANCES .... PAUL A. KAPLAN
PARTING GLANCES .... YORAM MANDEL
PARTNERS .... AARON RUSSO
PARTNERS .... FRANCIS VEBER
PARTY, THE .... KEN WALES
PARTY LINE .... KURT ANDERSON
PARTY LINE .... MONICA WEBB
PARTY LINE .... THOMAS S. BYRNES
PARTY LINE .... WILLIAM WEBB
PASCALI'S ISLAND .... CARY BROKAW
PASCALI'S ISLAND .... ERIC FELLNER
PASCALI'S ISLAND .... PAUL RAPHAEL
PASS THE AMMO .... DAVID STREIT
PASS THE AMMO .... HERB JAFFE
PASS THE AMMO .... MORT ENGELBERG
PASSAGE TO INDIA, A .... JOHN BRABOURNE
PASSAGE TO INDIA, A .... EDWARD SANDS
PASSAGE TO INDIA, A .... JOHN HEYMAN
PASSAGE TO INDIA, A .... RICHARD GOODWIN
PASSENGER, THE .... CARLO PONTI
PASSOVER PLOT, THE .... WOLF SCHMIDT
PAT GARRETT & BILLY THE KID .... GORDON CARROLL
PATERNITY .... HANK MOONJEAN
PATERNITY .... JERRY TOKOFSKY
PATERNITY .... LAWRENCE GORDON
PATHFINDER .... JULIE CORMAN
PATHS OF GLORY .... JAMES B. HARRIS
PATTI ROCKS .... GREGORY M. CUMMINS
PATTI ROCKS .... GWEN FIELD
PATTI ROCKS .... SAM GROGG
PATTY HEARST .... JAMES D. BRUBAKER
PATTY HEARST .... MARVIN WORTH
PATTY HEARST .... MICHAEL ROSENBLATT
PATTY HEARST .... THOMAS COLEMAN
PAWNBROKER, THE .... ELY LANDAU
PEE-WEE'S BIG ADVENTURE .... RICHARD GILBERT ABRAMSON
PEE-WEE'S BIG ADVENTURE .... WILLIAM E. MCEUEN
PEE-WEE'S BIG ADVENTURE .... ROBERT SHAPIRO
PEEPER .... IRWIN WINKLER
PEEPER .... ROBERT CHARTOFF
PEGGY SUE GOT MARRIED .... BARRIE M. OSBORNE
PEGGY SUE GOT MARRIED .... PAUL R. GURIAN
PEGGY SUE GOT MARRIED .... RAY STARK
PENITENT, THE .... MICHAEL FITZGERALD
PENN AND TELLER GET KILLED .... ARTHUR PENN
PENN AND TELLER GET KILLED .... TIMOTHY MARX
PENNIES FROM HEAVEN .... HERBERT ROSS
PENNIES FROM HEAVEN .... NORA KAYE†
PENNIES FROM HEAVEN .... RICK MCCALLUM
PEOPLE NEXT DOOR, THE .... KENNETH UTT
PERFECT .... JACK LARSON
PERFECT .... JAMES BRIDGES
PERFECT .... KIM KURUMADA
PERFECT COUPLE, A .... ROBERT ALTMAN
PERFECT COUPLE, A .... TOMMY THOMPSON
PERFECT COUPLE, A .... SCOTT BUSHNELL
PERFECT STRANGERS .... CARTER DE HAVEN
PERFECT STRANGERS .... PAUL KURTA
PERFORMANCE .... SANDY LIEBERSON
PERMANENT RECORD .... FRANK MANCUSO JR.
PERMANENT RECORD .... HERB RABINOWITZ
PERMANENT RECORD .... MARTIN HORNSTEIN
PERSONAL BEST .... DAVID GEFFEN
PERSONAL BEST .... ROBERT TOWNE
PERSONAL CHOICE .... JOSEPH PEREZ
PERSONAL CHOICE .... MIKE PLOTKIN
PERSONAL SERVICES .... TIM BEVAN
PERSONALS, THE .... PATRICK C. WELLS
PET SEMATARY .... MITCHELL GALIN
PET SEMATARY .... RALPH S. SINGLETON
PET SEMATARY .... RICHARD P. RUBINSTEIN
PET SEMATARY .... TIM ZINNEMANN
PETE 'N' TILLIE .... JULIUS J. EPSTEIN
PETE 'N' TILLIE .... JENNINGS LANG
PETER GUNN .... KEN WALES
PETER RABBIT & TALES OF BEATRIX POTTER .... JOHN BRABOURNE
PETER RABBIT & TALES OF BEATRIX POTTER .... RICHARD GOODWIN
PETE'S DRAGON .... JEROME COURTLAND
PETE'S DRAGON .... RON MILLER
PETULIA .... RAYMOND WAGNER
PETULIA .... DENIS O'DELL
PETULIA .... DON DEVLIN
PHANTASM II .... DAC COSCARELLI
PHANTASM II .... ROBERTO A. QUEZADA
PHANTOM INDIA .... ELLIOTT KASTNER
PHANTOM OF THE OPERA, THE .... HARRY ALAN TOWERS
PHANTOM OF THE OPERA, THE .... MENAHEM GOLAN
PHANTOM OF THE PARADISE .... GUSTAVE BERNE
PHANTOM OF THE PARADISE .... EDWARD R. PRESSMAN
PHAR LAP .... JOHN SEXTON
PHAR LAP .... RICHARD DAVIS
PHILADELPHIA EXPERIMENT, THE .... DOUGLAS CURTIS
PHILADELPHIA EXPERIMENT, THE .... JOEL B. MICHAELS
PHILADELPHIA EXPERIMENT, THE .... JOHN CARPENTER
PHOBIA .... LARRY SPIEGEL
PHYSICAL EVIDENCE .... MARTIN RANSOHOFF
PHYSICAL EVIDENCE .... DON CARMODY
PIAF - THE EARLY YEARS .... CY FEUER
PICASSO TRIGGER .... ARLENE SIDARIS
PICK-UP ARTIST, THE .... DAVID L. MACLEOD
PICKUP ALLEY .... ALBERT R. BROCCOLI
PICKUP ALLEY .... IRVING ALLEN†
PICNIC AT HANGING ROCK .... HAL MCELROY
PICNIC AT HANGING ROCK .... JAMES MCELROY
PICNIC AT HANGING ROCK .... PATRICIA LOVELL
PIECE OF THE ACTION, A .... MELVILLE TUCKER
PIED PIPER, THE .... DAVID PUTTNAM
PIED PIPER, THE .... SANDY LIEBERSON
PING PONG .... MALCOLM CRADDOCK
PING PONG .... MICHAEL GUEST
PINK CADILLAC .... DAVID VALDES
PINK CADILLAC .... MICHAEL GRUSKOFF
PINK FLAMINGOS .... JOHN WATERS
PINK FLOYD - THE WALL .... ALAN MARSHALL
PINK JUNGLE, THE .... TED MANN
PINK PANTHER, THE .... MARTIN JUROW
PINK PANTHER STRIKES AGAIN, THE .... BLAKE EDWARDS
PINK PANTHER STRIKES AGAIN, THE .... TONY ADAMS
PIRANHA .... JEFF SCHECHTMAN
PIRANHA .... JON DAVISON
PIRANHA .... ROGER CORMAN
PIRANHA II .... CHAKO VAN LEUWEN
PIRANHA II .... JEFF SCHECHTMAN
PIRANHA II .... OBIDIO G. ASSONITIS
PIRATES .... MARK LOMBARDO
PIRATES .... TARAK BEN AMMAR
PIRATES .... THOM MOUNT
PIRATES OF PENZANCE, THE .... EDWARD R. PRESSMAN
PIRATES OF PENZANCE, THE .... JOSEPH PAPP
PIRATES OF PENZANCE, THE .... TIMOTHY BURRILL
PIT AND THE PENDULUM, THE .... SAMUEL Z. ARKOFF
PIT AND THE PENDULUM, THE .... JAMES H. NICHOLSON†
PIT STOP .... ROGER CORMAN
PLACES IN THE HEART .... MICHAEL HAUSMAN
PLACES IN THE HEART .... ARLENE DONOVAN
PLAGUE DOGS, THE .... MARTIN ROSEN
PLAIN CLOTHES .... MICHAEL MANHEIM
PLAIN CLOTHES .... RICHARD WECHSLER
PLAIN CLOTHES .... STEVEN-CHARLES JAFFE
PLANES, TRAINS AND AUTOMOBILES .... JOHN HUGHES
PLANES, TRAINS, AND AUTOMOBILES .... MICHAEL CHINICH

PLANES, TRAINS, AND AUTOMOBILES ... NEIL A. MACHLIS
PLATOON ... A. KITMAN HO
PLATOON ... ARNOLD KOPELSON
PLATOON ... DEREK GIBSON
PLATOON ... JOHN DALY
PLAY DIRTY ... HARRY SALTZMAN
PLAY IT AGAIN, SAM ... CHARLES H. JOFFE
PLAY IT COOLER ... ALBERT R. BROCCOLI
PLAY IT COOLER ... IRVING ALLEN†
PLAY MISTY FOR ME ... JENNINGS LANG
PLAY MISTY FOR ME ... ROBERT DALEY
PLAYERS ... ARNOLD SCHULMAN
PLAYERS ... ROBERT EVANS
PLAYING FOR KEEPS ... ALAN BREWER
PLAYING FOR KEEPS ... BOB WEINSTEIN
PLAYING FOR KEEPS ... HARVEY WEINSTEIN
PLAYING FOR KEEPS ... JULIA PALAU
PLAYING FOR KEEPS ... MICHAEL RYAN
PLAYING FOR KEEPS ... PATRICK WACHSBERGER
PLAZA SUITE ... HOWARD W. KOCH
PLENTY ... EDWARD R. PRESSMAN
PLENTY ... JOSEPH PAPP
PLENTY ... MARK SEILER
PLENTY ... ROY STEVENS
PLOUGHMAN'S LUNCH, THE ... ANN SCOTT
PLOUGHMAN'S LUNCH, THE ... SIMON RELPH
PLOT AGAINST HARRY, THE ... MICHAEL ROEMER
PLOT AGAINST HARRY, THE ... ROBERT M. YOUNG
POCKET MONEY ... JOHN FOREMAN
POINT BLANK ... JUDD BERNARD
POINT BLANK ... ROBERT CHARTOFF
POLICE ACADEMY ... PAUL MASLANSKY
POLICE ACADEMY 2: THEIR FIRST ASSIGNMENT ... JOHN GOLDWYN
POLICE ACADEMY 2: THEIR FIRST ASSIGNMENT ... LEONARD KROLL
POLICE ACADEMY 2: THEIR FIRST ASSIGNMENT ... PAUL MASLANSKY
POLICE ACADEMY 3: BACK IN TRAINING ... DONALD WEST
POLICE ACADEMY 3: BACK IN TRAINING ... PAUL MASLANSKY
POLICE ACADEMY 4: CITIZENS ON PATROL ... DONALD WEST
POLICE ACADEMY 4: CITIZENS ON PATROL ... PAUL MASLANSKY
POLICE ACADEMY 5: ASSIGNMENT MIAMI BEACH ... DONALD WEST
POLICE ACADEMY 5: ASSIGNMENT MIAMI BEACH ... PAUL MASLANSKY
POLICE ACADEMY 6: CITY UNDER SIEGE ... DONALD WEST
POLICE ACADEMY 6: CITY UNDER SIEGE ... PAUL MASLANSKY
POLTERGEIST ... FRANK MARSHALL
POLTERGEIST ... KATHLEEN KENNEDY
POLTERGEIST ... STEVEN SPIELBERG
POLTERGEIST II: THE OTHER SIDE ... FREDDIE FIELDS
POLTERGEIST II: THE OTHER SIDE ... MARK VICTOR
POLTERGEIST II: THE OTHER SIDE ... MICHAEL GRAIS
POLTERGEIST III ... BARRY BERNARDI
POLTERGEIST III ... GARY SHERMAN
POLYESTER ... JOHN WATERS
POLYESTER ... ROBERT MAIER
POLYESTER ... ROBERT SHAYE
POLYESTER ... SARA RISHER
POOR COW ... JOSEPH JANNI
POPE OF GREENWICH VILLAGE, THE ... GENE KIRKWOOD
POPE OF GREENWICH VILLAGE, THE ... HOWARD W. KOCH JR.
POPEYE ... C.O. ERICKSON
POPEYE ... ROBERT EVANS
POPEYE ... SCOTT BUSHNELL
PORKY'S ... BOB CLARK
PORKY'S ... DON CARMODY
PORKY'S ... HAROLD GREENBERG
PORKY'S ... MELVIN SIMON
PORKY'S II: THE NEXT DAY ... ALAN LANDSBURG
PORKY'S II: THE NEXT DAY ... BOB CLARK
PORKY'S II: THE NEXT DAY ... DON CARMODY
PORKY'S II: THE NEXT DAY ... HAROLD GREENBERG
PORKY'S II: THE NEXT DAY ... MELVIN SIMON
PORKY'S REVENGE ... MELVIN SIMON
PORKY'S REVENGE ... MILTON GOLDSTEIN
PORKY'S REVENGE ... ROBERT L. ROSEN
PORTNOY'S COMPLAINT ... ERNEST LEHMAN
PORTNOY'S COMPLAINT ... SIDNEY BECKERMAN
POSEIDON ADVENTURE, THE ... IRWIN ALLEN
POSITIVE I.D. ... ANDY ANDERSON
POSITIVE I.D. ... VICTOR SHER
POSTCARDS FROM THE EDGE ... JOHN CALLEY
POSTCARDS FROM THE EDGE ... MIKE NICHOLS
POSTCARDS FROM THE EDGE ... NEIL A. MACHLIS
POSTCARDS FROM THE EDGE ... ROBERT GREENHUT
POSTMAN ALWAYS RINGS TWICE, THE ... ANDREW BRAUNSBERG
POSTMAN ALWAYS RINGS TWICE, THE ... BOB RAFELSON
POSTMAN ALWAYS RINGS TWICE, THE ... CHARLES B. MULVEHILL
POUND PUPPIES AND THE LEGEND OF BIG PAW ... DONALD KUSHNER
POUND PUPPIES AND THE LEGEND OF BIG PAW ... EDD GRILES
POUND PUPPIES AND THE LEGEND OF BIG PAW ... PETER LOCKE
POUND PUPPIES AND THE LEGEND OF BIG PAW ... RAY VOLPE
POWAQQATSI ... GODFREY REGGIO
POWAQQATSI ... LAWRENCE TAUB
POWAQQATSI ... MARCEL KAHN
POWAQQATSI ... MEL LAWRENCE
POWAQQATSI ... MENAHEM GOLAN
POWAQQATSI ... TOM LUDDY
POWAQQATSI ... YORAM GLOBUS
POWER ... MARK TARLOV
POWER ... REENE SCHISGAL
POWER ... WOLFGANG GLATTES
POWER PLAY ... RONALD I. COHEN
POWER, THE ... JEFFREY OBROW
POWER, THE ... STACEY GIACHINO
POWWOW HIGHWAY ... CARL KRAINES
POWWOW HIGHWAY ... DENIS O'BRIEN
POWWOW HIGHWAY ... GEORGE HARRISON
POWWOW HIGHWAY ... JAN WIERINGA
PRANCER ... GREG TAYLOR
PRANCER ... RAFFAELLA DE LAURENTIIS
PRANCER ... MIKE PETZOLD
PRANKS ... JEFFREY OBROW
PRAY FOR DEATH ... DON VAN ATTA
PRAY FOR DEATH ... MOSHE BARKAT
PRAY FOR DEATH ... MOSHE DIAMANT
PRAY FOR DEATH ... SUNIL SHAH
PRAYER FOR THE DYING, A ... PETER SNELL
PREDATOR ... JIM THOMAS
PREDATOR ... JOEL SILVER
PREDATOR ... JOHN A. DAVIS
PREDATOR ... LAURENCE P. PEREIRA
PREDATOR ... LAWRENCE GORDON
PRESIDENT'S ANALYST, THE ... HOWARD W. KOCH
PRESIDENT'S ANALYST, THE ... STANLEY RUBIN
PRESIDIO, THE ... D. CONSTANTINE CONTE
PRESIDIO, THE ... FRED CARUSO
PRESIDIO, THE ... JONATHAN A. ZIMBERT
PRESUMED INNOCENT ... MARK ROSENBERG
PRESUMED INNOCENT ... SUSAN SOLT
PRESUMED INNOCENT ... SYDNEY POLLACK
PRETTY BABY ... LOUIS MALLE
PRETTY IN PINK ... JOHN HUGHES
PRETTY IN PINK ... LAUREN SHULER-DONNER
PRETTY IN PINK ... MICHAEL CHINICH
PRETTY POISON ... JACK GROSSBERG
PRETTY POISON ... LAWRENCE TURMAN
PRETTY SMART ... JEFF BEGUN
PRETTY SMART ... JOSEPH MEDAWAR
PRETTY SMART ... KEN SOLOMON
PRETTY SMART ... MELANIE J. ALSCHULER
PRETTY WOMAN ... ARNON MILCHAN
PRETTY WOMAN ... STEVEN REUTHER
PRETTY WOMAN ... LAURA ZISKIN
PRETTYKILL ... JOHN R. BOWEY
PRETTYKILL ... MARTIN WALTERS
PRETTYKILL ... SANDY HOWARD
PRICK UP YOUR EARS ... ANDREW BROWN
PRICK UP YOUR EARS ... TIM BEVAN
PRICK UP YOUR EARS ... SARAH RADCLYFFE
PRIDE AND THE PASSION, THE ... STANLEY KRAMER
PRIME CUT ... JOE WIZAN
PRINCE OF DARKNESS ... LARRY J. FRANCO
PRINCE OF DARKNESS ... SHEP GORDON
PRINCE OF DARKNESS ... ANDRE BLAY
PRINCE OF PENNSYLVANIA, THE ... JOAN FISHMAN
PRINCE OF PENNSYLVANIA, THE ... KERRY ORENT
PRINCE OF THE CITY ... BURTT HARRIS
PRINCE OF THE CITY ... RAY HARTWICK
PRINCE OF THE CITY ... JAY PRESSON ALLEN
PRINCESS ACADEMY, THE ... FRED WEINTRAUB
PRINCESS ACADEMY, THE ... SANDRA WEINTRAUB ROLAND
PRINCESS BRIDE, THE ... ANDREW SCHEINMAN
PRINCESS BRIDE, THE ... JEFFREY STOTT
PRINCESS BRIDE, THE ... NORMAN LEAR
PRINCESS BRIDE, THE ... ROB REINER
PRINCESS BRIDE, THE ... STEVE NICOLAIDES
PRINCIPAL, THE ... THOMAS H. BRODEK
PRISON ... CHARLES BAND
PRISON ... IRWIN YABLANS
PRISONER OF ZENDA, THE ... PETER MACGREGOR-SCOTT
PRISONER OF ZENDA, THE ... WALTER MIRISCH
PRISONERS ... KEITH BARISH
PRIVATE BENJAMIN ... CHARLES SHYER
PRIVATE BENJAMIN ... GOLDIE HAWN
PRIVATE BENJAMIN ... HARVEY MILLER
PRIVATE BENJAMIN ... NANCY MEYERS
PRIVATE EYES, THE ... LANG ELLIOTT
PRIVATE EYES, THE ... WANDA DELL
PRIVATE FUNCTION, A ... DENIS O'BRIEN
PRIVATE FUNCTION, A ... GEORGE HARRISON
PRIVATE FUNCTION, A ... MARK SHIVAS
PRIVATE INVESTIGATIONS ... SIGURJON SIGHVATSSON
PRIVATE INVESTIGATIONS ... STEVEN GOLIN
PRIVATE LESSONS ... DAN ENRIGHT
PRIVATE LESSONS ... IRVING OSHMAN
PRIVATE LESSONS ... JACK BARRY
PRIVATE LESSONS ... R. BEN EFRAIM
PRIVATE LIFE OF SHERLOCK HOLMES, THE ... BILLY WILDER
PRIVATE PARTS ... GENE CORMAN
PRIVATE SCHOOL ... DON ENRIGHT
PRIVATE SCHOOL ... R. BEN EFRAIM
PRIVATES ON PARADE ... DENIS O'BRIEN
PRIVATES ON PARADE ... GEORGE HARRISON
PRIVATES ON PARADE ... SIMON RELPH
PRIVILEGE ... JOHN HEYMAN
PRIVILEGE ... TIMOTHY BURRILL
PRIVILEGED ... RICK STEVENSON
PRIZE OF GOLD ... ALBERT R. BROCCOLI
PRIZE OF GOLD ... IRVING ALLEN†
PRIZZI'S HONOR ... JOHN FOREMAN
PRODIGAL, THE ... KEN WALES
PRODUCERS, THE ... JACK GROSSBERG
PROJECT X ... C.O. ERICKSON
PROJECT X ... LAWRENCE LASKER
PROJECT X ... WALTER F. PARKES
PROJECTIONIST, THE ... HARRY HURWITZ
PROMISE, THE ... PAUL HELLER
PROMISE, THE ... FRED WEINTRAUB
PROMISED LAND ... ANDREW MEYER
PROMISED LAND ... RICK STEVENSON
PROMISED LAND ... ROBERT REDFORD
PROMISES IN THE DARK ... SHELDON SCHRAGER
PROMISES IN THE DARK ... JEROME HELLMAN
PROPHECY ... ROBERT L. ROSEN
PROTECTOR, THE ... DAVID CHAN
PROTECTOR, THE ... RAYMOND CHOW
PROTOCOL ... GOLDIE HAWN
PROTOCOL ... ANTHEA SYLBERT
PSYCHO II ... BERNARD SCHWARTZ
PSYCHO II ... HILTON A. GREEN
PSYCHO III ... HILTON A. GREEN
PULP ... MICHAEL KLINGER
PULSE ... PATRICIA STALLONE
PULSE ... WILLIAM E. MCEUEN
PUMPKINHEAD ... ALEX DE BENEDETTI
PUMPKINHEAD ... HOWARD SMITH
PUMPKINHEAD ... RICHARD C. WEINMAN
PUNCHLINE ... MICHAEL RACHMIL
PUNCHLINE ... DANIEL MELNICK
PUPPETOON MOVIE, THE ... ARNOLD LEIBOVIT
PURGATORY ... AMI ARTZI
PURGATORY ... DIMITRI VILLARD
PURGATORY ... ROBBY WALD
PURPLE HEARTS ... SIDNEY J. FURIE
PURPLE PEOPLE EATER ... BRAD KREVOY
PURPLE PEOPLE EATER ... STEVEN STABLER
PURPLE RAIN ... JOSEPH RUFFALO
PURPLE RAIN ... ROBERT CAVALLO
PURPLE RAIN ... STEVEN FARGNOLI
PURPLE ROSE OF CAIRO, THE ... CHARLES H. JOFFE
PURPLE ROSE OF CAIRO, THE ... MICHAEL PEYSER
PURPLE ROSE OF CAIRO, THE ... ROBERT GREENHUT
PURSUIT OF D. B. COOPER, THE ... DAN WIGUTOW
PURSUIT OF D. B. COOPER, THE ... DONALD KRANZE
PURSUIT OF D. B. COOPER, THE ... MICHAEL TAYLOR
PURSUIT OF D. B. COOPER, THE ... RON SHELTON

PURSUIT OF
D. B. COOPER, THE .... WILLIAM TENNANT
PUSS IN BOOTS .... MENAHEM GOLAN
PUSS IN BOOTS .... YORAM GLOBUS
PUZZLE OF A
DOWNFALL CHILD .... JENNINGS LANG
PUZZLE OF A
DOWNFALL CHILD .... JOHN FOREMAN

Q

Q .... DAN SANDBURG
Q .... LARRY COHEN
Q .... PAUL KURTA
Q & A .... BURTT HARRIS
Q & A .... PATRICK WACHSBERGER
Q & A .... ARNON MILCHAN
QUADROPHENIA .... ROY BAIRD
QUARTET .... ISMAIL MERCHANT
QUEEN OF BLOOD .... ROGER CORMAN
QUEEN OF HEARTS .... GRAHAM BENSON
QUEEN OF HEARTS .... JOHN HARDY
QUEST FOR FIRE .... DENIS HEROUX
QUEST FOR FIRE .... JOHN KEMENY
QUEST FOR FIRE .... MICHAEL GRUSKOFF
QUICK CHANGE .... BILL MURRAY
QUICK CHANGE .... FREDERIC GOLCHAN
QUICK CHANGE .... ROBERT GREENHUT
QUICKSILVER .... MICHAEL RACHMIL
QUICKSILVER .... DANIEL MELNICK
QUIET COOL .... ARTHUR M. SARKISSIAN
QUIET COOL .... GERALD T. OLSON
QUIET COOL .... LARRY THOMPSON
QUIET COOL .... PIERRE DAVID
QUIET COOL .... ROBERT SHAYE
QUIET COOL .... SARA RISHER
QUIET PLACE IN
THE COUNTRY, A .... ALBERTO GRIMALDI
QUIGLEY DOWN UNDER .... ALEXANDRA ROSE
QUIGLEY DOWN UNDER .... MEGAN ROSE
QUIGLEY DOWN UNDER .... STANLEY O'TOOLE
QUINTET .... ROBERT ALTMAN

R

R.P.M. .... STANLEY KRAMER
RABID .... ANDRE LINK
RABID .... JOHN DUNNING
RABID .... IVAN REITMAN
RACE TO GLORY .... DANIEL A. SHERKOW
RACE TO GLORY .... DAVID G. STERN
RACE TO GLORY .... JON GORDON
RACE WITH THE DEVIL .... PAUL MASLANSKY
RACHEL PAPERS, THE .... ANDREW S. KARSCH
RACHEL PAPERS, THE .... ERIC FELLNER
RACHEL PAPERS, THE .... JAMES T. ROE III
RACHEL PAPERS, THE .... PAUL RAPHAEL
RACHEL RIVER .... LINDSAY LAW
RACHEL RIVER .... TIMOTHY MARX
RACHEL, RACHEL .... PAUL NEWMAN
RACING WITH THE MOON .... ART LEVINSON
RACING WITH THE MOON .... JOHN KOHN
RACING WITH THE MOON .... STANLEY R. JAFFE
RACING WITH THE MOON .... ALAIN BERNHEIM
RACING WITH THE MOON .... SHERRY LANSING
RAD .... JACK SCHWARTZMAN
RAD .... ROBERT L. LEVY
RADIO DAYS .... EZRA SWERDLOW
RADIO DAYS .... JACK ROLLINS
RADIO DAYS .... ROBERT GREENHUT
RADIO DAYS .... CHARLES H. JOFFE
RADIOACTIVE DREAMS .... MOCTESUMA ESPARZA
RADIOACTIVE DREAMS .... TOM KARNOWSKI
RAFFERTY AND THE GOLD
DUST TWINS .... ART LINSON
RAFFERTY AND THE GOLD
DUST TWINS .... MICHAEL GRUSKOFF
RAFFERTY AND THE GOLD
DUST TWINS .... JERRY BRUCKHEIMER
RAGE OF HONOR .... DON VAN ATTA
RAGE OF HONOR .... MOSHE BARKAT
RAGE OF HONOR .... MOSHE DIAMANT
RAGE OF HONOR .... SUNIL R. SHAH
RAGGEDY MAN .... BURT WEISSBOURD
RAGGEDY MAN .... TERRY NELSON
RAGGEDY MAN .... WILLIAM D. WITTLIFF
RAGGEDY RAWNEY, THE .... BOB WEIS
RAGGEDY RAWNEY, THE .... DENIS O'BRIEN
RAGGEDY RAWNEY, THE .... GEORGE HARRISON
RAGING BULL .... IRWIN WINKLER
RAGING BULL .... ROBERT CHARTOFF
RAGTIME .... BERNARD WILLIAMS
RAGTIME .... DINO DE LAURENTIIS
RAGTIME .... MICHAEL HAUSMAN
RAIDERS OF THE LOST ARK .... FRANK MARSHALL
RAIDERS OF THE LOST ARK .... GEORGE LUCAS
RAIDERS OF THE LOST ARK .... ROBERT WATTS
RAIDERS OF THE
LOST ARK .... HOWARD KAZANJIAN
RAIN MAN .... GERALD R. MOLEN
RAIN MAN .... MARK JOHNSON
RAIN MAN .... PETER GUBER
RAIN MAN .... JON PETERS
RAIN PEOPLE, THE .... BART PATTON
RAIN PEOPLE, THE .... RONALD COLBY
RAINBOW, THE .... DAN IRELAND
RAINBOW, THE .... KEN RUSSELL
RAINBOW, THE .... RONALDO VASCONCELLOS
RAINBOW, THE .... WILLIAM J. QUIGLEY
RAISE THE TITANIC .... WILLIAM FRYE
RAISE THE TITANIC .... MARTIN STARGER
RAISING ARIZONA .... ETHAN COEN
RAISING ARIZONA .... JAMES JACKS
RAMBO: FIRST BLOOD PART II .... BUZZ FEITSHANS
RAMBO: FIRST BLOOD PART II .... MARIO KASSAR
RAMBO: FIRST BLOOD PART II .... ANDREW VAJNA
RAMBO III .... BUZZ FEITSHANS
RAMBO III .... MARIO KASSAR
RAMBO III .... ANDREW VAJNA
RAMPAGE .... DAVID SALVEN
RAN .... MASATO HARA
RAN .... SERGE SILBERMAN
RANCHO DELUXE .... ELLIOTT KASTNER
RAPPIN' .... JEFFREY SILVER
RAPPIN' .... MENAHEM GOLAN
RAPPIN' .... YORAM GLOBUS
RATBOY .... DAVID VALDES
RATBOY .... FRITZ MANES
RAVEN, THE .... SAMUEL Z. ARKOFF
RAVEN, THE .... JAMES H. NICHOLSON†
RAW COURAGE .... ROBERT L. ROSEN
RAW COURAGE .... RONNY COX
RAW DEAL .... MARTHA SCHUMACHER
RAW MEAT .... PAUL MASLANSKY
RAZOR'S EDGE, THE .... HARRY BENN
RAZOR'S EDGE, THE .... ROB COHEN
RAZOR'S EDGE, THE .... ROBERT P. MARCUCCI
RAZORBACK .... HAL MCELROY
REAL GENIUS .... ROBERT DALEY
REAL GENIUS .... BRIAN GRAZER
REAL MEN .... LOUIS A. STROLLER
REAL MEN .... MARTIN BREGMAN
REANIMATOR .... BRIAN YUZNA
RECKLESS .... SCOTT RUDIN
RECKLESS .... EDGAR J. SCHERICK
RECKONING, THE .... RONALD SHEDLO
RED BERET .... ALBERT R. BROCCOLI
RED BERET .... ANTHONY BUSHELL
RED BERET .... IRVING ALLEN†
RED DAWN .... BUZZ FEITSHANS
RED DAWN .... SIDNEY BECKERMAN
RED HEADED STRANGER .... WILLIAM D. WITTLIFF
RED HEADED STRANGER .... WILLIE NELSON
RED HEAT .... GORDON CARROLL
RED HEAT .... MARIO KASSAR
RED HEAT .... WALTER HILL
RED HEAT .... ANDREW VAJNA
RED SCORPION .... DANIEL SKLAR
RED SCORPION .... JACK ABRAMOFF
RED SCORPION .... PAUL ERICKSON
RED SCORPION .... ROBERT ABRAMOFF
RED SONJA .... A. MICHAEL LIEBERMAN
RED SONJA .... CHRISTIAN FERRY
REDS .... DAVID L. MACLEOD
REDS .... DEDE ALLEN
REDS .... WARREN BEATTY
REFLECTION OF FEAR, A .... HOWARD B. JAFFE
REIVERS, THE .... ROBERT E. RELYEA
RELENTLESS .... DAVID MADDEN
RELENTLESS .... HOWARD SMITH
RELENTLESS .... LISA M. HANSEN
RELENTLESS .... PAUL HERTZBERG
REMEMBER MY NAME .... ROBERT ALTMAN
REMO WILLIAMS: THE
ADVENTURE BEGINS .... DICK CLARK
REMO WILLIAMS: THE
ADVENTURE BEGINS .... MEL BERGMAN
REMO WILLIAMS: THE
ADVENTURE BEGINS... .... JUDY GOLDSTEIN
REMO WILLIAMS: THE
ADVENTURE BEGINS... .... LARRY SPIEGEL
REMOTE CONTROL .... MARK LEVINSON
REMOTE CONTROL .... SCOTT ROSENFELT
RENEGADES .... JAMES G. ROBINSON
RENEGADES .... JOE ROTH
RENEGADES .... PAUL SCHIFF
RENEGADES .... ROBERT W. CORT
RENEGADES .... TED FIELD
RENT CONTROL .... BENNI KORZEN
RENT-A-COP .... RAYMOND WAGNER
RENTED LIPS .... MARTIN MULL
RENTED LIPS .... MEL HOWARD
RENTED LIPS .... HERB JAFFE
RENTED LIPS .... MORT ENGELBERG
REPO MAN .... GERALD T. OLSON
REPO MAN .... MICHAEL NESMITH
REPO MAN .... PETER MCCARTHY
REQUIEM FOR A
HEAVYWEIGHT .... JACK GROSSBERG
RESCUE, THE .... JIM THOMAS
RESCUE, THE .... JOHN THOMAS
RESCUE, THE .... LAURA ZISKIN
RESCUERS, THE .... RON MILLER
RESTLESS .... ROBERT SINGER
RESTLESS NATIVES .... ANDY PATERSON
RESTLESS NATIVES .... MARK BENTLEY
RESTLESS NATIVES .... RICK STEVENSON
RESURRECTION .... RENEE MISSEL
RESURRECTION .... HOWARD ROSENMAN
RETRIBUTION .... BRIAN CHRISTIAN
RETRIBUTION .... GUY MAGAR
RETRIBUTION .... LEE WASSERMAN
RETRIBUTION .... SCOTT LAVIN
RETURN ENGAGEMENT .... CAROLYN PFEIFFER
RETURN FROM WITCH
MOUNTAIN .... JEROME COURTLAND
RETURN FROM WITCH MOUNTAIN .... RON MILLER
RETURN OF A MAN
CALLED HORSE .... SANDY HOWARD
RETURN OF SWAMP
THING, THE .... ANNETTE CIRILLO
RETURN OF SWAMP
THING, THE .... BENJAMIN MELNIKER
RETURN OF SWAMP
THING, THE .... CHARLES MITCHELL
RETURN OF SWAMP
THING, THE .... MICHAEL USLAN
RETURN OF SWAMP THING, THE .... TOM KUHN
RETURN OF THE JEDI .... GEORGE LUCAS
RETURN OF THE JEDI .... JIM BLOOM
RETURN OF THE JEDI .... ROBERT WATTS
RETURN OF THE JEDI .... HOWARD KAZANJIAN
RETURN OF THE LIVING DEAD .... TOM FOX
RETURN OF THE LIVING DEAD .... DEREK GIBSON
RETURN OF THE LIVING DEAD .... JOHN DALY
RETURN OF THE LIVING
DEAD PART II .... EUGENE C. CASHMAN
RETURN OF THE LIVING DEAD PART II .... TOM FOX
RETURN OF THE LIVING
DEAD PART II .... WILLIAM S. GILMORE
RETURN OF THE
MUSKETEERS, THE .... PIERRE SPENGLER
RETURN OF THE PINK PANTHER .... TONY ADAMS
RETURN OF THE
PINK PANTHER .... BLAKE EDWARDS
RETURN OF THE SOLDIER, THE .... ANN SCOTT
RETURN OF THE
SOLDIER, THE .... EDWARD SIMONS
RETURN OF THE
SOLDIER, THE .... J. GORDON ARNOLD
RETURN OF THE SOLDIER, THE .... JOHN QUESTED
RETURN OF THE SOLDIER, THE .... SIMON RELPH
RETURN TO OZ .... GARY KURTZ
RETURN TO OZ .... PAUL MASLANSKY
RETURN TO SALEM'S LOT .... PAUL KURTA
RETURN TO SNOWY RIVER .... GEOFF BURROWES
RETURN TO WATERLOO .... DENNIS WOOLF
REUBEN, REUBEN .... DAN ALLINGHAM
REUBEN, REUBEN .... JULIUS J. EPSTEIN
REUBEN, REUBEN .... WALTER SHENSON
REVENGE .... HUNT LOWRY
REVENGE .... KEVIN COSTNER
REVENGE .... STANLEY RUBIN
REVENGE OF THE NERDS .... DAVID OBST
REVENGE OF THE NERDS .... PETER BART
REVENGE OF
THE NERDS .... PETER MACGREGOR-SCOTT
REVENGE OF THE NERDS .... PETER SAMUELSON
REVENGE OF THE NERDS .... TED FIELD
REVENGE OF THE NERDS II:
NERDS IN PARADISE .... ROBERT W. CORT
REVENGE OF THE NERDS II:
NERD IN PARADISE .... TED FIELD
REVENGE OF THE NERDS II:
NERDS IN PARADISE .... JOE ROTH
REVENGE OF THE NERDS II:
NERDS IN PARADISE .... PAUL SCHIFF

REVENGE OF THE NERDS II:
NERDS IN PARADISE ..... PETER BART
REVENGE OF THE NINJA ..... MENAHEM GOLAN
REVENGE OF THE NINJA ..... YORAM GLOBUS
REVENGE OF THE PINK
PANTHER ..... BLAKE EDWARDS
REVENGE OF THE PINK PANTHER ..... TONY ADAMS
REVENGE OF THE PINK PANTHER ..... KEN WALES
REVERSAL OF
FORTUNE ..... EDWARD R. PRESSMAN
REVERSAL OF FORTUNE ..... OLIVER STONE
REVOLUTION ..... CHRIS BURT
REVOLUTION ..... HUGH HUDSON
REVOLUTION ..... IRWIN WINKLER
REVOLUTION ..... ROBERT CHARTOFF
REVOLUTIONARY, THE ..... EDWARD R. PRESSMAN
RHINESTONE ..... BILL BLAKE
RHINESTONE ..... HOWARD SMITH
RHINESTONE ..... JAMES D. BRUBAKER
RHINESTONE ..... RICHARD M. SPITALNY
RHINESTONE ..... MARVIN WORTH
RHINOCEROS ..... EDWARD LEWIS
RHINOCEROS ..... JACK GROSSBERG
RHINOCEROS ..... ELY LANDAU
RHINOCEROS ..... HENRY T. WEINSTEIN
RICH AND FAMOUS ..... WILLIAM ALLYN
RICH KIDS ..... MICHAEL HAUSMAN
RICH KIDS ..... ROBERT ALTMAN
RICH KIDS ..... GEORGE W. GEORGE
RICH KIDS ..... SCOTT BUSHNELL
RICHARD PRYOR LIVE ON
THE SUNSET STRIP ..... RICHARD PRYOR
RICHARD'S THINGS ..... MARK SHIVAS
RIDE A WILD PONY ..... JEROME COURTLAND
RIDE A WILD PONY ..... RON MILLER
RIDE IN THE WHIRLWIND ..... JACK NICHOLSON
RIDE IN THE WHIRLWIND ..... MONTE HELLMAN
RIDERS OF THE STORM ..... LAURIE KELLER
RIDERS OF THE STORM ..... PAUL COWAN
RIDING THE EDGE ..... WOLF SCHMIDT
RIGHT STUFF, THE ..... IRWIN WINKLER
RIGHT STUFF, THE ..... JAMES D. BRUBAKER
RIGHT STUFF, THE ..... ROBERT CHARTOFF
RIKKY AND PETE ..... BRYCE MENZIES
RIKKY AND PETE ..... DAVID PARKER
RIKKY AND PETE ..... NADIA TASS
RING OF BRIGHT WATER ..... EDGAR J. SCHERICK
RISKY BUSINESS ..... JON AVNET
RISKY BUSINESS ..... STEVE TISCH
RITA, SUE AND BOB TOO! ..... OSCAR LEWENSTEIN
RITA, SUE AND BOB TOO! ..... PATSY POLLOCK
RITA, SUE AND BOB TOO! ..... SANDY LIEBERSON
RITZ, THE ..... DENIS O'DELL
RIVER NIGER, THE ..... ISAAC L. JONES
RIVER NIGER, THE ..... SIDNEY BECKERMAN
RIVER OF DEATH ..... AVI LERNER
RIVER OF DEATH ..... HARRY ALAN TOWERS
RIVER RAT, THE ..... MICHAEL APTED
RIVER RAT, THE ..... ROBERT LARSON
RIVER'S EDGE ..... DAVID STREIT
RIVER'S EDGE ..... MIDGE SANFORD
RIVER'S EDGE ..... SARAH PILLSBURY
RIVER'S EDGE ..... DEREK GIBSON
RIVER'S EDGE ..... JOHN DALY
RIVER, THE ..... ROBERT CORTES
RIVER, THE ..... EDWARD LEWIS
ROAD GAMES ..... BARBI TAYLOR
ROAD GAMES ..... BERNARD SCHWARTZ
ROAD GAMES ..... RICHARD FRANKLIN
ROADHOUSE ..... JOEL SILVER
ROADHOUSE ..... STEVE PERRY
ROADHOUSE ..... TIM MOORE
ROADHOUSE 66 ..... MARK LEVINSON
ROADHOUSE 66 ..... MICHAEL ROSENBLATT
ROADHOUSE 66 ..... SCOTT ROSENFELT
ROADHOUSE 66 ..... THOMAS COLEMAN
ROADIE ..... ZALMAN KING
ROADIE ..... CAROLYN PFEIFFER
ROBIN AND MARIAN ..... DENIS O'DELL
ROBIN AND MARIAN ..... RICHARD SHEPHERD
ROBIN AND MARION ..... RAY STARK
ROBOCOP ..... EDWARD NEUMEIER
ROBOCOP ..... JON DAVISON
ROBOCOP ..... ARNE L. SCHMIDT
ROBOCOP II ..... JON DAVISON
ROBOCOP II ..... PATRICK CROWLEY
ROCK 'N' ROLL HIGH SCHOOL ..... MICHAEL FINNELL
ROCK 'N' ROLL HIGH SCHOOL ..... ROGER CORMAN
ROCK AND RULE ..... MICHAEL HIRSH
ROCK AND RULE ..... PATRICK LOUBERT
ROCKET GIBRALTAR ..... GEOFFREY MAYO
ROCKET GIBRALTAR ..... JEFF WEISS
ROCKET GIBRALTAR ..... MARCUS VISCIDI
ROCKET GIBRALTAR ..... MICHAEL ULICK
ROCKET GIBRALTAR ..... ROBERT FISHER
ROCKY ..... GENE KIRKWOOD
ROCKY ..... IRWIN WINKLER
ROCKY ..... ROBERT CHARTOFF
ROCKY II ..... IRWIN WINKLER
ROCKY II ..... ROBERT CHARTOFF
ROCKY III ..... IRWIN WINKLER
ROCKY III ..... HERB NANAS
ROCKY III ..... ROBERT CHARTOFF
ROCKY IV ..... ARTHUR CHOBANIAN
ROCKY IV ..... IRWIN WINKLER
ROCKY IV ..... JAMES D. BRUBAKER
ROCKY IV ..... ROBERT CHARTOFF
ROCKY HORROR
PICTURE SHOW, THE ..... JOHN GOLDSTONE
ROCKY HORROR
PICTURE SHOW, THE ..... LOU ADLER
ROGER AND ME ..... MICHAEL MOORE
ROLLER BOOGIE ..... BRUCE COHN CURTIS
ROLLER BOOGIE ..... IRWIN YABLANS
ROLLERBALL ..... PATRICK PALMER
ROLLERBALL ..... NORMAN JEWISON
ROLLERCOASTER ..... JENNINGS LANG
ROLLING THUNDER ..... NORMAN T. HERMAN
ROLLING THUNDER ..... LAWRENCE GORDON
ROLLOVER ..... BRUCE GILBERT
ROMANCING THE STONE ..... JACK BRODSKY
ROMANCING THE STONE ..... MICHAEL DOUGLAS
ROMANTIC COMEDY ..... MARVIN MIRISCH
ROMANTIC COMEDY ..... MORTON GOTTLIEB
ROMANTIC COMEDY ..... WALTER MIRISCH
ROMEO AND
JULIET ..... ANTHONY HAVELOCK-ALLAN
ROMEO AND JULIET ..... JOHN BRABOURNE
ROMERO ..... ELLWOOD E. KIESER
ROMERO ..... JOHN SACRET YOUNG
ROMERO ..... LAWRENCE MORTORFF
ROMERO ..... MIKE RHODES
ROOFTOPS ..... ALLAN GOLDSTEIN
ROOFTOPS ..... HOWARD W. KOCH JR.
ROOFTOPS ..... STUART BENJAMIN
ROOFTOPS ..... SUE JETT
ROOFTOPS ..... TAYLOR HACKFORD
ROOFTOPS ..... TONY MARK
ROOM AT THE TOP ..... JAMES WOOLF
ROOM AT THE TOP ..... SIR JOHN WOOLF
ROOM WITH A VIEW, A ..... ISMAIL MERCHANT
ROSA LUXEMBURG ..... EBERHARD JUNKERSDORF
ROSALIE GOES SHOPPING ..... ELEONORE ADLON
ROSALIE GOES SHOPPING ..... JILL GRIFFITH
ROSALIE GOES SHOPPING ..... PERCY ADLON
ROSARY MURDERS, THE ..... MICHAEL R. MIHALICH
ROSARY MURDERS, THE ..... ROBERT G. LAUREL
ROSE BOWL STORY, THE ..... WALTER MIRISCH
ROSE GARDEN, THE ..... MENAHEM GOLAN
ROSE GARDEN, THE ..... YORAM GLOBUS
ROSE GARDEN, THE ..... ARTUR BRAUNER
ROSE GARDEN, THE ..... CHRISTOPHER PEARCE
ROSE, THE ..... AARON RUSSO
ROSE, THE ..... TONY RAY
ROSE, THE ..... MARVIN WORTH
ROSEBUD BEACH HOTEL, THE ..... HARRY HURWITZ
ROSEBUD BEACH
HOTEL, THE ..... IRVING SCHWARTZ
ROSELAND ..... ISMAIL MERCHANT
ROUGH CUT ..... DAVID MERRICK
ROUND MIDNIGHT ..... IRWIN WINKLER
ROXANNE ..... DANIEL MELNICK
ROXANNE ..... MICHAEL RACHMIL
ROXANNE ..... STEVE MARTIN
ROYAL FLASH ..... DENIS O'DELL
ROYAL FLASH ..... DAVID V. PICKER
RUDE AWAKENING ..... AARON RUSSO
RUMBLE FISH ..... FRANCIS FORD COPPOLA
RUMBLE FISH ..... DOUG CLAYBOURNE
RUMBLE FISH ..... GRAY FREDERICKSON
RUMBLE FISH ..... FRED ROOS
RUMPLESTILTSKIN ..... ITZIK KOL
RUMPLESTILTSKIN ..... MENAHEM GOLAN
RUMPLESTILTSKIN ..... YORAM GLOBUS
RUNAWAY ..... MICHAEL RACHMIL
RUNAWAY TRAIN ..... HENRY T. WEINSTEIN
RUNAWAY TRAIN ..... MENAHEM GOLAN
RUNAWAY TRAIN ..... ROBERT A. GOLDSTON
RUNAWAY TRAIN ..... ROBERT WHITMORE
RUNAWAY TRAIN ..... YORAM GLOBUS
RUNNER STUMBLES, THE ..... STANLEY KRAMER
RUNNING ..... JOHN M. ECKERT
RUNNING ..... ROBERT COOPER
RUNNING ..... MICHAEL DOUGLAS
RUNNING ..... RONALD I. COHEN
RUNNING BRAVE ..... IRA ENGLANDER
RUNNING MAN, THE ..... GEORGE LINDER
RUNNING MAN, THE ..... KEITH BARISH
RUNNING MAN, THE ..... TIM ZINNEMANN
RUNNING MAN, THE ..... ROB COHEN
RUNNING ON EMPTY ..... AMY ROBINSON
RUNNING ON EMPTY ..... BURTT HARRIS
RUNNING ON EMPTY ..... GRIFFIN DUNNE
RUNNING ON EMPTY ..... NAOMI FONER
RUNNING SCARED ..... DAVID FOSTER
RUNNING SCARED ..... PETER HYAMS
RUNNING SCARED ..... JONATHAN A. ZIMBERT
RUNNING SCARED ..... LAWRENCE TURMAN
RUSSIA HOUSE, THE ..... FRED SCHEPISI
RUSSIA HOUSE, THE ..... PAUL MASLANSKY
RUSSIAN ROULETTE ..... ELLIOTT KASTNER
RUSSIAN ROULETTE ..... JERRY BICK
RUSSIANS ARE COMING,
THE RUSSIANS ARE
COMING, THE ..... NORMAN JEWISON
RUSSKIES ..... MARK LEVINSON
RUSSKIES ..... STEPHEN DEUTSCH
RUSSKIES ..... MORT ENGELBERG
RUSSKIES ..... SCOTT ROSENFELT
RUSTLER'S RHAPSODY ..... JOSE VICUNA
RUSTLER'S RHAPSODY ..... DAVID GILER
RUTHLESS PEOPLE ..... JOANNA LANCASTER
RUTHLESS PEOPLE ..... MICHAEL PEYSER
RUTHLESS PEOPLE ..... RICHARD WAGNER
RUTHLESS PEOPLE ..... WALTER YETNIKOFF
RYAN'S DAUGHTER ..... ANTHONY HAVELOCK-ALLAN
RYAN'S DAUGHTER ..... ROY STEVENS

S*P*Y*S ..... IRWIN WINKLER
S*P*Y*S ..... ROBERT CHARTOFF
S.O.B. ..... BLAKE EDWARDS
S.O.B. ..... MICHAEL B. WOLF
S.O.B. ..... TONY ADAMS
SABRINA ..... BILLY WILDER
SAFARI ..... IRVING ALLEN†
SAFARI ..... ALBERT R. BROCCOLI
SAFE PLACE, A ..... BERT SCHNEIDER
SAHARA ..... MENAHEM GOLAN
SAHARA ..... TERI SHIELDS
SAHARA ..... YORAM GLOBUS
SAILOR WHO FELL FROM GRACE
WITH THE SEA, THE ..... MARTIN POLL
SAINT JACK ..... EDWARD L. RISSIEN
SAINT JACK ..... HUGH M. HEFNER
SAINT JACK ..... ROGER CORMAN
SALAAM BOMBAY! ..... ANIL TEJANI
SALAAM BOMBAY! ..... CHERIE RODGERS
SALAAM BOMBAY! ..... GABRIEL AUER
SALAAM BOMBAY! ..... MICHAEL NOZIK
SALAAM BOMBAY! ..... MIRA NAIR
SALAAM BOMBAY! ..... MITCH EPSTEIN
SALAMANDER, THE ..... PAUL MASLANSKY
SALO: THE LAST 120 DAYS
OF SODOM ..... ALBERTO GRIMALDI
SALOME'S LAST DANCE ..... PENNY CORKE
SALOME'S LAST DANCE ..... ROBERT LITTMAN
SALOME'S LAST DANCE ..... WILLIAM J. QUIGLEY
SALON KITTY ..... ERMANNO DONATI
SALON KITTY ..... GIULIO SBARIGIA
SALSA ..... MENAHEM GOLAN
SALSA ..... YORAM GLOBUS
SALVADOR ..... DEREK GIBSON
SALVADOR ..... GERALD GREEN
SALVADOR ..... OLIVER STONE
SALVADOR ..... JOHN DALY
SALVATION! ..... BETH B
SALVATION! ..... IRVING ONG
SALVATION! ..... MICHAEL SHAMBERG
SALVATION! ..... MICHEL DUVAL
SALVATION! ..... NED RICHARDSON
SAME TIME, NEXT YEAR ..... MORTON GOTTLIEB
SAME TIME, NEXT YEAR ..... WALTER MIRISCH
SAMMY AND
ROSIE GET LAID ..... SARAH RADCLYFFE
SAMMY AND ROSIE GET LAID ..... TIM BEVAN
SAND PEBBLES, THE ..... ROBERT WISE
SANDPIPER, THE ..... MARTIN RANSOHOFF
SANTA CLAUS - THE MOVIE ..... ILYA SALKIND
SANTA CLAUS - THE MOVIE ..... PIERRE SPENGLER
SATISFACTION ..... AARON SPELLING
SATISFACTION ..... ALAN GREISMAN
SATISFACTION ..... ARMYAN BERNSTEIN
SATISFACTION ..... ROBERT ALDEN
SATURDAY NIGHT AND
SUNDAY MORNING ..... HARRY SALTZMAN
SATURDAY NIGHT FEVER ..... KEVIN MCCORMICK
SATURDAY NIGHT FEVER ..... ROBERT STIGWOOD
SATURDAY THE 14TH ..... JULIE CORMAN

SATURDAY THE 14TH STRIKES BACK ... JULIE CORMAN
SATURN 3 ... STANLEY DONEN
SATURN 3 ... MARTIN STARGER
SAVAGE BEACH ... ARLENE SIDARIS
SAVAGE IS LOOSE, THE ... ROBERT E. RELYEA
SAVAGE MESSIAH ... HARRY BENN
SAVAGE MESSIAH ... KEN RUSSELL
SAVAGE SAM ... BILL ANDERSON
SAVAGES ... ISMAIL MERCHANT
SAVE THE TIGER ... CHARLES R. MEEKER
SAVE THE TIGER ... STEVE SHAGAN
SAVE THE TIGER ... EDWARD S. FELDMAN
SAVE THE TIGER ... MARTIN RANSOHOFF
SAVING GRACE ... HERBERT F. SOLOW
SAY ANYTHING ... JAMES L. BROOKS
SAY ANYTHING ... POLLY PLATT
SAY ANYTHING ... RICHARD MARKS
SCANDAL ... BOB WEINSTEIN
SCANDAL ... HARVEY WEINSTEIN
SCANDAL ... JOE BOYD
SCANDAL ... TIM BEVAN
SCANDAL ... SARAH RADCLYFFE
SCANDAL ... NIK POWELL
SCANDAL ... STEPHEN WOOLLEY
SCANDALOUS ... ALEX WINITSKY
SCANDALOUS ... MARTIN C. SCHUTE
SCANDALOUS ... CARTER DE HAVEN
SCANDALOUS ... ARLENE SELLERS
SCANNERS ... CLAUDE HEROUX
SCANNERS ... PIERRE DAVID
SCANNERS ... VICTOR SOLNICKI
SCARECROW ... ROBERT M. SHERMAN
SCARED STIFF ... DANIEL F. BACANER
SCARFACE ... MARTIN BREGMAN
SCARFACE ... PETER SAPHIER
SCARFACE ... LOUIS A. STROLLER
SCAVENGER HUNT ... PAUL MASLANSKY
SCENES FROM THE CLASS STRUGGLE IN BEVERLY HILLS ... AMIR J. MALIN
SCENES FROM THE CLASS STRUGGLE IN BEVERLY HILLS ... IRA DEUTCHMAN
SCENES FROM THE CLASS STRUGGLE IN BEVERLY HILLS ... JAMES C. KATZ
SCHIZOID ... MENAHEM GOLAN
SCHIZOID ... YORAM GLOBUS
SCHLOCK ... GEORGE FOLSEY JR.
SCHOOL DAZE ... GRACE BLAKE
SCHOOL DAZE ... LORETHA C. JONES
SCHOOL DAZE ... MONTY ROSS
SCHOOL DAZE ... SPIKE LEE
SCORPIO ... WALTER MIRISCH
SCOTT JOPLIN ... ROB COHEN
SCOTT JOPLIN ... STAN HOUGH
SCREAM AND SCREAM AGAIN ... MAX ROSENBERG
SCREAM AND SCREAM AGAIN ... MILTON SUBOTSKY
SCREAM FOR HELP ... IRWIN YABLANS
SCREAM FOR HELP ... MICHAEL WINNER
SCROOGE ... ROBERT H. SOLO
SCROOGED ... ART LINSON
SCROOGED ... JENNIE LEW TUGEND
SCROOGED ... RAY HARTWICK
SCROOGED ... RICHARD DONNER
SCROOGED ... STEVE ROTH
SCRUBBERS ... DENIS O'BRIEN
SCRUBBERS ... DON BOYD
SCRUBBERS ... GEORGE HARRISON
SCUM ... CLIVE PARSONS
SCUM ... DAVINA BELLING
SEA AROUND US, THE ... IRWIN ALLEN
SEA GULL, THE ... SIDNEY LUMET
SEA OF LOVE ... LOUIS A. STROLLER
SEA OF LOVE ... MARTIN BREGMAN
SECOND HAND HEARTS ... JAMES WILLIAM GUERCIO
SECOND SIGHT ... JOSEPH M. CARACCIOLO
SECOND SIGHT ... MARK TARLOV
SECOND THOUGHTS ... DAVID FOSTER
SECOND THOUGHTS ... LAWRENCE TURMAN
SECOND WIND ... ALEXANDRA ROSE
SECONDS ... EDWARD LEWIS
SECRET ADMIRER ... C.O. ERICKSON
SECRET ADMIRER ... JIM KOUF
SECRET ADMIRER ... STEVE ROTH
SECRET CEREMONY ... JOHN HEYMAN
SECRET CEREMONY ... NORMAN PRIGGEN
SECRET CEREMONY ... PAUL HELLER
SECRET HONOR ... ROBERT ALTMAN
SECRET HONOR ... SCOTT BUSHNELL
SECRET LIFE OF AN AMERICAN WIFE, THE ... HANK MOONJEAN
SECRET OF MY SUCCESS, THE ... DAVID CHASMAN
SECRET OF MY SUCCESS, THE ... HERBERT ROSS
SECRET OF MY SUCCESS, THE ... JOSEPH M. CARACCIOLO
SECRET OF N.I.M.H., THE ... DON BLUTH
SECRET OF N.I.M.H., THE ... GARY GOLDMAN
SECRET OF N.I.M.H., THE ... JOHN POMEROY
SECRET OF SANTA VITTORIA, THE ... STANLEY KRAMER
SECRET PLACES ... SIMON RELPH
SECRETS ... CHRIS GRIFFIN
SECRETS ... DAVID PUTTNAM
SEDUCTION OF JOE TYNAN, THE ... MARTIN BREGMAN
SEDUCTION OF JOE TYNAN, THE ... LOUIS A. STROLLER
SEDUCTION, THE ... BRUCE COHN CURTIS
SEDUCTION, THE ... CHUCK RUSSELL
SEDUCTION, THE ... FRANK CAPRA JR.
SEDUCTION, THE ... IRWIN YABLANS
SEDUCTION, THE ... JOSEPH WOLF
SEE NO EVIL ... LESLIE LINDER
SEE NO EVIL ... MARTIN RANSOHOFF
SEE NO EVIL, HEAR NO EVIL ... ARNE SULTAN†
SEE NO EVIL, HEAR NO EVIL ... BURTT HARRIS
SEE NO EVIL, HEAR NO EVIL ... EARL BARRET
SEE NO EVIL, HEAR NO EVIL ... MARVIN WORTH
SEE YOU IN THE MORNING ... ALAN J. PAKULA
SEE YOU IN THE MORNING ... SUSAN SOLT
SEEMS LIKE OLD TIMES ... RAY STARK
SEMI-TOUGH ... DAVID MERRICK
SENDER, THE ... CHARLES R. MEEKER
SENDER, THE ... EDWARD S. FELDMAN
SENIOR PROM ... STEVE TISCH
SENIORS ... CARTER DE HAVEN
SENIORS ... RIC R. ROMAN
SENIORS ... STANLEY SHAPIRO
SEPARATE VACATIONS ... ANDRAS HAMORI
SEPARATE VACATIONS ... ROBERT LANTOS
SEPARATE VACATIONS ... STEPHEN J. ROTH
SEPTEMBER ... CHARLES H. JOFFE
SEPTEMBER ... JACK ROLLINS
SEPTEMBER ... ROBERT GREENHUT
SERIAL ... SIDNEY BECKERMAN
SERPENT AND THE RAINBOW, THE ... DAVID LADD
SERPENT AND THE RAINBOW, THE ... DOUG CLAYBOURNE
SERPENT AND THE RAINBOW, THE ... KEITH BARISH
SERPENT AND THE RAINBOW, THE ... ROB COHEN
SERPENT'S EGG, THE ... DINO DE LAURENTIIS
SERPICO ... MARTIN BREGMAN
SESAME STREET PRESENTS: FOLLOW THAT BIRD ... JOAN GANZ COONEY
SESAME STREET PRESENTS: FOLLOW THAT BIRD ... TONY GARNETT
SEVEN HOURS TO JUDGMENT ... HELEN SARLUI-TUCKER
SEVEN HOURS TO JUDGMENT ... MORT ABRAHAMS
SEVEN HOURS TO JUDGMENT ... PAUL MASON
SEVEN MAGNIFICENT GLADIATORS ... MENAHEM GOLAN
SEVEN MAGNIFICENT GLADIATORS ... YORAM GLOBUS
SEVEN MINUTES IN HEAVEN ... FRED ROOS
SEVEN PERCENT SOLUTION, THE ... STANLEY O'TOOLE
SEVEN-PERCENT SOLUTION, THE ... ARLENE SELLERS
SEVEN-PERCENT SOLUTION, THE ... ALEX WINITSKY
SEVEN-PERCENT SOLUTION, THE ... HERBERT ROSS
SEVEN-UPS, THE ... PHILIP D'ANTONI
SEVEN-UPS, THE ... KENNETH UTT
SEVEN YEAR ITCH, THE ... BILLY WILDER
SEVENTH SIGN, THE ... KATHY HALLBERG
SEVENTH SIGN, THE ... PAUL R. GURIAN
SEVENTH SIGN, THE ... ROBERT W. CORT
SEVENTH SIGN, THE ... TED FIELD
SEX, LIES, AND VIDEOTAPE ... JOHN HARDY
SEX, LIES, AND VIDEOTAPE ... MORGAN MASON
SEX, LIES, AND VIDEOTAPE ... NANCY TENENBAUM
SEX, LIES, AND VIDEOTAPE ... NICK WECHSLER
SEX, LIES, AND VIDEOTAPE ... ROBERT NEWMYER
SGT. PEPPER'S LONELY HEARTS CLUB BAND ... DEE ANTHONY
SGT. PEPPER'S LONELY HEARTS CLUB BAND ... ROBERT STIGWOOD
SHADEY ... OTTO PLASCHKES
SHADOW OF THE HAWK ... JOHN KEMENY
SHAFT ... JOEL FREEMAN
SHAG: THE MOVIE ... DEREK GIBSON
SHAG: THE MOVIE ... JEFFREY SILVER
SHAG: THE MOVIE ... JOHN DALY
SHAG: THE MOVIE ... JULIA CHASMAN
SHAG: THE MOVIE ... NIK POWELL
SHAG: THE MOVIE ... STEPHEN WOOLLEY
SHAGGY D.A., THE ... BILL ANDERSON
SHAGGY D.A., THE ... RON MILLER
SHAKEDOWN ... ALAN SOLOMON
SHAKEDOWN ... J. BOYCE HARMAN JR.
SHAKEDOWN ... LEONARD SHAPIRO
SHAKESPEARE WALLAH ... ISMAIL MERCHANT
SHAMPOO ... WARREN BEATTY
SHANGHAI SURPRISE ... DENIS O'BRIEN
SHANGHAI SURPRISE ... GEORGE HARRISON
SHANGHAI SURPRISE ... JOHN KOHN
SHANGHAI SURPRISE ... ROBIN DOUET
SHARKEY'S MACHINE ... EDWARD TEETS
SHARKEY'S MACHINE ... HANK MOONJEAN
SHARMA AND BEYOND ... CHRIS GRIFFIN
SHARMA AND BEYOND ... DAVID PUTTNAM
SHE DANCES ALONE ... EARLE MACK
SHE DANCES ALONE ... FEDERICO DE LAURENTIIS†
SHE DANCES ALONE ... MARION HUNT
SHE'S BACK ... CYNTHIA DEPAULA
SHE'S BACK ... LAWRENCE KASANOFF
SHE'S BACK ... RICHARD KESTINGE
SHE'S GOTTA HAVE IT ... SPIKE LEE
SHE'S HAVING A BABY ... JOHN HUGHES
SHE'S HAVING A BABY ... RONALD COLBY
SHE'S OUT OF CONTROL ... JOHN G. WILSON
SHE'S OUT OF CONTROL ... ROBERT KAUFMAN
SHE'S OUT OF CONTROL ... STEPHEN DEUTSCH
SHE-DEVIL ... G. MAC BROWN
SHE-DEVIL ... JONATHAN BRETT
SHE-DEVIL ... SUSAN SEIDELMAN
SHEENA ... CHRISTIAN FERRY
SHEENA ... PAUL ARATOW
SHEENA ... YORAM BEN-AMI
SHEER MADNESS ... EBERHARD JUNKERSDORF
SHELTERING SKY, THE ... JEREMY THOMAS
SHINING, THE ... STANLEY KUBRICK
SHIP OF FOOLS ... STANLEY KRAMER
SHIRLEY VALENTINE ... JOHN DARK
SHIRLEY VALENTINE ... LEWIS GILBERT
SHIRLEY VALENTINE ... WILLY RUSSELL
SHOCK TO THE SYSTEM, A ... LESLIE MORGAN
SHOCK TO THE SYSTEM, A ... ALICE ARLEN
SHOCK TO THE SYSTEM, A ... PATRICK MCCORMICK
SHOCK TREATMENT ... JOHN GOLDSTONE
SHOCK TREATMENT ... LOU ADLER
SHOCK TREATMENT ... MICHAEL WHITE
SHOCKER ... BARIN KUMAR†
SHOCKER ... MARIANNE MADDALENA
SHOCKER ... SHEP GORDON
SHOCKER ... WES CRAVEN
SHOES OF THE FISHERMAN, THE ... GEORGE ENGLUND
SHOOT ... DICK BERG
SHOOT ... HARVE SHARMAN
SHOOT THE MOON ... ALAN MARSHALL
SHOOT THE MOON ... STUART MILLAR
SHOOT THE MOON ... EDGAR J. SCHERICK
SHOOT TO KILL ... DANIEL PETRIE JR.
SHOOT TO KILL ... PHILLIP ROGERS
SHOOT TO KILL ... RON SILVERMAN
SHOOTING PARTY, THE ... GEOFFREY REEVE
SHOOTING PARTY, THE ... JEREMY SAUNDERS
SHOOTING, THE ... JACK NICHOLSON
SHOOTING, THE ... MONTE HELLMAN
SHOOTIST, THE ... DINO DE LAURENTIIS
SHORT CIRCUIT ... DAVID FOSTER
SHORT CIRCUIT ... DENNIS JONES
SHORT CIRCUIT ... GREGG CHAMPION
SHORT CIRCUIT ... JOHN HYDE
SHORT CIRCUIT ... MARK DAMON
SHORT CIRCUIT ... LAWRENCE TURMAN
SHORT CIRCUIT II ... DAVID FOSTER
SHORT CIRCUIT II ... GARY FOSTER
SHORT CIRCUIT II ... MICHAEL MACDONALD
SHORT CIRCUIT II ... LAWRENCE TURMAN
SHORT TIME ... JOE WIZAN
SHORT TIME ... MALCOLM R. HARDING
SHORT TIME ... MICKEY BOROFSKY
SHORT TIME ... TODD BLACK
SHOW OF FORCE ... FRED WEINTRAUB
SHY PEOPLE ... MENAHEM GOLAN
SHY PEOPLE ... YORAM GLOBUS
SICILIAN, THE ... JOANN CARELLI
SICILIAN, THE ... SIDNEY BECKERMAN
SICILIAN, THE ... MICHAEL CIMINO
SID & NANCY ... ERIC FELLNER
SID & NANCY ... PETER MCCARTHY
SIDE OUT ... GARY FOSTER

SIDE OUT ..... JAY WESTON
SIDE OUT ..... JOHN ZANE
SIDEWALK STORIES ..... CHARLES LANE
SIDEWALK STORIES ..... HOWARD M. BRICKNER
SIDEWALK STORIES ..... VICKI LEBENBAUM
SIDEWINDER ..... ELMO WILLIAMS
SIDNEY SHELDON'S BLOODLINE ..... DAVID V. PICKER
SIDNEY SHELDON'S BLOODLINE ..... SIDNEY BECKERMAN
SIESTA ..... CHRIS BROWN
SIESTA ..... GARY KURFIRST
SIESTA ..... JULIO CARO
SIESTA ..... NIK POWELL
SIESTA ..... ZALMAN KING
SIGN O' THE TIMES ..... JOSEPH RUFFALO
SIGN O' THE TIMES ..... ROBERT CAVALLO
SIGN O' THE TIMES ..... SIMON FIELDS
SIGN O' THE TIMES ..... STEVEN FARGNOLI
SIGN OF ZORRO, THE ..... BILL ANDERSON
SIGNAL 7 ..... BEN MYRON
SIGNAL 7 ..... DON TAYLOR
SIGNS OF LIFE ..... ANDREW REICHSMAN
SIGNS OF LIFE ..... CARY BROKAW
SIGNS OF LIFE ..... LINDSAY LAW
SIGNS OF LIFE ..... MARCUS VISCIDI
SILENCE OF THE LAMBS, THE ..... RON BOZMAN
SILENCE OF THE NORTH ..... MURRAY SHOSTAK
SILENCE OF THE NORTH ..... ROBERT BAYLIS
SILENT MOVIE ..... MICHAEL HERTZBERG
SILENT PARTNER, THE ..... GARTH DRABINSKY
SILENT PARTNER, THE ..... JOEL B. MICHAELS
SILENT RUNNING ..... MICHAEL GRUSKOFF
SILKWOOD ..... BUZZ HIRSCH
SILKWOOD ..... JOEL TUBER
SILKWOOD ..... LARRY CANO
SILKWOOD ..... MIKE NICHOLS
SILKWOOD ..... MICHAEL HAUSMAN
SILVER BEARS, THE ..... ARLENE SELLERS
SILVER BEARS, THE ..... ALEX WINITSKY
SILVER DREAM RACER ..... RENE DUPONT
SILVER STREAK ..... EDWARD K. MILKIS
SILVER STREAK ..... FRANK YABLANS
SILVER STREAK ..... MARTIN RANSOHOFF
SILVER STREAK ..... ROBERT BOYETT
SILVER STREAK ..... THOMAS L. MILLER
SILVERADO ..... CHARLES OKUN
SILVERADO ..... LAWRENCE KASDAN
SILVERADO ..... MICHAEL GRILLO
SIMON ..... MARTIN BREGMAN
SIMON ..... LOUIS A. STROLLER
SINFUL DAVEY ..... WALTER MIRISCH
SINFUL LIFE, A ..... DANIEL RASKOV
SINFUL LIFE, A ..... MILES A. COPELAND III
SINFUL LIFE, A ..... PAUL COLICHMAN
SING ..... CRAIG ZADAN
SING ..... NEIL MERON
SING ..... WOLFGANG GLATTES
SISTER, SISTER ..... GABE SUMNER
SISTER, SISTER ..... J. DAVID MARKS
SISTER, SISTER ..... WALTER COBLENZ
SISTERS ..... EDWARD R. PRESSMAN
SISTERS, OR THE BALANCE OF HAPPINESS ..... EBERHARD JUNKERSDORF
SIX PACK ..... MICHAEL TRIKILIS
SIX PACK ..... TED WITZER
SIX PACK ..... CHARLES R. MEEKER
SIX PACK ..... EDWARD S. FELDMAN
SIX WEEKS ..... JON PETERS
SIX WEEKS ..... PETER GUBER
SIXTEEN CANDLES ..... HILTON A. GREEN
SIXTEEN CANDLES ..... MICHELLE MANNING
SIXTEEN CANDLES ..... NED TANEN
SKI PATROL ..... DONALD L. WEST
SKI PATROL ..... PAUL MASLANSKY
SKI PATROL ..... PHILLIP B. GOLDFINE
SKIN DEEP ..... JAMES G. ROBINSON
SKIN DEEP ..... JOE ROTH
SKIN DEEP ..... TONY ADAMS
SKINHEADS ..... DAVID RESKIN
SKINHEADS ..... GREYDON CLARK
SKY BANDITS ..... RICHARD HERLAND
SLAMDANCE ..... BARRY OPPER
SLAMDANCE ..... CARY BROKAW
SLAMDANCE ..... RUPERT HARVEY
SLAMS, THE ..... GENE CORMAN
SLAP SHOT ..... ROBERT J. WUNSCH
SLAP SHOT ..... STEPHEN J. FRIEDMAN
SLAP SHOT ..... ROBERT L. CRAWFORD
SLAUGHTERHOUSE FIVE ..... PAUL MONASH
SLAUGHTERHOUSE-FIVE ..... JENNINGS LANG
SLAVES OF NEW YORK ..... ISMAIL MERCHANT
SLAYGROUND ..... BOB MERCER
SLAYGROUND ..... GOWER FROST
SLAYGROUND ..... JOHN DARK
SLEEPER ..... CHARLES H. JOFFE
SLEEPER ..... JACK GROSSBERG
SLEEPER ..... JACK ROLLINS
SLEUTH ..... EDGAR J. SCHERICK
SLIPPING INTO DARKNESS ..... DON SCHAIN
SLIPPING INTO DARKNESS ..... JONATHAN D. KRANE
SLIPPING INTO DARKNESS ..... LYDIA DEAN PILCHER
SLIPPING INTO DARKNESS ..... SIMON R. LEWIS
SLIPPING INTO DARKNESS ..... WILLIAM J. ROUHANA JR.
SLITHER ..... JACK SHER
SLUGGER'S WIFE, THE ..... RAY STARK
SLUGGER'S WIFE, THE ..... MARGARET BOOTH
SMALL CIRCLE OF FRIENDS, A ..... TIM ZINNEMANN
SMASH PALACE ..... ROGER DONALDSON
SMILE ..... MARION DOUGHERTY
SMILE ..... MICHAEL RITCHIE
SMILE ..... TIM ZINNEMANN
SMILE ..... DAVID V. PICKER
SMITH! ..... BILL ANDERSON
SMITHEREENS ..... SUSAN SEIDELMAN
SMOKEY AND THE BANDIT ..... MORT ENGELBERG
SMOKEY AND THE BANDIT ..... ROBERT L. LEVY
SMOKEY AND THE BANDIT II ..... HANK MOONJEAN
SMOKEY AND THE BANDIT II ..... PETER BURRELL
SMOKEY AND THE BANDIT PART 3 ..... MORT ENGELBERG
SMOKEY BITES THE DUST ..... GALE ANNE HURD
SMOKEY BITES THE DUST ..... ROGER CORMAN
SMOOTH TALK ..... LINDSAY LAW
SMOOTH TALK ..... MARTIN ROSEN
SMOOTH TALK ..... TIMOTHY MARX
SMORGASBORD ..... ARNOLD ORGOLINI
SMORGASBORD ..... PETER NELSON
SNIPER, THE ..... STANLEY KRAMER
SNOWBALL EXPRESS ..... RON MILLER
SNOW JOB ..... EDWARD L. RISSIEN
SO FINE ..... MICHAEL LOBELL
SO FINE ..... RAY HARTWICK
SOGGY BOTTOM U.S.A. ..... ELMO WILLIAMS
SOLARBABIES ..... IRENE WALZER
SOLARBABIES ..... JACK FROST SANDERS
SOLARBABIES ..... MEL BROOKS
SOLDIER BLUE ..... GABRIEL KATZKA†
SOLDIER BLUE ..... HAROLD LOEB
SOLDIER BLUE ..... WILLIAM S. GILMORE
SOLDIER IN THE RAIN ..... MARTIN JUROW
SOLDIER'S STORY, A ..... PATRICK PALMER
SOLDIER'S STORY, A ..... RONALD L. SCHWARY
SOLDIER'S STORY, A ..... NORMAN JEWISON
SOME CALL IT LOVING ..... JAMES B. HARRIS
SOME CALL IT LOVING ..... RAMSEY THOMAS
SOME GIRLS ..... RICK STEVENSON
SOME GIRLS ..... ROBERT REDFORD
SOME KIND OF HERO ..... HOWARD W. KOCH
SOME KIND OF NUT ..... WALTER MIRISCH
SOME KIND OF WONDERFUL ..... JOHN HUGHES
SOME KIND OF WONDERFUL ..... RONALD COLBY
SOME KIND OF WONDERFUL ..... RONALD I. COHEN
SOME KIND OF WONDERFUL ..... MICHAEL CHINICH
SOME LIKE IT HOT ..... BILLY WILDER
SOMEBODY KILLED HER HUSBAND ..... MARTIN POLL
SOMEONE TO LOVE ..... JUDITH WOLINSKY
SOMEONE TO LOVE ..... M. H. SIMONSONS
SOMEONE TO WATCH OVER ME ..... HAROLD SCHNEIDER
SOMEONE TO WATCH OVER ME ..... THIERRY DE GANAY
SOMEONE TO WATCH OVER ME ..... RIDLEY SCOTT
SOMETHING WICKED THIS WAY COMES ..... PETER DOUGLAS
SOMETHING WILD ..... EDWARD SAXON
SOMETHING WILD ..... JONATHAN DEMME
SOMETHING WILD ..... KENNETH UTT
SOMETHING WILD ..... RON BOZMAN
SOMETIMES A GREAT NOTION ..... JOHN FOREMAN
SOMEWHERE IN TIME ..... STEPHEN DEUTSCH
SON OF FLUBBER ..... BILL WALSH†
SON OF FLUBBER ..... RON MILLER
SONGWRITER ..... MICHAEL MODER
SONGWRITER ..... SYDNEY POLLACK
SOPHIE'S CHOICE ..... ALAN J. PAKULA
SOPHIE'S CHOICE ..... KEITH BARISH
SOPHIE'S CHOICE ..... WILLIAM C. GERRITY
SOPHIE'S CHOICE ..... MARTIN STARGER
SORORITY HOUSE MASSACRE ..... RON DIAMOND
SOUL MAN ..... CAROL BLACK
SOUL MAN ..... DONNA SMITH
SOUL MAN ..... NEAL MARLENS
SOUL MAN ..... STEVE TISCH
SOUND OF MUSIC, THE ..... ROBERT WISE
SOUND OF MUSIC, THE ..... SAUL CHAPLIN
SOUNDER ..... ROBERT B. RADNITZ
SOUP FOR ONE ..... MARVIN WORTH
SOUTHERN COMFORT ..... DAVID GILER
SOUTHERN COMFORT ..... WILLIAM J. IMMERMAN
SPACE RAGE ..... PATRICK C. WELLS
SPACE RAIDERS ..... ROGER CORMAN
SPACEBALLS ..... EZRA SWERDLOW
SPACEBALLS ..... MEL BROOKS
SPACECAMP ..... DAVID SALVEN
SPACECAMP ..... LEONARD J. GOLDBERG
SPACECAMP ..... PATRICK BAILEY
SPACECAMP ..... WALTER COBLENZ
SPACED INVADERS ..... LUIGI CONGOLANI
SPACED INVADERS ..... GEORGE ZECEVIC
SPACEHUNTER: ADVENTURES IN THE FORBIDDEN ZONE ..... ANDRE LINK
SPACEHUNTER: ADVENTURES IN THE FORBIDDEN ZONE ..... DON CARMODY
SPACEHUNTER: ADVENTURES IN THE FORBIDDEN ZONE ..... JOHN DUNNING
SPACEHUNTER: ADVENTURES IN THE FORBIDDEN ZONE ..... IVAN REITMAN
SPARKLE ..... BERYL VERTUE
SPARKLE ..... PETER BROWN
SPARKLE ..... HOWARD ROSENMAN
SPARTACUS ..... EDWARD LEWIS
SPARTACUS ..... KIRK DOUGLAS
SPASMS ..... MARTIN ERLICHMAN
SPECIAL DAY, A ..... CARLO PONTI
SPECIAL EFFECTS ..... CARTER DE HAVEN
SPECIAL EFFECTS ..... PAUL KURTA
SPEED ZONE ..... ALBERT S. RUDDY
SPEED ZONE ..... ANDRE MORGAN
SPEED ZONE ..... MURRAY SHOSTAK
SPEED ZONE ..... VIVIENNE LEEBOSH
SPEED ZONE ..... WENDY GREAN
SPELLBINDER ..... BRIAN RUSSELL
SPELLBINDER ..... HOWARD L. BALDWIN
SPELLBINDER ..... JOE WIZAN
SPELLBINDER ..... KATE BENTON
SPELLBINDER ..... MICKEY BOROFSKY
SPELLBINDER ..... RICHARD COHEN
SPELLBINDER ..... STEVEN E. BERMAN
SPELLBINDER ..... TODD BLACK
SPHINX ..... STANLEY O'TOOLE
SPIES LIKE US ..... BERNIE BRILLSTEIN
SPIES LIKE US ..... GEORGE FOLSEY JR.
SPIES LIKE US ..... LESLIE BELZBERG
SPIES LIKE US ..... BRIAN GRAZER
SPIKE OF BENSONHURST ..... DAVID WEISMAN
SPIKE OF BENSONHURST ..... NELSON LYON
SPIKES GANG, THE ..... WALTER MIRISCH
SPIRITS OF THE DEAD ..... ALBERTO GRIMALDI
SPLASH ..... BRIAN GRAZER
SPLASH ..... JOHN THOMAS LENOX
SPLIT DECISIONS ..... JOE WIZAN
SPLIT DECISIONS ..... MICKEY BOROFSKY
SPLIT DECISIONS ..... TODD BLACK
SPLIT IMAGE ..... JEFF YOUNG
SPLIT IMAGE ..... TED KOTCHEFF
SPLIT, THE ..... IRWIN WINKLER
SPLIT, THE ..... ROBERT CHARTOFF
SPRING BREAK ..... BARBARA DE FINA
SPRING BREAK ..... SEAN S. CUNNINGHAM
SPY WHO LOVED ME, THE ..... ALBERT R. BROCCOLI
SQUARE DANCE ..... CHARLES HAID
SQUARE DANCE ..... DANIEL PETRIE
SQUARE DANCE ..... JANE ALEXANDER
SQUEEZE, THE ..... DAVID SHAMROY HAMBURGER
SQUEEZE, THE ..... HARRY COLOMBY
SQUEEZE, THE ..... MICHAEL TANNEN
SQUEEZE, THE ..... RUPERT HITZIG
SQUEEZE, THE ..... STANLEY O'TOOLE
SSSSSSSS ..... RICHARD D. ZANUCK
SSSSSSSS ..... DAVID BROWN
ST. ELMO'S FIRE ..... BERNARD SCHWARTZ
ST. ELMO'S FIRE ..... LAUREN SHULER-DONNER
ST. ELMO'S FIRE ..... NED TANEN
ST. HELENS ..... MICHAEL TIMOTHY MURPHY
ST. HELENS ..... PETER S. DAVIS
ST. HELENS ..... WILLIAM N. PANZER
ST. IVES ..... PANCHO KOHNER
ST. IVES ..... STANLEY S. CANTER
STACKING ..... LINDSAY LAW
STACKING ..... MARTIN ROSEN
STACKING ..... PETER BURRELL
STAKEOUT ..... CATHLEEN SUMMERS
STAKEOUT ..... GREGG CHAMPION
STAKEOUT ..... JIM KOUF
STAKEOUT ..... JOHN BADHAM
STAKEOUT ON DOPE STREET ..... ROGER CORMAN
STALAG 17 ..... BILLY WILDER
STALKING MOON, THE ..... ALAN J. PAKULA
STAND ALONE ..... DANIEL P. KONDOS

STAND ALONE .... DAVID C. THOMAS
STAND ALONE .... GEORGE KONDOS
STAND ALONE .... LEON WILLIAMS
STAND ALONE .... TAMAR SIMON HOFFS
STAND AND DELIVER .... LINDSAY LAW
STAND AND DELIVER .... TOM MUSCA
STAND BY ME .... ANDREW SCHEINMAN
STAND BY ME .... BRUCE A. EVANS
STAND BY ME .... RAYNOLD GIDEON
STANLEY & IRIS .... ARLENE SELLERS
STANLEY & IRIS .... ALEX WINITSKY
STANLEY & IRIS .... PATRICK PALMER
STAR 80 .... GRACE BLAKE
STAR 80 .... KENNETH UTT
STAR 80 .... WOLFGANG GLATTES
STAR CHAMBER, THE .... FRANK YABLANS
STAR CHAMBER, THE .... JONATHAN A. ZIMBERT
STAR CHAMBER, THE .... MICHAEL DOUGLAS
STAR IS BORN, A .... BARBRA STREISAND
STAR IS BORN, A .... JON PETERS
STAR SPANGLED GIRL .... HOWARD W. KOCH
STAR TREK II: THE WRATH OF KHAN .... HARVE BENNETT
STAR TREK II: THE WRATH OF KHAN .... ROBERT SALLIN
STAR TREK III: THE SEARCH FOR SPOCK .... GARY NARDINO
STAR TREK III:THE SEARCH FOR SPOCK .... HARVE BENNETT
STAR TREK IV: THE VOYAGE HOME .... RALPH WINTER
STAR TREK IV:THE VOYAGE HOME .... HARVE BENNETT
STAR TREK V: THE FINAL FRONTIER .... MEL EFROS
STAR TREK V: THE FINAL FRONTIER .... RALPH WINTER
STAR TREK V:THE FINAL FRONTIER .... HARVE BENNETT
STAR WARS .... GARY KURTZ
STAR! .... SAUL CHAPLIN
STARDUST .... SANDY LIEBERSON
STARDUST .... DAVID PUTTNAM
STARDUST .... ROY BAIRD
STARDUST MEMORIES .... JACK ROLLINS
STARDUST MEMORIES .... ROBERT GREENHUT
STARDUST MEMORIES .... CHARLES H. JOFFE
STARMAN .... BARRY BERNARDI
STARMAN .... BRUCE A. EVANS
STARMAN .... LARRY J. FRANCO
STARMAN .... RAYNOLD GIDEON
STARMAN .... MICHAEL DOUGLAS
STARS AND BARS .... SHELDON SCHRAGER
STARS AND BARS .... SUSAN RICHARDS
STARS AND BARS .... SANDY LIEBERSON
STARSHIP INVASIONS .... EARL GLICK
STARSHIP INVASIONS .... ED HUNT
STARSHIP INVASIONS .... KEN GORD
STARSHIP INVASIONS .... NORMAN GLICK
START THE REVOLUTION WITHOUT ME .... BUD YORKIN
START THE REVOLUTION WITHOUT ME .... NORMAN LEAR
STARTING OVER .... ALAN J. PAKULA
STARTING OVER .... JAMES L. BROOKS
STATE OF GRACE .... MICHAEL HAUSMAN
STATE OF GRACE .... NED DOWD
STATE OF GRACE .... RANDY OSTROW
STATE OF GRACE .... RON ROTHOLZ
STATE OF THINGS, THE .... CHRIS SIEVERNICH
STATIC .... AMY NESS
STATIC .... JULIO CARO
STAY HUNGRY .... HAROLD SCHNEIDER
STAY HUNGRY .... BOB RAFELSON
STAYING ALIVE .... BILL OAKES
STAYING ALIVE .... ROBERT STIGWOOD
STAYING ALIVE .... SYLVESTER STALLONE
STAYING TOGETHER .... DEREK GIBSON
STAYING TOGETHER .... JOHN DALY
STAYING TOGETHER .... JOSEPH FEURY
STAYING TOGETHER .... MILTON JUSTICE
STEALING HEAVEN .... ANDROS EPAMINONDAS
STEALING HEAVEN .... SIMON MACCORKINDALE
STEALING HEAVEN .... SUSAN GEORGE
STEALING HOME .... THOM MOUNT
STEALING HOME .... HANK MOONJEAN
STEEL .... LEE MAJORS
STEEL .... PETER S. DAVIS
STEEL .... WILLIAM N. PANZER
STEEL DAWN .... CONRAD HOOL
STEEL DAWN .... EDGAR BOLD
STEEL DAWN .... LANCE HOOL
STEEL DAWN .... LARRY SUGAR
STEEL DAWN .... WILLIAM J. QUIGLEY
STEEL JUSTICE .... JOHN STRONG
STEEL JUSTICE .... MICHAEL ROSENBLATT
STEEL JUSTICE .... THOMAS COLEMAN
STEEL MAGNOLIAS .... RAY STARK
STEEL MAGNOLIAS .... VICTORIA WHITE
STEELYARD BLUES .... JULIA PHILLIPS
STEELYARD BLUES .... MICHAEL PHILLIPS
STEELYARD BLUES .... TONY BILL
STELLA .... DAVID V. PICKER
STELLA .... SAMUEL GOLDWYN JR.
STEPFATHER, THE .... JAY BENSON
STEPFATHER II .... CAROL LAMPMAN
STEPFATHER II .... DARIN SCOTT
STEPFATHER II .... WILLIAM BURR
STEPFORD WIVES, THE .... EDGAR J. SCHERICK
STEPHEN KING'S CAT'S EYE .... MARTHA SCHUMACHER
STEPHEN KING'S CAT'S EYE .... MILTON SUBOTSKY
STEPHEN KING'S SILVER BULLET .... MARTHA SCHUMACHER
STERILE CUCKOO, THE .... ALAN J. PAKULA
STEWARDESS SCHOOL .... ANDREW FOGELSON
STEWARDESS SCHOOL .... JERRY A. BAERWITZ
STEWARDESS SCHOOL .... MICHAEL KANE
STEWARDESS SCHOOL .... PHIL FELDMAN
STICK .... JENNINGS LANG
STICK .... ROBERT DALEY
STICK .... WILLIAM GORDEAN
STICK .... HANK MOONJEAN
STICKY FINGERS .... CATLIN ADAMS
STICKY FINGERS .... JOHN RYAN
STICKY FINGERS .... JONATHAN OLSBERG
STICKY FINGERS .... MELANIE MAYRON
STILL OF THE NIGHT .... ARLENE DONOVAN
STILL OF THE NIGHT .... KENNETH UTT
STILL OF THE NIGHT .... WOLFGANG GLATTES
STING, THE .... RICHARD D. ZANUCK
STING, THE .... JULIA PHILLIPS
STING, THE .... TONY BILL
STING, THE .... ROBERT L. CRAWFORD
STING, THE .... MICHAEL PHILLIPS
STING, THE .... DAVID BROWN
STING II, THE .... JENNINGS LANG
STIR CRAZY .... MELVILLE TUCKER
STONE BOY, THE .... IVAN BLOCH
STONE BOY, THE .... JAMES G. ROBINSON
STONE BOY, THE .... JOE ROTH
STONY ISLAND .... ANDREW DAVIS
STONY ISLAND .... TAMAR SIMON HOFFS
STOP MAKING SENSE .... GARY GOETZMAN
STOP MAKING SENSE .... GARY KURFIRST
STORIES FROM A FLYING TRUNK .... RICHARD GOODWIN
STORIES FROM A FLYING TRUNK .... JOHN BRABOURNE
STORMY MONDAY .... NIGEL STAFFORD-CLARK
STORY OF MANKIND, THE .... IRWIN ALLEN
STRAIGHT TIME .... HOWARD PINE
STRAIGHT TIME .... STANLEY BECK
STRAIGHT TIME .... TIM ZINNEMANN
STRAIGHT TO HELL .... CARY BROKAW
STRAIGHT TO HELL .... ERIC FELLNER
STRAIGHT TO HELL .... SCOTT MILLANEY
STRANDED .... MARK LEVINSON
STRANDED .... ROBERT SHAYE
STRANDED .... SCOTT ROSENFELT
STRANGE BEHAVIOR .... ANTONY I. GINNANE
STRANGE BEHAVIOR .... DAVID HEMMINGS
STRANGE BEHAVIOR .... DEREK GIBSON
STRANGE BEHAVIOR .... JOHN BARNETT
STRANGE BEHAVIOR .... WILLIAM FAYMAN
STRANGE BEHAVIOR .... JOHN DALY
STRANGE BREW .... BRIAN FRANKISH
STRANGE BREW .... JACK GROSSBERG
STRANGE BREW .... LOUIS M. SILVERSTEIN
STRANGE INVADERS .... WALTER COBLENZ
STRANGER IS WATCHING, A .... JACK GROSSBERG
STRANGER IS WATCHING, A .... SIDNEY BECKERMAN
STRANGER THAN PARADISE .... OTTO GROKENBERGER
STRANGER THAN PARADISE .... SARA DRIVER
STRANGER, THE .... HUGO LAMONICA
STRANGER, THE .... MICHAEL NOLIN
STRANGERS IN PARADISE .... RON NORMAN
STRANGERS KISS .... DOUGLAS DILGE
STRANGERS KISS .... HERCULES BELLVILLE
STRANGERS KISS .... MICHAEL WHITE
STRANGERS KISS .... SEAN FERRER
STRAPLESS .... RICK MCCALLUM
STRAW DOGS .... DANIEL MELNICK
STRAWBERRY STATEMENT, THE .... ROBERT CHARTOFF
STRAWBERRY STATEMENT, THE .... IRWIN WINKLER
STREAMERS .... NICK J. MILETI
STREAMERS .... ROBERT ALTMAN
STREAMERS .... SCOTT BUSHNELL
STREET SMART .... EVZEN W. KOLAR
STREET SMART .... MENAHEM GOLAN
STREET SMART .... YORAM GLOBUS
STREETS OF FIRE .... GENE LEVY
STREETS OF FIRE .... JOEL SILVER
STREETS OF FIRE .... LAWRENCE GORDON
STREETS OF FIRE .... WALTER HILL
STREETS OF GOLD .... DEZSO MAGYAR
STREETS OF GOLD .... HARRY UFLAND
STREETS OF GOLD .... JOE ROTH
STREETS OF GOLD .... PATRICK MCCORMICK
STREETWALKIN' .... ROBERT ALDEN
STREETWALKIN' .... ROGER CORMAN
STREETWISE .... CHERYL MCCALL
STRIKE IT RICH .... CHRISTINE OESTRICHER
STRIKE IT RICH .... BOB WEINSTEIN
STRIKE IT RICH .... HARVEY WEINSTEIN
STRIKE IT RICH .... GRAHAM EASTON
STRIKING BACK .... JAMES MARGELLOS
STRIKING BACK .... R. BEN EFRAIM
STRIPES .... DAN GOLDBERG
STRIPES .... JOE MEDJUCK
STRIPES .... MICHAEL C. GROSS
STRIPES .... IVAN REITMAN
STRIPPED TO KILL .... ANDY RUBEN
STRIPPED TO KILL .... MARK BYERS
STRIPPED TO KILL .... MATT LEIPZIG
STRIPPED TO KILL .... ROGER CORMAN
STRIPPED TO KILL 2 .... RODMAN FLENDER
STRIPPED TO KILL 2 .... ROGER CORMAN
STRIPPED TO KILL 2 .... ANDY RUBEN
STRIPPER .... ARNON MILCHAN
STRIPPER .... GEOF BARTZ
STRIPPER .... JEROME GARY
STRIPPER .... MELVYN J. ESTRIN
STRIPPER .... MICHAEL NOLIN
STRIPPER .... THOM TYSON
STROKER ACE .... HANK MOONJEAN
STRONGEST MAN IN THE WORLD, THE .... BILL ANDERSON
STUDENT BODIES .... HARVEY MILLER
STUDENT BODIES .... JERRY BELSON
STUDENT NURSES, THE .... ROGER CORMAN
STUFF, THE .... BARRY SHILS
STUFF, THE .... LARRY COHEN
STUFF, THE .... PAUL KURTA
STUNT MAN, THE .... MELVIN SIMON
STUNT MAN, THE .... RICHARD RUSH
STUNTS .... PETER S. DAVIS
STUNTS .... ROBERT SHAYE
STUNTS .... WILLIAM N. PANZER
SUBJECT WAS ROSES, THE .... KENNETH UTT
SUBMARINE X-1 .... WALTER MIRISCH
SUBURBIA .... BERT DRAGIN
SUBURBIA .... ROGER CORMAN
SUCCESS .... DANIEL H. BLATT
SUCCESS .... EDGAR J. SCHERICK
SUDDEN IMPACT .... CLINT EASTWOOD
SUDDEN IMPACT .... FRITZ MANES
SUDDEN TERROR .... PAUL MASLANSKY
SUGARLAND EXPRESS, THE .... RICHARD D. ZANUCK
SUGARLAND EXPRESS, THE .... DAVID BROWN
SUMMER HEAT .... MICHAEL ROSENBLATT
SUMMER HEAT .... PATRICIA STALLONE
SUMMER HEAT .... THOMAS COLEMAN
SUMMER HEAT .... WILLIAM TENNANT
SUMMER LOVERS .... JOEL DEAN
SUMMER LOVERS .... MICHAEL MODER
SUMMER MAGIC .... RON MILLER
SUMMER OF '42 .... RICHARD A. ROTH
SUMMER RENTAL .... GEORGE SHAPIRO
SUMMER RENTAL .... BERNIE BRILLSTEIN
SUMMER SCHOOL .... GEORGE SHAPIRO
SUMMER SCHOOL .... HOWARD WEST
SUMMER SCHOOL .... JEFF FRANKLIN
SUMMER SCHOOL .... MARC TRABULUS
SUMMER STORY, A .... DANTON RISSNER
SUMMER WISHES, WINTER DREAMS .... JACK BRODSKY
SUNBURN .... GERALD GREEN
SUNBURN .... JAY BERNSTEIN
SUNBURN .... JOHN QUESTED
SUNBURN .... DEREK GIBSON
SUNBURN .... JOHN DALY
SUNDAY BLOODY SUNDAY .... JOSEPH JANNI
SUNDAY LOVERS .... LEO L. FUCHS
SUNDOWNERS, THE .... FRED ZINNEMANN
SUNNYSIDE .... ROBERT L. SCHAFFEL

SUNSET ... TONY ADAMS
SUNSHINE BOYS, THE ... RAY STARK
SUPERDAD ... BILL ANDERSON
SUPERGIRL ... TIMOTHY BURRILL
SUPERGIRL ... ILYA SALKIND
SUPERMAN ... PIERRE SPENGLER
SUPERMAN ... ILYA SALKIND
SUPERMAN II ... PIERRE SPENGLER
SUPERMAN II ... ILYA SALKIND
SUPERMAN III ... PIERRE SPENGLER
SUPERMAN III ... ILYA SALKIND
SUPERMAN IV: THE QUEST FOR PEACE ... MENAHEM GOLAN
SUPERMAN IV: THE QUEST FOR PEACE ... MICHAEL J. KAGAN
SUPERMAN IV: THE QUEST FOR PEACE ... YORAM GLOBUS
SUPERNATURALS, THE ... DON LEVIN
SUPERNATURALS, THE ... JOEL SOISSON
SUPERNATURALS, THE ... MEL PEARL
SUPERNATURALS, THE ... MICHAEL S. MURPHEY
SUPERSTITION ... ANDREW VAJNA
SUPERSTITION ... MARIO KASSAR
SURE THING, THE ... ANDREW SCHEINMAN
SURE THING, THE ... HENRY WINKLER
SURE THING, THE ... ROGER BIRNBAUM
SURF II ... FRANK D. TOLIN
SURF II ... GEORGE BRAUNSTEIN
SURF II ... LOU GEORGE
SURF II ... RON HAMADY
SURRENDER ... AARON SPELLING
SURRENDER ... ALAN GREISMAN
SURRENDER ... MENAHEM GOLAN
SURRENDER ... YORAM GLOBUS
SURVIVAL GAME ... GIDEON AMIR
SURVIVAL GAME ... MOSHE DIAMANT
SURVIVAL QUEST ... DAC COSCARELLI
SURVIVAL QUEST ... ROBERTO A. QUEZADA
SURVIVAL RUN ... MEL BERGMAN
SURVIVAL RUN ... RUBEN BROIDO
SURVIVORS, THE ... HOWARD PINE
SURVIVORS, THE ... WILLIAM SACKHEIM
SUSPECT ... DANIEL A. SHERKOW
SUSPECT ... JENNIFER OGDEN
SUSPECT ... JOHN VEITCH
SUZANNE ... ROBERT LANTOS
SUZANNE ... STEPHEN J. ROTH
SWAMP THING ... BENJAMIN MELNIKER
SWAMP THING ... MICHAEL USLAN
SWARM, THE ... IRWIN ALLEN
SWASHBUCKLER ... ELLIOTT KASTNER
SWASHBUCKLER ... JENNINGS LANG
SWEET DREAMS ... BERNARD SCHWARTZ
SWEET DREAMS ... CHARLES B. MULVEHILL
SWEET HEARTS DANCE ... GABRIELLE MANDELIK
SWEET HEARTS DANCE ... JEFFREY LURIE
SWEET HEARTS DANCE ... LAUREN WEISSMAN
SWEET HEARTS DANCE ... ROBERT GREENWALD
SWEET KILL ... TAMARA ASSEYEV
SWEET LIBERTY ... LOUIS A. STROLLER
SWEET LIBERTY ... MARTIN BREGMAN
SWEET LORRAINE ... ANGELIKA SALEH
SWEET LORRAINE ... IAIN PATERSON
SWEET LORRAINE ... JOSEPH SALEH
SWEET LORRAINE ... STEVE GOMER
SWEET REVENGE ... BRAD KREVOY
SWEET REVENGE ... ROGER CORMAN
SWEET REVENGE ... STEVEN STABLER
SWEETIE ... JOHN MAYNARD
SWEETIE ... WILLIAM MACKINNON
SWIMMING TO CAMBODIA ... AMIR J. MALIN
SWIMMING TO CAMBODIA ... EDWARD SAXON
SWIMMING TO CAMBODIA ... IRA DEUTCHMAN
SWIMMING TO CAMBODIA ... LEWIS ALLEN
SWIMMING TO CAMBODIA ... PETER NEWMAN
SWIMMING TO CAMBODIA ... R.A. SHAFRANSKY
SWING SHIFT ... CHARLES B. MULVEHILL
SWING SHIFT ... JERRY BICK
SWING SHIFT ... ALEX WINITSKY
SWING SHIFT ... ARLENE SELLERS
SWISS FAMILY ROBINSON ... BILL ANDERSON
SWITCHING CHANNELS ... DON CARMODY
SWITCHING CHANNELS ... MARTIN RANSOHOFF
SWORD OF THE VALIANT ... MENAHEM GOLAN
SWORD OF THE VALIANT ... MICHAEL J. KAGAN
SWORD OF THE VALIANT ... PHILIP M. BREEN
SWORD OF THE VALIANT ... YORAM GLOBUS
SYLVESTER ... MARTIN JUROW
SYLVESTER ... RAY STARK
SYLVIA ... MARTIN POLL

T

T-BIRD GANG ... ROGER CORMAN
TABLE FOR FIVE ... ROBERT L. SCHAFFEL
TAFFIN ... ALLAN SCOTT
TAFFIN ... JOHN A. DAVIS
TAFFIN ... PETER SHAW
TAKE DOWN ... KEITH MERRILL
TAKE THE MONEY AND RUN ... CHARLES H. JOFFE
TAKE THE MONEY AND RUN ... JACK GROSSBERG
TAKE THIS JOB AND SHOVE IT ... GREGORY S. BLACKWELL
TAKE THIS JOB AND SHOVE IT ... J. DAVID MARKS
TAKE THIS JOB AND SHOVE IT ... WILLIAM J. IMMERMAN
TAKING OF PELHAM 1-2-3, THE ... GABRIEL KATZKA†
TAKING OF PELHAM 1-2-3, THE ... STEPHEN F. KESTEN
TAKING OF PELHAM 1-2-3, THE ... EDGAR J. SCHERICK
TALES FROM THE DARKSIDE - THE MOVIE ... RICHARD P. RUBINSTEIN
TALES OF TERROR ... SAMUEL Z. ARKOFF
TALES OF TERROR ... JAMES H. NICHOLSON†
TALK RADIO ... A. KITMAN HO
TALK RADIO ... EDWARD R. PRESSMAN
TALK RADIO ... GREG STRANGIS
TALK RADIO ... SAM STRANGIS
TALL GUY, THE ... PAUL WEBSTER
TALL GUY, THE ... TIM BEVAN
TAMARIND SEED, THE ... KEN WALES
TANGO AND CASH ... JON PETERS
TANGO AND CASH ... LARRY J. FRANCO
TANGO AND CASH ... PETER GUBER
TANGO AND CASH ... PETER MACDONALD
TANK ... IRWIN YABLANS
TANK FORCE ... ALBERT R. BROCCOLI
TAP GARY ADELSON
TAP RICHARD VANE
TAPEHEADS ... MICHAEL NESMITH
TAPEHEADS ... PETER MCCARTHY
TAPEHEADS ... ROBERT S. LECKY
TAPS ... HOWARD B. JAFFE
TAPS ... STANLEY R. JAFFE
TARGET ... DAVID BROWN
TARGET ... RICHARD D. ZANUCK
TARGET: HARRY ... GENE CORMAN
TARGET: HARRY ... ROGER CORMAN
TARGETS ... PETER BOGDANOVICH
TARGETS ... ROGER CORMAN
TARZAN, THE APE MAN ... BO DEREK
TATTOO ... JOSEPH E. LEVINE†
TATTOO ... RICHARD P. LEVINE
TATTOO ... ROBERT F. COLESBERRY
TAXI DRIVER ... JULIA PHILLIPS
TAXI DRIVER ... MICHAEL PHILLIPS
TEACHERS ... AARON RUSSO
TEENAGE MUTANT NINJA TURTLES ... DAVID CHAN
TEENAGE MUTANT NINJA TURTLES ... KIM DAWSON
TEENAGE MUTANT NINJA TURTLES ... GRAHAM COTTLE
TEENAGE MUTANT NINJA TURTLES ... RAYMOND CHOW
TEENAGE MUTANT NINJA TURTLES ... SIMON FIELDS
TEEN WITCH ... ALANA H. LAMBROS
TEEN WITCH ... EDUARD SARLUI
TEEN WITCH ... MOSHE DIAMANT
TEEN WITCH ... RAFAEL EISENMAN
TEEN WOLF ... MARK LEVINSON
TEEN WOLF ... MICHAEL ROSENBLATT
TEEN WOLF ... SCOTT ROSENFELT
TEEN WOLF ... THOMAS COLEMAN
TEEN WOLF TOO ... KENT BATEMAN
TEEN WOLF TOO ... MICHAEL ROSENBLATT
TEEN WOLF TOO ... THOMAS COLEMAN
TELEFON ... JAMES B. HARRIS
TELEPHONE, THE ... MOCTESUMA ESPARZA
TELEPHONE, THE ... ROBERT KATZ
TELL THEM WILLIE BOY IS HERE ... JENNINGS LANG
TEMPEST ... PATO GUZMAN
TEMPEST ... PAUL MAZURSKY
TEMPEST ... STEVEN BERNHARDT
TEN FROM YOUR SHOW OF SHOWS ... JULIAN SCHLOSSBERG
TEN LITTLE INDIANS ... AVI LERNER
TEN LITTLE INDIANS ... HARRY ALAN TOWERS
TENANT, THE ... ANDREW BRAUNSBERG
TENDER MERCIES ... HORTON FOOTE
TENDER MERCIES ... PHILIP S. HOBEL
TENDER MERCIES ... ROBERT DUVALL
TENTH VICTIM, THE ... CARLO PONTI
TEQUILA SUNRISE ... THOM MOUNT
TEQUILA SUNRISE ... TOM SHAW
TERMINAL MAN, THE ... MICHAEL DRYHURST
TERMINAL MAN, THE ... MIKE HODGES
TERMINATOR, THE ... DEREK GIBSON
TERMINATOR, THE ... JOHN DALY
TERMINATOR, THE ... GALE ANNE HURD
TERMS OF ENDEARMENT ... JAMES L. BROOKS
TERMS OF ENDEARMENT ... MARTIN JUROW
TERMS OF ENDEARMENT ... PENNY FINKELMAN COX
TERROR IN THE AISLES ... ANDREW J. KUEHN
TERROR IN THE AISLES ... STEPHEN J. NETBURN
TERROR WITHIN, THE ... REID SHANE
TERROR WITHIN, THE ... RODMAN FLENDER
TERROR WITHIN, THE ... ROGER CORMAN
TERROR, THE ... FRANCIS FORD COPPOLA
TERRORVISION ... ALBERT BAND
TERRORVISION ... CHARLES BAND
TESS ... TIMOTHY BURRILL
TEST OF LOVE, A ... DON MURRAY
TESTAMENT ... JONATHAN BERNSTEIN
TEX ... RON MILLER
TEX ... TIM ZINNEMANN
TEXAS CHAINSAW MASSACRE, THE ... TOBE HOOPER
TEXAS CHAINSAW MASSACRE PART 2, THE ... HENRY HOLMES
TEXAS CHAINSAW MASSACRE PART 2, THE ... JAMES JORGENSEN
TEXAS CHAINSAW MASSACRE PART 2, THE ... MENAHEM GOLAN
TEXAS CHAINSAW MASSACRE PART 2, THE ... TOBE HOOPER
TEXAS CHAINSAW MASSACRE PART 2, THE ... YORAM GLOBUS
TEXASVILLE ... BILL PEIFFER
TEXASVILLE ... HENRY T. WEINSTEIN
TEXASVILLE ... JAKE EBERTS
TEXASVILLE ... PETER BOGDANOVICH
TEXASVILLE ... ROBERT WHITMORE
THANK GOD IT'S FRIDAY ... ROB COHEN
THANK YOU ALL VERY MUCH ... EDGAR J. SCHERICK
THAT CHAMPIONSHIP SEASON ... MENAHEM GOLAN
THAT CHAMPIONSHIP SEASON ... ROBERT F. LEVINE
THAT CHAMPIONSHIP SEASON ... YORAM GLOBUS
THAT DARN CAT! ... BILL WALSH†
THAT DARN CAT! ... RON MILLER
THAT MAN BOLT ... BERNARD SCHWARTZ
THAT MAN FROM RIO ... ALEXANDRE MNOUCHKINE
THAT MAN FROM RIO ... GEORGES DANCIGERS
THAT SINKING FEELING ... BILL FORSYTH
THAT SUMMER ... CLIVE PARSONS
THAT SUMMER ... DAVINA BELLING
THAT WAS THEN...THIS IS NOW ... ALAN BELKIN
THAT WAS THEN... THIS IS NOW ... BRANDON K. PHILLIPS
THAT WAS THEN... THIS IS NOW ... GARY R. LINDBERG
THAT WAS THEN...THIS IS NOW ... JOHN M. ONDOV
THAT'LL BE THE DAY ... ROY BAIRD
THAT'LL BE THE DAY ... SANDY LIEBERSON
THAT'LL BE THE DAY ... DAVID PUTTNAM
THAT'S ADEQUATE ... HARRY HURWITZ
THAT'S ADEQUATE ... IRVING SCHWARTZ
THAT'S DANCING! ... DAVID NIVEN JR.
THAT'S DANCING! ... GENE KELLY
THAT'S DANCING! ... JACK HALEY JR.
THAT'S ENTERTAINMENT! ... JACK HALEY JR.
THAT'S ENTERTAINMENT! ... DANIEL MELNICK
THAT'S ENTERTAINMENT, PART 2 ... DANIEL MELNICK
THAT'S ENTERTAINMENT, PART 2 ... SAUL CHAPLIN
THAT'S LIFE! ... JONATHAN D. KRANE
THAT'S LIFE! ... TONY ADAMS
THELONIOUS MONK: STRAIGHT NO CHASER ... BRUCE RICKER
THELONIOUS MONK: STRAIGHT NO CHASER ... CHARLOTTE ZWERIN
THELONIOUS MONK: STRAIGHT, NO CHASER ... CLINT EASTWOOD
THERE WAS A CROOKED MAN ... C.O. ERICKSON
THEY ALL LAUGHED ... BLAINE NOVAK
THEY ALL LAUGHED ... GEORGE MORFOGEN
THEY ALL LAUGHED ... RUSSELL SCHWARTZ
THEY ALL LAUGHED ... MICHAEL MODER
THEY CALL ME MISTER TIBBS! ... WALTER MIRISCH
THEY CAME FROM WITHIN ... ALFRED PARISER

THEY CAME FROM WITHIN ..... ANDRE LINK
THEY CAME FROM WITHIN ..... JOHN DUNNING
THEY CAME FROM WITHIN ..... IVAN REITMAN
THEY LIVE ..... ANDRE BLAY
THEY LIVE ..... LARRY J. FRANCO
THEY LIVE ..... SHEP GORDON
THEY MIGHT BE GIANTS ..... PAUL NEWMAN
THEY MIGHT BE GIANTS ..... JENNINGS LANG
THEY MIGHT BE GIANTS ..... JOHN FOREMAN
THEY SHOOT HORSES, DON'T THEY? ..... ROBERT CHARTOFF
THEY SHOOT HORSES, DON'T THEY? ..... IRWIN WINKLER
THEY SHOOT HORSES, DON'T THEY? ..... SYDNEY POLLACK
THIEF ..... JERRY BRUCKHEIMER
THIEF ..... RONNIE CAAN
THIEF OF HEARTS ..... DON SIMPSON
THIEF OF HEARTS ..... JERRY BRUCKHEIMER
THIEF OF HEARTS ..... TOM JACOBSON
THIEF WHO CAME TO DINNER, THE ..... BUD YORKIN
THIEVES LIKE US ..... GEORGE LITTO
THIEVES LIKE US ..... JERRY BICK
THIN BLUE LINE, THE ..... LINDSAY LAW
THIN BLUE LINE, THE ..... MARK LIPSON
THING, THE ..... DAVID FOSTER
THING, THE ..... LARRY J. FRANCO
THING, THE ..... WILBUR STARK
THING, THE ..... LAWRENCE TURMAN
THINGS ARE TOUGH ALL OVER ..... HOWARD BROWN
THINGS CHANGE ..... NED DOWD
THINGS CHANGE ..... MICHAEL HAUSMAN
THINK BIG ..... BRAD KREVOY
THINK BIG ..... STEPHEN STABLER
THIRD MAN ON THE MOUNTAIN ..... BILL ANDERSON
THIRST ..... ANTONY I. GINNANE
THIS IS ELVIS ..... ANDREW SOLT
THIS IS ELVIS ..... DAVID L. WOLPER
THIS IS ELVIS ..... MALCOLM LEO
THIS IS SPINAL TAP ..... KAREN MURPHY
THOSE GLORY, GLORY DAYS ..... CHRIS GRIFFIN
THOSE GLORY, GLORY DAYS ..... DAVID PUTTNAM
THOSE LIPS, THOSE EYES ..... HERB JAFFE
THOSE LIPS, THOSE EYES ..... MICHAEL PRESSMAN
THOSE LIPS, THOSE EYES ..... STEVEN-CHARLES JAFFE
THOSE MAGNIFICENT MEN IN THEIR FLYING MACHINES ..... TED MANN
THOSE MAGNIFICENT MEN IN THEIR FLYING MACHINES ..... ELMO WILLIAMS
THRASHIN' ..... ALAN SACKS
THRASHIN' ..... CHARLES FRIES
THRASHIN' ..... MIKE ROSENFELD
THREE AMIGOS ..... STEVE MARTIN
THREE AMIGOS ..... GEORGE FOLSEY JR.
THREE AMIGOS ..... LORNE MICHAELS
THREE FOR THE ROAD ..... HERB JAFFE
THREE FOR THE ROAD ..... MORT ENGELBERG
THREE FUGITIVES ..... FRANCIS VEBER
THREE FUGITIVES ..... LAUREN SHULER-DONNER
THREE KINDS OF HEAT ..... MICHAEL J. KAGAN
THREE MEN AND A BABY ..... EDWARD TEETS
THREE MEN AND A BABY ..... JEAN FRANCOIS LEPETIT
THREE MEN AND A BABY ..... ROBERT W. CORT
THREE MEN AND A BABY ..... TED FIELD
THREE MEN AND A CRADLE ..... JEAN FRANCOIS LEPETIT
THREE MUSKETEERS , THE ..... ALEXANDER SALKIND
THREE MUSKETEERS, THE ..... ILYA SALKIND
THREE MUSKETEERS, THE ..... PIERRE SPENGLER
THREE O'CLOCK HIGH ..... AARON SPELLING
THREE O'CLOCK HIGH ..... ALAN GREISMAN
THREE O'CLOCK HIGH ..... DAVID E. VOGEL
THREE O'CLOCK HIGH ..... JOHN A. DAVIS
THREE O'CLOCK HIGH ..... NEIL ISRAEL
THREE SISTERS, THE ..... JOHN GOLDSTONE
THREE WARRIORS ..... SY GOMBERG
THREE WARRIORS ..... SAUL ZAENTZ
THRESHOLD ..... JON SLAN
THRESHOLD ..... MICHAEL BURNS
THROW MOMMA FROM THE TRAIN ..... ARNE L. SCHMIDT
THROW MOMMA FROM THE TRAIN ..... KRISTINE JOHNSON
THROW MOMMA FROM THE TRAIN ..... LARRY BREZNER
THUMB TRIPPING ..... IRWIN WINKLER
THUMB TRIPPING ..... ROBERT CHARTOFF
THUNDER AND LIGHTNING ..... ROGER CORMAN
THUNDERBALL ..... KEVIN MCCLORY
THUNDERBALL ..... ALBERT R. BROCCOLI
THUNDERBOLT AND LIGHTFOOT ..... ROBERT DALEY
THX 1138 ..... FRANCIS FORD COPPOLA
THX 1138 ..... LAWRENCE STURHAHN
TICKET TO HEAVEN ..... ALAN SIMMONS
TICKET TO HEAVEN ..... RONALD I. COHEN
TICKET TO HEAVEN ..... VIVIENNE LEEBOSH
TIGER WALKS, A ..... BILL ANDERSON
TIGER WARSAW ..... AMIN Q. CHAUDHRI
TIGER WARSAW ..... GAY MAYER
TIGER WARSAW ..... NAVIN DESAI
TIGER WARSAW ..... WATSON WARRINER
TIGER'S TALE, A ..... PETER DOUGLAS
TIGHTROPE ..... FRITZ MANES
TIGHTROPE ..... BUZZ FEITSHANS
TIGHTROPE ..... CLINT EASTWOOD
TILTMELVIN SIMON
TILTRUDY DURAND
TIME AFTER TIME ..... HERB JAFFE
TIME BANDITS ..... DENIS O'BRIEN
TIME BANDITS ..... GEORGE HARRISON
TIME BANDITS ..... TERRY GILLIAM
TIME OF DESTINY, A ..... ANNA THOMAS
TIME OF DESTINY, A ..... CAROLYN PFEIFFER
TIME OF DESTINY, A ..... SHEP GORDON
TIME OF THE BEAST ..... JOHN R. BOWEY
TIME OF THE BEAST ..... RUSSELL D. MARKOWITZ
TIME WALKER ..... DIMITRI VILLARD
TIME WALKER ..... JASON WILLIAMS
TIME WALKER ..... ROBBY WALD
TIME WALKER ..... ROBERT SHAFTER
TIMERIDER: THE ADVENTURE OF LYLE SWANN ..... HARRY GITTES
TIMERIDER: THE ADVENTURE OF LYLE SWANN ..... MICHAEL NESMITH
TIMES OF HARVEY MILK, THE ..... RICHARD SCHMIECHEN
TIMES SQUARE ..... JACOB BRACKMAN
TIMES SQUARE ..... JOHN NICOLELLA
TIMES SQUARE ..... KEVIN MCCORMICK
TIMES SQUARE ..... ROBERT STIGWOOD
TIN MEN ..... MARK JOHNSON
TO BE OR NOT TO BE ..... HOWARD JEFFREY
TO BE OR NOT TO BE ..... IRENE WALZER
TO BE OR NOT TO BE ..... MEL BROOKS
TO DIE FOR ..... GREG H. SIMS
TO DIE FOR ..... LEE CAPLIN
TO DIE FOR ..... BARIN KUMAR†
TO FIND A MAN ..... MORT ABRAHAMS
TO KILL A MOCKINGBIRD ..... ALAN J. PAKULA
TO KILL A PRIEST ..... JEAN-PIERRE ALESSANDRI
TO KILL A PRIEST ..... TIMOTHY BURRILL
TO LIVE AND DIE IN L.A. ..... IRVING H. LEVIN
TO LIVE AND DIE IN L.A. ..... SAMUEL SCHULMAN
TO SLEEP WITH ANGER ..... CALDECOTT CHUBB
TO SLEEP WITH ANGER ..... EDWARD R. PRESSMAN
TOGETHER BROTHERS ..... ROBERT L. ROSEN
TOKYO POP ..... JOEL TUBER
TOKYO POP ..... JONATHAN OLSBERG
TOKYO POP ..... KAZ KUZUI
TOM HORN ..... FRED WEINTRAUB
TOM HORN ..... MICHAEL RACHMIL
TOM HORN ..... SANDRA WEINTRAUB ROLAND
TOM JONES ..... TONY RICHARDSON
TOMB, THE ..... FRED OLEN RAY
TOMB, THE ..... PAUL HERTZBERG
TOMB, THE ..... RICHARD KAYE
TOMB, THE ..... RONNIE HADAR
TOMMY ..... BERYL VERTUE
TOMMY ..... CHRISTOPHER STAMP
TOMMY ..... HARRY BENN
TOMMY ..... KEN RUSSELL
TOMMY ..... ROBERT STIGWOOD
TOMORROW ..... HARRY SALTZMAN
TONIGHT FOR SURE ..... FRANCIS FORD COPPOLA
TOO MUCH ..... MENAHEM GOLAN
TOO MUCH ..... YORAM GLOBUS
TOO MUCH ..... YOSUKE MIZUNO
TOO OUTRAGEOUS! ..... ROY KROST
TOO SOON TO LOVE ..... RICHARD RUSH
TOOTSIE ..... CHARLES EVANS
TOOTSIE ..... DICK RICHARDS
TOOTSIE ..... RONALD L. SCHWARY
TOOTSIE ..... SYDNEY POLLACK
TOP GUN ..... BILL BADALATO
TOP GUN ..... JERRY BRUCKHEIMER
TOP GUN ..... WARREN SKAAREN
TOP GUN ..... DON SIMPSON
TOP SECRET! ..... HUNT LOWRY
TOP SECRET! ..... JON DAVISON
TOP SECRET! ..... TOM JACOBSON
TORA! TORA! TORA! ..... ELMO WILLIAMS
TORCH SONG TRILOGY ..... HOWARD GOTTFRIED
TORCH SONG TRILOGY ..... RONALD K. FIERSTEIN
TORCHLIGHT ..... JOEL DOUGLAS
TOTAL RECALL ..... RONALD SHUSETT
TOUCH AND GO ..... HARRY COLOMBY
TOUCH AND GO ..... STEPHEN J. FRIEDMAN
TOUCH AND GO ..... JACK GROSSBERG
TOUGH ENOUGH ..... ANDREW D.T. PFEFFER
TOUGH ENOUGH ..... MICHAEL C. LEONE
TOUGH ENOUGH ..... WILLIAM S. GILMORE
TOUGH GUYS ..... JANA SUE MEMEL
TOUGH GUYS ..... JOE WIZAN
TOUGH GUYS ..... RICHARD HASHIMOTO
TOUGH GUYS DON'T DANCE ..... FRANCIS FORD COPPOLA
TOUGH GUYS DON'T DANCE ..... MENAHEM GOLAN
TOUGH GUYS DON'T DANCE ..... TOM LUDDY
TOUGH GUYS DON'T DANCE ..... YORAM GLOBUS
TOUGHER THAN LEATHER ..... RICK RUBIN
TOUGHER THAN LEATHER ..... RUSSELL SIMMONS
TOUGHER THAN LEATHER ..... VINCENT GIORDANO
TOWERING INFERNO, THE ..... IRWIN ALLEN
TOY, THE ..... PHIL FELDMAN
TOYS IN THE ATTIC ..... WALTER MIRISCH
TRACK 29 ..... DENIS O'BRIEN
TRACK 29 ..... GEORGE HARRISON
TRACK 29 ..... RICK MCCALLUM
TRACKDOWN ..... BERNARD SCHWARTZ
TRACKS ..... BERT SCHNEIDER
TRACKS ..... HOWARD ZUCKER
TRACKS ..... NORMAN IRVING COHEN
TRACKS ..... TED SHAPIRO
TRADING HEARTS ..... HERB JAFFE
TRADING HEARTS ..... MORT ENGELBERG
TRADING PLACES ..... AARON RUSSO
TRADING PLACES ..... GEORGE FOLSEY JR.
TRAIL OF THE PINK PANTHER ..... JONATHAN D. KRANE
TRAIL OF THE PINK PANTHER ..... BLAKE EDWARDS
TRAIL OF THE PINK PANTHER ..... TONY ADAMS
TRANSYLVANIA 6-5000 ..... THOMAS H. BRODEK
TRANSYLVANIA 6-5000 ..... MACE NEUFELD
TRANSYLVANIA 6-5000 ..... ARNOLD FISHMAN
TRANSYLVANIA 6-5000 ..... PAUL LICHTMAN
TRANSYLVANIA TWIST ..... ROGER KORMAN
TRANSYLVANIA TWIST ..... ALIDA CAMP
TRAVELLING NORTH ..... BEN GANNON
TRAXX ..... GARY DEVORE
TREASURE OF MATECUMBE ..... BILL ANDERSON
TREASURE OF MATECUMBE ..... RON MILLER
TREMORS ..... BRENT MADDOCK
TREMORS ..... GALE ANNE HURD
TREMORS ..... S.S. WILSON
TREMORS ..... GINNY NUGENT
TRENCHCOAT ..... JERRY LEIDER
TRIAL OF BILLY JACK, THE ..... TOM LAUGHLIN
TRIALS OF OSCAR WILDE, THE ..... ALBERT R. BROCCOLI
TRIALS OF OSCAR WILDE, THE ..... IRVING ALLEN†
TRIBUTE ..... DAVID FOSTER
TRIBUTE ..... GARTH DRABINSKY
TRIBUTE ..... JOEL B. MICHAELS
TRIBUTE ..... RICHARD S. BRIGHT
TRIBUTE ..... LAWRENCE TURMAN
TRICK OR TREAT ..... JOEL SOISSON
TRICK OR TREAT ..... MICHAEL S. MURPHEY
TRIP TO BOUNTIFUL, THE ..... GEORGE YANEFF
TRIP TO BOUNTIFUL, THE ..... HORTON FOOTE
TRIP TO BOUNTIFUL, THE ..... SAM GROGG
TRIP TO BOUNTIFUL, THE ..... STERLING VAN WAGENEN
TRIUMPH OF THE SPIRIT ..... ARNOLD KOPELSON
TRIUMPH OF THE SPIRIT ..... SHIMON ARAMA
TRIUMPHS OF A MAN CALLED HORSE ..... DEREK GIBSON
TRIUMPHS OF A MAN CALLED HORSE ..... SANDY HOWARD
TROLL ..... ALBERT BAND
TRON ..... DONALD KUSHNER
TRON ..... RON MILLER
TROOP BEVERLY HILLS ..... AVA OSTERN FRIES
TROOP BEVERLY HILLS ..... CHARLES FRIES
TROOP BEVERLY HILLS ..... MARTIN MICKELSON
TROUBLE IN MIND ..... CARY BROKAW
TROUBLE IN MIND ..... DAVID BLOCKER
TROUBLE IN MIND ..... CAROLYN PFEIFFER
TROUBLE MAN ..... JOEL FREEMAN
TROUBLE WITH DICK, THE ..... BOB AUGUR
TROUBLE WITH DICK, THE ..... GARY WALKOW
TROUBLE WITH SPIES, THE ..... BURT KENNEDY
TROUBLE WITH SPIES, THE ..... CONSTANTINE P. KAROS
TRUCK TURNER ..... FRED WEINTRAUB
TRUCK TURNER ..... PAUL HELLER
TRUE BELIEVER ..... LAWRENCE LASKER
TRUE BELIEVER ..... PATRICK CROWLEY
TRUE BELIEVER ..... PETER ROSTEN

TRUE BELIEVER ... WALTER F. PARKES
TRUE BLOOD ... PETER MARIS
TRUE CONFESSIONS ... IRWIN WINKLER
TRUE CONFESSIONS ... JAMES D. BRUBAKER
TRUE CONFESSIONS ... ROBERT CHARTOFF
TRUE LOVE ... RICHARD GUAY
TRUE LOVE ... SHELLEY HOUIS
TRUE STORIES ... GARY KURFIRST
TRUE STORIES ... KAREN MURPHY
TRUE STORIES ... EDWARD R. PRESSMAN
TRUST ME ... CURT BEUSMAN
TRUST ME ... GEORGE EDWARDS
TUCKER - THE MAN AND HIS DREAM ... FRED FUCHS
TUCKER - THE MAN AND HIS DREAM ... FRED ROOS
TUCKER - THE MAN AND HIS DREAM ... GEORGE LUCAS
TUFF TURF ... DONALD P. BORCHERS
TUFF TURF ... PAT KEHOE
TULIPS ... DON CARMODY
TULIPS ... HAROLD GREENBERG
TULIPS ... JOHN B. BENNETT
TUNNELVISION ... NEIL ISRAEL
TUNNELVISION ... JOE ROTH
TURK 182 ... PETER SAMUELSON
TURK 182 ... RENE DUPONT
TURK 182 ... ROBERT W. CORT
TURK 182 ... TED FIELD
TURNER & HOOCH ... MICHAEL HERTZBERG
TURNER & HOOCH ... MICHELE ADER
TURNER & HOOCH ... DANIEL PETRIE JR.
TURNER & HOOCH ... RAYMOND WAGNER
TURNING POINT, THE ... ARTHUR LAURENTS
TURNING POINT, THE ... HERBERT ROSS
TURTLE DIARY ... PETER SNELL
TURTLE DIARY ... RICHARD JOHNSON
TWELVE ANGRY MEN ... HENRY FONDA†
TWELVE ANGRY MEN ... REGINALD ROSE
TWELVE CHAIRS, THE ... MICHAEL HERTZBERG
TWICE IN A LIFETIME ... BUD YORKIN
TWICE IN A LIFETIME ... DAVID SALVEN
TWICE UPON A TIME ... BILL COUTURIE
TWICE UPON A TIME ... GEORGE LUCAS
TWILIGHT ZONE - THE MOVIE ... GEORGE FOLSEY JR.
TWILIGHT ZONE - THE MOVIE ... STEVEN SPIELBERG
TWILIGHT ZONE - THE MOVIE ... FRANK MARSHALL
TWILIGHT ZONE - THE MOVIE ... JOHN LANDIS
TWILIGHT ZONE - THE MOVIE ... JON DAVISON
TWILIGHT ZONE - THE MOVIE ... MICHAEL FINNELL
TWILIGHT ZONE - THE MOVIE ... KATHLEEN KENNEDY
TWILIGHT'S LAST GLEAMING ... HELMUT JEDELE
TWILIGHT'S LAST GLEAMING ... MERV ADELSON
TWINKY ... JOHN HEYMAN
TWINS ... IVAN REITMAN
TWINS ... JOE MEDJUCK
TWINS ... MICHAEL C. GROSS
TWISTED NERVE ... FRANK GRANAT
TWISTED NERVE ... GEORGE W. GEORGE
TWISTER ... DAN IRELAND
TWISTER ... WIELAND SCHULZ-KEIL
TWISTER ... WILLIAM J. QUIGLEY
TWO FOR THE ROAD ... STANLEY DONEN
TWO FOR THE SEESAW ... WALTER MIRISCH
TWO JAKES, THE ... HAROLD SCHNEIDER
TWO JAKES, THE ... ROBERT EVANS
TWO MINUTE WARNING ... CHARLES R. MEEKER
TWO MINUTE WARNING ... EDWARD S. FELDMAN
TWO MOON JUNCTION ... DON LEVIN
TWO MOON JUNCTION ... DONALD P. BORCHERS
TWO MOON JUNCTION ... MEL PEARL
TWO OF A KIND ... JOE WIZAN
TWO OF A KIND ... ROGER M. ROTHSTEIN†
TWO-LANE BLACKTOP ... MICHAEL S. LAUGHLIN

U

U2: RATTLE AND HUM ... MICHAEL HAMLYN
U2: RATTLE AND HUM ... PAUL MCGUINNESS
UFORIA ... BARRY KROST
UFORIA ... GORDON WOLF
UFORIA ... MELVIN SIMON
UFORIA ... SUSAN SPINKS
UHF ... DEREN GETZ
UHF ... GENE KIRKWOOD
UHF ... GRAY FREDERICKSON
UHF ... JOHN HYDE
UHF ... KEVIN BRESLIN
ULZANA'S RAID ... CARTER DE HAVEN
UNBEARABLE LIGHTNESS OF BEING, THE ... BERTIL OHLSSON
UNBEARABLE LIGHTNESS OF BEING, THE ... SAUL ZAENTZ
UNCLE BUCK ... JOHN HUGHES
UNCLE BUCK ... TOM JACOBSON
UNCLE JOE SHANNON ... GENE KIRKWOOD
UNCLE JOE SHANNON ... IRWIN WINKLER
UNCLE JOE SHANNON ... ROBERT CHARTOFF
UNCOMMON VALOR ... JOHN MILIUS
UNCOMMON VALOR ... BUZZ FEITSHANS
UNDER COVER ... MENAHEM GOLAN
UNDER COVER ... YORAM GLOBUS
UNDER FIRE ... ANNA ROTH
UNDER FIRE ... EDWARD TEETS
UNDER FIRE ... JONATHAN T. TAPLIN
UNDER THE BOARDWALK ... DAVID SAUNDERS
UNDER THE BOARDWALK ... GREGORY S. BLACKWELL
UNDER THE BOARDWALK ... MATTHEW IRMAS
UNDER THE BOARDWALK ... STEVEN H. CHANIN
UNDER THE CHERRY MOON ... JOSEPH RUFFALO
UNDER THE CHERRY MOON ... ROBERT CAVALLO
UNDER THE CHERRY MOON ... STEVEN FARGNOLI
UNDER THE CHERRY MOON ... GRAHAM COTTLE
UNDER THE VOLCANO ... MICHAEL FITZGERALD
UNDER THE VOLCANO ... MORITZ BORMAN
UNDER THE VOLCANO ... WIELAND SCHULZ-KEIL
UNDERGROUND ACES ... JAY WESTON
UNDERGROUND ACES ... SAMUEL Z. ARKOFF
UNFAITHFULLY YOURS ... JACK B. BERNSTEIN
UNFAITHFULLY YOURS ... DANIEL MELNICK
UNFAITHFULLY YOURS ... JOE WIZAN
UNFAITHFULLY YOURS ... MARVIN WORTH
UNHOLY, THE ... WILLIAM J. QUIGLEY
UNIDENTIFIED FLYING ODDBALL ... RON MILLER
UNION CITY ... GRAHAM BELIN
UNMARRIED WOMAN, AN ... TONY RAY
UNMARRIED WOMAN, AN ... PAUL MAZURSKY
UNNAMEABLE, THE ... DEAN RAMSER
UNNAMEABLE, THE ... JEAN-PAUL OUELETTE
UNNAMEABLE, THE ... PAUL WHITE
UNTIL SEPTEMBER ... MICHAEL GRUSKOFF
UNTOUCHABLES, THE ... ART LINSON
UNTOUCHABLES, THE ... RAY HARTWICK
UP IN SMOKE ... LOU ADLER
UP IN SMOKE ... LOU LOMBARDO
UP THE CREEK ... FRED BAUM
UP THE CREEK ... LOUIS S. ARKOFF
UP THE CREEK ... MICHAEL MELTZER
UP THE CREEK ... SAMUEL Z. ARKOFF
UP THE DOWN STAIRCASE ... ALAN J. PAKULA
UP THE SANDBOX ... IRWIN WINKLER
UP THE SANDBOX ... MARTIN ERLICHMAN
UP THE SANDBOX ... ROBERT CHARTOFF
UPTOWN SATURDAY NIGHT ... MELVILLE TUCKER
URANIUM CONSPIRACY, THE ... FRANCESCO CORTI
URANIUM CONSPIRACY, THE ... YORAM GLOBUS
URBAN COWBOY ... IRVING AZOFF
URBAN COWBOY ... C.O. ERICKSON
URBAN COWBOY ... ROBERT EVANS
URGH! A MUSIC WAR ... MICHAEL WHITE
USED CARS ... BOB GALE
USED CARS ... JOHN MILIUS
USED CARS ... STEVEN SPIELBERG

V

VALACHI PAPERS, THE ... DINO DE LAURENTIIS
VALENTINO ... IRWIN WINKLER
VALENTINO ... ROBERT CHARTOFF
VALENTINO RETURNS ... DAVID WISNIEVITZ
VALENTINO RETURNS ... PETER HOFFMAN
VALLEY GIRL ... ANDREW LANE
VALLEY GIRL ... MICHAEL ROSENBLATT
VALLEY GIRL ... THOMAS COLEMAN
VALLEY GIRL ... WAYNE CRAWFORD
VALMONT ... MICHAEL HAUSMAN
VALMONT ... PAUL RANNAM
VAMP ... DONALD P. BORCHERS
VAMPIRE'S KISS ... BARBARA ZITWER
VAMPIRE'S KISS ... BARRY SHILS
VAMPIRE'S KISS ... DEREK GIBSON
VAMPIRE'S KISS ... JOHN DALY
VARIETY ... R.A. SHAFRANSKY
VENOM ... MARTIN BREGMAN
VENOM ... RICHARD R. ST. JOHNS
VENOM ... LOUIS A. STROLLER
VERDICT, THE ... BURTT HARRIS
VERDICT, THE ... DAVID BROWN
VERDICT, THE ... RICHARD D. ZANUCK
VERNON, FLORIDA ... ERROL MORRIS
VERONIKA VOSS ... THOMAS SCHUEHLY
VIBES ... DEBORAH BLUM
VIBES ... RAY HARTWICK
VIBES ... RON HOWARD
VIBES ... TONY GANZ
VICE SQUAD ... BOB REHME
VICE SQUAD ... BRIAN FRANKISH
VICE SQUAD ... FRANK CAPRA JR.
VICE SQUAD ... FRANK E. HILDEBRAND
VICE SQUAD ... SANDY HOWARD
VICE VERSA ... ALAN LADD JR.
VICE VERSA ... DICK CLEMENT
VICE VERSA ... IAN LA FRENAIS
VICIOUS ... CHARLES HANNAH
VICIOUS ... DAVID HANNAY
VICIOUS ... LYNN BARKER
VICIOUS ... TOM BROADBRIDGE
VICTOR/VICTORIA ... BLAKE EDWARDS
VICTOR/VICTORIA ... TONY ADAMS
VICTORY ... FREDDIE FIELDS
VICTORY ... GORDON MCLENDON
VIDEODROME ... CLAUDE HEROUX
VIDEODROME ... LAWRENCE NESIS
VIDEODROME ... PIERRE DAVID
VIDEODROME ... VICTOR SOLNICKI
VIEW TO A KILL, A ... ALBERT R. BROCCOLI
VIGILANTE FORCE ... GENE CORMAN
VILLAIN ... ALAN LADD JR.
VILLAIN ... ELLIOTT KASTNER
VILLAIN ... JAY KANTER
VILLAIN, THE ... PAUL MASLANSKY
VILLAIN, THE ... MORT ENGELBERG
VIOLETS ARE BLUE ... MARYKAY POWELL
VIOLETS ARE BLUE ... RICHARD A. ROTH
VIPER ... PETER MARIS
VISION QUEST ... PETER GUBER
VISION QUEST ... STAN WESTON
VISION QUEST ... ADAM FIELDS
VISION QUEST ... JON PETERS
VISIONS OF EIGHT ... DAVID L. WOLPER
VISIONS OF EIGHT ... STAN MARGULIES
VISIONS OF EIGHT ... TED MANN
VISITING HOURS ... CLAUDE HEROUX
VISITING HOURS ... PIERRE DAVID
VISITING HOURS ... VICTOR SOLNICKI
VITAL SIGNS ... CATHLEEN SUMMERS
VITAL SIGNS ... LAURIE PERLMAN
VOICES ... JOE WIZAN
VOLUNTEERS ... RICHARD SHEPHERD
VOLUNTEERS ... THEODORE R. PARVIN
VOLUNTEERS ... WALTER F. PARKES
VON RICHTOFEN AND BROWN ... GENE CORMAN
VOYAGE TO THE BOTTOM OF THE SEA ... IRWIN ALLEN

W

W.C. FIELDS AND ME ... JAY WESTON
WAIT UNTIL SPRING, BANDINI ... AMADEO PAGANI
WAIT UNTIL SPRING, BANDINI ... CHRISTIAN CHARRET
WAIT UNTIL SPRING, BANDINI ... CYRIL DE ROUVRE
WAIT UNTIL SPRING, BANDINI ... ERWIN PROVOOST
WAIT UNTIL SPRING, BANDINI ... FRED ROOS
WAIT UNTIL SPRING, BANDINI ... GIORGIO SILVAGO
WAIT UNTIL SPRING, BANDINI ... TOM LUDDY
WAITING FOR THE LIGHT ... CALDECOTT CHUBB
WAITING FOR THE LIGHT ... EDWARD R. PRESSMAN
WAITING FOR THE LIGHT ... RON BOZMAN
WAITING FOR THE MOON ... FREDERIC BOURBOULON
WAITING FOR THE MOON ... LINDSAY LAW
WAITING FOR THE MOON ... SANDRA SCHULBERG
WALK LIKE A MAN ... LEONARD KROLL
WALK LIKE A MAN ... ROBERT KLANE
WALK ON THE MOON, A ... DINA SILVER
WALK WITH LOVE AND DEATH, A ... CARTER DE HAVEN
WALKABOUT ... SI LITVINOFF
WALKER ... ANGEL FLORES-MARINI
WALKER ... CARLOS ALVAREZ
WALKER ... EDWARD R. PRESSMAN
WALKING STICK, THE ... ALAN LADD JR.
WALKING STICK, THE ... ELLIOTT KASTNER
WALL STREET ... A. KITMAN HO
WALL STREET ... EDWARD R. PRESSMAN
WALL TIME ... HOWARD ROSENMAN
WALTZ ACROSS TEXAS ... MARK LEVINSON
WALTZ ACROSS TEXAS ... MARTIN JUROW
WALTZ ACROSS TEXAS ... SCOTT M. ROSENFELT

WANDA NEVADA .... NEAL DOBROFSKY
WANDA NEVADA .... WILLIAM HAYWARD
WANDERERS, THE .... MARTIN RANSOHOFF
WANDERERS, THE .... RICHARD R. ST. JOHNS
WANTED DEAD OR ALIVE .... MICHAEL PATRICK GOODMAN
WANTED DEAD OR ALIVE .... ARTHUR M. SARKISSIAN
WANTED DEAD OR ALIVE .... BARRY BERNARDI
WANTED DEAD OR ALIVE .... ROBERT C. PETERS
WAR OF THE ROSES, THE .... ARNON MILCHAN
WAR OF THE ROSES, THE .... JAMES L. BROOKS
WAR OF THE ROSES, THE .... DOUG CLAYBOURNE
WAR OF THE ROSES, THE .... POLLY PLATT
WAR PARTY .... BERNARD WILLIAMS
WAR PARTY .... CHRIS CHESSER
WAR PARTY .... DEREK GIBSON
WAR PARTY .... FRANC RODDAM
WAR PARTY .... JOHN DALY
WARGAMES .... HAROLD SCHNEIDER
WARGAMES .... LEONARD J. GOLDBERG
WARLOCK .... ARNOLD KOPELSON
WARLOCK .... STEVE MINER
WARLORDS OF THE 21ST CENTURY .... LLOYD PHILLIPS
WARLORDS OF THE 21ST CENTURY .... ROBERT WHITEHOUSE
WARM DECEMBER, A .... MELVILLE TUCKER
WARM SUMMER RAIN .... CASSIAN ELWES
WARM SUMMER RAIN .... LIONEL WIGRAM
WARM SUMMER RAIN .... PATRICIA FOULKROD
WARNING SIGN .... JIM BLOOM
WARNING SIGN .... MATTHEW ROBBINS
WARRIOR AND THE SORCERESS .... ROGER CORMAN
WARRIOR QUEEN .... HARRY ALAN TOWERS
WARRIORS OF THE LOST WORLD .... FRANK E. HILDEBRAND
WARRIORS OF THE LOST WORLD .... ROBERTO BESSI
WARRIORS, THE .... FRANK MARSHALL
WARRIORS, THE .... JOEL SILVER
WARRIORS, THE .... LAWRENCE GORDON
WASH, THE .... CALVIN SKAGGS
WASH, THE .... LINDSAY LAW
WATCHER IN THE WOODS, THE .... RON MILLER
WATCHER IN THE WOODS, THE .... TOM LEETCH
WATCHERS .... DAMIAN LEE
WATCHERS .... DAVID MITCHELL
WATCHERS .... ROGER CORMAN
WATER .... DAVID WIMBURY
WATER .... DENIS O'BRIEN
WATER .... GEORGE HARRISON
WATER .... IAN LA FRENAIS
WATERHOLE #3 .... KEN WALES
WATERLOO .... DINO DE LAURENTIIS
WATERSHIP DOWN .... MARTIN ROSEN
WATTSTAX .... DAVID L. WOLPER
WAVELENGTH .... JAMES ROSENFIELD
WAVELENGTH .... MAURICE ROSENFIELD
WAXWORK .... DAN IRELAND
WAXWORK .... GREGORY CASCANTE
WAXWORK .... MARIO SOTELA
WAXWORK .... STAFAN AHRENBERG
WAXWORK .... WILLIAM J. QUIGLEY
WAY WE WERE , THE .... RAY STARK
WAY WE WERE, THE .... RICHARD ROTH
WE ARE THE LAMBETH BOYS .... LEON CLORE
WE THINK THE WORLD OF YOU .... HUGH STODDART
WE THINK THE WORLD OF YOU .... PAUL COWAN
WE THINK THE WORLD OF YOU .... TOMASSO JANDELLI
WE'RE NO ANGELS .... ART LINSON
WE'RE NO ANGELS .... FRED CARUSO
WE'RE NO ANGELS .... ROBERT DE NIRO
WEDDING, A .... ROBERT ALTMAN
WEDDING, A .... TOMMY THOMPSON
WEDDING, A .... SCOTT BUSHNELL
WEDNESDAY'S CHILD .... TONY GARNETT
WEEDS .... BILL BADALATO
WEEDS .... BILLY CROSS
WEEDS .... MEL PEARL
WEEKEND AT BERNIE'S .... MALCOLM R. HARDING
WEEKEND AT BERNIE'S .... ROBERT KLANE
WEEKEND AT BERNIE'S .... VICTOR DRAI
WEIRD SCIENCE .... JOEL SILVER
WELCOME HOME .... DON CARMODY
WELCOME HOME .... MARTIN RANSOHOFF
WELCOME HOME, ROXY CARMICHAEL .... PENNY FINKELMAN COX
WELCOME TO 18 .... BRUCE W. BROWN
WELCOME TO 18 .... DAVID C. THOMAS
WELCOME TO L.A. .... ROBERT ALTMAN
WEST SIDE STORY .... ROBERT WISE
WETHERBY .... SIMON RELPH
WHALES OF AUGUST, THE .... CAROLYN PFEIFFER
WHALES OF AUGUST, THE .... MIKE KAPLAN
WHALES OF AUGUST, THE .... SHEP GORDON
WHAT COMES AROUND .... JERRY REED
WHAT COMES AROUND .... TED EVANSON
WHAT'S THE MATTER WITH HELEN? .... CHARLES R. MEEKER
WHAT'S THE MATTER WITH HELEN? .... EDWARD S. FELDMAN
WHAT'S UP TIGER LILY? .... HENRY G. SAPERSTEIN
WHAT'S UP, DOC? .... PETER BOGDANOVICH
WHAT? .... ANDREW BRAUNSBERG
WHATEVER IT TAKES .... BOB DEMCHUK
WHEELS OF FIRE .... ROGER CORMAN
WHEN A STRANGER CALLS .... BARRY KROST
WHEN A STRANGER CALLS .... MELVIN SIMON
WHEN A STRANGER CALLS .... STEVE FEKE
WHEN A STRANGER CALLS .... DOUG CHAPIN
WHEN EIGHT BELLS TOLL .... ELLIOTT KASTNER
WHEN HARRY MET SALLY... .... ANDREW SCHEINMAN
WHEN HARRY MET SALLY... .... JEFFREY STOTT
WHEN HARRY MET SALLY... .... ROB REINER
WHEN HARRY MET SALLY... .... STEVE NICOLAIDES
WHEN THE WHALES CAME .... GEOFFREY WANSELL
WHEN THE WHALES CAME .... SIMON CHANNING-WILLIAMS
WHEN TIME RAN OUT .... IRWIN ALLEN
WHEN YOU COMIN' BACK, RED RYDER .... PAUL MASLANSKY
WHERE ARE THE CHILDREN .... ZEV BRAUN
WHERE EAGLES DARE .... ELLIOTT KASTNER
WHERE THE BOYS ARE '84 .... ALLAN CARR
WHERE THE BUFFALO ROAM .... ART LINSON
WHERE THE HEART IS .... EDGAR F. GROSS
WHERE THE HEART IS .... JOHN BOORMAN
WHERE THE LILIES BLOOM .... ROBERT B. RADNITZ
WHERE THE RIVER RUNS BLACK .... BRUNO BARRETO
WHERE THE RIVER RUNS BLACK .... DAN FARRELL
WHERE THE RIVER RUNS BLACK .... FLAVIO R. TAMBELLINI
WHERE THE RIVER RUNS BLACK .... HARRY UFLAND
WHERE THE RIVER RUNS BLACK .... JAMES G. ROBINSON
WHERE THE RIVER RUNS BLACK .... JOE ROTH
WHERE'S JACK? .... MICHAEL DEELEY
WHERE'S POPPA .... JERRY TOKOFSKY
WHERE'S POPPA? .... MARVIN WORTH
WHISTLE BLOWER, THE .... GEOFFREY REEVE
WHISTLE BLOWER, THE .... JAMES REEVE
WHITE BUFFALO, THE .... PANCHO KOHNER
WHITE DAWN, THE .... MARTIN RANSOHOFF
WHITE DOG .... JON DAVISON
WHITE DOG .... EDGAR J. SCHERICK
WHITE GIRL, THE .... DWIGHT WILLIAMS
WHITE GIRL, THE .... JAMES CANNADY
WHITE HUNTER, BLACK HEART .... CLINT EASTWOOD
WHITE HUNTER, BLACK HEART .... DAVID VALDES
WHITE LINE FEVER .... JOHN KEMENY
WHITE MISCHIEF .... MICHAEL WHITE
WHITE MISCHIEF .... SIMON PERRY
WHITE NIGHTS .... BILL BORDEN
WHITE NIGHTS .... TAYLOR HACKFORD
WHITE NIGHTS .... WILLIAM S. GILMORE
WHITE OF THE EYE .... BRAD WYMAN
WHITE OF THE EYE .... CASSIAN ELWES
WHITE WATER SUMMER .... MARK TARLOV
WHITE WATER SUMMER .... WOLFGANG GLATTES
WHO FRAMED ROGER RABBIT .... STEVEN SPIELBERG
WHO FRAMED ROGER RABBIT .... FRANK MARSHALL
WHO FRAMED ROGER RABBIT .... ROBERT WATTS
WHO FRAMED ROGER RABBIT .... KATHLEEN KENNEDY
WHO IS KILLING THE GREAT CHEFS OF EUROPE? .... MERV ADELSON
WHO IS KILLING THE GREAT CHEFS OF EUROPE? .... LEE RICH
WHO IS KILLING THE GREAT CHEFS OF EUROPE? .... WILLIAM ALDRICH
WHO'LL STOP THE RAIN .... GABRIEL KATZKA†
WHO'LL STOP THE RAIN .... HERB JAFFE
WHO'S AFRAID OF VIRGINIA WOOLF? .... ERNEST LEHMAN
WHO'S HARRY CRUMB? .... ARNON MILCHAN
WHO'S HARRY CRUMB? .... JOHN CANDY
WHO'S THAT GIRL .... BERNARD WILLIAMS
WHO'S THAT GIRL .... JON PETERS
WHO'S THAT GIRL .... PETER GUBER
WHO'S THAT GIRL .... ROGER BIRNBAUM
WHO'S THAT GIRL .... ROSILYN HELLER
WHOLLY MOSES! .... DAVID BEGELMAN
WHOLLY MOSES! .... FREDDIE FIELDS
WHOOPEE BOYS, THE .... DAVID OBST
WHOOPEE BOYS, THE .... JEFF BUHAI
WHOOPEE BOYS, THE .... PETER MACGREGOR-SCOTT
WHOOPEE BOYS, THE .... STEVE ZACHARIAS
WHOOPEE BOYS, THE .... ADAM FIELDS
WHOOPS APOCALYPSE .... BRIAN EASTMAN
WHOSE LIFE IS IT ANYWAY? .... LAWRENCE P. BACHMANN
WHOSE LIFE IS IT ANYWAY? .... MARTIN C. SCHUTE
WHOSE LIFE IS IT ANYWAY? .... RAY COONEY
WHY ME? .... IRWIN YABLINS
WHY ME? .... MARJORIE ISRAEL
WHY WOULD I LIE? .... JAMES L. STEWART
WHY WOULD I LIE? .... PANCHO KOHNER
WHY WOULD I LIE? .... RICH IRVINE
WICHITA .... WALTER MIRISCH
WICKED LADY, THE .... MENAHEM GOLAN
WICKED LADY, THE .... YORAM GLOBUS
WICKED STEPMOTHER .... ROBERT LITTMAN
WICKER MAN, THE .... PETER SNELL
WILD AT HEART .... MONTY MONTGOMERY
WILD AT HEART .... SIGURJON SIGHVATSSON
WILD AT HEART .... STEVEN GOLIN
WILD BUNCH, THE .... PHIL FELDMAN
WILD COUNTRY, THE .... RON MILLER
WILD HORSES .... GARY HAUNAN
WILD HORSES .... JOHN BARNETT
WILD LIFE, THE .... CAMERON CROWE
WILD LIFE, THE .... DON PHILLIPS
WILD LIFE, THE .... ART LINSON
WILD LIFE, THE .... C.O. ERICKSON
WILD ONE, THE .... STANLEY KRAMER
WILD PACK, THE .... HALL BARTLETT
WILD PAIR, THE .... HELEN SARLUI-TUCKER
WILD PAIR, THE .... PAUL MASON
WILD PAIR, THE .... RANDALL TORNO
WILD PARTY, THE .... ISMAIL MERCHANT
WILD RACERS, THE .... TAMARA ASSEYEV
WILD RACERS, THE .... ROGER CORMAN
WILD RIDE, THE .... ROGER CORMAN
WILD ROVERS, THE .... BLAKE EDWARDS
WILD ROVERS, THE .... TONY ADAMS
WILD SEED , THE .... ALBERT S. RUDDY
WILD THING .... DAVID CALLOWAY
WILD THING .... MICHAEL ROSENBLATT
WILD THING .... NICOLAS CLERMONT
WILD THING .... THOMAS COLEMAN
WILDCATS .... ANTHEA SYLBERT
WILDCATS .... GORDON A. WEBB
WILDFIRE .... HUNT LOWRY
WILDFIRE .... IRVIN KERSHNER
WILDFIRE .... JERRY TOKOFSKY
WILDFIRE .... STANLEY R. ZUPNIK
WILDROSE .... JOHN HANSON
WILDROSE .... SANDRA SCHULBERG
WILL VINTON'S FESTIVAL OF CLAYMATION .... WILL VINTON
WILLIE AND PHIL .... PAUL MAZURSKY
WILLIE AND PHIL .... TONY RAY
WILLIE DYNAMITE .... DAVID BROWN
WILLIE DYNAMITE .... RICHARD D. ZANUCK
WILLOW .... NIGEL WOOLL
WILLOW .... GEORGE LUCAS
WILLY WONKA AND THE CHOCOLATE FACTORY .... TED MANN
WILLY WONKA AND THE CHOCOLATE FACTORY .... DAVID L. WOLPER
WILLY WONKA AND THE CHOCOLATE FACTORY .... STAN MARGULIES
WIND AND THE LION, THE .... HERB JAFFE
WINDOWS .... JOHN NICOLELLA
WINDOWS .... MICHAEL LOBELL
WINDY CITY .... ALAN GREISMAN
WINNERS TAKE ALL .... CHRISTOPHER W. KNIGHT
WINNERS TAKE ALL .... DAVID R. AXELROD
WINNERS TAKE ALL .... TOM TATUM
WINNING .... JENNINGS LANG
WINNING .... JOHN FOREMAN
WINTER FLIGHT .... ROBIN DOUET
WINTER FLIGHT .... SUSAN RICHARDS
WINTER FLIGHT .... DAVID PUTTNAM
WINTER KILLS .... FRED CARUSO
WINTER KILLS .... LEONARD J. GOLDBERG
WINTER KILLS .... ROBERT STERLING
WINTER PEOPLE .... ROBERT H. SOLO
WINTER TAN, A .... LOUISE CLARK
WIRED .... CHARLES R. MEEKER
WIRED .... EDWARD S. FELDMAN
WIRED .... P. MICHAEL SMITH

WIRED .... PAUL CARRAN
WISDOM .... BERNARD WILLIAMS
WISDOM .... ROBERT WISE
WISE BLOOD .... KATHY FITZGERALD
WISE BLOOD .... MICHAEL FITZGERALD
WISE GUYS .... AARON RUSSO
WISE GUYS .... IRWIN RUSSO
WISE GUYS .... PATRICK MCCORMICK
WISH YOU WERE HERE .... SARAH RADCLYFFE
WITCHBOARD .... RON MITCHELL
WITCHBOARD .... WALTER JOSTEN
WITCHES, THE .... DUSTY SYMONDS
WITCHES, THE .... JIM HENSON
WITCHES, THE .... MARK SHIVAS
WITCHES OF EASTWICK, THE .... JON PETERS
WITCHES OF EASTWICK, THE .... NEIL CANTON
WITCHES OF EASTWICK, THE .... PETER GUBER
WITHNAIL AND I .... DAVID WIMBURY
WITHNAIL AND I .... LAWRENCE KIRSTEIN
WITHNAIL AND I .... PAUL HELLER
WITHOUT A CLUE .... MARC STIRDIVANT
WITHOUT A TRACE .... STANLEY R. JAFFE
WITNESS .... DAVID BOMBYK†
WITNESS .... EDWARD S. FELDMAN
WITNESS .... CHARLES R. MEEKER
WIZ, THE .... KEN HARPER
WIZ, THE .... ROB COHEN
WIZARD OF LONELINESS, THE .... LINDSAY LAW
WIZARD OF LONELINESS, THE .... PHILIP PORCELLA
WIZARD OF LONELINESS, THE .... THOM TYSON
WIZARD OF SPEED AND TIME, THE .... DEVEN CHIERIGHINO
WIZARD OF SPEED AND TIME, THE .... DON ROCHANBEAU
WIZARD OF SPEED AND TIME, THE .... RICHARD KAYE
WIZARD, THE .... DAVID CHISOLM
WIZARD, THE .... KEN TOPOLSKY
WIZARD, THE .... LINDSLEY PARSONS JR.
WIZARDS .... RALPH BAKSHI
WIZARDS OF THE LOST KINGDOM .... ALEX SESSA
WIZARDS OF THE LOST KINGDOM .... FRANK ISAAC
WOLFEN .... RUPERT HITZIG
WOLFEN .... ALAN KING
WOMAN IN RED, THE .... JACK FROST SANDERS
WOMAN IN RED, THE .... VICTOR DRAI
WOMAN UNDER THE INFLUENCE, A .... SAM SHAW
WOMEN IN LOVE .... LARRY KRAMER
WOMEN IN LOVE .... ROY BAIRD
WOMEN'S CLUB, THE .... FRED WEINTRAUB
WOMEN'S CLUB, THE .... MARTIN HORNSTEIN
WON TON TON, THE DOG WHO SAVED HOLLYWOOD .... ARNOLD SCHULMAN
WON TON TON, THE DOG WHO SAVED HOLLYWOOD .... MICHAEL WINNER
WON TON TON, THE DOG WHO SAVED HOLLYWOOD .... DAVID V. PICKER
WONDERLAND .... STEVE MORRISON
WONDERLAND .... ROBIN DOUET
WONDERWALL .... ANDREW BRAUNSBERG
WORKING GIRL .... DOUGLAS WICK
WORKING GIRL .... LAURENCE MARK
WORKING GIRL .... ROBERT GREENHUT
WORKING GIRLS .... ANDI GLADSTONE
WORKING GIRLS .... LIZZIE BORDEN
WORLD ACCORDING TO GARP, THE .... GEORGE ROY HILL
WORLD ACCORDING TO GARP, THE .... PATRICK KELLEY
WORLD ACCORDING TO GARP, THE .... ROBERT L. CRAWFORD
WORLD APART, A .... GRAHAM BRADSTREET
WORLD APART, A .... SARAH RADCLYFFE
WORLD APART, A .... TIM BEVAN
WORLD GONE WILD .... ROBERT L. ROSEN
WORLD OF HENRY ORIENT, THE .... JEROME HELLMAN
WORLD OF SUZIE WONG, THE .... RAY STARK
WORTH WINNING .... DALE POLLOCK
WORTH WINNING .... GIL FRIESEN
WORTH WINNING .... TOM JOYNER
WRAITH, THE .... JOHN KEMENY
WRONG GUYS, THE .... CHARLES GORDON
WRONG GUYS, THE .... PAUL DEMEO
WRONG GUYS, THE .... RONALD E. FRAZIER
WRONG IS RIGHT .... ANDREW FOGELSON
WRONG IS RIGHT .... RICHARD BROOKS
WUSA .... PAUL NEWMAN
WUSA .... JOHN FOREMAN
WUSA .... HANK MOONJEAN
WUTHERING HEIGHTS .... SAMUEL Z. ARKOFF

X

X - THE MAN WITH X-RAY EYES .... JAMES H. NICHOLSON†
X - THE MAN WITH X-RAY EYES .... SAMUEL Z. ARKOFF
X, Y, AND ZEE .... ALAN LADD JR.
X, Y, AND ZEE .... JAY KANTER
X, Y, AND ZEE .... ELLIOTT KASTNER
XANADU .... LAWRENCE GORDON
XANADU .... LEE KRAMER
XANADU .... JOEL SILVER
XTRO .... MARK FORSTATER
XTRO .... ROBERT SHAYE

Y

YAKUZA, THE .... SYDNEY POLLACK
YANKS .... JOSEPH JANNI
YANKS .... LESTER PERSKY
YEAR OF LIVING DANGEROUSLY, THE .... JAMES MCELROY
YEAR OF THE DRAGON .... DINO DE LAURENTIIS
YELLOWBEARD .... CARTER DE HAVEN
YELLOWBEARD .... DEREK GIBSON
YELLOWBEARD .... JOHN DALY
YENTL .... BARBRA STREISAND
YENTL .... RUSTY LEMORANDE
YENTL .... LARRY DE WAAY
YES, GIORGIO .... ALAIN BERNHEIM
YES, GIORGIO .... HERBERT H. BRESLIN
YES, GIORGIO .... PETER FETTERMAN
YES, GIORGIO .... TERRY CARR
YESTERDAY'S HERO .... ELLIOTT KASTNER
YESTERDAY'S HERO .... KEN REGAN
YESTERDAY'S HERO .... OSCAR S. LERMAN
YOU CAN'T HURRY LOVE .... ELLEN STELOFF
YOU CAN'T HURRY LOVE .... JONATHAN D. KRANE
YOU CAN'T HURRY LOVE .... LAWRENCE KASANOFF
YOU CAN'T WIN 'EM ALL .... GENE CORMAN
YOU ONLY LIVE TWICE .... ALBERT R. BROCCOLI
YOU ONLY LIVE TWICE .... HARRY SALTZMAN
YOU TALKIN' TO ME? .... MICHAEL POLAIRE
YOU'RE A BIG BOY NOW .... PHIL FELDMAN
YOUNG DOCTORS IN LOVE .... GARRY MARSHALL
YOUNG DOCTORS IN LOVE .... JERRY BRUCKHEIMER
YOUNG DOCTORS IN LOVE .... NICK ABDO
YOUNG DOCTORS, THE .... LAWRENCE TURMAN
YOUNG DOCTORS, THE .... STUART MILLAR
YOUNG EINSTEIN .... DAVID ROACH
YOUNG EINSTEIN .... GRAHAM BURKE
YOUNG EINSTEIN .... RAY BEATTIE
YOUNG EINSTEIN .... WARWICK ROSS
YOUNG EINSTEIN .... YAHOO SERIOUS
YOUNG FRANKENSTEIN .... MICHAEL GRUSKOFF
YOUNG GUNS .... CHRISTOPHER CAIN
YOUNG GUNS .... IRBY SMITH
YOUNG GUNS .... JAMES G. ROBINSON
YOUNG GUNS .... JOE ROTH
YOUNG GUNS .... JOHN FUSCO
YOUNG GUNS .... PAUL SCHIFF
YOUNG REBEL , THE .... HENRY T. WEINSTEIN
YOUNG SHERLOCK HOLMES .... STEVEN SPIELBERG
YOUNG SHERLOCK HOLMES .... HARRY BENN
YOUNG SHERLOCK HOLMES .... MARK JOHNSON
YOUNG SHERLOCK HOLMES .... FRANK MARSHALL
YOUNG SHERLOCK HOLMES .... KATHLEEN KENNEDY
YOUNG TOSCANINI .... TARAK BEN AMMAR
YOUNG WARRIORS .... VICTORIA MEYERINK
YOUNGBLOOD .... PATRICK C. WELLS
YOUNGBLOOD .... PETER BART
YOUNGBLOOD .... PETER GUBER
YOUNGBLOOD .... JON PETERS

Z

ZACHARIAH .... GEORGE ENGLUND
ZACHARIAH .... LAWRENCE KUBIK
ZARAK .... ALBERT R. BROCCOLI
ZARAK .... IRVING ALLEN†
ZARDOZ .... JOHN BOORMAN
ZELIG .... CHARLES H. JOFFE
ZELIG .... JACK ROLLINS
ZELIG .... ROBERT GREENHUT
ZELLY AND ME .... ELLIOTT LEWITT
ZELLY AND ME .... SUE JETT
ZELLY AND ME .... TINA RATHBORNE
ZELLY AND ME .... TONY MARK
ZOMBIE HIGH .... AZIZ GHAZAL
ZOMBIE HIGH .... CASSIAN ELWES
ZOMBIE HIGH .... MARC TOBEROFF
ZONE TROOPERS .... PAUL DEMEO
ZONE TROOPERS .... CHARLES BAND
ZOO GANG, THE .... JOHN WATSON
ZOO GANG, THE .... PEN DENSHAM
ZOO GANG, THE .... RICHARD B. LEWIS
ZOOT SUIT .... GORDON DAVIDSON
ZOOT SUIT .... PETER BURRELL
ZORRO, THE GAY BLADE .... GEORGE HAMILTON
ZORRO, THE GAY BLADE .... C.O. ERICKSON

STUDIO

STUDIOS

A

A & M FILMS, INC.
1416 N. La Brea Ave.
Hollywood, CA 90028
213/469-2411

President .... Jerry Moss
Executive Vice President - Production ..... Dale Pollock
Senior Executive - Production .... Lianne Halfon
Development Executive .... George Kemblith
Story Editor .... Ross Canter

ABC
CAPITAL CITIES/ABC, INC.
24 E. 51st St.
New York, NY 10022-6887
212/421-9595

Chairman .... Thomas S. Murphy
President & CEO .... Daniel B. Burke
President - ABC Communications .... Phillip J. Meek
Executive Vice President .... Joseph P. Dougherty
Senior Vice President & Chief Financial Officer .... Ronald J. Doerfler
Senior Vice President & General Counsel .... Stephen A. Weiswasser
Senior Vice President - European Operations .... Richard Spinner
Vice President - Policy & Standards .... Alfred R. Schneider
Vice President - Corporate Communications .... Patricia J. Matson

ABC Network Division
1330 Avenue of the Americas
New York, NY 10019
212/887-7777

4151 Prospect Ave.
Los Angeles, CA 90027
213/557-7777

President .... John B. Sias
President - ABC Entertainment .... Robert A. Iger
Group President - ABC News & Sports/President - ABC News .... Roone Arledge
President - ABC Sports .... Dennis Swanson
President - ABC Television Network .... Mark Mandala
President - Daytime, Children's & Late-Night Entertainment .... Michael Brockman
President - Broadcast Operations & Engineering .... Robert Siegenthaler
Senior Vice President - Network Group .... James J. Allegro
Senior Vice President - Affiliate Relations .... George M. Newi
Senior Vice President -Finance ...... Warren D. Schaub
Senior Vice President - Marketing & Research Services .... Alan Wurtzel
Senior Vice President - Sales .... H. Weller Keever
Vice President -Public Relations ... Richard J. Connelly
Vice President - Public Relations, West Coast .... Robert J. Wright
Vice President - Broadcast Standards & Practices, West Coast .... Brett A. White
Vice President - Eastern Division Sales .... William Harmond
Vice President - Western Division Sales .... Peter McCarthy
Vice President - Operations .... Mark Roth

ABC Broadcasting Division
President .... Michael P. Mallardi
President - Broadcast Operations & Engineering .... Julius Barnathan
President - ABC Video Enterprises .... Herbert A. Granath
President - Television Stations, East .... Lawrence J. Pollock
President - Television Stations, West .... Kenneth M. Johnson
President - ABC National Television Sales .... John B. Watkins
President - ABC Radio .... James B. Arcara
President - Radio Stations .... Don P. Bouloukos
President - Radio Networks .... Aaron M. Daniels

ABC Entertainment: West Coast
President .... Robert A. Iger
Executive Vice President .... Stuart Bloomberg
Executive Vice President - Primetime .... Ted Harbert
Executive Vice President - Movies for Television/Miniseries .... Allen Sabinson
Senior Vice President - Business Affairs & Contracts .... Ronald B. Sunderland
Vice President - ABC Novels for Television & Limited Series .... Christy Welker
Vice President - Production Administration .... Deirdre A. Paulino
Vice President - Broadcast Standards & Practices .... Christine Hikawa

Vice President - Business Affairs ...... Gavin B. Gordon
Vice President - Business Affairs & Administration ...... Ronald Pratz
Vice President - Children's Programming ...... Jennie Trias
Vice President - Comedy Series Development ...... Kim Fleary
Vice President - On-Air Promotion ...... Stuart Brower
Vice President - Primetime Programming ...... John Barber
Vice President - Dramatic Series Development ...... Gary Levine
Vice President - Entertainment Research ...... Roy Rothstein
Vice President - Finance ...... Thomas Van Schaick
Vice President - Marketing ...... Mark Zakarin
Vice President - Mini-Series ...... Judd Parkin
Vice President - Program Administration ...... Stephen K. Nenno
Vice President - Program Planning & Scheduling ...... George Keramidas
Vice President - Special Programs ...... John Hamlin
Vice President - Casting & Talent ...... Donna L. Rosenstein
Vice President - Tape Production ...... Edgar Hirst

ABC Entertainment: East Coast

Senior Vice President - Daytime Programming ...... Jo Ann Emmerich
Vice President - Early Morning Programs ...... Philip R. Beuth
Vice President - Motion Pictures Post Production ...... Andre De Szekely
Vice President & General Manager - Broadcast Operations ...... Joseph D. Giovanni

ABC DISTRIBUTION

825 Seventh Ave.
New York, NY 10019

Senior Vice President ...... Archie C. Purvis
Vice President - Worldwide Cable & Home Video Marketing ...... Michael Dragotto
Vice President - Program Acquisitions & Development ...... Paul Coss

ABC PRODUCTIONS

2040 Avenue of the Stars
Los Angeles, CA 90067
213/557-7777

President ...... Brandon Stoddard
Executive Vice President ...... Jerry Offsay
Vice President - Production Administration ...... Deirdre A. Paulino

ACT III COMMUNICATIONS INC.

1800 Century Park East, Suite 200
Los Angeles, CA 90067
213/553-3636

Chairman & Chief Executive Officer ...... Norman Lear
President & Chief Operating Officer ...... Thomas B. McGrath
Senior Vice President & General Counsel ...... Michael E. Cahill
Vice President - Corporate Development ...... Janet Schoff
Vice President - Public Affairs ...... Betsy Kenny

Act III Productions

President ...... Andrew Meyer
Senior Vice President ...... Sarah Ryan Black
Senior Vice President - Production ...... Nancy Klopper
Executive Vice President ...... Mark E. Pollack

Act III Television

President ...... Deborah Aal
Vice President ...... James A. Miller

ALLIANCE ENTERTAINMENT CORP.

8439 Sunset Blvd. #404
Los Angeles, CA 90046
213/654-9488

920 Yonge St. #400
Toronto, Ontario, Canada M4W 3C7
416/967-1174

Co-Chairman ...... Denis Heroux
Co-Chairman ...... Robert Lantos
President ...... Susan Cavan
Chief Financial Officer ...... Jay Firestone
Senior Vice President - Production ...... Michael Nolin
Vice President - Development ...... Steven DeNure
Vice President - Legal Affairs ...... John Robinson

Alliance Releasing Corporation

President ...... Victor Loewy
General Manager ...... Joe Brown
Advertising ...... Mary Pat Gleeson

AMBLIN ENTERTAINMENT

100 Universal Plaza, Bungalow 477
Universal City, CA 91608
818/777-4600

President ...... Steven Spielberg
Executive Producer ...... Frank Marshall
Executive Producer ...... Kathleen Kennedy
Senior Vice President ...... Deborah Newmyer
Vice President - Marketing ...... Brad Globe

Vice President - TV Division ....Carole Kirschner
Story Editor ....Bettina Viviano
Special Consultant ....Marvin J. Levy
Special Consultant ....Gerry Lewis

AMERICAN PLAYHOUSE
1776 Broadway, 9th Floor
New York, NY 10019
212/757-4552

Executive Director & President ....David M. Davis
Executive Producer ....Lindsay Law
Vice President - Business &
Legal Affairs ....Roberta Lynn Tross
Director of Program Development ....Lynn Holst

ANGELIKA FILMS
1974 Broadway
New York, NY 10023
212/769-1400

Chairman ....Angelika T. Saleh
President & Chief
Executive Officer ....Joseph J.M. Saleh
Executive Vice President -
International Marketing ....Alex Massis
Vice President - Foreign Sales ....Richard Salzburg
Vice President - Acquisitions ....Jessica Saleh-Hunt

APOLLO PICTURES
6071 Bristol Parkway
Culver City, CA 90230
213/568-8282

President & Chief Executive Officer ......Ron Beckman
Executive Vice President - Production ..Jere Henshaw
Vice President - Physical Production .....Robert Rosen
Director of Creative Affairs ....Russell Chesley
Director of Development.......................Greg Johnson

AVENUE PICTURES
12100 Wilshire Blvd., Suite 1650
Los Angeles, CA 90025
213/207-1150

Chairman & Chief Executive Officer ....Cary Brokaw
Vice President - Finance &
Chief Financial Officer ....Sheri Halfon
Executive Vice President &
Chief Operations Officer ....Patrick Murray
Executive VicePresident -
Marketing & Distribution ....Bingham Ray
Vice President - Production ....Anna Gross
Vice President - Production &
Acquisitions......................................Claudia Lewis

B

STEVEN BOCHCO PRODUCTIONS
20th Century-Fox
10201 W. Pico Blvd.
Los Angeles, CA 90035
213/203-1711

Chairman & Chief Executive Officer ....Steven Bochco
President & Chief
Financial Officer ....Franklin B. Rohner
Executive Vice President -
Creative Affairs ....Dayna Flanagan
Vice President - Administration ......Marilyn Fiebelkorn
Vice President - Business Affairs ....Wilton M. Haff
Vice President - Finance ....James A. Roach
Vice President - Production ....Phillip Goldfarb
Vice President - Public Relations .....James A. Gordon

C

THE CANNELL STUDIOS
7083 Hollywood Blvd.
Los Angeles, CA 90028
213/465-5800

Chairman & Chief
Executive Officer.......................Stephen J. Cannell
President ....Michael Dubelko
Senior Vice President - Legal &
Business Affairs ....Howard D. Kurtzman
Senior Vice President ....Jo Swerling Jr.
Vice President & Chief
Financial Officer ....Joe Kaczorowski
Vice President & Controller ....Andrew R. Hubsch

Stephen J. Cannell Productions
President ....Peter Roth
Executive Vice President ....Mathew N. Herman
Vice President - Cannell Films, Ltd. ....Alex Beaton
Vice President - Post Production ....Gary Winter
Vice President - Talent ....Simon Ayer
Vice President - Telefilms,
Miniseries & Off-Network ....Brenda Friend

CANNON PICTURES
(see PATHE Entertainment Co.)

CAROLCO PICTURES INC.
8800 Sunset Blvd.
Los Angeles, CA 90069
213/850-8800

Chairman .... Mario Kassar
President .... Peter Hoffman
President - Licensing .... Danny Simon
Executive Vice President & CFO .... Louis Weiss
Executive Vice President - Foreign Sales .... Rocco Viglietta
Senior Vice President - Business Affairs .... Lynwood Spinks
Vice President & Head of Production .... Buzz Feitshans
Vice President & European Representative .... Gabriella Martin
Vice President - Business Affairs .... Barbara Zipperman
Vice President - Business Affairs .... Lorin Brennan
Vice President - Corporate Development .... Thomas Levine
Vice President - Finance .... Karen Taylor
Vice President - Music .... Steve Love
Vice President - Post Production .... Michael R. Sloan
Vice President - Sales .... Chris Bialek
Director of Development .... Kathryn Sommer

CASTLE ROCK ENTERTAINMENT
335 N. Maple Dr., Suite 135
Beverly Hills, CA 90210
213/285-2300

Partner .... Alan Horn
Partner .... Glenn Padnick
Partner .... Rob Reiner
Partner .... Martin Shafer
Partner .... Andrew Scheinman
Chief Financial Officer .... Al Linton
Senior Vice President - Business .... Greg Paul
Vice President - Business Affairs .... Jess Wittenberg
Vice President - Creative Affairs .... Liz Glotzer
Vice President - Production .... Rachel Pfeffer
Vice President - Publicity & Promotion .... John DeSimio
Vice President - TV Production .... Lynn Deegan
Executive Story Editor .... Mary Woods
Executive Story Editor .... Caitlin Scanlon
Director of Creative Affairs - TV .... Robin Green

CBS INC.
7800 Beverly Blvd.
Los Angeles, CA 90036
213/852-2345

51 W. 57th St.
New York, NY 10019
212/975-4321

Chairman .... William S. Paley
President & Chief Executive Officer .... Laurence A. Tisch

CBS Broadcast Group
President - Broadcast Group .... Howard Stringer
President - Marketing Division .... Thomas F. Leahy
President - CBS Enterprises .... Jim Warner
President - CBS Entertainment .... Jeff Sagansky
President - CBS News .... David Burke
President - CBS Radio .... Nancy Widmann
President - CBS Sports .... Neal H. Pilson
President - CBS Television Stations .... Eric Ober
President - Affiliate Relations Division .... Anthony C. Malara
Senior Vice President - Communications .... George Schweitzer
Senior Vice President - Planning & Research .... David Poltrack
Vice President & Assistant to President .... Beth Waxman Bressan
Vice President - Creative Services .... Jerold Goldberg
Vice President - Media Relations .... Ann Morfogen

CBS Entertainment: Hollywood
President .... Jeff Sagansky
Senior Vice President - Program Planning .... Peter F. Tortorici
Senior Vice President - Business Affairs .... William B. Klein
Vice President - Advertising & Promotion .... Michael Mischler
Vice President - Affiliate Advertising & Promotion .... Brad Crum
Vice President - Business Affairs, Administration .... James F. McGowan
Vice President - Business Affairs, Long Form Contracts & Acquisitions .... Sid Lyons
Vice President - Business Affairs, Music Operations .... Harry Heitzer
Vice President - Business Affairs, Talent & Guild Negotiations .... Leola Gorius

Vice President - Business Affairs, West Coast .... Layne Britton
Vice President - Children's Program & Daytime Specials .... Judy Price
Vice President - Comedy Program Development .... Tim Flack
Vice President - Current Programs .... Charles Schnebel
Vice President - Current Programs .... Maddy Horne
Vice President - Daytime Programs .... Lucy Johnson
Vice President - Dramatic Program Development .... Jonathan Levin
Vice President - Dramatic Specials ..... Marion Brayton
Vice President - Entertainment & Informational Specials .... Fred Rappoport
Vice President - International Program Development .... John Matoian
Vice President - Late Night Programs .... Rod Perth
Vice President - Media Planning, Advertising & Promotion .... Kathie Culleton
Vice President - Motion Pictures for TV & Mini-Series .... Pat Faulstich
Vice President - Motion Pictures for TV, Miniseries .... Steve Mills
Vice President - On-Air Promotion ..... Steve Jacobson
Vice President - Program Planning & Current Programs .... Herbert Gross
Vice President - Publicity .... Susan Tick
Vice President - Special Projects .... Steve Warner
Vice President - Talent & Casting .... Lisa Freiberger
Vice President - Talent & Guild Negotiations .... Leola Govins

CBS Broadcast Group: Hollywood

Vice President - TV Research .... Arnold Becker
Vice President - Program Practices ...... Carol A. Altieri

CBS Entertainment Productions

Vice President .... Norman S. Powell
Vice President - Series Development .... Mary Mazur

CINECOM

(see ODYSSEY/Cinecom International)

CINETEL FILMS INC.

3800 W. Alameda, Suite 825
Burbank, CA 91505
818/955-9551

President & Chief Executive Officer ..... Paul Hertzberg
Chief Financial Officer .... Nick Gorenc
Executive Vice President .... Lisa M. Hansen
Vice President - Business Affairs .... Judith Jecmen
Vice President - Creative Affairs .... Melanie Friesen
Vice President - Domestic & International Distribution .... John Rubinich
Vice President - Marketing .... Anne W. Cochran
Vice President - Theatrical Distribution .... Ed Cruea
Vice President .... David Jackson

DICK CLARK PRODUCTIONS

3003 W. Olive Ave.
Burbank, CA 91505
818/841-3003

President .... Dick Clark
Senior Vice President - Creative Affairs ... Neil Stearns
Vice President - Creative Affairs .... Ellen Glick
Vice President & Chief Labor Counsel .... Joel M. Grossman
Director of Development .... Pat Troise

COLUMBIA PICTURES ENTERTAINMENT INC.

Studio Plaza
3400 Riverside Drive
Burbank, CA 91505
818/954-6000

President - Columbia Pictures International TV .... Nicholas Bingham
President - RCA/Columbia Worldwide Video .... W. Patrick Campbell
President - Music Publishing Division .... Robert Holmes
Executive Vice President- Legal Affairs .... Jared Jussim
Vice President .... David Rosenfelt
Vice President - Regulatory Affairs ..... Vicki R. Solmon

Motion Picture Group

Co-Chairman .... Peter Guber
Co-Chairman .... Jon Peters
Chief Operating Officer .... Lewis J. Korman
Executive Vice President .... David Matalon
Vice President - Columbia Tri-Star Film Distribution .... Marie M. Collins
Vice President - Office of the Chairmen ... Cary Woods

Columbia Pictures

Chairman .... Frank Price
Chief Financial Officer .... Lawrence J. Ruisi
President - Marketing .... Buffy Shutt
President - Domestic Distribution .... James Spitz
President - Production Administration .... Gary Martin
President - Worldwide Production .... Michael Nathanson

Executive Vice President .... Arnold W. Messer
Executive Vice President .... Roger Faxon
Executive Vice President .... Gary Schrager
Executive Vice President - Marketing ...... Kathy Jones
Executive Vice President - Operations .... David L. Kennedy
Executive Vice President - Production ..... Darris Hatch
Executive Vice President - Production ...... Amy Pascal
Executive Vice President - Worldwide Post Production .... Thomas McCarthy
Senior Vice President .... M. Jay Wilkingshaw
Senior Vice President - Advertising & Director of Creative Services .... Kenneth Stewart
Senior Vice President - Advertising .... William Loper
Senior Vice President - Business Affairs & Administration .... Christie Rothenberg
Senior Vice President - Business Affairs .... Lee N. Rosenbaum
Senior Vice President - Creative Advertising .... Howard Russo
Senior Vice President & General Counsel .... Ronald N. Jakobi
Senior Vice President & General Sales Manager .... Jerry Jorgensen
Senior Vice President - Legal Affairs .... Beth Burke
Senior Vice President - Legal Affairs & Assistant General Counsel .... Mark Resnick
Senior Vice President - Legal Affairs, Distribution .... Vicki R. Solmon
Senior Vice President - Marketing .... Eddie Egan
Senior Vice President - Media .... John Butkovich
Senior Vice President - Publicity, Promotion & Field Operations .... Edward Russell
Senior Vice President - Research .... Lenore Cantor
Senior Vice President - West Coast Administration .... Barbara Cline
Vice President - Advertising, Publicity & Promotion .... Janice E. Glaser
Vice President - Assistant Controller .... Richard Bengloff
Vice President - Assistant Treasurer .... Joseph W. Kraft
Vice President - Business Affairs Administration .... Thomas R. Stack
Vice President - Business Affairs, Music Group .... Keith C. Zajic
Vice President - Controller .... Edgar H. Howells Jr.
Vice President - Controller .... Jay M. Green
Vice President - East Coast Publicity .... Dennis Higgins
Vice President - Legal Affairs ...... Joan Salzman Grant
Vice President - Legal Affairs .... Phyllis Olmes
Vice President - Marketing & Distribution Administration .... Patrick D. Walters
Vice President - Music .... Bones Howe
Vice President - Operations .... Conrad K. Steely
Vice President - Operations .... David Holman
Vice President - Operations & Administration .... Mark Zucker
Vice President - Personnel .... Susan B. Ganelli
Vice President - Post Production .... Jim Honore
Vice President - Production .... Dennis Greene
Vice President - Production .... Barry Sabath
Vice President - Publicity & Special Events .... Hollace G. Davids
Vice President - Publicity .... Ann-Marie Stein
Vice President - Research .... Ariel Diaz
Vice President - Sales Planning .... Richard B. Elliott
Vice President - Studio Publicity .... Mark Gill
Vice President - Treasurer .... Kenneth S. Williams
Vice President - West Coast Administration .... Frederick J. Garcia
Vice President .... Claire Bisceglia
Executive Story Editor .... John B. Carls

Tri-Star Pictures

Studio Plaza
3400 Riverside Dr.
Burbank, CA 91505
818/972-7700

Chairman .... Mike Medavoy
Executive Vice President - Business Affairs .... Kenneth Lemberger
Executive Vice President - Domestic Distribution .... William Soady
Executive Vice President & General Counsel .... Leslie H. Jacobson
Senior Vice President & Production Controller .... Donald B. Miller
Senior Vice President - Creative Advertising .... Dallas Garred
Senior Vice President - General Sales Manager .... Robert Capps
Senior Vice President - Legal Affairs .... Lisbeth Aschenbrenner
Senior Vice President - National Advertising & Research .... Mark Kristol
Senior Vice President - Production .... Richard Fischoff
Senior Vice President - Production ...... Shelly Hochron
Senior Vice President - Production ..... Katherine Lingg
Senior Vice President - Production .... Alan Riche
Senior Vice President - Production .... Stephen F. Randall

Vice President - Administration ..... Gerald Iannaccone
Vice President - Ancillary Markets .... Glen Meredith
Vice President & Assistant Controller - Theatrical .... Winston van Buitenen
Vice President - Business Affairs Administration .... Grant Gullickson
Vice President - Business Affairs .... John Sansone
Vice President - Creative Advertising .... Stephanie Allen
Vice President & Division Manager - Central .... Jack Simmons
Vice President & Division Manager - Eastern .... Howard Mahler
Vice President & Division Manager - Southern .... Joe Kennedy
Vice President & Division Manager - Western .... Rory Bruer
Vice President - Field Publicity & Promotion .... Ellen Kroner
Vice President - Legal Affairs .... Jon Gibson
Vice President - Legal Affairs .... Rebecca Nunberg
Vice President - Legal Affairs, Distribution & Marketing .... Surie Rudoff
Vice President - Management Information Systems .... James J. Dileo
Vice President - National Publicity .... Cara White
Vice President - National Publicity .... Marcy Granata
Vice President - Production .... Christopher Lee
Vice President - Production Management .... Steven Saeta
Vice President & Treasurer .... Elizabeth Burnett
Story Editor .... Stan Chervin

Columbia Pictures Television

Chairman & Chief Executive Officer .... Gary Lieberthal
President .... Scott Siegler
Executive Vice President - Business Affairs .... Valerie Cavanaugh
Senior Vice President - Business Affairs .... Jan Abrams
Senior Vice President - Corporate Communications & Publicity .... Don Demesquita
Senior Vice President - Drama Development .... James Veres
Senior Vice President - Legal Affairs ... Gregory Boone
Senior Vice President - Marketing .... Michael Zucker
Senior Vice President - Research .... David Mumford
Senior Vice President .... Andrew J. Kaplan
Vice President - Business Affairs Administration .... Stephanie Knauer
Vice President - Business Affairs .... Harvey Harrison
Vice President - Business Affairs .... Jeffrey S. Weiss
Vice President - Business Affairs .... Richard Frankie
Vice President - Comedy Development .... Marla Ginsburg
Vice President - Comedy Development .... Steven Mendelson
Vice President - Production .... Ed Lammi
Vice President - Research .... Douglas Roth
Vice President - Talent & Casting .... Rick Jacobs

Columbia Pictures International Television

President .... Nicholas Bingham

RCA/Columbia Home Video Worldwide

President & Chief Executive Officer .... W. Patrick Campbell
Executive Vice President & Chief Financial Officer .... William Chardavoyne
Executive Vice President & Chief Operating Officer .... Paul Culberg
Executive Vice President - International Sales & Marketing .... Chris Deering
Executive Vice President .... James Tauber
Vice President - Worldwide Acquisitions & Business Affairs .... Gina Resnick
Vice President - Acquisitions & Programming .... Larry Estes
Vice President - Business & Legal Affairs .... Monica Lipkin

Triumph Releasing

President .... J. Edward Shugrue
Executive Vice President - International .... S. Anthony Manna
Senior Vice President - Administration .... Milton Fishman
Senior Vice President -Marketing ...... Duncan C. Clark
Vice President - Administration .... Louis P. Mont
Vice President - Domestic Sales & Distribution .... Linda Ditrinco
Vice President - Legal Affairs .... Sherry E. Sherman
Vice President - Marketing .... Stephen Klein

CONCORDE PICTURES/ NEW HORIZONS

11600 San Vicente Blvd.
Los Angeles, CA 90049
213/826-0978

President .... Roger Corman
President - Concorde International .... Brad Krevoy
Vice President .... Julie Corman
Vice President - Ancillary Rights .... Pamela A. Abraham

Vice President - Finance .... Catherine Sanders
Vice President - Finance .... Dennis Manders
Vice President - Operations .... Catherine Cyran
Vice President - Production .... Rodman Flender
Vice President - Southern Division ... Mary Lou Lanaux
Director of Business Affairs .... Douglas Bull
Director of International Marketing &
Services .... Pamela Vlastas
Director of Acquisitions .... Lynn Whitney
General Sales Manager .... Harry Gilg
Development .... Sally Mattison

D

WALT DISNEY CO.

500 S. Buena Vista St.
Burbank, CA 91521
818/560-1000

Chairman of the Board & Chief
Executive Officer .... Michael D. Eisner
Vice Chairman .... Roy E. Disney
President & Chief Operating Officer ..... Frank G. Wells
Senior Vice President &
Chief Financial Officer .... Judson Green
Senior Vice President &
General Counsel .... Joe Shapiro
Senior Vice President -
International Marketing .... Kevin Hyson
Senior Vice President - Strategic
Planning & Development .... Lawrence P. Murphy
Vice President & Counsel .... Jon Richmond
Vice President & Counsel .... Joseph F. Santaniello
Vice President & Counsel .... Peter F. Nolan
Vice President & Counsel .... Richard F.X. Clair
Vice President & Secretary .... Doris A. Smith
Vice President & Treasurer .... John H. Forsgren
Vice President - Corporate
Communications .... Erwin Okun
Vice President - Corporate Projects .... Linda Warren
Vice President - Environmental Policy ..... Kym Murphy
Vice President - Information
Services .... Bernard F. Mathaisel
Vice President - Management &
Audit .... Gerald L. Swider
Vice President - Tax
Administration/Counsel .... Jerry Kavulic

Walt Disney Studios

Chairman .... Jeffrey Katzenberg
President .... Richard Frank
President - Network TV Production .... Garth Ancier
Executive Vice President .... Randy Reiss
Senior Vice President - Finance .... Chris McGurk
Vice President - Production &
Resources .... Scott Dorman
Vice President - Post Production .... David McCann
Vice President - Studio
Operations .... Harry Grossman
Vice President - Casting .... Gretchen Rennell
Vice President - Music .... Chris Montan

Walt Disney Pictures

President - Production .... David Hoberman
President - Worldwide Marketing .... Robert B. Levin
Executive Vice President -Business &
Legal Affairs .... Helene Hahn
Senior Vice President -Business &
Legal Affairs .... Robin Russell
Senior Vice President -
Creative Services .... Robert Jahn
Senior Vice President - Domestic
Marketing .... Gary Kalkin
Senior Vice President - Feature
Animation .... Peter Schneider
Senior Vice President - Motion
Picture Financing .... Ronald J. Cayo
Vice President - Creative Services .... Robert Jahn
Vice President - Media .... Bobbi Blair
Vice President - Post Production .... Don Hall
Vice President - Production .... Don DeLine
Vice President - Production .... Jane Goldenring
Vice President - Production .... Adam Leipzig
Vice President - Production .... David Vogel

Touchstone Pictures

President - Production .... David Kirkpatrick
Vice President - Production .... Bridget Johnson
Vice President - Production .... Michael Roberts
Vice President - Production .... Romi Straussman

Hollywood Pictures

President - Production .... Ricardo Mestres
Senior Vice President - Business &
Legal Affairs .... Bernardine Brandis
Senior Vice President - Production ..... Michael Peyser
Vice President - Business Affairs .... Alan Myerson
Vice President - Legal Affairs .... Steve Bardwill
Vice President - Post Production .... Art Repola
Vice President - Production .... Kathryn F. Galan
Vice President - Production .... Charles Hirschorn
Vice President - Production .... Sam Mercer
Vice President - Production .... Amanda Stern
Vice President - Production & Casting .... Paula Herold
Vice President - Theatrical Distribution ... Chuck Viane

Theatrical Animation Division
Senior Vice President .... Peter Schneider
Vice President - Creative Affairs .... Charles Fink
Vice President - Production & Finance .... Tim Engel

Walt Disney Television
President - Network Television .... Randy Reiss
Executive Vice President - Animation .... Gary Krisel
Executive Vice President - Business & Legal Affairs .... Bill Kerstetter
Senior Vice President - Business Affairs .... Laurie Younger
Senior Vice President - Business & Legal Affairs .... John Reagan
Senior Vice President - Pay TV .... Hal Richardson
Vice President - Animation .... Michael Webster
Vice President - Business Affairs .... Jere Haustater
Vice President - Business Affairs .... Kenneth D. Werner
Vice President - Finance .... Lawrence R. Rutkowski
Vice President - Legal Affairs .... Lawrence Kaplan
Vice President - Legal Counsel .... David Mayer
Vice President - Network Legal Affairs .... Scottye Hedstrom

Buena Vista Television
Senior Vice President .... Robert Jacquemin
Senior Vice President - BVTV Productions .... Jamie Bennett
Senior Vice President - Marketing .... Carol Black
Vice President & General Manager .... Mark Zoradi
Vice President - Creative Services .... Sal Sardo
Vice President - Distribution & Finance .... John Elia
Vice President - Marketing .... Catherine Schulte
Vice President - Programming & Production .... Mary Kellogg-Joslyn
Vice President - Programming .... Bruno Cohen
Vice President - Publicity .... Ed Pine
Vice President - Research .... Michael Mellon

The Disney Channel
President .... John F. Cooke
Senior Vice President - Original Programming .... Stephen D. Fields
Vice President - Consumer Marketing ... Tom Wzsalek
Vice President - Finance & Treasurer ... Patrick Lopker
Vice President - Original Programming ..... Gary Marsh
Vice President - Programming .... Bruce Rider
Vice President - Sales & Affiliate Marketing .... Mark Handler
Vice President .... Patrick Davidson

Buena Vista Distribution
President .... Richard Cook
Senior Vice President & General Sales Manager .... Phillip Barlow
Vice President & Assistant General Sales Manager, West .... Roger Lewin
Vice President & General Counsel ... Bob Cunningham
Vice President - Finance & Administration .... Lynne Snyder
Vice President - Production .... Daniel Jason Heffner
Vice President - Promotions .... Brett Dicker

Buena Vista Home Video
Vice President - Brand Marketing .... Kelley Avery
Vice President - Domestic Sales .... Bob Roberts
Vice President - International Home Video .... Richard B. Cohen
Vice President - Pay TV & Acquisitions .... Hal Richardson
Vice President - Sales .... Dick Longwell

Buena Vista International
President - Television .... Etienne de Villiers
Senior Vice President - Theatrical Distribution & Marketing .... Kevin Hyson
Vice President & Supervisor of Productions -South America & Latin America .... Ivan Genit
Vice President & Supervisor - Far East & Australasia .... Rolf Mittweg
Vice President - International Marketing .... David Gross
Vice President - Walt Disney Prods. France .... Richard Dassonville
Vice President - Worldwide Service .... Jeffrey S. Miller
Vice President - International Publicity ...... Hilary Clark

E

EPIC PRODUCTIONS INC.
3339 W. Cahuenga Blvd., Suite 500
Los Angeles, CA 90068
213/969-2800

Co-Chair .... Moshe Diamant
Co-Chair .... Eduard Sarlui
President & Chief Operating Officer .... Andrew D.T. Pfeffer
President - Marketing & Distribution .... Elliot Slutzky
President - Home Video .... Don Rosenberg
Chief Financial Officer .... Nancy Halloran

Senior Vice President - Advertising .... Andy Foster
Senior Vice President - Business Affairs & General Counsel .... Richard Reiner
Senior Vice President - Theatrical Distribution .... David Garber
Vice President - National Publicity .... Jeff Freedman

F

FRIES ENTERTAINMENT INC.

6922 Hollywood Blvd.
Los Angeles, CA 90028
213/466-2266

Chairman & Chief Executive Officer & President .... Charles W. Fries
Senior Executive Vice President - Administration .... Charles M. Fries
Executive Vice President - Corporate Development .... James A. Parsons
Executive Vice President - Fries Television .... Clifford Alsberg
Executive Vice President - Motion Picture Development .... Michael Rosenfeld
Executive Vice President - Theatrical Production & Acquisitions .... Henry Seggerman
Senior Vice President - Promotion & Marketing .... Tony Habeeb
Vice President - Administration .... William Roland
Vice President - Business Affairs ...... Robert L. Chasin
Vice President - Corporate Development .... Kent Cristensen
Vice President - Development .... Christopher Fries
Vice President - Development, TV Series .... Terry Allen
Vice President - Motion Picture Development .... Judith Boasberg
Vice President - Production .... Andrea Newman
Vice President - Production Supervision .... S. Bryan Hickox
Vice President - Production .... Tom Fries
Vice President - TV Movies & Mini-series .... Thomas Nunnan

Fries Theatrical

Executive Vice President - International Distribution .... Larry Friedricks
Executive Vice President .... Maurice Singer
Vice President - International Distribution .... Paula Fierman
Director of Foreign Distribution .... Tracy Levin

Fries Home Video

Vice President - Advertising & Publicity .... Cathy Mantegna

Fries Distribution

Executive Vice President - Domestic Distribution .... Ave Butensky
Executive Vice President .... James Dudelson
Senior Vice President & General Sales Manager .... Peter Schmid
Senior Vice President - Distribution .... Richard H. Askin Jr.
Vice President - Firstrun Syndication & Daytime Development .... Allan Schwartz
Vice President - Advertising & Promotion .... Lou Wexner
Director of Advertising & Promotion .... Terri Kilroy

G

GLADDEN ENTERTAINMENT CORPORATION

10100 Santa Monica Blvd., Suite 600
Los Angeles, CA 90067
213/282-7500

Chairman .... Bruce McNall
President & Chief Executive Officer .... David Begelman
Vice President & Chief Financial Officer .... Suzan Waks
Controller .... Patricia Linden
Vice President - Business Affairs .... Ezra J. Doner
Vice President - Post Production .... Norman Wallerstein
Marketing & Distribution Consultant .... Richard Kahn

THE SAMUEL GOLDWYN COMPANY

10203 Santa Monica Blvd., Suite 500
Los Angeles, CA 90067
213/552-2255

Chairman & Chief Executive Officer .... Samuel Goldwyn Jr.
President & Chief Operating Officer ..... Meyer Gottlieb
President - Marketing .... Alan Freeman
Senior Vice President - Worldwide Production .... Thomas Rothman
Senior Vice President - Business Affairs .... Norman Flicker
Senior Vice President - Finance .... Hans Turner
Senior Vice President - International Theatrical Sales .... Ann Dubinet
Senior Vice President - Operations ..... J. Michael Byrd

Vice President - Acquisitions .... Ann Templeton
Vice President - Creative Affairs .... Rene Missel
Vice President - East Coast
Development & Acquisitions .... Nancy Star
Vice President - Marketing .... Cliff Hauser
Vice President - Production .... Howard Cohen
Vice President - TV Programming &
Ancillary Sales .... Gary Marenzi

Television

President .... Dick Askin
Vice President - Development .... Ray Solley

H

HEMDALE FILM CORPORATION

1118 N. Wetherly Dr.
Los Angeles, CA 90069
213/550-6894

Chairman .... John Daly
President .... Derek Gibson
Executive Vice President -
Worldwide Marketing .... Martin Rabinovitch
Executive Vice President -
International .... Kathy Morgan
Executive Vice President .... Terence Hustedt
Senior Vice President .... Steve Rothman
Vice President - Advertising .... Ed McKenna
Director - Business Affairs .... Ron Aikin
Director - Creative Advertising .... David Zimmerman
Director - Foreign Sales &
Acquisitions, London .... George Miller
Director - Publicity .... Amy Sexton
General Sales Manager .... Dick Miller
Development .... Dorian Langdon
Acquisitions .... Ann Marie Gillen

Hemdale Releasing Corp.

Chairman .... John Daly
President - Worldwide Distribution .... Andy Gruenberg
Executive Vice President .... Derek Gibson

HOME BOX OFFICE, INC.

1100 Avenue of the Americas
New York, NY 10036
212/512-1000

2049 Century Park East, Suite 4100
Los Angeles, CA 90067
213/201-9200

Chairman & Chief Executive Officer ..... Michael Fuchs
President .... Joe Collins
Executive Vice President - Affiliate
Sales & Operations .... Peter Frame
Senior Vice President & Chief
Financial Officer .... Jeff Bewkes
Senior Vice President &
General Counsel .... John Redpath
Senior Vice President - Business
Affairs .... Harold Akselrad
Senior Vice President - Film
Programming & Home Video ... Stephen J. Scheffer
Senior Vice President - Film
Programming .... Leslie Jacobson
Senior Vice President - Marketing .... John Billock
Senior Vice President - Network
Operations .... Larry Carlson
Senior Vice President - Original
Programming .... Bridget Potter
Senior Vice President - Program
Operations & Sports .... Seth G. Abraham
Vice President - Affiliate Operations ... Steve Davidson
Vice President - Corporate Affairs .... Jim Noonan
Vice President - Media &
Corporate Affairs .... Quentin Schaffer
Vice President - Original
Programming .... Sasha Emerson
Vice President - Production,
East Coast .... Marjorie Kalins
Vice President - Program Planning .... David Baldwin
Vice President - Program Promotion .... Tim Braine

HBO Pictures

Senior Vice President .... Robert Cooper
Senior Vice President - Business
Affairs .... Glenn Whitehead
Senior Vice President - Legal .... Horace Collins
Senior Vice President - Original
Programming .... Chris Albrecht
Vice President - Business
Affairs .... Michael Lombardo
Vice President - Business
Affairs/Production .... Cathy Fitzpatrick
Vice President - Business
Affairs/Production .... Tom Hammel
Vice President - Film Acquisitions .... Neil Brown
Vice President - Media Relations ...... Quentin Schaffer
Vice President - Media Relations,
West Coast .... Richard Licata
Vice President - Operations .... Holly Dworsky
Vice President - Original Programming .... Bill Sanders
Vice President - Original Programming ... Jeff Bricmont
Vice President - Program Publicity .... Ellen Rubin
Vice President .... Ilene Kahn

HBO Video

President .... Eric Kessler
Senior Vice President - Marketing .... Tracy Dolgin
Vice President - Direct Marketing & New Business Development .... Ellen Stolzman

I

IMAGE ORGANIZATION INC.

9000 Sunset Blvd., Suite 915
Los Angeles, CA 90069
213/278-8751

Chairman & Chief Executive Officer .... Pierre David
Executive Vice President .... Lawrence Goebel
Senior Vice President - International Distribution .... Mark A. Horowitz
Vice President - Distribution .... David Carson
Vice President - Marketing .... Paula Fierman
Director of Acquisitions .... James Botko

IMAGINE FILMS ENTERTAINMENT INC.

1925 Century Park East, Suite 2300
Los Angeles, CA 90067
213/277-1665

Chairman & Chief Executive Officer .... Ron Howard
Chairman & Chief Executive Officer .... Brian Grazer
President .... Tony Ludwig
Executive Vice President .... Melinda Benedek
Senior Vice President - Business Affairs .... Peter Bachman
Senior Vice President - Motion Pictures .... David Friendly
Senior Vice President - Motion Pictures .... Tova Laiter
Senior Vice President - Television .... Joyce Brotman
Senior Vice President - Television .... Dori Weiss
Vice President - Television .... Todd Bergensen
Vice President - Physical Production ...... Terry Spazek
Vice President - Controller .... Adene Walter
Vice President - Production Finance .... Jerry L. Rife
Vice President - Motion Pictures .... Karen Kehela

Second City Entertainment

Andrew Alexander
Michael Rollens

INTERSCOPE COMMUNICATIONS

10900 Wilshire Blvd., Suite 1400
Los Angeles, CA 90024
213/208-8525

President .... Robert W. Cort
Executive Vice President - Production .... Ted Field
Executive Vice President-Television .... Patricia Clifford
Vice President - Creative Affairs .... David Madden
Production Executive .... Cynthia Sherman

ISLAND PICTURES

9000 Sunset Blvd., Suite 700
Los Angeles, CA 90069
213/276-4500

Chief Executive Officer .... Chris Blackwell
Co-President .... Mark Burg
Co-President .... Chris Zarpas
Senior Vice President - Financial Affairs .... Mel Klein
Vice President - Creative Affairs .... Cathy Yoneda
Vice President - Distribution .... Jill Zignego
Vice President - Operations .... Dan Genetti
Director of Creative Advertising .... Alex Swart

ITC ENTERTAINMENT GROUP

12711 Ventura Blvd.
Studio City, CA 91604
818/760-2110

115 E. 57th St.
New York, NY 10022
212/371-6660

45 Seymour St.
London, England W1A 1AG
44/1-262-8040

President & Chief Executive Officer .... Chris Gorog
Chief Financial Officer .... James T. Johnson
Executive Vice President - Motion Pictures & TV .... Peter Frankovich
Executive Vice President - Production .... Dennis Brown
Executive Vice President & General Counsel .... John Huncke
Senior Vice President - International .... James P. Marrinan
Vice President - Worldwide Acquisitions .... Paul Almond
Vice President - Business & Legal Affairs .... Ed Gilbert
Vice President - International Theatrical Sales .... Larry Garrett
Vice President - International Theatrical Sales .... Paul Borno
Vice President - Motion Pictures .... Lisa Lieberman
Vice President - Television .... Glenda Grant

M

MANAGEMENT COMPANY ENTERTAINMENTGROUP INC.

2400 Broadway, Suite 100
Santa Monica, CA 90404
213/315-7800

575 Fifth Ave., Suite 24C
New York, NY 10017
212/l983-5799

Chairman & Chief Executive Officer .... Jonathan D. Krane
Executive Vice President - Chief Financial Officer .... Mark Huggins
Executive VicePresident - Distribution .... Michael Bisio
Executive Vice President - Motion Pictures & Talent .... William Tennant
Senior Vice President - Office of the Chairman .... Leah Palco
Vice President - Business & Legal Affairs .... Janet L. Stott
Vice President - Communications .... Debra Stein
Vice President - Development .... Dan Berk
Vice President - International Communications .... Judy McGuinn
Vice President - International Sales .... John Alexander
Vice President - Motion Picture Operations .... David Enson

Independent Production Resources

President .... Stuart B. Rekant
Executive Vice President .... Malcolm A. Birnbaum
Vice President .... Jeffrey Calman

Manson International

Chairman of the Board .... William J. Rouhana
Executive Vice President & Chief Operating Officer .... Peter Elson
Senior Vice President - International Sales .... Michael J. Werner
Vice President - Finance .... Judith Goldstein
Vice President - International Sales .... John Alexander
Vice President - Sales .... Maura Hoy

MCA INC.

(see UNIVERSAL Pictures)

METRO-GOLDWYN-MAYER/UNITED ARTISTS TELECOMMUNICATIONS INC.

10202 W. Washington Blvd.
Culver City, CA 90232
213/280-6000

Chairman of the Board & Chief Executive Officer .... Jeffrey Barbakow
President & Chief Operating Officer .... Norman Horowitz
Executive Vice President .... Kevin Spivak
Senior Executive Vice President .... Sidney H. Sapsowitz
Senior Vice President .... Trevor Fetter
Senior Vice President & Corporate General Counsel & Secretary .... William Allen Jones
Senior Vice President - Finance & Chief Financial Officer .... Thomas P. Carson
Senior Vice President - Labor Relations .... Benjamin B. Kahane
Senior Vice President - Production & General Counsel .... Chris Ann Maxwell
Vice President - Administration .... David Millington
Vice President - Corporate Communications .... Peter Graves
Vice President - Corporate Business Affairs .... Thomas J. Taylor
Vice President - Film & Tape Production Services .... Claudia Gray
Vice President - Human Resources .... Steven Shaw
Vice President - Management Information Systems .... John Sanders

MGM/UA Film Group

President & Chief Executive Officer .... Richard Gerber
President - International Distribution .... Jack Gordon
President - Worldwide Marketing .... David M. Forbes
Executive Vice President - Worldwide Production .... John Goldwyn
Executive Vice President - Marketing .... Barrie Lorie
Executive Vice President - Production .... Richard Berger
Executive Vice President - Theatrical Business Affairs .... Robert Geary
Senior Vice President - Worldwide Production .... Jack B. Bernstein
Senior Vice President - Business Affairs .... Darcie Denkert
Senior Vice President - Production .... Karen Rosenfelt
Senior Vice President - Publicity .... Barry Glasser

Vice President & Controller .... Kathleen A. Coughlan
Vice President & Treasurer .... Walter C. Hoffer
Vice President - Acquisitions .... Laurence Roth
Vice President - Advertising .... William Loper
Vice President - Creative Affairs ... Christopher Bomba
Vice President - Creative Affairs .... June Petrie
Vice President - Creative Affairs .... Wendy Dytman
Vice President - East Coast Production .... Karen Lerner
Vice President - East Coast Publicity & Promotion .... Donna Dickman
Vice President - Market Research .... Gregory A. Foster
Vice President - Media .... Richard Porter
Vice President - Post Production .... Fred Nolting
Vice President - Post Production .... Gary Bell

MGM/UA Marketing Services Division

Senior Vice President - Marketing .... Don Barrett
Senior Vice President .... William Laper
Vice President - Marketing .... Jack Smith

MGM/UA Music Division

Senior Vice President & General Manager .... Bob Greenberg
Senior Vice President .... Lionel Newman
Vice President .... Harry Lojewski
Vice President - Music Business Affairs .... Ira Selsky

MGM/UA Legal Division

Senior Vice President .... Nancy Niederman
Senior Vice President .... Molly Wilson
Vice President & Senior Production Counsel .... Marcia Spielholz
Vice President & Senior Production Counsel .... Deanna J. Heath
Vice President .... Mary Craig Calkins
Vice President .... Alexandra Denman
Vice President .... John Drinkwater
Vice President .... Judy Jason
Vice President .... Frank Montalbano
Vice President .... Michael Smarinsky
Vice President .... Sally Suchil

MGM/UA Television Production Group

Chairman & Chief Executive Officer .... David Gerber
President .... Lynn Loring
Senior Vice President - Business Affairs & Administration .... Mark Pedowitz
Senior Vice President - Network Series Programming .... Susan Harbert
Senior Vice President - Production .... Christopher Seitz
Vice President - Administration .... Leslie H. Frends
Vice President - Business Affairs .... J.A. (Ted) Baer
Vice President - Business Affairs .... Steve Knisely
Vice President - Casting .... Mary Jo Slater
Vice President - Current Programming .... Ron Levinson
Vice President - Development .... Harriet Brown
Vice President - Development .... Judy Palnick
Vice President - Longform Programming .... Jeff Ryder
Vice President - Post Production .... Bruce Pobjoy
Vice President - Production .... Dennis Judd II
Vice President - Production .... Ron Von Schimmelmann
Vice President - Program Development .... George Paris

MGM/UA Distribution Co.

President .... David M. Forbes
Senior Vice President & General Sales Manager .... John Jay Peckos
Senior Vice President - Distribution .... Jack Foley
Senior Vice President - Distribution .... Lewis O'Neil
Senior Vice President - Marketing Administration .... Budd Filippo
Vice President - Administration .... Richard Parness
Vice President - Classics .... Ben Y. Cammack, Jr.
Vice President - Distribution .... Joseph Griffin
Vice President - Marketing Administration .... Nancy Ong
Vice President - Media & Co-op Advertising .... Maryanne Coury

MIRAMAX

375 Greenwich Street
New York, NY 10013
212/941-3800

President - Production .... Fred Milstein
Co-Chairman .... Harvey Weinstein
Co-Chairman .... Bob Weinstein
Chief Financial Officer .... John Schmidt
Executive Vice President - Production & Acquisitions .... Fred Milstein
Executive Vice President .... Russell Schwartz
Vice President - Acquisitions & Development .... Michael Spielberg
Vice President - Distribution .... Martin Zeidman
Vice President - Marketing .... Adam Rogers
Vice President - Publicity .... Christina Kounelias

MORGAN CREEK PRODUCTIONS
1801 Century Park East, 19th Floor
Los Angeles, CA 90067
213/284-8884

Chairman .... James G. Robinson
President .... David Nicksay
Executive Vice President & Chief
Operating Officer .... Gary Barber
Vice President & Controller .... Russ Gubler
Vice President - Business Affairs .... Gary Stutman
Vice President - Business
Affairs & Legal .... Jay Doughtery
Vice President - Production .... Larry Katz
Vice President - Production .... Paul Schiff

Morgan Creek International
President .... Gary Barber
Senior Vice President .... Julian Levin

MOTOWN PRODUCTIONS
345 N. Maple Dr., Suite 235
Beverly Hills, CA 90210
213/281-2675

President .... Suzanne de Passe
Executive Vice President -
Television .... Burt Hechtman
Senior Vice President - Production .... Carol A. Caruso
Vice President - Business
Affairs .... Joan Whitehead Evans
Vice President - Business Affairs ..... Ronnie Goldstein
Vice President - Creative Affairs .... Brenda Antin
Vice President - Musical Features,
Stage & TV .... Suzanne Coston

MTM ENTERPRISES INC.
4024 Radford Ave.
Studio City, CA 91604
818/760-5942

President - Television .... Peter Grad
President - Motion Pictures .... Marianne Moloney
Senior Executive Vice President .... Mel Blumenthal
Executive Vice President &
General Counsel .... Ken Meyer
Executive Vice President - International
Co-Production .... Tim Buxton
Executive Vice President .... William Allen
Senior Vice President -
Talent .... Geri Windsor-Fischer
Vice President - Business Affairs ...... Patricia Ahmann
Vice President - Business Affairs .... Jim Goodman

Vice President - Comedy
Development .... Lynn Deegan
Vice President - Post Production .... Ted Rich
Vice President - Production .... Bernie Oseransky
Vice President - Public Relations .... Larry Bloustein

N

NBC, INC.
3000 W. Alameda Ave.
Burbank, CA 91523
818/840-4444

30 Rockefeller Plaza
New York, NY 10020
212/664-4444

Chairman of the Board .... John F. Welch Jr.
President & Chief
Executive Officer .... Robert C. Wright
Vice Chairman of the Board .... Irwin Segelstein
President - NBC Television
Network .... Pierson Mapes
President - NBC Cable &
Business Development .... Thomas S. Rogers
President - NBC Enterprises .... Jerome Wexler
President - NBC News .... Michael Gartner
President - NBC Sports .... Dick Ebersol
President - Operations &
Technical Services .... Michael Sherlock
President - Television Stations .... Albert Jerome
Group Executive Vice President .... Robert C. Butler
Group Executive Vice President .... Robert Walsh
Executive Vice President &
General Counsel .... Richard Cotton
Executive Vice President .... Albert F. Barber
Vice President - Business
Development & Planning .... Susan C. Greene
Vice President - Program Standards -
Community Relations .... Rosalyn Weinman

NBC Entertainment
President .... Brandon Tartikoff
Executive Vice President -
Primetime Programs .... Warren Littlefield
Senior Vice President - East Coast
Programs & Program Planning .... Lee Curlin
Senior Vice President - Series
Programs .... Perry Simon
Senior Vice President - Motion Pictures
for Television & Mini-Series .... Anthony Masucci

Vice President - Children's & Family Programs .... Phyllis Tucker Vinson
Vice President - Comedy Development ..... Leslie Lurie
Vice President - Comedy Programs .... Michele Brustin
Vice President - Current Comedy Programs .... Edward Frank
Vice President - Current Drama Programs .... Barry Pike
Vice President - Daytime Drama .... Susan Lee
Vice President - Daytime Programs .... Jacqueline S. Smith
Vice President - Drama Development .... Dan Filie
Vice President - Entertainment Production .... Tim Quealy
Vice President - Family Programs .... Winifred White
Vice President - Finance & Administration .... Joseph Cicero
Vice President - Game Programs .... Joel Stein
Vice President - Mini-Series .... Ruth Slawson
Vice President - Program Planning .... Alan Sternfeld
Vice President - Program Production .... Perry Massey Jr.
Vice President - Research .... William Rubens
Vice President - Specials & Variety Programs .... Richard Ludwin
Vice President - Talent & Casting .... Lori Openden
Vice President - Talent .... Joel Thurm

NBC Business Affairs

Executive Vice President - Business Affairs .... John Agoglia
Senior Vice President - Finance .... Donald Carswell
Vice President - Business Affairs, Primetime Programs .... Gary Newman
Vice President - Business Affairs, Primetime Programs .... Leigh Brecheen
Vice President - Corporate Planning .... Ellen Agress
Vice President - Program Acquisitions .... Joseph Bures
Vice President - Program Marketing & Administration .... Alan Gerson
Vice President - Program Marketing & Administration .... Joseph Candido
Vice President - Strategic Planning ... Barbara Watson

NBC Corporate Communications

Executive Vice President - Marketing .... John Miller
Senior Vice President - Corporate Communications .... Betty Hudson
Vice President - Advertising & Promotion, East Coast .... Tim Miller
Vice President - Advertising & Promotion, West Coast .... Vince Manzeia
Vice President - Advertising Operations & Administration .... Paul Wang
Vice President - Corporate Communications .... Joseph Rutledge
Vice President - International Marketing ..... Gary Wald
Vice President - Media Relations, East Coast .... Curtis Block
Vice President - Media Relations, NBC Productions .... Gene Walsh
Vice President - Media Relations, West Coast .... Kathleen Tucci
Vice President - On-Air Promotion .... John Luma
Vice President - Print Advertising .... Jenness Brewer
Vice President - Special Promotion Projects .... Charles Stepner

NBC Productions

330 Bob Hope Drive
Burbank, CA 91523
818/840-7500

President .... Brandon Tartikoff
Executive Vice President .... John Agoglia
Senior Vice President .... Todd Leavitt
Vice President - Business Affairs .... Albert Spevak
Vice President - Creative Affairs .... Ivan Fecan
Vice President - Creative Affairs .... Brian Frons
Vice President - Film Production .... William Phillips
Vice President - Post Production ...... Dorothy J. Bailey

NELSON ENTERTAINMENT GROUP

335 N. Maple Dr., Suite 350
Beverly Hills, CA 90210
213/285-6000

8 Queen St.
London W1X 7PH

Chairman & Chief Executive Officer .... F. Richard Northcott
President & Chief Operating Officer ..... Barry Spikings
President - Production .... Rick Finkelstein
Chief Financial Officer .... Ron Cushey
Senior Vice President - Nelson Films .... Rick Finkelstein
Senior Vice President - Production ...... Donna Dubrow
Vice President - Production .... Graham Henderson

Nelson International

President & Chief Executive Officer .... Ian Jessel
Executive Vice President - Sales & Marketing .... Ian Scorer

Senior Vice President - International
Sales & Marketing .... Massimo Graziosi
Vice President - Business Affairs .... Kevin Koloff

Embassy Home Entertainment
President & Chief Operating Officer ..... Richard Childs
President - EHE International .... Ian Jessel
Executive Vice President &
Chief Financial Officer . ... Ron Cushy
Executive Vice President -
Corporate Affairs .... Walter Olesiuk
Executive Vice President -
Nelson Home Video .... Rand Bleimeister
Senior Vice President - In-House
Public Relations & Marketing .... Peter Graves
Vice President - Finance &
Administration, EHE
International. .... Malcolm Reeve

NEW LINE CINEMA CORP.
116 N. Robertson Blvd., 2nd Floor
Los Angeles, CA 90048
213/854-5811

575 8th Ave.
New York, NY 10018
212/239-8880

President & Chief Executive Officer .... Robert Shaye
President - International Affairs .... Rolf Mittweg
Senior Vice President - Advertising .... Theresa Collins
Senior Vice President -
Business Affairs .... Donna Bascom
Senior Vice President &
Treasurer .... Stephen Abramson
Vice President - Administration .... Randy Gardner
Vice President - Business Affairs .... Phillip L. Rosen
Vice President - Sales
Control & Auditing .... Nestor Nieves
Vice President - Sales &
Marketing - International .... Canela Gelano

New Line Productions Inc.
President .... Sara Risher
Executive Vice President -
Production .... Deborah Moore
Vice President - Acquisitions .... Tony Safford
Vice President - Creative Affairs .... Marjorie Lewis
Vice President - Creative
Development .... Michael DeLuca
Vice President - Post Production .... Joe Fineman

New Line Distribution Inc.
President & Chief
Executive Officer .... Mitchell Goldman
Co-President - Marketing .... Michael Harpster
Co-President - Marketing .... Sandra Ruch
Senior Vice President - Distribution .... Al Shapiro
Senior Vice President -
Marketing & Publicity .... Alison Emilio
Vice President - Marketing
Operations .... Ellen Eisenberg

O

ODYSSEY/CINECOM INTERNATIONAL
1250 Broadway, 33rd Floor
New York, NY 10001
212/239-8360

6500 Wilshire Blvd., Suite 400
Los Angeles, CA 90048
213/655-9335

Chairman & Co-Chief
Executive Officer .... Stephen Swid
President & Co-Chief
Executive Officer .... Amir Jacob Malin
President & Chief
Operating Officer .... Patrick Wachsberger
Senior Executive Vice President .... Veronica Maingard
Executive Vice President & Chief
Financial Officer .... John F. Levy
Executive Vice President -
Advertising & Marketing .... Thomas Moody
Executive Vice President -
Sales & Marketing .... Richard Abramawitz
Executive Vice President .... Bart Walker
Senior Vice President - Marketing ...... Johnny Friedkin
Senior Vice President - Production &
Acquisitions .... Leon Falk
Vice President - Acquisitions .... Shelby Stone
Vice President - Production .... Eric Steel
Vice President - Sales .... Dawn Hendler

ORION PICTURES CORP.
1888 Century Park East
Los Angeles, CA 90067
213/282-0550

9 W. 57th St.
New York, NY 10019
212/980-1117

Chairman of the Board .... Arthur Krim
President & Chief Executive Officer .... Eric Pleskow

Executive Vice President .... William Bernstein
Executive Vice President - Production .... Marc E. Platt
Senior Vice President & Chief Financial Officer & Treasurer .... Melvin Woods
Senior Vice President & General Counsel & Secretary .... Leonard Pack
Senior Vice President - Business Affairs .... Rachel Blachman
Senior Vice President - Finance ... Lawrence Bernstein
Senior Vice President - Operations & Finance .... Neil R. McCarthy
Vice President & Chief Accounting Officer & Controller .... Joel Grossman
Vice President - Administration ... Wendy Smith Stover
Vice President - Advertising .... Tami Masuda
Vice President - Human Resources .... Robin Berlin
Vice President - Production & Management .... Stan Neufeld
Vice President - Production Finance, East Coast .... Eric Shonz
Vice President - Production Finance, West Coast .... Merryl Salenger
Vice President - Production Management .... Ron Lynch
Vice President - Production Finance .... Julie Landau
Vice President - Production .... Lawrence E. Jackson
Vice President - Production .... Michael Barlow
Vice President - Production .... Hutch Parker
Story Editor .... Pat Morrison

Orion Pictures Distribution

Chairman of the Board .... David M. Forbes
Chief Executive Officer .... Eric Pleskow
Executive Vice President - Marketing .... Charles O. Glenn
Executive Vice President - Sales & Distribution .... Bernard (Buddy) Golden
Senior Vice President & Chief Financial Officer & Treasurer .... Melvin F. Woods
Senior Vice President & General Counsel & Secretary .... Leonard Pack
Senior Vice President & General Sales Manager .... Robert A. Schein
Senior Vice President - Post Production .... Solomon Lomita
Vice President & Chief Accounting Officer & Controller .... Joel Grossman
Vice President & Counsel .... John W. Hester
Vice President & Director of Media Services .... Susan K. Taylor
Vice President - Advertising .... Tina Tanen
Vice President - Creative Advertising .... Jeffrey Arter
Vice President - Media Services ..... Beverly Weinstein
Vice President - Promotion & Field Activities .... Carl J. Ferrazza
Vice President - Publicity & Promotion, West Coast .... Fred Skidmore
Vice President - Publicity .... Gail B. Brownstein
Vice President - Western Division .... Terry Kierzek

Orion Pictures International

President .... Robert Meyers
President - Television .... John Laing
Senior Vice President - International Video .... Diane Keating
Vice President - Worldwide Theatrical, Nontheatrical & TV Services .... Glaister Kerr
Vice President - Administration .... Arnold I. Adirim
Vice President - Europe & Africa .... Stuart Salter
Vice President - International Advertising & Publicity .... Susan Dambra
Vice President - International Operations .... Richard Plattsman
Vice President - Japan & the Far East .... Robert Chow
Vice President - Latin America .... Bob Girard
Vice President - Operations .... Vincent Famulari

Orion Classics

President .... Eric Pleskow
Vice President - Acquisitions .... Donna Gigliotti
Vice President - Business Affairs .... John Logigian
Vice President - Marketing & Distribution .... Tom Bernard
Vice President - Sales & Marketing .... Michael Barker

Orion Home Entertainment

Chairman & Chief Executive Officer .... Lawrence B. Hilford
Senior Vice President - Administration & Operations .... Gerald Sobczak
Senior Vice President - Business Affairs .... Robert A. Mirisch
Vice President - Business Affairs .... Kimberle Aronzon

Orion Television Entertainment

Chariman & Chief Executive Officer .... Gary Nardino
President .... Gary Randall
Senior Vice President - Business Affairs, Legal & Finance .... Irwin Moss
Senior Vice President - Development ..... Jeff Watchell
Senior Vice President - Marketing .... Larry Lynch
Senior Vice President - Production .... Rick Rosen
Vice President - Business Affairs .... Edward A. Hoffman
Vice President - Current Programs .... Gary Randall
Vice President - Production .... Bob Sanitsky

P

PARAMOUNT PICTURES CORP.

5555 Melrose Ave.
Hollywood, CA 90038
213/956-5000

Chairman & CEO - Paramount Communications .... Martin S. Davis
Chairman & Chief Executive Officer .... Frank G. Mancuso, Sr.
Executive Vice President & General Counsel .... A. Robert Pisano
Executive Vice President .... Richard Zimbert
Executive Vice President .... M. Kenneth Suddleson
Executive Vice President - Finance & Administration .... Patrick B. Purcell
Executive Vice President - Finance & Administration, Famous Music .... Sidney Herman
Senior Vice President & Assistant General Counsel .... Paul Springer
Senior Vice President & Deputy General Counsel .... Joshua Wattles
Senior Vice President & Treasurer .... Alan J. Bailey
Senior Vice President - Contract Accounting .... Allen S. Gottlieb
Senior Vice President - Corporate Communications .... Deborah Rosen
Senior Vice President - Financial Planning & Analysis .... John Bailey
Senior Vice President - Human Resources .... William A. Hawkins
Senior Vice President - Industrial Relations .... Stephen Koppekin
Senior Vice President - Management Information Systems .... Warren Ferriter
Senior Vice President - Theatrical Exhibition Group .... Larry Gleason
Vice President - Administration ...... Rosemary DiPietra
Vice President - Contract Accounting .... Carmen G. Desiderio
Vice President - Corporate Controller .... Thomas Zimmerman
Vice President - Employee Relations Legal Services .... Rina Wallack
Vice President - Financial Planning .... Steven J. Kowaliw
Vice President - Financial Planning & Analysis .... Bruce Churchill
Vice President - Human Resources .... Joanne Adams Griffith
Vice President - Labor Relations .... Richard P. Schonland
Vice President - Management Information Systems .... Gary Naiman
Vice President - Motion Picture Planning .... Mark J. Badagliacca
Vice President - Publicity .... Blaise J. Noto
Vice President - Systems Planning ..... Robert E. Zolan

Paramount Motion Picture Group

President .... Sidney Ganis
President .... Barry L. London
President - Worldwide Marketing .... Arthur Cohen
President - Domestic Distribution ...... Wayne Lewellen
Executive Vice President .... Robert Beitcher
Executive Vice President - General Sales Manager .... Jeffrey Blake
Executive Vice President - Marketing & Creative Affairs .... Nancy Goliger
Executive Vice President - International Marketing & Distribution .... Martin Kutner
Executive Vice President - Marketing .... Mardi Marans
Senior Vice President - Worldwide Publicity & Promotion .... Diana Widom
Senior Vice President - Advertising .... Thomas Campanella
Senior Vice President - Business Affairs .... Richard Fowkes
Senior Vice President - Business Affairs .... Gregory Gelfan
Senior Vice President - Legal Affairs ..... Ralph Kamon
Senior Vice President - Publicity .... Cheryl Boone Isaacs
Senior Vice President - Publicity & Advertising .... Robert Dorfman
Senior Vice President - Sales Operations .... Steven J. Rapaport
Vice President - Acquisitions .... John Ferraro
Vice President - Business Affairs - Music .... Gary Culpepper
Vice President - Creative Advertising .... Lucia Ludovico
Vice President - Creative Advertising .... Michael D. Camp
Vice President - Exhibitor Services .... Alan Cordover
Vice President - International Marketing .... Leslie Pound
Vice President - Legal Affairs .... David Rosenbaum
Vice President - Legal Affairs .... Robert B. Cohen
Vice President - Marketing .... Jerry A. Meadors
Vice President - Marketing Administration .... Ron Hein

Vice President - Merchandising & Licensing .... Andrea Hein
Vice President - Music Legal Affairs .... Linda Wohl
Vice President - Music .... Lonnie Sill
Vice President - Promotion & Field Publicity .... Michael Battaglia
Vice President - Sales Administration .... Bernard Spannagel

Paramount Production Division
President .... Gary Lucchesi
Senior Vice President .... Thomas Barad
Senior Vice President - European Production .... Ileen Maisel
Senior Vice President - Feature Production Management .... Robert Relyea
Senior Vice President - Production .... Lance Young
Vice President - Feature Production Management .... Larry Albucher
Vice President - Production .... William Horberg
Vice President - Production .... Constance Kaplan
Vice President - Production .... Teddy Zee
Vice President - Production Finance .... Frank Bodo

Paramount Studio Group
President .... Earl Lestz
Senior Vice President - Post Production .... Paul Haggar
Senior Vice President - Operations .... David Mannix
Vice President - Planning & Development .... Christine Essel
Vice President - Post Production .... Fred Chandler
Vice President - Studio & Community Relations .... Eunice Chesler
Vice President - Studio Administration .... Larry A. Owens
Vice President - Videotape Operations ..... Tom Bruehl

Paramount Television Group
President .... Mel Harris
President - Domestic Television ...... Lucille S. Salhany
President - Network Television .... John S.Pike
President - Video .... Robert Klingensmith
Senior Vice President - Business Development .... Alan Cole-Ford
Vice President & Controller .... Mark Lebowitz
Vice President - International Operations .... Joseph Lucas
Vice President - Latin American Sales .... Ramon Perez
Vice President - Operations .... Philip E. Murphy
Vice President - Planning .... Jack Waterman

Domestic Television Division
President .... Lucille S. Salhany
Executive Vice President .... Steven A. Goldman
Executive Vice President - Programming .... Frank H. Kelly
Executive Vice President - General Sales Manager .... R. Gregory Meidel
Senior Vice President - Advertising & Promotion .... Meryl Cohen
Senior Vice President - Business Affairs & Finance .... Robert Sheehan
Senior Vice President - Business Affairs .... Vance Scott Van Petten
Vice President - Administration .... Howard Green
Vice President - Creative Affairs ... Steven Nalevansky
Vice President - Eastern Regional Manager .... R. Edward Wilson
Vice President - Finance .... Emeline F. Davis
Vice President - Legal Affairs .... Thomas M. Fortuin
Vice President - Off-Network, Basic Cable, & Advertising Sales .... Joel Berman
Vice President - Production .... Cliff Lachman
Vice President - Production .... Jack Wartlieb
Vice President - Programming .... Charlotte Koppe
Vice President - Research & Sales Development .... James E. Martz
Vice President - Western Regional Manager .... Richard Montgomery

Network Television Division
President .... John S.Pike
Executive Vice President - Business Affairs .... Cecilia R. Andrews
Executive Vice President - Creative Affairs .... John Symes
Senior Vice President - Development ..... Paul J. Heller
Senior Vice President - Legal Affairs ... Howard Barton
Senior Vice President - Production .... Michael P. Schoenbrun
Vice President - Advertising & Publicity .... John A. Wentworth
Vice President - Business Affairs .... Ronald J. Jacobson
Vice President - Finance .... Gerald Goldman
Vice President - Programs .... Timothy Iacofano
Vice President - Programs .... Thomas Mazza
Vice President - Talent & Casting .... Helen Mossler-Herman

Paramount Video Division
President .... Robert Klingensmith
Executive Vice President .... Timothy Clott

Senior Vice President &
General Manager .... Eric Doctorow
Senior Vice President - Business &
International Affairs .... James Gianopulos
Senior Vice President - Finance &
Operations .... Jay Heifetz
Vice President - Advertising &
Sales Promotion .... Hollace Brown
Vice President - Legal Affairs .... Steven Madoff
Vice President - Marketing .... Alan Perper
Vice President - Sales .... Jack Kanne

PATHE ENTERTAINMENT CO.
640 N. San Vicente Blvd.
Los Angeles, CA 90048
213/658-2100

Co-Chairman & Chief
Executive Officer .... Giancarlo Parretti
Co-Chairman & Chief
Operating Officer .... Liliana Avincola
Chairman .... Alan Ladd Jr.
Chairman - Production .... Jay Kanter
President - International
Production .... Sanford Lieberson
President - Worldwide Marketing .... Greg Morrison
Senior Executive Vice President -
Business Affairs .... Frank I. Davis
Executive Vice President -
Business Affairs .... Alan Krieger
Executive Vice President - Production
Management .... Leonard Kroll
Vice President - Business Affairs .... Ronni Goldstein
Vice President - Business
Affairs .... Chris Ann Maxwell
Vice President - Marketing .... Katherine Orloff
Vice President - Production .... David Ladd
Vice President - Production .... Rebecca Pollack

Cannon Entertainment
5757 Wilshire Blvd., Suite 721
Los Angeles, CA 90036
213/965-0901

Chairman & Chief Executive
Officer & President .... Yoram Globus
Chief Financial Officer .... Aurelio Germes

Cannon Pictures
Chairman .... Ovidio Assonitis
Vice Chairman .... William J. Immerman
President .... Christopher Pearce
Senior Vice President - Production ..... Peter Shepherd
Vice President - Administration .... Allan Greenblatt

R

RASTAR/INDIEPROD.
Columbia Plaza West
Burbank, CA 91505
818/954-6000

Co-Chairman .... Ray Stark
Co-Chairman .... Daniel Melnick
Vice Chairman .... William Nestel
Vice Chairman .... Allen Shapiro
President - Production, Rastar .... John Fielder
President - Production, Indieprod .... John Fiedler
Executive Vice President -
Television .... David Sontag
Senior Vice President - Marketing .... Dan Safran
Vice President - Production .... Cathy Rabin
Vice President - Production .... Nancy Graham
Vice President .... Elizabeth Fox
Vice President .... Janet Garrison

REPUBLIC PICTURES CORP.
12636 Beatrice Street
Los Angeles, CA 90066
213/306-4040

Chairman .... Russell Goldsmith
President .... Aubrey (Bud) Groskopf
President - International
Distribution .... Joe Levinsohn
Executive Vice President .... Laurie Levit
Senior Vice President .... Steven Beeks
Vice President & Chief
Financial Officer .... David Kirchheimer
Vice President & National
Sales Manager .... Dick Jolliffe
Vice President & International
Sales Manager .... Joe Levinsohn
Vice President - Acquisitions .... Mel Layton
Vice President - Business
Affairs & Legal .... Richard Kurshner
Vice President - East Coast .... Elaine Cohen
Vice President - Marketing .... Vallery Kountze

S

SCOTTI BROTHERS ENTERTAINMENT INDUSTRIES
2114 Pico Blvd.
Santa Monica, CA 90405
213/450-3193

Chairman & Chief Executive Officer .... Tony Scotti
Co-Chairman .... Ben Scotti
Co-Chairman .... Fred Scotti
President - Scotti Bros. Distribution ...... Jerry Pickman
President - Scotti Bros. Records .... Johnny Musso
President - Scotti/Vinnedge TV .... Syd Vinnedge
Chief Financial Officer .... Tom Bradshaw
Executive Vice President - Production ..... Hilton Green
Vice President - Administration ...... Barbara Herburger

SHAPIRO GLICKENHAUS ENTERTAINMENT CORPORATION
12001 Ventura Place, Suite 404
Studio City, CA 91604
818/766-8500

1619 Broadway, Suite 306
New York, NY 10019
212/265-1150

Chairman .... James M. Glickenhaus
President & Chief Executive Officer .... Leonard Shapiro
Executive Vice President .... Alan M. Solomon
Senior Vice President & General Manager, Home Video .... Peter Pidutti
Senior Vice President & General Sales Manager .... Robert Berney Jr.
Senior Vice President - Acquisition & Production .... Frank Isaac
Vice President - Domestic Distribution & Marketing .... Jerry Landesman

SKOURAS PICTURES INC.
1040 N. Las Palmas Ave.
Hollywood, CA 90038
213/467-3000

President & Chief Executive Officer .... Dimitri (Tom) Skouras
President - Motion Picture Division .... Jeffrey Lipsky
Senior Vice President - Business & Legal Affairs .... Jeffrey Holmes
Senior Vice President - Finance & Administration .... John Kendrick
Senior Vice President - International .... Sigrid Ann Davison
Vice President - Acquisitions .... Majorie Skouras
Vice President - Corporate Projects .... B.J. Miller
Vice President - International .... Midge Barnett

SOVEREIGN PICTURES INC.
11845 W. Olympic Blvd., Suite 1055
Los Angeles, CA 90064
213/312-1001

Chairman & Chief Executive Officer .... Ernst Goldschmidt
President .... Barbara Boyle
Executive Vice President .... David Lamping
Senior Vice President & Chief Financial Officer .... Craig Staley
Senior Vice President .... Michael Helfant
Vice President & Controller .... Judith Garinger
Vice President - Advertising & Publicity .... Andrew Foster
Vice President - Production .... Ron Yerxa

SPELLING ENTERTAINMENT CO.
1041 N. Formosa Ave.
Los Angeles, CA 90046
213/850-2413

Chairman .... Aaron Spelling
President & Chief Executive Officer .... Jules Haimovitz
Executive Vice President .... Ronald Lightstone
Senior Vice President & Chief Financial Officer .... John Brady

Spelling Productions
President - Theatrical Division .... Alan Greisman
Executive Supervising Producer .... E. Duke Vincent
Senior Vice President - Business & Finance .... Tony Colabraro
Senior Vice President - Business & Legal Affairs .... Art Frankel
Vice President - Business Affairs .... Barbara M. Rubin
Vice President - Program Development .... Marcia Basichis
Vice President - Talent & Casting .... Tony Shepherd
Vice President - Movies for Television & Miniseries .... Andy Siegel

T

TRANS WORLD ENTERTAINMENT
3330 Cahuenga Blvd. West, Suite 500
Los Angeles, CA 90068
213/969-2800

Co-Chairman .... Moshe Diamant
Co-Chairman .... Eduard Sarlui
President - Motion Picture Division .... Paul Mason
President - Distribution & Marketing .... Elliot Slutsky
President - Domestic Distribution .... Yoram Pelman
Senior Vice President - Creative Advertising .... Steve Segal
Vice President - Foreign Sales .... Chris Davis
Vice President - Publicity .... Zbigniew Kozlowski

Emerald Films International
President .... Ernst (Etchie) Stroh
Vice President - International Marketing & Publicity. .... Jamie Midgley
Vice President - Operations .... Luz Moretti
Vice President - Sales .... Sergio Aguero

TRI-STAR PICTURES
(see COLUMBIA Pictures Entertainment)

TURNER ENTERTAINMENT
1050 Techwood Drive
Atlanta, GA 30318
404/827-1434

10100 Venice Blvd.
Culver City, CA 90232
213/558-7300

Chairman & Chief Executive Officer .... Ted Turner

Turner Network Television
President .... Gerry Hogan
Executive Vice President .... Scott Sassa
Senior Vice President - Original Programming .... Linda Berman
Vice President - Creative Services .... Betty Cohen
Vice President - Marketing & Communications .... Arthur Sando
Vice President - Program Development .... Gerry Clard
Vice President - Public Relations .... Michael Oglesby

Turner Entertainment Company
10100 Venice Blvd.
Culver City, CA 90232
213/558-7300

President & Chairman - Turner Program Services .... Jack Petrick
Vice President & General Manager .... Steve Chamberlain
Vice President - Home Entertainment .... Ellen Wander
Vice President - Program Development .... Laurie Pozmantier

TWENTIETH CENTURY FOX FILM CORPORATION
10201 W. Pico Blvd.
Los Angeles, CA 90035
213/277-2211

40 W. 57th St., 8th Floor
New York, NY 10019
212/977-5500

Mailing Address
P.O. Box 900
Beverly Hills, CA 90213

Owner .... Rupert Murdoch
Chairman & Chief Executive Officer .... Barry Diller
Chairman - Fox Film Corporation .... Joe Roth
President & Chief Operating Officer .... Strauss Zelnick
President - Fox Inc. .... Jonathan Dolgen
Executive Vice President .... Chase Carey
Senior Vice President & Deputy General Counsel .... Lyman S. Gronemeyer
Senior Vice President & Assistant General Counsel .... Mary Anne Harrison
Senior Vice President - Banking & Taxes .... John P. Meehan
Senior Vice President - Employee Relations & Administration .... Dean S. Ferris
Senior Vice President - External Legal Affairs .... David Y. Handelman
Senior Vice President - Finance .... Harvey Finkel
Senior Vice President - Studio & Broadcast Operations .... Andrew Setos
Vice President & Assistant to the Chairman. .... Beth Colloty
Vice President & Controller .... Harvey Finkel
Vice President - Administration & Strategic Planning .... Robert Fleming

Vice President - Labor Relations .... Pam DiGiovanni
Vice President - Personnel .... Leslee Perlstein
Vice President - Taxes .... Earl Hammond
Vice President - TV Production
Legal Affairs .... Walter Swanson

Motion Picture Division Production

President - Worldwide Production ..... Roger Birnbaum
Executive Vice President - Business Affairs .... Leon Brachman
Executive Vice President - Production .... Tom Jacobson
Senior Vice President - Music .... Elliot Lurie
Senior Vice President - Post Production .... Gary Gerlich
Senior Vice President - Production .... Melissa Bachrach
Senior Vice President - Production .... Elizabeth Brand-Gabler
Senior Vice President - Production .... Riley Ellis
Senior Vice President - Production .... Jon Landau
Senior Vice President - Production ..... Michael London
Senior Vice President - Production ..... Margery Simkin
Senior Vice President - Production Management .... Michael Joyce
Vice President - Business Affairs .... Cappy Cagan
Vice President - Business Affairs .... Charles Holland
Vice President - Finance .... John Pearson
Vice President - Media .... Nancy Utley-Jacobs
Vice President - Production .... Susan Cartsonis
Vice President - Production .... Nancy Neufeld

Marketing & Distribution

President - Domestic Distribution & Marketing .... Thomas Sherak
President - Domestic Distribution .... Bruce Snyder
President - Marketing .... Robert Harper
Executive Vice President & General Sales Manager .... Richard Myerson
Executive Vice President - Marketing ..... Cynthia Wick
Senior Vice President - Marketing .... Jeff Ammer
Vice President - Creative Advertising .... Christopher Pula
Vice President - Creative Advertising ..... Roland Mesa
Vice President - Licensing & Merchandising .... Albert Ovadia
Vice President - Publicity .... Susan Culley
Vice President - Sales Administration & Branch Operations .... Morris Stermer
Vice President - Sales Operations & Administration .... Harvey Applebaum

International Division

President - Foreign Distribution & Marketing .... Jean-Louis Rubin
Vice President - Europe & Middle East .... Jorge G. Canizares
Vice President - Far East & Australia .... Jacob Shapiro
Vice President - Finance & Administration .... James Langsbard
Vice President - International Advertising, Publicity & Promotion .... Joel Coler
Vice President - International Operations, Latin America .... Francisco (Paco) Rodriguez

Fox Broadcasting Co.

Chairman & Chief Executive Officer .... Barry Diller
President & Chief Operating Officer .... Jamie Kellner
Senior Vice President - Affiliate Relations .... Preston Padden
Vice President - Affiliate Relations, Central Region .... Robert Mariano
Vice President - Affiliate Relations, Eastern Region .... Greg Gush
Vice President - Affiliate Relations, Western Region .... David Ferrara

FBC Entertainment

President .... Peter Chernin
President, Fox Night at the Movies .... Lawrence A. Jones
Executive Vice President - Series Programming .... Paul Stupin
Senior Vice President - Advertising & Promotion .... Sandy Grushow
Senior Vice President - Business Affairs ..... Ira Kurgan
Senior Vice President - Development ... Rob Kenneally
Senior Vice President - Publicity & Corporate Creative Services .... Brad Turrell
Vice President - Advertising & Promotion .... Michael Peikoff
Vice President - Current Programming .... Christopher Davidson
Vice President - Current Programming .... Michael Lansbury
Vice President - Development .... Joe Davola
Vice President - Movies & Miniseries .... Paul Nagel
Vice President - National Sales .... Jean Rossi
Vice President - Research & Marketing ... Andy Fessel
Vice President - Sales Development & Marketing .... Hank Close
Vice President - Talent & Casting .... Robert Harbin

Fox Inc.
President .... Jonathan Dolgen
President - Production .... Harris L. Katleman
Executive Vice President - Production & Finance .... Charles Goldstein
Senior Vice President - Business Affairs .... Gary S. Newman
Senior Vice President - Creative Affairs .... Stuart Sheslow
Senior Vice President - Production Management .... Robert Gros
Vice President - Business Affairs .... Benson Begun
Vice President - Corporate Taxes .... Raymond L. Parrish
Vice President - Current Programming & Planning .... Steven Gelber
Vice President - Post Production .... Edward Nassour
Vice President - Tape Production .... Joel Hornstock

Television Distribution Division
President - Domestic Syndication ..... Michael Lambert
President - International Syndication .... Williams Saunders
Executive Vice President - Administration & Operations .... Leonard Grossi
Senior Vice President - Domestic Syndication & Marketing .... Fred Bierman
Vice President - Adminstration & Strategic Planning .... Robert T. Fleming
Vice President - European Operations .... Malcolm Vaughn
Vice President - Labor Relations .... Hugo Rossitter
Vice President - Legal Affairs .... David Witus
Vice President - Research .... George Gubert
Vice President - Syndicated Programming .... Joel Cheatwood

21ST CENTURY FILM CORP.
8200 Wilshire Blvd.
Beverly Hills, CA 90211
213/658-3000

156 W. 56th St., 20th Floor
New York, NY 10019
212/765-5656

Chairman of the Board & Chief Executive Officer .... Menahem Golan
President .... Ami Artzi
Executive Vice President & Chief Operating Officer .... Alain Jakubowicz
Executive Vice President - Worldwide Motion Picture Production .... Gene Corman
Senior Vice President & General Sales Manager .... Jerry Jorgensen
General Counsel .... Rowland W. Day II
Vice President & Chief Financial Officer .... Robert E. Younger
Vice President - Worldwide Motion Picture Production .... Bram Roos
Vice President - Administration .... Hanan Adaki
Vice President - Creative Affairs .... Jerry Felix
Vice President - Distribution .... Allen Elrod
Vice President - Distribution .... David L. Garel
Vice President - Distribution .... Daniel Marks
Vice President - East Coast Production .... David Gil
Vice President - International Acquisitions .... Alain Berger
Vice President - International Operations .... Avraham Berman
Vice President - International Sales .... Carole DeLosSantos
Vice President - Legal Affairs .... William S. Weiner
Vice President & Managing Director, Italy .... Anna Dunn
Vice President - Production .... Marc S. Fischer
Vice President - Publicity .... Priscilla McDonald

U

UNIVERSAL PICTURES
100 Universal City Plaza
Universal City, CA 91608
818/777-1000
MCA Inc.

Chairman & Chief Executive Officer .... Lew R. Wasserman
President & Chief Operating Officer .... Sidney Jay Sheinberg
Executive Vice President .... Thomas Wertheimer
Vice President & Controller .... Richard E. Baker
Vice President & President/Chief Executive Officer - MCA Records ..... Alvin N. Teller
Vice President - Human Resources .... Janet Wood

MCA Motion Picture Group
Chairman .... Thomas P. Pollock
Senior Vice President .... Fred Bernstein
Senior Vice President .... Joseph Fischer
Senior Vice President - Music Creative Affairs .... Burt Berman
Vice President .... Ann Busby
Vice President - Business Affairs .... Mel Sattler

Vice President - Business Affairs .... Gerald Barton
Vice President - Business Affairs .... Mark Halloran
Vice President - Music Business Affairs, Filmed Entertainment Group .... Roxanne Lippel

Universal Pictures Production
President - Worldwide Production .... Casey Silver
Executive Vice President - Production .... Joshua Donen
Senior Vice President - Production & Post Production .... Donna Smith
Vice President - Creative Affairs .... Julia Chasman
Vice President - Feature Casting .... Nancy Nayor
Vice President - Production .... Hal Lieberman
Vice President - Production .... Tom Craig
Vice President - Production .... Fred Brost
Vice President - Production & Acquisitions .... James Jacks
Vice President - Talent Relations .... Linda Berken

Universal Pictures Marketing
Executive Vice President - Worldwide Marketing .... Simon Kornblit
Senior Vice President - Marketing .... Perry Katz
Senior Vice President - Marketing & Creative Advertising .... David Sameth
Senior Vice President - Marketing, Publicity & Promotion .... Sally Van Slyke
Vice President & Director of Research .... Roger Seltzer
Vice President - Creative Advertising/ Creative Director .... Carol McMillan
Vice President - Creative Affairs .... Peter Frankfurt
Vice President - International Advertising & Publicity .... Nadia Alves-Bronson
Vice President - Media & Co-op Advertising .... Teri Korban-Seide
Vice President - Media & Co-op Advertising .... Vic Fondrk
Vice President - Planning & Marketing .... Charlotte Reith

Universal Pictures Distribution
President .... Fred Mound
Vice President .... Dave Richoux
Vice President .... Phil Sherman
Vice President .... Nikki Rocco
Vice President - Acquisitions .... Robert A. Sherwood

Universal City Studios
Senior Vice President & General Manager .... Donald E. Slusser

Senior Vice President - Post Production .... James A. (Skip) Lusk
Vice President - Legal & Business Affairs .... Jerry Blair

Universal Television
President .... Kerry McCluggage
Executive Vice President - Administration .... Irv Sepkowitz
Senior Vice President - Dramatic & Longform Programming .... Charmaine Balian
Senior Vice President - Music .... Roxanne Lippel
Vice President - Casting .... Joan Sittenfield
Vice President - Comedy Development .... Brad Johnson

MCA Television Entertainment
President .... Shelly Schwab
Executive Vice President - Administration .... Edward Masket
Executive Vice President - Creative Affairs .... Ned Nalle
Executive Vice President - Production ...... Jim Watters
Senior Vice President - Business Affairs .... Bob Kelley
Senior Vice President - Program Development .... Kenneth J. Arber
Vice President - Research & Development .... Gerald T. Farrell

MCA Home Entertaiment Group
President - MCA Home Video .... Robert Blattner
Executive Vice President .... Sondra Berchin
Senior Vice President - Business Affairs & Administration .... Blair M. Westlake
Vice President - Creative Services .... Craig Relyea
Vice President - Marketing .... Andrew Kairey

V

VIACOM INC.
1211 Avenue of the Americas
New York, NY 10036
212/575-5175

10 Universal City Plaza
Universal City, CA 91608
818/505-7500

Chairman & Chief Executive Officer ...... Henry Schleiff
President .... Arthur Kananack
President - Acquisitions & First-Run Programming .... Michael Gerber

President - Domestic Syndication ....Joe Zelski
President - International Sales ....Raul Lefcovich
Executive Vice President & General Counsel ....Gregory J. Ricca
Executive Vice President & General Sales Manager ....Paul Kalvin
Executive Vice President - Marketing ....Dennis Gillespie
Senior Vice President - Programs ....Toby Martin
Senior Vice President ....Scott Davis
Senior Vice President...........................Peter Newman
Vice President & Counsel ....Andrew E. Suser
Vice President - Marketing & News Media ....Judith Pless

Viacom International
President & Chief Executive Officer ....Frank J. Biondi Jr.
Senior Vice President & Chief Financial Officer.......................George S. Smith Jr.
Senior Vice President & Secretary ....Mark M. Weinstein
Senior Vice President - Corporate Relations ....Raymond A. Boyce
Senior Vice President...................Edward D. Horowitz
Vice President - Corporate Development.....................................Leslie Schine
Vice President - Human Resources .....William Roskin

Viacom Pictures
Chairman ....Neil S. Braun
President & Chief Executive Officer ....Frederick Schneier
Vice President ....Barbara Title

Viacom Productions Inc.
President ....Thomas D. Tannenbaum
Senior Vice President - Business Affairs ....Roger P. Kirman
Senior Vice President - Production ......Michael Moder
Senior Vice President ....Robert Greenfield
Vice President - Development ....Steven D. Gordon
Vice President - Drama ....David Auerbach

MTV Networks, Inc.
1775 Broadway
New York, NY 10019
212/713-6400
213/505-7812

Chairman & Chief Executive Officer ....Tom Freston
President - HA! ....Ed Bennett
President - MTV ....John Reardon
President - Nickelodeon/ Nick At Nite ....Geraldine Laybourne
President - VH-1 ....Edward Bennett
Chief Financial Officer ....James Shaw
Executive Vice President & General Manager ....Lee Masters
Executive Vice President - Corporate Affairs & Communications ....Marshall Cohen
Executive Vice President - New Business Development ....Sara Levinson
Senior Vice President - Law & Business Affairs ....Lois Peel Eisenstein

Showtime Networks Inc.
Chairman & Chief Executive Officer ....Winston (Tony) Cox
Executive Vice President - Programming ....Fred Schneier
Senior Vice President - Business Affairs ....William F. Rogers
Senior Vice President - Corporate Affairs ....McAdory Lipscomb Jr.
Senior Vice President - Original Programs & Production ....Steve Hewitt
Senior Vice President - Strategic Planning ....Angela B. Gerkin
Vice President - Business Affairs ....Jeff Silberman
Vice President - Corporate Communications ....Nancy Glauberman
Vice President - Direct Marketing ......Mark Greenberg
Vice President - Marketing Strategy ...William Fowkes
Vice President - Program Administration...................................Robert Nitkin
Vice President - Program Research ....Joanne Bouffard
Vice President - Consumer Public Relations ....Lee Tenebruso
Vice Preident & Counsel ....Andrea Simon

W

WARNER BROS. INC.
4000 Warner Blvd.
Burbank, CA 91522
818/954-6000

Special Counsel - Warner Communications ....Steve Ross
Chairman & Chief Executive Officer .....Robert A. Daly
President & Chief Operating Officer ....Terry Semel
Executive Vice President ....Barry M. Meyer

Executive Vice President - Aquisitions .... James R. Miller
Executive Vice President .... Charles McGregor
Executive Vice President - Marketing & Planning .... Sanford Reisenbach
Senior Vice President & General Counsel .... John A. Schulman
Senior Vice President .... David G. Stanley
Vice President - Production .... William L. Young
Vice President - Worldwide Video Acquisitions .... Elyse Eisenberg
Vice President - Business Affairs .... Steven Bersch

Warner Bros. Production

President - Theatrical Production .... Bruce Berman
Executive Vice President .... Mark Canton
Senior Vice President - Business Affairs .... James R. Miller
Senior Vice President - Theatrical Production .... Lucy Fisher
Senior Vice President & Treasurer .... Ralph Peterson
Vice President - Contract Administration .... Pat Hopkins
Vice President - Creative Affairs .... Kimberly Brent
Vice President - Creative Affairs, East Coast .... Susan Dalsimer
Vice President - Film Acquisition .... Diane Maddox
Vice President - Post Production .... Fred Talmadge
Vice President - Production .... Allyn Stewart
Vice President - Production .... Bill Gerber
Vice President - Production .... Lisa Henson
Vice President - Production .... Robert Guralnick
Vice President - Production .... Tom Lassally
Vice President - Talent .... Marion Dougherty
Vice President - Theatrical Production .... Robert Brassel
Vice President - Worldwide Acquisitions .... Mitch Horwits

Warner Bros. Advertising & Publicity

President - Worldwide Theatrical Advertising & Publicity .... Robert Friedman
Senior Vice President - Worldwide Creative Advertising .... Joel Wayne
Senior Vice President - Worldwide Publicity .... Joe Hyams
Senior Vice President - Marketing Research Worldwide .... Richard Del Belso
Vice President - Worldwide Advertising & Publicity Services .... Lori Drazen
Vice President - Media .... John Jacobs
Vice President - National Publicity .... Carl Samrock
Vice President - Publicity & Promotion .... Charlotte Gee
Vice President - Publicity .... Dawn McElwaine
Vice President - Publicity .... John Dartigue

Warner Bros. International

President - International .... Richard J. Fox
Senior Vice President - International .... Wayne Duband
Vice President - London .... Eric Senat
Vice President - Studio Administration Offices - International Division .... Peter Howard
Vice President - International Marketing - Home Video .... Brian Jamieson
Vice President - Canadian Advertising & Publicity .... Dianne Schwalm
Vice President - European Advertising & Publicity .... Julian Senior
Vice President - International Advertising & Publicity .... Irving N. Ivers
Vice President - Theatrical Distribution - International .... Edward E. Frumkes

Warner Bros. Distribution

President - Domestic Distribution .... D. Barry Reardon
Senior Vice President & General Sales Manager .... Daniel R. Fellman
Vice President - Sales Operations .... Don Tannenbaum
Vice President - Sales Operation .... Richard A. Shiff

Warner Bros. Administration

Executive Vice President & Treasurer .... Ralph Peterson
Senior Vice President & Corporate Controller .... Edward A. Romano
Vice President & General Counsel .... John Schulman
Vice President & General Counsel - Theatrical Legal .... Jeremy Williams
Vice President & Deputy General Counsel - Air Division .... Sheldon Presser
Vice President - Administrative Services & Operations .... Sebastian Pasqua
Vice President - Business Affairs .... Keith Fleer
Vice President - Business Affairs .... Patti Connolly
Vice President - Business Affairs .... Steven S. Spira
Vice President - National Field Operations .... Stuart Gottesman
Vice President - Human Resources .... Adrienne J. Gary
Vice President - Industrial Relations .... Alan H. Raphael
Vice President - Labor Relations .... J.R. Ballance

Vice President - Production Accounting .... Lawrence W. Schneider
Vice President - Theatrical Business Affairs Administration ..... Virginia Tweedy
Vice President - Worldwide Merchandising .... Dan Romanelli
Consultant .... Stanley Belkin

Warner Bros. Music

President .... Gary Lemel
Vice President - Music Administration ...... Bill Schrank
Vice President - Music Administration .... Doug Frank

Warner Bros. Television

President - TV .... Harvey Shephard
President - Pay-TV & Network Feature Film Sales .... Edward Bleier
Senior Vice President - Business Affairs .... Beverly Nix
Vice President - Film & Tape Productions .... Steve Papazian
Vice President - Marketing - Pay TV, Animation, Network Features .... Eric Frankel
Vice President - Movies & Mini-Series .... Gregg Maday
Vice President - Pay-TV Sales & Administration .... Stanley Solson
Vice President - Research, Off-Network, Cable & Features .... Robert Jennings
Vice President - Sales Planning, Pay-TV & Network .... Jeffrey Calman
Vice President - Talent & Casting .... Marcia S. Ross
Vice President - TV Production .... Gary Credle

Warner Bros. Animation

President - Network & Pay TV .... Edward Bleier
Vice President - Animation .... Kathleen Helppie

Time Warner Enterprises

President & CEO .... Robert Pittman

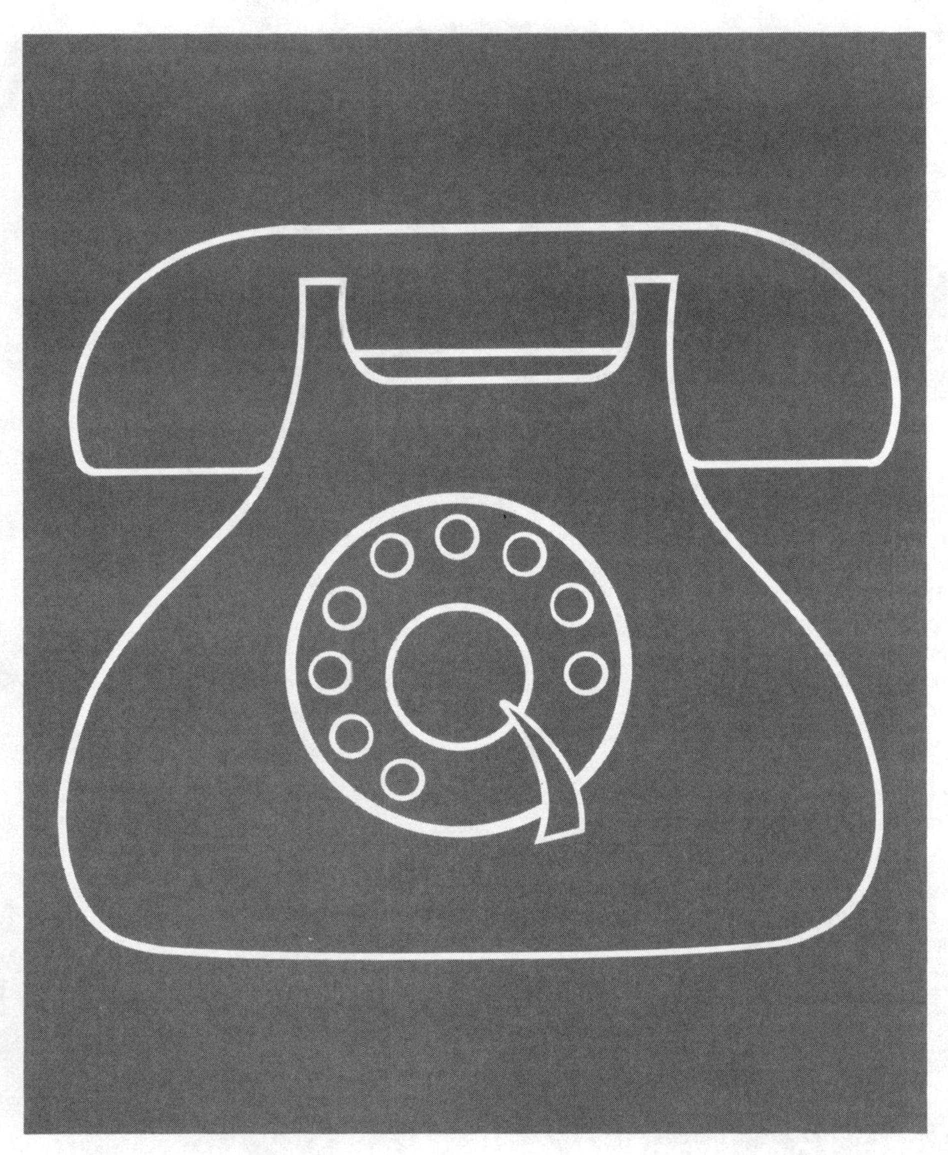

AGENTS

A

ABRAMS ARTISTS & ASSOCIATES
9200 Sunset Blvd., Suite 625
Los Angeles, CA 90069
213/859-0625

420 Madison Avenue
Suite 1400
New York, NY 10017
212/935-8980

Harry Abrams
Toni Benson
Martin Lesak
Nina Pakula
Joseph Rice

BRET ADAMS, LTD.
448 West 44th St.
New York, NY 10036
212/765-5630

Bret Adams
Nancy Curtis
Mary Harden
Margi Rountree

ADDIS-WECHSLER & ASSOCIATES
8444 Wilshire Blvd., 5th Floor
Beverly Hills, CA 90211
213/653-8867

Keith Addis
Gerald Harrington
Danny Heeps
Eli Johnson
Nick Wechsler

THE ADLER AGENCY
9056 Santa Monica Blvd.
West Hollywood, CA
213/278-3456

Jerry Adler

THE AGENCY
10351 Santa Monica Blvd., Suite 211
Los Angeles, CA 90025
213/551-3000

Larry Becsey
Dick Berman
Caron Champoux
Bill Danziger
Nevin Dolcefino
Christine Foster
Ellen Fuchs
Michael Packingham
Jerry Ryben
Irv Schwartz
Laura Sutten
Jerry Zeitman

AGENCY FOR THE PERFORMING ARTS
9000 Sunset Blvd.,12th Floor
Los Angeles, CA 90069
213/273-0744

888 Seventh Ave.
New York, NY 10016
212/582-1500

Casey Bierer
Jon Brown
Lee Dintsman
John Gaines
Hal Gefsky
Emily Gerson (NY)
Dick Gilmore
Jim Gosnell
Rick Greenstein
David Kalodner (NY)
Kenneth Kaplan (NY)
Lee Kappelman
Marty Klein
Tom Korman
Rick Leed (NY)
Harvey Litwin (NY)
Larry Masser
Stuart Miller
Dan Pietragaloo
Danny Robinson
Ellen Seidman
Bonnie Sugarman
Burt Taylor
Steve Tellez
Doug Warner

BUDDY ALTONI TALENT AGENCY
P.O. Box 1022
Newport Beach, CA 92660
714/851-1711

Buddy Altoni

CARLOS ALVARADO AGENCY
8820 Sunset Blvd., Suites A & B
Los Angeles, CA 90069
213/652-0272

Carlos Alvarado
Monalee Schilling

AMERICAN ARTISTS, INC.
6994 El Camino Real, #208
Carlsbad, CA 92009

Ronald E. Matonak

FRED AMSEL & ASSOCIATES, INC.
6310 San Vicente Blvd., Suite 407
Los Angeles, CA 90048
213/939-1188

Fred Amsel
Mike Eisenstadt
John Frazier

IRVIN ARTHUR ASSOCIATES
9363 Wilshire Blvd., Suite 212
Beverly Hills, CA 90210
213/278-5934

Irvin Arthur
Michael Green
Anne McDermott
Lloyd Segan
Robyn Stevens
Jeff Sullivan

THE ARTISTS AGENCY
10000 Santa Monica Blvd., Suite 305
Los Angeles, CA 90067
213/277-7779

Jim Cota
Mickey Freiberg
Merrily Kane
Ginger Lawrence
Michael Livingston
Richard A. Shepherd
Bruce Tuseld
Don Wolff

ARTISTS AGENCY, INC.
(In Association with Favored Artists)
230 West 55th St., #29D
New York, NY 10019
212/245-6960

Stacie Rausch
Jonathan Russo
Barry Weiner

ARTISTS ALLIANCE
(In Association with the Anne Geddes Agency)
8457 Melrose Pl., #200
Los Angeles, CA 90069
213/651-2401

Audrey Caan
Karen Frank
Jack Panell
Rodney Sheldon

THE ARTISTS GROUP
1930 Century Park West, Suite 403
Los Angeles, CA 90067
213/552-1100

Gordon Berry
Cory Eglash
Susan Grant
Nancy Moon
Barry Saloman
Arnie Soloway
Hal Stalmaster

ASHER/KROST MANAGEMENT
644 N. Doheny Dr.
Los Angeles, CA 90069
213/273-9433

Peter Asher
Barry Krost

HOWARD J. ASKENASE
217 Glen Airy Dr.
Los Angeles, CA 90068
213/464-4114

Howard J. Askenase

ASSOCIATED MANAGEMENT CO.
9200 Sunset Blvd., PH-20
Los Angeles, CA 90069
213/550-0570

Harold Cohen
Jerry Levy

ASSOCIATED TALENT AGENCY, INC.
9744 Wilshire Blvd., Suite 312
Los Angeles, CA 90212
213/271-4662

Bud Kenneally
Patrick White
Martin Zitter

B

BARRETT, BENSON, McCARTT & WESTON
2121 Avenue of the Stars, Suite 2450
Los Angeles, CA 90067
213/277-4998

Christopher Barrett
Jeffrey A. Benson
Dianne Fraser
Ben Freiberger
Scott Lambert
Bettye McCartt
Steve Rose
Sara Schedeen

Bettina Viviano
Richard A. Weston
Tory Whipple

THE BARSKIN AGENCY
120 S. Victory Blvd., Suite 104-A
Burbank, CA 91502
818/848-5536

David Barskin

BART-MILANDER ASSOCIATES INC.
4146 Lankershim Blvd., Suite 300
North Hollywood, CA 91602
818/761-4040

Al Bart
Jeff H. Kaufman
Stan Milander
Cathy Schleussmer

BAUER BENEDEK AGENCY
9255 Sunset Blvd., Suite 716
Los Angeles, CA 90069
213/275-2421

Marty Bauer
Peter Benedek
Dan Halsted
Martin Hurwitz
David J. Kanter
John Lesher
Gavin Palone
Cynthia Shelton
Jeremy Zimmer

BAUMAN, HILLER & ASSOCIATES
250 West 57th St.
New York, NY 10019
212/757-0098

Richard Bauman
Walter Hiller
Victor Latino
Kay Liberman
Mark Redanty
Chris Schmidt

BDP & ASSOCIATES
10637 Burbank Blvd.
North Hollywood, CA 91601
818/506-7615

Samuel Gelfman

GEORGES BEAUME
3 Quai Malaquais
Paris, 75006 France
325-2837

Georges Beaume

THE BENNETT AGENCY
150 S. Barringston Ave., Suite 1
Los Angeles, CA 90049
213/471-2251

Carole Bennett

LOIS BERMAN
240 West 44th St.
New York, NY 10036
212/575-5114

Lois Berman

J. MICHAEL BLOOM
233 Park Avenue South, 10th Floor
New York, NY 10003
212/529-6500

9200 Sunset Blvd., Suite 710
Los Angeles, CA 90069
213/275-6800

Ric Beddingfield
J. Michael Bloom
Heidi Powers (NY)
Robert Risher
Marilyn Szatmary

BORMAN ENTERTAINMENT
9220 Sunset Blvd., Suite 320
Los Angeles, CA 90069
213/859-9292

Gary Borman

BRANDON & DWORSKI
9046 Sunset Blvd.
Los Angeles, CA 90069
213/273-6173

Eric Anders
Paul Brandon
David Dworski

BRESLER, KELLY & KIPPERMAN
15760 Ventura Blvd., Suite 1730
Encino, CA 91436
818/905-1155

111 West 57th St., Suite 1409
New York, NY 10019
212/265-1980

Sandy Bresler
John Kelly
Perri Kipperman (NY)

THE BRILLSTEIN COMPANY
9200 Sunset Blvd., Suite 428
Los Angeles, CA 90069
213/275-6135

Bernie Brillstein
Brad Grey
Marc Gurvitz
Howard Klein
Sandy Wernick

BRODER-KURLAND-WEBB-UFFNER AGENCY
8439 Sunset Blvd., Suite 402
Los Angeles, CA 90069
213/656-9262

Bob Broder
Norman Kurland
Beth Uffner
Elliot Webb

CURTIS BROWN LTD.
10 Astor Place
New York, NY 10003
212/473-5400

606 N. Larchmont, Suite 309
Los Angeles, CA 90004
213/461-0148

Jeanine Edmunds (NY)
Peter Ginsberg (NY)
Aemilie Jacobson (NY)
Timothy Knowlton (NY)
Marilyn Marlowe (NY)
Jeff Melnick
Steven Pevner (NY)
Irene Skolnick (NY)
Clyde Taylor (NY)
Maureen Walters (NY)
Walter Wood

NED BROWN AGENCY
407 N. Maple Dr.
Beverly Hills, CA 90210
213/276-1131

John Brown
Ned Brown

DON BUCHWALD & ASSOCIATES
10 East 44th St.
New York, NY 10017
212/867-1070

Richard Basch
Don Buchwald
David Elliott
Michael Katz
Steven Kaye
Scott Linder
Ana Mouradian
Joanne Nici
Ricki Olshan
Michael Raymen
David Riva
Randi Ross
David Williams

BRETT CALDER AGENCY
17420 Ventura Blvd., Suite 4
Encino, CA 91316
818/906-2825

Maury Calder

CAMDEN ARTISTS
2121 Avenue of the Stars, Suite 410
Los Angeles, CA 90067
213/556-2022

Merritt Blake
Joel Dean
Brian Taylor
David Wardlow

CAMERON'S MANAGEMENT
120 Victoria St.
Potts Point, NSW 2011
Australia

JUNE CANN MANAGEMENT
203 Alfred St. North
North Sydney, NSW 2060
Australia

CARLYLE MANAGEMENT
639 N. Larchmont Dr., 2nd Floor
Los Angeles, CA 90038
213/469-3086

Phyllis Carlyle
Sheri Martin
Erik McGrath

CAVALLO, RUFFALO & FARGNOLI MANAGEMENT
11355 W. Olympic Blvd., Suite 555
Los Angeles, CA 90064
213/473-1564

One Lansdown Walk
London W11 3LN
England
01/221-2110

Robert Cavallo
Steven Fargnoli
Joseph Ruffalo

CENTURY ARTISTS, LTD.
9744 Wilshire Blvd., Suite 308
Beverly Hills, CA 90212
213/273-4366

Louis Bershad

CHARTER MANAGEMENT
9000 Sunset Blvd., Suite 1112
Los Angeles, CA 90069
213/278-1690

Toni Cosentino
Michael Greenfield
Dan Moulthrop

THE CHASIN AGENCY
190 N. Canon Drive, Suite 201
Beverly Hills, CA 90210
213/278-7505

Laurie Apelian
Tom Chasin

CHATTO & LINNIT
Prince of Wales Theatre
Coventry Street
London, W1 England

CINEMA TALENT INTERNATIONAL
7906 Santa Monica Blvd., Suite 212
Los Angeles, CA 90067
213/656-1937

George Rumanes

CIRCLE TALENT ASSOCIATES
9465 Wilshire Blvd., Suite 725
Beverly Hills, CA 90212
213/281-3765

Siegfried Hodel
Jon Klane
Donna Lee

KINGSLEY COLTON & ASSOCIATES
16661 Ventura Blvd., Suite 400
Encino, CA 91436
818/788-6043

Kingsley Colton

CONTEMPORARY ARTISTS, LTD.
132 Lasky Drive
Beverly Hills, CA 90212
213/278-8250

Neil Baggs
Gary Fuchs
Carmella Gallion
Bill Hart
Ronnie Leif
Al Melnick
Christopher Schiffrin

CONWAY & ASSOCIATES
999 N. Doheny Dr., Suite 403
Los Angeles, CA 90069
213/271-8133

Ben Conway
Scott Penney
Mary Rader

THE COOPER AGENCY
10100 Santa Monica Blvd., Suite 310
Los Angeles, CA 90067
213/277-8422

Frank Cooper
Jeff Cooper
Christine D'Angelo

CREATIVE ARTISTS AGENCY
9830 Wilshire Blvd.
Beverly Hills, CA 90212
213/288-4545

Dan Adler
Martin Baum
Glen Bickel
Nan Blitman
Bob Bookman
Bobby Brooks
Eric Carlson
Leslie Castanuala
Donna Chavous
Sandy Climan
Justin Connolly
Al Duncan
Lee Gabler
Robert Graham
Amy Grossman
Bill Haber
Ken Hardy
Rand Holston
Phil Kent
Tony Krantz
Richard Kurtzman
Steven Lafferty
John Levin
Josh Lieberman
Brian Loucks
Richard Lovett
Mike Marcus
Michael Menchel
Ron Meyer
Rick Nicita
Tina Nides
David O'Connor
Michael Ovitz
Rowland Perkins
Michael Piranian
Pam Prince
Jack Rapke
Mitch Rose
Sonia Rosenfeld

Tom Ross
Rob Scheidlinger
Jane Sindell
Bradford Smith
Fred Specktor
Abby Spigel
Rosalie Swedlin
John Sykes
Adam Venit
Bruce Vinokur
Paula Wagner
Jonathan Weisgal
Sally Willcox
Michael Wimer

CREATIVE TECHNIQUE
Box 311, Station F
Toronto, Ontario M4Y 2L7
Canada
416/466-4173

Suzanne De Poe

PETER CROUCH & ASSOCIATES
59 Frith St.
London, W1 England
01/734-2167

D

JUDY DAISH AGENCY
122 Wigmore St.
London, W1H England
01/486-5405

LARRY DALZELL ASSOCIATES
Three Goodwin Court
St. Martin's Lane
London, W1 England
01/734-7311

DIAMOND ARTISTS, LTD.
9200 Sunset Blvd.
Los Angeles, CA 90069
213/278-8146

Abby Greshler
Lillian Micely
Guy Steiner

D.R.M.
28 Charing Cross Road
London, WC2H 0DB England
01/836-3903

STEPHEN DUBRIDGE AGENCY
London, England
01/734-7311

E

ROBERT EISENBACH AGENCY
9000 Sunset Blvd., Suite 611
Los Angeles, CA 90069
213/273-0801

Robert Eisenbach

EMERALD ARTISTS, INC.
6565 Sunset Blvd., Suite 310
Los Angeles, CA 90028
213/465-2974

Nancy Chaidez
Ida Fisher
Debbie Parker

F

CAROL FAITH AGENCY
[Music)
280 S. Beverly Dr., Suite 411
Beverly Hills, CA 90212
213/274-0776

FAVORED ARTISTS
8150 Beverly Blvd., Suite 201
Los Angeles, CA 90048
213/653-3191

George Goldey
Scott Henderson
Paul Yamamoto

FILM ARTISTS ASSOCIATES
470 S. San Vicente Blvd.
Los Angeles, CA 90069
213/651-1700

Chris Dennis
Penn Dennis

FLICK EAST-WEST TALENTS, INC.
1608 Las Palmas
Hollywood, CA 90028
213/463-6333

881 Seventh Ave., Rm. 1110
New York, NY 10019
212/307-1850

Peg Donegan (NY)
Alan Mindel
Adam Schroeder (NY)
Denise Shaw
Hilary Shore

FRASER & DUNLAP
91 Regent Street
London, W1 England
01/734-7311

Tim Corrie
Robin Daulton
Ken Ewing

KURT FRINGS AGENCY, INC.
328 S. Beverly Dr.
Beverly Hills, CA 90210
213/277-1103

Kurt Frings

THE GAGE GROUP
9255 Sunset Blvd., Suite 515
Los Angeles, CA 90069
213/859-8777

1650 Broadway, Suite 406
New York, NY 10019
212/541-5250

Rick Ax
Caren Borhman
Martin Gage
Jerry Koch
David Windsor

GALLIN-MOREY ASSOCIATES
8730 Sunset Blvd.
Penthouse West
Los Angeles, CA 90069
213/659-5593

Danny Davis
Sandy Gallin
Todd Headlee
Barry Josephson
Nancy Louis
Linda Lyon
Jim Morey
Kayla Pressman
Michael Rotenberg
Susan Shore

ANNE GEDDES AGENCY
8457 Melrose Pl., #200
Los Angeles, CA 90069
213/651-2401

Anne Geddes

GELFAND, RENNERT & FELDMAN
1880 Century Park East, Suite 900
Los Angeles, CA 90067
213/553-1707

GENERAL MANAGEMENT CORPORATION
9000 Sunset Blvd., Suite 400
Los Angeles, CA 90069
213/274-8805

Helen Kushnick

PAUL GERARD TALENT AGENCY
2918 Alta Vista Dr.
Newport Beach, CA 92660
714/644-7950

ROY GERBER & ASSOCIATES
9046 Sunset Blvd., Suite 208
Los Angeles, CA 90069
213/550-0100

Roy Gerber

THE GERSH AGENCY
232 N. Canon Dr.
Beverly Hills, CA 90210
213/274-6611

130 W. 42nd St., Suite 2400
New York, NY 10036
212/997-1818

Ron Bernstein
Ellen Curren (NY)
David DeCatrillo
Bob Duva (NY)
Bob Gersh
Dave Gersh
Phil Gersh
David Guc (NY)
Barbara Halprin
Donald Ingram (NY)
Leslie Latkin
Mary Meagher (NY)
Susan Morris (NY)
Nancy Nigrosh
Diane Roberts
Natalie Rosson
Scott Yoselow (NY)
Peter Young

J. CARTER GIBSON
9000 Sunset Blvd., Suite 801
Los Angeles, CA 90069
213/274-8813

J. Carter Gibson

JAY GILBERT TALENT AGENCY
8400 Sunset Blvd., Suite 2A
Hollywood, CA 90069
213/656-5906

PHILLIP B. GITTELMAN
1221 N. Kings Rd., PH-405
Los Angeles, CA 90059
213/656-9215

Phillip B. Gittelman

HARRY GOLD & ASSOCIATES
12725 Ventura Blvd., Suite E
Studio City, CA 91604
818/769-5003

Francine Gersh
Harry Gold
Ruth Hansen
Bonnie Liedtke

GOLDSTEIN & COMPANY, INC.
10100 Santa Monica Blvd., Suite 200
Los Angeles, CA 90067
213/557-2507

Terry Goldstein
Ron Nadell

GORES/FIELDS AGENCY
10100 Santa Monica Blvd., Suite 700
Los Angeles, CA 90067
213/277-4400

Jack Fields
Sam Gores
Linda Howard
Stan Jacob
Judith Neff
Arthur Toretzky

GORFAINE/SCHWARTZ/ROBERTS
(In Association with The Lantz Office)
9255 Sunset Blvd., Suite 505
Los Angeles, CA 90069
213/858-1144

Michael Gorfaine
Lou Malacarne
Nancy Roberts
Samuel Schwartz
Vasi Vangelos

GRAY/GOODMAN, INC.
205 S. Beverly Dr., Suite 210
Beverly Hills, CA 90212
213/276-7070

Mark Goodman
Stephen Gray
Walter Partos

HAROLD R. GREENE, INC.
8455 Beverly Blvd., Suite 309
Los Angeles, CA 90048
213/852-4959

Harold R. Greene

LARRY GROSSMAN & ASSOCIATES
211 S. Beverly Drive, Suite 206
Beverly HIlls, CA 90212
213/550-8127

Janet Grossman
Larry Grossman

THE GURIAN AGENCY
3900 Cross Creek Rd., Suite 6
Malibu, CA 90265
213/550-0400

Naomi Gurian

H

REECE HALSEY AGENCY
8733 Sunset Blvd., Suite 101
Los Angeles, CA 90069
213/652-2409

Reece Halsey

THE MITCHELL J. HAMILBURG AGENCY
292 S. La Cienega Blvd., Suite 312
Beverly Hills, CA 90211
213/657-1501

Michael Hamilburg

HARRIS & GOLDBERG TALENT AND LITERARY AGENCY
2121 Avenue of the Stars, Suite 950
Los Angeles, CA 90067
213/553-5200

Howard Goldberg
Michelle Grant
Scott Harris
Jodi Levine
Steve Lovett
Nicholas Stevens
Frank Wuliger

HATTON & BAKER
18 Jermyn St.
London, W1 England
01/439-2971

Terence Baker

DUNCAN HEATH & ASSOCIATES
162 Wardour Street
London, W1 England
01/439-1471

Duncan Heath

THE HELLER AGENCY
706 Hollywood Blvd., Suite 818
Hollywood, CA 90028
213/462-7151

Robin Elliott
Seymour Heller

HENDERSON/HOGAN AGENCY, INC.
247 S. Beverly Drive, Suite 102
Beverly Hills, CA 90212
213/274-7815

405 W. 44th St.
New York, NY 10036
212/765-5190

Margaret Henderson
Jerry Hogan (NY)
Karen Kirsch (NY)
Matthew Lesher
Joan Pardis
Jean Walton (NY)

HERMAN & LEWIS TALENT AGENCY
9601 Wilshire Blvd., Suite 333
Beverly Hills, CA 90210
213/550-8913

Richard Herman
Michael Lewis

ROBERT G. HUSSONG AGENCY
721 N. La Brea Ave., Suite 201
Los Angeles, CA 90038
213/652-2893

Robert Hussong

I

MICHAEL IMISON PLAYWRIGHTS
01/354-3174 (London)
212/874-2671 (New York)

Alan Brodie (London)
Michael Imison (London)
Abbe Levin (NY)

INTERNATIONAL CREATIVE MANAGEMENT
8899 Beverly Blvd.
Los Angeles, CA 90048
213/550-4000

40 West 57th Street
New York, NY 10019
212/556-5600

38 Via Siacci
Rome, Italy
806-041

388-396 Oxford Street
London, W1 England
01/629-8080

Bridget Aschenberg (NY)
Ben Benjamin
Jeff Berg
Alan Berger
Michael Black
Leigh Brillstein
Steve Carbone
Diane Cairns
Sam Cohn (NY)
Patty Detroit
Arlene Donovan (NY)
Steve Dontaville
Bill Douglas
Sandi Dudek
Jack Dytman
Andrea Eastman (NY)
George Freeman
Joe Funicello
Nancy Geller
Jack Gilardi
Sylvia Gold
Bob Gomer
Hildy Gottlieb
Alan Greenspan
Iris Grossman
Richard Heller
Scott Hudson (NY)
Richard Kraft
Robert Levinson
David Lewis (NY)
Ed Limato
David Lonner
Lisa Loosemore (NY)
Martha Luttrell
Paul Martino (NY)
Guy McElwaine
Lou Pitt
Pat Quinn
Steve Rabineau
Lynn Radmin
Diana Rathbun
Bill Robinson
Sheila Robinson
Joe Rosenberg
Michael Schulman
Scott Schwartz
Paul Schwartzman
Eric Shepard (NY)
Jim Wiatt
David Wirtschatter

INTERTALENT AGENCY
9200 Sunset Blvd., Penthouse 25
Los Angeles, CA 90069
213/271-0600

Bill Block
David Greenblatt

J. J. Harris
Judy Hofflund
Adam Isaacs
Mark Rossen
David Schiff
Danny Sexton
Tom Strickler

J

JANKLOW & NESBITT ASSOCIATES
598 Madison Ave.
New York, NY 10022
212/421-1700

Morton Janklow
Lynn Nesbitt

MELINDA JASON
Columbia Pictures
Studio Plaza, 3400 Riverside Dr.
Burbank, CA 91505

THE THOMAS JENNINGS AGENCY
427 N. Canon Dr., Suite 205
Beverly Hills, CA 90210
213/274-5418

Tom Jennings

ANTHONY JONES
01/839-2556

K

THE KAPLAN-STAHLER AGENCY
8383 Wilshire Blvd., Suite 923
Beverly Hills, CA 90211
213/653-4483

Mitchell Kaplan
Elliot Stahler

PATRICIA KARLAN AGENCY
4425 Riverside Dr., Suite 102
Burbank, CA 91505
818/846-8666

THE KEENER ORGANIZATION
9121 Sunset Blvd.
Los Angeles, CA 90069
213/273-9876

Matt Keener

PAUL KOHNER, INC.
9169 Sunset Blvd.
Los Angeles, CA 90069
213/550-1060

Josh Baser
Gary Salt
Robert A. Schwartz
Neal Stevens
Pearl Wexler

KOPALOFF COMPANY
1930 Century Park West, Suite 403
Los Angeles, CA 90067
213/203-8430

Don Kopaloff

LUCY KROLL
390 West End Ave.
New York, NY 10024
212/877-0556

Barbara Hogenson
Lucy Kroll
Holly Lebed

L

LAKE & DOUROUX
445 S. Beverly Dr., Suite 310
Beverly Hills, CA 90212
213/557-0700

Michael Douroux
Candace Lake

THE LANTZ OFFICE
888 7th Ave., 25th Floor
New York, NY 10106
212/586-0200

Ed Betz (NY)
Robert Duva (NY)
Joy Harris (NY)
Robert Lantz (NY)

IRVING PAUL LAZAR AGENCY
120 El Camino Dr.
Beverly Hills, CA 90212
213/275-6153

One East 66th Street
New York, NY 10021
212/355-1177

Irving Paul Lazar
Alan Nevins

LEADING ARTISTS
445 N. Bedford Dr., Penthouse
Beverly Hills, CA 90210
213/858-1999

Jim Berkus
Dana Cioffi
Gary Cosay
Pat Dollard
Ilene Feldman
Chris Harbert
Toby Jaffe
Tory Metzger
Robb Rothman
Robert Stein

LEADING PLAYERS MANAGEMENT
29 Kings Rd.
London, SW3 England

JACK LENNY ASSOCIATES
9454 Wilshire Blvd., Suite 600
Beverly Hills, CA 90212
213/271-2174

100 W. 57th St., Suite 3-I
New York, NY 10019
212/582-0270

Jim Lenny

THE LIBERTY AGENCY
10845 Lindbrook Dr., Suite 200
Los Angeles, CA 90024
213/824-7937

Glynnis Liberty

LITKE/GALE/MADDEN
10390 Santa Monica Blvd., Suite 300
Los Angeles, CA 90025
213/785-9200

Barbara Gale
Marty Litke
Molly Madden

THE ROBERT LITTMAN COMPANY, INC.
409 N. Camden Dr., Suite 105
Beverly Hills, CA 90210
213/278-1572

Robert Littman

LONDON MANAGEMENT
235/241 Regent St.
London, W1 England
01/493-1610

STERLING LORD LITERISTIC
One Madison Ave.
New York, NY 10010
212/696-2800

Philippa Brophy
Susan Lee Cohen
Don Cutler
Lizzie Grossman
Jody Hotchkiss
Elizabeth Kaplan
Stuart Krichevsky
Sterling Lord
Peter Matson

LUND AGENCY
8606 Wonderland Ave.
Los Angeles, CA 90046
213/656-5310

Cara Lund

GRACE LYONS AGENCY
8380 Melrose Blvd., Suite 202
Los Angeles, CA 90069
213/655-5100

Grace Lyons

M

CHRISTOPHER MANN, LTD.
39 Davies St.
London, W1 England
01/493-2810

Christopher Mann

STEPHANIE MANN REPRESENTATION
8323 Blackburn Ave., Suite 5
Los Angeles, CA 90048
213/653-7130

Stephanie Mann

SANDRA MARSH MANAGEMENT
14930 Ventura Blvd., Suite 200
Sherman Oaks, CA 91403
818/905-6961

Sandra Marsh

KIRBY McCAULEY
432 Park Ave. South, Suite 1509
New York, NY 10016
212/683-7561

JAMES McHUGH AGENCY
8150 Beverly Blvd., Suite 303
Los Angeles, CA 90048
213/651-2770

James McHugh

MEDIA ARTISTS GROUP
6255 Sunset Blvd., Suite 627
Hollywood, CA 90028
213/463-5610

Barbara Alexander
Myra Berger
Raphael Berko
Keith Driscoll
David List
Carolyn Thompson
Debora LaVere

HELEN MERRILL, LTD.
435 West 23rd St., Suite 1-A
New York, NY 10011
212/691-5326

THE MILLER AGENCY
23560 Lyons Ave., Suite 209
Santa Clarita, CA 91321
805/255-7173

Tom Miller

THE MISHKIN AGENCY
2355 Benedict Canyon
Beverly Hills, CA 90201
213/274-5261

Meyer Mishkin

WILLIAM MORRIS AGENCY
151 El Camino Drive
Beverly Hills, CA 90212
213/274-7451

1350 Avenue of the Americas
New York, NY 10019
212/586-5100

2325 Crestmoore Road
Nashville, TN 37215
615/385-0310

31-32 Soho Square
London W1, England
01/434-2191

Via Giosue Carducci, 10
Rome, Italy
011-48-608-1234

Lamonstrasse 9
Munich 27, West Germany
011-47-608-1234

Larry Auerbach
Arthur Axelman
Mel Berger (NY)
Adam Berkowitz (NY)
Pam Bernstein (NY)
Boaty Boatwright (NY)
Leo Bookman (NY)
Norman Brokaw
Bruce Brown
John Burnham
Michael Carlisle (NY)
Lee Cohen
James Crabbe
Bob Crestani
Ames Cushing
Roger Davis
Brian Dubin (NY)
Alan Eisman
Tony Fantozzi
Jeff Field
Alan Gasmer
Steve Glick
Christopher Godsick
Dodie Gold
Robert Gottlieb
Leonard Hirshan
Andrew Howard
Toni Howard
Joan Hyler
George Lane (NY)
Owen Laster (NY)
Ned Leavitt (NY)
Biff Liff (NY)
Ron Mardigian
Sue Mengers
Lenny Noveck
Gilbert Parker (NY)
Mike Peretzian
John Ptak
Gary Rado
Leonard Rosenberg
Hal Ross
Katy Rothacker (NY)
Marc Schwartz
Judy Scott-Fox
Mike Simpson
Steven Starr (NY)
Jim Stein (NY)
Beth Swofford
Mark Teitelbaum
Bobbi Thompson
Peter Turner
Irene Webb
Fred Westheimer
Carol Yumkas
Scott Zimmerman

THE MORTON AGENCY
1103 1/2 Glendon Avenue
Los Angeles, CA 90024
213/824-4089

Michael Werner

N

CHRISTOPHER NASSIF & ASSOCIATES
1801 Avenue of the Stars, Suite 1250
Los Angeles, CA 90067
213/556-4343

Marty Barkan
Christopher Nassif
Adrienne Spitze

DICK ODGERS
London, England
01/262-1611

Peter Murphy
Dick Odgers

FIFI OSCARD AGENCY
19 W. 44th St.
New York, NY 10036
212/764-1100

Phyllis Black
Francis Del Duca
Ivy Fischer-Stone
Dee Gray
Richard Kurtzman
Carmen LaVia
Kevin McShane
John Medeiros
Nancy Murray
Fifi Oscard
Peter Sawyer

THE DANIEL OSTROFF AGENCY
9200 Sunset Blvd., Suite 402
Los Angeles, CA 90069
213/278-2020

Dan Ostroff

P

BARRY PERELMAN AGENCY
9200 Sunset Blvd., Suite 531
Los Angeles, CA 90069
213/274-5999

Douglas A. Brodax
Barry Perelman

A.D. PETERS AND CO., LTD.
10 Buchingham St.
London, WC2 England
01/580-9592

Anthony Jones Peters

LYNN PLESHETTE AGENCY
2700 N. Beachwood Dr.
Los Angeles, CA 90068
213/465-0428

Lynn Pleshette
Richard Green

PREFERRED ARTISTS
16633 Ventura Blvd., Suite 1421
Encino, CA 91436
818/990-0305

Richard Brustein
Sy Fischer
Robert Goldfarb
Sylvia Hirsch
Randall Skolnik
Roger Strull
Michele Wallerstein
Lew Weitzman

JIM PREMINGER AGENCY
1650 Westwood Blvd., Suite 201
Los Angeles, CA 90024
213/475-9491

Harvey Harrison
Jim Preminger
Monica Riordan

PROGRESSIVE ARTISTS AGENCY
400 S. Beverly Drive, Suite 216
Beverly Hills, CA 90212
213/553-8561

Bernie Carneol
Belle Zwerdling

R

DOUGLAS RAE MANAGEMENT
28 Charing Cross Road
London WC2, England
01/836-3903

Jenny Cassarotto
Douglas Rae

MARGARET RAMSEY AGENCY
London, England
01/240-0601

JOHN REDWAY & ASSOCIATES
16 Berners St.
London, W1 England
01/580-9592

THE RICHLAND/WUNSCH AGENCY
9220 Sunset Blvd., Suite 311
Los Angeles, CA 90069
213/278-1955

Dan Richland
Joe Richland
Bob Wunsch
Rafe Wunsch

RISKY BUSINESS MANAGEMENT
10966 Le Conte Avenue, Suite A
Los Angeles, CA 90024
213/478-7609

Ronnie Kaye
Jim Rissmiller
Pat Walsh
Victor Roccki

ROBINSON, WEINTRAUB, GROSS & ASSOCIATES, INC.
8428 Melrose Place, Suite C
Los Angeles, CA 90069
213/653-5802

Judith Everett
Ken Gross
Nancy Jones
Stuart Robinson
Bernie Weintraub

STEPHANIE ROGERS & ASSOCIATES
3855 Lankershim Blvd., Suite 218
North Hollywood, CA 91614
818/509-1010

Stephanie Rogers

ROLLINS, MORRA & BREZNER INC.
801 Westmount Dr.
Los Angeles, CA 90069
213/657-5404

130 W. 57th St., Suite 11-D
New York, NY 10019
212/582-1940

Larry Brezner
Buddy Morra
Roger Nygard
Jack Rollins (NY)
David Steinberg

JACK ROSE AGENCY
6430 Sunset Blvd., Suite 1203
Hollywood, CA 90028
213/463-7300

Dave Baratta
Eddie Barnes
Tanya Chasman
Carol DeTanna-Dean
Eddie Keyes
Tracey Moschel
Karen Rae
Jack Rose
Bette Schwartz

THE ROSEN/TURTLE GROUP
15010 Ventura Blvd., Suite 219
Sherman Oaks, CA 91403
818/907-9891

Michael Rosen
Cindy Turtle

THE MARION ROSENBERG OFFICE
(In Association with Robinson, Weintraub, Gross & Associates)
8428 Melrose Place, Suite C
Los Angeles, CA 90069
213/653-5802

Marion Rosenberg

ROSENSTONE/WENDER
3 E. 48th St.
New York, NY 10017
212/832-8330

Howard Rosenstone
Phyllis Wender

S

SANFORD-BECKETT-SKOURAS
1015 Gayley Avenue, Suite 301
Los Angeles, CA 90024
213/208-2100

Brenda Beckett
Rick Berg
Cynthia Campos-Greenberg
Brad Gross
Geoffrey Sanford
Spyros Skouras

THE IRV SCHECTER COMPANY
9300 Wilshire Blvd., Suite 410
Beverly Hills, CA 90212
213/278-8070

Elinor Berger
Doug Draizin
Merril Jonas
Stu Kaplan
Debbie Klein
Don Klein
Russ Lyster
Michael Margules
Victorla Michaels
Todd Moyer
Irv Schecter
Dan Shaner

SCHIOWITZ & ASSOCIATES, INC.
291 S. La Cienega Blvd., Suite 306
Beverly Hills, CA 90211
213/657-0480

Charles Clay
Josh Schiowitz

SUSAN SCHULMAN LITERARY AGENCY, INC.
454 W. 44th St.
New York, NY 10036
212/713-1633

Susan Schulman

DON SCHWARTZ & ASSOCIATES
8749 Sunset Blvd., Suite 200
Los Angeles, CA 90069
213/657-8910

Al Criado
Carey Gosa
Mimi Laurita
Don Schwartz

SELECT ARTISTS
337 W. 43rd St.
New York, NY 10036
212/586-4300

Cindy Alexander
Alan Willig

SELECTED ARTISTS AGENCY
13111 Ventura Blvd., Suite 204
Studio City, CA 91604
213/877-0055
818/905-5744

Flo Joseph
David Kainer

SELWYN TALENT AGENCY
P.O. Box 69623
Los Angeles, CA 90069
213/463-3700

Mike Selwyn

DAVID SHAPIRA & ASSOCIATES
15301 Ventura Blvd., Suite 345
Sherman Oaks, CA 91403
818/906-0322

Bob Goldfarb
David Shapira

SHAPIRO-LICHTMAN, INC.
8827 Beverly Blvd.
Los Angeles, CA 90048
213/859-8877

Mark Lichtman
Mike Robins
Bob Shapiro
Marty Shapiro
Mitchel E. Stein

SHAPIRO/WEST & ASSOCIATES
141 El Camino Dr., Suite 205
Beverly Hills, CA 90212
213/278-8896

Diane Barnett
George Shapiro
Howard West

SHARR ENTERPRISES
P.O. Box 69453
Los Angeles, CA 90069
213/278-1981

Ina Bernstein Sharr

LEW SHERRELL AGENCY, LTD.
7060 Hollywood Blvd., Suite 610
Los Angeles, CA 90028
213/461-9955

Jo Martin
Lew Sherrell

SHORR/STILLE & ASSOCIATES
800 S. Robertson Blvd, Suite 6
Los Angeles, CA 90035
213/659-6160

Fred Shorr
Lucy Stille
Lucy Stutz
Jeniifer Sudarsky

LINDA SIEFERT & ASSOCIATES
8A Brunswick Gardens
London, W8 4AJ England
01/229-5163

GERALD K. SMITH & ASSOCIATES
P.O. Box 7430
Burbank, CA 91510
213/849-5388

Gerald K. Smith

SUSAN SMITH & ASSOCIATES
121 N. San Vicente Blvd.
Beverly Hills, CA 90211
213/852-4777

Jim Carnahan
Justen Dardis
Patricia Hacker
Sandra Lucchessi
Judy Page
Kevin Riley
Susan Smith

SMITH/GOSNELL/NICHOLSON & ASSOCIATES
P.O. Box 1166
Pacific Palisades, CA 90272
213/459-0307

Cecilia Bank
Ray Gosnell
Debbie Haeusler
Skip Nicholson
Creighton Smith

STE REPRESENTATION, LTD.
9301 Wilshire Blvd., Suite 312
Beverly Hills, CA 90210
213/550-3982

888 Seventh Ave.
New York, NY 10109
213/246-1030

Alisa Adler
Tex Bena (NY)
Susan Calogerakis
David Eidenberg
Roberta Kent
Joel Rudnick
Jerilyn Scott
Clifford Stevens (NY)

CHARLES H. STERN AGENCY, INC.
11755 Wilshire Blvd., Suite 2320
Los Angeles, CA 90025
213/479-1788

Charles H. Stern

STONE MANNERS TALENT AGENCY
9113 Sunset Blvd.
Los Angeles, CA 90069
213/275-9599

Matt de Ganon
Scott Manners
Lynn Rawlins
Tim Stone
Victoria Wisdom
Christopher Wright

THE SHIRLEY STRICK AGENCY
9220 Sunset Blvd., Suite 204
Los Angeles, CA 90069
213/273-0919

Shirley Strick
Cory Taylor

H.N. SWANSON, INC. AGENCY
8523 Sunset Blvd.
Los Angeles, CA 90069
213/652-5385

Ben Kamsler
Michael Siegel
H.N. Swanson

T

TALENT GROUP, INC.
9250 Wilshire Blvd.
Beverly Hills, CA 90212
213/273-9559

David Brady
Pat Brannon
Carole Fields
Judy Rich

TRIAD ARTISTS
10100 Santa Monica Blvd., 16th Floor
Los Angeles, CA 90067
213/556-2727

888 Seventh Ave.
New York, NY 10106
212/489-8100

Tim Angle (NY)
Ben Bernstein
Judy Cech
Nicole David
Jenny Delaney
Brad Gersh
Mark Grayson
Peter Grosslight
Todd Harris
Scott Henderson
Bob Hohman
Jeff Hunter (NY)
Diane Kamp (NY)
Michael Kane
Bruce Kaufman
John Kimble
Tracy Kramer
Rob Lee
Devra Lieb
Pat Magnorella
Bayard Maybank
Joel Milner
Lawrence Mirisch
Ken Neisser
Gene Parseghian
Ronda Gomez Quinones
Marshall Resnick
Arnold Rifkin
Frank Riley
Lee Rosenberg
Richard Rosenberg
Joanna Ross (NY)
Michele Sacharow
Paul Alan Smith
Brian Swardstrom
Lloyd Weintraub
Cynthia Wilkerson
Ted Wilkins (NY)

TWENTIETH CENTURY ARTISTS
3800 Barham Blvd., Suite 303
Los Angeles, CA 90068
213/850-5516

Jerry Davidson
Cindy Davis
Diane Davis
Estelle Hertzberg
Vivian Hollander
Stevie Nelson
Steven Stevens

WARDEN/WHITE/VAN DUREN
3000 Olympic Blvd., Suite 2408
Santa Monica, CA 90404
213/315-4725

Annette Van Duren
David Warden
Steve White

ELLIOT WAX & ASSOCIATES
9255 Sunset Blvd., Suite 612
Los Angeles, CA 90069
213/273-8217

Elliot Wax
Marc A. Wax

THE WELTMAN COMPANY
425 S. Beverly Dr.
Beverly Hills, CA 90212
213/556-2801

Philip Weltman

PENNY WESSON
London, England
01/722-6607

MICHAEL WHITEHALL
125 Gloucester Rd.
London, W7 4TE England
01/244-8466

WILE ENTERPRISES, INC.
200 N. Robertson Blvd.
Beverly Hills, CA 90211
213/288-3070

Shelly Wile

THE WRIGHT CONCEPT
1015 N. Cahuenga Blvd.
Hollywood, CA 90038
213/461-3844

Marcie Wright

WRITERS & ARTISTS AGENCY
11726 San Vicente Blvd., Suite 300
Los Angeles, CA 90049
213/820-2240

70 West 36th St., Suite 501
New York, NY 10018
212/947-8765

John Barkworth
Marti Blumenthal

William Craver (NY)
Rima Bauer Greer
Paul Haas
Michael Lazo
Susan Leibman (NY)
Molly McCarthy (NY)
Virginia Raymond (NY)
Lori Rothman
Joan Scott
Kitty Shields (NY)
Jeanne St. Calbre
Michael Stipanich
Trevor Walton
Hillary Wayne

Z

ZIEGLER & ASSOCIATES
1222 Sixth St.
Santa Monica, CA 90401
213/278-0070

CASTINGDIRECTORS

* Casting Society of America

A

JANE ALDERMAN*
c/o WLS-TV
190 N. State St.
Chicago, IL 60601
312/899-4250

ROBIN ALLAN
The Casting Company
7319 Beverly Blvd., Suite 1
Los Angeles, CA 90036
213/938-2170

SANDY ALLISON
1759 Orchid
Los Angeles, CA 90028
213/874-3631

ANDERSON/McCOOK/WHITE CASTING
3855 Lankershim Blvd.
North Hollywood, CA 91614
818/760-3934

Catherine White

Nancy McCook

SIMON AYER
Vice President of Talent
Stephen J. Cannell Productions, Inc.
7083 Hollywood Blvd.
Los Angeles, CA 90028
213/856-7571

B

LINDA BACA
6557 Bellaire Ave.
North Hollywood, CA 91606
818/762-1230

BAKER/NISBET
451 N. LaCienega Blvd. #12
Los Angeles, CA 90048
213/657-5687

BARBARA BALDAVIN*
c/o CSA
6565 Sunset Blvd., Suite 306
Los Angeles, CA 90028
213/463-1925

ANTHONY BARNAO
Director of Casting
CBS Entertainment
7800 Beverly Blvd., Suite 284
Los Angeles, CA 90036
213/852-2835

MARY ANN BARTON
930 N. Westbourne
Los Angeles, CA 90069
213/854-6635

BARYLSKI/PATTON CASTING
Sunset Gower Studios
1438 N. Gower St.
Los Angeles, CA 90028
213/460-7375

Deborah Barylski*

Cami Patton*

FRAN BASCOM*
Columbia Pictures Television
Columbia Plaza East, Suite 148
Burbank, CA 91505
818/954-2675

PAMELA BASKER*
Champion/Basker Casting
7060 Hollywood Blvd., Suite 808
Hollywood, CA 90028
213/466-1884

LISA BEACH
Director of Casting
Hollywood Pictures
500 S. Buena Vista St.
Burbank, CA 91521
818/560-2085

JUDY BELSHE
5514 Satsuma Ave.
North Hollywood, CA 90601
818/760-1380

ANNETTE BENSON*
Perry/Benson Casting
11350 Ventura Blvd., Suite 201
Studio City, CA 91604
818/766-3896

BERGERON/LAWSON CASTING
P.O. Box 1489
La Canada, CA 91011
818/790-9832

Elza Bergeron*

Judie Lawson

SHARON BIALY*
Pagano/Bialy Casting
1680 N. Vine St., Suite 904
Los Angeles, CA 90028
213/871-0051

LACY BISHOP
Los Angeles Theatre Center
514 S. Spring St.
Los Angeles, CA 90013
213/627-6500

SUSAN BLUESTEIN*
4063 Radford, Suite 105
Studio City, CA 91604
818/505-6636

EUGENE BLYTHE*
Vice President of Talent
Walt Disney Studios
500 S. Buena Vista St.
Burbank, CA 91521
818/560-7625

RISA BRAMON*
Bramon & Hopkins Casting
8265 Sunset Blvd., Suite 207
Los Angeles, CA 90046
213/650-2545

JACOV BRESLER
5330 Lankershim Blvd. #205
North Hollywood, CA 91601
818/760-1391

JACKIE BRISKEY*
Lorimar Television
3970 Overland Ave.
Culver City, CA 90232
213/280-8810

BROWN/WEST CASTING
7319 Beverly Blvd., Suite 10
Los Angeles, CA 90036
213/938-2575

Ross Brown*

Mary West*

BUCK/EDELMAN CASTING
4051 Radford Ave., Suite B
Studio City, CA 91604
818/506-7328

Mary Buck*

Susan Edelman*

PERRY BULLINGTON
Bullington/MacDonald Casting
9200 Sunset Blvd., Suite 530
West Hollywood, CA 90069
213/859-1089

JACKIE BURCH*
20th Century Fox
10201 W. Pico Blvd., Trailer 714
Los Angeles, CA 90035
213/203-3650

WHITNEY BURNETT-VOSS*
c/o C.S.A.
311 W. 43rd St.
New York, NY 10036
212/333-4552

BURROWS/TILLMAN CASTING
Paramount Studios
5555 Melrose Ave., Wilder 210
Los Angeles, CA 90038
213/468-5921

Victoria Burrows*

Mark Tillman*

BUSTLES CASTING
11634 Moorpark Ave.
Studio City, CA 91604
818/980-2924

IRENE CAGEN*
Liberman/Hirschfeld Casting
Sunset-Gower Studios
1438 N. Gower St., Suite 1410
Los Angeles, CA 90028
213/460-7258

REUBEN CANNON & ASSOCIATES
Raleigh Studios
5300 Melrose Ave., Suite 309-E
Los Angeles, CA 90038
213/960-4502

Reuben Cannon*

Carol Dudley*

MATT CASELLA
Walt Disney Studios
500 S. Buena Vista St.
Western Bldg. 3, Suite 4
Burbank, CA 91521
818/560-1159

ALICE CASSIDY*
Lorimar
3970 Overland Ave.
Prod. Bldg., Suite 230
Culver City, CA 90232
213/280-8810

THE CASTING COMPANY
7319 Beverly Blvd., Suite 1
Los Angeles, CA 90036
213/938-2170

Robin Allan
Janet Hirshenson*
Jane Jenkins*
Roger Mussenden

CASTING SOCIETY OF AMERICA
6565 Sunset Blvd. #306
Los Angeles, CA 90028
213/463-1925

311 W. 43rd St.
New York, NY 10036
212/333-4552

CENTRAL CASTING
2600 W. Olive St., 5th Floor
Burbank, CA 91505
818/569-5200

CHAMPION/BASKER CASTING
7060 Hollywood Blvd., Suite 808
Hollywood, CA 90028
213/466-1884

Pamela Basker*
Fern Champion*
Sue Swan

ALETA CHAPPELLE*
311 W. 43rd St., Suite 700
New York, NY 10036
212/582-1101

ELLEN CHENOWETH*
c/o Werthemer, Armstrong & Hirsch
1888 Century Park East, Suite 1888
Los Angeles, CA 90067
213/333-4552

BARBARA CLAMAN, INC.
6565 Sunset Blvd., Suite 412
Los Angeles, CA 90028
213/466-3400

Barbara Claman*
Vicki Goggin
Jan Powell
Mark Saks*

DAVID COHN*
9060 Santa Monica Blvd., Suite 202
West Hollywood, CA 90069
213/859-4812

MARY COLQUHOUN*
c/o C.S.A.
311 W. 43rd St.
New York, NY 10036
212/333-4552

RUTH CONFORTE*
P.O. Box 5718
Sherman Oaks, CA 91403
818/760-8220

KATHLEEN CONNER*
c/o C.S.A.
6565 Sunset Blvd., Suite 306
Los Angeles, CA 90028
213/463-1925

ELEANOR COOKE*
c/o C.S.A.
6565 Sunset Blvd., Suite 306
Los Angeles, CA 90028
213/463-1925

DENNIS CORNELL
Vice President - Talent & Casting
Columbia Pictures Television
1438 N. Gower St.
Los Angeles, CA 90028
213/460-7254

ALLISON COWITT
Fenton/Taylor Casting
100 Universal City Plaza, Bungalow 477
Universal City, CA 91423
818/777-4610

ELAINE CRAIG VOICE CASTING
6565 Sunset Blvd., Suite 418
Hollywood, CA 90028
213/469-8773

MARGUERITE CRAVATT
Creative Casting
1680 N. Vine St., Suite 709
Hollywood, CA 90028
213/466-7319

D

GLENN DANIELS*
Warner Bros.
4000 Warner Blvd.
Burbank, CA 91522
818/954-1495

ANITA DANN*
P.O. Box 2041
Beverly Hills, CA 90213
213/278-7765

ERIC DAWSON
Ulrich/Dawson Casting
100 Universal City Plaza, Bldg. 466
Universal City, CA 91608
818/777-7802

PAUL DECKER
NBC
3000 W. Alameda Ave.
Burbank, CA 91523
818/840-3500

DENNISON/SELZER CASTING
3000 Olympic Blvd.
Santa Monica, CA 90404
213/315-4850
Sally Dennison*
Justine Jacoby*
Julie Selzer*

JOAN D'INCECCO*
ABC Entertainment
101 W. 67th St.
New York, NY 10023
212/887-3844

DIANE DIMEO*
12725 Ventura Blvd., Suite H
Studio City, CA 91604
818/505-0945

DICK DINMAN*
1350 N. Highland Ave., Suite 6
Los Angeles, CA 90028
213/469-2283

PAM DIXON*
P.O. Box 672
Beverly Hills, CA 90213
213/271-8064

DONNA DOCKSTADER*
Universal Studios
100 Universal Plaza #463-110
Universal City, CA 91608
818/777-1961

CHRISTIE DOOLEY
7800 Beverly Blvd. Suite 3371
Los Angeles, CA 90036
213/852-4501

KIM DORR*
The Arthur Company
100 Universal City Plaza, Bldg. 447
Universal City, CA 91608
818/505-1200

MARION DOUGHERTY
Vice President - Talent
Warner Bros.
4000 Warner Blvd.
Burbank, CA 91522
818/954-3021

CAROL DUDLEY*
Reuben Cannon & Associates
100 Universal City Plaza, Bldg. 466
Universal City, CA 91608
818/777-7801

NAN DUTTON*
1340 E. 6th St.
Los Angeles, CA 90021
213/629-0938

E

SUSAN EDELMAN*
Buck/Edelman Casting
4051 Radford Avenue, Suite B
Studio City, CA 91604
818/506-7328

PENNY ELLERS*
Robinson/Ellers Casting
7080 Hollywood Blvd., Suite 606
Los Angeles, CA 90028
213/962-9735

JO EVANS
P.O. Box 10704
Glendale, CA 91209
818/956-7048

CODY MICHAEL EWELL*
20th Century Fox
10201 W. Pico Blvd., Bldg. 63, Suite 10
Los Angeles, CA 90035
213/203-2232

F

RACHELLE FARBERMAN*
The Kushner-Locke Company
11601 Wilshire Blvd., 21st Floor
Los Angeles, CA 90025
213/445-1111

BETTY FARROW
13338 McCormick
Van Nuys, CA 91401
818/986-7113

FENTON/TAYLOR CASTING
100 Universal City Plaza, Bungalow 477
Universal City, CA 91423
818/777-4610

Allison Cowitt
Mike Fenton*
Lynda Gordon
Valorie Massalas
Judy Taylor*

STEVEN FERTIG
Rubin/Fertig Casting
5750 Wilshire Blvd., #222
Los Angeles, CA 90036
213/965-1500

HOWARD FEUER*
477 Madison Ave., 5th Floor
New York, NY 10019
212/735-5342

LEONARD FINGER*
1501 Broadway, Suite 1511
New York, NY 10036
212/944-8611

NANCY FOY*
c/o C.S.A.
6565 Sunset Blvd., Suite 306
Los Angeles, CA 90029
213/960-4575

LINDA FRANCIS*
c/o C.S.A.
6565 Sunset Blvd., Suite 306
Los Angeles, CA 90029
213/960-4575

JEROLD FRANKS
Onorato/Franks Casting
1717 N. Highland Ave., Suite 904
Los Angeles, CA 90028
213/468-8833

FRAZIER/GINSBERG CASTING
5555 Melrose Ave., Chevalier 117
Los Angeles, CA 90038
213/468-4475

Carrie Frazier*
Shani Ginsberg*

LISA FREIBERGER
Vice President - Talent & Casting
CBS Entertainment
7800 Beverly Blvd., Suite 244
Los Angeles, CA 90036
213/852-2335

JEAN FROST*
3000 Olympic Blvd., Suite 1470
Los Angeles, CA 90404
213/315-4720

G

MELINDA GARTZMAN*
330 Bob Hope Dr., Suite C-113
Burbank, CA 91523
818/840-7660

JEFF GERRARD
10661 Whipple St.
Toluca Lake, CA 91602
818/508-8665

SHANI GINSBERG*
Frazier/Ginsberg Casting
5555 Melrose Ave., Chevalier 117
Los Angeles, CA 90038
213/468-4475

JAN GLASER*
MGM/UA
10125 W. Washington Blvd.
Culver City, CA 90230
213/204-0474

LAURA GLEASON*
c/o C.S.A.
311 W. 43rd St., Suite 700
New York, NY 10036
212/333-4552

SUSAN GLICKSMAN*
P.O. Box 1168-962
Studio City, CA 91614
818/766-2610

VICKI GOGGIN
Barbara Claman, Inc.
6565 Sunset Blvd., Suite 412
Los Angeles, CA 90028
213/466-3400

THE GOLDEN CASTING COMPANY
133 W. 72nd St., 6th Floor
New York, NY 10023
212/496-0146

Patricia Golden*
John McCabe

PETER GOLDEN*
Vice President - Casting
GTG Productions
9336 W. Washington Blvd.
Bldg. O, Suite 204
Los Angeles, CA 90230
213/202-3209

DANNY GOLDMAN
1006 N. Cole Ave.
Los Angeles, CA 90038
213/463-1600

ALIXE GORDIN*
129 W. 12th St.
New York, NY 10011
212/627-0472

LYNDA GORDON
Fenton/Taylor Casting
100 Universal City Plaza, Bungalow 477
Universal City, CA 91423
818/777-4610

CHRISTOPHER GORMAN*
Senior Director of Casting
CBS Entertainment
7800 Beverly Blvd., Suite 244
Los Angeles, CA 90036
213/852-2975

DAVID GRAHAM*
590 N. Rossmore Ave., Suite 2
Los Angeles, CA 90004
213/871-2012

MARILYN GRANAS
220 S. Palm Dr.
Beverly Hills, CA 90212
213/278-3773

KELLYE GREEN
9903 Santa Monica Blvd., Suite 102
Beverly Hills, CA 90212
213/277-9619

JEFF GREENBERG*
5555 Melrose Ave., Marx Bros. 102
Los Angeles, CA 90038
213/468-4886

GLENIS GROSS
Stokes/Gross Casting
11969 Ventura Blvd., Suite 302
Studio City, CA 91604
818/508-6485

DAN GUERRERO
625 N. Flores St.
Los Angeles, CA 90048
213/655-2417

H

JILL HABERMAN*
c/o C.S.A.
311 W. 43rd St., Suite 700
New York, NY 10036
212/333-4552

PEG HALLIGAN*
c/o C.S.A.
6565 Sunset Blvd., Suite 306
Los Angeles, CA 90028
818/840-7628

MILT HAMERMAN*
100 Universal City Plaza
Bldg. 507, Suite 4-A
Universal City, CA 91608
818/777-1711

ROBERT HARBIN*
Vice President - Talent & Casting
20th Century Fox
10201 W. Pico Blvd.
Executive Bldg., Suite 335
Los Angeles, CA 90035
213/203-3847

GENO HAVENS
P.O. Box 69277
Los Angeles, CA 90069
213/394-1495

PATTI HAYES
419 N. Larchmont Ave., Suite 249
Los Angeles, CA 90004
213/I933-0116

PAT HEALY
650 N. Bronson Ave.
Los Angeles, CA 90004
213/464-7968

KAREN HENDEL*
2049 Century Park East, Suite 4100
Los Angeles, CA 90067
213/201-9309

CATHY HENDERSON*
Kings Road Entertaiment
1901 Ave. of the Stars, Suite 605
Century City, CA 90067
213/552-0057

JUDY HENDERSON*
330 W. 89th St.
New York, NY 10024
212/877-0225

PAULA HEROLD*
Vice President of Production & Casting
Hollywood Pictures
500 S. Buena Vista St., ROD Bldg. 171
Burbank, CA 91521
818/560-1532

MARC HIRSCHFELD*
Liberman-Hirschfeld Casting
Sunset-Gower Studios
1438 N. Gower St., Suite 1410
Los Angeles, CA 90028
213/460-7258

JANET HIRSHENSON*
The Casting Company
7319 Beverly Blvd., Suite 1
Los Angeles, CA 90036
213/938-2170

HOFFMAN/FISHBAUGH CASTING
1020 N. Cole Ave., Suite 4370
Hollywood, CA 90038
213/463-7986

Bobby Hoffman*

JUDITH HOLSTRA*
4043 Radford Ave.
Studio City, CA 91604
818/761-9420

BILLY HOPKINS*
Bramon & Hopkins Casting
Lincoln Center Theater
150 W. 65th St.
New York, NY 10023
212/362-7600

STUART HOWARD*
215 Park Ave. South
New York, NY 10003
212/477-2323

VICKI HUFF*
20th Century Fox
10201 W. Pico Blvd.
Admin. Bldg. 12, Suite 153
Los Angeles, CA 90035
213/203-3475

PHYLLIS HUFFMAN*
Warner Bros.
75 Rockefeller Plaza, 23rd Floor
New York, NY 10019
212/484-6371

HUGHES/MOSS CASTING
c/o C.S.A.
311 W. 43rd St., Suite 700
New York, NY 10036
212/333-4552

Julie Hughes*
Barry Moss*

BETH HYMSON*
20th Century-Fox TV
10201 W. Pico Blvd.
Los Angeles, CA 90035
213/203-2662

I

DONNA ISAACSON*
Lyons/Isaacson Casting
453 W. 16th St., 2nd Floor
New York, NY 10011
212/691-8555

J

RICK JACOBS
Senior Vice President of Talent & Casting
Columbia Pictures TV
Studio Plaza
3400 Riverside Dr., Suite 8-56
Burbank, CA 91505
818/972-8591

JUSTINE JACOBY*
Dennison/Selzer Casting
11500 Tennessee Ave.
Los Angeles, CA 90064
213/444-7542

JANE JENKINS*
The Casting Company
7319 Beverly Blvd., Suite 1
Los Angeles, CA 90036
213/938-2170

JOHNSON & BUCKINGHAM CASTING
6362 Hollywood Blvd., Suite 320
Hollywood, CA 90028
213/463-4401

JOHNSON/LIFF CASTING
1501 Broadway, Suite 1400
New York, NY 10036
212/391-2680

Geoffrey Johnson*
Vincent G. Liff*
Tara Jayne Rubin*
Andrew M. Zerman*

MEL JOHNSON*
P.O. Box 4640
Universal City, CA 91608
818/760-3012

ED JOHNSTON
Director of Casting
Walt Disney Studios
500 S. Buena Vista St., Casting 1
Burbank, CA 91521
818/560-7875

ALLISON JONES
5555 Melrose Ave.
Cooper 103
Los Angeles, CA 90038
213/468-4850

CARO JONES*
5858 Hollywood Blvd., Suite 220
Los Angeles, CA 90028
213/464-9216

ROSALIE JOSEPH*
165 W. 46th St.
New York, NY 10003
212/921-5781

K

DARLENE KAPLAN*
Universal Studios
100 Universal City Plaza
Bldg. 463, Suite 104
Universal City, CA 91608
818/777-1114

KELLY CASTING
3859 Lankershim Blvd.
Studio City, CA 91604
818/762-0500

MALLORY KENNEDY
6815 Willoughby, Suite 105
Los Angeles, CA 90038
213/462-4561

RODY KENT*
5422 Vickery Blvd.
Dallas, TX 75206
214/827-3418

SUSIE KITTLESON
1302 N. Sweetzer, Suite 503
Los Angeles, CA 90069
213/652-7011

MARSHA KLEINMAN*
704 N. Gardner St., Suite 2
Los Angeles, CA 90046
213/852-1521

NANCY KLOPPER
Senior Vice President of Production
Act III Communications Inc.
1800 Century Park East, Suite 200
Los Angeles, CA 90067
213/553-3636

EILEEN KNIGHT*
5300 Melrose Ave., East Bldg. 309E
Los Angeles, CA 90038
213/960-4502

KATHY KNOWLES
709 21st St.
Santa Monica, CA 90402
213/394-4145

JOANNE KOEHLER
New World Television
1440 S. Sepulveda Blvd., Suite 110
Los Angeles, CA 90025
213/444-8535

STEVE KOLZAK
1438 N. Gower St.
Los Angeles, CA 90028
213/460-7245

KORDOS & CHARBONNEAU CASTING
445 E. Ohio, Suite 410
Chicago, IL 60611
312/527-4455

Nan Charbonneau*
Richard Kordos*

ANNAMARIE KOSTURA*
NBC Entertainment
3000 W. Alameda Ave., Suite 233
Burbank, CA 91523
818/840-4410

LYNN KRESSEL*
111 W. 57th St., Suite 1422
New York, NY 10019
212/581-6990

FRAN KUMIN*
Simon & Kumin Casting
1600 Broadway, Suite 609
New York, NY 10019
212/245-7670

DEBORAH KURTZ
1600 N. Highland Ave., Suite 4
Los Angeles, CA 90028
213/461-3800

L

JUDY LANDAU
1006 N. Cole Ave.
Los Angeles, CA 90038
213/464-0437

SHANA LANDSBURG
Director of Casting
3000 W. Alameda Ave., Suite 233
Burbank, CA 91523
818/840-4142

JASON LA PADURA*
39 W. 19th St., 12th Floor
New York, NY 10011
212/206-6420

ELIZABETH LARROQUETTE*
P.O. Box 6303
Malibu, CA 90264
818/954-2605

BARBARA LAUREN
P.O. Box 5271
Beverly Hills, CA 90210
818/506-6111

JUDIE LAWSON
Bergeron/Lawson Casting
P.O. Box 1489
La Canada, CA 91011
818/790-9832

GERALDINE LEDER
5555 Melrose Ave., Sternberg 201
Los Angeles, CA 90038
213/468-4703

KATHLEEN LETTERIE*
c/o C.S.A.
6565 Sunset Blvd., Suite 306
Los Angeles, CA 90028
818/760-5278

ELIZABETH LEUSTIG*
1173 N. Ardmore, Suite 1
Los Angeles, CA 90029
213/667-2103

JOHN LEVEY*
Director of Talent
Warner Bros. Television
4000 Warner Blvd.
Burbank, CA 91522
818/954-4080

GAIL LEVIN
5555 Melrose Ave.
Dressing Rm. Bldg., Suite 227
Los Angeles, CA 90038
213/468-8565

JODI LEVIN
1428 N. Gower
Los Angeles, CA 90028
213/460-7258

LIBERMAN/HIRSCHFELD CASTING
Sunset-Gower Studios
1438 N. Gower St., Suite 1408
Los Angeles, CA 90028
213/460-7258

Irene Cagen*
Marc Hirschfeld*
Meg Liberman*

AMY LIBERMAN
Viacom
100 Universal City Plaza, Bldg. 157
Universal City, CA 91608
818/777-4820

VINCE LIEBHART*
524 W. 57th St., Suite 5330
New York, NY 10019
212/757-4350

TERRY LIEBLING*
8407 Coreyell Place
Los Angeles, CA 90046
213/656-6803

MICHAEL LIEN CASTING
7461 Beverly Blvd., Suite 203
Los Angeles, CA 90036
213/937-0411

VINCENT LIFF*
Johnson/Liff Casting
1501 Broadway, Suite 1400
New York, NY 10036
212/391-2680

ROBIN LIPPIN*
500 S. Buena Vista St., Suite 1020
Burbank, CA 91505
818/560-6627

LISA LONDON*
CBS/MTM Studios
4024 Radford Ave.
Administration Bldg., Suite 319
Studio City, CA 91604
818/760-6283

BEVERLY LONG
Crossroads of the World
6671 Sunset Blvd., Suite 1584-A
Los Angeles, CA 90028
213/466-0770

MOLLY LOPATA*
4043 Radford Ave.
Studio City, CA 91604
818/753-8086

LEESA LORD
7058 Worster Ave.
North Hollywood, CA 91605
818/765-8080

DEBORAH LUCCHESI
P.O. Box 900
Beverly Hills, CA 90213
213/203-2583

LYONS/ISAACSON CASTING
435 W. 16th St., 2nd Floor
New York, NY 10019
212/691-8555

Donna Isaacson*
John S. Lyons*
Christine Sheaks

M

MacDONALD/BULLINGTON CASTING
9200 Sunset Blvd., Suite 530
West Hollywood, CA 90069
213/859-1089

Perry Bullington
Bob MacDonald

AMANDA MACKEY
517 N. Robertson Blvd.
Los Angeles, CA 90048
213/278-5816

MAGIC CASTING AGENCY
439 S. La Cienega Blvd., Suite 215
Los Angeles, CA 90048
213/276-8024

FRANCINE MAISLER
Manager of Casting
NBC Entertainment
3000 W. Alameda Ave.
Burbank, CA 91523
818/840-3835

MARK MALIS
Universal Studios
100 Universal Plaza, Suite 463-100
Universal City, CA 91608
818/777-1101

ANN REMSEN MANNERS
Barbara Remsen & Associates
Raleigh Studios
650 N. Bronson Ave., Suite 124
Los Angeles, CA 90004
213/464-7968

SHEILA MANNING
508 S. San Vicente, Suite 101
Los Angeles, CA 90048
213/852-1046

MARGARETTE & KENNEDY CASTING
6815 Willoughby Ave., Suite 105
Los Angeles, CA 90038
213/462-4561

Susan Margarette

IRENE MARIANO*
Lorimar Telepictures
3970 Overland Ave., Producers Bldg. 230
Culver City, CA 90232
213/280-8810

MINDY MARIN*
5555 Melrose Ave., Gower-Mill 106
Los Angeles, CA 90038
213/468-5163

VALORIE MASSALAS
Fenton/Taylor Casting
100 Universal City Plaza, Bungalow 477
Universal City, CA 91423
818/777-4610

VALERIE McCAFFREY
Director, Feature Casting
Universal Studios
100 Universal City Plaza
Universal City, CA 91608
818/777-3566

NANCY McCOOK
Anderson/McCook/White Casting
3855 Lankershim Blvd.
North Hollywood, CA 91614
818/760-3934

PAT McCORKLE*
264 W. 40th St.
New York, NY 10018
212/840-0992

BEVERLY McDERMOTT*
923 N. Golf Dr.
Hollywood, FL 33021
305/625-5111

DODIE McLEAN*
8033 Sunset Blvd., Suite 810
West Hollywood, CA 90046
213/876-7999

VIVIAN McRAE*
P.O. Box 1351
Burbank, CA 91507
818/848-9590

MARGARET McSHARRY
Director of Casting
CBS Entertainment
7800 Beverly Blvd., Suite 284
Los Angeles, CA 90036
213/852-2862

VIRGINIA McSWAIN*
11909 Weddington St., Suite 202
N. Hollywood, CA 91607
213/463-1925

JOAN MELLINI
8281 Melrose Ave., Suite 201
Los Angeles, CA 90046
213/653-9240

JOANNA MERLIN*
440 West End Ave.
New York, NY 10024
212/724-8575

MERRILL & PARTNERS
Los Angeles, CA 90048
213/659-2273

JEFF MESHEL
Manager of Casting
NBC Entertainment
3000 W. Alameda Ave.
Burbank, CA 91523
818/840-4729

ELLEN MEYER*
P.O. Box 2147
Malibu, CA 90265
213/444-1818

BARBARA MILLER*
Lorimar Telepictures
3970 Overland Ave., Producers Bldg. 230
Culver City, CA 90232
213/280-8810

LISA MIONIE*
Viacom
10 Universal City Plaza, 32nd Floor
Universal City, CA 91608
818/505-7661

PAT MOCK*
c/o C.S.A.
6565 Sunset Blvd., Suite 306
Los Angeles, CA 90028
213/463-1925

BOB MORONES*
733 N. Seward St.
Hollywood, CA 90038
213/467-2834

BOBBI MORRIS
8150 Beverly Blvd., Suite 204
Los Angeles, CA 90048
213/653-4031

HELEN MOSSLER*
Vice President - Talent & Casting
Paramount Television
5555 Melrose Ave., Bluhdorn 128
Los Angeles, CA 90038
213/468-5578

DREW MURPHY
Ahmanson Theatre
135 N. Grand Ave.
Los Angeles, CA 90012
213/972-7401

JANE MURRAY
P.O. Box 64161
Los Angeles, CA 90064
213/462-2301

ROGER MUSSENDEN
The Casting Company
7319 Beverly Blvd., Suite 1
Los Angeles, CA 90036
213/938-2170

N

ROBIN STOLTZ NASSIF*
Director of Casting
ABC Entertainment
2040 Ave. of the Stars, 5th Floor
Los Angeles, CA 90067
213/557-6423

NANCY NAYOR*
Vice President - Casting
100 Universal City Plaza, Bldg. 500
Universal City, CA 91608
818/777-3566

DEBRA NEATHERY
4820 N. Cleon Ave.
North Hollywood, CA 91601
818/506-5524

NEW STAR CASTING
8489 W. 3rd St., Suite 16
Los Angeles, CA 90048
213/655-2565

MARK NICLAS CASTING
656 N. Harper
Los Angeles, CA 90048
213/658-1066

ELLEN NOVACK*
20 Jay St., Suite 9B
New York, NY 10013
212/431-3939

PATRICIA O'BRIEN
3701 W. Oak St.
Burbank, CA 91505
818/954-3000

PAULINE O'CON
Manager of Casting
ABC Entertainment
2040 Ave. of the Stars, 5th Floor
Los Angeles, CA 90067
213/557-6425

MERYL O'LOUGHLIN*
Imagine Entertainment
1925 Century Park East, 23rd Floor
Los Angeles, CA 90067
213/277-1665

ONORATO/FRANKS CASTING
1717 N. Highland Ave., Suite 709
Los Angeles, CA 90028
213/468-8833

Jerry Franks*

Al Onorato*

LORI OPENDEN*
Vice President - Talent & Casting
NBC Entertainment
3000 W. Alameda Ave., Suite 233
Burbank, CA 91523
818/840-3774

JEFFREY OSHEN*
Republic Pictures
335 N. Maple Dr., Suite 354
Beverly Hills, CA 90210
213/285-6210

JESSICA OVERWISE*
17250 Sunset Blvd., Suite 304
Pacific Palisades, CA 90272
213/459-2686

P

PAGANO/BIALY CASTING
Pagano/Bialy Casting
1680 N. Vine St., Suite 904
Los Angeles, CA 90028
213/871-0051

Sharon Bialy*

Richard Pagano*

MARVIN PAIGE*
P.O. Box 69964
Los Angeles, CA 90028
213/760-3040

PARADOXE CASTING
7441 Sunset Blvd., Suite 205
Los Angeles, CA 90046
213/851-6110

JENNIFER J. PART*
100 Universal City Plaza
Bldg. 507, Suite 4-F
Universal City, CA 91608
818/560-6196

CAMI PATTON*
Barylski/Patton Casting
Sunset Gower Studios
1438 N. Gower St.
Los Angeles, CA 90028
213/460-7375

MERCEDES PENNEY
5000 Lankershim Blvd., Suite 3
North Hollywood, CA 91601
818/763-1067

SALLY PERLE & ASSOCIATES
12178 Ventura Blvd., Suite 201
Studio City, CA 91604
818/762-8752

PERRY/BENSON CASTING
11350 Ventura Blvd., Suite 201
Studio City, CA 91604
818/766-3896

Annette Benson*

Penny Perry

SHANCY PIERCE
948 N. Fairfax
Los Angeles, CA 90046
213/654-2103

LOIS PLANCO*
1600 Broadway, Suite 909
New York, NY 10019
212/245-8620

PAM POLIFRONI*
3000 W. Alameda Ave.
Studio 11, 2nd Floor
Burbank, CA 91523
818/840-4641

HOLLY POWELL*
Stone/Powell Casting
Sunset-Gower Studios
1438 N. Gower St., Casting #2407
Los Angeles, CA 90028
213/460-7391

JAN POWELL
Barbara Claman, Inc.
6565 Sunset Blvd., Suite 412
Los Angeles, CA 90028
213/466-3400

SALLY POWERS*
c/o C.S.A.
6565 Sunset Blvd., Suite 306
Los Angeles, CA 90028
213/463-1925

PRODUCERS CASTING AGENCY
6331 Hollywood Blvd., Suite 1103
Hollywood, CA 90028
213/464-8233

R

JOHANNA RAY*
941-A N. Mansfield Ave.
Los Angeles, CA 90038
213/463-7177

KAREN REA*
8985 Venice Blvd.
Los Angeles, CA 90230
213/202-6900

JOE REICH*
c/o C.S.A.
6565 Sunset Blvd., Suite 306
Los Angeles, CA 90028
818/840-3244

BARBARA REMSEN & ASSOCIATES
Raleigh Studios
650 N. Bronson Ave., Suite 124
Los Angeles, CA 90004
213/464-7968

Ann Remsen Manners

Barbara Remsen*

SHIRLEY RICH*
200 E. 66th St., Sutie E-1202
New York, NY 10021
212/688-9540

DAVID ROACH
10202 W. Washington Blvd., Taylor 206
Los Angeles, CA 90232
213/280-5678

ROBINSON/ELLERS CASTING
7080 Hollywood Blvd., Suite 606
Los Angeles, CA 90028
213/962-9735

Penny Ellers*

Joyce Robinson*

JEFF ROSEN
1600 N. Highland Ave., Suite 1
Los Angeles, CA 90028
213/461-3800

VICKI ROSENBERG & ASSOCIATES
Columbia Pictures Television
300 Avon St., Trailer 74
Burbank, CA 91505
818/954-2793

Vicki Rosenberg*

Sharon Soble

DONNA ROSENSTEIN*
Vice President - Casting & Talent
ABC Entertainment
2040 Ave. of the Stars, 5th Floor
Los Angeles, CA 90067
213/557-6532

MARCIA ROSS*
Vice President - Talent & Casting
Warner Bros. Television
4000 Warner Blvd.
Burbank, CA 91522
818/954-1123

RENEE ROUSSELOT*
Director of Casting
Walt Disney Pictures
500 S. Buena Vista St.
Casting Bldg., Suite 6
Burbank, CA 91521
818/560-7509

RUBIN/FERTIG CASTING
5750 Wilshire Blvd., Suite 276
Los Angeles, CA 90036
213/965-1500

Ben Rubin*

Steven Fertig

DAVID RUBIN CASTING
c/o C.S.A.
6565 Sunset Blvd., Suite 306
Los Angeles, CA 90028
818/777-9670

David Rubin*

Debra Zane

DEBRA RUBINSTEIN*
Raleigh Studios
5300 Melrose Ave., Suite 303-E
Los Angeles, CA 90038
213/960-4503

S

DORIS SABBAGH
Columbia Pictures Television
Columbia Plaza East, Suite 148
Burbank, CA 91505
818/954-2985

MARK SAKS*
Barbara Claman, Inc.
6565 Sunset Blvd., Suite 412
Los Angeles, CA 90028
213/466-3400

DAVID J. SCHACKER & ASSOCIATES
463 S. Robertson Blvd.
Beverly Hills, CA 90211
213/273-8834

GUS SCHIRMER
1403 N. Orange Grove Ave.
Los Angeles, CA 90046
213/876-5044

JANE SCHWARTZ
1717 N. Highland Ave., Suite 909
Los Angeles, CA 90028
213/460-4414

JEAN SCOCCIMARRO*
Orion Television
11500 Tennessee Ave.
Los Angeles, CA 90064
213/444-7434

SUSAN SCUDDER*
7083 Hollywood Blvd.
Los Angeles, CA 90028
213/856-7574

JOE SCULLY*
5642 Etiwanda Ave., Suite 8
Tarzana, CA 91356
818/763-2028

LILA SELIK CASTING
4117 McLaughlin, Suite 9
Los Angeles, CA 90066
213/391-9986

JULIE SELZER*
Dennison/Selzer Casting
11500 Tennessee Ave.
Los Angeles, CA 90064
213/444-7542

CARL SHAIN
921 S. Curson
Los Angeles, CA 90036
213/935-6631

BONNIE SHANE
1238 S. Glendale Ave.
Glendale, CA 91205
818/502-5370

SARI SHAPIRO
P.O. Box 69277
Los Angeles, CA 90069
213/874-1719

KIYO GLENN SHARP
4567 Nagle Ave.
Sherman Oaks, CA 91423
818/789-7842

SUSAN SHAW*
20th Century Fox
10201 W. Pico Blvd., Trailer 732
Los Angeles, CA 90035
213/203-3692

BILL SHEPARD*
c/o C.S.A.
6565 Sunset Blvd., Suite 306
Los Angeles, CA 90028
818/789-4776

TONY SHEPHERD*
Vice President - Talent & Casting
Aaron Spelling Productions
1041 N. Formosa Ave.
Hollywood, CA 90046
213/850-2875

MELANIE SHERWOOD
6305 Yucca, 6th Floor
Los Angeles, CA 90028
213/462-6817

JENNIFER SHULL*
c/o C.S.A.
6565 Sunset Blvd., Suite 306
Los Angeles, CA 90028
213/463-1925

MARGERY SIMKIN*
c/o C.S.A.
311 W. 43rd St., Suite 700
New York, NY 10036
213/203-1530

JOAN SIMMONS
P.O. Box 832
Tarzana, CA 91356
818/996-5131

SIMON & KUMIN CASTING
1600 Broadway, Suite 1005
New York, NY 10019
212/245-7670

Fran Kumin*

Meg Simon*

MELISSA SKOFF*
11684 Ventura Blvd., Suite 5141
Studio City, CA 91604
818/760-2058

MARY JO SLATER*
Vice President - Casting
MGM/UA TV
10000 W. Washington Blvd., Suite 4011
Culver City, CA 90232
213/280-6128

KATHY SMITH
12001 Valleyheart Dr.
Studio City, CA 91604
818/508-2058

SHARON SOBLE
Vicki Rosenberg & Associates
Columbia Pictures Television
300 Avon St., Trailer 74
Burbank, CA 91505
818/954-2793

STANLEY SOBLE*
Mark Taper Forum
135 N. Grand Ave.
Los Angeles, CA 90012
213/972-7374

CAROL SOSKIN CASTING
P.O. Box 480106
Los Angeles, CA 90048
213/473-7044

LYNN STALMASTER*
9911 W. Pico Blvd., Suite 1580
Los Angeles, CA 90035
213/552-0983

JANE STAUGUS CASTING, INC.
10153 1/2 Riverside Dr., Suite 108
Toluca Lake, CA 91602
818/508-8868

RON STEPHENSON*
Director of Casting
Universal Television
100 Universal City Plaza
Bldg. 463, Suite 106
Universal City, CA 91608
818/777-3498

SALLY ANN STINER*
12228 Venice Blvd., Suite 503
Los Angeles, CA 90066
213/827-9796

STOKES/GROSS CASTING
c/o C.S.A.
6565 Sunset Blvd., Suite 306
Los Angeles, CA 90028
213/460-7391

Glenis Gross

Stanzi Stokes*

STONE/POWELL CASTING
Sunset-Gower Studios
1438 N. Gower St., Casting #2407
Los Angeles, CA 90028
213/460-7391

Holly Powell*

Randy Stone*

GILDA STRATTON*
4000 Warner Blvd.
N. Admin. Bldg., Suite 18
Burbank, CA 91522
818/954-2843

SUE SWAN
Champion/Basker Casting
7060 Hollywood Blvd., Suite 808
Hollywood, CA 90028
213/466-1884

MONICA SWANN*
5300 Melrose Ave., Suite 309E
Los Angeles, CA 90038
213/856-1702

T

JUDY TAYLOR*
Fenton/Taylor Casting
100 Universal City Plaza, Bungalow 477
Universal City, CA 91423
818/777-4610

JULIET TAYLOR*
130 W. 57th St., Suite 12E
New York, NY 10019
212/245-4635

TEITLBAUM/HEIT
2000 W. Magnolia Blvd., Suite 209
Burbank, CA 91506
818/845-9041

TEPPER/GALLEGOS
7033 Sunset Blvd., Suite 208
Los Angeles, CA 90028
213/469-3577

Estelle Tepper

JOEL THURM
Vice President - Talent
NBC Entertainment
3000 W. Alameda Ave., Suite 233
Burbank, CA 91523
818/840-3835

ROSEMARIE TICHLER*
New York Shakespeare Festival
425 Lafayette St.
New York, NY 10003
212/598-7100

BONNIE TIMMERMAN*
c/o C.S.A.
311 W. 43rd St.
New York, NY 10036
212/333-4552

TLC/BOOTH
6521 Homewood Ave.
Los Angeles, CA 90028
213/464-2788

JOY TODD*
37 E. 28th St., Suite 700
New York, NY 10016
212/685-3537

SUSAN TYLER
3859 Lankershim Blvd.
Studio City, CA 91604
818/506-0400

U

ULRICH/DAWSON CASTING
100 Universal City Plaza, Bldg. 466
Universal City, CA 91608
818/777-7802

Eric Dawson
Robert Ulrich*

UNIQUE CASTING
540 NW 165th St. Road
Miami, FL 33169
305/947-9339

Ed Arenas
Yonit Hamer*

KAREN VICE*
20th Century Fox
10201 W. Pico Blvd.
Bldg. 38, Suite 229
Los Angeles, CA 90035
213/203-1900

JOSE VILLAVERDE*
c/o C.S.A.
6565 Sunset Blvd., Suite 306
Los Angeles, CA 90028
213/463-1925

BRAD WAISBREN ENTERPRISES
P.O. Box 8741
Universal City, CA 91608
818/506-3000

SAMUEL WARREN & ASSOCIATES INTL.
2244 4th Ave., Suite D
San Diego, CA 92101
213/857-8230

APRIL WEBSTER*
c/o C.S.A.
6565 Sunset Blvd., Suite 306
Los Angeles, CA 90028
818/954-3352

MARY WEST*
Brown/West Casting
7319 Beverly Blvd., Suite 10
Los Angeles, CA 90036
213/938-2575

MEGAN WHITAKER
Lorimar
3970 Overland Ave., Suite P-230
Culver City, CA 90232
213/288-8810

CATHERINE WHITE
Anderson/McCook/White Casting
3855 Lankershim Blvd.
North Hollywood, CA 91614
818/760-3934

NICK WILKINSON
Director of Casting
ABC Entertainment
2040 Ave. of the Stars, 5th Floor
Los Angeles, CA 90067
213/577-6547

TAMMY WINDSOR
14001 Peach Grove
Sherman Oaks, CA 91423
818/501-3510

GERI WINDSOR-FISCHER*
Senior Vice President - Talent
MTM Enterprises
4024 Radford Ave., Bldg. 1, Suite 390
Studio City, CA 91604
818/760-5233

LIZ WOODMAN*
c/o C.S.A.
311 W. 43rd St., Suite 700
New York, NY 10036
212/787-3782

GERRIE WORMSER
P.O. Box 6449
Beverly Hills, CA 90210
213/277-3281

Y

DIANE C. YOUNG*
c/o C.S.A.
6565 Sunset Blvd., Suite 306
Los Angeles, CA 90028
818/954-5418

Z

JOANNE ZALUSKI*
9348 Civic Center Dr., Suite 407
Beverly Hills, CA 90210
213/456-5160

DEBRA ZANE
David Rubin Casting
c/o C.S.A.
6565 Sunset Blvd., Suite 306
Los Angeles, CA 90028
818/777-9670

INDEX OF ADVERTISERS

A special thanks to our advertisers whose support makes it possible for us to bring you this **Second Edition of FILM PRODUCERS, STUDIOS, AGENTS & CASTING DIRECTORS GUIDE**

J & M Entertainment .... Cover 2
Colorado Motion Picture & TV Commission .... Cover 3
Agfa-Gevaert .... Cover 4
Robert Easton VI
Amnesty International USA 168
Film & Video 170
A Catered Creation 206
Samuel French 236
Drama Books 236
Chicago Film Office 236
United Way 238
AIDS Project Los Angeles 258

ABOUT THE EDITORS

JACK LECHNER'S firmly held belief that no fact is too trivial has vexed his friends and family since childhood. Nonetheless, he has constructed crossword puzzles and word games for various publications; written the unfortunately titled *Ivy League Rock & Roll Quiz Book;* and set an unbreakable record for losing the most money on *Final Jeopardy.* He has also worked as a development executive for film production companies in New York and Los Angeles.

Jack lives in Hollywood with his wife Sam Maser and their enormous cat, Flora Turnpike.

★★★

SUSAN AVALLONE was a magazine editor for four years before entering the entertainment industry. She has worked as an assistant to a development excecutive and is currently an assistant to a writer/producer. She is also editor of the FILM WRITERS GUIDE and CINEMATOGRAPHERS, PRODUCTION DESIGNERS, COSTUME DESIGNERS & FILM EDITORS GUIDE, also published by Lone Eagle Publishing.

A native of New York City, Susan has resided in Los Angeles for two years with her husband Carr D'Angelo.

PRODUCERS AWARDS AND NOMINATIONS 1977-1989

★★ = Winner in the category

1977
ANNIE HALL .... Charles H. Joffe★★
THE GOODBYE GIRL .... Ray Stark
JULIA .... Richard Roth
STAR WARS .... Gary Kurtz
THE TURNING POINT .... Herbert Ross and Arthur Laurents

1978
COMING HOME .... Jerome Hellman
THE DEER HUNTER .... Barry Spikings, Michael Deeley, Michael Cimino and John Peverall★★
HEAVEN CAN WAIT .... Warren Beatty
MIDNIGHT EXPRESS .... Alan Marshall and David Puttnam
AN UNMARRIED WOMAN .... Paul Mazursky and Tony Ray

1979
ALL THAT JAZZ .... Robert Alan Aurthur
APOCALYPSE NOW .... Francis Coppola
BREAKING AWAY .... Peter Yates
KRAMER VS. KRAMER .... Stanley R. Jaffe★★
NORMA RAE .... Tamara Asseyev and Alex Rose

1980
COAL MINER'S DAUGHTER .... Bernard Schwartz
THE ELEPHANT MAN .... Jonathan Sanger
ORDINARY PEOPLE .... Ronald L. Schwary★★
RAGING BULL .... Irwin Winkler and Robert Chartoff
TESS .... Claude Berri and Timothy Burrill

1981
ATLANTIC CITY .... Denis Heroux and John Kemeny
CHARIOTS OF FIRE .... David Puttnam★★
ON GOLDEN POND .... Bruce Gilbert
RAIDERS OF THE LOST ARK .... Frank Marshall
REDS .... Warren Beatty

1982
E.T. THE EXTRA-TERRESTRIAL .... Steven Spielberg and Kathleen Kennedy
GANDHI .... Richard Attenborough★★
MISSING .... Edward Lewis and Mildred Lewis
TOOTSIE .... Sydney Pollack and Dick Richards
THE VERDICT ... Richard D. Zanuck and David Brown

1983
THE BIG CHILL .... Michael Shamberg
THE DRESSER .... Peter Yates
THE RIGHT STUFF .... Irwin Winkler and Robert Chartoff
TENDER MERCIES .... Philip S. Hobel
TERMS OF ENDEARMENT .... James L. Brooks★★

1984
AMADEUS .... Saul Zaentz★★
THE KILLING FIELDS .... David Puttnam
A PASSAGE TO INDIA .... John Brabourne and Richard Goodwin
PLACES IN THE HEART .... Arlene Donovan
A SOLDIER'S STORY .... Norman Jewison, Ronald L. Schwary and Patrick Palmer

1985
THE COLOR PURPLE .... Steven Spielberg, Kathleen Kennedy, Frank Marshall and Quincy Jones
KISS OF THE SPIDER WOMAN .... David Weisman
OUT OF AFRICA .... Sydney Pollack★★
PRIZZI'S HONOR .... John Foreman
WITNESS .... Edward S. Feldman

1986
CHILDREN OF A LESSER GOD .... Burt Sugarman and Patrick Palmer
HANNAH AND HER SISTERS .... Robert Greenhut
THE MISSION ...... Fernando Ghia and David Puttnam
PLATOON .... Arnold Kopelson★★
A ROOM WITH A VIEW .... Ismail Merchant

1987
BROADCAST NEWS .... James L. Brooks
FATAL ATTRACTION .... Stanley R. Jaffe and Sherry Lansing
HOPE AND GLORY .... John Boorman
THE LAST EMPEROR .... Jeremy Thomas★★
MOONSTRUCK .... Norman Jewison

1988
THE ACCIDENTAL TOURIST .... Lawrence Kasdan, Charles Okun and Michael Grillo
DANGEROUS LIAISONS .... Norma Heyman and Hank Moonjean
MISSISSIPPI BURNING .... Frederick Zollo and Robert F. Colesberry
RAIN MAN .... Mark Johnson★★
WORKING GIRL .... Douglas Wick

1989
BORN ON THE FOURTH OF JULY .... Oliver Stone and A. Kitman Ho
DEAD POETS SOCIETY .... Steven Haft, Tony Thomas and Paul Junger Witt
DRIVING MISS DAISY .... Lili Fini Zanuck and Richard D. Zanuck★★
FIELD OF DREAMS .... Charles Gordon and Lawrence Gordon
MY LEFT FOOT .... Noel Pearson and Arthur Lappin